, Ireland
ia@lero.ie

ny
-dortmund.de

e-ISSN 1611-3349
-45233-2   e-ISBN 978-3-662-45234-9
8-3-662-45234-9
berg New York Dordrecht London

gress Control Number: Applied for

ary: SL 1 – Theoretical Computer Science and General Issues

Lecture Notes in Computer Science   8802

T0224358

Tiziana Margar.

Leveragin
of Formal
Verificatio

Technologies fo

6th International Symp
Imperial, Corfu, Greece
Proceedings, Part I

Volume Editors

Tiziana Margaria
University of Limerick
E-mail: tiziana.margar

Bernhard Steffen
TU Dortmund, Germa
E-mail: steffen@cs.tu

ISSN 0302-9743
ISBN 978-3-662
DOI 10.1007/97
Springer Heide

Library of Con

LNCS Sublibr

Typesetting

Printed on

Springer i

 Springer

Introduction

Welcome to the proceedings of ISoLA 2014, the 6th International Symposium on Leveraging Applications of Formal Methods, Verification and Validation, that was held in Imperial, Corfu (Greece) during October 8–11, 2014, endorsed by EASST, the European Association of Software Science and Technology.

This year's event was at the same time ISoLA's tenth anniversary. It also followed the tradition of its symposia forerunners held 2004 and 2006 in Cyprus, 2008 in Chalkidiki, and 2010 as well as 2012 in Crete, and the series of ISoLA Workshops in Greenbelt (USA) in 2005, Poitiers (France) in 2007, Potsdam (Germany) in 2009, in Vienna (Austria) in 2011, and 2013 in Palo Alto (USA).

As in the previous editions, ISoLA 2014 provided a forum for developers, users, and researchers to discuss issues related to the adoption and use of rigorous tools and methods for the specification, analysis, verification, certification, construction, test, and maintenance of systems from the point of view of their different application domains. Thus, since 2004 the ISoLA series of events serves the purpose of bridging the gap between designers and developers of rigorous tools on one side, and users in engineering and in other disciplines on the other side. It fosters and exploits synergetic relationships among scientists, engineers, software developers, decision makers, and other critical thinkers in companies and organizations. By providing a specific, dialogue-oriented venue for the discussion of common problems, requirements, algorithms, methodologies, and practices, ISoLA aims in particular at supporting researchers in their quest to improve the usefulness, reliability, flexibility, and efficiency of tools for building systems, and users in their search for adequate solutions to their problems.

The symposium program consisted of a collection of *special tracks* devoted to the following hot and emerging topics:

- Statistical Model Checking, Past Present and Future (K. Larsen, A. Legay)
- Formal Methods and Analysis in Software Product Line Engineering (I. Schäfer, M. ter Beck)
- Risk-Based Testing (M. Felderer, M. Wendland, I. Schieferdecker)
- Scientific Workflows (J. Kok, A. Lamprecht, K. Turner, K. Wolstencroft)
- Medical Cyber Physical Systems (E. Bartocci, S. Gao, S. Smolka)
- Evaluation and Reproducibility of Program Analysis (M. Schordan, W. Lowe, D. Beyer)
- Automata Learning (F. Howar, B. Steffen)
- Rigorous Engineering of Autonomic Ensembles (R. de Nicola, M. Hölzl, M. Wirsing)
- Engineering Virtualized Services (R. Hähnle, E. Broch Johnsen)
- Security and Dependability for Resource Constrained Embedded Systems (B. Hamid, C. Rudolph)
- Semantic Heterogeneity in the Formal Development of Complex Systems (I. Ait Sadoune, J.P. Gibson)

- Evolving Critical Systems (M. Hinchey, T. Margaria)
- Model-Based Code-Generators and Compilers (J. Knoop, W. Zimmermann, U. Assmann)
- Processes and Data Integration in the Networked Healthcare (J. Mündler, T. Margaria, C. Rasche)

The symposium also featured:

- Tutorial: Automata Learning in Practice (B. Steffen, F. Howar)
- RERS: Challenge on Rigorous Examination of Reactive Systems (F. Howar, J. van de Pol, M. Schordan, M. Isberner, T. Ruys, B. Steffen)
- Doctoral Symposium and Poster Session (A.-L. Lamprecht)
- Industrial Day (A. Hessenkämper)

Co-located with the ISoLA Symposium was:

- STRESS 2014 - Third International School on Tool-Based Rigorous Engineering of Software Systems (J. Hatcliff, T. Margaria, Robby, B. Steffen)

We thank the track organizers, the members of the Program Committee and their subreferees for their effort in selecting the papers to be presented, the local organization chair, Petros Stratis, and the Easyconference team for their continuous precious support during the week as well as during the entire two-year period preceding the events. We also thank Springer for being, as usual, a very reliable partner for the proceedings production. Finally, we are grateful to Horst Voigt for his Web support, and to Dennis Kühn, Maik Merten, Johannes Neubauer, and Stephan Windmüller for their help with the online conference service (OCS).

Special thanks are due to the following organizations for their endorsement: EASST (European Association of Software Science and Technology), and our own institutions, TU Dortmund, and the University of Potsdam.

October 2014   Tiziana Margaria
                                                            Bernhard Steffen

Organization

Symposium Chair

Bernhard Steffen

Program Chair

Tiziana Margaria

Program Committee:

Yamine Ait Ameur	ISAE-ENSMA, France
Idi Ait-Sadoune	SUPÉLEC, France
Uwe Assmann	TU Dresden, Germany
Ezio Bartocci	TU Wien, Austria
Dirk Beyer	University of Passau, Germany
Rocco De Nicola	IMT Lucca, Italy
Michael Felderer	University of Innsbruck, Austria
Sicun Gao	Carnegie Mellon University, USA
J. Paul Gibson	Télécom SudParis, France
Kim Guldstrand Larsen	Aalborg University, Denmark
Reiner Hähnle	TU Darmstadt, Germany
Brahim Hamid	IRIT, France
Mike Hinchey	Lero, Ireland
Matthias Hölzl	Ludwig-Maximilians-University Munich, Germany
Falk Howar	Carnegie Mellon University, USA
Einar Broch Johnsen	University of Oslo, Norway
Jens Knoop	TU Wien, Austria
Joost Kok	LIACS Leiden University, The Netherlands
Anna-Lena Lamprecht	University of Potsdam, Germany
Axel Legay	Inria, France
Welf Löwe	Linnaeus University, Sweden
Tiziana Margaria	University of Limerick, Ireland
Christoph Rasche	University of Potsdam, Germany
Carsten Rudolph	Fraunhofer SIT, Germany
Ina Schäfer	TU Braunschweig, Germany
Ina Schieferdecker	FU Berlin, Germany
Markus Schordan	Lawrence Livermore National Laboratory, USA

Table of Contents – Part I

Automata Learning

Formal Methods and Analysis in Software Product Line Engineering

Model-Based Code Generators and Compilers

Tutorial: Automata Learning in Practice

LNCS Transactions on Foundations for Mastering Change

Table of Contents – Part II

Engineering Virtualized Systems

Statistical Model Checking

Risk-Based Testing

Medical Cyber-Physical Systems

Scientific Workflows

Evaluation and Reproducibility of Program Analysis

Processes and Data Integration in the Networked Healthcare

Semantic Heterogeneity in the Formal Development of Complex Systems

Industrial Track

Doctoral Symposium and Poster Session

Evolving Critical Systems - Track Introduction

Mike Hinchey[1] and Tiziana Margaria[2]

[1] Lero—The Irish Software Engineering Research Centre,
University of Limerick, Ireland
mike.hinchey@lero.ie

[2] Chair of Service and Software Engineering, University Potsdam, Germany
margaria@cs.uni-potsdam.de

The need is becoming evident for a software engineering research community that focuses on the development and maintenance of Evolving Critical Systems (ECS). The software and systems engineering community must concentrate its efforts on the techniques, methodologies and tools needed to design, implement, and maintain critical software systems that evolve successfully (without risk of failure or loss of quality). Critical systems are systems where failure or malfunction will lead to significant negative consequences. These systems may have strict requirements for security and safety, to protect the user or others. Alternatively, these systems may be critical to the organization's mission, product base, profitability or competitive advantage.

Lero—the Irish Software Engineering Research Centre, along with many of its collaborators has been leading the effort in defining and addressing an Evolving Critical Systems research agenda, with more focus on predictability, quality, and the ability to change. This work has been supported by a Dagstuhl workshop, a special issue of *Computer* (May 2010), and now this special track at ISoLA 2014.

The fundamental research question underlying ECS is how do we design, implement and maintain critical software systems. These systems must be highly reliable while maintaining this reliability as they evolve. This must be done without incurring prohibitive costs [3].

We must maintain the quality of critical software despite constant change in its teams, processes, methods and toolkits. We must improve our existing software development methodologies so that they facilitate and support the maintenance of ECS.

We must specify what we want to achieve during an evolution cycle and confirm that we have achieved the intended result (verification) and only the intended result (validation). We must elicit and represent requirements for change so that we ensure the changes are made correctly. In addition, we must develop techniques for better estimating specific evolution activities before they begin, so that we only attempt software change when we know that the benefits will outweigh costs.

All of these requirements demand us to develop strategies that will make model-drive automatic evolution a better alternative to manual change. Where change cannot be automated, or where it is not appropriate to do so, we must develop heuristics for determining that change is viable. When humans must perform the change, we must develop support tools to mitigate risk.

T. Margaria and B. Steffen (Eds.): ISoLA 2014, Part I, LNCS 8802, pp. 1–3, 2014.
© Springer-Verlag Berlin Heidelberg 2014

Given the tensions between the need for software change and the implicit danger is changing critical software, the pressing issue is which are the appropriate tools, processes and techniques to evolve critical systems in a cost-effective and low-risk manner.

A concerted effort from the research community to overcome these challenges is needed. The papers in this track address several dimensions of these needs:

- *Statistical Abstraction Boosts Design and Test Efficiency of Evolving Critical Systems* [6] shows how to improve the efficiency of Monte Carlo simulations, that are used to efficiently estimate critical properties of complex evolving systems but are computationally intensive. In order to not repeat the costly simulations every time something changes, the idea is to resort to behaviour-preserving statistical abstractions of its environment. A frequency domain metric helps to judge the a priori performance of an abstraction and provide an a posteriori indicator to aid construction of abstractions optimised for critical properties.
- *Combinatory Logic Synthesizer* [2] describes features and architecture of a tool to automatically compose larger systems from repositories of components based on combinatory logic with intersection types. It is used to support evolution by simplifying the synthesis for Object Oriented Software.
- *Incremental Syntactic-Semantic Reliability Analysis of Evolving Structured Workflows* [1] addresses the flexibilization of workflow-based software composition, in order to cope with changing business processes. The proposed incremental verification approach focuses on the probabilistic verification of reliability requirements of structured workflows. It is based on a syntactic-semantic approach that uses operator-precedence grammars enriched with semantic attributes.
- *DyWA* Prototype-driven development of web applications with DyWA [4] introduces an approach to the user-driven development of process-oriented web applications where application experts model the domain-specific data models according to their professional knowledge and understanding, and the business process models that act on these automatically generated elementary data operations. The resulting business processes are directly complete *executable prototypes* of the resulting web application, without coding. [4]
- *Domain-Specific Languages for Enterprise Systems* [5] describes POETS, a software architecture for enterprise resource planning systems that uses domain-specific languages for specifying reports and contracts. This allows succinct declarative specifications, and rapid adaptability and customisation that supports run-time changes to the data model, reports and contracts, while retaining full auditability.

References

1. Bianculli, D., Filieri, A., Ghezzi, C., Mandrioli, D.: Incremental syntactic-semantic reliability analysis of evolving structured workflows. In: Margaria, T., Steffen, B. (eds.) ISoLA 2014, Part I. LNCS, vol. 8802, pp. 41–55. Springer, Heidelberg (2014)

2. Bessai, J., Dudenhefner, A., Düdder, B., Martens, M., Rehof, J.: Combinatory logic synthesizer. In: Steffen, B., Margaria, T. (eds.) ISoLA 2014, Part I. LNCS, vol. 8802, pp. 26–40. Springer, Heidelberg (2014)
3. Nuseibeh, L.C.M.H.B., Fiadeiro, J.L.: Evolving critical systems. Computer 43(5), 28–33 (2010)
4. Neubauer, J., Frohme, M., Steffen, B., Margaria, T.: Prototype-driven development of web applications with DyWA. In: Steffen, B., Margaria, T. (eds.) ISoLA 2014, Part I. LNCS, vol. 8802, pp. 56–72. Springer, Heidelberg (2014)
5. Andersen, J., Bahr, P., Henglein, F., Hvitved, T.: Domain-specific languages for enterprise systems. In: Steffen, B., Margaria, T. (eds.) ISoLA 2014, Part I. LNCS, vol. 8802, pp. 73–95. Springer, Heidelberg (2014)
6. Sedwards, A.L.S.: Statistical abstraction boosts design and test efficiency of evolving critical systems. In: Steffen, B., Margaria, T. (eds.) ISoLA 2014, Part I. LNCS, vol. 8802, pp. 4–25. Springer, Heidelberg (2014)

Statistical Abstraction Boosts Design and Test Efficiency of Evolving Critical Systems

Axel Legay and Sean Sedwards

Inria Rennes – Bretagne Atlantique

Abstract. Monte Carlo simulations may be used to efficiently estimate critical properties of complex evolving systems but are nevertheless computationally intensive. Hence, when only part of a system is new or modified it seems wasteful to re-simulate the parts that have not changed. It also seems unnecessary to perform many simulations of parts of a system whose behaviour does not vary significantly.

To increase the efficiency of designing and testing complex evolving systems we present simulation techniques to allow such a system to be verified against behaviour-preserving statistical abstractions of its environment. We propose a frequency domain metric to judge the a priori performance of an abstraction and provide an a posteriori indicator to aid construction of abstractions optimised for critical properties.

1 Introduction

The low cost of hardware and demand for increased functionality make modern computational systems highly complex. At the same time, such systems are designed to be extensible and adaptable, to account for new functionality, increased use and new technology. It is usually cost-efficient to allow a system to evolve piece-wise, rather than replace it entirely, such that over time it may not respect its original specification. A key challenge is therefore to ensure that the critical performance of evolving systems is maintained up to the point of their obsolescence.

The basic challenge has been addressed by robust tools and techniques developed in the field of software engineering, which allow designers to specify and verify the performance of complex systems in terms of data flow. The level of abstraction of these techniques often does not include the precise dynamical behaviour of the implementation, which may critically affect performance. Hence, to guarantee that the implementation of a system respects its specification it is necessary to consider detailed dynamical models. In particular, it is necessary to consider dynamics that specifically model the uncertainty encountered in real deployment.

1.1 Our Approach

To address the problem of designing and testing evolving critical systems [16] we focus on efficient ways to construct and formally verify large dynamical models

T. Margaria and B. Steffen (Eds.): ISoLA 2014, Part I, LNCS 8802, pp. 4–25, 2014.

whose structure evolves over time. In particular, we consider systems comprising components whose dynamics may be represented by continuous time Markov chains (CTMC). CTMCs model uncertainty by probabilistic distributions and may also include deterministic behaviour (i.e., that happens with probability 1 in a given state). Importantly, CTMCs allow the verification and quantification of properties that include real time.

We consider verification of dynamical properties using *model checking*, where properties are specified in temporal logic [6]. Importantly, such logics typically include an *until* operator, which expresses properties that include temporal causality. To quantify uncertainty and to consider events in real time, *numerical* model checking extends this idea to probabilistic systems, such as modelled by CTMCs. Current numerical model checking algorithms are polynomial in the size of the state space [1,6], but the state space scales exponentially with respect to the number of interacting variables, i.e., the intuitive notion of the size of the system. Techniques such as *symbolic* model checking [5], *partial order reduction* [14], *bounded* model checking [3] and *abstraction refinement* [7] have made model checking much more efficient in certain cases, but the majority of real systems remain intractable.

Statistical model checking (SMC) is a Monte Carlo technique that avoids the 'state explosion problem' [6] of numerical model checking by estimating the probability of a property from the proportion of simulation traces that individually satisfy it. SMC is largely immune to the size of the state space and takes advantage of Bernoulli random variable theory to provide confidence bounds for its estimates [20,25]. Since SMC requires independent simulation runs, verification can be efficiently divided on parallel computing architectures. SMC can thus offer a tractable approximate solution to industrial-scale numerical model checking problems that arise during design or certification of a system. SMC may nevertheless be computationally expensive with rare properties (which are often critical) and when high precision is required.

SMC relies on simulation, so in this work we propose a technique of *statistical abstraction* to boost the efficiency of simulation. We show how to construct adequate statistical abstractions of external systems and we provide a corresponding stochastic simulation algorithm that maintains existing optimisations and respects the causality of the original system. We demonstrate that it is possible to make useful gains in performance with suitable systems. We provide a metric to judge a priori that an abstraction is good and an indicator to warn when the abstraction is not good in practice. Importantly, we show that a statistical abstraction may be optimised for critical rare properties, such that overall performance is better than simulation without abstraction.

The basic assumption of our approach is that we wish to apply SMC to a system comprising a *core* system in an environment of non-trivial *external* systems. In particular, we assume that properties of the external systems are not of interest, but that the environment nevertheless influences and provides input to the core. In this context, we define an external system to be one whose behaviour is not affected by the behaviour of the core or other external systems.

This may seem like a severe restriction, but this topology occurs frequently because it is an efficient and reliable way to construct large systems from modules. A simple example is a network of sensing devices feeding a central controller. Our case study is a complex biological signalling network that has this topology. To consider more general interactions would eliminate the modularity that makes statistical abstraction feasible.

Our idea is to replace the external systems with simple characterisations of their output, i.e., of the input to the core system. To guarantee the correct time-dependent behaviour of the environment, we find the best approach is to construct an abstraction based on an empirical distribution of traces, created by independent simulations of the external systems. During subsequent investigation, the core system is simulated against traces chosen uniformly at random from the empirical distributions of each of the external systems. The abstractions are constructed according to a metric based on frequency domain analysis. We make gains in performance because (i) the external systems are simulated in the absence of other parts of the system, (ii) the empirical distributions contain only the transitions of the variables that affect the core and (iii) the empirical distributions contain the minimum number of traces to adequately represent the observed behaviour of the variables of interest.

SMC generally has very low memory requirements, so it is possible to take advantage of the unused memory to store distributions of pre-simulated traces. Such distributions can be memory intensive, so we also consider memory-efficient abstractions using Gaussian processes, to approximates the external system on the fly. We give results that demonstrate the potential of this approach, using frequency domain analysis to show that it is possible to construct abstractions that are statistically indistinguishable from empirical abstractions.

Although our idea is simple in concept, we must show that we can achieve a gain in performance and that our algorithm produces correct behaviour. The first challenge arises because simulation algorithms are optimised and SMC already scales efficiently with respect to system size. We must not be forced to use inefficient simulation algorithms and the cost of creating the abstractions must not exceed the cost of just simulating the external systems. The second challenge arises because, to address the first challenge, we must adapt and interleave the simulation algorithms that are most efficient for each part of the system.

1.2   Related Work

Various non-statistical abstractions have been proposed to simplify the formal analysis of complex systems. These include partial order reduction [14], abstract interpretation [8] and lumping [19]. In this work we assume that such behaviour-preserving simplifications have already been applied and that what remains is a system intractable to numerical techniques. Such systems form the majority.

Approximating the dynamical behaviour of complex systems with statistical processes is well established in fields such as econometrics and machine learning. Using ideas from these fields, we show in Section 4.2 that abstracting external systems as Gaussian processes may be a plausible approach for SMC. We do not attempt to survey the considerable literature on this subject here, but mention some recent work [4] that, in common with our own, links continuous time Markov chains, temporal logic and Gaussian processes. The authors of [4] address a different problem, however. They use a Gaussian process to parametrise a CTMC that is not fully specified, according to temporal logic constraints.

Of greatest relevance to our approach is that of [2], which considers a complex heterogeneous communication system (HCS) comprising multiple peripheral devices (sensors, switches, cameras, audio devices, displays, etc.), that communicate bidirectionally via a central server. The authors of [2] use SMC to verify the correct communication timing of the HCS. To increase efficiency they replace the peripherals with *static* empirical distributions of their respective communication timings, generated by simulating the entire system. In contrast to our approach, (*i*) the quality of the statistical abstractions is not specified or measured, (*ii*) the distributions of the statistical abstractions are static (not varying with time) and (*iii*) the statistical abstractions are generated by simulating the entire system. The consequence of (*i*) is that it is not possible to say whether the abstractions adequately encapsulate the behaviour of the peripherals. The consequence of (*ii*) is that the abstractions do not allow for different behaviour at different times: a sequence of samples from the abstraction does not in general represent samples of typical behaviour, hence the abstraction does not preserve the behaviour of the original system. The consequence of (*iii*) is that the abstractions are generated at the cost of simulating the entire system, thus only allowing significant gains with multiple queries. A further consequence of (*ii*), in common with our own approach, is that the approach of [2] cannot model bidirectional communication. This remains an open problem.

1.3   Structure of the Paper

In Section 2 we use the equivalence of classic stochastic simulation algorithms to show how the simulation of a complex system may be correctly decomposed. We then present the compositional stochastic simulation algorithm we use for abstraction. In Section 3 we motivate the use of empirical distributions as abstractions and show how they may be validated using frequency domain analysis. In Section 3.2 we provide a metric to judge the a priori quality of an abstraction and in Section 3.3 we provide an a posteriori metric to help improve the critical performance of an abstraction. In Section 4 we give a brief overview of our biological case study and present results using empirical abstractions. In Section 4.2 we present promising results using Gaussian process abstractions. We conclude with Section 5. Appendix A gives full technical details of our case study.

2   Stochastic Simulation Algorithms

We consider systems generated by the parallel composition of *stochastic guarded commands* over state variables. A state of the system is an assignment of values to the state variables. A stochastic guarded command (referred to simply as a command) is a guarded command [9] with a stochastic rate, having the form (*guard, action, rate*). The *guard* is a logical predicate over the state, enabling the command; the *rate* is a function of the state, returning a positive real-valued *propensity*; the *action* is a function that assigns new values to the state variables. The semantics of an individual command is a continuous time Markov jump process, with an average stochastic rate of making jumps (transitions from one state to another) equal to its propensity. The semantics of a parallel composition of commands is a Markov jump process where commands compete to execute their actions. An evolution of the system proceeds from an initial state at time zero to a sequence of new states at monotonically increasing times, until some time bound or halting state is reached. The time between states is referred to as the delay. A halting state is one in which no guard is enabled or in which the propensities of all enabled commands are zero. Since the effect is equivalent, in what follows we assume, without loss of generality, that a disabled command has zero propensity.

In the following subsections we use the equivalence of classic stochastic simulation algorithms to formulate our compositional simulation algorithm.

2.1 Direct Method

Each simulation step comprises randomly choosing a command according to its probability and then independently sampling from an exponential distribution to find the delay. Given a system containing n commands whose propensities in a state are $p_1, \ldots, p_n$, the probability of choosing command i is $p_i / \sum_{j=1}^{n} p_j$. Command ν is thus chosen by finding the minimum value of ν that satisfies

$$\mathcal{U}(0, \sum_{j=1}^{n} p_j) \leq \sum_{i=1}^{\nu} p_i. \tag{1}$$

$\mathcal{U}(0, \sum_{j=1}^{n} p_j)$ denotes a value drawn uniformly at random from the interval $(0, \sum_{j=1}^{n} p_j)$. The delay time is found by sampling from an exponential probability density with amplitude equal to the sum of the propensities of the competing commands. Hence,

$$t = \frac{-\ln(\mathcal{U}(0, 1])}{\sum_{j=1}^{n} p_j}. \tag{2}$$

$\mathcal{U}(0, 1]$ denotes a value drawn uniformly at random from the interval $(0, 1]$.

2.2 First Reaction Method

In each visited state a 'tentative' delay time is generated for every command, by randomly sampling from an exponential distribution having probability density function $p_i e^{-p_i t}$, where p_i is the propensity of command i. The concrete delay time of this step is set to the smallest tentative time and the action to execute belongs to the corresponding command. Explicitly, the tentative delay time of command i is given by $t_i = -\ln(\mathcal{U}_i(0, 1])/p_i$. $\mathcal{U}_i(0, 1]$ denotes sample i drawn uniformly at random from the interval $(0, 1]$. Commands with zero propensity are assigned infinite times. It is known that the FRM is equivalent to the DM [12], but for completeness we give a simple proof.

Let $P_i = p_i e^{-p_i t}$ be the probability density of the tentative time t_i of command i. Since the tentative times are statistically independent, the joint probability density of all tentative times is simply the product of the n individual densities with respect to n time variables. The marginal density of tentative time t_i when it is the minimum is given by

$$P_i^{\min} = \int_{t_i}^{\infty} dt_1 \cdots \int_{t_i}^{\infty} dt_{i-1} \int_{t_i}^{\infty} dt_{i+1} \cdots \int_{t_i}^{\infty} dt_n \, P_1 \cdots P_n$$
$$= p_i e^{-t \sum_{j=1}^{n} p_j}.$$

Since only one command can have the minimum tentative time (the probability of two samples having the same value is zero), the overall density of times of the FRM is the sum of the marginal densities

$$\sum_{i=1}^{n} P_i^{\min} = \sum_{j=1}^{n} p_j e^{-t \sum_{k=1}^{n} p_k}.$$

This is the same density used by the DM (2).   ∎

2.3   Simulating Subsystems

A system described by a parallel composition of commands may be decomposed into a disjoint union of subsets of commands, which we call *subsystems* to be precise. By virtue of the properties of minimum and the equivalence of the DM and FRM, in what follows we reason that it is possible to simulate a system by interleaving the simulation steps of its subsystems, allowing each subsystem to be simulated using the most efficient algorithm.

Using the FRM, if we generate tentative times for all the commands in each subsystem and thus find the minimum tentative time for each, then the minimum of such times is also the minimum of the system considered as a whole. This time corresponds to the command whose action we must execute. By the equivalence of the DM and FRM, we can also generate the minimum tentative times of subsystems using (2) applied to the subset of propensities in each subsystem. Having chosen the subsystem with the minimum tentative time, thus also defining the concrete delay time, the action to execute is found by applying (1) to the propensities of the chosen subsystem. Similarly, we may select the subsystem by applying (1) to combined propensities $q_1, \ldots, q_i, \ldots$, where each q_i is the sum of the propensities in subsystem i. Having selected the subsystem, we can advance the state of the whole system by applying either the DM or FRM (or any other equivalent algorithm) to just the subsystem.

We define an *external* subsystem to be a subsystem whose subset of state variables are not modified by any other subsystem. We define a *core* subsystem to be a subsystem that does not modify the variables of any other subsystem.

Given a system that may be decomposed into a core subsystem and external subsystems, it is clear that traces of the external subsystems may be generated independently and then interleaved with simulations of the core subsystem. Simulations of the core subsystem, however, are dependent on the modifications to its state variables made by the external subsystems.

By virtue of the memoryless property of exponential distributions, the FRM will produce equivalent results using *absolute* times instead of relative delay times. This is the basis of the 'next reaction method' (NRM, [10]). Precisely, if a command is unaffected by the executed action, its tentative absolute time may be carried forward to the next step by subtracting the absolute tentative time of the selected command. Intuitively, the actions of commands that are momentarily independent are interleaved with the actions of the other commands. Since, by assumption, no action of the core or any other subsystem may affect the commands of the external subsystems, it is correct to simulate the core subsystem in conjunction with the interleaved absolute times of events in the simulations of the external subsystems. Moreover, it is only necessary to include transitions in the abstractions that modify the propensities of the commands in the core.

2.4 Compositional Stochastic Simulation Algorithm

Given a system comprising a core subsystem and external subsystems, the pseudo-code of our compositional simulation algorithm is given in Algorithm 1. The basic notion is intuitive: at each step the algorithm chooses the event that happens next. To account for the fact that the core is not independent of the external subsystems, the algorithm "backtracks" if the simulated time of the core exceeds the minimum next state time of the external subsystems.

Algorithm 1. Compositional stochastic simulation algorithm

Initialise all subsystems and set their times to zero
Generate the next state and time of all external subsystems
Let t_{core} denote the time of the core subsystem
while *new states are required and there is no deadlock* **do**
  Let ext_{min} be the external subsystem with minimum next state time
  Let t_{min} be the next state time of ext_{min}
  while $t_{core} < t_{min}$ **do**
    Generate the next state and time of the core
    Output the global state at time t_{core}
  Disregard the last state and time of the core
  Output the global state according to ext_{min} at t_{min}
  Generate the next state and time of ext_{min}

Algorithm 1 does not specify how the next states of each subsystem will be generated. Importantly, we have shown that it is correct to simulate external subsystems independently, so long as the chosen simulation algorithms produce traces equivalent to those of the FRM and DM. Algorithm 1 thus provides the flexibility to use the best method to simulate each part of the system. With a free choice of algorithm, worst case performance for an arbitrary subsystem of n commands is $\mathcal{O}(n)$ per step. If a subsystem has low update dependence between commands, asymptotic performance could be as low as $\mathcal{O}(\log_2 n)$ using the NRM [10].

Algorithm 1 is our abstraction simulation algorithm, using statistical abstractions to provide the next states of the external subsystems. In the case of empirical distribution abstractions, this amounts to reading the next state of a randomly selected stored trace. In the case of Gaussian process abstractions, new states need only be generated when old states are consumed.

3   Empirical Distribution Abstraction

We propose the use of a relatively small number of stored simulation traces as an empirical distribution abstraction of an external subsystem, where the traces need only contain the changes of the output variables.

The output trace of a stochastic simulation is a sequence of states, each labelled with a monotonically increasing time. The width of the trace is equal to the number of state variables, plus one for time. Each new state in the full trace corresponds to the execution of one of the commands in the model. Typically, the action of a single command updates only a small subset of the state variables. Hence, the value of any variable in the trace is likely to remain constant for several steps. Given that the core system is only influenced by a subset of the variables in the external system, it is possible to reduce the width of the abstraction by ignoring the irrelevant variables. Moreover, it is possible to reduce the length of the trace by ignoring the steps that make no change to the output variables.

We argue that we may adequately approximate an external subsystem by a finite number of stored traces, so long as their distribution adequately "covers" the variance of behaviour produced by the subsystem. To ensure that a priori the empirical distribution encapsulates the majority of typical behaviour, in Section 3.2 we provide a metric based on frequency domain analysis. Recognising that some (rare) properties may be critically dependent on the external system (i.e., depend on properties that are rare in the empirical distribution of the external subsystem), in Section 3.3 we provide an indicator to alert the user to improve the abstraction. The user may then create abstractions that favour rare (critical) properties and perform better than standard simulation.

3.1   Frequency Domain Analysis

Characterising the "average" empirical behaviour of stochastic systems is challenging. In particular, the mean of a set of simulation traces is not adequate because random phase shifts between traces cause information to be lost. Since delay times between transitions are drawn from exponential random variables, two simulations starting from the same initial state may drift out of temporal synchronisation, even if their sequences of transitions are identical. For example, in the case of an oscillatory system, the maxima of one simulation trace may eventually coincide with the minima of another, such that their average is a constant non-oscillatory value.

To characterise the behaviour of our abstractions we therefore adopt the frequency domain technique proposed in [23] and used in [17]. In particular, we apply the discrete Fourier transform (DFT) to simulation traces, in order to transform them from the time domain to the frequency domain. The resulting individual frequency spectra, comprising ordered sets of frequency components, may be combined into a single average spectrum. Once the behaviour has been characterised in this way, it is possible to compare it with the average spectra of other systems or abstractions.

The Fourier transform is linear and reversible, hence the resulting complex frequency spectra (i.e., containing both amplitude and phase angle components) are an adequate dual of what is seen in the time domain. Amplitude spectra (without considering phase) are common in the physics and engineering literature because the effects of phase are somewhat non-intuitive and phase is not in general independent of amplitude (i.e., the phase is partially encoded in the amplitude). We have found that the phase component of spectra generated by simulations of CTMCs is uninformative (in the information theoretic sense) and that by excluding the phase component we are able to construct an average frequency spectrum that does not suffer the information loss seen in the time domain. This provides a robust and sensitive empirical characterisation of the average behaviour of a system or of a statistical abstraction.

Our technique can be briefly summarised as follows. Multiple simulation traces are sampled at a suitable fixed time interval δt and converted to complex frequency spectra using an efficient implementation of the DFT:

$$f_m = \sum_{n=0}^{N-1} x_n e^{-i\frac{2\pi mn}{N}} \tag{3}$$

Here i denotes $\sqrt{-1}$, f_m is the mth frequency component (of a total of N) and x_n is the nth time sample (of N) of a given system variable. By virtue of consistent sampling times, the N frequencies in each complex spectrum are the same and may be combined to give a mean distribution. Since the DFT is a linear transformation, the mean of the complex spectra is equivalent to the DFT of the mean of the time series. Hence, to avoid the information loss seen in the time domain, we calculate the mean of the *amplitudes* of the complex spectra, thus excluding phase.

The values of N and δt must be chosen such that the resulting average spectrum encapsulates all the high and low frequencies seen in the interesting behaviour. In practice, the values are either pre-defined or learned from the behaviour seen in a few initial simulations, according to the following considerations.

$N\delta t$ is the overall time that the system is observed and must obviously be sufficiently long to see all behaviour of interest. Equivalently, $(N\delta t)^{-1}$ is the minimum frequency resolution (the difference between frequencies in the spectrum) and must be small enough to adequately capture the lowest interesting frequency in the behaviour. To make low frequency spectral components appear more distinct (and be more significant in the average spectrum), it may be useful to make $N\delta t$ much longer than the minimum time to see all behaviour (e.g., double), however this must be balanced against the cost of simulation and the cost of calculating (3) (typically $O(N \log N)$).

The quantity $(2\delta t)^{-1}$ defines the maximum observable frequency (the Nyquist frequency) and must be chosen to capture the highest frequency of interest in the behaviour. The theoretical spectrum of an instant discrete transition has frequency components that extend to infinity, however the amplitude of the spectrum decreases with increasing frequency. In a stochastic context, the highest frequency components are effectively hidden below the noise floor created by the stochasticity. The practical consequence is that δt may be made much greater than the minimum transition time in the simulation, without losing information about the average behaviour.

In summary, to encapsulate the broadest range of frequencies in the average spectrum it is generally desirable to decrease δt and increase $N\delta t$. However, setting the value of δt too low may include a lot of uninteresting noise in the spectrum, while setting $N\delta t$ too large may include too much uninteresting low frequency behaviour. In both cases there is increased computational cost.

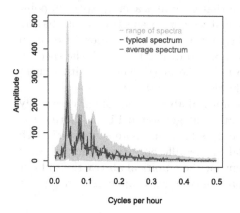

Fig. 1. Frequency spectra of protein complex (C) in genetic oscillator [24]

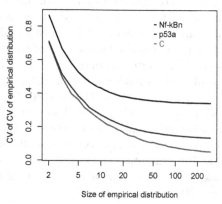

Fig. 2. Convergence of empirical distribution abstractions

To quantify similarity of behaviour, in this paper we use the discrete space version of the Kolmogorov-Smirnov (K-S) statistic [21] to measure the distance between average amplitude spectra. Intuitively, the K-S statistic is the maximum absolute difference between two cumulative distributions. This gives a value in the interval $[0,1]$, where 0 corresponds to identical distributions. Heuristically, we consider two distributions to be "close" when the K-S statistic is less than 0.1.

Fig. 1 illustrates our technique of frequency domain analysis applied to 1000 simulations of the protein complex (denoted C) in the genetic oscillator of [24].

3.2   Adequacy of Empirical Abstractions

In Fig. 1 we see that spectrum of an individual simulation trace is noisy, but the mean is apparently smooth. In fact, the average frequency spectrum comprises discrete points, but because of random phase shifts between simulation traces of CTMCs, there is a strong correlation between adjacent frequencies. To formalise this, using the notation of (3), we denote a frequency magnitude spectrum as $\bigcup_{m=0}^{N-1} |f_m|$, where $|f_m|$ is the magnitude of frequency component m. The mean spectrum of an empirical abstraction containing M simulation traces is thus written $\bigcup_{m=0}^{N-1} \frac{1}{M} \sum_{j=1}^{M} |f_m^{(j)}|$, where $|f_m^{(j)}|$ is the magnitude of frequency component m in spectrum j. Using the notion of *coefficient of variation* (CV, defined as the standard deviation divided by the mean), to quantify the a priori adequacy of an empirical distribution abstraction we define the metric

$$\mathrm{CV}(\bigcup_{m=0}^{N-1} \mathrm{CV}(\bigcup_{j=1}^{M} |f_m^{(j)}|)) \tag{4}$$

The CV is a normalised measure of dispersion (variation). $\mathrm{CV}(\bigcup_{j=1}^{M} |f_m|)$ is then the normalised dispersion of the data that generates average spectral point m. Normalisation is necessary to give equal weight to spectral points having high and low values, which have equal significance in this context. Equation (4) is the normalised dispersion of the normalised dispersions of all the spectral points. The outer normalisation aims to make the metric neutral with respect to subsystems having different absolute levels of stochasticity.

Figure 2 illustrates (4) applied to the empirical abstractions of our case study (NF-kBn and p53a), as well as to the data that generated Fig. 1. Noting the logarithmic x-scale, we observe that the curves have an apprent "corner", such that additional simulations eventually make little difference. The figure suggests that 100 simulation traces will be sufficient for the empirical abstractions of our case study. An empirical abstraction of protein complex C appears to require at least 200 simulation traces.

3.3   Critical Abstractions

Our metric allows us to construct empirical abstractions that encapsulate a notion of the typical behaviour of an external system, in an incremental way. However, certain properties of the core system may be critically dependent on behaviour that is atypical in a "general purpose" abstraction. To identify when it is necessary to improve an empirical abstraction, we provide the following indicator.

We consider the empirical abstraction of an arbitrary external subsystem and assume that it contains N_A independently generated simulation traces. After performing SMC with N simulations of the complete system, we observe that n

satisfy the property, giving n/N as the estimate of the probability that the system satisfies the property. Each simulation requires a sample trace to be drawn from the empirical distribution, hence n samples from the empirical abstraction were "successful". These n samples are not necessarily different (they cannot be if $n > N_A$), so by n_A we denote the number of different samples that were successful. Assuming N to be sufficiently large, we can say that if $n_A/N_A > n/N$ the external subsystem is relatively unimportant and the abstraction is adequate. Intuitively, the core "restricts" the probability of the external subsystem. If $n_A/N_A \leq n/N$, however, the property may be critically dependent on the external subsystem, because a smaller proportion of the behaviour of the subsystem satisfies the property than the system as a whole. This condition indicates that the abstraction may not be adequate for the particular property. Moreover, if the absolute value of n_A is low, the statistical confidence of the overall estimate is reduced. To improve the abstraction, as well as the overall efficiency with respect to the property, we borrow techniques from *importance splitting* [18].

The general idea is to increase the occurrence of traces in the abstraction that satisfy the property, then compensate the estimate by the amount their occurrence was increased. If the property of the subsystem that allows the core system to satisfy the property is known (call it the 'subproperty'), we may construct an efficient empirical abstraction that guarantees $n_A/N_A \geq n/N$ in the following way. SMC is performed on the subsystem using the subproperty, such that only traces that satisfy the subproperty are used in the abstraction. Any properties of the core using this abstraction are conditional on the subproperty and any estimates must be multiplied by the estimated probability of the subproperty with respect to the subsystem (call this the 'subprobability'). In the case of multiple subsystems with this type of abstraction, the final estimate must be multiplied by the product of all subprobabilities.

Using these ideas it is possible to create a set of high performance abstractions optimised to verify rare critical behaviour of complex evolving systems.

4   Case Study

Biological systems are an important and challenging area of interest for formal verification (e.g., [15]). The challenges arise from complexity, scale and the lack of complete information. In contrast to the verification of man-made systems, where it is usual to check behaviour with respect to an intended specification, formal verification of biological systems is often used to find out how they work or to hypothesise unknown interactions. Hence, it is not the actual system that evolves, but the model of the system, and the task is to ensure that modifications do not affect the critical function of existing parts.

To demonstrate our techniques we consider a biological model of coupled oscillatory systems [17]. The model pre-dates the present work and was constructed to hypothesise elemental reactions linking important biological subsystems, based on available experimental evidence. A core model of the *cell cycle* receives external oscillatory signals from models of protein families NF-κB and p53. Although the semantics of the model is chemical reactions, it is nevertheless typical of many computational systems. The model contains 93 commands and a crude estimate of the total number of states is 10^{174} (estimated from the range of values seen in simulations). An overview of the model is given in Appendix A, with precise technical details given in Tables 1 to 5. A more detailed biological description is given in [17].

4.1 Results

The external subsystems in our biological case study are themselves simplifications of very much larger systems, but we are nevertheless able to make substantial improvements in performance by abstraction. The improvements would be greater still if we were to consider the unsimplified versions of the external subsystems. The following numerical results are the average of hundreds of simulations and may be assumed to be within $\pm 5\%$ of the extreme values.

The behavioural phenomena in the case study require simulations of approximately 67 hours of simulated time, corresponding to approximately 72×10^6 simulation steps in the complete model. Of this, approximately 40×10^6 steps are due to the p53 system and approximately 20×10^6 steps are due to the NF-κB system. The abstracted traces of p53a are approximately 5.2×10^6 steps, while the abstracted traces of NF-kBn are approximately 1.3×10^6 steps. Hence, an equivalent simulation using these abstractions with Algorithm 1 requires only about 18.5×10^6 steps. Moreover, because we remove 41 commands from the model, each step takes approximately 52/93 as much time. Overall, we make a worthwhile seven-fold improvement in simulation performance.

On the basis of the results presented in Fig. 2, we suppose that 100 traces are adequate for our empirical distributions. This number is likely to be more than an order of magnitude fewer than the number of simulations required for SMC, so there is a saving in the cost of checking a single property, even when the cost of creating the abstractions is included. Subsequent savings are greater. By considering only the output variables p53a and NF-kBn, the size of each trace is reduced by factors of approximately 27 and 85, respectively. Without compression, the empirical abstractions for p53a and NF-kBn occupy approximately 2.4 and 0.6 gigabytes of memory, respectively. This is tractable with current hardware, however we anticipate that a practical implementation will compress the empirical abstractions using an algorithm optimised for fast decompression, e.g., using the Lempel-Ziv-Oberhumer (LZO) library.[1]

4.2 Gaussian Process Abstraction

In this section we report promising results using a memory-efficient form of statistical abstraction based on *Gaussian processes*. If we can generate traces that are statistically indistinguishable from samples of the original distribution, we can avoid the storage costs of an empirical distribution. Gaussian processes are popular in machine learning [22] and work by constructing functions that

---

[1] www.oberhumer.com/opensource/lzo

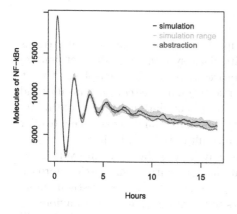
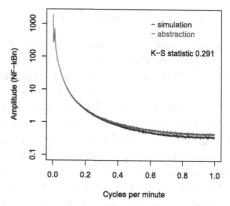

Fig. 3. Traces of NF-kBn generated by simulation and abstraction

Fig. 4. Average spectra of simulation and abstraction of NF-kBn

model the time evolution of the mean and covariance of multivariate Gaussian random variables.

Since we wish to judge our abstraction with frequency domain analysis, we construct a simple process that generates sampled traces directly. This is suffi-cient to reveal the potential and shortfalls of the approach. We assume a train-ing set of M sampled simulation traces of the output variable of a subsystem, denoted $\bigcup_{j=1}^{M}(x_n^{(j)})_{n=0}^{N-1}$, where $x_n^{(j)}$ is the nth sample of variable x in simula-tion trace j. From this we construct a sequence of Gaussian random variables $(X_n)_{n=1}^{N-1}$, where $X_n \sim \mathcal{N}(\text{Mean}_{j\in\{1,...M\}}(x_n^{(j)} - x_{n-1}^{(j)}), \text{Variance}_{j\in\{1,...,M\}}(x_n^{(j)} - x_{n-1}^{(j)}))$. Each X_n thus models the change in values from sample $n-1$ to sample n. A trace $(y)_{n=0}^{N-1}$ may be generated from this abstraction by setting $y_0 = x_0$ (the initial value) and iteratively calculating $y_n = y_{n-1} + \xi_n$, where ξ_n is a sample from X_n.

To judge the performance of our abstraction we measure the K-S distance between empirical distributions generated by the original system and by the Gaussian processes. We then compare this with the K-S distance between two empirical distributions generated by the original system (the 'self distance'). In this investigation all distributions contain 100 traces. With infinitely large distri-butions the expected self distance is zero, but the random variation between finite distributions causes the value to be higher. With 100 traces the self distances for p53a and NF-kBn are typically 0.02 ± 0.01. The K-S distances between the Gaussian process abstractions and empirical distributions of simulations form the original systems are typically 0.03 for p53a and 0.3 for NF-kBn. Using this metric, the p53a abstraction is almost indistinguishable from the original, but the abstraction for NF-kBn is not adequate. Figs. 3 and 4 illustrate the per-formance of the Gaussian process abstraction for NF-kBn. At this scale the p53a abstraction is visually indistinguishable from the original and is therefore not shown.

5 Challenges and Prospects

Empirical distribution abstractions are simple to construct, provide sample traces that are correct with respect to the causality of the systems they abstract, but are memory-intensive. In contrast, Gaussian processes offer a memory-efficient away to abstract external systems, but do not implicitly guarantee correct causality and their parameters must be learned from no fewer simulations than would be required for an empirical distribution. Despite this, Gaussian processes seem to offer the greatest potential for development, as a result of their scalability.

Our preliminary results suggest that it may be possible to create very good abstractions with Gaussian processes, but that our current simplistic approach will not in general be adequate. Our ongoing work will therefore investigate more sophisticated processes, together with ways to guarantee that their behaviour respects the causality of the systems they abstract. Their increased complexity will necessarily entail more sophisticated learning techniques, whose computational cost must also be included when considering efficiency.

A substantial future challenge is to adapt our techniques to systems with bidirectional communication between components. In this context empirical distributions are unlikely to be adequate, since the abstractions would be required to change in response to input signals. One plausible approach is to construct Gaussian processes parametrised by functions of input signals.

References

1. Baier, C., Haverkort, B., Hermanns, H., Katoen, J.: Model-checking algorithms for continuous-time markov chains. IEEE Transactions on Software Engineering 29(6), 524–541 (2003)
2. Basu, A., Bensalem, S., Bozga, M., Caillaud, B., Delahaye, B., Legay, A.: Statistical abstraction and model-checking of large heterogeneous systems. In: Hatcliff, J., Zucca, E. (eds.) FMOODS 2010, Part II. LNCS, vol. 6117, pp. 32–46. Springer, Heidelberg (2010)
3. Biere, A., Cimatti, A., Clarke, E., Zhu, Y.: Symbolic model checking without bDDs. In: Cleaveland, W.R. (ed.) TACAS 1999. LNCS, vol. 1579, pp. 193–207. Springer, Heidelberg (1999)
4. Bortolussi, L., Sanguinetti, G.: Learning and designing stochastic processes from logical constraints. In: Joshi, K., Siegle, M., Stoelinga, M., D'Argenio, P.R. (eds.) QEST 2013. LNCS, vol. 8054, pp. 89–105. Springer, Heidelberg (2013)
5. Burch, J.R., Clarke, E.M., McMillan, K.L., Dill, D.L., Hwang, L.-J.: Symbolic model checking: 10^{20} states and beyond. Information and Computation 98(2), 142–170 (1992)
6. Clarke, E.M., Emerson, E.A., Sifakis, J.: Model checking: algorithmic verification and debugging. ACM Commun. 52(11), 74–84 (2009)
7. Clarke, E.M., Grumberg, O., Long, D.E.: Model checking and abstraction. ACM Transactions on Programming Languages and Systems (TOPLAS) 16(5), 1512–1542 (1994)
8. Cousot, P., Cousot, R.: Abstract interpretation: a unified lattice model for static analysis of programs by construction or approximation of fixpoints. In: Proceedings of the 4th ACM SIGACT-SIGPLAN Symposium on Principles of Programming Languages, pp. 238–252. ACM (1977)

9. Dijkstra, E.W.: Guarded commands, nondeterminacy and formal derivation of programs. ACM Commun. 18, 453–457 (1975)
10. Gibson, M., Bruck, J.: Efficient exact stochastic simulation of chemical systems with many species and many channels. J. of Physical Chemistry A 104, 1876 (2000)
11. Gillespie, D.T.: Stochastic simulation of chemical kinetics. Annual Review of Physical Chemistry 58(1), 35–55 (2007)
12. Gillespie, D.T.: A general method for numerically simulating the stochastic time evolution of coupled chemical reactions. Journal of Computational Physics 22(4), 403–434 (1976)
13. Gillespie, D.T.: A rigorous derivation of the chemical master equation. Physica A 188, 404–425 (1992)
14. Godefroid, P.: Using partial orders to improve automatic verification methods. In: Clarke, E., Kurshan, R.P. (eds.) CAV 1990. LNCS, vol. 531, pp. 176–185. Springer, Heidelberg (1991)
15. Heath, J., et al.: Probabilistic model checking of complex biological pathways. Theoretical Computer Science 391, 239–257 (2008)
16. Hinchey, M., Coyle, L.: Evolving critical systems. In: 2010 17th IEEE International Conference and Workshops on Engineering of Computer Based Systems (ECBS), p. 4 (March 2010)
17. Ihekwaba, A., Sedwards, S.: Communicating oscillatory networks: frequency domain analysis. BMC Systems Biology 5(1), 203 (2011)
18. Jegourel, C., Legay, A., Sedwards, S.: Importance splitting for statistical model checking rare properties. In: Sharygina, N., Veith, H. (eds.) CAV 2013. LNCS, vol. 8044, pp. 576–591. Springer, Heidelberg (2013)
19. Kemeny, J.G., Knapp, A.W., Snell, J.L.: Denumerable markov chains. Springer (1976)
20. Okamoto, M.: Some inequalities relating to the partial sum of binomial probabilities. Annals of the Institute of Statistical Mathematics 10, 29–35 (1959)
21. Pettitt, A.N., Stephens, M.A.: The Kolmogorov-Smirnov Goodness-of-Fit Statistic with Discrete and Grouped Data. Technometrics 19(2), 205–210 (1977)
22. Rasmussen, C.E., Williams, C.K.I.: Gaussian Processes for Machine Learning. MIT Press (2006)
23. Sedwards, S.: A Natural Computation Approach To Biology: Modelling Cellular Processes and Populations of Cells With Stochastic Models of P Systems. PhD thesis, University of Trento (2009)
24. Vilar, J.M.G., Kueh, H.Y., Barkai, N., Leibler, S.: Mechanisms of noise-resistance in genetic oscillators. Proceedings of the National Academy of Sciences 99(9), 5988–5992 (2002)
25. Wald, A.: Sequential Tests of Statistical Hypotheses. Annals of Mathematical Statistics 16(2), 117–186 (1945)

A   Model of Coupled Oscillatory Systems

Fig. 5 illustrates the direct effect that one chemical species in the model has on another. Each node represents a state variable, whose value records the instantaneous number of molecules of a chemical species. The edges in the graph are directional, having a source and destination node. Influence that acts in both directions is represented by a bi-directional edge. Positive influence implies that increasing the number of source molecules will increase the number of destination molecules. The presence of an edge in the diagram indicates the existence of a command in which the source species variable appears in the *rate* and the destination species variable appears in the *action*. The variables that we use to abstract the external systems, namely p53a and NF-kBn, are highlighted in red.

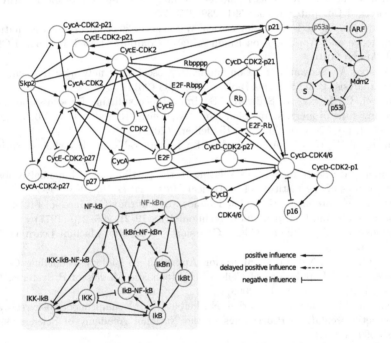

Fig. 5. Direct influence of variables in the case study. External systems are shown on grey backgrounds. Variables in red are used in abstractions.

The precise technical details of the model are given in Tables 1 to 5. Table 2 gives the reaction scheme of the core system (the cell cycle). Tables 1 and 3 contain the reactions schemes of the external systems (NF-κB and p53, respectively). Table 4 gives the initial numbers of molecules of each species and Table 5 gives the values of the constants used.

The model is given in terms of chemical reactions for compactness and to be compatible with previous work on these systems. Reactions have the form *reactants* → *products*, where *reactants* and *products* are possibly empty multisets of chemical species, described by the syntax $\emptyset$ | S { "+" S }, in which $\emptyset$ denotes the empty multiset and S is the name of a chemical species. The semantics of reactions assumes that the system contains a multiset of molecules. A reaction is enabled if *reactants* is a subset of this multiset. An enabled reaction is executed by removing *reactants* from the system and simultaneously adding *products*.

The rate at which a reaction is executed is stochastic. The majority of the reactions in our model are 'elemental' [11], working by 'mass action kinetics' according to fundamental physical laws [13]. Hence, under the assumption that the system is 'well stirred' [13], the rate at which a reaction is executed is given by the product of some rate constant k and the number of ways that *reactants* may be removed from the system. Elemental reactions in our model are thus converted to commands according to the following table.

Reaction pattern	Command (*guard, rate, action*)
$\emptyset \to A$	$(true, k, A = A + 1)$
$A \to B$	$(A > 0, kA, A = A - 1; B = B + 1)$
$A \to B + C$	$(A > 0, kA, A = A - 1; B = B + 1; C = C + 1)$
$A + B \to C$	$(A > 0 \wedge B > 0, kAB, A = A - 1; B = B - 1; C = C + 1)$
$A + B \to C + D$	$(A > 0 \wedge B > 0, kAB, A = A - 1; B = B - 1; C = C + 1; D = D + 1)$

A few of the reactions are abstractions of more complex mechanisms, using Michaelis-Menten dynamics, Hill coefficients or delays. The semantics of their execution is the same, so the *guard* and *action* given above are correct, but the *rate* is given by an explicit function. Delays appear in the rate as a function of a molecular species S and a delay time τ. The value of this function at time t is the number of molecules of S at time $t - \tau$.

The reaction rate constants and initial values have been inferred using ODE models that consider concentrations, rather than numbers of molecules. To convert the initial concentrations to molecules, they must be multiplied by a discretisation constant, alpha, having the dimensions of volume. Specifically, alpha is the product of Avogadro's number and the volume of a mammalian cell. The rate constants must also be transformed to work with numbers of molecules. The rate constants of reactions of the form $\emptyset \to \cdots$ must be multiplied by alpha. The rate constants of reactions of the form $A + B \to \cdots$ must be divided by alpha. The rate constants of reactions of the form $A \to \cdots$ may be used unaltered. In the case of explicit functions that are the product of a rate constant and a number of molecules raised to some power h, the value of the constant must be divided by alpha^{h-1}.

Table 1. NF-κB reactions

Reaction	Rate constant or [function]
IkB → ∅	kdeg1
IkB → IkBn	ktp1
IkB + NFkB → IkBNFkB	la4
IkBt → IkB + IkBt	ktr1
IkBn → IkB	ktp2
IkBn + NFkBn → nIkBNFkB	la4
IkBn → ∅	kdeg1
nIkBNFkB → IkBn + NFkBn	kd4
nIkBNFkB → IkBNFkB	k2
nIkBNFkB → NFkBn	kdeg5
IkBNFkB → nIkBNFkB	k3
IkBt → ∅	ktr3
∅ → IkBt	tr2a
∅ → IkBt	$[tr2 \times (NFkBn)^h]$
IkBNFkB → IkB + NFkB	kd4
IkBNFkB → NFkB	kdeg4
IKK + IkB → IKKIkB	la1
IKK + IkBNFkB → KIkBNFkB	la7
IKK → ∅	k02
IKKIkB → IKK + IkB	kd1
IKKIkB → IKK	kr1
IKKIkB + NFkB → KIkBNFkB	la4
KIkBNFkB → IKK + IkBNFkB	kd2
KIkBNFkB → IKKIkB + NFkB	kd4
KIkBNFkB → NFkB + IKK	kr4
NFkB → NFkBn	k1
NFkBn → NFkB	k01

Table 2. Cell cycle reactions

Reaction	Rate constant or [function]
CycDCDK46 → CDK46	R1
CycDCDK46 + p16 → CycDCDp16	R29
CycDCDK46 + p27 → CycDCDp27	R6
CycDCDK46 → CDK46 + CycD	R21b
CycD + CDK46 → CycDCDK46	R21a
CDK46 → ∅	R32
CycACDK2 + E2F → CycACDK2	R15
∅ → E2F	R43
E2F → E2F + E2F	R42
CycE → ∅	R26
E2F → CycE + E2F	R2
CycECDK2 → CDK2	R3
CycECDK2 → CDK2 + CycE	R24b
CDK2 + CycE → CycECDK2	R24a
CDK2 + CycA → CycACDK2	R25a
CDK2 → ∅	R33
CycA → ∅	R27
E2F → CycA + E2F	R4
CycACDK2 → CDK2	R5
CycACDK2 → CycA + CDK2	R25b
p27 + CycECDK2 → CycECDp27	R7
p27 + CycACDK2 → CycACDp27	R8
∅ → p27	R20
CycECDp27 + Skp2 → Skp2 + CycECDK2	R9
CycACDp27 + Skp2 → Skp2 + CycACDK2	R10
Skp2 → ∅	R34
∅ → Skp2	R31
Rb → ∅	R18
Rb + E2F → E2FRb	R11
∅ → Rb	R17
Rbpppp → Rb	R16
CycDCDK46 + E2FRb → E2FRbpp + CycDCDK46	R12
CycDCDp27 + E2FRb → E2FRbpp + CycDCDp27	R13
CycDCDp21 + E2FRb → E2FRbpp + CycDCDp21	R41
E2FRbpp + CycECDK2 → CycECDK2 + Rbpppp + E2F	R14
CycDCDp16 → p16	R19
p16 → ∅	R23
∅ → p16	R28
CycD → ∅	R22
E2F → CycD + E2F	R44
∅ → CycD	R30a
p21 + CycDCDK46 → CycDCDp21	R35a
p21 + CycECDK2 → CycECDp21	R36a
p21 + CycACDK2 → CycACDp21	R37a
∅ → p21	R40a
CycDCDp21 → p21 + CycDCDK46	R35b
CycECDp21 → p21 + CycECDK2	R36b
Skp2 + CycECDp21 → CycECDK2 + Skp2	R38
CycACDp21 → p21 + CycACDK2	R37b
Skp2 + CyCACDp21 → CycACDK2 + Skp2	R39
∅ → CycD	$[\text{R30b} \times (\text{NFkBn})^h]$
p53a → p21 + p53a	R40b

Table 3. p53 reactions

Reaction	Rate constant or [function]
p53i + Mdm2 → Mdm2	kap53i
∅ → p53i	kbp53i
p53a + Mdm2 → Mdm2	kap53a
p53i → p53a	[w×(Sn/(Sn+Ts))×p53i]
ARF + p53a → 2 p53a	R46
Mdm2 → ∅	kaMdm2
Mdm2 + ARF → ∅	R48
∅ → Mdm2	[kbMdm2×delay(p53a,tau)]
I → ∅	kai
∅ → I	[kbi×(delay(p53a,tau)+delay(p53i,tau))]
ARF → ∅	R47
∅ → ARF	R45a
S + I → I	kas
∅ → S	kbs×e

Table 4. Initial number of molecules

Species	Amount	Species	Amount
p53i	0	CycECDK2	0
p53a	0.1×alpha	CDK2	2.0×alpha
Mdm2	0.15×alpha	CycA	0
I	0.1×alpha	CycACDK2	0
S	0	p27	1.0×alpha
ARF	0	CycDCDp27	0.001×alpha
IkB	0	CycECDp27	0
IkBn	0	CycACDp27	0
nIkBNFkB	0	Skp2	1.0×alpha
IkBt	0	Rb	1.0×alpha
IkBNFkB	0.2×alpha	E2FRb	1.95×alpha
IKK	0.2×alpha	E2FRbpp	$1.0×10^{-3}$×alpha
IKKIkB	0	Rbpppp	1.02×alpha
KIkBNFkB	0	CycDCDp16	$1.0×10^{-5}$×alpha
NFkB	0	p16	1.0×alpha
NFkBn	0.025×alpha	CycD	0
CycDCDK46	0	p21	0
CDK46	5.0×alpha	CycDCDp21	0
E2F	0	CycECDp21	0
CycE	0	CycACDp21	0

Table 5. Values of constants

Name	Value	Name	Value	Name	Value
alpha	100000	R8	7.0×10^{-2}/alpha	R35b	5.0×10^{-3}
h	2	R9	0.225/alpha	R36a	1.0×10^{-2}/alpha
kdeg1	0.16	R10	2.5×10^{-3}/alpha	R36b	1.75×10^{-4}
ktp1	0.018	R11	5.0×10^{-5}/alpha	R37a	7.0×10^{-2}/alpha
ktp2	0.012	R12	1.0×10^{-4}/alpha	R37b	1.75×10^{-4}
ktr1	0.2448	R13	1.0×10^{-2}/alpha	R38	0.225/alpha
kd4	0.00006	R14	0.073/alpha	R39	2.5×10^{-3}/alpha
la1	0.1776/alpha	R15	0.022/alpha	R40a	5.0×10^{-5}×alpha
kd1	0.000888	R16	5.0×10^{-8}	R40b	1.0×10^{-3}
la4	30/alpha	R17	5.0×10^{-5}×alpha	R41	1.0×10^{-2}/alpha
k2	0.552	R19	5.0×10^{-2}/alpha	R42	1.0×10^{-4}
k3	0.00006	R20	1.0×10^{-4}×alpha	R43	5.0×10^{-5}×alpha
tr2a	0.000090133×alpha	R21a	2.0×10^{-3}/alpha	R44	3.0×10^{-4}
ktr3	0.020733	R21b	8.0×10^{-3}	R45a	8.0×10^{-5}×alpha
tr2	$0.5253/\text{alpha}^{(h-1)}$	R22	7.5×10^{-3}	R45b	0.008
kdeg4	0.00006	R23	5.0×10^{-3}	R46	2.333×10^{-5}/alpha
kdeg5	0.00006	R24a	8.0×10^{-3}/alpha	R47	0.01167
la7	6.06/alpha	R24b	3.9×10^{-3}	R48	1.167×10^{-5}/alpha
kd2	0.095	R25a	8.0×10^{-3}/alpha	kbp53i	0.015×alpha
kr1	0.012	R25b	4.0×10^{-3}	kbMdm2	0.01667
kr4	0.22	R26	2.5×10^{-3}	kap53i	2.333/alpha
k1	5.4	R27	5.0×10^{-4}	kaMdm2	0.01167
k01	0.0048	R28	2.0×10^{-4}×alpha	tau	80
k02	0.0072	R29	5.0×10^{-4}/alpha	kap53a	0.02333/alpha
R1	5.0×10^{-6}	R30a	0.004×alpha	kas	0.045/alpha
R2	4.5×10^{-3}	R30b	$0.9961/\text{alpha}^{(h-1)}$	kbi	0.01667
R3	5.0×10^{-3}	R31	5.0×10^{-4}×alpha	kai	0.01167
R4	2.5×10^{-3}	R32	8.0×10^{-4}	kbs	0.015×alpha
R5	5.0×10^{-4}	R33	8.0×10^{-4}	e	1
R6	5.0×10^{-4}/alpha	R34	9.0×10^{-4}	n	4
R7	1.0×10^{-2}/alpha	R35a	5.0×10^{-4}/alpha	w	11.665
				Ts	$1 \times \text{alpha}^{n}$

Combinatory Logic Synthesizer

Jan Bessai, Andrej Dudenhefner, Boris Düdder, and Moritz Martens,
and Jakob Rehof

Technical University of Dortmund, Department of Computer Science,
Dortmund, Germany

Abstract. We present Combinatory Logic Synthesizer (CL)S, a type-based tool to automatically compose larger systems from repositories of components. We overview its underlying theory, combinatory logic with intersection types, and exemplify its application to synthesis. We describe features and architecture of the tool and our plans for its ongoing and future development. Finally, we present some use cases in ongoing work, especially in the context of synthesis for Object Oriented Software.

1 Introduction

Combinatory logic synthesis [1] is a type-theoretic approach towards synthesis from specified components in a repository. Components are represented by typed combinators $(X : \rho)$ where X is the component name and ρ is an intersection type [2] representing both the compontent's actual interface type and semantic information describing the component's intended usage. The question whether there is a composition e of components in the repository such that e satisfies a certain goal specification τ corresponds to the *relativized inhabitation problem* in combinatory logic — given a set Γ of typed combinators and a goal type τ, does there exist an applicative term e (referred to as an *inhabitant*) of type τ under the type assumptions in Γ? Algorithms solving the relativized inhabitation problem for certain combinatory logics have been given [3,4,5], thus laying the foundation for a tool-realization of combinatory logic synthesis.

In this paper we report on current work on and on experiments with Combinatory Logic Synthesizer, (CL)S,[1] an end-to-end prototypical tool, providing user-support in design of repositories, a core inhabitation routine based on the above mentioned inhabitation algorithms, optimizing heuristics of the inherently complex core algorithms, and means of translating synthesized compositions into executable code in various implementation languages.

The paper is structured as follows. Section 2 develops background information on combinatory logic synthesis, provides an overview of related work and discusses a motivating example. In Section 3 we describe the architecture and the current state of development of (CL)S. In Section 4 we discuss ongoing work and plans for future development. Section 5 concludes by presenting some examples from ongoing work on applications of our tool, particularly within the context of Object Oriented software by means of Java Virtual Machine languages.

---

[1] http://www-seal.cs.tu-dortmund.de/seal/pages/research/cls_en.shtml

T. Margaria and B. Steffen (Eds.): ISoLA 2014, Part I, LNCS 8802, pp. 26–40, 2014.
© Springer-Verlag Berlin Heidelberg 2014

2 Background and Related Work

The work presented in this paper is closely related to current movements[2] towards component-based synthesis, where synthesis is considered relative to a given collection (library, repository) of components rather than aiming at construction of a system "from scratch". Possible benefits of relativizing synthesis to component collections include the exploitation of design intelligence and abstraction (in the form of abstract component interfaces) embodied by components. Moreover, modern development scenarios increasingly depend on extended usage of components. However, for component-oriented synthesis to work well, components presumably need to be designed for composition.

Synthesis approaches can be distinguished by the model of computation as well as the methods of specification assumed. One line of work is characterized by the usage of temporal logic and automata theoretic models, whereas another is characterized by the usage of deductive methods in program logics (e.g., [6]) and in type theory. A recent comprehensive introduction and survey on program synthesis is presented in [7] providing a categorization scheme for synthesis methods. Within this scheme combinatory logic synthesis is classifiable as functional synthesis with semantic candidate spaces.

Recently, component-orientation was promoted in the automata theoretic approach by Lustig and Vardi [8]. Combinatory logic synthesis was proposed in [1] as a deductive, type-based approach to synthesis from components in a repository, where repositories are regarded as type environments in combinatory logic [9]. Component interfaces are specified semantically using intersection types [2]. The logical basis for combinatory logic synthesis is the relativized inhabitation problem, in that algorithms for solving this problem can be used to automatically synthesize component compositions (inhabitants).

The pioneering work on synthesizing linear process models (sequential composition of calls to components) in [10] combines temporal constraints with types and subtyping to capture taxonomic hierarchies. Combinatory logic synthesis is related to adaptation synthesis via proof counting discussed in [11,12], where semantic types are combined with proof search in a specialized proof system. In particular, we follow the approach in [11,12] in using semantic specifications at the interface level, where semantic specifications are assumed to correctly describe properties of the component (checking that this is indeed so is regarded as an orthogonal issue). The idea of adaptation synthesis in [11] is related to our notion of composition synthesis, however our logic is different, our design of semantic types with intersection types is novel, and the algorithmic methods are different. Semantic intersection types can be compared to refinement types [13], but semantic types do not need to stand in a refinement relation to implementation types. Still, refinement types are a great source of inspiration for how semantic types can be used in specifications in many interesting situations.

---

[2] http://www.dagstuhl.de/de/programm/kalender/semhp/?semnr=14232.

2.1 Composition Synthesis

In its minimal form, composition synthesis consists of a single logical rule:

$$\frac{\Gamma \vdash F : \tau' \to \tau \quad \Gamma \vdash G : \tau'}{\Gamma \vdash (F\ G) : \tau}(\to\text{E})$$

The ($\to$E)-rule (viewed logically, under the Curry-Howard isomorphism, this is modus ponens) forms the simplest logical model of applicative composition of *named component specifications* $(X : \rho) \in \Gamma$ from a *repository* Γ, satisfying *goal* τ. With fixed Γ and τ as part of the input, the *inhabitation problem* is the decision problem

$$\exists e.\ \Gamma \vdash e : \tau?$$

— does there exist a composition e from repository Γ with $\Gamma \vdash e : \tau$? An inhabitation algorithm is used to *construct* or synthesize a composition e from Γ and τ. The inhabitation problem is the foundation for *automatic synthesis* and is inherently *component-oriented*.

In a type-oriented approach to composition synthesis, types (τ) take the role of specifications of named components represented by terms (e):

$$\text{Types } \tau, \tau' ::= a \mid \alpha \mid \tau \to \tau'$$
$$\text{Terms } e, e' ::= X \mid (e\ e')$$

Types are constructed from constants (a), variables (α), or function types ($\tau \to \tau'$). Terms are constructed by using named components or combinators X and using application of e to e', ($e\ e'$). An additional rule (var) is added to allow schematic instantiations of combinator types (component specifications) using substitutions.

$$\frac{\text{Substitution } S}{\Gamma, (X : \tau) \vdash X : S(\tau)}(\text{var}) \qquad \frac{\Gamma \vdash e : \tau' \to \tau \quad \Gamma \vdash e' : \tau'}{\Gamma \vdash (e\ e') : \tau}(\to \text{E})$$

From a logical point of view, this system is a Hilbert-style presentation of a minimal propositional logic based on implicit schematism (var) and modus ponens ($\to$E).

2.2 Example for Combinatory Logic Synthesis

The idea of combinatory logic synthesis is demonstrated by the following example presenting a scenario for tracking containers in logistics (see also [1] where this example was introduced). Figure 1 presents a repository Γ containing existing (API-)functions for tracking containers, where R is the data-type real. Function O returns a tracking object TrObj. Given a tracking object TrObj, function Tr returns a triple of which the first entry is a coordinate of the tracking object, followed by time information, and the current temperature of the tracking object. The function pos projects the position and time from such a triple. Function cdn projects the coordinate and functions fst and snd project the first resp. second

```
0     : TrObj
Tr    : TrObj → D((R, R), R, R)
pos   : D((R, R), R, R) → ((R, R), R)
cdn   : ((R, R), R) → (R, R)
fst   : (R, R) → R
snd   : (R, R) → R
tmp   : D((R, R), R, R) → R
cc2pl : ((R, R), R) → ((R, R), R)
cl2fh : R → R
```

Fig. 1. Repository Γ containing functions for tracking containers in logistics

entry in a pair like a coordinate. Function tmp returns the temperature. Two additional conversion functions cc2pl and cl2fh are contained, that convert Cartesian to polar coordinates and temperature from Celsius to Fahrenheit.

Figure 2 presents a taxonomy that describes semantic concepts, noted in blue, in our scenario. Dashed lines denote a *has-a* relationship whereas continuous lines denote an *is-a* relationship. In particular, *Trackdata* contains a position *Pos* and a temperature *Temp* that can be measured in Celsius *Cel* or Fahrenheit *Fh*.

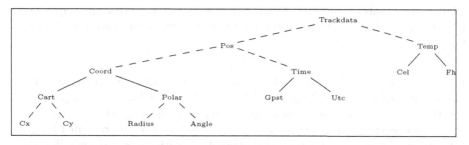

Fig. 2. Taxonomy describing semantic concepts for tracking containers.

None of the semantic information is explicitly included in Γ but only in its verbose description. A central idea in our approach to combinatory logic synthesis is that intersection types, introduced in [2], can be used to semantically refine the specification of functions contained in the repository Γ, for example by adding abstract conceptual information from a taxonomy. Figure 3 presents such a refined repository $\mathcal{C}$. Native types, such as R, are intersected with semantic types, such as *Cel* or *Fh*, to specify meaning, e.g. in cl2fh the type $\mathrm{R} \cap Cel$ describes a temperature represented by a real number w.r.t. the Celsius scale whereas the type $\mathrm{R} \cap Fh$ describes a temperature represented by a real number w.r.t. the Fahrenheit scale. Type variables (α, α') facilitate generic combinators like tmp which is applicable to temperatures in both measurement systems.

We can now find a meaningful composition that returns a temperature in Fahrenheit by constructing the inhabitant cl2fh (tmp (Tr 0)) of the type $\mathrm{R} \cap Fh$, formally:

```
0      : TrObj
Tr     : TrObj → D((R, R)∩Cart, R∩Gpst, R∩Cel)
pos    : D((R, R)∩α, R∩α′, R) → ((R, R)∩α, R∩α′)∩Pos
cdn    : ((R, R)∩α, R)∩Pos → (R, R)∩α
fst    : ((R, R)∩Coord → R)∩(Cart → Cx)∩(Polar → Radius)
snd    : ((R, R)∩Coord → R)∩(Cart → Cy)∩(Polar → Angle)
tmp    : D((R, R), R, R∩α) → R∩α
cc2pl  : (R, R)∩Cart → (R, R)∩Polar
cl2fh  : R∩Cel → R∩Fh
```

Fig. 3. Semantically refined repository $\mathcal{C}$

$$\mathcal{C} \vdash \text{cl2fh (tmp (Tr 0))} : \text{R} \cap Fh$$

In general, the situation in combinatory logic synthesis is the following. We are *given* a repository of component names X_i (regarded as combinator symbols in combinatory logic) with associated implementations C_i of type τ_i in a native implementation language L1

$$X_1 \triangleq C_1 : \tau_1, \ldots, X_n \triangleq C_n : \tau_n$$

Thus, a combinator symbol X_i is used as a placeholder for a concrete implementation C_i. In addition, we are *given* an associated repository as a combinatory type environment

$$\mathcal{C} = \{X_1 : \phi_1, \ldots, X_n : \phi_n\}$$

where ϕ_i represents τ_i augmented by semantic information describing the type of the implementation of C_i in L1. Then, we *ask for* combinatory compositions e with $\mathcal{C} \vdash e : \phi$ such that e satisfies, in addition, the property of *implementation type correctness* requiring that e be a well-typed program in L1 after substituting all occurring combinator symbols X_i with their corresponding implementations C_i.

Since repositories $(\Gamma, \mathcal{C})$ may change, we consider the *relativized inhabitation* problem: given $\mathcal{C}$ and ϕ, does there exist e such that $\mathcal{C} \vdash e : \phi$? Later on, we will use the abbreviating notation $\mathcal{C} \vdash ? : \phi$. In the tracking example above such an $e = \text{cl2fh (tmp (Tr 0))}$ is the synthesized composition for the request $\phi = \text{R} \cap Fh$. Even in simple types, relativized inhabitation is undecidable (as explained in [1], this can be traced to the Linial-Post theorem [14]) and can be considered a Turing-complete logic programming language for generating compositions (see [1]). Here, $\mathcal{C}$ can be viewed as a logic program, the types of combinators $(X : \phi) \in \mathcal{C}$ are its rules, ϕ its input goal, and search for inhabitants its execution semantics.

2.3 Staged Extension

In order to flexibilize combinatory logic synthesis, staged composition synthesis (SCS) was proposed in [5]. SCS introduces a metalanguage, L2, in which L1-code can be manipulated. The metalanguage is essentially the $\lambda_e^{\square\rightarrow}$-calculus of Davies and Pfenning [15] which introduces a modal type operator, $\square$, to inject L1-types into the type-language of L2. Intuitively, a type $\square\tau$ can be understood to describe L1-code of L1-type τ. A second repository containing *composition components* with implementations in L2 is introduced. Then, synthesis automatically composes both L1- and L2-components, resulting in more flexible and powerful forms of composition since complex L1-code-maniualations, including substitutions of code into L1-templates, may be encapsulated in composition components. It is a nice consequence of the operational semantic theory of $\lambda_e^{\square\rightarrow}$ that computation can be *staged*. For a composition e of type $\square\tau$, it is guaranteed that all L2-operations can be computed away in a first *composition time* stage, leaving a well typed L1-program of type τ to be executed in a following *runtime* stage.

3 Combinatory Logic Synthesizer

In order to make composition synthesis feasible and accessible for experiments, and for application to realistic synthesis scenarios, we implemented the synthesis tool (CL)S. The core synthesis algorithm implements an optimized version of the inhabitation procedure [4] in Microsoft™ F# and C# using the Microsoft™ .NET-framework. In the following we discuss various features of (CL)S. Note also, that we extended (CL)S for conducting synthesis within SCS (cf. Sec. 2.3).

3.1 Tool

Input: To allow a user to specify component repositories, we defined an input language for (CL)S which is closely related to the mathematical notation of intersection types. To aid the user in specifying repositories (CL)S provides editor-extensions (for Microsoft™ Visual Studio 2013 and Notepad++) with syntax-highlighting, code completion, etc. For convenience and more concise representation of types we extended the input language by covariant type constructors, e.g., the type (R, R) represents a pair of real numbers where $(\cdot, \cdot)$ is a type constructor for a pair of types. Furthermore, we allow variable kinding, where type variables, e.g. α in the example in Sect. 2.2, can be kinded by restricting the range of values (type constants) that the variable can be instantiated with, e.g., $\alpha_{\text{temp}}\sim>\{Cel, Fh\}$ states that α_{temp} can be instantiated by the type constants Cel or Fh (but not by $Cart$). In order to represent taxonomic structures (cf. Sec. 2.2) on the semantic concepts describing intended usage of various components, (CL)S allows for explicit introduction of atomic subtyping constraints, e.g., $\text{int} \leq R$, expressing the fact that the type of integers is a subtype of the type of reals.

Processing: Processing of a synthesis question can be represented as a graph. This graph is called execution graph and contains two kinds of nodes. The first kind represents the choices of the algorithm and the other kind represents additionally generated synthesis tasks. Edges represent control flow. We implemented a data structure for internal representation of the execution graph where the nodes are decorated with additional information concerning performance, processing, etc. In contrast to the algorithm presented in [4], which only decides if there is a solution to a given synthesis request, (CL)S also enumerates all (if the solution space is finite — otherwise the user is informed that cyclic solutions have been found) possible solutions. This last feature of (CL)S is essential concerning the applicability of composition synthesis.

(CL)S supports two different processing modes that have both been compiled for Windows as well as for Linux (using Mono). These are a batch-mode processing a synthesis request from a local file and a webservice-mode for synthesis requests on a remote server. The webservice exposes endpoints offering access via SOAP and REST. To this end, there are two hosting solutions of the webservice. First, there is a stand-alone server, mainly intended for usage in experiments. Second, there is a hosted version for application servers (IIS), intended for usage in industrial settings.

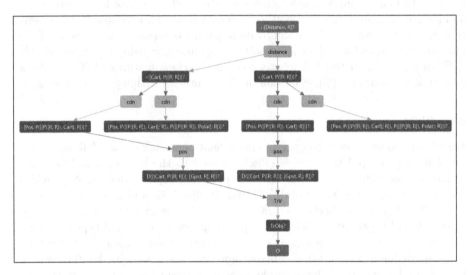

Fig. 4. Example of Execution Graph

Output: (CL)S provides various output formats depending on the intended usage of the results. First and foremost, there exists an XML-representation of the solutions to a given synthesis request for further processing. Also note that the XML-representation, among others, includes a human readable representation. Second, it is possible to export the execution graph corresponding to a given synthesis request to various formats, which can then be displayed visually (cf. Fig. 4). This feature is particularly important for an in depth analysis of a synthesis process. It supports both with regard to error-detection in the design of repositories as well as for conducting experiments, allowing to apply graph-analysis and -processing tools.

Finally, various configurable logging functionalities are provided by (CL)S which is a crucial feature with regard to debugging and analyzing experiments.

3.2 Optimizations

To increase efficiency of the synthesis algorithm we implemented various optimizations that aim for acceleration of synthesis with respect to orthogonal aspects. First, in order to allow for scale-up and scale-out, we moved from a sequential implementation of the core synthesis algorithm to a concurrent one. Parallelization of the algorithm was necessary to exploit computation facilities in contemporary multi-core and cluster computing environments. Concurrency of the algorithm is facilitated by the above mentioned execution graph controlling synthesis. Parallelization needed sophisticated algorithm engineering as well as distributed techniques, like work-stealing queues and distributed message queues.

It has been shown that the simplest decision problems underlying combinatory logic synthesis (relativized inhabitation in bounded combinatory logic) is superexponential (EXPTIME-complete for monomorphic combinator types [3] and $(k+2)$-EXPTIME-complete for k-bounded combinatory logic [4]). Thus, heuristics for optimizing inhabitation is essential for application in practical scenarios. We implemented one such heuristic (which is based on the type theoretical problem of intersection type matching [16]) which formulates a necessary condition (referred to as "lookahead-strategy") for newly generated synthesis requests to be solvable. We experimentally compared the impact of the lookahead-strategy to the performance of the initial synthesis-algorithm of (CL)S. One experiment does arithmetic in $\mathbb{Z}_n$ and is parameterized by two integers, m and n (cf. Sec. 4.1 for details). Timing results for both implementations and different values of n and m can be found in Tab. 1 (cf. Sec. 4.1).

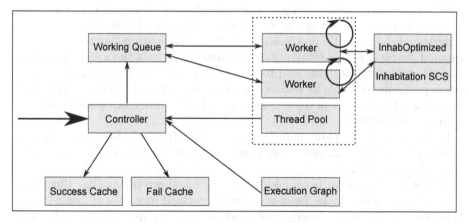

Fig. 5. Dependency Diagram for (CL)S

Using caches for successful and failed synthesis requests showed improvement. Cycle-detection in the execution graph allows for avoidance of cyclic inhabitants.

3.3 Architecture

The core architecture of (CL)S is depicted in Fig. 5. It is a modular master-slave architecture with a controller as master and thread-pooled slaves processing the synthesis requests with modular algorithms (e.g. the lookahead algorithm InhabOptimized). A work-stealing queue contains the synthesis tasks for each slave and the execution graph is the computation and synchronization data-structure. The success and fail caches are used by the controller for pruning unnecessary computations. The main challenges in design and implementation are concurrency issues imposed by the distribution of the algorithm.

4 Current and Future Work

Currently, our (CL)S implementation is undergoing major structural changes. We integrate, on a more fundamental level, existing features that are currently added-on, such as type constants, variable kinding and covariant type constructors, and we tune the integration for performance.

In the current redesign cycle we emphasize maintainability of (CL)S and extend it by new features. From a user perspective, the most important new feature extends cycle detection to cycle analysis. In many applications, cyclic structures both on type- and on term level are essential for meaningful constructions. The current framework presents the whole solution space, including cycles, in a concise data structure. From a performance perspective, the single most important new feature extends the lookahead-strategy by utilizing inherent monotonicity of several inhabitation subroutines.

We simplify existing type theoretic algorithms and improve their cooperation by introducing pre- and postconditions to enhance overall efficiency of (CL)S. Additionally, we prove tight upper complexity bounds of several type theoretic problems that are utilized by the inhabitation procedure. During the analysis of underlying type theoretic problems, we identify combinatorial subroutines (e.g. minimal set cover in inhabitation) and separate them from the main algorithm. The new theoretical insights lead to a more profound understanding of inhabitation performance limits as well as improvement in specialized cases. The next step forward will be to develop a more systematic theory of optimization for composition synthesis.

In future work we plan to further extend the theoretic foundation of our framework needed to expand it into important application areas such as object-oriented code synthesis.

Although we work with complexity classes far above polynomial time, our approach has proven to be feasible in many practical scenarios of limited size. Therefore, it is essential to analyze and understand the sources of complexity and non-determinism in (CL)S. In order to improve practical performance, we plan to algorithmically inspect and restructure user provided repositories to detect special cases. Furthermore, we see great potential in developing further heuristics to improve the lookahead-strategy.

4.1   Experimental Evaluation

In order to evaluate heuristic optimizations, we created a parameterized repository Γ_n^m for arithmetic in $\mathbb{Z}_n$, exploiting the fact that finite function tables can be coded by means of intersection types [2]. Γ_n^m consists of the identity-, successor- and predecessor-function in $\mathbb{Z}_n$ as well as an m-ary combinator to compose $\mathbb{Z}_n$-functions. For a $\mathbb{Z}_n$-function coded by an intersection type τ_n, we ask the inhabitation question $\Gamma_n^m \vdash? : \tau_n$, i.e., we synthesize the particular $\mathbb{Z}_n$-function. The runtime performance of the initial (CL)S implementation, of a version of (CL)S using lookahead, and of the redesigned (CL)S are captured in Tab. 1. Practically infeasible tasks are marked with "–". The lookahead-strategy provides a considerable improvement over the initial implementation, making inhabitation questions that often appear in practice solvable. Further experience with the framework led to substantial performance gains with the redesigned (CL)S which allows for new practical applications.

Table 1. Experimental Runtime Performance for Γ_n^m

(n, m)	Initial (CL)S	Lookahead-(CL)S	Redesigned (CL)S
$(2, 3)$	210 ms	111 ms	93 ms
$(3, 2)$	12504 ms	124 ms	98 ms
$(3, 3)$	–	354 ms	110 ms
$(4, 4)$	–	$7.5 * 10^6$ ms	121 ms
$(7, 7)$	–	–	1063 ms
$(10, 10)$	–	–	54250 ms
$(43, 3)$	–	–	8813 ms

4.2   Interfaces and Language Abstraction

The staged extension described in Sect. 2.3 is a valuable addition to our tool. Thus, it is an important part of our work to find encodings of L1-languages which are suitable for synthesis using L2-implementations. Our current language for L2-implementations is the $\lambda_e^{\square \to}$-calculus extended with a string based templating mechanism. We treat L1-code fragments as strings and allow L2-implementations to concatenate them and to fill in variables. After reduction no template variables are left and the resulting string is embedded into the XML reply format. This approach is easy to understand and very powerful, but it can be desirable to use tools more specialized for the structure of a given L1-language. Practical applications show the diversity of possible L1-targets. They include classical programming languages like F# or Java, workflow description languages like BPMN and even highly specialized domain specific languages for tasks such as the configuration of nodes in a cloud computing environment. To gain a more structured view than the one provided by plain strings, without losing generality, we plan to change our templating system to use XML encodings of abstract L1-syntax trees. This would not only allow to reason about reusable combinators for tree transformations, but also enables a standardized interface for postprocessors. These can parse the synthesized XML code fragment and translate it to any desirable representation. They can be implemented in any high level programming language and make use of the best available tools for the task at hand. The XML encoding would allow to incorporate a limited form of static model checking directly into the synthesis process: additionally to type checking, XPath could be used to assert structural properties of the generated L1-code and to sort out unwanted solutions early.

Figure 6 summarizes our envisioned synthesis pipeline. It starts with users providing source code fragments, possibly even as diagrams. These fragments are then (semi-automatically) translated to typed combinators with XML fragments and templating abstractions over XML fragments as implementations. Types (depicted as puzzle pieces for L1 and puzzle pieces with holes for L2) are intersected with user provided semantic types that guide the inhabitation process (depicted as colors). The typed combinator repository is then used as input for SCS. Combinators for L2 are reduced and the result will be XML fragments describing the abstract syntax tree of the synthesized programs. In a final step those syntax trees are postprocessed to real programs or possibly graphical representations of real programs. Pre- and postprocessing steps require careful design tailored for each individual inhabitation language. They build the bridge to the problem independent interface exposed by our inhabitation web service depicted as the SCS screw driver tool.

4.3   Software Engineering Process

The software engineering process plays a major role in the design of a complex tool like (CL)S. Currently, we mainly develop research prototypes with a focus on understandable and correct implementations demonstrating our theoretical results. In future, we plan to introduce a more formal development model in order to facilitate the growth of our team and to react to the short periods in which student members join us for their own project work. To this end, we plan to turn our research demonstrations into integration tests, which are automatically executed by a continuous integration server. This also involves an automatic build and deployment process, which has the additional benefit of simplifying cloud installations. Furthermore, we are currently reevaluating existing and creating new guidelines for our code structure. We explicitly leave open release and versioning policies to be able to catch up with new research results.

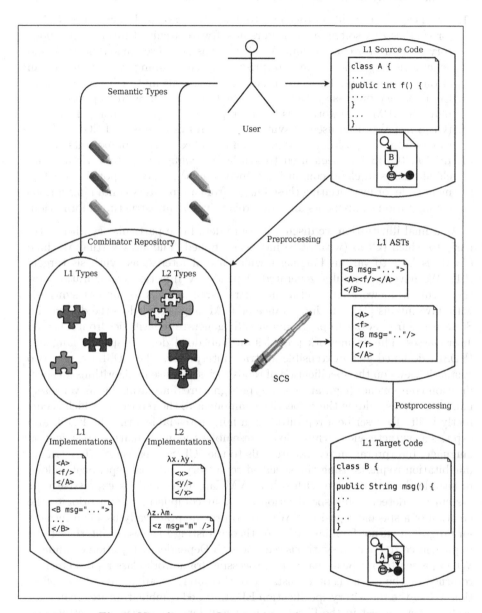

Fig. 6. Visualization of our envisioned process pipeline

5   Applications

(CL)S has already been applied to a variety of synthesis scenarios.

1. ArchiType[3], a rapid-prototyping tool for software architects, uses (CL)S for synthesizing software connectors in software architectures from a repository of connector components. ArchiType has been used in synthesizing and generating C#-code for an enterprise resource planning system and for an eCommerce system. These are relatively large-scale and realistic scenarios.
2. Combinatory process synthesis [17] uses (CL)S (with SCS) to generate deployable BPMN 2.0 workflows from a repository of process components.
3. (CL)S has also been used to synthesize control programs for LEGO® NXT robots from a repository of atomic and complex control components [18].
4. In [19], (CL)S has been used to synthesize configurations for virtual machine images in cloud computing (OpenNebula) and corresponding deployment code for instantiating these images from a repository containing various configuration components and comprehensive IT infrastructure information.

As a final illustration we discuss in more detail one particular synthesis scenario to which (CL)S (with SCS) has been applied. The Java Virtual Machine (JVM) is host to various languages which are of interest as synthesis targets (L1). We have successfully generated Dependency Injection configurations for the Spring framework [20] and a current research focus is to support synthesis with Java mixins [21]. The importance of JVM languages led to the design of a Scala based framework to programmatically generate repositories from reflected Java classes. This framework provides an embedded domain specific language (EDSL) designed as an extensible abstract interpreter. The EDSL exposes two syntactic views on the specification of repositories. For use in algorithms all specification components (e.g., arrows in type signatures) are available as verbosely named methods, adding the respective component to the repository which is currently built. To describe a repository in a human readable form, the EDSL also exposes a syntactic view, which closely resembles the mathematical specification language. Interpretation results are calls to the (CL)S webservice. They trigger inhabitation requests using the specified repository and goal type. Scala allows to seamlessly interoperate with other JVM languages and its expressive type system can detect many specification errors at compiletime, even prior to the creation of a specific repository. We aim to provide practically usable interfaces for programmers not familiar with type theory. Listing 1 shows the interface to be implemented to create a synthesis request for a Dependency Injection candidate. When passed to our Scala based preprocessing framework class representations returned by the methods of an instance of this interface are analyzed via reflection. Using the repository specification EDSL, typed combinators are created for each existing object in the library context and for all constructor-, setter- and factory-methods of the library classes. For example, a class `EmployeeController` with a constructor requiring a data access object (DAO) to obtain information about employees, triggers the creation of the following combinator

---

[3] http://www-seal.cs.tu-dortmund.de/seal/pages/research/architype_en.shtml

EmployeeController :($\Box$Scope $\cap\ \alpha$) $\rightarrow \Box$(EmployeeDAO $\cap\ \alpha$)

$\rightarrow \Box$(EmployeeController $\cap\ \alpha \cap$ setterTarget)

EmployeeController :λScope. letbox **scope** = Scope in

λDAO. letbox **dao** = DAO in

box "<bean xsi:type='cls:Constructor'>"

"<name>EmployeeController</name>"

"<typeName>EmployeeController</typeName>"

"<scope>"**scope**"</scope>"

"<argument>"

"<typeName>EmployeeDAO</typeName>"

"<reference>"**dao**"</reference>"

"</argument>"

"</bean>"

```
1  public interface InhabitationRequest {
2      public Class [] libraryClasses ();
3      public ConfigurableApplicationContext
          libraryContext ();
4      public String classNameExclusionRegexp ();
5      public Class targetType ();
6      public String targetScope ();
7  }
```

Listing 1. Interface to request Spring Dependency Injection candidates

The combinator takes two arguments, a scope supplying lifecycle information to Spring, and the data access object. It operates on boxed L1-terms, where L1 is an XML based representation of Spring Beans translatable to a Dependency Injection configuration via postprocessing. Its result is an L1-term describing how to instantiate an EmployeeController. Semantic constant setterTarget in the combinator result type indicates that setter-methods of the object may be used to inject more dependencies into it. The above mentioned extended $\lambda_e^{\Box\rightarrow}$-implementation already creates XML, but still treats it as strings, making it a candidate for the planned enhancements described in Sect. 4.2. Synthesis results for the described scenario and two given existing database connections are available online[4].

Compared to earlier versions [20], our recent developments allow more succinct combinator types, because cyclic scenarios can be addressed within the algorithm. Repository creation as well as calls to the webservice are automatized and wrapped into a Maven[5] plug-in, enabling the synthesis of Spring configurations at the click of a mouse button.

---

[4] http://www-seal.cs.tu-dortmund.de/seal/pages/research/DI-example.zip
[5] http://maven.apache.org/

References

1. Rehof, J.: Towards Combinatory Logic Synthesis. In: 1st International Workshop on Behavioural Types, BEAT 2013. ACM (2013)
2. Barendregt, H., Coppo, M., Dezani-Ciancaglini, M.: A Filter Lambda Model and the Completeness of Type Assignment. Journal of Symbolic Logic 48, 931–940 (1983)
3. Rehof, J., Urzyczyn, P.: Finite Combinatory Logic with Intersection Types. In: Ong, L. (ed.) Typed Lambda Calculi and Applications. LNCS, vol. 6690, pp. 169–183. Springer, Heidelberg (2011)
4. Düdder, B., Martens, M., Rehof, J., Urzyczyn, P.: Bounded Combinatory Logic. In: Proceedings of CSL 2012. LIPIcs, vol. 16, pp. 243–258. Schloss Dagstuhl (2012)
5. Düdder, B., Martens, M., Rehof, J.: Staged Composition Synthesis. In: Shao, Z. (ed.) ESOP 2014 (ETAPS). LNCS, vol. 8410, pp. 67–86. Springer, Heidelberg (2014)
6. Manna, Z., Waldinger, R.: Fundamentals Of Deductive Program Synthesis. IEEE Transactions on Software Engineering 18, 674–704 (1992)
7. Bodik, R., Jobstmann, B.: Algorithmic Program Synthesis: Introduction. International Journal on Software Tools for Technology Transfer 15, 397–411 (2013)
8. Lustig, Y., Vardi, M.Y.: Synthesis from Component Libraries. In: de Alfaro, L. (ed.) FOSSACS 2009. LNCS, vol. 5504, pp. 395–409. Springer, Heidelberg (2009)
9. Hindley, J.R., Seldin, J.P.: Lambda-calculus and Combinators, an Introduction. Cambridge University Press (2008)
10. Steffen, B., Margaria, T., von der Beeck, M.: Automatic Synthesis of Linear Process Models from Temporal Constraints: An Incremental Approach. In: In ACM/SIGPLAN Int. Workshop on Automated Analysis of Software, AAS 1997 (1997)
11. Haack, C., Howard, B., Stoughton, A., Wells, J.B.: Fully Automatic Adaptation of Software Components Based on Semantic Specifications. In: Kirchner, H., Ringeissen, C. (eds.) AMAST 2002. LNCS, vol. 2422, pp. 83–98. Springer, Heidelberg (2002)
12. Wells, J.B., Yakobowski, B.: Graph-Based Proof Counting and Enumeration with Applications for Program Fragment Synthesis. In: Etalle, S. (ed.) LOPSTR 2004. LNCS, vol. 3573, pp. 262–277. Springer, Heidelberg (2005)
13. Freeman, T., Pfenning, F.: Refinement Types for ML. In: Proceedings of PLDI 1991, pp. 268–277. ACM (1991)
14. Linial, L., Post, E.L.: Recursive Unsolvability of the Deducibility, Tarski's Completeness and Independence of Axioms Problems of Propositional Calculus. Bulletin of the American Mathematical Society 50 (1949)
15. Davies, R., Pfenning, F.: A Modal Analysis of Staged Computation. Journal of the ACM 48, 555–604 (2001)
16. Düdder, B., Martens, M., Rehof, J.: Intersection Type Matching with Subtyping. In: Hasegawa, M. (ed.) TLCA 2013. LNCS, vol. 7941, pp. 125–139. Springer, Heidelberg (2013)
17. Vasileva, A.: Synthese von Orchestrationscode für Cloud-basierte Dienste. Diploma thesis, Technical University of Dortmund, Department of Computer Science (2013)
18. Wolf, P.: Entwicklung einer Adapters mit VI Scripting (LabVIEW) zur Synthese von LEGO® NXT-VIs aus einem Repository. Bachelor's thesis, Technical University of Dortmund, Department of Computer Science (2013)
19. Plate, S.: Automatische Generierung einer Konfiguration für virtuelle Maschinen unter Zuhilfenahme eines Inhabitationsalgorithmus. Bachelor's thesis, Technical University of Dortmund, Department of Computer Science (2013)
20. Bessai, J.: Synthesizing Dependency Injection Configurations for the Spring Framework. Master's thesis, TU Dortmund, Department of Computer Science (2013)
21. Bracha, G.: The Programming Language Jigsaw: Mixins, Modularity and Multiple Inheritance. PhD thesis, University of Utah, Salt Lake City, UT, USA (1992)

Incremental Syntactic-Semantic Reliability Analysis of Evolving Structured Workflows

Domenico Bianculli[1], Antonio Filieri[2], Carlo Ghezzi[3], and Dino Mandrioli[3]

[1] University of Luxembourg
`domenico.bianculli@uni.lu`
[2] University of Stuttgart
`antonio.filieri@informatik.uni-stuttgart.de`
[3] Politecnico di Milano
`{carlo.ghezzi,dino.mandrioli}@polimi.it`

Abstract. Modern enterprise information systems are built following the paradigm of service-orientation. This paradigm promotes workflow-based software composition, where complex business processes are realized by orchestrating different, heterogenous components. These workflow descriptions evolve continuously, to adapt to changes in the business goals or in the enterprise policies. Software verification of evolving systems is challenging mainstream methodologies and tools. Formal verification techniques often conflict with the time constraints imposed by change management practices for evolving systems. Since changes in these systems are often local to restricted parts, an incremental verification approach could be beneficial.

In this paper we focus on the probabilistic verification of reliability requirements of structured workflows. We propose a novel incremental technique based on a syntactic-semantic approach. Reliability analysis is driven by the syntactic structure (defined by an operator-precedence grammar) of the workflow and encoded as semantic attributes associated with the grammar. Incrementality is achieved by coupling the evaluation of semantic attributes with an incremental parsing technique. The approach has been implemented in a prototype tool; preliminary experimental evaluation confirms the theoretical speedup over a non-incremental approach.

1 Introduction

Enterprise information systems are realized nowadays by leveraging the principles of service-oriented architecture [31]. This paradigm fosters the design of systems that rely on *workflow-based* composition mechanisms, like those offered by BPEL, where complex applications are realized by integrating different, heterogenous services, possibly from different divisions within the same organization or even from third-party organizations. These workflows often realize crucial business functions; their correctness and reliability is of ultimate importance for the enterprises.

Moreover, these systems represent an instance of *open-world software* [4] where, because of the intrinsic dynamicity and decentralization, service behaviors and interactions cannot be fully controlled or predicted. These characteristics, when bundled with the inherent need for enterprise software to evolve (e.g., to adapt to changes in the

T. Margaria and B. Steffen (Eds.): ISoLA 2014, Part I, LNCS 8802, pp. 41–55, 2014.

business goals or in the enterprise policies), require to rethink the various engineering phases, for dealing with the phenomenon of software evolution; in this paper we focus on the verification aspect.

Incremental verification has been suggested as a possible approach to dealing with evolving of software [36]. An incremental verification approach tries to reuse as much as possible the results of a previous verification step, and accommodates within the verification procedure—possibly in a "smart" way—the changes occurring in the new version. By avoiding re-executing the verification process from scratch, incremental verification may considerably reduce the verification time. This may be appealing for adoption within agile development processes. Incremental verification may speed up change management, which may be subject to severe time constraints. Moreover, incremental verification helps software engineers reason on and understand the effects and the implications of changes.

In this paper we propose a novel incremental technique for performing probabilistic verification of reliability requirements of structured workflows. Our technique follows a syntactic-semantic approach: reliability verification is *driven* by the structure of the workflow (prescribed by a formal grammar) and *encoded* as synthesis of semantic attributes [32], associated with the grammar and evaluated by traversing the syntax tree of the workflow. The technique is realized on top of SiDECAR [5,6] (Syntax-DrivEn inCrementAl veRification), our general framework to define verification procedures, which are automatically enhanced with incrementality by the framework itself. The framework is based on operator precedence grammars [21], which allow for re-parsing, and hence semantic re-analysis, to be confined within an inner portion of the input that encloses the changed part [3]. This property is the key for an efficient incremental verification procedure: since the verification procedure is encoded within attributes, their evaluation proceeds incrementally, hand-in-hand with parsing. We report on the preliminary evaluation of the tool implementing the proposed technique; the results shows a significant speedup over a non-incremental approach.

The rest of the paper is structured as follows. Section 2 introduces some background concepts on operator precedence grammars and attribute grammars. Section 3 shows how our framework exploits operator precedence grammars to support syntactic-semantic incremental verification. Section 4 details our incremental reliability verification technique. In Sect. 5 we present the preliminary experimental evaluation of the approach. Section 6 surveys related work. Section 7 provides some concluding remarks.

2 Background

Hereafter we briefly recall the definitions of operator precedence grammars and attribute grammars. For more information on formal languages and grammars, we refer the reader to [26] and [11].

2.1 Operator Precedence Grammars

A *context-free (CF)* grammar G is a tuple $G = \langle V_N, V_T, P, S \rangle$, where V_N is a finite set of non-terminal symbols; V_T is a finite set of terminal symbols, disjoint from V_N;

$$\begin{array}{lll}
\langle S\rangle & ::= \langle A\rangle & \{value(\langle S\rangle) = value(\langle A\rangle)\} \\
\langle S\rangle & ::= \langle B\rangle & \{value(\langle S\rangle) = value(\langle B\rangle)\} \\
\langle A_0\rangle & ::= \langle A_1\rangle \text{ `+' } \langle B\rangle & \{value(\langle A_0\rangle) = value(\langle A_1\rangle) + value(\langle B\rangle)\} \\
\langle A\rangle & ::= \langle B_1\rangle \text{ `+' } \langle B_2\rangle & \{value(\langle A\rangle) = value(\langle B_1\rangle) + value(\langle B_2\rangle)\} \\
\langle B_0\rangle & ::= \langle B_1\rangle \text{ `*' 'n'} & \{value(\langle B_0\rangle) = value(\langle B_1\rangle) * eval(\text{'n'})\} \\
\langle B\rangle & ::= \text{'n'} & \{value(\langle B\rangle) = eval(\text{'n'})\}
\end{array}$$

	'n'	'*'	'+'
'n'		$>$	$>$
'*'	$\doteq$		
'+'	$<$	$<$	$>$

(b)

(a)

Fig. 1. (a) Example of an operator grammar ('n' stands for any natural number), extended with semantic attributes; (b) its operator precedence matrix

$P \subseteq V_N \times (V_N \cup V_T)^*$ is a relation whose elements represent the rules of the grammar; $S \in V_N$ is the axiom or start symbol. We use the following naming convention, unless otherwise specified: non-terminal symbols are enclosed within chevrons, such as $\langle A\rangle$; terminal ones are enclosed within single quotes, such as '+' or are denoted by lowercase letters at the beginning of the alphabet $(a, b, c, \ldots)$; lowercase letters at the end of the alphabet $(u, v, x, \ldots)$ denote terminal strings; ε denotes the empty string. For the notions of *immediate derivation* ($\Rightarrow$), *derivation* ($\overset{*}{\Rightarrow}$), and the language $L(G)$ generated by a grammar G please refer to the standard literature, e.g., [26].

A rule is in *operator form* if its right hand side (rhs) has no adjacent non-terminals; an *operator grammar (OG)* contains only rules in operator form.

Operator precedence grammars (OPGs) [21] are defined starting from operator grammars by means of binary relations on V_T named *precedence*. Given two terminals, the precedence relations between them can be of three types: *equal-precedence* ($\doteq$), *takes-precedence* ($>$), and *yields-precedence* ($<$). The meaning of precedence relations is analogous to the one between arithmetic operators and is the basic driver of deterministic parsing for these grammars. Precedence relations can be computed in an automatic way for any operator grammar. We represent the precedence relations in a $V_T \times V_T$ matrix, named *operator precedence matrix (OPM)*. An entry $m_{a,b}$ of an OPM represents the set of operator precedence relations holding between terminals a and b. For example, Fig. 1b shows the OPM for the grammar of arithmetic expressions depicted at the left side of Fig. 1a. Precedence relations have to be neither reflexive, nor symmetric, nor transitive, nor total. If an entry $m_{a,b}$ of an OPM M is empty, the occurrence of the terminal a followed by the terminal b represents a malformed input, which cannot be generated by the grammar.

Definition 1 (Operator Precedence Grammar). *An operator grammar G is an operator precedence grammar if and only if its OPM is a conflict-free matrix, i.e., for each $a, b \in V_T, |m_{a,b}| \leq 1$.*

Definition 2 (Fischer Normal Form, from [11]). *An OPG is in Fischer Normal Form (FNF) if it is invertible, the axiom $\langle S\rangle$ does not occur in the right-hand side of any rule, no empty rule exists except possibly $\langle S\rangle \Rightarrow \varepsilon$, the other rules having $\langle S\rangle$ as left-hand side (lhs) are renaming, and no other renaming rules exist.*

The grammar of Fig. 1a is in FNF. In the sequel, we assume, without loss of generality, that OPGs are in FNF. Also, as is customary in the parsing of OPGs, the input strings are implicitly enclosed between two '#' special characters, such that '#' yields precedence to any other character and any character takes precedence over '#'. The key feature of OPG parsing is that a sequence of terminal characters enclosed within a pair $\lessdot \gtrdot$ and separated by $\doteq$ uniquely determines a rhs to be replaced, with a shift-reduce algorithm, by the corresponding lhs. Notice that in the parsing of these grammars non-terminals are "transparent", i.e., they are not considered for the computation of the precedence relations. For instance, consider the syntax tree of Fig. 2a generated by the grammar of Fig. 1a: the leaf '6' is preceded by '+' and followed by '*'. Because '+' $\lessdot$ '6' $\gtrdot$ '*', '6' is reduced to $\langle B \rangle$. Similarly, in a further step we have '+' $\lessdot$ $\langle B \rangle$ '*' $\doteq$ '7' $\gtrdot$ '*' and we apply the reduction $\langle B \rangle \Rightarrow \langle B \rangle$ '*' '7' (notice that non-terminal $\langle B \rangle$ is "transparent") and so on.

2.2 Attribute Grammars

Attribute Grammars (AGs) have been proposed by Knuth as a way to express the semantics of programming languages [32]. AGs extend CF grammars by associating *attributes* and semantic functions to the rules of a CF grammar; attributes define the "meaning" of the corresponding nodes in the syntax tree. In this paper we consider only *synthesized* attributes, which characterize an information flow from the children nodes (of a syntax tree) to their parents; more general attribute schemas do not add semantic power [32].

An AG is obtained from a CF grammar G by adding a finite set of attributes SYN and a set SF of semantic functions. Each symbol $X \in V_N$ has a set of (synthesized) attributes $SYN(X)$; $SYN = \bigcup_{X \in V_N} SYN(X)$. We use the symbol α to denote a generic element of SYN; we assume that each α takes values in a corresponding domain T_α. The set SF consists of functions, each of them associated with a rule p in P. For each attribute α of the lhs of p, a function $f_{p\alpha} \in SF$ synthesizes the value of α based on the attributes of the non-terminals in the rhs of p. For example, the grammar in Fig. 1a can be extended to an attribute grammar that computes the value of an expression. All nodes have only one attribute called *value*, with $T_{value} = \mathbb{N}$. The set of semantic functions SF is defined as in the right side of Fig. 1a, where semantic functions are enclosed in braces next to each rule. The $+$ and $*$ operators appearing within braces correspond, respectively, to the standard operations of arithmetic addition and multiplication, and $eval(\cdot)$ evaluates its input as a number. Notice also that, within a rule, different occurrences of the same grammar symbol are denoted by distinct subscripts.

3 Syntactic-Semantic Incrementality

Our incremental technique for probabilistic verification of reliability requirements of structured workflows is realized on top of SiDECAR [5,6], our general framework for incremental verification. The framework exploits a syntactic-semantic approach to define verification procedures that are encoded as semantic functions associated with an attribute grammar. In this section we show how OPGs, equipped with a suitable attribute schema, can support incrementality in such verification procedures in a natural and efficient way.

3.1 The Locality Property and Syntactic Incrementality

The main reason for the choice of OPGs is that, unlike more commonly used grammars that support deterministic parsing, they possess and benefit from the *locality property*, i.e., the possibility of starting the parsing from any arbitrary point of the sentence to be analyzed, independent of the context within which the sentence is located. In fact for OPGs the following proposition holds.

Proposition 1. If $a\langle A\rangle b \overset{*}{\Rightarrow} asb$, then, for every t, u, $\langle S\rangle \overset{*}{\Rightarrow} tasbu$ iff $\langle S\rangle \overset{*}{\Rightarrow} ta\langle A\rangle bu \overset{*}{\Rightarrow}$ *tasbu*. As a consequence, if s is replaced by v in the context $[\![ta, bu]\!]$, and $a\langle A\rangle b \overset{*}{\Rightarrow} avb$, then $\langle S\rangle \overset{*}{\Rightarrow} ta\langle A\rangle bu \overset{*}{\Rightarrow} tavbu$, and (re)parsing of *tavbu* can be stopped at $a\langle A\rangle b \overset{*}{\Rightarrow} avb$.

Hence, if we build—with a bottom-up parser—the derivation $a\langle A\rangle b \overset{*}{\Rightarrow} avb$, we say that a *matching condition* with the previous derivation $a\langle A\rangle b \overset{*}{\Rightarrow} asb$ is satisfied and we can replace the old subtree rooted in $\langle A\rangle$ with the new one, independently of the global context $[\![ta, bu]\!]$ (only the local context $[\![a, b]\!]$ matters for the incremental parsing).

For instance, consider the string and syntax tree of Fig. 2a. Assume that the expression is modified by replacing the term '6*7*8' with '7*8'. The corresponding new subtree can clearly be built independently within the context $[\![$'+', '#'$]\!]$. The matching condition is satisfied by '+'$\langle B\rangle$'#' $\overset{*}{\Rightarrow}$ '+''6''*''7''*''8''#' and '+'$\langle B\rangle$'#' $\overset{*}{\Rightarrow}$ '+''7''*''8''#'; thus the new subtree can replace the original one without affecting the remaining part of the global tree. If, instead, we replace the second '+' by a '*', the affected portion of syntax tree would be larger and more re-parsing would be necessary[1].

In general, the incremental parsing algorithm, for any replacement of a string w by a string w' in the context $[\![t, u]\!]$, automatically builds the minimal "sub-context" $[\![t_1, u_1]\!]$ such that for some $\langle A\rangle$, $a\langle A\rangle b \overset{*}{\Rightarrow} at_1wu_1b$ and $a\langle A\rangle b \overset{*}{\Rightarrow} at_1w'u_1b$.

The locality property[2] has a price in terms of generative power. For example, the LR grammars traditionally used to describe and parse programming languages do not enjoy it. However they can generate all the deterministic languages. OPGs cannot; this limitation, however, is more of theoretical interest than of real practical impact. Large parts of the grammars of many computer languages are operator precedence [26, p. 271]; a complete OPG is available for Prolog [8]. Moreover, in many practical cases one can obtain an OPG by minor adjustments to a non operator-precedence grammar [21].

In the current SiDECAR prototype, we developed an incremental parser for OPGs that exhibits the following features: linear complexity in the length of the string, in case of parsing from scratch; linear complexity in the size of the *modified subtree(s)*, in case of incremental parsing; $O(1)$ complexity of the matching condition test.

3.2 Semantic Incrementality

In a bottom-up parser, semantic actions are performed during a reduction. This allows the re-computation of semantic attributes after a change to proceed hand-in-hand with

---

[1] Some further optimization could be applied by integrating the matching condition with techniques adopted in [24] (not reported here for brevity).

[2] The locality property has also been shown to support an efficient parallel parsing technique [3], which is not further exploited here.

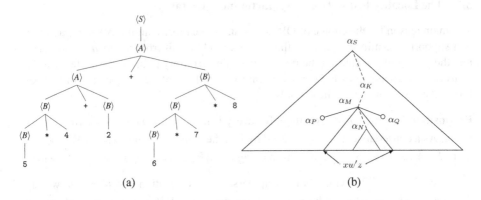

Fig. 2. (a) Abstract syntax tree of the expression '5*4+2+6*7*8'; (b) Incremental evaluation of semantic attributes on a generic syntax tree

the re-parsing of the modified substring. Suppose that, after replacing substring w with w', incremental re-parsing builds a derivation $\langle N \rangle \stackrel{*}{\Rightarrow} xw'z$, with the same non-terminal $\langle N \rangle$ as in $\langle N \rangle \stackrel{*}{\Rightarrow} xwz$, so that the matching condition is verified. Assume also that $\langle N \rangle$ has an attribute α_N. Two situations may occur related to the computation of α_N:

1) The α_N attribute associated with the new subtree rooted in $\langle N \rangle$ has the same value as before the change. In this case, all the remaining attributes in the rest of the tree will not be affected, and no further analysis is needed.

2) The new value of α_N is different from the one it had before the change. In this case (see Fig. 2b) only the attributes on the path from $\langle N \rangle$ to the root $\langle S \rangle$ (e.g., $\alpha_M, \alpha_K, \alpha_S$) may change and in such case they need to be recomputed. The values of the other attributes not on the path from $\langle N \rangle$ to the root (e.g., α_P and α_Q) do not change: there is no need to recompute them.

4   Incremental Reliability Analysis of Structured Workflows

In this section we define our procedure for incremental reliability analysis of structured workflows. As mentioned in the previous section, SiDECAR requires the verification procedure to be encoded as an attribute grammar schema. We assume that the structured workflows are written in a tiny and simple language called *Mini*, whose OPG is shown in Fig. 3. It is a minimalistic language that includes the major constructs of structured programming and allows for expressing the *sequence*, *exclusive choice*, *simple merge*, and *structured loops* patterns, from van der Aalst's workflow patterns collection [1].

The verification procedure is based on our previous work [14], which supports the analysis of workflow constructs similar to those in *Mini*, in a non-incremental way; we refer the reader to [14] for the technical choice behind the analysis itself. Moreover, for the sake of readability and to reduce the complexity of attribute schemas, *Mini* workflows support only (global) boolean variables; we model invocation of external services as boolean functions with no input parameters. We remark that more complex analyses and workflow languages (see, for example, the extension of [14] in [13] for support of BPEL business processes, including parallelism and nested workflows) could be supported with richer attribute schemas.

Reliability is a "user-oriented" property [9]; i.e., a software may be more or less reliable depending on its use. If user inputs do not activate a fault, a failure may never occur even in a software containing defects [2]; on the other hand, users may stress a faulty component, leading to a high frequency of failure events. Here we consider reliability as the probability of successfully accomplishing an assigned task, when requested.

To show the benefits of incrementality, we will apply the verification procedure to analyze two versions of the same example workflow (shown in Fig. 4a). They differ in the assignment at line 3, which determines the execution of the subsequent *if* statement, with implications on the results of the two analyses. Figure 4b depicts the syntax tree of version 1 of the workflow, as well as the subtree that is different in version 2; nodes of the tree have been numbered for quick reference. The following notation is introduced to specify the attribute schema of the verification procedure. For a *Mini* workflow, let F be the set of functions modeling invocations to external services; V the set of variables defined within the workflow; E the set of boolean expressions that can appear as the condition of an *if* or a *while* statement in the workflow. An expression $e \in E$ is either a combination of boolean predicates on variables or a placeholder predicate labeled $*$.

To model the probabilistic verification procedure, first we assume that each function $f \in F$ has a probability $Pr_S(f)$ of successfully completing its execution. If successfully executed, the function returns a boolean value. We are interested in the value returned by a function in case it appears as the rhs of an assignment because the assigned variable may appear in a condition. The probability of assigning *true* to the lhs variable of the statement is the probability that the function returns *true*, which is the product $Pr_S(f) \cdot Pr_T(f)$, where $Pr_T(f)$ is the *conditioned* probability that f returns *true* given that it has been successfully executed. For the sake of readability, we make the simplifying assumption that all functions whose return value is used in an assignment are always successful, i.e., have $Pr_S(f) = 1$. Thanks to this assumption the probability of f returning *true* coincides with $Pr_T(f)$ and allows us to avoid cumbersome, though conceptually simple, formulae in the following development.

For the conditions $e \in E$ of *if* and *while* statements, $Pr_T(e)$ denotes the probability of e to be evaluated to *true*. In case of an *if* statement, the evaluation of a condition e leads to a probability $Pr_T(e)$ of following the *then* branch, and $1 - Pr_T(e)$ of following the

$\langle S \rangle ::=$ 'begin' $\langle stmtlist \rangle$ 'end'
$\langle stmtlist \rangle ::= \langle stmt \rangle$ ';' $\langle stmtlist \rangle \mid \langle stmt \rangle$ ';'
$\langle stmt \rangle ::= \langle function\text{-}id \rangle$ '(' ')' $\mid \langle var\text{-}id \rangle$ ':=' 'true' $\mid \langle var\text{-}id \rangle$ ':=' 'false'
$\quad \mid \langle var\text{-}id \rangle$ ':=' $\langle function\text{-}id \rangle$ '(' ')'
$\quad \mid$ 'if' $\langle cond \rangle$ 'then' $\langle stmtlist \rangle$ 'else' $\langle stmtlist \rangle$ 'endif'
$\quad \mid$ 'while' $\langle cond \rangle$ 'do' $\langle stmtlist \rangle$ 'endwhile'
$\langle var\text{-}id \rangle ::= \ldots$
$\langle function\text{-}id \rangle ::= \ldots$
$\langle cond \rangle ::= \ldots$

Fig. 3. The grammar of the *Mini* language

```
1   begin
2    opA();
3    x := true;
4    if (x==true)
5      then opB();
6      else opA();
7    endif;
8   end
```

```
1   begin
2    opA();
3    x := false;
4    if (x==true)
5      then opB();
6      else opA();
7    endif;
8   end
```

(a) Version 1 (top)
Version 2 (bottom)

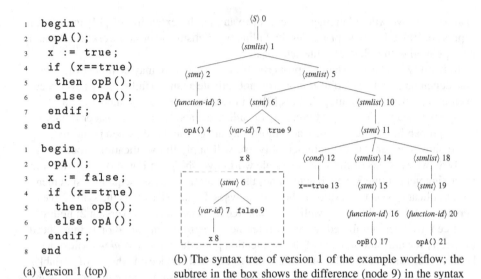

(b) The syntax tree of version 1 of the example workflow; the subtree in the box shows the difference (node 9) in the syntax tree of version 2

Fig. 4. The two versions of the example workflow and their syntax tree(s)

else branch. For *while* statements, $Pr_T(e)$ is the probability of executing one iteration of the loop. The probability of a condition to be evaluated to *true* or *false* depends on the current usage profile and can be estimated on the basis of the designer's experience, the knowledge of the application domain, or gathered from previous executions or running instances by combining monitoring and statistical inference techniques [19].

The value of $Pr_T(e)$ is computed as follows. If the predicate is the placeholder $*$, the probability is indicated as $Pr_T(*)$. If e is a combination of boolean predicates on variables, the probability value is defined with respect to its atomic components (assuming probabilistic independence among the values of the variables in V):

- $e = $ "v==true" $\implies Pr_T(e) = Pr_T(v)$
- $e = $ "v==false" $\implies Pr_T(e) = 1 - Pr_T(v)$
- $e = e_1 \land e_2 \implies Pr_T(e) = Pr_T(e_1) \cdot Pr_T(e_2)$
- $e = \neg e_1 \implies Pr_T(e) = 1 - Pr_T(e_1)$

The initial value of $Pr_T(v)$ for a variable $v \in V$ is undefined; after the variable is assigned, it is defined as follows:

- v:=true $\implies Pr_T(v) = 1$
- v:=false $\implies Pr_T(v) = 0$
- v:=f() $\implies Pr_T(v) = Pr_T(f)$

The reliability of a workflow is computed as the *expected probability value* of its successful completion. To simplify the mathematical description, we assume independence among all the failure events.

The reliability of a sequence of statements is essentially the probability that all of them are executed successfully. Given the independence of the failure events, it is the product of the reliability value of each statement.

For an *if* statement with condition *e*, its reliability is the reliability of the *then* branch weighted by the probability of *e* to be *true*, plus the reliability of the *else* branch weighted by the probability of *e* to be *false*. This intuitive definition is formally grounded on the law of total probability and the previous assumption of independence.

The reliability of a *while* statement with condition *e* and body *b* is determined by the number of iterations *k*. We also assume that $Pr_T(e) < 1$, i.e., there is a non-zero probability of exiting the loop, and that $Pr_T(e)$ does not change during the iterations. The following formula is derived by applying well-known properties of probability theory:

$$E(Pr_S(\langle while \rangle)) = \sum_{k=0}^{\infty} (Pr_T(e) \cdot Pr_S(b))^k \cdot (1 - Pr_T(e)) = \frac{1 - Pr_T(e)}{1 - Pr_T(e) \cdot Pr_S(b)}$$

A different construction of this result can be found in [14].

We are now ready to encode this analysis through the following attributes:
- $SYN(\langle S \rangle) = SYN(\langle stmlist \rangle) = SYN(\langle stmt \rangle) = \{\gamma, \vartheta\}$;
- $SYN(\langle cond \rangle) = \{\delta\}$;
- $SYN(\langle function\text{-}id \rangle) = SYN(\langle var\text{-}id \rangle) = \{\eta\}$;
where:
  - γ represents the reliability of the execution of the subtree rooted in the node the attribute corresponds to.
  - ϑ represents the knowledge acquired after the execution of an assignment. Precisely, ϑ is a set of pairs $\langle v, Pr_T(v) \rangle$ with $v \in V$ such that there are no two different pairs $\langle v_1, Pr_T(v_1) \rangle, \langle v_2, Pr_T(v_2) \rangle \in \vartheta$ with $v_1 = v_2$. If $\nexists \langle v_1, Pr_T(v_1) \rangle \in \vartheta$ no knowledge has been gathered concerning the value of a variable v_1. If not differently specified, ϑ is empty.
  - δ represents $Pr_T(e)$, with *e* being the expression associated with the corresponding node.
  - η is a string corresponding to the literal value of an identifier.

The actual value of γ in a node has to be evaluated with respect to the information possibly available in ϑ. For example, let us assume that for a certain node n_1, $\gamma(n_1) = .9 \cdot Pr_T(v)$. This means that the actual value of $\gamma(n_1)$ depends on the value of the variable *v*. The latter can be decided only after the execution of an assignment statement. If such assignment happens at node n_2, the attribute $\vartheta(n_2)$ will contain the pair $\langle v, Pr_T(v) \rangle$. For example, let us assume $Pr_T(v) = .7$; after the assignment, the actual value of $\gamma(n_1)$ is refined considering the information in $\vartheta(n_2)$, assuming the numeric value .63. We use the notation $\gamma(\cdot) \mid \vartheta(\cdot)$ to describe the operation of refining the value of γ with the information in ϑ. Given that $\gamma(\cdot) \mid \emptyset = \gamma(\cdot)$, the operation will be omitted when $\vartheta(\cdot) = \emptyset$.

The attribute schema for the Mini language is defined as follows:

1. $\langle S \rangle ::=$ 'begin' $\langle stmlist \rangle$ 'end'
   $\gamma(\langle S \rangle) := \gamma(\langle stmlist \rangle)$
2. (a) $\langle stmlist_0 \rangle ::= \langle stmt \rangle$ ';' $\langle stmlist_1 \rangle$
       $\gamma(\langle stmlist_0 \rangle) := (\gamma(\langle stmt \rangle) \cdot \gamma(\langle stmlist_1 \rangle)) \mid \vartheta(\langle stmt \rangle)$
   (b) $\langle stmlist \rangle ::= \langle stmt \rangle$ ';'
       $\gamma(\langle stmlist \rangle) := \gamma(\langle stmt \rangle)$
3. (a) $\langle stmt \rangle ::= \langle function\text{-}id \rangle$ '(' ')'
       $\gamma(\langle stmt \rangle) := Pr_S(f)$ with $f \in F$ and $\eta(\langle function\text{-}id \rangle) = f$

(b) $\langle stmt \rangle ::= \langle var\text{-}id \rangle$ ':=' 'true'
$\quad \gamma(\langle stmt \rangle) := 1,$
$\quad \vartheta(\langle stmt \rangle) := \{ \langle \eta(\langle var\text{-}id \rangle), 1 \rangle \}$

(c) $\langle stmt \rangle ::= \langle var\text{-}id \rangle$ ':=' 'false'
$\quad \gamma(\langle stmt \rangle) := 1, \; \vartheta(\langle stmt \rangle) := \{ \langle \eta(\langle var\text{-}id \rangle), 0 \rangle \}$

(d) $\langle stmt \rangle ::= \langle var\text{-}id \rangle$ '=' $\langle function\text{-}id \rangle$ '(' ')'
$\quad \gamma(\langle stmt \rangle) := 1, \; \vartheta(\langle stmt \rangle) := \{ \langle \eta(\langle var\text{-}id \rangle), Pr_T(\eta(\langle function\text{-}id \rangle)) \rangle \}$ with $f \in F$
$\quad$ and $\eta(\langle function\text{-}id \rangle) = f$

(e) $\langle stmt \rangle \quad ::=$ 'if' $\langle cond \rangle$ 'then' $\langle stmtlist_0 \rangle$ 'else' $\langle stmtlist_1 \rangle$ 'endif'
$\quad \gamma(\langle stmt \rangle) := \gamma(\langle stmtlist_0 \rangle) \cdot \delta(\langle cond \rangle) + \gamma(\langle stmtlist_1 \rangle) \cdot (1 - \delta(\langle cond \rangle))$

(f) $\langle stmt \rangle ::=$ 'while' $\langle cond \rangle$ 'do' $\langle stmtlist \rangle$ 'endwhile'
$$\gamma(\langle stmt \rangle) := \frac{1 - \delta(\langle cond \rangle)}{1 - \delta(\langle cond \rangle) \cdot \gamma(\langle stmtlist \rangle)}$$

4. $\langle cond \rangle \quad ::= \ldots$
$\quad \delta(\langle cond \rangle) := Pr_T(e),$ with $\eta(\langle cond \rangle) = e$

We now show how to perform probabilistic verification of reliability properties with SiDECAR on the two versions of the example workflow of Fig. 4a. In the steps of attribute synthesis, for brevity, we use numbers to refer to corresponding nodes in the syntax tree of Fig. 4b. As for the reliability of the two functions used in the workflow, we assume $Pr_S(opA) = .97, Pr_S(opB) = .99.$

Example Workflow - Version 1 Given the abstract syntax tree in Fig. 4b, evaluation of attributes leads to the following values (shown top to bottom, left to right, with η attributes omitted):

$\gamma(2) := .97;$

$\gamma(6) := 1;$

$\vartheta(6) := \{ \langle x, 1 \rangle \};$

$\delta(12) := Pr_T(\text{"x==true"});$

$\gamma(15) := .99;$

$\gamma(14) := \gamma(15);$

$\gamma(19) := .97;$

$\gamma(18) := \gamma(19);$

$\gamma(11) := .99 \cdot \delta(12)$
$\quad + .97 \cdot (1 - \delta(12));$

$\gamma(10) := \gamma(11);$

$\gamma(5) := (\gamma(6) \cdot \gamma(10)) \mid \vartheta(6) = .99;$

$\gamma(1) := \gamma(2) \cdot \gamma(5) = .9603;$

$\gamma(0) := \gamma(1) = .9603.$

The resulting value for $\gamma(0)$ represents the reliability of the workflow, i.e., each execution has a probability equal to .9603 of being successfully executed.

Example Workflow - Version 2 Version 2 of the example workflow differs from version 1 only in the assignment at line 3, which leads the incremental parser to build the subtree shown in the box of Fig. 4b. Because the matching condition is satisfied, this subtree is hooked into node 6 of the original tree. Re-computation of the attributes proceeds upward to the root, leading to the following final values (shown top to bottom, left to right, with η attributes omitted):

$\gamma(6) := 1;$

$\vartheta(6) := \{ \langle x, 0 \rangle \};$

$\gamma(5) := (\gamma(6) \cdot \gamma(10)) \mid \vartheta(6) = .97;$

$\gamma(1) := \gamma(2) \cdot \gamma(5) = .9409;$

$\gamma(0) := \gamma(1) := .9409.$

Thus, our incremental approach requires to reparse only 3 nodes and reevaluate only 5 attributes instead of the 13 ones computed in a full, non-incremental (re)parsing (as for Version 1).

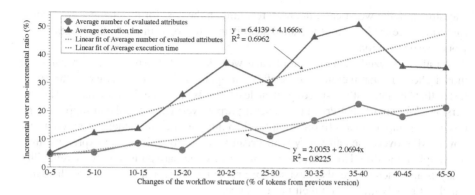

Fig. 5. Comparison between the incremental verification approach and the non-incremental one

5 Evaluation

To show the effectiveness of our approach, we performed a preliminary experimental evaluation using a prototype developed in Java, on a Intel Xeon E31220 3.10Ghz CPU, with 32Gb of RAM, running Ubuntu Server 12.04 64bit. We generated 56 random *Mini* workflows, each one with about 10000 tokens. For each workflow we randomly generated 30 subsequent versions, applying a series of deletions and/or insertions of syntactically valid code snippets, ranging in total from 5% to 50% of the workflow size. We run the probabilistic verification procedure defined above on all generated versions, both in an incremental way and in a non-incremental one. For each run, we measured the *number of evaluated attributes* and the *execution time*. Figure 5 shows the average of the ratio between the performance of the incremental approach over the non-incremental one, for both metrics. The results show that the execution time of our incremental approach is linear with respect to the size of the change(s), as expected from Sect. 3.1: the smaller the changes on the input program are, the faster the incremental approach is than the non-incremental one. This preliminary evaluation shows a 20x speedup of the incremental approach over the non-incremental one, for changes affecting up to 5% of the input artifact (having a total size of just 10^4 tokens); in the case of changes affecting about 50% of the code, we measured a 3x speedup. Since for large, long-lasting systems it is expected that most changes only involve a small fraction of the code, the gain of applying our incremental approach can be significant.

The parsing algorithm used within our framework has a temporal complexity (on average) linear in the size of the modified portion of the syntax tree. Hence any change in the workflow has a minimal impact on the adaptation of the abstract syntax tree too. Semantic incrementality allows for minimal (re)evaluation of the attributes, by proceeding along the path from the node corresponding to the change to the root, whose length is normally logarithmic with respect to the length of the workflow description. Notice that even if the change in a statement affects the execution of another location of the code (e.g., an assignment to a global variable), such dependency would be automatically handled in the least common ancestor of the two syntactic nodes. Such common ancestor is, in the worst case, the root, resulting in the cost for the change propagation (in terms of re-evaluation of the attributes) being still logarithmic in the length of the workflow description.

We also analyzed each version of each workflow with Prism v.4.1, a probabilistic model checker. Our incremental verification approach was, on average, 4268 times faster than Prism, with a speedup of at least 1000x in about 35% of the workflows versions. We remark that Prism is a general-purpose verification tool that supports various types of input models (more complex than those needed to model structured workflows). Moreover, one can verify with Prism several properties more expressive than the simple reliability. However, the reason for this comparison is that many reliability analysis approaches (see also next section) make use of probabilistic model checking, which ultimately impacts on their performance.

6 Related Work

Reliability analysis of workflow has been widely investigated in the last decade. Most of the proposed approaches are based on algebraic methods [29], graph manipulation [12], or stochastic modeling [25,34,22,9,35,28]. To the best of our knowledge, the only approach explicitly formalized by means of an attribute grammar is [14]. Nevertheless, only few approaches provide incrementality, at least to some extent; they are mainly grounded in the concepts of change encapsulation and of change anticipation [23].

Incrementality by *change encapsulation* is achieved by applying compositional reasoning to a modularized system using the assume-guarantee [30] paradigm. This paradigm views systems as a collection of cooperating modules, each of which has to guarantee certain properties. The verification methods based on this paradigm are said to be compositional, since they allow reasoning about each module separately and deducing properties about their integration. If the effect of a change can be localized inside the boundaries of a module, the other modules are not affected, and their verification does not need to be redone. This feature is for example exploited in [10], which proposes a framework for performing assume-guarantee reasoning in an incremental and fully automatic fashion.

Approaches based on *change anticipation* assume that the artifact under analysis can be divided into static (unchangeable) parts and variable ones, and rely on *partial evaluation* [15] to postpone the evaluation of the variable parts. Partial evaluation can be seen as a transformation from the original version of the program to a new version called *residual program*, where the properties of interest have been partially computed against the static parts, preserving the dependency on the variable ones. As soon as a change is observed, the computation can be moved a further step toward completion by fixing one or more variable parts according to the observations.

The above approaches, however, are based on the assumption that engineers know a priori the parts that are most likely subject to future evolution and can encapsulate them within well-defined borderlines. Our approach, instead, does not make any hypothesis on where changes will occur during system's life: it simply evaluates a posteriori their scope within system's structure as formalized by the syntax tree. This should be particularly beneficial in most modern systems that evolve in a fairly unpredictable way, often without a unique design responsibility.

Focusing on incremental probabilistic verification, the three main techniques supporting incremental verification of stochastic models (e.g., Markov Chains) are *decomposition* [33], which belongs to the class of change encapsulation, and *parametric analysis* [12,27] and *delta evaluation* [34], which can be classified as change anticipation techniques. The first decomposes the input model into its strongly connected components (SCCs), allowing verification subtasks to be carried on within each SCC; local results are then combined to verify the global property. By defining a dependency relation among SCCs, when a change occurs, only the SCCs depending on the changed one have to be verified. The benefits of incrementality in this case depend on the quality of the SCC partition and the corresponding dependency relation. In the case of parametric analysis the probability value of the transitions in the model that are supposed to change are labeled with symbolic parameters. The model is then verified providing results in the form of closed mathematical formulae having the symbolic parameters as unknowns. As the actual values for the parameters become available (e.g., during the execution of the system), they are replaced in the formulae, providing a numerical estimation of the desired property (e.g., system reliability). Whenever the values of the parameters change, the closed formula obtained by the preprocessing phase can be reused, with significant improvements of the verification time [18,16]. The main limitation of this approach is that a structural change in the software (i.e., not describable by a parameters assignment) invalidates the results of the preprocessing phase, requiring the verification to start from scratch, with consequent degradation of the analysis performance. Delta evaluation is concerned with incremental reliability analysis based on conveniently structured Discrete Time Markov Chains (DTMC). The structure of those model follows the proposal by [9], where each software module (represented by a state of the DTMC), can transfer the control to another module, or fail by making a transition toward an absorbing failure state, or complete the execution by moving toward an absorbing success state. Assuming that a single module failure probability changes at a time, only few arithmetic operations are needed to correct the previous reliability value. Despite its efficiency, delta evaluation can only deal with changes in a modules failure probability, providing no support for both structural changes and changes in the interaction probabilities among modules. Finally, in [29] service compositions are formalized through a convenient algebraic structure and an incremental framework is used to compose local results into a global quantitative property, in an assume-guarantee flavor. The approach is widely applicable for verification of component-based systems, and it has been applied for reliability analysis. The compositionality entailed by the assume-guarantee infrastructure can be recasted into our syntactic-semantic approach.

7   Conclusion and Future Work

Incrementality is one of the most promising means to dealing with software evolution. In this paper we addressed the issue of incrementality in the context of the probabilistic verification of reliability requirements of structured workflows. We defined a novel incremental technique based on a syntactic-semantic approach: the verification procedure is encoded as synthesis of semantic attributes associated with the grammar defining the structure of workflows. As confirmed by the preliminary experimental evaluation, the execution time of our incremental approach is linear with respect to the size of the change(s). When changes involve only a small fraction of the artifact to analyze, our approach can provide a significant speedup over a non-incremental approach.

In the future, we plan to extend our approach to support richer workflow languages, such as BPEL and BPMN, as well as other types of verification procedures. The first direction will require to express the grammar of the workflow languages in an OPG form, with the possible caveat of reducing the readability of the grammar and impacting on the definition of the attribute schemas. As for the second direction, we plan to investigate richer attribute schemas, to support both new language features and different verification algorithms (e.g., to support more realistic assumptions on the system under verification as well as state-of-the-art optimizations and heuristics). Finally, we plan to apply our approach to the related problem of probabilistic symbolic execution [20,7,17]. In all these scenarios incrementality would be automatically provided by our SiDECAR framework, without any further effort for the developer.

Acknowledgments. This work has been partially supported by the European Community under the IDEAS-ERC grant agreement no. 227977-SMScom and by the National Research Fund, Luxembourg (FNR/P10/03). We thank Alessandro Maria Rizzi for helping with the implementation of the prototype.

References

1. van der Aalst, W.M.P., Ter Hofstede, A.H.M., Kiepuszewski, B., Barros, A.P.: Workflow patterns. Distrib. Parallel Databases 14(1), 5–51 (2003)
2. Avizienis, A., Laprie, J.-C., Randell, B., Landwehr, C.: Basic concepts and taxonomy of dependable and secure computing. IEEE Trans. Dependable Secure Comput. 1(1), 11–33 (2004)
3. Barenghi, A., Viviani, E., Crespi Reghizzi, S., Mandrioli, D., Pradella, M.: PAPAGENO: A parallel parser generator for operator precedence grammars. In: Czarnecki, K., Hedin, G. (eds.) SLE 2012. LNCS, vol. 7745, pp. 264–274. Springer, Heidelberg (2013)
4. Baresi, L., Di Nitto, E., Ghezzi, C.: Toward open-world software: Issues and challenges. IEEE Computer 39(10), 36–43 (2006)
5. Bianculli, D., Filieri, A., Ghezzi, C., Mandrioli, D.: A syntactic-semantic approach to incremental verification (2013), http://arxiv.org/abs/1304.8034
6. Bianculli, D., Filieri, A., Ghezzi, C., Mandrioli, D.: Syntactic-semantic incrementality for agile verification. Sci. Comput. Program (2013), doi:10.1016/j.scico.2013.11.026
7. Borges, M., Filieri, A., d'Amorim, M., Păsăreanu, C.S., Visser, W.: Compositional solution space quantification for probabilistic software analysis. In: Proc. of PLDI 2014, pp. 123–132. ACM (2014)
8. de Bosschere, K.: An operator precedence parser for standard Prolog text. Softw. Pract. Exper. 26(7), 763–779 (1996)
9. Cheung, R.C.: A user-oriented software reliability model. IEEE Trans. Softw. Eng. SE-6(2), 118–125 (1980)
10. Cobleigh, J.M., Giannakopoulou, D., Păsăreanu, C.S.: Learning assumptions for compositional verification. In: Garavel, H., Hatcliff, J. (eds.) TACAS 2003. LNCS, vol. 2619, pp. 331–346. Springer, Heidelberg (2003)

11. Reghizzi, S.C., Mandrioli, D.: Operator precedence and the visibly pushdown property. J. Comput. Syst. Sci. 78(6), 1837–1867 (2012)
12. Daws, C.: Symbolic and parametric model checking of discrete-time markov chains. In: Liu, Z., Araki, K. (eds.) ICTAC 2004. LNCS, vol. 3407, pp. 280–294. Springer, Heidelberg (2005)
13. Distefano, S., Ghezzi, C., Guinea, S., Mirandola, R.: Dependability assessment of web service orchestrations. IEEE Trans. Rel. (2014) (PrePrint), doi:10.1109/TR.2014.2315939
14. Distefano, S., Filieri, A., Ghezzi, C., Mirandola, R.: A compositional method for reliability analysis of workflows affected by multiple failure modes. In: Proc. of CBSE 2011, pp. 149–158. ACM (2011)
15. Ershov, A.: On the partial computation principle. Inform. Process. Lett. 6(2), 38–41 (1977)
16. Filieri, A., Ghezzi, C.: Further steps towards efficient runtime verification: Handling probabilistic cost models. In: Proc. of FormSERA 2012, pp. 2–8. IEEE (2012)
17. Filieri, A., Păsăreanu, C.S., Visser, W., Geldenhuys, J.: Statistical symbolic execution with informed sampling. In: Proc. of SIGSOFT 2014/FSE-22, ACM (2014)
18. Filieri, A., Ghezzi, C., Tamburrelli, G.: Run-time efficient probabilistic model checking. In: Proc. of ICSE 2011, pp. 341–350. ACM (2011)
19. Filieri, A., Ghezzi, C., Tamburrelli, G.: A formal approach to adaptive software: continuous assurance of non-functional requirements. Formal Asp. Comput. 24(2), 163–186 (2012)
20. Filieri, A., Păsăreanu, C.S., Visser, W.: Reliability analysis in symbolic pathfinder. In: Proc. of ICSE 2013, pp. 622–631. IEEE Press (2013)
21. Floyd, R.W.: Syntactic analysis and operator precedence. J. ACM 10, 316–333 (1963)
22. Gallotti, S., Ghezzi, C., Mirandola, R., Tamburrelli, G.: Quality prediction of service compositions through probabilistic model checking. In: Becker, S., Plasil, F., Reussner, R. (eds.) QoSA 2008. LNCS, vol. 5281, pp. 119–134. Springer, Heidelberg (2008)
23. Ghezzi, C.: Evolution, adaptation, and the quest for incrementality. In: Calinescu, R., Garlan, D. (eds.) Monterey Workshop 2012. LNCS, vol. 7539, pp. 369–379. Springer, Heidelberg (2012)
24. Ghezzi, C., Mandrioli, D.: Incremental parsing. ACM Trans. Program. Lang. Syst. 1(1), 58–70 (1979)
25. Goseva-Popstojanova, K., Mathur, A., Trivedi, K.: Comparison of architecture-based software reliability models. In: Proc. of ISSRE 2001, pp. 22–31. IEEE (2001)
26. Grune, D., Jacobs, C.J.H.: Parsing Techniques - a practical guide, 2nd edn. Springer (2008)
27. Hahn, E., Hermanns, H., Zhang, L.: Probabilistic reachability for parametric markov models. STTT 13(1), 3–19 (2011)
28. Immonen, A., Niemela, E.: Survey of reliability and availability prediction methods from the viewpoint of software architecture. Software and Systems Modeling 7(1), 49–65 (2008)
29. Johnson, K., Calinescu, R., Kikuchi, S.: An incremental verification framework for component-based software systems. In: Proc. of CBSE 2013, pp. 33–42. ACM (2013)
30. Jones, C.B.: Tentative steps toward a development method for interfering programs. ACM Trans. Program. Lang. Syst. 5(4), 596–619 (1983)
31. Josuttis, N.: SOA in Practice: The Art of Distributed System Design. O'Reilly (2007)
32. Knuth, D.E.: Semantics of context-free languages. Theory of Computing Systems 2, 127–145 (1968)
33. Kwiatkowska, M., Parker, D., Qu, H.: Incremental quantitative verification for Markov decision processes. In: Proc. of DSN 2011, pp. 359–370. IEEE (2011)
34. Meedeniya, I., Grunske, L.: An efficient method for architecture-based reliability evaluation for evolving systems with changing parameters. In: Proc. of ISSRE 2010, pp. 229–238. IEEE (2010)
35. Pham, H.: System software reliability. Springer (2006)
36. Sistla, P.: Hybrid and incremental model-checking techniques. ACM Comput. Surv. 28(4es) (1996)

Prototype-Driven Development
of Web Applications with DyWA

Johannes Neubauer[1], Markus Frohme[1], and Bernhard Steffen[1],
and Tiziana Margaria[2]

[1] Chair of Programming Systems, TU Dortmund, Germany
{johannes.neubauer,markus.frohme,steffen}@cs.tu-dortmund.de
[2] Chair Service and Software Engineering, Universität Potsdam, Germany
margaria@cs.uni-potsdam.de

Abstract. In this paper we present an approach to the user-driven
development of process-oriented web applications that combines *business process modeling* with user-side application domain evolution. In the
center is the DyWA framework that accompanies the prototype-driven
web-application development from the domain modeling through the development and deployment phase to the actual runtime and later product evolution: Using DyWA, application experts without programming
knowledge are able to model (according to their professional knowledge
and understanding) both domain-specific data models and the business
process models that act on the data via automatically generated elementary data operations. The resulting business processes integrate data
access and manipulation, and directly constitute *executable prototypes*
of the resulting web application. All this is illustrated for OCS-lite, a
cut-down version of Springer's online editorial system.

Keywords: prototyping, metadata and data definition. business process
modeling, domain modeling, automated software engineering.

1 Software Evolution in Web Applications

In today's world, web applications serve billions of users worldwide. They are
already now the easiest and most widespread way of IT use for the broad public, not requiring downloads, installations, configurations or specific infrastructure preparation: access "anywhere, anytime" from any device has become true.
From the provider's side, web applications allow processing user requests in an
automated manner at any given time from arbitrary locations, making them a
valuable medium for companies to offer their services. Companies such as Ama-
zon.com Inc., eBay Inc. and in particular Facebook could not exist without the
Web, and their success largely depends on their ability to quickly react to cus-
tomer/user needs. Continuous evolution, the sense of continuous model-driven
engineering [19], is critical to the business model of these giants.

Two distinct system design practices evolved from this need:

T. Margaria and B. Steffen (Eds.): ISoLA 2014, Part I, LNCS 8802, pp. 56–72, 2014.

- *Agile Software development* methods such as Scrum [30] or Extreme Programming (XP) [3] base their development style on a very close informal cooperation between the application expert and the software developer. Here, it is the software developer who constructs the application in small, prioritized increments for frequent intermediate inspection by the application expert.
- *Business process modeling* [27,28,1] aims at involving the application expert directly in the process design phase of the software development: with the introduction of BPMN 2.0 [1], requirement specifications in terms of business processes are considered part of the actual software development process. The ultimate goal here is that these process models are directly executable.

These two schools of practice deal in different fashions with the typical *semantic gap* of software engineering [16]. Agile software development stresses the user-in-the-loop philosophy: it requires the continuous and close cooperation between the application expert and the developer, but leaves the full technical solution in the hands of the developer. Conventional business process modeling is inherently closer to the expert's application domain, but it lacks built-in ways to handle the required business activities at the user level: e.g. to deal with new resources and data types, such activities have to be manually implemented by IT experts.

To truly enable end users to be first -class citizens in the application design, a new form of *executable prototyping* needs to give application experts full control over the complete (iterative) creation process, including the business activities required to introduce, control, and manage new business objects and resources. In the past [31] we already combined methods of agile software development with (business) process modeling via eXtreme Model-Driven Design (XMDD) [20], and its incarnation the Java Application Building Center (jABC) framework [33]. This prototype-driven development process for web applications overcomes in particular most service integration problems of current BPM approaches [6], by offering an easy to use design of the business logic for an application. However, this alone is not sufficient to close the entire gap, because it needs a similar ease of definition and management for the data and objects that occur in the applications, and it needs efficient and robust support for evolution and change.

In this paper we introduce this holistic approach. There, the Dynamic Web Application (DyWA) provides the web based user-friendly definition of domain entities as well as the final execution environment, and behind the scenes it integrates with the newest iteration of the reference implementation of XMDD, the Java Application Building Center 4 (jABC4), that provides the process definition facility [24,22]. As a result, DyWA becomes for the user a web-based definition facility for application domains in terms of a *type schema*, which delivers also a generic, fully functional web-based *evolving prototype* of the resulting application that accompanies the development right from the beginning.

We are going to introduce a small case study, the Online Conference Service (OCS)-lite, model its types in DyWA, create the necessary processes in jABC, and export them back into DyWA in order to offer to the end users a running web application obtained entirely without manual coding. We are then going to change the requirements, impacting both the data types and the business logic of the application, and show how the application can be accordingly evolved by the users without writing new code.

In the following, Sect. 2, we locate our approach in the context of the behavioral programming school of thought. Then, in Sect. 3 we present the running case study, the OCS-lite, with sample requirements and changes we want to illustrate. Sect. 4 summarizes the basic principles of modeling business processes with the jABC4. In Sect. 5 we show DyWA's concepts and architecture, further developed stepwise along the case study. The central trait (and strength) of DyWA is then illustrated in Sec. 6: the ease of system evolution with changes in the domain model and the business logic. Finally, Sect. 7 sheds light on related work and Sect. 8 summarizes our results and experiences so far.

2   Behavioral Model-Driven Design

The incrementally arising prototype stores descriptions of the domain specific data types, their associations, and corresponding data objects all in the same database. This way of organizing the definition, management, integration and evolution of data and behavior (in form of processes) is consistent with the philosophy underlying the behavioral programming paradigm put forward by David Harel [8], where incremental specifications are considered a core element of application development.

In our case, we talk more specifically of behavioral model-driven design: based on the defined types and corresponding Create, Read, Update, Delete (CRUD) operations, application experts are able to model domain specific business processes in our modeling environment jABC4, which are directly executable. This way the prototype can be augmented or modified stepwise by acting on one or more types in the type schema, the corresponding data-objects, and the executable process models, while maintaining executability at all times. As every step is automated via a corresponding code generator, no manual coding is required at all. This opens the whole development process, including the domain modeling, to *application experts* who can control the development of their application at any time by 'playing' with the executable prototype.

The agility of the prototypes is supported via features like asynchronous type schema where changes to types are reflected instantly in the running prototype and online data-migration for reestablishing a stable type schema after each development iteration. These concepts allow to integrate other approaches, such as the behavioral programming paradigm. Furthermore, making the mentioned layers accessible (in a semantic way) to application experts, the claims for *natural* development environments like in behavioral programming can be satisfied.

3   Case Study: The OCS-Lite

The Online Conference Service (OCS) online manuscript submission and review service is part of a long-lived software product line for the Springer Verlag started

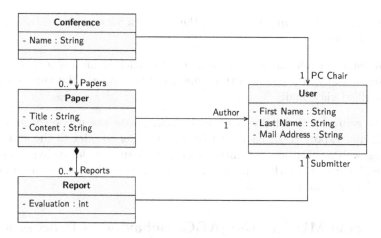

Fig. 1. Fragment of the domain model of the OCS-lite, showing the main entities and relations of the application domain

in 1999 [13]. The OCS/OJS product line evolved over time to also include diversified journal and volume production preparation services. The new line, started in 2009, is specifically designed for verifiability, as described in [23].

The service appropriately handles a wealth of independent but often indirectly related user interactions, where accomplishing a task may have consequences for other participants [12] or shared objects. From this point of view, the OCS is a user- and context-driven reactive system with a web interface. Users can decide whether to reject a task, which typically consists of performing small workflows, when to execute it, and in case of multiple tasks in which order to process them. The large number of involved participants, roles (like author or PC chair), interaction styles, and the high degree of freedom in choosing individual tasks makes the OCS a challenge for conventional business process modeling approaches.

Figure 1 shows a small fragment of the class diagram of the OCS-lite's basic concepts, that we call *types*.

The OCS deals with named `Conference`s with a PC chair managing the program committee and the paper submissions. Type `User` represents people registered to the OCS. It has a first and a last name, and an e-mail address, useful to distinguish homonymous users. A PC chair can be represented by an object of type `User`. In this simplified fragment, a paper has a title, an author (also of type `User`) and its content – a string representation of the printed text. Papers receive several `Reports` that rate their quality through an evaluation grade. Reports are in general submitted by reviewers, who are again of type `User`.

Initial requirements: application experts require the OCS-lite to

(R1) allow to submit a report to a paper, and
(R2) new reports should specify a paper, a reviewer and an evaluation value.

Once the initial prototype for these requirements is deployed, we introduce

Change of requirements: to improve the feedback for a paper, instead of just an evaluation value,

(C1) the reviewers should provide an actual feedback in form of a text.
(C2) Additionally, if a new report is submitted to a paper, the author should be notified via e-mail.

We are going to model the types in DyWA, create the necessary processes in jABC, and export them back into DyWA in order to offer to the end users a running web application obtained entirely without manual coding. Because DyWA is designed to work with jABC, we start with a short description of the DyWA-relevant aspects of jABC.

4   eXtreme MDD in the jABC: Behavior as Processes

The executable process models of the OCS are realized in the *jABC* [18,17,33], a framework for service-oriented design and development that follows the XMDD of [20]. XMDD combines ideas from service orientation, model-driven design and extreme programming and enables application experts to control the design and evolution of processes during their whole life-cycle on the basis of Lightweight Process Coordination (LPC) [17].

We have presented how to realize Higher-Order Processes in jABC in [25] and in [24], therefore we describe here only the aspects in direct connection with the DyWA. The jABC allows users to develop services and applications easily by composing reusable building blocks into (flow-)graph structures that are both formally well-defined and easy to read and build. These building blocks are called Service Independent Building Blocks (SIBs) in analogy to the original telecommunication terminology [31], and in the spirit of the service-oriented computing paradigm [16] and of the One-Thing Approach (OTA) [15], an evolution of the model-based Lightweight Coordination approach of [17] specifically applied to services. The OTA provides the conceptual modeling infrastructure (one thing for all) that enables all the stakeholders (application experts, designer, component experts, implementer, quality insurers, . . .) to closely cooperate working on models as primary "things". In particular it enables immediate *user experience* and *seamless acceptance*, which is a central constituent of the One Thing Approach (OTA): The fact that all stakeholders work on and modify one and the same thing allows every stakeholder to observe the progress of the development and the implications of decisions at their own level of expertise.

On the basis of a large library of such SIBs, which come in domain-specific collections as well as in domain-independent collections, the user builds behavioral models for the desired system in terms of hierarchical Service Logic Graphs (SLGs) [32]. These graphs form the modeling backbone of the OTA: All the information concerning documentation, role, rights, consistency conditions, animation code, execution code, semantic annotations, etc. comes here together. Immediate user experience results from the XMDD approach, where already the initial graphical models are executable, be it as the basis for interactive 'what/if

games', documentation browsing, or simple interpreted animation. This allows
to "feel" the behavior and detect conceptual errors already very early in the
requirement models.

SLGs are formal models: they are semantically interpreted as Kripke Transition Systems (KTSs), a generalization of both Kripke structures and Labeled
Transition Systems (LTSs) [21] that allows labels both on nodes and edges. Nodes
in the SLG represent activities (or services/components, depending on the application domain). Once one has the SIB libraries, it is easy to create business
process models by composing and configuring SIBs in processes/workflows.

The central open question for an application expert is how to automatically
produce SIBs that manipulate data, if all the expert knows is the structure of
his/her business objects. DyWA solves exactly this problem.

5 DyWA

The DyWA framework is designed to support the application experts and programmers in various aspects of the software development process. We

- provide a *running web application prototype* from the very first moment of
  the software development process. This allows us to maintain a running
  prototype during the complete development process.
- make it possible to *modify and adapt the application domain at runtime*. This
  allows us to extend the XMDD paradigm and the One-Thing Approach and
  delegate the domain modeling to the application experts.
- *automatically provide the modeled domain* in the jABC as a new SIB collection. This allows a seamless modeling experience, because the application
  experts model both the application domain and the business process within
  their cognitive world. It also mitigates the costs of a manual implementation
  and provision, and reduces the semantic gap.
- further automate the reintegration of the modeled business processes in the
  DyWA web application, that offers them to end users via an execution facility.

The *persistence layer*, realized in a database, holds the flexible *type and object
schema* that allows to model an application domain via its domain specific data
dynamically at runtime. The *presentation layer* (Editors, Views) of the DyWA
framework is realized in a web interface, allowing application experts to easily
edit the application domain themselves and modify and update it at any time.
These two layers are domain-independent, therefore they come with the DyWA
framework. Accordingly, users have a running (yet empty) prototype right from
the beginning. The domain experts use this prototype to create and alter the domain information continuously, throughout the development and entire lifetime
of the application. In this sense, there is no distinction between prototype and
real product, as called for by the modern agile culture, that encourages so called
dev-ops teams, where developers and operations team together and co-evolve the
software products.

To link the data definitions in DyWA to the service-oriented functionality necessary in jABC for the manipulation of actual data, a *code generator* generates

for each type a corresponding collection of management SIBs (CRUD operations on the types). These SIBs are domain specific Java classes (i.e. the transformation layer) from the modeled domain. Once all the processes are orchestrated to a web application, this application can be plugged-in to the existing (initially empty) DyWA environment. According to our ready-to-use principle, it is now directly ready for execution.

5.1 Agile Domain Modeling for Runtime Migration during Evolution

Basing the user's running prototype on a *meta schema* distinct from the concrete implementation of the SIBs and of the processes also allows to manage different versions of the application domain simultaneously. This eases migrating between different versions of prototypes at runtime: all that is needed is to bind the models to a new implementation, or to switch from one model (with its version of the type schema, concrete generated SIB collection, corresponding processes, and their code) to a different one. We discuss the evolution specifically in Sect. 5.4. Here we first apply the domain modeling to the OCS-lite case study.

Business processes refer to business objects and act upon them by means of operations on their elements. In our OCS-lite, for example, the term "User" refers to the association of a first name, a last name and an e-mail address. These must be made accessible to the business process activities. In terms of the semantic gap,

- either one has a user-side, informal definition of these elements, as common in the business process modeling community, with the subsequent need for programming experts to understand what they mean and to implement them by means of specific data types,
- or one has from the beginning a precise definition in terms of programming-level types, that makes it possible to develop a static collection of domain specific services that the application experts can use during their process modeling.

Depending on the size and complexity of the domain, as well as on the initial depth of knowledge of it, the initial creation and continuous maintenance of data definitions on one side and corresponding domain specific services on the other side may cost a significant amount of resources. To satisfy both sides, and keep them automatically aligned, we developed the following two-level approach.

The web application runs on a *meta schema*, that describes data in terms of *MS-types* and *MS-objects*, which are both stored in the meta schema database. A MS-type is used to model the concrete types and associations of an application domain, whereas MS-objects hold the actual data of the application and thus constitute instantiations of the respective MS-Types. Objects are linked to a type, yielding a concept of typed domain specific data. This organization allows to save domain unspecific, arbitrary data, as far as they can be described with the type schema.

As shown in Figure 1(right), in DyWA we natively support primitive types, which can be used in the initial model. Non-primitive types are defined during the domain modeling process and become available from then on to later stages of the application's evolution.

Primitive types: String, Long, Double, Boolean, and **Timestamp** and lists of such types, e.g. lists of strings **List<String>**.

Complex types: Abstract reference to a modeled domain type, as in the OCS-lite business objects include a reference to a paper or report. Complex attributes are themselves well-defined modeled types. One may also specify a **List<Complex>** attribute, that is again (single-)typed. E.g., the OCS can use a list of papers, or a list of reports, but no list of mixed papers and reports.

OCS-lite Example

We create first the type User, whose attributes "First Name", "Last Name" and "Mail Address" can be described with the primitive type String. For the type Conference, the field "Name" can be again described with the primitive type String, and the attribute "PC Chair" with the recently modeled type User. For application experts familiar with the OCS it is easy to model the domain presented in Figure 1 with the provided type schema, even for complex type structures. For example, if each PC Chair should also know his/her conferences, a User should have an additional reference to a Conference, which is a dependency easily modeled in a following step. So the evolutionary approach of the type schema allows also complex type structures such as cyclic references.

5.2   Managing Data with Dynamic Types

In the DyWA database, type schema and data objects coexist, shaping the meta schema. To maintain the agility throughout the whole persistence layer, we need to store application data with similar flexibility to the types, taking into account that the type schema allows flexible remodeling at runtime, and thus we must know to which version of the type schema the data belongs.

Figure 2 shows the core functionality of our object storage and the connection between objects and types for a concrete instance of the OCS-lite.

We implement the objects by linking them dynamically to the structure of their types, allowing flexible storage of data: each object instance references exactly one type, and based on the attributes of the type, each object instance can save a value in a separated property per attribute. These properties allow the same loose coupling as the attributes of a type. By combining types and objects we can validate the integrity of the application data.

In the OCS-lite, once the type "Conference" is defined the application experts can create new conference objects in the DyWA object editor. If later on it is decided to add the "Name" field, it is then possible to add a name to all existing conferences, although this attribute was not initially present. This allows a flexible evolution of the data model of an application domain.

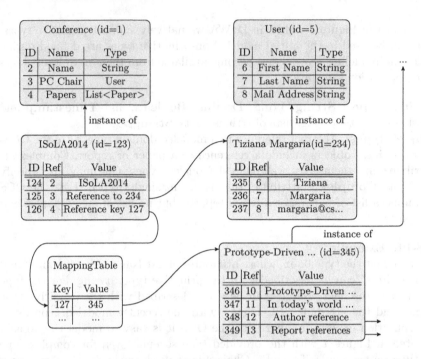

Fig. 2. Schematic layout of the OCS-lite business objects. Objects (green) reference their specific types and fields (blue), and hold references to other objects.

5.3   Provision of the Application Domain to the Business Logic Design

To allow a seamless interaction between business processes and the domain data model, we need to

- integrate the modeled domain in the business process modeling framework, and
- enable a fluid interaction between these two layers, to yield an overall seamless and agile development process.

So far, the abstract types only *describe* an application domain and not necessarily *represent* it, because the information is stored as generic key-value pairs in the database, but is not known to the processes that define the business logic.

DyWA provides a code generator that produces Java-classes corresponding to the modeled domain in the database. This highly automated approach to the business-to-IT layer connection minimizes the effort and time to achieve a fully functional and domain specific modeling environment. No manual coding is needed. As an example, Figure 3 shows a sketch of the generated class for the type `Conference`. The granularity of the encapsulation chosen while modeling the domain is preserved in the Java classes that will be used during process

```
 1  @IdRef(id = 12L)
 2  @OriginalName(name = "Conference")
 3  public class Conference {
 4
 5      private DBObject delegate;
 6
 7      Conference(DBObject obj) {
 8          this.delegate = obj;
 9      }
10      @IdRef(id = 13L)
11      @OriginalName(name = "Name")
12      public String getName() {
13          return delegate.getStringProperty(13);
14      }
15      @IdRef(id = 15L)
16      @OriginalName(name = "PC Chair")
17      public User getPC_Chair() {
18          return new User(delegate.getObjectProperty(15));
19      }
20      //remaining getters and setters
21  }
```

Fig. 3. A sketch of the generated `Conference` class: A thin domain-specific wrapper of the meta-schema

modeling: here, the generator creates a single class for the modeled type "Conference". An `@OriginalName` annotation preserves the original information in the generated classes, necessitated by the special treatment of whitespaces and special characters that guarantees valid Java identifiers. To connect information between the meta schema and the generated schema the `IdRef` annotation stores the database id of the modeled type. This referential integrity that is independent from the names of types and fields is important for our concept and is one reason why we did not choose existing approaches, such as e.g. Teneo [7], a project combining Eclipse Modeling Framework (EMF) with a persistence provider such as Hibernate [10]. The attributes of a "Conference" that model the name, the PC chair and multiple papers are translated by the code generator to getter- and setter methods in the same fashion.

Once the modeled domain is available in form of Java classes, it can be readily integrated in the jABC4: the domain specific entities are retrievable via domain-specific controllers in jABC.

5.4 Modeling Domain Specific Business Processes

Besides the plain Java classes, the generator also generates the domain specific services for basic CRUD operations that may be used dynamically as SIBs in the jABC. For the `Conference`, the generated `ConferenceController` provides methods for creating a conference and saving its data in the database, reading

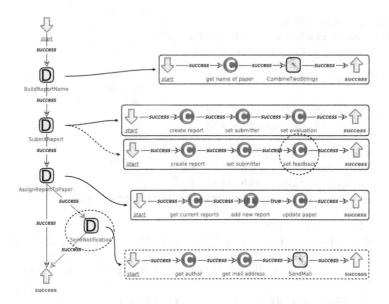

Fig. 4. The "SubmitReportToPaper" process. Changes to the original process are high-lighted with a dashed outline. In the updated process, we changed the "SubmitReport" process and added a new "SendNotification" process.

existing conferences from the database and deleting conferences. The controllers and entities allow a service-oriented manipulation on the business objects of the web application.

With the generated domain classes and the corresponding domain-specific CRUD services application experts can themselves model the required business processes in their own domain specific environment. Figure 4 shows sample business process(es) for the "SubmitPaperToConference" example from Section 3.

The main "SubmitReportToPaper" process (on the left) adds a new report to a given paper, and has submitter and evaluation as input parameter of the process model. Internally it contains three sub-processes:

- the "BuildReportName" sub-process takes the paper name "X" (input parameter of the process) and returns the string "Submitted report for paper: X". Receiving the actual name of the paper uses a dynamic SIB created from the "getName()" method of the generated Paper class. The external sub process "CombineTwoStrings" connects both parts of the required string. The result is returned via the end SIB "success" and saved in the context of the original process.
- the sub-process "SubmitReport" creates a new report with this computed report name, sets its submitter and evaluation, and saves this data into the database. All these operations communicate with the database: the corresponding SIBs are dynamically created from the generated ReportController. The "success" SIB returns the created report.

– "AssignReportToPaper" combines both concepts. It fetches the current reports of a given paper via a dynamic SIB created from the "getReports()" method of the Paper class and saves the returned collection in the process context. The new value is added to this collection with a dynamic SIB created from the Java Collections Interface, using the former list as an instance for this method call. Finally, a method of the generated PaperController stores the new collection in the database.

This model so far is a hierarchical orchestration of processes. The SIBs have executable Java code, but the SLGs are "just" models and their process-level code generation is the next step.

5.5 Integrating Business Processes into the Enterprise Environment

The code generator of the jABC generates the code for this process as a Java class named SubmitReportToPaper, whose execute method starts the process. This code could be deployed in the standard way on a server, but we instead wish to not have to deal with Java source code – a too technical level for the user friendly service oriented approach we are following. Instead, DyWA generates a web application interface based on the modeled processes in form of a *controller*. This last step makes the ready to use process available again to end users in the DyWA website: the web application is ready, and no manual coding has been required.

6 Evolution and Development Cycles

In general, a prototype-driven development style for real dev-ops style development and operations cycles through multiple stages of refinement and enhancement. In iterative software development by prototyping, as common in Continuous Model-Driven Engineering, changes happen often but with modest increments. However, when considering modification and evolution, anything can change over time.

6.1 Changes That do not Affect the Domain

If new requirements force an update of the business processes, but the domain model is untouched, the processes that implement the new requirements can be modeled within the jABC while the previous version is running. An updated version of the web application is created with the code generators of the jABC and the DyWA framework, all in an off-line fashion, so that the currently deployed web application still runs and is not affected by these changes. Applying the changes and meeting the new requirements only needs a redeployment of the updated web application as a drop-in replacement. Since we are focusing on short-running processes, i.e collections of separated use cases that are triggered via user interaction, this redeployment mechanism allows us to minimize the impact on the availability of the application and therefore on the users. This ease of update encourages constant updates of the application and enables a modern, incremental prototype driven experimentation.

6.2   Update to the Domain

In case some requirement changes lead to an update of the domain of the web application, the separation of off-line and on-line stages comes into play. When the DyWA code generator generates the domain classes and services, it creates a snapshot of the type schema at that point of time: this is the fixed snapshot later used by the processes of the prototype. Because the web application is running on a meta schema, the modeled types only constitute a specific parametrization of this meta schema, and are maintained separately. This means that the domain information may be changed independently of the currently active prototype, because the meta schema and the prototype are only loosely linked by the transformation layer. Due to our implementation of the meta schema[1] and our approach that the entire application's behavior is defined in the processes, domain changes do not impact the executability of the currently active version of the prototype.

Domain experts can therefore frequently and swiftly update also the requirements of their domain without impacting the current prototype. Changes of the domain will only take effect if and when the processes are correspondingly updated as well, as described before, delivering an updated running prototype. This updated prototype can be used as a drop-in replacement too, because the business layer uses the "transformation" layer, which is capable of handling arbitrary domains, and the controllers offering the necessary operations to communicate with the database.

However, if the updated processes require new information elements that extend the data from previous prototypes, it is necessary to first migrate the application data between the different domains (or domain versions). This migration can be done online (while the application is running) in a step-by-step fashion. There is no need for a complex migration script that does it all at once. Some migration steps can even be done by the users themselves.

6.3   Evolving the OCS-Lite

For our OCS-lite, we wish to apply the requirement changes described in section 3 to the currently deployed web application. Requirements C1) and C2) need a domain extension: with the DyWA type editor we update the domain adding to the type "Report" the new attribute "Feedback" and marking the now obsolete attribute "Evaluation" as *deleted*.

Starting the jABC per script, one can now automatically re-execute the preceding steps of the domain generator on the updated type schema, and update the business processes in order to handle the new data elements. The updated

---

[1] Especially when deleting types/fields, we only mark those types/fields as deleted, allowing existing processes to still access the old data

"SubmitReportToPaper" process is shown in fig. 4. It uses the new `setFeedback` method of the `ReportController` as well as a technical process which calls an external service to send the mail.

With the updated processes, we automatically create a new prototype that now allows the users to execute the new business process, which requires a textual feedback and sends this feedback to the author of the paper.

7 Related Work

The definition facility of our approach abstracts from technical details enabling to exchange the respective database implementation. This is true for many abstraction layers like object relational mappers [10] (which we base on in our approach), too. In addition, DyWA allows to exchange the class of database, i.e., whether a NoSQL, relational, or any other class of database is used.

Moreover, DyWA relies on a considerable Java EE [11] tool stack, which made it possible to build the framework with manageable effort. The definition of the domain and the processes is completely independent from the target language as well as the underlying technologies used. Hence, it would be possible to exchange the complete tool stack (e.g. to the .Net platform with C# [35]) of a prototype at any point in its lifetime as long as there is a DyWA conform implementation available as well as corresponding generators.

The modeling language WebML [5] and its successor IFML [4] adopted from the Object Management Group (OMG) in march 2014, focus on incorporating the application expert into defining the content, the interaction with the user, and the control behavior of the front-end of software applications [26]. They integrate with UML class diagrams for the domain model. Binding to the business logic is realized via connectors to UML dynamic diagrams (e.g., state charts and sequence diagrams) and BPMN. Hence, IFML provides a new modeling fragment for front-end design facilities and heavily relies on existing solutions like UML and BPMN for domain- and process modeling. The IFML approach and the underlying frameworks do not focus on prototype-driven development and merging domain- and business process modeling as they, e.g., have completely separated modeling and implementation phases. BPMN even lacks support for sophisticated service integration [6]. In our approach we natively include the general purpose process modeling framework jABC4, which allows us to provide a domain-specific, yet feature-rich modeling environment.

Another aspect that is handled differently across state-of-the-art approaches is the support for iterative prototyping and the ability to transition a prototype into a production-ready application. The issue with approaches like Spring Roo [29] that allow managing an application domain is that evolving the application domain is a non-trivial aspect. Existing solutions to this problem [37,36] show that, depending on where the domain information is realized, migrating an application domain might be quite cumbersome. To our knowledge the Process-Oriented Event-Driven Transaction Systems (POETS) [9] architecture is hereof the most related approach to DyWA regarding the mindset. In particular, the generalized and extended variant described in [2] starts with an 'empty' Enterprise Resource Planning (ERP) system, which is then at runtime filled with a data model, reports (data aggregations), and contracts (business logic). The definitions are done in Domain-Specific Languages (DSLs) mostly based on Haskell. Hence from the application experts perspective, the online data model definition in DyWA and the process-oriented definition of the business logic in our approach is quite different from POETS. Furthermore, POETS currently does not support data migration and non-additive changes to the data model.

In our approach we embrace a generic meta schema which reflects changes to the domain model and offers at the same time access to old and new type schema in the running application until a development iteration has finished. This simplifies and unfolds the migration process, and enables us to offer a service with near-zero downtime due to online migration. Nevertheless, we are able to maintain an interface to the application expert that acts like he or she is developing a native, domain-specific application. The structure of our meta-schema resembles the *ECore* model underlying the EMF [34] modeling framework.

8 Conclusions

We have shown how application experts can gain the full control over the complete (iterative) development process of web applications by combining agile, prototype-driven development with (business) process modeling via XMDD. The DyWA framework provides right from the beginning a fully functional prototype of a data model, where application experts can directly define a type schema for their domain of expertise. The type schema is automatically generated to executable domain specific entity classes and corresponding CRUD operations. On this basis, application experts model business processes, which are directly executable within the prototype. As every step is automated via a corresponding code generator, we open the whole development process, including the domain modeling, to the application expert. Domain model (in form of a type schema) and data coexist in one database. As we showed on our OCS-lite example, the stored data may even adhere to different versions of a type schema. This enables extremely short downtime phases and data migration at runtime. Due to a comparatively high degree of automation we are able to shrink the semantic gap concerning the provision of domain specific services and we can cope elegantly with the agility of agile development processes.

The experience so far with our prototype-driven approach turned out to be very promising. We have first external users [14], that right now are in the course of modeling a complex data and process models landscape for interdisciplinary experiments concerning cachexia in cancer metabolism [14] coordinated at the Universidade de São Paulo in Brazil. As the researchers are healthcare and life science experts (altogether, over 60 scientists) without computer science background, the ease of data management and process management is essential, in particular in the context of a continuously expanding network of international partners which requires ongoing adaptations.

References

1. Allweyer, T.: BPMN 2.0-Business Process Model and Notation. Bod (2009)
2. Collet, P.: Domain Specific Languages for Managing Feature Models: Advances and Challenges. In: Steffen, B., Margaria, T. (eds.) ISoLA 2014, Part I. LNCS, vol. 8802, pp. 273–288. Springer, Heidelberg (2014)
3. Beck, K.: Extreme Programming Explained: Embrace Change. The XP Series. Addison-Wesley (2000)
4. Brambilla, M., Fraternali, P.: Interaction Flow Modeling Language: Model-Driven UI Engineering of Web and Mobile Apps with IFML. The MK/OMG Press, Elsevier Science (2014)
5. Brambilla, M., Comai, S., Fraternali, P., Matera, M.: Designing Web Applications with Webml and Webratio. In: Rossi, G., Pastor, O., Schwabe, D., Olsina, L. (eds.) Web Engineering. Human-Computer Interaction Series, pp. 221–261. Springer (2008)
6. Doedt, M., Steffen, B.: An Evaluation of Service Integration Approaches of Business Process Management Systems. In: 2012 35th Annual IEEE on Software Engineering Workshop (SEW), pp. 158–167 (2012)
7. Eclipse Foundation: Teneo website (2013), www.eclipse.org/emft/projects/teneo (visited on May 16, 2013)
8. Harel, D., Marron, A., Weiss, G.: Behavioral programming. Commun. ACM 55(7), 90–100 (2012)
9. Henglein, F., Larsen, K.F., Simonsen, J.G., Stefansen, C.: Poets: Process-Oriented Event-Driven Transaction Systems. Journal of Logic and Algebraic Programming 78(5), 381–401 (2009), The 1st Worksh. on Formal Languages and Analysis of Contract-Oriented Software (FLACOS 2007)
10. JBoss Inc.: Hibernate website (2013), http://www.hibernate.org/ (visited on May 17, 2013)
11. Jendrock, E., Evans, I., Gollapudi, D., Haase, K., Cervera-Navarro, R., Srivathsa, C., Markito, W.: Java EE 7 Tutorial, vol. 2. Pearson Education (2014)
12. Karusseit, M., Margaria, T.: A Web-Based Runtime-Reconfigurable Role Management Service (2007)
13. Karusseit, M., Margaria, T.: Feature-based Modelling of a Complex, Online-Reconfigurable Decision Support Service. Electr. Notes Theor. Comput. Sci. 157(2), 101–118 (2006)
14. Margaria, T., Floyd, B., Camargo, R.G., Lamprecht, A.-L., Neubauer, J., Seelaender, M.: Simple management of high assurance data in long-lived interdisciplinary healthcare research: A proposal. In: Steffen, B., Margaria, T. (eds.) ISoLA 2014. LNCS, vol. 8803, pp. 529–547. Springer, Heidelberg (2014)
15. Margaria, T., Steffen, B.: Business Process Modeling in the jABC: The One-Thing Approach. In: Handbook of Research on Business Process Modeling, pp. 1–26. IGI Global (2009)
16. Margaria, T.: Service is in the Eyes of the Beholder. IEEE Computer (November 2007)
17. Margaria, T., Steffen, B.: Lightweight coarse-grained coordination: a scalable system-level approach. STTT 5(2-3), 107–123 (2004)
18. Margaria, T., Steffen, B.: Agile it: Thinking in user-centric models. In: Margaria, T., Steffen, B. (eds.) ISoLA 2008. CCIS, vol. 17, pp. 490–502. Springer, Heidelberg (2009)

19. Margaria, T., Steffen, B.: Continuous Model-Driven Engineering. IEEE Computer 42, 106–109 (2009)
20. Margaria, T., Steffen, B.: Service-Orientation: Conquering Complexity with XMDD. In: Hinchey, M., Koyle, L. (eds.) Conquering Complexity, Springer (2012)
21. Müller-Olm, M., Schmidt, D.A., Steffen, B.: Model-Checking: A Tutorial Introduction. SAS, 330–354 (1999)
22. Neubauer, J.: Higher-Order Process Engineering. Phd thesis, Technische Universität Dortmund (2014), http://hdl.handle.net/2003/33479
23. Neubauer, J., Margaria, T., Steffen, B.: Design for Verifiability: The OCS Case Study. In: Formal Methods for Industrial Critical Systems: A Survey of Applications. John Wiley & Sons (2011) (in print)
24. Neubauer, J., Steffen, B.: Plug-and-Play Higher-Order Process Integration. Computer 46(11), 56–62 (2013)
25. Neubauer, J., Steffen, B.: Second-order servification. In: Zoeppritz, M., Blaser, A. (eds.) IBM 1983. LNBIP, vol. 150, pp. 13–25. Springer, Heidelberg (1983)
26. Object Management Group, Inc., Ifml website (2014), http://www.ifml.org(visited on July 25, 2014)
27. Pasley, J.: How BPEL and SOA are changing Web services development. IEEE Internet Computing 9(3), 60–67 (2005)
28. Recker, J., Mendling, J.: On the translation between BPMN and BPEL: Conceptual mismatch between process modeling languages. In: CAiSE Proc. of Workshops and Doctoral Consortium, pp. 521–532. Namur Uni. Press (2006)
29. Rimple, K., Penchikala, S., Alex, B.: Spring Roo in action. Manning (2012)
30. Schwaber, K.: Agile Project Management with Scrum. Microsoft Press (2009)
31. Steffen, B., Margaria, T.: METAFrame in practice: Design of intelligent network services. In: Olderog, E.-R., Steffen, B. (eds.) Correct System Design. LNCS, vol. 1710, pp. 390–415. Springer, Heidelberg (1999)
32. Steffen, B., Margaria, T., Braun, V., Kalt, N.: Hierarchical Service Definition. In: Annual Review of Communication, pp. 847–856. Int. Engineering Consortium Chicago (USA), IEC (1997)
33. Steffen, B., Margaria, T., Nagel, R., Jörges, S., Kubczak, C.: Model-Driven Development with the jABC. In: Bin, E., Ziv, A., Ur, S. (eds.) HVC 2006. LNCS, vol. 4383, pp. 92–108. Springer, Heidelberg (2007)
34. Steinberg, D., Budinsky, F., Paternostro, M., Merks, E.: EMF: Eclipse Modeling Framework 2.0, 2nd edn. Addison-Wesley Professional (2009)
35. Troelsen, A.: C# and the. NET Platform, vol. 1. Apress (2001)
36. Vermolen, S.D., Wachsmuth, G., Visser, E.: Generating Database Migrations for Evolving Web Applications. In: Proc. 10th ACM Int. Conf. on Generative Programming and Component Engineering, GPCE 2011, pp. 83–92. ACM, New York (2011)
37. Wimmer, M., Moreno, N., Vallecillo, A.: Systematic Evolution of WebML Models by Coupled Transformations. In: Brambilla, M., Tokuda, T., Tolksdorf, R. (eds.) ICWE 2012. LNCS, vol. 7387, pp. 185–199. Springer, Heidelberg (2012)

Domain-Specific Languages
for Enterprise Systems

Jesper Andersen[2], Patrick Bahr[1], Fritz Henglein[1], and Tom Hvitved[1]

[1] Department of Computer Science, University of Copenhagen, Universitetsparken 5,
2100 Copenhagen, Denmark
{bahr,henglein,hvitved}@diku.dk
[2] Configit A/S, Kristianiagade 7, 2100 Copenhagen, Denmark
ja@configit.com

Abstract. The process-oriented event-driven transaction systems (PO-ETS) architecture introduced by Henglein et al. is a novel software architecture for enterprise resource planning (ERP) systems. POETS employs a pragmatic separation between (i) transactional data, that is, what has happened; (ii) reports, that is, what can be derived from the transactional data; and (iii) contracts, that is, which transactions are expected in the future. Moreover, POETS applies domain-specific languages (DSLs) for specifying reports and contracts, in order to enable succinct declarative specifications as well as rapid adaptability and customisation. In this paper we present an implementation of a generalised and extended variant of the POETS architecture. The extensions amount to a customisable data model based on nominal subtyping; support for run-time changes to the data model, reports and contracts, while retaining full auditability; and support for referable data that may evolve over time, also while retaining full auditability as well as referential integrity. Besides the revised architecture, we present the DSLs used to specify data definitions, reports, and contracts respectively. Finally, we illustrate a use case scenario, which we implemented in a trial for a small business.

1 Introduction

Enterprise Resource Planning (ERP) systems are comprehensive software systems used to integrate and manage business activities in enterprises. Such activities include—but are not limited to—financial management (accounting), production planning, supply chain management and customer relationship management. ERP systems emerged as a remedy to heterogeneous systems, in which data and functionality are spread out—and duplicated—amongst dedicated subsystems. Instead, an ERP system it built around a central database, which stores all information in one place.

Traditional ERP systems such as Microsoft Dynamics NAV[1], Microsoft Dynamics AX[2], and SAP[3] are three-tier architectures with a client, an application

---

[1] http://www.microsoft.com/en-us/dynamics/products/nav-overview.aspx.
[2] http://www.microsoft.com/en-us/dynamics/products/ax-overview.aspx.
[3] http://www.sap.com.

T. Margaria and B. Steffen (Eds.): ISoLA 2014, Part I, LNCS 8802, pp. 73–95, 2014.
© Springer-Verlag Berlin Heidelberg 2014

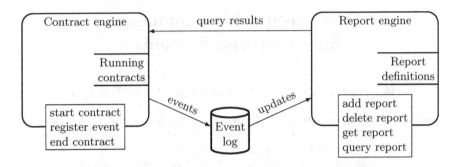

Fig. 1. Bird's-eye view of the POETS architecture (diagram copied from [6])

server, and a centralised relational database system. The central database stores information in tables, and the application server provides the business logic, typically coded in a general purpose, imperative programming language.

The process-oriented event-driven transaction systems (POETS) architecture introduced by Henglein et al. [6] is a qualitatively different approach to ERP systems. Rather than storing both transactional data and implicit process state in a database, POETS employs a pragmatic separation between transactional data, which is persisted in an *event log*, and *contracts*, which are explicit representations of business processes, stored in a separate module. Moreover, rather than using general purpose programming languages to specify business processes, POETS utilises a declarative domain-specific language (DSL) [1]. The use of a DSL not only enables compositional construction of formalised business processes, it minimises the semantic gap between requirements and a running system, and it facilitates treating processes as data for analysis. Henglein et al. take it as a goal of POETS that "[...] the formalized requirements *are* the system" [6, page 382].

The bird's-eye view of the POETS architecture is presented in Figure 1. At the heart of the system is the event log, which is an append-only list of transactions. Transactions represent "things that take place" such as a payment by a customer, a delivery of goods by a shipping agency, or a movement of items in an inventory. The append-only restriction serves two purposes. First, it is a legal requirement in ERP systems that transactions, which are relevant for auditing, are retained. Second, the report engine utilises monotonicity of the event log for optimisation, as shown by Nissen and Larsen [19].

Besides the radically different software architecture, POETS distinguishes itself from existing ERP systems by abandoning the double-entry bookkeeping (DEB) accounting principle [28] in favour of the Resources, Events, and Agents (REA) accounting model of McCarthy [13].

1.1 Outline and Contributions

The motivation for our work is to assess the POETS architecture in terms of a prototype implementation. During the implementation process we have added features for dynamically managing values and entities to the original architecture. Moreover, in the process we found that the architecture need not be tied to the REA ontology—indeed to ERP systems—but can be viewed as a discrete event modelling framework. Its adequacy for other domains remains future research, however.

Our contributions are as follows:

- We present a generalised and extended POETS architecture (Section 2) that has been fully implemented.
- We present domain-specific languages for data modelling (Section 2.1), report specification (Section 2.4), and contract specification (Section 2.5).
- We illustrate small use case that we have implemented in our system as part of a trial for a small business (Section 3).

The POETS server system has been implemented in Haskell. Its client code has been developed in Java, primarily for Android. The choice of Haskell, specifically the Glasgow Haskell Compiler (GHC), is due to: the conciseness, affinity and support of functional programming for enterprise software [14] and declarative DSL implementation; its expressive type system, which supports statically typed solutions to the Expression Problem [3,2]; and competitive run-time performance due to advanced compiler optimisations in GHC. The use of Java on the client side (not further discussed in this paper) arises from POETS, conceived to be cloud-based and mobile from the outset, targeting low-cost mobile devices and a practical desire to reuse code as much as possible across smartphones, tablets, portables and desktops.

The source code of this implementation is available from the repository at https://bitbucket.org/jespera/poets/. In addition, the repository also includes the full source code for the use case presented in Section 3.

2   Revised POETS Architecture

Our generalised and extended architecture is presented in Figure 2. Compared to the original architecture in Figure 1, the revised architecture sees the addition of three new components: a *data model*, an *entity store*, and a *rule engine*. The rule engine is currently not implemented, and we will therefore not return to this module until Section 4.2.

As in the original POETS architecture, the event log is at the heart of the system. However, in the revised architecture the event log plays an even greater role, as it is the *only* persistent state of the system. This means that the states of all other modules are also persisted in the event log, hence the flow of information from all other modules to the event log in Figure 2. For example, whenever a contract is started or a new report is added to the system, then an event reflecting this operation is persisted in the event log. This, in turn, means that the state of each module can—in principle—be derived from the event log. However, for performance reasons each module—including the event log—maintains its own state in memory.

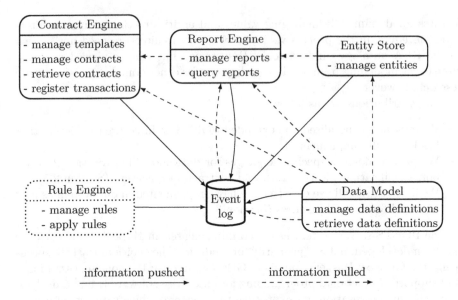

Fig. 2. Bird's-eye view of the generalised and extended POETS architecture

Data Model		
Function	**Input**	**Output**
addDataDefs	ontology specification	
getRecordDef	record name	type definition
getSubTypes	record name	list of record names

Fig. 3. Data model interface

We describe each module of the revised architecture in the following subsections. Since we will focus on the revised architecture in the remainder of the text, we will refer to said architecture simply as POETS.

2.1   Data Model

The data model is a core component of the extended architecture, and the interface it provides is summarised in Figure 3. The data model defines the *types* of data that are used throughout the system, and it includes predefined types such as events. Custom types such as invoices can be added to the data model at run-time via *addDataDefs*. For simplicity we currently only allow addition of types, not updates and deletions, which can be supported by suitable namespace management.

Types define the structure of the data in a running POETS instance manifested as *values*. A value—such as a concrete invoice—is an instance of the data specified by a type. Values are not only communicated between the system and its environment but they are also stored in the event log, which is simply a list of values of a certain type.

Types. Structural data such as payments and invoices are represented as *records*, that is, typed finite mappings from field labels to values. Record types define the structure of such records by listing the constituent field labels and their associated types. In order to form a hierarchical ontology of record types, we use a nominal subtyping system [22]. That is, each record type has a unique name, and one type is a subtype of another if and only if stated so explicitly or by transitivity. For instance, a customer can be defined as a subtype of a person, which means that a customer contains all the data of a person, similar to inheritance in object oriented programming.

The choice of nominal types over structural types [22] is justified by the domain: the nominal type associated with a record may have a semantic impact. For instance, the type of customers and premium customers may be structurally equal, but a value of one type is considered different from the other, and clients of the system may for example choose to render them differently. Moreover, the purpose of the rule engine, which we return to in Section 4.2, is to define rules for values of a particular semantic domain, such as invoices. Hence it is wrong to apply these rules to data that happens to have the same structure as invoices. Although we use nominal types to classify data, the DSLs support full record polymorphism [20] in order to minimise code duplication. That is, it is possible for instance to use the same piece of code with customers and premium customers, even if they are not related in the subtyping hierarchy.

The grammar for types is as follows:

$$T ::= \mathbf{Bool} \mid \mathbf{Int} \mid \mathbf{Real} \mid \mathbf{String} \mid \mathbf{Timestamp} \mid \mathbf{Duration} \quad \text{(type constants)}$$
$$\mid \mathit{RecordName} \quad \text{(record type)}$$
$$\mid [T] \quad \text{(list type)}$$
$$\mid \langle \mathit{RecordName} \rangle \quad \text{(entity type)}$$

Type constants are standard types Booleans, integers, reals, and strings, and less standard types timestamps (absolute time) and durations (relative time). Record types are named types, and the record typing environment—which we will describe shortly—defines the structure of records. For record types we assume a set $\mathit{RecordName} = \{\mathsf{Customer}, \mathsf{Address}, \mathsf{Invoice}, \dots\}$ of record names ranged over by r. Concrete record types are typeset in sans-serif and begin with a capital letter. Likewise, we assume a set $\mathit{FieldName}$ of all field names ranged over by f. Concrete field names are typeset in sans-serif beginning with a lower-case letter.

List types $[\tau]$ represent lists of values, where each element has type τ, and it is the only collection type currently supported. Entity types $\langle r \rangle$ represent entity values that have associated data of type r. For instance, if the record type Customer describes the data of a customer, then a value of type $\langle \mathsf{Customer} \rangle$ is a (unique) customer entity, whose associated Customer data may evolve over time. The type system ensures that a value of an entity type will have associated data of the given type, similar to referential integrity in database systems [4]. We will return to how entities are created and modified in Section 2.3.

All data are type checked before they enter the system, both in order to check that record values conform with the record typing environment, but also to check that entity values have valid associated data. In particular, events are type checked before they are persisted in the event log. We will explain what this means in detail in Section 2.2 and 2.3. The typing judgement has the form $\mathcal{R}, \mathcal{E} \vdash v : \tau$, where $\mathcal{R}$ is a record typing environment, which contains record type definitions, $\mathcal{E}$ is an entity typing environment, which maps each defined entity to its declared type, v is a value, and τ is a type. Both $\mathcal{R}$ and $\mathcal{E}$ are given by the data model and the entity store, respectively. The POETS system has a type checker that checks whether a value v has type τ in the context of $\mathcal{R}$ and $\mathcal{E}$.

Ontology Language. In order to specify record types, we use a variant of Attempto Controlled English [5] due to Jønsson Thomsen [10], referred to as the *ontology language*. The approach is to define data types in near-English text, in order to minimise the gap between requirements and specification. A simple example in the ontology language is given below:

Person is abstract.   *Address has a String called road.*
Person has a String called name.   *Address has an Int called no.*

Customer is a Person.
Customer has an Address.

Predefined Ontology. Unlike the original POETS architecture [6], our generalised architecture is not fixed to an enterprise resource planning (ERP) domain. However, we require a set of predefined record types.

The predefined ontology defines five root concepts in the data model, that is, record types maximal with respect to the subtyping relation. Each of these five root concepts Data, Event, Transaction, Report, and Contract are abstract and only Event and Contract define record fields. Custom data definitions added via *addDataDefs* are only permitted as subtypes of Data, Transaction, Report, and Contract. In contrast to that, Event has a predefined and fixed hierarchy.

Data types represent elements in the domain of the system such as customers, items, and resources.
Transaction types represent events that are associated with a contract, such as payments, deliveries, and issuing of invoices.
Report types are result types of report functions, that is, the data of reports, such as inventory status, income statement, and list of customers. The Report structure does not define *how* reports are computed, only *what kind* of result is computed. We will describe the report engine in Section 2.4.
Contract types represent the different kinds of contracts, such as sales, purchases, and manufacturing procedures. Similar to Report, the structure does not define what the contract dictates, only what is required to instantiate the contract. The purpose of Contract is hence dual to the purpose of Report: the former determines an input type, and the latter determines an output type. We will return to contracts in Section 2.5.

Event types form a fixed hierarchy and represent events that are logged in the system. Events are conceptually separated into *internal* events and *external* events, which we describe further in the following section.

2.2   Event Log

The event log is the only persistent state of the system, and it describes the complete state of a running POETS instance. The event log is an append-only list of records of the type Event. Each event reflects an atomic interaction with the running system. This approach is also applied at the "meta level" of POETS: in order to allow agile evolution of a running POETS instance, changes to the data model, reports, and contracts are reflected in the event log as well.

The monotonic nature of the event log—data is never overwritten or deleted from the system—means that the state of the system can be reconstructed at any previous point in time. In particular, transactions are never deleted, which is a legal requirement for ERP systems. The only component of the architecture that reads directly from the event log is the report engine (compare Figure 2), hence the only way to access data in the log is via a report.

All events are equipped with an internal timestamp (internalTimeStamp), the time at which the event is registered in the system. Therefore, the event log is always monotonically decreasing with respect to internal timestamps, as the newest event is at the head of the list. Conceptually, events are divided into *external* and *internal* events.

External events are events that are associated with a contract, and only the contract engine writes external events to the event log. The event type TransactionEvent models external events, and it consists of three parts: (i) a contract identifier (contractId), (ii) a timestamp (timeStamp), and (iii) a transaction (transaction). The identifier associates the external event with a contract, and the timestamp represents the time at which the external event takes place. Note that the timestamp need not coincide with the internal timestamp. For instance, a payment in a sales contract may be registered in the system the day after it takes place. There is hence no a priori guarantee that external events have decreasing timestamps in the event log—only external events that pertain to the same contract are required to have decreasing timestamps. The last component, transaction, represents the actual action that takes place, such as a payment from one person or company to another. The transaction is a record of type Transaction, for which the system makes no assumptions.

Internal events reflect changes in the state of the system at a meta level. This is the case for example when a contract is instantiated or when a new record definition is added. Internal events are represented by the remaining subtypes of the Event record type. Figure 4 provides an overview of all non-abstract record types that represent internal events.

A common pattern for internal events is to have three event types to represent creation, update, and deletion of respective components. For instance, when a report is added to the report engine, a CreateReport event is persisted to the log, and when it is updated or deleted, UpdateReport and DeleteReport events

Event	Description
AddDataDefs	A set of data definitions is added to the system. The field defs contains the ontology language specification.
CreateEntity	An entity is created. The field data contains the data associated with the entity, the field recordType contains the string representation of the declared type, and the field ent contains the newly created entity value.
UpdateEntity	The data associated with an entity is updated.
DeleteEntity	An entity is deleted.
CreateReport	A report is created. The field code contains the specification of the report, and the fields description and tags are meta data.
UpdateReport	A report is updated.
DeleteReport	A report is deleted.
CreateContractDef	A contract template is created. The field code contains the specification of the contract template, and the fields recordType and description are meta data.
UpdateContractDef	A contract template is updated.
DeleteContractDef	A contract template is deleted.
CreateContract	A contract is instantiated. The field contractId contains the newly created identifier of the contract and the field contract contains the name of the contract template to instantiate, as well as data needed to instantiate the contract template.
UpdateContract	A contract is updated.
ConcludeContract	A contract is concluded.

Fig. 4. Internal events

are persisted accordingly. This means that previous versions of the report specification can be retrieved, and more generally that the system can be restarted simply by replaying the events that are persisted in the log on an initially empty system. Another benefit to the approach is that the report engine, for instance, does not need to provide built-in functionality to retrieve, say, the list of all reports added within the last month—such a list can instead be computed as a report itself!

Since we allow the data model of the system to evolve over time, we must be careful to ensure that the event log, and thus all data in it, remains well-typed at any point in time. Let $\mathcal{R}_t$, $\mathcal{E}_t$, and l_t denote the record typing environment, entity typing environment, and event log, respectively at time t. Since an entity might be deleted over time, and thus is removed from the entity typing environment, the event log may not be well-typed with respect to the current entity typing environment. To this end, we type the event log with respect to the *accumulated entity typing environment* $\widehat{\mathcal{E}}_t = \bigcup_{t' \leq t} \mathcal{E}_{t'}$ at time t. That is, $\widehat{\mathcal{E}}_t(e) = r$ iff there is some time $t' \leq t$ with $\mathcal{E}_{t'}(e) = r$. The *stable type* invariant, which we will discuss in Section 2.3, guarantees that $\widehat{\mathcal{E}}_t$ is indeed well-defined.

Entity Store		
Function	**Input**	**Output**
createEntity	record name, record	entity
updateEntity	entity, record	
deleteEntity	entity	

Fig. 5. Entity store interface

For changes to the record typing environment, we require the following invariants for any points in time t, t' and the event log l_t at time t:

$$\text{if } t' \leq t \text{ then } \mathcal{R}_{t'} \subseteq \mathcal{R}_t, \text{ and} \qquad \text{(monotonicity)}$$

$$\mathcal{R}_t, \widehat{\mathcal{E}_t} \vdash l_t : [\text{Event}] . \qquad \text{(log typing)}$$

Note that the *log typing* invariant follows from the *monotonicity* invariant and the type checking $\mathcal{R}_t, \mathcal{E}_t \vdash e : \text{Event}$ for each new incoming event, provided that for each record name r occurring in the event log, no additional record fields are added to r, and r is not made an abstract record type. We will refer to the two invariants above collectively as *record typing invariants*. They will become crucial in the following section.

2.3 Entity Store

The entity store provides very simple functionality, namely creation, deletion and updating of entities, respectively. To this end, the entity store maintains an entity environment ϵ_t that maps each defined entity e to its value $\epsilon_t(e)$. In addition, the entity store also maintains a compact representation of the history of entity environments $\epsilon_0, \ldots, \epsilon_t$. The interface of the entity store is summarised in Figure 5.

In order to type check entities, the entity store also maintains an *entity typing environment* $\mathcal{E}_t$, that is, a finite partial mapping from entities to record names. Intuitively, an entity typing environment maps an entity to the record type that it has been declared to have upon creation.

The entity store checks a number of invariants that ensure the integrity of the system. Specifically, the entity store ensures the following invariants, where we use the notation $\mathcal{E}_t$, $\mathcal{R}_t$ and ϵ_t, for the entity typing environment, the record typing environment, and the entity environment, respectively at time t:

$$\text{if } \mathcal{E}_t(e) = r \text{ and } \mathcal{E}_{t'}(e) = r', \text{ then } r = r', \qquad \text{(stable type)}$$

$$\text{if } \mathcal{E}_t(e) \text{ is defined, then so is } \epsilon_t(e), \text{ and} \qquad \text{(well-definedness)}$$

$$\text{if } \epsilon_t(e) = v, \text{ then } \mathcal{E}_t(e) = r \text{ and } \mathcal{R}_{t'}, \mathcal{E}_{t'} \vdash v : r \text{ for some } t' \leq t. \quad \text{(well-typing)}$$

We refer to the three invariants above collectively as the *entity integrity invariants*. The *stable type* invariant states that each entity can have at most one declared type throughout its lifetime. The *well-definedness* invariant guarantees that every entity that is given a type also has an associated record value. Finally, the *well-typing* invariant guarantees that the record value associated with an entity *was* well-typed at some earlier point in time t'.

The creation of a new entity via *createEntity* at time $t+1$ requires a declared type r and an initial record value v, and it is checked that $\mathcal{R}_t, \mathcal{E}_t \vdash v : r$. If the value type checks, a *fresh* entity value $e \notin \bigcup_{t' \leq t} \mathrm{dom}(\epsilon_{t'})$ is created, and the entity environment and the entity typing environment are updated accordingly:

$$\epsilon_{t+1}(x) = \begin{cases} v & \text{if } x = e, \\ \epsilon_t(x) & \text{otherwise,} \end{cases} \qquad \mathcal{E}_{t+1}(x) = \begin{cases} r & \text{if } x = e, \\ \mathcal{E}_t(x) & \text{otherwise.} \end{cases}$$

Moreover, a CreateEntity event is persisted to the event log containing e, r, and v for the relevant fields.

Similarly, if the data associated with an entity e is updated to the value v at time $t+1$, then it is checked that $\mathcal{R}_t, \mathcal{E}_t \vdash v : \mathcal{E}_t(e)$, and the entity store is updated like above. Note that the entity typing environment is unchanged, that is, $\mathcal{E}_{t+1} = \mathcal{E}_t$. A corresponding UpdateEntity event is persisted to the event log containing e and v for the relevant fields.

Finally, if an entity e is deleted at time $t+1$, then it is removed from both the entity store and the entity typing environment:

$$\epsilon_{t+1}(x) = \epsilon_t(x) \text{ iff } x \in \mathrm{dom}(\epsilon_t) \setminus \{e\}$$
$$\mathcal{E}_{t+1}(x) = \mathcal{E}_t(x) \text{ iff } x \in \mathrm{dom}(\mathcal{E}_t) \setminus \{e\}.$$

A corresponding DeleteEntity event is persisted to the event log containing e for the relevant field.

Note that, by default, $\epsilon_{t+1} = \epsilon_t$ and $\mathcal{E}_{t+1} = \mathcal{E}_t$, unless one of the situations above apply. It is straightforward to show that the *entity integrity invariants* are maintained by the operations described above (the proof follows by induction on the timestamp t). Internally, that is, for the report engine compare Figure 2, the entity store provides a lookup function $\mathrm{lookup}_t : Ent \times [0, t] \rightharpoonup_{\mathrm{fin}} Record$, where $\mathrm{lookup}_t(e, t')$ provides the latest value associated with the entity e at time t', where t is the current time. Note that this includes the case in which e has been deleted at or before time t'. In that case, the value associated with e just before the deletion is returned. Formally, lookup_t is defined in terms of the entity environments as follows:

$$\mathrm{lookup}_t(e, t_1) = v \text{ iff } \exists t_2 \leq t_1 : \epsilon_{t_2}(e) = v \text{ and } \forall t_2 < t_3 \leq t_1 : e \notin \mathrm{dom}(\epsilon_{t_3}).$$

In particular, we have that if $e \in \mathrm{dom}(\epsilon_{t_1})$, then $\mathrm{lookup}_t(e, t_1) = \epsilon_{t_1}(e)$.

From this definition and the invariants of the system, we can derive the following fundamental safety property for the entity store:

Proposition 1. *Given timestamps $t \leq t_1 \leq t_2$ and entity e, the following holds:*

If $\mathcal{R}_t, \widehat{\mathcal{E}}_t \vdash e : \langle r \rangle$, then $\mathrm{lookup}_{t_2}(e, t_1) = v$ for some v and $\mathcal{R}_{t_2}, \widehat{\mathcal{E}}_{t_2} \vdash v : r$.

Report Engine		
Function	**Input**	**Output**
addReport	name, type, description, tags, report definition	
updateReport	name, type, description, tags, report definition	
deleteReport	name	
queryReport	name, list of values	value

Fig. 6. Report engine interface

That is, if an entity value previously entered the system, and hence type checked, then all future dereferencing will not get stuck, and the obtained value will be well-typed with respect to the accumulated entity typing environment.

2.4 Report Engine

The purpose of the report engine is to provide user-definable views, called *reports*, of the system's event log.[4] Conceptually, a report is compiled from the event log by a *report function*, a function of type [Event] → Report. The *report language* provides a means to specify such a report function in a declarative manner. The interface of the report engine is summarised in Figure 6.

The Report Language. The report language is—much like the query fragment of *SQL*—a functional language *without side effects*. It only provides operations to non-destructively manipulate and combine values. Since the system's storage is based on a shallow event log, the report language must provide operations to relate, filter, join, and aggregate pieces of information. Moreover, as the data stored in the event log is inherently heterogeneous—containing data of different kinds—the report language offers a comprehensive type system that allows us to safely operate in this setting.

The report language is based on the simply typed lambda calculus extended with polymorphic (non-recursive) let expressions as well as type case expressions. The core language is given by the following grammar:

$$e ::= x \mid c \mid \lambda x.e \mid e_1\,e_2 \mid \textbf{let } x = e_1 \textbf{ in } e_2 \mid \textbf{type } x = e \textbf{ of } \{r \to e_1; \_ \to e_2\},$$

where x ranges over variables, and c over constants which include integers, Booleans, tuples and list constructors as well as operations on them like +, *if-then-else* etc. In particular, we assume a fold operation **fold** of type $(\alpha \to \beta \to \beta) \to \beta \to [\alpha] \to \beta$. This is the only operation of the report language that permits recursive computations on lists. However, the full language provides syntactic sugar to express operations on lists more intuitively in the form of list comprehensions [26].

---

[4] The term "report" often conflates the data computed and their visual rendering; here "report" denotes only the computed data.

The extended list comprehensions of the report language also allows the programmer to filter according to run-time type information, which builds on type case expressions of the form **type** $x = e$ **of** $\{r \to e_1; \_ \to e_2\}$ in the core language. In such a type case expression, an expression e of some record type r_e gets evaluated to record value v which is then bound to a variable x. The record type r that the record value v is matched against can be any subtype of r_e. Further evaluation of the type case expression depends on the type r_v of the record value v. This type can be any subtype of r_e. If r_v is a subtype of r, then the evaluation proceeds with e_1, otherwise with e_2. Binding e to a variable x allows us to use the stricter type r in the expression e_1.

Another important component of the report language consists of the dereferencing operators ! and @, which give access to the lookup operator provided by the entity store. Given an expression e of an entity type $\langle r \rangle$, both dereferencing operators provide a value v of type r. That is, both ! and @ are unary operators of type $\langle r \rangle \to r$ for any record type r. In the case of the operator !, the resulting record value v is the latest value associated with the entity to which e evaluates. More concretely, given an entity value v, the expression $v!$ evaluates to the record value $\text{lookup}_t(v, t)$, where t is the current time ("now").

On the other hand, the *contextual* dereference operator @ yields the value of an entity at the time of the event it is extracted from. Concretely, every entity v that enters the event log is annotated with the timestamp of the event it occurs in. That is, each entity value embedded in an event e in the event log, occurs in an annotated form (v, s), where s is the value of e's internalTimeStamp field. Given such an annotated entity value (v, s), the expression $(v,s)@$ evaluates to $\text{lookup}_t(v, s)$ and given a bare entity value v the expression $v@$ evaluates to $\text{lookup}_t(v, t)$.

Note that in each case for either of the two dereference operators, Proposition 1 guarantees that the lookup operation yields a record value of the right type. That is, they are total functions of type $\langle r \rangle \to r$ that never get stuck.

Lifecycle of Reports. Like entities, the set of reports registered in a running POETS instance—and thus available for querying—can be changed via the external interface to the report engine. To this end, the report engine interface provides the operations *addReport*, *updateReport*, and *deleteReport*. The former two take a *report specification* that contains the name of the report, the definition of the report function that generates the report data and the type of the report function. Optionally, it may also contain further meta information in the form of a description text and a list of tags.

The remaining operation provided by the report engine—*queryReport*—constitutes the core functionality of the reporting system. Given a name of a registered report and a list of arguments, this operation supplies the given arguments to the corresponding report function and returns the result.

Contract Engine		
Function	**Input**	**Output**
createTemplate	name, type, description, specification	
updateTemplate	name, type, description, specification	
deleteTemplate	name	
createContract	meta data	contract ID
updateContract	contract ID, meta data	
concludeContract	contract ID	
getContract	contract ID	contract state
registerTransaction	contract ID, timestamp, transaction	

Fig. 7. Contract engine interface

2.5   Contract Engine

The role of the contract engine is to determine which transactions—that is, external events, compare Section 2.2—are expected by the system. Transactions model events that take place according to an *agreement*, for instance a delivery of goods in a sale, a payment in a lease agreement, or a movement of items from one inventory to another in a production plan. Such agreements are referred to as *contracts*, although they need not be legally binding contracts. The purpose of a contract is to provide a detailed description of *what* is expected, by *whom*, and *when*. A sales contract, for example, may stipulate that first the company sends an invoice, then the customer pays within a certain deadline, and finally the company delivers goods within another deadline.

The interface of the contract engine is shown in Figure 7.

Contract Templates. In order to specify contracts such as the aforementioned sales contract, we use an extended variant of the contract specification language (CSL) of Hvitved et al. [9], which we will refer to as the POETS contract specification language (PCSL) in the following. For reusability, contracts are always specified as *contract templates* rather than as concrete contracts. A contract template consists of four parts: (i) a template name, (ii) a template type, which is a subtype of the Contract record type, (iii) a textual description, and (iv) a PCSL specification. We describe PCSL in Section 2.5.

The template name is a unique identifier, and the template type determines the parameters that are available in the contract template.

Example 1. We may define the following type for sales contracts in the ontology language (assuming that the record types Customer, Company, and Goods have been defined):

Sale is a Contract.
Sale has a Customer entity.
Sale has a Company entity.

Sale has a list of Goods.
Sale has an Int called amount.

With this definition, contract templates of type Sale are parametrised over the fields customer, company, goods, and amount of types $\langle$Customer$\rangle$, $\langle$Company$\rangle$, [Goods], and Int, respectively.

The contract engine provides an interface to add contract templates (*createTemplate*), update contract templates (*updateTemplate*), and remove contract templates (*deleteTemplate*) from the system at run-time. The structure of contract templates is reflected in the external event types CreateContractDef, UpdateContractDef, and DeleteContractDef, compare Section 2.2. A list of (non-deleted) contract templates can hence be computed by an appropriate report.

Contract Instances. A contract template is instantiated via *createContract* by supplying a record value v of a subtype of Contract. Besides custom fields, which depend on the type at hand, such a record always contains the fields templateName and startDate inherited from the Contract record type. The field templateName contains the name of the template to instantiate, and the field startDate determines the start date of the contract. The fields of v are substituted into the contract template in order to obtain a *contract instance*, and the type of v must therefore match the template type. For instance, if v has type Sale then the field templateName must contain the name of a contract template that has type Sale. We refer to the record v as *contract meta data*.

When a contract c is instantiated by supplying contract meta data v, a *fresh* contract identifier i is created, and a CreateContract event is persisted in the event log with with contract $= v$ and contractId $= i$. Hereafter, transactions t can be registered with the contract via *registerTransaction*, which will update the contract to a *residual contract* c', written $c \xrightarrow{t} c'$, and a TransactionEvent with transaction $= t$ and contractId $= i$ is written to the event log. The state of the contract can be acquired from the contract engine at any given point in time via *getContract*, which enables run-time analyses of contracts, for instance in order to generate a list of expected transactions.

Registration of a transaction $c \xrightarrow{t} c'$ is only permitted if the transaction is expected in the current state c. That is, there need not be a residual state for all transactions. After zero or more successful transactions, $c \xrightarrow{t_1} c_1 \xrightarrow{t_2} \cdots \xrightarrow{t_n} c_n$, the contract may be concluded via *concludeContract*, provided that the residual contract c_n does not contain any outstanding obligations. This results in a ConcludeContract event to be persisted in the event log.

The lifecycle described above does not take into account that contracts may have to be updated at run-time, for example if it is agreed to extend the payment deadline in a sales contract. To this end, running contracts are allowed to be updated, simply by supplying new contract meta data (*updateContract*). The difference in the new meta data compared to the old meta data may not only be a change of, say, items to be sold, but it may also be a change in the field templateName. The latter makes it is possible to replace the old contract by a qualitatively different contract, since the new contract template may describe a different workflow. There is, however, an important restriction: a contract can only be updated if any previous transactions registered with the contract also conform with the new contract. That is, if the contract has evolved like $c \xrightarrow{t_1} c_1 \xrightarrow{t_2} \cdots \xrightarrow{t_n} c_n$, and an update to a new contract c' is requested, then only if $c' \xrightarrow{t_1} c'_1 \xrightarrow{t_2} \cdots \xrightarrow{t_n} c'_n$, for some $c'_1, \ldots, c'_n$, is the update permitted. A successful update results in an UpdateContract event to be written to the event log with the new meta data.

For simplicity, we only allow the updates described above. Another possibility is to allow updates where the current contract c is replaced directly by a new contract c'. This effect can be attained by prefixing c' with $[t_1, \ldots, t_n]$ as contract actions.

As for contract templates, a list of (non-concluded) contract instances can be computed by a report that inspects CreateContract, UpdateContract, and ConcludeContract events respectively.

The Contract Language. The fourth component of contract templates—the PCSL specification—is the actual normative content of contract templates. PCSL extends Hvitved's CSL [9] mainly at the level of expressions E, by adding support for the value types in POETS, as well as lambda abstractions and function applications. At the level of clauses C, PCSL is similar to CSL, albeit with a slightly altered syntax. Typing of PCSL expressions is more challenging since we have added (record) polymorphism as well as subtyping.

We do not present PCSL formally here; instead, it is illustrated in the use case in Section 3 below.

3   Use Case: Legejunglen

We outline a use case that we implemented in a trial with a small business called *Legejunglen*, an indoor playground for children.

The user interface to the POETS system is provided by a client application for the Android operating system. The application is suitable for both phone and tablet devices. Although, for this trial we focused on the tablet user experience. The client application communicates with the POETS system running on a server via the APIs of individual subsystems as described in Section 2. The client provides a generic user interface guided by the ontology. There is functionality to visualise ontology elements as well as allowing user input of ontology elements. Additionally, a simple mechanism for compile-time specialised visualisations is provided. The generic visualisations handle ontology changes without any changes needed on the client. The central part of the user interface provides an overview of the state of currently instantiated contract templates as well as allowing users to interact with running contracts.

In the following, we present the final results of an iterative refinement process on modelling the *Legejunglen* business. We conclude with some reflections on using the DSLs for iterative model evolution.

The most important functionality for day-to-day use at *Legejunglen* is to (1) register bookings for customers and (2) to get an overview of the scheduled events for a single day. Apart from that, the system should provide standard accounting functionality.

The main workflow that we needed to implement is the booking system, that is, the system according to which a customer reserves a time at the playground. This workflow is encoded in a contract template Appointment. The data associated with this contract are defined in the following ontology definition:

Appointment is a Contract.
Appointment is abstract.
Appointment has a DateTime called arrivalDate.
Appointment has Food.
Appointment has a Location called placement.
Appointment has a Participants.
Appointment has an Int called numberOfTableSettings.
Appointment has a String called comments.
Appointment has an Adult entity called contactPerson.

The full ontology also contains declarations that define the auxiliary concepts Food, Location, Participants and Adult, which we have elided here. The fields that are associated with the Appointment record type have to be provided in order to instantiate the corresponding *Appointment* contract template. These fields are then directly accessible in the definition of the contract template.

Figure 8 details the definition of the contract template that describes the workflow for booking an appointment at *Legejunglen*. The full contract is defined at the very bottom by referring to the *confirm* clause. Note that we directly reference the arrivalDate, numberOfTableSettings and contactPerson field of the Appointment record. The three clauses of the contract template roughly correspond to three states an active *Appointment* contract may be in: first, in the *confirm* clause we wait for confirmation from the customer until one day before the expected arrival. After that we wait for the arrival of the customer at the expected time (plus a one hour delay). Finally, we expect the payment within one day.

Next we turn to the reporting functionality of POETS. For daily planning purposes, *Legejunglen* requires an overview of the booked appointments of any given day. This functionality is easily implemented in the reporting language. Firstly, we define the record type that contains the result of the desired report:

Schedule is a Report.
Schedule has a list of Appointment called appointments.

Secondly, we define the actual report function that searches the event log for the creation of *Appointment* contracts with a given arrivalDate. The report definition is given in Figure 9.

A more complex report specification is given in Figure 10. This report compiles an overview of all appointments made during a month as well as the sum of all payments that were registered by the system during that time. This report

name: *appointment*
type: Appointment
description: "Contract for handling a appointment."

// A reference to the designated entity that represents the company
val *me = reports.me* ()

clause *confirm*(*expectedArrival* : **Duration**, *numberOfTableSettings* : **Int**)
⟨*me* : ⟨Me⟩, *contact* : ⟨Adult⟩⟩ =
  when ContactConfirms
    due within *expectedArrival* ⟨−⟩ 1*D*
    remaining *newDeadline*
  then
    arrival(*newDeadline*)⟨*me, contact*⟩
  else *arrival*(*expectedArrival*)⟨*me, contact*⟩

clause *arrival*(*expectedArrival* : **Duration**)⟨*me* : ⟨Me⟩, *contact* : ⟨Adult⟩⟩ =
⟨*me*⟩ GuestsArrive
    due within *expectedArrival* ⟨+⟩ 1*H*
  then *payment*(*me*)⟨*contact*⟩

clause *payment*(*me* : ⟨Me⟩)⟨*contact* : ⟨Adult⟩⟩ =
⟨*contact*⟩ Payment(*sender s, receiver r*)
      where *r ≡ me ∧ s ≡ contact*
      due within 1*D*

contract = *confirm*(*subtractDate arrivalDate contractStartDate,*
        numberOfTableSettings)⟨*me, contactPerson*⟩

Fig. 8. Contract template for booking an appointment

name: DailySchedule
description:
  Returns *a* **list of** *appointments for which the expected*
    arrival is the same as the given date.
tags: *legejunglen*

report : Date → Schedule
report *expectedArrival* =
  Schedule { *appointments* = [*arra* |
      putC : PutContract ← **events**,
      arra : Appointment = *putC.contract*,
      expectedArrival ≡ arra.arrivalDate.date] }

Fig. 9. Report definition for compiling a daily schedule

specification uses an explicit *fold* in order to accumulate the payment and appointment information that are spread throughout the event log.

Although *Legejunglen* is a relatively simple business, a significant amount of the work done in the trial involved refining the workflows implicitly in use and formalising what reports were needed. The ability to specify a workflow using the contract language and then immediately try it out in the Android client, helped the modelling process tremendously. A basic contract template for keeping track of bookings was made quickly, which facilitated the process of iterative evaluation and refinement to precisely capture the way *Legejunglen* worked. Changes on the POETS side were quite easy to perform. Changes are typically isolated. That is, support for new workflows or reports does not require a change to the data model and only amounts to adding new contract templates respectively report specifications. This can be performed while the system is up and running, without any downtime. In addition, the subtyping discipline employed in POETS' data model is a key feature in enabling extending the ontology of at run time without compromising the integrity of its state or the semantics of its reports and contracts.

The effort for implementing changes in the data model and the workflow is quite modest. Minor changes in the requirements tended to require little changes in the ontology and contract specifications. Typically, this is also the case for changes in the report specifications. However, changes in report specifications turned out to be quite complicated in some instances. Reports have the ability to produce highly structured information from the flat-structured event log. Unfortunately, this ability is reflected in the complexity of the corresponding report specifications. Nonetheless, from the report specifications we have written, we can extract a small set of high-level patterns that cover most common use cases. Integrating these high-level patterns into the reporting language should greatly reduce the effort for writing reports and further increase readability.

Changes in the underlying modelling on the POETS side were rather easy to propagate to the Android client software. As mentioned, the client application provides a generic user interface to the POETS system that allows it to reflect any changes made in the modelling in the POETS system. However, this generic interface does not always provide the optimal user experience and therefore needs manual refinement to reflect changes in the modelling. Additionally, there have also been specific requirements to the client software, which had to be implemented.

4   Conclusion

We have presented an extended and generalised version of the POETS architecture [6], which we have fully implemented. It is based on declarative domain-specific languages for specifying the data model, reports, and contracts of a POETS instance, which offer enterprise domain concepts and encapsulate important invariants that facilitate safe run-time changes to data types, reports and contracts; full recoverability and auditability of any previous system state;

MonthlyOverview is a Report.
MonthlyOverview has a Real called total.
MonthlyOverview has a list of AppointmentInfo called appointments.

name: MonthlyOverview
description:
 Get *information about payments received for given month.*
tags: legejunglen

allContracts : [PutContract]
allContracts = [*pc* |
  cc : CreateContract ← **events**,
  pc = *first cc* [*uc* | *uc* : UpdateContract ← **events**, *uc.contractId* ≡ *cc.contractId*]]

allPayments : Date → [(Payment, PutContract)]
allPayments date =
 [(*pay, putC*) |
   putC ← *allContracts*,
   arra : Appointment = *putC.contract*,
   arra.arrivalDate.month ≡ *date.month*,
   arra.arrivalDate.year ≡ *date.year*,
   tr : TransactionEvent ← *transactionEvents*,
   tr.contractId ≡ *putC.contractId*,
   pay : Payment = *tr.transaction*]

initialOverview = MonthlyOverview { *total*   = 0,
                      appointments = [] }

addAppointment : (Payment, Appointment) → [AppointmentInfo] → [AppointmentInfo]
addAppointment payArr arrs = *insertProj*
 (λ*pa* → *pa.appointment.arrivalDate*)
 (AppointmentInfo {*appointment* = *payArr*.2, *payment* = *payArr*.1})
 arrs

calc payPut overv =
  type *x* = *payPut*.2.*contract* **of**
   Appointment → *overv* {
    total   = *overv.total* + *payPut*.1.*money.amount*,
    appointments = *addAppointment* (*payPut*.1, *x*) *overv.appointments* }
   _ → *overv*

report : Date → MonthlyOverview
report *date* = **fold** *calc initialOverview* (*allPayments date*)

Fig. 10. Report definition for compiling a monthly payment overview

and strict separation of logged raw data and efficiently computed user-specified derived data. In particular, in contrast to its predecessor, any historical system state is reestablishable for auditing since also master data, contract and report changes are logged, not only transactional data.

The use case presented illustrates the conciseness of POETS DSLs and support for rapid exploratory process and report design since the "specification is the implementation" approach made it easy to make an initial model of the business as well as evolve it to new requirements. While no significant conclusions for usability and fitness for use in complex commercial settings can be drawn without a suitable experimental design, we believe the preliminary results justify hypothesising that domain specialists should be able to read, understand and specify data models (types) and, with suitable training in *formalisation*, eventually contract and report specifications without having to worry about programming or system specifics.

4.1 Related work

This paper focuses on the radical *use* of declarative domain-specific languages in POETS motivated by the Resources, Event, Agents accounting model [13,6]. The syntactic and semantic aspects of its domain modelling language [25], its contract language [9] (evolved from [1]) and functional reporting[5] [19,18] are described elsewhere.

ERP systems relate broadly to and combine aspects of discrete event simulation, workflow modelling, choreography and orchestration, run-time monitoring, process specification languages (such as LTL), process models (such as Petri nets), and report languages (such as the query sublanguage of SQL and reactive functional programming frameworks), which makes a correspondingly extensive review of related work from a general ERP systems point of view a difficult and expansive task.

More narrowly, POETS can be considered an example of *language-oriented programming* [27] applied to the business modelling domain. Its contract language specifies detailed real-time and value constraints (e.g. having to pay the cumulatively correct amount by some deadline, not just some amount at some time) on contract partners, neither supporting nor fixing a particular business process. See [8, Chapter 1] and [7] for a survey of *contract* models and languages.

A hallmark of POETS is its enforcement of static invariants that guarantee auditability and type correctness even in the presence of run-time updates to data types, processes and reports. Recently the jABC approach [23,12] has added support for types, data-flow modelling and processes as first-class citizens. The resulting DyWA (Dynamic Web Application) approach [15,17,16] offers support for step-by-step run-time enhancement with data types and corresponding business processes until an application is ready for execution and for its subsequent evolution.

---

[5] Automatic incrementalisation is not implemented in the present version.

Automatic incrementalisation of report functions in POETS can be thought of as translating bulk-oriented queries that conceptually inspect the complete event log every time they are run to continuous queries on streams [24], based on formal differentiation techniques [21,11].

4.2 Future Work

Expressivity A possible extension of the data model is to introduce finite maps, which will enable a modelling of resources that is closer in structure to that of Henglein et al. [6]. Another possible extension is to allow types as values in the report language. There are instances where we currently use a string representation of record types rather than the record types themselves. This representation is, of course, suboptimal: we would like such runtime represenations of types machine checked and take subtyping into account.

Rules A rule engine is a part of our extended architecture (Figure 2), however it remains to be implemented. The purpose of the rule engine is to provide rules—written in a separate domain-specific language—that can constrain the values that are accepted by the system. For instance, a rule might specify that the items list of a Delivery transaction always be non-empty.

More interestingly, the rule engine will enable values to be *inferred* according to the rules in the engine. For instance, a set of rules for calculating VAT will enable the field vatPercentage of an OrderLine to be inferred automatically in the context of a Sale record. That is, based on the information of a sale and the items that are being sold, the VAT percentage can be calculated automatically for each item type.

The interface to the rule engine will be very simple: a record value with zero or more *holes* is sent to the engine, and the engine will return either (i) an indication that the record cannot possibly fulfil the rules in the engine, or (ii) a (partial) substitution that assigns inferred values to (some of) the holes of the value as dictated by the rules. Hence when we, for example, instantiate the sale of a bicycle. then we first let the rule engine infer the VAT percentage before passing the contract meta data to the contract engine.

Forecasts A feature of the contract engine, or more specifically of the reduction semantics of contract instances, is the possibility to retrieve the state of a running contract at any given point in time. The state is essentially the AST of a contract clause, and it describes what is currently expected in the contract, as well as what is expected in the future.

Analysing the AST of a contract enables the possibility to do *forecasts*, for instance to calculate the expected outcome of a contract or the items needed for delivery within the next week. Forecasts are, in some sense, dual to reports. Reports derive data from transactions, that is, facts about what has previously happened. Forecasts, on the other hand, look into the future, in terms of calculations over running contracts. We have currently implemented a single forecast, namely a forecast that lists the set of immediately expected transactions for a given contract. A more ambitious approach is to devise (yet another) language for writing forecasts, that is, functions that operate on contract ASTs.

Practicality In order to make POETS useful in practice, many features are still missing. However, we see no inherent difficulties in adding them to POETS compared to traditional ERP architectures. To mention a few: (i) security, that is, authorisation, users, roles, etc.; (ii) module systems for the report language and contract language, that is, better support for code reuse; and (iii) check-pointing of a running system, that is, a dump of the memory of a running system, so the event log does not have to be replayed from scratch when the system is restarted.

Acknowledgements. Morten Ib Nielsen and Mikkel Jønsson Thomsen both contributed to our implementation and design of POETS, for which we are thankful. We thank the participants of the DIKU course "POETS Summer of Code" and Lejejunglen for testing, use and valuable input to POETS. This work has been made possible by a grant by the Danish National Advanced Technology Foundation (Højteknologifonden) for Project 3gERP.

References

1. Andersen, J., Elsborg, E., Henglein, F., Simonsen, J.G., Stefansen, C.: Compositional specification of commercial contracts. International Journal on Software Tools for Technology Transfer (STTT) 8(6), 485–516 (2006)
2. Bahr, P., Hvitved, T.: Compositional data types. In: Proc. 7th ACM SIGPLAN Workshop on Generic Programming (WGP), pp. 83–94. ACM (2011)
3. Bahr, P., Hvitved, T.: Parametric compositional data types. In: Proc. Mathematically Structured Functional Programming, MSFP (2012)
4. Bernstein, A.J., Kifer, M.: Databases and Transaction Processing: An Application-Oriented Approach, 1st edn. Addison-Wesley Longman Publishing Co., Inc., Boston (2001)
5. Fuchs, N.E., Kaljurand, K., Kuhn, T.: Attempto Controlled English for Knowledge Representation. In: Baroglio, C., Bonatti, P.A., Małuszyński, J., Marchiori, M., Polleres, A., Schaffert, S. (eds.) Reasoning Web. LNCS, vol. 5224, pp. 104–124. Springer, Heidelberg (2008)
6. Henglein, F., Larsen, K.F., Simonsen, J.G., Stefansen, C.: POETS: Process-oriented event-driven transaction systems. Journal of Logic and Algebraic Programming 78(5), 381–401 (2009)
7. Hvitved, T.: A survey of formal languages for contracts. In: Fourth Workshop on Formal Languages and Analysis of Contract–Oriented Software (FLACOS 2010), pp. 29–32 (2010)
8. Hvitved, T.: Contract Formalisation and Modular Implementation of Domain-Specific Languages. PhD thesis, Department of Computer Science, University of Copenhagen (DIKU) (November 2011)
9. Hvitved, T., Klaedtke, F., Zălinescu, E.: A trace-based model for multiparty contracts. The Journal of Logic and Algebraic Programming 81(2), 72–98 (2012); Preliminary version presented at 4th Workshop on Formal Languages and Analysis of Contract-Oriented Software (FLACOS 2010) (2010)

10. Thomsen, M.J.: Using Controlled Natural Language for specifying ERP Requirements. Master's thesis, University of Copenhagen, Department of Computer Science (2010)
11. Liu, Y.A.: Efficiency by incrementalization: An introduction. Higher-Order and Symbolic Computation 13(4) (2000)
12. Margaria, T., Steffen, B.: Business process modelling in the jabc: the one-thing-approach. In: Handbook of Research on Business Process Modeling, pp. 1–26. IGI Global (2009)
13. McCarthy, W.E.: The REA Accounting Model: A Generalized Framework for Accounting Systems in a Shared Data Environment. The Accounting Review LVII(3), 554–578 (1982)
14. Murthy, C.: Advanced programming language design in enterprise software: A lambda-calculus theorist wanders into a datacenter. In: Proc. ACM Symp. on Principles of Programming Languages (POPL), ACM SIGPLAN Notices, vol. 42(1), pp. 263–264. ACM (2007)
15. Neubauer, J., Steffen, B.: Plug-and-play higher-order process integration. Computer 46(11), 56–62 (2013)
16. Neubauer, J., Steffen, B., Frohme, M., Margaria, T.: Prototype-driven development of web applications with dywa. In: These Proceedings (2014)
17. Neubauer, J., Steffen, B., Margaria, T.: Higher-order process modeling: Product-lining, variability modeling and beyond. Electronic Proceedings in Theoretical Computer Science (EPTCS) 129, 259–283 (2013)
18. Nissen, M.: Reporting technologies. In: 2nd 3gERP Workshop, Frederiksberg, Denmark (2008)
19. Nissen, M., Larsen, K.F.: FunSETL — Functional Reporting for ERP Systems. In: Chitil, O. (ed.) 19th International Symposium on Implementation and Application of Functional Languages, IFL 2007, pp. 268–289 (2007)
20. Ohori, A.: A Polymorphic Record Calculus and Its Compilation. ACM Trans. Program. Lang. Syst. 17, 844–895 (1995)
21. Paige, R., Koenig, S.: Finite differencing of computable expressions. ACM TOPLAS 4(3), 402–454 (1982)
22. Pierce, B.C.: Types and Programming Languages. The MIT Press (2002)
23. Steffen, B., Margaria, T., Nagel, R., Jörges, S., Kubczak, C.: Model-driven development with the jABC. In: Bin, E., Ziv, A., Ur, S. (eds.) HVC 2006. LNCS, vol. 4383, pp. 92–108. Springer, Heidelberg (2007)
24. Terry, D., Goldberg, D., Nichols, D., Oki, B.: Continuous queries over append-only databases. In: Proc. SIGMOD Conference, vol. 21(2). ACM (1992)
25. Thomsen, M.J.: Using controlled natural language for specifying ERP requirements. Master's thesis, Department of Computer Science (DIKU), University of Copenhagen (July 2010)
26. Wadler, P.: Comprehending monads. Mathematical Structures in Computer Science 2(04), 461–493 (1992)
27. Ward, M.P.: Language-oriented programming. Software-Concepts and Tools 15(4), 147–161 (1994)
28. Weygandt, J.J., Kieso, D.E., Kimmel, P.D.: Financial Accounting, with Annual Report. Wiley (2004)

Introduction to "Rigorous Engineering of Autonomic Ensembles"– Track Introduction

Martin Wirsing[1], Rocco De Nicola[2], and Matthias Hölzl[1]

[1] Ludwig-Maximilians-Universität München
{martin.wirsing,matthias.hoelzl}@ifi.lmu.de
[2] IMT Institute for Advanced Studies Lucca
rocco.denicola@imtlucca.it

Today's software systems are becoming increasingly distributed and decentralized and have to adapt autonomously to dynamically changing, open-ended environments. Often their nodes partake in complex interactions with other nodes or with humans. We call these kinds of distributed, complex systems operating in open-ended and changing environments, ensembles.

To facilitate analysis and reasoning about their properties, the static structure and interactions in ensembles should be strictly layered and highly constrained, and their interface to the environment should follow a precisely specified protocol. In practice, however, none of these conditions is satisfied: ensembles are typically complex, multi-layered networks of interconnected parts, where different layers interact and influence each other in intricate and sometimes unforeseen ways. The environment in which they operate is highly dynamic, with frequent short-term and long-term changes. For example, individual nodes in a network may experience intermittent connection problems requiring short-term adaptation until connectivity is restored. On the other hand, with systems depending on services from a multitude of other providers it is not uncommon for services to be discontinued or for providers to go out of business. This necessitates changes of the system that persist in the long run.

It is infeasible for human operators to constantly monitor interactions in an ensembles and to adjust it to cope with unexpected circumstances; similarly it is not possible to rewrite the software for every change in operational or environmental conditions. Instead of static software that operates without knowledge about its environment and hence relies on manual configuration and optimization we have to build systems with self-aware, intelligent components that posseses features such as adaptation, self-organization, and both autonomous and collective behavior. Ensembles have to adapt autonomously to dynamically changing situations while still respecting their design constraints and requirements.

Because of their distributed and decentralized nature, ensembles usually have to achieve this by simultaneous adaptation of multiple nodes. But in open systems exhibiting this kind of distributed adaptation, unforeseen events and properties can arise. Modelling and engineering techniques for ensembles have to take into account such "emergent" properties in addition to satisfying functional and quantitative requirements.

T. Margaria and B. Steffen (Eds.): ISoLA 2014, Part I, LNCS 8802, pp. 96–98, 2014.

Current software engineering methods are not adequate for dealing with these challenges: these methods, both agile and heavyweight, rely to a large degree on code inspection and testing, approaches which are not adequate for reliably developing large concurrent systems, let alone self-aware, adaptive systems. Formal methods have successfully been employed in an ever increasing number of projects; however, they generally cannot deal with the dynamic and open-ended nature of the systems we are interested in, and they are difficult to scale to the size of industrial-scale projects. Approaches from autonomic and multi-agent systems address aspects such as self-configuration and self-optimization, but they lack necessary guarantees for reliability, dependability and security and are therefore not appropriate for critical systems.

Finding new ways to understand, design and build ensembles, and to predict their behaviour, is therefore a difficult but important endeavour. The ISoLA track on "Rigorous Engineering of Autonomic Ensembles" presents techniques for modelling and analysing systems that adapt collectively to dynamically changing environment conditions and requirements. In many cases, these models and analysis techniques not only capture qualitative properties of the system, such as absence of deadlocks, they are also be able to express quantitative properties such as quality of service.

In "Helena@Work: Modeling the Science Cloud Platform" [4], A. Klarl et al. present a role-based modeling approach for dynamically composed, adaptive, heterogeneous systems and apply this method to a cloud-computing platform. The paper "Formalizing Self-Adaptive Clouds with KnowLang" [6] by E. Vassev et al. formalizes a knowledge-based perspective on the same problem domain using the KnowLang language for knowledge representation. In their contribution "Performance-Aware Engineering of Autonomic Component Ensembles" [2], T. Bures et al. propose a method for integrating performance monitoring and awareness in different stages of the development process. The paper "Self-Expression and Dynamic Attribute-based Ensembles in SCEL" [3] by G. Cabri et al. shows how the SCEL language can provide a rigorous mechanism for changing the coordination patterns used in an ensemble to adapt to different circumstances. A version of SCEL that includes a policy-specification language is introduced by M. Loreti et al. in "On Programming and Policing Autonomic Computing Systems" [5]. S. Bensalem et al. show how the BIP language and verification tools can be used to guarantee safety properties for complex systems by means of several case studies from the field of (swarm) robotics in "Rigorous System Design Flow for Autonomous Systems" [1].

The results presented in this track were developed as part of the ASCENS project.[1] The goal of ASCENS is to build ensembles in a way that combines the maturity and wide applicability of traditional software-engineering approaches with the assurance about functional and non-functional properties provided by formal methods and the flexibility, low management overhead, and optimal utilization of resources promised by autonomic, self-aware systems. To this end ASCENS is researching new concepts for the design and development of autonomous,

---

[1] http://www.ascens-ist.eu/

self-aware systems with parallel and distributed components. ASCENS has developed sound, formal reasoning and verification techniques to support the specification and development of these systems as well as their analysis at run-time. The project goes beyond the current state of the art in solving difficult problems of self-organization, self-awareness, autonomous and collective behavior, and resource optimization in a complex system setting.

References

1. Bensalem, S., Bozga, M., Combaz, J., Triki, A.: Rigorous System Design Flow for Autonomous Systems. In: Margaria, T., Steffen, B. (eds.) ISoLA 2014, Part I. LNCS, vol. 8802, pp. 184–198. Springer, Heidelberg (2014)
2. Bureš, T., Horký, V., Kit, M., Marek, L., Tůma, P.: Towards Performance-Aware Engineering of Autonomic Component Ensembles. In: Margaria, T., Steffen, B. (eds.) ISoLA 2014, Part I. LNCS, vol. 8802, pp. 131–146. Springer, Heidelberg (2014)
3. Cabri, G., Capodieci, N., Cesari, L., De Nicola, R., Pugliese, R., Tiezzi, F., Zambonelli, F.: Self-expression and Dynamic Attribute-based Ensembles in SCEL. In: Margaria, T., Steffen, B. (eds.) ISoLA 2014, Part I. LNCS, vol. 8802, pp. 147–163. Springer, Heidelberg (2014)
4. Klarl, A., Mayer, P., Hennicker, R.: HelenaatWork: Modeling the Science Cloud Platform. In: Margaria, T., Steffen, B. (eds.) ISoLA 2014, Part I. LNCS, vol. 8802, pp. 99–116. Springer, Heidelberg (2014)
5. Loreti, M., Margheri, A., Pugliese, R., Tiezzi, F.: On Programming and Policing Autonomic Computing Systems. In: Margaria, T., Steffen, B. (eds.) ISoLA 2014, Part I. LNCS, vol. 8802, pp. 164–183. Springer, Heidelberg (2014)
6. Vassev, E., Hinchey, M., Mayer, P.: Formalizing Self-Adaptive Clouds with KnowLang. In: Margaria, T., Steffen, B. (eds.) ISoLA 2014, Part I. LNCS, vol. 8802, pp. 117–130. Springer, Heidelberg (2014)

HELENA@Work:
Modeling the Science Cloud Platform[*]

Annabelle Klarl, Philip Mayer, and Rolf Hennicker

Ludwig-Maximilians-Universität München, Germany

Abstract. Exploiting global interconnectedness in distributed systems, we want autonomic components to form teams to collaborate for some global goal. These teams have to cope with heterogeneity of participants, dynamic composition, and adaptation. HELENA advocates a modeling approach centered around the notion of roles which components can adopt to take part in task-oriented teams called ensembles. By playing roles, the components dynamically change their behavior according to their responsibilities in the task. In this paper, we report on the experiences of using HELENA in modeling and developing a voluntary peer-2-peer cloud computing platform. We found that the design with roles and ensembles provides a reasonable abstraction of our case study. The model is well-structured, easy to understand and helps to identify and eliminate collaboration mismatches early in the development.

1 Introduction

The development of distributed software systems, i.e. systems in which individual parts run on different machines connected via some sort of communication network, has always been a challenge for software engineers. Special care has to be taken to the unique requirements concerning concurrency and sharing of responsibilities. In this area, difficult issues arise particularly in those systems in which the individual distributed software components have a certain degree of autonomy and interact in a non-centralized and non-trivial manner.

Such systems are investigated in the EU project ASCENS [1], where the individual distributed artifacts are components which provide the basic capabilities for collaborating teams. These components dynamically form *ensembles* to perform collective tasks which are directed towards certain goals. We believe that the execution and interaction of entities in such ensembles is best described by what we call *roles*. They are an abstraction of the part an individual component plays in a collaboration. We claim that separating the behavior of components into individual roles leads to an easier understanding, modeling, and programming of ensemble-based systems. Our modeling approach HELENA [9,12] thus extends existing component-based software engineering methods by modeling roles. Each role (more precisely role type) adds particular capabilities to the basic functionalities of a component which are only relevant when performing the

---

[*] This work has been partially sponsored by the EU project ASCENS, 257414.

T. Margaria and B. Steffen (Eds.): ISoLA 2014, Part I, LNCS 8802, pp. 99–116, 2014.
© Springer-Verlag Berlin Heidelberg 2014

role. Exploiting these role-specific capabilities, we specify *role behaviors* which the component dynamically adopts when taking over a role. For the specification of role behaviors we extend [9] by introducing a process language which allows to describe dynamic creation of role instances on selected component instances. The structural characteristics of collaborations are defined in *ensemble structures* capturing the contributing role types and potential interactions.

In this paper, we report on the experiences of using HELENA in modeling and developing a larger software system. As our case study we have selected the *Science Cloud Platform (SCP)* [14] which is one of the three case studies used in the ASCENS project. The SCP is, in a nutshell, a platform of distributed, voluntarily provided computing nodes. The nodes interact in a peer-to-peer manner to execute, keep alive, and allow use of user-defined software applications. The goal of applying HELENA to the SCP is to find a reasonable abstraction that serves as clear documentation, analysis model, and guideline for the implementation. We experienced that the HELENA model helps to rigorously describe the concepts of the SCP. During analysis of the models, collaboration mismatches can be eliminated at early stages. As we shall discuss, the implementation also benefits from the encapsulation in roles. However, during implementation some additional effort is required to provide an infrastructure which supports the role concept on top of the component-based system. Lastly, special care has to be taken to make the system robust against communication failures and to provide communication facilities between ensembles and the outside world which is not yet tackled in HELENA.

In the following sections, we first describe the case study in Sec. 2. Afterwards, we summarize the HELENA modeling approach in Sec. 3 and apply it to the case study in Sec. 4. Sec. 5 describes the realization of the HELENA model on the infrastructure of the SCP and Sec. 6 discusses some related work. Lastly, we report on experiences and give an outlook in Sec. 7.

2   Case Study

One of the three case studies in the ASCENS project is the *Science Cloud Platform (SCP)* [14]. The SCP employs a network of distributed, voluntarily provided computing nodes, in which users can deploy user-defined software applications. To achieve this functionality, the SCP reuses ideas from three usually separate computing paradigms: cloud computing, voluntary computing, and peer-to-peer computing. In a nutshell, the SCP implements a platform-as-a-service in which individual, voluntarily provided computing nodes interact using a peer-to-peer protocol to deploy, execute, and allow usage of user-defined applications. The SCP takes care to satisfy the requirements of the applications, keeps them running even if nodes leave the system, and provides access to the deployed applications. For a full description of the SCP, we refer to [14]. In the following, we only discuss those parts relevant for this paper.

The SCP is formed by a network of computers which are connected via the Internet, and on which the SCP software is installed (we call these *nodes*).

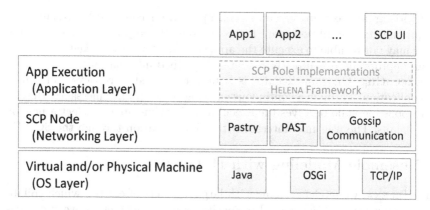

Fig. 1. SCP architecture (new parts in dashed boxes)

The layout of an SCP node is shown in Fig. 1, along with the technologies involved. The dashed boxes are those parts contributed in the current work.

The bottom layer shows the infrastructure: The SCP is a Java application and thus runs in the Java VM; it also uses the OSGi component framework to dynamically deploy and run applications (as bundles). In general, plain TCP/IP networking is used to communicate between nodes on this level.

The second layer implements the basic networking logic. The SCP uses the distributed peer-to-peer overlay networking substrate Pastry [16] for communication. Pastry works similarly to a Distributed Hash Table (DHT) in that each node is represented by an ID. Node IDs are organized to form a ring along which messages can be routed to a target ID. Pastry manages joining and leaving nodes and contains various optimizations for fast routing. On top of this mechanism, the DHT PAST allows storage of data at specific IDs. On this layer, a gossip protocol [7] is used to spread information about the nodes through the network; this information includes node abilities (CPU, RAM), but also information about applications. Each node slowly builds its own picture of the network, pruning information where it becomes outdated.

The third layer (from the bottom) is presented in this paper, and implements the application execution logic based on HELENA. The dashed boxes describe the intended implementation which are discussed throughout the paper. The required functionality of the application layer is that of reliable application execution given the application requirements on the one hand and the instability of the network on the other hand. This process is envisioned as follows:

1. **Deploying and undeploying:** A user deploys an application using the SCP UI (top right). The application is assigned an ID (based on its name) and stored using the DHT (PAST) at the closest node according to the ID; this ensures that exactly one node is responsible for the application, and this node can always be retrieved based on the application name (we call this node the *app-responsible node*). If this node leaves, the next adjacent node based on ID proximity takes its place.

2. **Finding an executor:** Since each application comes with execution requirements and all nodes are heterogeneous, the app-responsible node may or may not be able to execute the application. Thus, it is tasked with *finding* an appropriate executor (based on the gossiped information).
3. **Executing:** Once an executor is found, it is asked to retrieve and run the application. Through a continuous exchange of keep-alive messages, the app-responsible node observes the executor and is thus able to select a new one if it fails. The user may interact with the application through the SCP UI.

3   Ensemble Modeling with HELENA

With HELENA, we model systems with large numbers of entities which collaborate in teams (*ensembles*) towards a specific goal. In this section, we summarize the basic ideas and ingredients of the HELENA approach [9,12]. It is centered around the notion of roles which components can adopt to form ensembles. The idea is that components can only collaborate under certain roles.

3.1   Ensemble Structures

The foundation for the aforementioned systems are components. To classify components we use *component types*. A component type defines a set of attributes (more precisely attribute types) representing basic information that is useful in all roles the component can adopt. Formally, a *component type ct* is a tuple $ct = (nm, attrs)$ such that nm is the name of the component type and $attrs$ is a set of attribute types. For the SCP case study we use a single component type Node; its attributes are not relevant for the sequel.

For performing certain tasks, components team up in *ensembles*. Each participant in the ensemble contributes specific functionalities to the collaboration, we say, the participant plays a certain role in the ensemble which we classify by role types. A role type determines the types of the components that are able to adopt this role. It also defines role-specific attributes (to store data that is only relevant for performing the role) and it defines message types for incoming, outgoing, and internal messages. Formally, a *message type* is of the form $msg = msgnm(riparams)(dataparams)$ such that $msgnm$ is the name of the message type, $riparams$ is a list of typed formal parameters to pass role instances, and $dataparams$ is a list of (for simplicity untyped) formal parameters for data.

Given a set CT of component types, a *role type rt* over CT is a tuple $rt = (nm, compTypes, roleattrs, rolemsgs)$ such that nm is the name of the role type, $compTypes \subseteq CT$ is a finite, non-empty subset of component types (whose instances can adopt the role), $roleattrs$ is a set of role specific attribute types, and $rolemsgs$ is a set of message types for incoming, outgoing, and internal messages supported by the role type rt. Fig. 2 shows a graphical representation of the role type for potential executors which will be needed and explained in the SCP case study later on; see Sec. 4. The notation PotentialExecutor:{Node} indicates that any component instance of type Node can play this role.

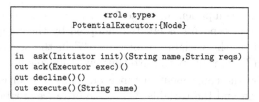

Fig. 2. Role type `PotentialExecutor`

Role types form the basic building blocks for collaboration in an ensemble. An *ensemble structure* determines the type of an ensemble that is needed to perform a certain task. It specifies which role types are needed in the collaboration, how many instances of each role type may contribute and which kind of messages can be exchanged between instances of the given role types.

Definition 1 (Ensemble Structure). *Let CT be a set of component types. An ensemble structure Σ over* CT *is a pair $\Sigma = (roleTypes, roleConstraints)$ such that roleTypes is a set of role types over* CT *and for each $rt \in roleTypes$, $roleConstraints(rt) \in Mult$ and Mult is the set of multiplicities available in UML, like 0..1, 1, $*$, 1..$*$, etc.*

For simplicity, we do not use explicit role connector types here opposed to [9] and assume that between (instances of) role types rt and rt' the messages with the same name that are output on one side and input on the other side can be exchanged. The ensemble structure for the SCP case study is visualized in Fig. 3. How it is derived from the requirements will be explained in Sec. 4.

3.2 Role Behavior Specifications

After having modeled the structural aspects of ensembles, we focus on the specification of behaviors for each role type of an ensemble structure. A role behavior is given by a process expression built from the null process, action prefix, nondeterministic choice, and recursion. In the following, we use X, Y for role instance variables, RT for role types, x for data variables[1], e for data expressions and ci for component instances (assuming a given repository of those); $\vec{z}$ denotes a list of z. There are five different kinds of actions. A send action is of the form $X!msgnm(\vec{Y})(\vec{e})$. It expresses that a message with name $msgnm$ and actual parameters $\vec{Y}$ and $\vec{e}$ is sent to a role instance named by variable X. The first parameter list $\vec{Y}$ consists of variables which name role instances to be passed to the receiver; with the second parameter list $\vec{e}$, data is passed to the receiver. A receive action is of the form $?msgnm(\vec{X} : \vec{RT})(\vec{x})$. It expresses the reception of a message with name $msgnm$. The values received on the parameters are bound to the variables $\vec{X}$ for role instances and to $\vec{x}$ for data. Internal actions are represented by $msgnm(\vec{Y})(\vec{e})$ denoting an internal computation with actual parameters. Internal computations can be used, e.g., to model the access of a role

---

[1] We distinguish between role instance variables and data variable since role instance variables can be used as recipients for messages later on, for instance for callbacks.

instance to its owning component instance. With the action $X \leftarrow \mathbf{create}(RT, ci)$ a new role instance of type RT is created, adopted by the component instance ci, and referenced by the variable X of type RT in the sequel. Similarly the action $X \leftarrow \mathbf{get}(RT, ci)$ retrieves an arbitrary existing role instance of type RT already adopted by the component instance ci. Thus, the variables $\vec{X}, \vec{x}$ used in message reception and the variable X for role instance creation and retrieval open a scope which binds the open variables with the same names in the successive process expression. The bound variables receive a type as declared by the role types $\vec{RT}, RT$ resp.

Definition 2 (Role Behavior). *Let Σ be an ensemble structure and rt be a role type in Σ. A role behavior $RoleBeh_{rt}$ for rt is a process expression built from the following abstract syntax:*

$$
\begin{array}{llll}
P & ::= & \mathbf{nil} & \textit{(null process)} \\
  & | & a.P & \textit{(action prefix)} \\
  & | & P_1 + P_2 & \textit{(nondeterministic choice)} \\
  & | & \mu V.P & \textit{(recursion)} \\
a & ::= & X!msgnm(\vec{Y})(\vec{e}) & \textit{(sending a message)} \\
  & | & ?msgnm(\vec{X}:\vec{RT})(\vec{x}) & \textit{(receiving a message)} \\
  & | & msgnm(\vec{Y})(\vec{e}) & \textit{(interal computation)} \\
  & | & X \leftarrow \mathbf{create}(RT, ci) & \textit{(role instance creation)} \\
  & | & X \leftarrow \mathbf{get}(RT, ci) & \textit{(role instance retrieval)}
\end{array}
$$

To be well-formed a role behavior $RoleBeh_{rt}$ must satisfy some obvious conditions: 1) For sending a message $X!msgnm(\vec{Y})(\vec{e})$ the role type rt must support the message type $msgnm(riparams)(dataparams)$ as outgoing message and the actual parameters must fit to the formal ones. Moreover, X must be a variable of some role type RT which supports the same message type as incoming message. Similarly, well-formedness of incoming and internal messages is defined. 2) Role instance creation $X \leftarrow \mathbf{create}(RT, ci)$ and role instance retrieval $X \leftarrow \mathbf{get}(RT, ci)$ are well-formed if RT is a role type in Σ, and if the component instance ci if of a type whose instances can adopt a role of type RT.

Definition 3 (Ensemble specification). *An ensemble specification is a pair $EnsSpec = (\Sigma, RoleBeh)$ such that Σ is an ensemble structure, and $RoleBeh$ is a family of role behaviors $RoleBeh_{rt}$ for each role type rt occurring in Σ.*

The ensemble specification for the SCP case study will be made up by the ensemble structure in Fig. 3 and by the role behavior specifications described in Sec. 4. Three concrete examples of role behavior specifications, translated to their graphical LTS representation, are shown in Fig. 4.

In this paper, we do not define a formal semantics of ensemble specifications which must take into account the form of process terms defined above; this is left to future work. However, some hints on the envisaged approach may be helpful. As a semantic basis to describe the evolution of ensembles we will use *ensemble automata* as defined in [9]. The states of an ensemble automaton show 1) the currently existing role instances of each role type occurring in Σ, 2) for each existing role instance, a unique component instance which currently adopts this role, 3) the data currently stored by each role instance, and 4) the current control state of each role instance showing its current progress of execution according to the specified role behavior. Ensemble automata model role instance creation as expected by introducing a fresh role instance which starts in the initial state of its associated role behavior. Retrieval of role instances delivers an existing role instance of appropriate type played by the specified component instance if there is one. Otherwise it is blocked. Concerning communication between role instances first an underlying communication paradigm must be chosen. The ensemble automata in [9] formalize synchronous communication such that sending and receiving of a message is performed simultaneously. If the recipient is not (yet) ready for reception of the message the sender is blocked. However, it is important to note that the communication style is not determined by an ensemble specification since the role behaviors specify local behaviors and thus support decentralized control which is typical for the systems under investigation. In particular, an asynchronous communication pattern can be chosen as well for the realization of an ensemble specification and this is indeed the case for the ensembles running on the SCP.

4   Modeling the SCP with HELENA

Let us revisit our case study from Sec. 2 to explain the benefits of the role-based modeling approach for such a system. In the SCP, distributed computing nodes interact to execute software applications. For one app, several computing nodes need to collaborate: They have to let a user deploy the app in the system, to execute (and keep alive) the app on a node satisfying the computation requirements of the app, and to let a user request a service from the app. For each of these responsibilities we can derive a specific behavior, but at design time it is unclear which node will be assigned with which responsibility. Additionally, each node must also be able to take over the same or different responsibilities for the execution of different apps in parallel. In a standard component-based design, we would have to come up with a single component type for a computing node which is able to combine the functionalities for each responsibility in one complex behavior. This is the case in the previous "all-in-one" implementation of the SCP [14]. The HELENA modeling approach, however, offers the possibility to model systems in terms of collaborating roles and ensembles. Firstly, roles allow to separate the definition of the capabilities and behavior required for a specific responsibility from the underlying component. Secondly, adopting different roles allows components to change their behavior on demand. Thirdly, concurrently running ensembles support the parallel execution of several tasks possibly sharing the same participants under different roles.

In the SCP, we assume given the basic infrastructure for communication between nodes (Pastry), storing data (PAST), and deploying and executing apps
(OSGi) (two bottom layers in Fig. 1). We apply HELENA for modeling the whole
process of application execution on top of this infrastructure. Computation nodes
represent the components underlying the HELENA model.

Ensemble Structure. The first step is to identify the required role types from
the stated requirements in Sec. 2.

1. **Deploying and undeploying:** For this subtask, we envision two separate
   role types. The `Deployer` provides the interface for deploying and undeploying an app and is responsible for the selection of the app-responsible node
   for storing the app code. The app-responsible node adopts the `Storage` role
   taking care for the actual storage and deletion of the app code and initiates
   the execution of the app.
2. **Finding an executor:** Three further roles are required for finding the appropriate execution node. The app-responsible node in the role `Initiator`
   determines the actual `Executor` from a set of `PotentialExecutors` and
   takes care that it is kept running until the user requests to undeploy the
   app. A `PotentialExecutor` is a node which the `Initiator` believes is able
   to execute the app based on the requirements of the app. However, it might
   currently not be able to do so, e.g., due to its current load. The actual
   `Executor` is selected from the set of `PotentialExecutors` and is responsible
   for app execution.
3. **Executing:** Once started, the app needs to be available for user requests.
   The `Requester` provides the interface between the user and the `Executor`
   and forwards requests and responses. The `Executor` from the previous sub-
   task gives access to the executed app.

In Fig. 3, we summarize the ensemble structure composed of these six roles
graphically. Each role can be supported by the components of type `Node`. The
multiplicities of the role types express that a running ensemble contains just one
role instance per role type except for `PotentialExecutor` and `Requester`. Labels at the connections between roles depict which messages can be exchanged
between these roles for collaboration. For instance, the incoming arrows on the
role type `PotentialExecutor` show the incoming message types specified in
Fig. 2 and similarly for the outgoing messages. We explain the exchanged messages in more detail when we focus on role behaviors. For each deployed app,
one instance of this ensemble structure is employed. Different components may
take over the required roles in one ensemble, but a single component may also
adopt different roles in the same ensemble. Moreover, different components can
take part at the same time in different ensembles under different roles.

Role Behavior Specifications. On the basis of this ensemble structure, we
specify a behavior for each role. For the roles `Deployer` and `Storage` taking

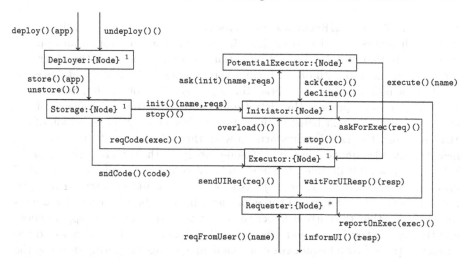

Fig. 3. Ensemble structure for app execution in the SCP

part in the first subtask, the role behaviors are rather straightforward and we give only an informal description. In the initial state the Deployer waits for the user to ask for app deployment and forwards the app code to the Storage for archiving and vice versa for undeployment. The Storage role starts by waiting for a request to store an app. Upon storage, it issues the creation of an Initiator which takes care that the app is executed. Afterwards the Storage is ready to provide the app code to an Executor or to delete it.

What is interesting about these two role types is which component instances are selected to adopt the roles. The Deployer is automatically played by the component instance where the user actually places her deployment request. When the Deployer creates a Storage it selects the component whose ID according to Pastry (cf. Sec. 2) is next to the ID of the app (given by the hash value of the app name). The uniqueness of component selection is essential since for any later communication with the Storage, e.g., for code retrieval, it must be possible to identify the owning component instance just from the app's name. For the same reason, we choose the owning component of the Storage to additionally adopt the Initiator role.

The behavior of the Requester is also straightforward and is again informally described. In the initial state, a Requester waits for the user to request a service from the app. It retrieves a reference to the Executor from the Initiator[2] and forwards the request to the Executor. It gets back a response from the Executor which it routes to the user. The part played by the Executor in this collaboration is depicted in Fig. 4c by the loop between states e5 and e6.

The most interesting behavior concerns the selection of an appropriate executor. In Fig. 4, we translated the process terms of the role behaviors for

---

[2] Note that for communication with the Initiator its owning component must be uniquely identifiable as mentioned before.

Initiator, PotentialExecutor and Executor into a labeled transition system which makes it easier to explain. Concerning the initiator of an app the main idea is that it asks a set of potential executors, one after the other, for execution of the app until one of them accepts. Since each node maintains a list of all other nodes and their abilities through a gossip protocol (cf. Sec. 2), the initiator can easily prepare this list of nodes satisfying the requirements of the app based on its current belief of the network. Triggered by the reception of the init message, the Initiator starts to walk through the list. It first creates a new PotentialExecutor on the next node satisfying the requirements and asks it for execution. If it declines, the next node satisfying the requirements is asked until one accepts (states i1 to i4). As soon as a PotentialExecutor accepts, the Initiator waits for one of three messages in state i4: 1) an overload message meaning that the current Executor is not able to execute the app anymore and the Initiator has to find a new one, 2) a request for the reference to the Executor (issued by a Requester), or 3) a stop message triggering stopping the execution of the app on the Executor.

The behavior of a PotentialExecutor starts with waiting for a request for app execution. If it does not satisfy the requirements of the app (like current load), it internally decides to refuse and sends back a decline message. Otherwise, it creates a new Executor on its owner, issues the execution, and acknowledges execution to the Initiator. An Executor starts by waiting for an execute message. Then the Executor retrieves a reference to the Storage, requests and gets the app code from it and starts execution of the app (states e1 to e5). As soon as the app has been started, the Executor can answer user requests or stop execution due to internal overload or an external stop request.

Analysis. The role behaviors provided by an ensemble specification can be used to analyze the dynamic behaviors of ensembles before implementing the system. A particularly important aspect concerns the avoidance of collaboration mismatches (collaboration errors) when role instances work together. Two types of errors can be distinguished. Firstly, an instance expects the arrival of a message which never has been issued. Secondly, an instance sends a message, but the recipient is not ready to receive. Let us analyze the latter type of collaboration error by considering the cooperation between Initiator and PotentialExecutor. The only output action occurring in $RoleBeh_{Initiator}$ which is addressed to a PotentialExecutor is the message ask occurring in state i2. It is sent to the PotentialExecutor, named by the variable pot, which has just been created in state i1. This potential executor starts in its initial state p0 in which it is obviously ready to accept the message ask. Afterwards, the Initiator is in state i3 and is ready to receive either a decline or an ack message which both can only be sent from the PotentialExecutor. After the reception of ask the PotentialExecutor is in state p1 and it has two options: 1) It can decide to refuse the request and sends the message decline which the Initiator accepts being back in state i1. In this case, the current PotentialExecutor terminates, a new one is created, the Initiator goes to state i2, and we are in a situation which we have already analyzed. 2) The other option in state p1 is to accept the execution request, to create an Executor, to cause the Executor to start execution and then to send the message ack to the Initiator who is still in state i3 and takes the message. So the instances of both roles, Initiator and PotentialExecutor, work well together. Interestingly this holds whether one uses synchronous or asynchronous communication in the implementation. How such an analysis can be performed on the basis of formal verification is a challenging issue of future research.

Limitations. At this point, we want to mention some restrictions underlying the current HELENA approach. Firstly, we rely on binary communication and do not support broadcast yet. Though broadcast sending could be easily integrated in our process expressions, to collect corresponding answers would still be an issue. Secondly, we build ensemble specifications on a given set of components such that we cannot model situations in which components fail. However, we are aware that one of the main characteristics of our case study is that nodes may fail and leave the network at any time. We wish that such failovers are handled transparently from the role behaviors. The idea is that components are monitored such that when failing all adopted roles are transparently transferred to another component and restarted there. A further issue concerns robustness since we assume reliable network transmission in our models. We do not want to include any mechanisms for resending messages in the role behavior specifications. Like failover mechanisms, this should be handled transparently by an appropriate infrastructure.

5   Using the HELENA Model for the SCP Implementation

In this section, we report on the experimental realization of the HELENA model[3]. HELENA separates between base components and roles running on top of them. The SCP is already built on components (the *SCP Node* layer in Fig. 1); thus, the HELENA implementation can build on the given infrastructure and realize the *application layer* shown by the dashed boxes in Fig. 1 by a role-based implementation as envisioned in the HELENA approach.

This HELENA *framework* amounts to around 1000 LOC and offers role-related functionality, such as the ability to create and retrieve roles via the network, and routing messages between roles by using Pastry. (This layer implements the same basic ideas already presented in the HELENA framework [12], but is based on the SCP and thus, Pastry). In a second step, we have translated the behavioral specifications of the six roles to Java code using the previously created framework. Each of the role implementations stays below 150 LOC with another 400 LOC in message classes. In the following two subsections we discuss the framework and role implementations, respectively, stressing where direct translation of the

---

[3] The code can be retrieved from http://svn.pst.ifi.lmu.de/trac/scp, version v3 of the node core implementation with gossip strategy.

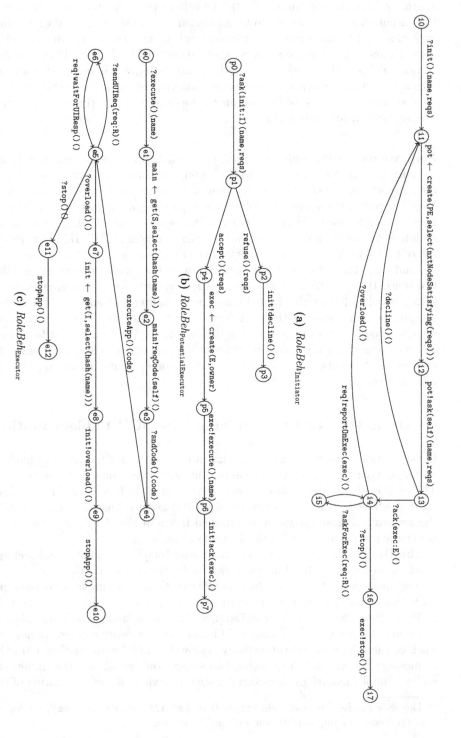

Fig. 4. Role behaviors for Initiator, PotentialExecutor, and Executor (all role types are abbreviated)

HELENA model was possible and where special care had to be taken to make the realization robust.

5.1 Implementing the HELENA Framework

A framework for implementing role behaviors needs to offer several features to role implementors.

Structural Aspects. The most important concept in HELENA are *roles*. Thus, the framework must offer the ability to create role types, and to instantiate and execute them. This maps quite naturally to using one Java class per role type, and instantiating this class for role instances. A registry on each node stores all instances currently adopted by the node and allows their retrieval. To enable concurrent execution, each role instance is realized as a Java thread, running locally in the OSGi container of the current node.

The framework provides means to create, retrieve, and address existing roles on other nodes; this requires a way of addressing roles. Thus, the second important structural aspect is addressing. In Pastry, each node is already identified by a unique 160-bit identifier. It is relatively straightforward to add a similar unique identifier for roles. However, there is also another kind of structuring element which is not directly visible in the behavioral specifications: The ensemble which constitutes the environment for the roles. This can clearly be seen when looking at the functions the framework needs to offer for role handling – these are the create and the get functions. Both require knowledge about which ensemble is addressed for creating a new role or where to look for an existing role. We have thus three identifiers in use in the HELENA framework: The node identifier (for addressing nodes using Pastry), the ensemble identifier (for creating new roles and retrieving existing roles) and the role identifier (which uniquely identifies one role instance).

Behavioral Aspects. This discussion already brings us to the behavioral aspects of the framework. Two functions of the framework were already mentioned – create and get. They are implemented as the Java methods (createRoleInstance and getRoleInstance) which both perform a full network round-trip between two Pastry nodes: They require a node and an ensemble ID as well as the class of the required role as input. The target node is instructed to create and start the new role (or retrieve it, in the second case). A role identifier as discussed above is returned which can then be used for role-to-role message routing.

The behavioral specifications make heavy use of role-to-role communication. A role must be able to send a message and to expect to receive a certain message in its behavior. For this purpose the framework provides the two methods sendMessage() and waitForMessage() for communication between roles.

The method sendMessage() takes a message and a target role; the message is routed between Pastry nodes to an input buffer in the target role. The method only returns when this has been successfully completed (i.e., an internal acknowledge is sent back upon which the sendMessage() function returns normally).

Otherwise, an exception is raised. Of course, correct collaboration requires that any message is finally consumed from the buffer. Moreover, any consumed message should also be expected by the target role as an input message in accordance with its role behavior specification. For this purpose we perform behavioral compatibility checks between role behaviors already during the ensemble modeling phase as discussed in Sec. 4.

The second method is `waitForMessage()` which instructs the framework to wait for a message of a certain type, or a selection of certain different types. The latter is required, for example, in the `Initiator` role when waiting for one of three possible messages in state i4 in Fig. 4a. The `waitForMessage()` function also takes a timeout value; an exception is raised if a message does not arrive in the given time (though specifying `INFINITY` is an option).

Given the basic infrastructure for role management and the communication functions above, we can now proceed to the role implementations.

5.2   Implementing Roles

As discussed above, role (types) are implemented in Java using classes. Thus, for each of the six roles above, a class is created, inheriting from an abstract role template for easier access to framework methods. Each role is instantiated within a certain ensemble and node. Upon startup, the main method implementing the role behavior is called.

The actions in role behavior specifications are translated to message exchanges. For each message type, a message class with an appropriate name is created, and equipped with the required parameters as indicated in the role types. For example, the `execute` message shared between `PotentialExecutor` and `Executor` is implemented by an instance of the `ExecuteMessage` class which carries the application name as a field.

A role behavior is translated into Java as follows:

- Transitions with incoming messages, e.g. `?store()(app)`, are translated into a `waitForMessage()` framework call for the corresponding message class, e.g. `StoreApplicationMessage`. The `waitForMessage()` method returns an instance of the message once received, which can be queried for the actual app.
- Transitions with an outgoing message, e.g. `!init()(name,reqs)`, are translated into a `sendMessage()` framework call. The message to be sent must be given as a parameter.
- Transitions referring to the two framework functions `get` and `create` are directly translated to calls to the corresponding framework methods `getRoleInstance()` and `createRoleInstance()`. They return role IDs which can then be used for communication.
- All other transitions, as well as loops and decisions are translated into their appropriate Java counterparts.

With this basic description, most of the role behaviors are directly translatable into Java code. As an example Fig. 5 shows (in condensed form) the

```
 1  public void run() {
 2      RAskForExecutionMessage askMsg =
 3          waitForIncomingMessage(INFINITY,RAskForExecutionMessage.class);
 4      if (refuseToExecute(askMsg.getAppInfo().getReqs())) {
 5          sendMessage(
 6              new RDeclineExecutionMessage(getRoleId(),askMsg.getInit()));
 7      }
 8      else {
 9          RoleId exec = createLocalRoleInstance(ExecutorRole.class);
10          sendMessage(
11              new RExecuteAppMessage(getRoleId(),exec,askMsg.getAppInfo()));
12          sendMessage(
13              new RAckExecutionMessage(getRoleId(),askMsg.getInit(),exec));
14      }
15  }
```

Fig. 5. Behavior implementation for `PotentialExecutor`

run-method of the `PotentialExecutor` role which is directly derived from its behavior specification in Fig. 4b. Thus, many collaboration errors are avoidable by a careful analysis of the ensemble model. Nevertheless, we were interested in a robust system implementation and hence we followed a defensive strategy such that not only semantic errors are taken into account.

One issue in the implementation is that each of the framework methods may fail for various reasons, and the resulting exceptions must be handled. Firstly, in all operations, timeouts may occur if a message could not be delivered. Secondly, role-to-role messages may fail if the target node does not (yet) participate in the expected ensemble or does not (yet) play an expected role; this also applies to the `getRoleInstance()` method. The `createRoleInstance()` may fail if the role class could not be instantiated or started. These errors are not captured in the role behaviors, but may occur in practice (in particular, they may occur during development if the implementation is not yet fully complete and stable).

A second issue is bootstrapping, both of HELENA ensembles and of basic node identification. At each ensemble startup, at least one role needs to be instantiated by an outside party before messages can be received. In this case study, the main entry point is the `Deployer` role; a second entry point is the `Requester` role. The bootstrapping point cannot be deduced from the local behavior specifications and therefore must be treated individually outside of the framework. In the case of the SCP, this part is played by the SCP UI (top right in Fig. 1).

There are also some points where the roles need to return information to an outside party. For example, the `Requester` role is invoked each time a UI request is made for an app; the response from the application must be presented to the user. This is exactly the opposite of the bootstrapping problem and requires explicit invocation of an outside party from the role. One could think of specialized actions for this; or introduce answers a role in general gives to users.

Basic node identification is another topic of interest: To create a role, the ID of the target node must be known. In the case of the SCP, we heavily rely on the fact that the `Initiator` and `Storage` node ID can always be found using the app name (as explained in Sec. 2). This makes both of these roles communication hubs. If such a mechanism is not available, other forms of node ID retrieval need to be found; one example is the `Initiator` role which uses the underlying, gossip-provided node information as an ID source. A similar problem applies to finding ensembles: A node which does not currently have a role in an ensemble does not know the ensemble ID and thus cannot route messages, which might occur in a formerly non-associated node on which a `Requester` is instantiated. We solve this again by using the app name as a hash for the ensemble ID, but this might be difficult in other settings.

6   Related Work

Combining the three paradigms of cloud computing, voluntary computing, and peer-to-peer computing has started to attract attention in recent years. Most approaches bridge volunteer and cloud computing for infrastructure-as-a-service systems. Cunsolo et al. [5], and Chandra and Weissman [4], they propose to use distributed voluntary resources with an architecture similar to our three-layered approach, but with a centralized management subsystem. Advocating a "fully decentralized p2p cloud", Babaoglu et al. [2] implement a system very similar to the SCP. They also introduce the idea of partitioning the system in slices matching a user's request. The idea is to create a subcloud in the system providing resources for one task. This resembles our approach of assembling nodes in task-oriented ensembles.

With HELENA, we offer a rigorous modeling method for describing such task-oriented groups. Modeling evolving objects with roles as perspectives on the objects has been proposed by various authors [13,17], but they do not see them as autonomic entities with behavior as we do in HELENA. For describing dynamic behaviors, we share ideas with different process calculi [6,8], but we use dynamic instance creation for roles on selected components. The idea to describe structures of interacting objects without having to take the entire system into consideration was already introduced by several authors [11,3,15], but they do not tackle concurrently running ensembles of autonomic entities. For a more detailed comparison of the HELENA ideas with the literature see [9]. Finally, let us stress that the SCEL approach [6] supports ensembles via group communication. After discussion with the authors of SCEL it seems straightforward to represent roles and the message passing communication paradigm also in SCEL. Then one could also experiment with the jRESP platform of SCEL for executing HELENA ensemble specifications.

7   Conclusion

We have shown how the HELENA modeling approach can be applied to a larger software system. Starting from the description of our case study, the Science Cloud Platform, we developed an ensemble specification based on six collaborating roles. An instance of this specification is able to deploy and execute a software application in a voluntary peer-to-peer network. Splitting the task of app execution in several independent roles was quite natural and helped to understand the individual subtasks. Compared to the development of one big component which combines all behaviors at one place, it was straightforward to derive behaviors for each role individually. However, we experienced that the granularity when deciding which roles to introduce was not always clear. Using the HELENA modeling approach allowed us to examine the modeled system for communication errors before implementation. During implementation of the model, translating the role behaviors to Java code has proven to be straightforward. To gain this complexity reduction, first a (reusable) HELENA framework layer was needed to provide HELENA-specific functionalities. The encapsulation of responsibilities in separate roles helped to make the SCP code clean and easy to understand. Special care had to be taken in four areas: Handling faults during communication, node identification for role creation and retrieval, handling node failures, and communication between ensembles and the outside world.

In the future, we want to pursue different research directions. In [9], we have given a formal semantics for ensemble specifications in terms of ensemble automata. In a next step we want to define rules for the generation of an ensemble automaton from an ensemble specification based on the new process expressions for role behaviors. Secondly, based on the ensemble automaton, we want to define when an ensemble can be considered communication-safe (for static architectures, called assemblies, this has been considered in [10]). We want to investigate conditions under which communication-safety of an ensemble automaton can be derived from pairwise behavioral compatibility of role behaviors. Thirdly, we want to support the composition of large ensembles from smaller ones and to study which properties can be guaranteed for the composed system. Lastly, we want to construct an infrastructure for HELENA models that can cope with unreliable systems and failing components.

References

1. The ASCENS Project, http://www.ascens-ist.eu
2. Babaoglu, Ö., Marzolla, M., Tamburini, M.: Design and implementation of a P2P Cloud system. In: Symposium on Applied Computing, pp. 412–417. ACM (2012)
3. Baldoni, M., Studi, U., Italy, T.: Interaction between Objects in powerJava. Journal of Object Technology 6, 7–12 (2007)
4. Chandra, A., Weissman, J.: Nebulas: Using Distributed Voluntary Resources to Build Clouds. In: Conf. on Hot Topics in Cloud Computing. USENIX Association (2009)
5. Cunsolo, V.D., Distefano, S., Puliafito, A., Scarpa, M.: CloudHome: Bridging the Gap between Volunteer and Cloud Computing. In: Huang, D.-S., Jo, K.-H., Lee, H.-H., Kang, H.-J., Bevilacqua, V. (eds.) ICIC 2009. LNCS, vol. 5754, pp. 423–432. Springer, Heidelberg (2009)
6. De Nicola, R., Ferrari, G., Loreti, M., Pugliese, R.: A Language-Based Approach to Autonomic Computing. In: Beckert, B., Damiani, F., de Boer, F.S., Bonsangue, M.M. (eds.) FMCO 2011. LNCS, vol. 7542, pp. 25–48. Springer, Heidelberg (2012)

7. Demers, A.J., Greene, D.H., Hauser, C., Irish, W., Larson, J., Shenker, S., Sturgis, H.E., Swinehart, D.C., Terry, D.B.: Epidemic algorithms for replicated database maintenance. In: Symposium on Principles of Distributed Computing, pp. 1–12. ACM (1987)
8. Deniélou, P.M., Yoshida, N.: Dynamic Multirole Session Types. In: Symposium on Principles of Programming Languages, pp. 435–446. ACM (2011)
9. Hennicker, R., Klarl, A.: Foundations for Ensemble Modeling - The Helena Approach - Handling Massively Distributed Systems with ELaborate ENsemble Architectures. In: Iida, S., Meseguer, J., Ogata, K. (eds.) Specification, Algebra, and Software. LNCS, vol. 8373, pp. 359–381. Springer, Heidelberg (2014)
10. Hennicker, R., Knapp, A., Wirsing, M.: Assembly theories for communication-safe component systems. In: Bensalem, S., Lakhneck, Y., Legay, A. (eds.) From Programs to Systems. LNCS, vol. 8415, pp. 145–160. Springer, Heidelberg (2014)
11. Herrmann, S.: Object Teams: Improving Modularity for Crosscutting Collaborations. In: Akşit, M., Mezini, M., Unland, R. (eds.) NODe 2002. LNCS, vol. 2591, pp. 248–264. Springer, Heidelberg (2003)
12. Klarl, A., Hennicker, R.: Design and Implementation of Dynamically Evolving Ensembles with the Helena Framework. In: Australasian Software Engineering Conf. IEEE (to appear, 2014)
13. Kristensen, B.B., Østerbye, K.: Roles: Conceptual Abstraction Theory and Practical Language Issues. Theor. Pract. Object Syst. 2(3), 143–160 (1996)
14. Mayer, P., Klarl, A., Hennicker, R., Puviani, M., Tiezzi, F., Pugliese, R., Keznikl, J., Bureš, T.: The Autonomic Cloud: A Vision of Voluntary, Peer-2-Peer Cloud Computing. In: Wshp. on Challenges for Achieving Self-Awareness in Autonomic Systems, pp. 1–6. IEEE (2013)
15. Reenskaug, T.: Working with objects: the OOram Framework Design Principles. Manning Publications (1996)
16. Rowstron, A., Druschel, P.: Pastry: Scalable, decentralized object location, and routing for large-scale peer-to-peer systems. In: Guerraoui, R. (ed.) Middleware 2001. LNCS, vol. 2218, pp. 329–350. Springer, Heidelberg (2001)
17. Steimann, F.: On the representation of roles in object-oriented and conceptual modelling. Data Knowl. Eng. 35(1), 83–106 (2000)

Formalizing Self-adaptive Clouds with KnowLang

Emil Vassev, Mike Hinchey, and Philip Mayer

[1] Lero–The Irish Software Engineering Research Centre,
University of Limerick, Limerick, Ireland
emil.vassev@lero.ie
[2] Lero–The Irish Software Engineering Research Centre,
University of Limerick, Limerick, Ireland
mike.hinchey@lero.ie
[3] Ludwig-Maximilian University, Munich, Germany
mayer@pst.ifi.lmu.de

Abstract. Cloud computing emerged as a paradigm offering new benefits to both social networking and IT business. However, to keep up with the increasing workload demand and to ensure that their services will be provided in a fail-safe manner and under consideration of their service-level agreement, contemporary cloud platforms need to be autonomous and self-adaptive. The development of self-adaptive clouds is a very challenging task, which is mainly due to their non-deterministic behavior, driven by service-level objectives that must be achieved despite the dynamic changes in the cloud environment. This paper presents a formal approach to modeling self-adaptive behavior for clouds. The approach relies on the KnowLang language, a formal language dedicated to knowledge representation for self-adaptive systems. A case study is presented to demonstrate the formalization of Science Clouds, a special class of self-adaptive clouds providing a cloud-scientific platform.

1 Introduction

Cloud platforms emerged as service providers promising major societal and business benefits. However, such benefits require that provided services are cost-effective and users are confident that services are efficient and released at reasonable risk. However, the increasing workload demand introduces risks to the aforementioned benefits, which led the software engineering communities to investigate new ways of developing and managing cloud systems. Hence, self-adaptation emerged as an important paradigm introducing self-adaptive clouds as systems capable of modifying their own behavior and/or structure in response to increasing workload demands and service failures. A common characteristic of self-adaptive clouds is emphasizing self-adaptations required to ensure that services will be provided in a fail-safe manner and under consideration of their service-level agreement (SLA).

The development of self-adaptive clouds is a very challenging task, which is mainly due to their non-deterministic behavior, driven by service-level objectives (SLOs) that must be achieved despite the dynamic changes in the cloud environment. In this paper, we present a formal approach to modeling self-adaptive behavior of Science Clouds, a cloud scientific platform for application execution and data storage [3]. In this endeavor,

T. Margaria and B. Steffen (Eds.): ISoLA 2014, Part I, LNCS 8802, pp. 117–130, 2014.

we used KnowLang, a formal framework under development within the ASCENS FP7 Project's [1] mandate. KnowLang's notation is a formal language dedicated to knowledge representation for self-adaptive systems and so, the framework provides both a notation and reasoner to deal with self-adaptation.

The rest of this paper is organized as follows. Section 2 presents the so-called ARE approach helping us capture the requirements for self-adaptive behavior. Section 3 presents our approach to specifying with KnowLang the self-adaptive behavior of Science Clouds. Finally, Section 4 provides brief concluding remarks and a summary of our future goals.

2 Capturing Requirements for Self-adaptive Behavior

The self-adaptive behavior is what makes the difference in Science Clouds. In this endeavor, we strive to capture this very behavior, so it can be properly designed and consecutively, implemented. To do so, we consider that self-adaptive behavior extends upstream the regular objectives of a system with special self-managing objectives, also called self-* objectives [6]. Basically, the self-* objectives provide autonomy features in the form of systems ability to automatically discover, diagnose, and cope with various problems. This ability depends on the systems degree of autonomicity, quality and quantity of knowledge, awareness and monitoring capabilities, and quality characteristics such as adaptability, dynamicity, robustness, resilience, and mobility. The approach for capturing all these requirements is called Autonomy Requirements Engineering (ARE) [6,5,4]. This approach strives to provide a complete and comprehensive solution to the problem of autonomy requirements elicitation and specification. Note that the approach targets exclusively the self-* objectives as the only means to explicitly determine and define autonomy requirements. Thus, it is not meant to handle the regular functional and non-functional requirements of the systems, presuming that those might by tackled by the traditional requirements engineering approaches, e.g., use case modeling, domain modeling, constraints modeling, etc. Hence, functional and nonfunctional requirements might be captured by the ARE approach only as part of the self-* objectives elicitation.

The ARE approach starts with the creation of a goals model that represents system objectives and their interrelationships for the system in question. For this, we use GORE (Goal-Oriented Requirements Engineering) where ARE goals are generally modeled with intrinsic features such as type, actor, and target, with links to other goals and constraints in the requirements model. Goals models might be organized in different ways copying with the system's specifics and engineers understanding about the system's goals. Thus we may have hierarchical structures where goals reside different level of granularity and concurrent structures where goals are considered as being concurrent to each other.

The next step in the ARE approach is to work on each one of the system goals along with the elicited environmental constraints to come up with the self-* objectives providing the autonomy requirements for this particular systems behavior. In this phase, we apply a special Generic Autonomy Requirements model to a system goal to derive autonomy requirements in the form of goals supportive and alternative self-* objectives along with the necessary capabilities and quality characteristics.

Finally, the last step after defining the autonomy requirements per systems objectives is the formalization of these requirements, which can be considered as a form of formal specification or requirements recording. The formal notation used to specify the autonomy requirements is KnowLang [8]. The process of requirements specification with KnowLang goes over a few phases:

1. Initial knowledge requirements gathering - involves domain experts to determine the basic notions, relations and functions (operations) of the domain of interest.
2. Behavior definition - identifies situations and behavior policies as control data helping to identify important self-adaptive scenarios.
3. Knowledge structuring - encapsulates domain entities, situations and behavior policies into KnowLang structures like concepts, properties, functionalities, objects, relations, facts and rules.

To specify self-* objectives with KnowLang, we use special policies associated with goals, special situations, actions (eventually identified as system capabilities), metrics, etc.[8]. Hence, self-* objectives are represented as policies describing at an abstract level what the system will do when particular situations arise. The situations are meant to represent the conditions needed to be met in order for the system to switch to a self-* objective while pursuing a system goal. Note that the policies rely on actions that are a-priori-defined as functions of the system. In case, such functions have not been defined yet, the needed functions should be considered as autonomous functions and their implementation will be justified by the AREs selected self-* objectives.

According to the KnowLang semantics, in order to achieve specified goals (objectives), we need to specify policy-triggering *actions* that will eventually change the system states, so the desired ones, required by the goals, will become effective [8]. Note that KnowLang policies allow the specification of autonomic behavior (autonomic behavior can be associated with self-* objectives), and therefore, we need to specify at least one policy per single goal, i.e., a policy that will provide the necessary behavior to achieve that goal. Of course, we may specify multiple policies handling same goal (objective), which is often the case with the self-* objectives and let the system decides which policy to apply taking into consideration the current situation and conditions. The following is a formal presentation of a KnowLang policy specification [8].

Policies (Π) are at the core of autonomic behavior (autonomic behavior can be associated with autonomy requirements). A policy π has a goal (g), policy situations (Si_π), policy-situation relations (R_π), and policy conditions (N_π) mapped to policy actions (A_π) where the evaluation of N_π may eventually (with some degree of probability) imply the evaluation of actions (denoted with $N_\pi \xrightarrow{[Z]} A_\pi$ (see Definition 2). A condition is a Boolean function over ontology (see Definition 4), e.g., the occurrence of a certain event.

Definition 1. $\Pi := \{\pi_1, \pi_2, ..., \pi_n\}, n \geq 0$ *(Policies)*

Definition 2. $\pi :=< g, Si_\pi, [R_\pi], N_\pi, A_\pi, map(N_\pi, A_\pi, [Z]) >$
$\quad A_\pi \subset A, N_\pi \xrightarrow{[Z]} A_\pi \quad$ *(A_π - Policy Actions)*
$\quad Si_\pi \subset Si, Si_\pi := \{si_{\pi_1}, si_{\pi_2}, ..., si_{\pi_n}\}, n \geq 0$

$$R_\pi \subset R, R_\pi := \{r_{\pi_1}, r_{\pi_2}, ..., r_{\pi_n}\}, n \geq 0$$
$$\forall r_\pi \in R_\pi \bullet (r_\pi := < si_\pi, [rn], [Z], \pi >), si_\pi \in Si_\pi$$
$$Si_\pi \overset{[R_\pi]}{\rightarrow} \pi \rightarrow N_\pi$$

Definition 3. $N_\pi := \{n_1, n_2, ..., n_k\}, k \geq 0$ *(Conditions)*

Definition 4. $n := be(O)$ *(Condition - Boolean Expression)*

Definition 5. $g := \langle \Rightarrow s' \rangle | \langle s \Rightarrow s' \rangle$ *(Goal)*

Definition 6. $s := be(O)$ *(State)*

Definition 7. $Si := \{si_1, si_2, ..., si_n\}, n \geq 0$ *(Situations)*

Definition 8. $si := < s, A \overset{\leftarrow}{si}, [E \overset{\leftarrow}{si}], A_{si} >$ *(Situation)*
    $A \overset{\leftarrow}{si} \subset A$ *(A $\overset{\leftarrow}{si}$ - Executed Actions)*
    $A_{si} \subset A$ *(A_{si} - Possible Actions)*
    $E \overset{\leftarrow}{si} \subset E$ *(E $\overset{\leftarrow}{si}$ - Situation Events)*

Policy situations (Si_π) are situations that may trigger (or imply) a policy π, in compliance with the policy-situations relations R_π (denoted with $Si_\pi \overset{[R_\pi]}{\rightarrow} \pi$), thus implying the evaluation of the policy conditions N_π (denoted with $\pi \rightarrow N_\pi$)(see Definition 2). Therefore, the optional policy-situation relations (R_π) justify the relationships between a policy and the associated situations (see Definition 2). In addition, the self-adaptive behavior requires relations to be specified to connect policies with situations over an optional probability distribution (Z) where a policy might be related to multiple situations and vice versa. Probability distribution is provided to support *probabilistic reasoning* and to help the KnowLang Reasoner choose the most probable situation-policy "pair". Thus, we may specify a few relations connecting a specific situation to different policies to be undertaken when the system is in that particular situation and the probability distribution over these relations (involving the same situation) should help the KnowLang Reasoner decide which policy to choose (denoted with $Si_\pi \overset{[R_\pi]}{\rightarrow} \pi$ - see Definition 2).

A goal g is a desirable transition to a state or from a specific state to another state (denoted with $s \Rightarrow s'$) (see Definition 5). A state s is a Boolean expression over ontology ($be(O)$)(see Definition 6), e.g., "a specific property of an object must hold a specific value". A situation is expressed with a state (s), a history of actions ($A \overset{\leftarrow}{si}$) (actions executed to get to state s), actions A_{si} that can be performed from state s and an optional history of events $E \overset{\leftarrow}{si}$ that eventually occurred to get to state s (see Definition 8).

Ideally, policies are specified to handle specific situations, which may trigger the application of policies. A policy exhibits a behavior via actions generated in the environment or in the system itself. Specific conditions determine, which specific actions (among the actions associated with that policy - see Definition 2) shall be executed. These conditions are often generic and may differ from the situations triggering the policy. Thus, the behavior not only depends on the specific situations a policy is specified to handle, but also depends on additional conditions. Such conditions might be organized in a way allowing for synchronization of different situations on the same policy. When a policy is applied, it checks what particular conditions are met and performs the mapped actions (see $map(N_\pi, A_\pi, [Z])$) - see Definition 2). An optional probability distribution can additionally restrict the action execution. Although initially specified, the probability distribution at both mapping and relation levels is recomputed after the execution of any involved action. The re-computation is based on the consequences of the action execution, which allows for reinforcement learning.

3 Formalizing Science Clouds with KnowLang

Science Clouds is a cloud computing scientific platform for application execution and data storage [3]. Individual users or universities can join a cloud to provide (and consume of course) resources to the community. A science cloud is a collection of cloud machines - notebooks, desktops, servers, or virtual machines, running the so-called Science Cloud Platform (SCP). Each machine is usually running one instance of the Science Cloud Platform (Science Cloud Platform instance or SCPi). Each SCPi is considered to be a Service Component (SC) in the ASCENS sense. To form a cloud, multiple SCPis communicate over the Internet by using the IP protocol. Within a cloud, a few SCPis might be grouped into a Service Component Ensemble (SCE), also called a Science Cloud Platform ensemble (SCPe). The relationships between the SCPis are dynamic and the formation of a SCPe depends mainly on the properties of the SCPis.

The common characteristic of an ensemble is SCPis working together to run one application in a fail-safe manner and under consideration of the Service Level Agreement (SLA) of that application, which may require a certain number of active SCPis, certain latency between the parts, or have restrictions on processing power or memory. The SCP is a platform as a service (PaaS), which provides a platform for application execution [3]. Thus, SCP provides an execution environment where special applications might be run by using the SCPs application programming interface (API) and SCPs library. These applications provide a software as a service (SaaS) cloud solution to users. The data storage service is provided in the same manner, i.e., via an application.

Based on the rationale above, we may deduct that the Science Clouds main objective is to provide a scientific platform for application execution and data storage [3]. Being a cloud computing approach, the Science Clouds approach extends the original cloud computing goal to provide services (or resources) to the community of users. Note that cloud computing targets three main types of service (or resource):

1. Infrastructure as a Service (IaaS): a solution providing resources such as virtual machines, network switches and data storage along with tools and APIs for management (e.g., starting VMs).
2. Platform as a Service (PaaS): a solution providing development and execution platforms for cloud applications.
3. Software as a Service (SaaS): a solution providing software applications as a resource.

The three different services above can be defined as three main goals of cloud computing, and their realization by Science Clouds will define the main Science Clouds goals. In addition, from the rationale above we may deduct that an underlying system goal is to optimize application execution by minimizing resource usage along with providing

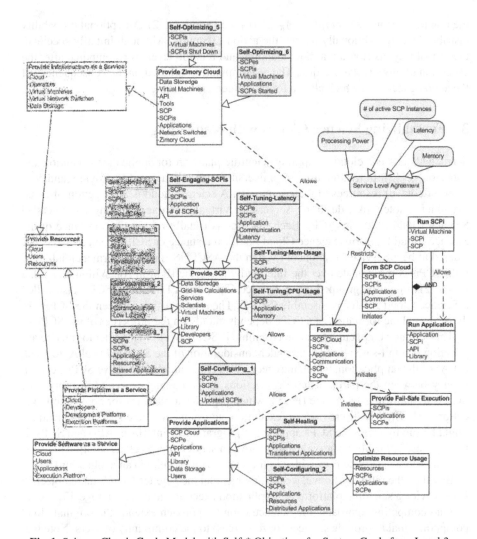

Fig. 1. Science Clouds Goals Model with Self-* Objectives for System Goals from Level 3

a fail-safe execution environment. Figure 1 depicts the ARE goals model for Science Clouds where goals are organized hierarchically at four different levels. As shown, the goals from the first three levels are main system goals captured at different levels of abstraction. The 3rd level is resided by goals directly associated with Science Clouds and providing a concrete realization of the cloud computing goals outlined at the first two levels. Finally, the goals from the 4th level are supporting and preliminary goals that need to be achieved before proceeding with the goals from the 3rd level. In addition, Figure 1 depicts the self-* objectives (depicted in gray color) derived for the Level 3 cloud goals. Basically, these objectives inherit the system goals they assist by providing behavior alternatives with respect to these system goals. The Science Clouds system switches to one of the assisting self-* objectives when alternative autonomous behavior is required (e.g., an SCPi fails to perform).

Note that the required analysis and process of building the goals model for Science Clouds along with the process of deriving the adaptation-supporting self-* objectives is beyond the scope of this paper. The interested reader is advised to refer to [7] where these are well described and discussed.

3.1 Specifying Cloud Ontology

In order to specify the autonomy requirements for Science Clouds, the first step is to specify a knowledge base (KB) representing the cloud in question, i.e., SCPes, SCPis, applications, etc. To do that, we need to specify ontology structuring the knowledge domains of the cloud. Note that these domains are described via domain-relevant concepts and objects (concept instances) related through relations. To handle explicit concepts like situations, goals, and policies, we grant some of the domain concepts with explicit state expressions where a state expression is a Boolean expression over the ontology (see Definition 6 in Section 2). Note that being part of the autonomy requirements, knowledge plays a very important role in the expression of all the autonomy requirements (see Section 2).

Figure 2, depicts a graphical representation of the Science Clouds ontology relating most of the domain concepts within a cloud. Note that the relationships within a concept tree are is-a (inheritance), e.g., the Latency concept is a Phenomenon and the Action concept is a Knowledge and consecutively Phenomenon, etc. Most of the concepts presented in Figure 2 were derived from the Science Clouds Goals Model (see Figure 1). Other concepts are considered as explicit and were derived from the KnowLangs specification model [9].

The following is a sample of the KnowLang specification representing two important concepts: the SCP concept and the Application concept (partial specification only). As specified, the concepts in a concept tree might have properties of other concepts, functionalities (actions associated with that concept), states (Boolean expressions validating a specific state), etc. The IMPL specification directive refers to the implementation of the concept in question, i.e., in the following example SCPImpl is the software implementation (presuming a C++ class) of the SCP concept.

```
// Science Cloud Platform
CONCEPT SCP {
  CHILDREN {}
  PARENTS { SCCloud.Thing..Cloud_Platform }
  STATES {
    STATE Running { this.PROPS.platform_API. STATES.Running AND this.PROPS.platform_Library.STATES.Running }
    STATE Executing { IS_PERFORMING(this.FUNCS.runApp) }
    STATE Observing { IS_PERFORMING(this.FUNCS.runApp) AND SCCloud.Thing..Application.PROPS.initiator=this }
    STATE Down { NOT this.STATES.Running }
    STATE Overloaded { this.STATES.OverloadedCPU OR this.STATES.OverloadedStorage
                       OR this.STATES.OverloadedMemory }
    STATE OverloadedCPU { SCCloud.Thing..Metric.CPU_Usage.VALUE > 0.95 }
    STATE OverloadedMemory { SCCloud.Thing..Metric.Memory_Usage.VALUE > 0.95 }
    STATE OverloadedStorage { SCCloud.Thing..Metric.Hard_Disk_Usage.VALUE > 0.95 }
    STATE ApplicationTransferred { LAST_PERFORMED(this, this.FUNCS.transferApp) }
    STATE InCommunication { this.FUNCS.hasActiveCommunication }
    STATE InCommunicationLatency { this.STATES.InCommunication AND this.FUNCS.getCommunicationLatency >0.5 }
    STATE InLowTrafic { this.FUNCS.getDataTrafic <= 0.5 }
    STATE Started { LAST_PERFORMED(this, this.FUNCS.start) }
    STATE Stopped { LAST_PERFORMED(this, this.FUNCS.stop) }
  }
  PROPS {
    PROP platform_API { TYPE {SCCloud.Thing..API} CARDINALITY {1} }
    PROP platform_Library { TYPE {SCCloud.Thing..Library} CARDINALITY {1} }
```

```
    PROP platform_CPU { TYPE {SCCloud.Thing..CPU} CARDINALITY {1} }
    PROP platform_Memory { TYPE {SCCloud.Thing..Memory} CARDINALITY {1} }
    PROP platform_Storage { TYPE {SCCloud.Thing..Data_Storage} CARDINALITY {1} }
    PROP platform_Applications { TYPE {SCCloud.Thing..Application} CARDINALITY {*} }
    }
    FUNCS {
    FUNC run { TYPE { SCCloud.Thing..Action.RunSCP } }
    FUNC down { TYPE { SCCloud.Thing..Action.StopSCP } }
    FUNC runApp { TYPE { SCCloud.Thing..Action.RunApplication } }
    FUNC startApp { TYPE { SCCloud.Thing..Action.StartApplication } }
    FUNC stopApp { TYPE { SCCloud.Thing..Action.StopApplication } }
    FUNC transferApp { TYPE { SCCloud.Thing..Action.TransferApplication } }
    FUNC startNewCommunication { TYPE { SCCloud.Thing..Action.StartCommunication } }
    FUNC stopNewCommunication { TYPE { SCCloud.Thing..Action.StopCommunication } }
    FUNC hasActiveCommunication { TYPE { SCCloud.Thing..Action.HasActiveCommunication } }
    FUNC getCommunicationLatency { TYPE { SCCloud.Thing..Action.GetCommunicationLatency } }
    FUNC getDataTraffic { TYPE { SCCloud.Thing..Action.GetTraffic } }
    }
    IMPL { SCCloud.SCPImpl }
    }

// Science Cloud Application
  CONCEPT Application {
    CHILDREN {}
        PARENTS { SCCloud.Thing..Software }
    STATES {
        STATE Running { PERFORMED(this.FUNCS.Started)  AND NOT PERFORMED(this.FUNCS. Stopped)  }
        STATE Started { LAST_PERFORMED(this, this.FUNCS.start) }
        STATE Stopped { LAST_PERFORMED(this, this.FUNCS.stop) }
    }
    PROPS {
        PROP needed_CPU_Power { TYPE {SCCloud.Thing..CPU_Power} CARDINALITY {1} }
        PROP needed_Memory { TYPE {SCCloud.Thing..Capacity} CARDINALITY {1} }
        PROP needed_Storage { TYPE {SCCloud.Thing..Storage} CARDINALITY {1} }
        PROP distributiveness { TYPE {Boolean} CARDINALITY {1} }
        PROP requiredSCPis { TYPE {Integer} CARDINALITY {1} }
        PROP requiredLatency { TYPE { SCCloud.Thing..Latency } CARDINALITY {1} }
        PROP initiator { TYPE {SCCloud.Thing..SCP} CARDINALITY {1} }
    }
    FUNCS {...}
    IMPL { SCCloud.ApplicationImpl }
    }
```

As mentioned above, the states are specified as Boolean expressions. For example, the state Executing is true while the SCP is performing the runApp function. The KnowLang operator *IS_PERFORMING* evaluates actions and returns true if an action

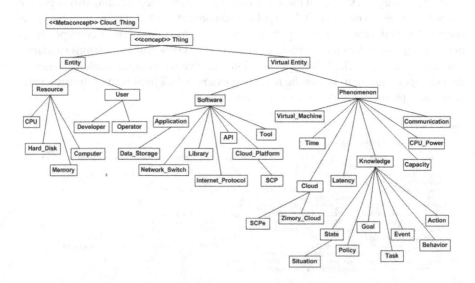

Fig. 2. Science Clouds Ontology Specified with KnowLang

is currently performing. Similarly, the operator *LAST_PERFORMED* evaluates actions and returns true if an action is the last successfully performed action by the concept realization. A concept realization is an object instantiated from that concept, e.g., a SCP instance (SCPi). A complex state might be expressed as a Boolean function of other states. For example, the Running state is expressed as a Boolean function of two other states, particularly, states of concepts properties, e.g., the SCP is running if both its API and Library are running:

```
STATE Running { this.PROPS.platform\_API.STATES.Running AND this.PROPS.platform\_Library.STATES.Running }
```

States are extremely important to the specification of goals (objectives), situations, and policies. For example, states help the KnowLang Reasoner determine at runtime whether the system is in a particular situation or a particular goal (objective) has been achieved.

3.2   Specifying Self-adaptive Behavior

To specify self-* objectives with KnowLang, we use *goals*, *policies*, and *situations*. These are defined as explicit concepts in KnowLang and for the Cloud Ontology we specified them under the concepts *Virtual_entity→Phenomenon→Knowledge* (see Figure 2). Figure 3, depicts a concept tree representing the specified Science Clouds goals. Note that most of these goals were directly interpolated from the goals model (see Figure 1).

Recall that KnowLang specifies goals as functions of states where any combination of states can be involved (see Section 2). A goal has an arriving state (Boolean function of states) and an optional departing state (another Boolean function of states) (see Definition 6 in Section 2). A goal with departing state is more restrictive, i.e., it can be achieved only if the system departs from the specific goals departing state.

The following code samples present the specification of two simple goals. Note that their arriving and departing states can be either single SCP states or sequences of states. Recall that the states used to specify these goals are specified as part of the SCP concept.

```
//
//==== Cloud Goals ========================================================================
//
CONCEPT_GOAL Self-optimizing_1 {
   SPEC {
      DEPART { SCP.STATES.OverloadedCPU  }
      ARRIVE { SCP.STATES.ApplicationTransferred AND NOT SCP.STATES.OverloadedCPU }
   }
}
CONCEPT_GOAL Self-optimizing_3 {
   SPEC {
      DEPART { SCP.STATES.InCommunicationLatency }
      ARRIVE { SCP.STATES.InLowTrafic AND NOT SCP.STATES.InCommunicationLatency }
   }
}
```

The following is a specification sample showing a simple policy called *ReduceCPU-Overhead* - as the name says, this policy is intended to reduce the CPU overhead of a SCPi. As shown, the policy is specified to handle the goal *Self_Opimizing_1* and is triggered by the situation *HighCPUUsage*. Further, the policy triggers conditionally (the *CONDITONS* directive requires that a SCPi is executing an application) the execution of a sequence of actions.

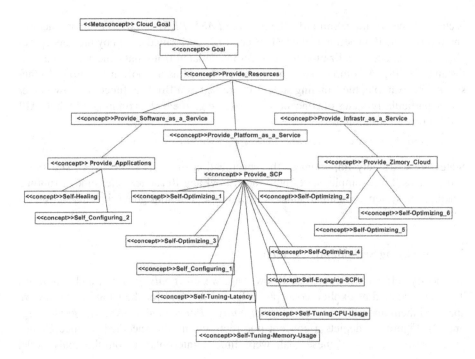

Fig. 3. Science Cloud Ontology: Cloud Goal Concept Tree

```
CONCEPT_POLICY ReduceCPUOverhead {
  SPEC {
    POLICY_GOAL { SCCloud.Thing..Self_Optimizing_1 }
    POLICY_SITUATIONS { SCCloud.Thing..HighCPUUsage }
    POLICY_RELATIONS { SCCloud.Thing..Policy_Situation_1 }
    POLICY_ACTIONS {SCCloud.Thing..Action.StartCommunication, SCCloud.Thing..Action.TransferApplication,
                    SCCloud.Thing..Action.StopCommunication }
    POLICY_MAPPINGS {
      MAPPING {
        CONDITIONS { SCCloud.Thing..SCP.STATES.Executing }
        DO_ACTIONS { SCCloud.Thing..SCP.Action.StartCommunication, SCCloud.Thing..SCP.Action.TransferApplication,
                     SCCloud.Thing..SCP.Action.StopCommunication }
      }
    }
  }
}
```

As mentioned above, policies are triggered by situations. Therefore, while specifying policies handling system objectives, we need to think of important situations that may trigger those policies. These situations shall be eventually outlined by scenarios. A single policy requires to be associated with (related to) at least one situation (see Section 2), but for polices handling self-* objectives we eventually need more situations. Actually, because the policy-situation relation is bidirectional, it is maybe more accurate to say that a single situation may need more policies, those providing alternative behaviors or execution paths from that situation. The following code represents the specification of the *HighCPUUsage* situation, used for the specification of the *ReduceCPUOverhead* policy.

Recall that situations are related to policies via relations (see Definition 2 in Section 2). The following code demonstrates how we related the *HighCPUUsage* situation to two different policies: *ReduceCPUOverhead* and *AIReduceCPUOverhead*.

```
//
//==== Cloud Relations =========================================================================
//
RELATIONS {
  RELATION Policy_Situation_1 {
    RELATION_PAIR { SCCloud.Thing..HighCPUUsage, SCCloud.Thing..ReduceCPUOverhead } PROBABILITY {0.5}
  }
  RELATION Policy_Situation_2 {
    RELATION_PAIR { SCCloud.Thing..HighCPUUsage, SCCloud.Thing..AIReduceCPUOverhead} PROBABILITY {0.4}
  }
}
```

As specified, the probability distribution gives initial designer's preference about what policy should be applied if the system ends up in the *HighCPUUsage* situation. Note that at runtime, the KnowLang Reasoner maintains a record of all the action executions and re-computes the probability rates every time when a policy has been applied. Thus, although initially the system will apply the *ReduceCPUOverhead* policy (it has the higher probability rate of 0.5), if that policy cannot achieve its goal due to action fails (e.g., the communication link with another SCPi is broken and application transfer is not possible), then the probability distribution will be shifted in favor of the *AIReduceCPUOverhead* policy and the system will try to apply that policy. Note that in this case both policies share the same goal.

Probability distribution at the level of situation-policy relation can be omitted, presuming the relationship will not change over time. It is also possible to assign probability distribution within a policy where the probability values are set at the level of action execution, e.g., see the specification of the *AIReduceCPUOverhead* policy above. As specified, the *AIReduceCPUOverhead* policy is intended to handle the *HighCPUUsage* situation by providing alternative execution paths with similar probability distribution. Here, probabilities are recomputed after every action execution, and thus the behavior change accordingly. Moreover, to increase the goal-oriented autonomicity, in this policy's specification, we used the special KnowLang operator *GENER-ATE_NEXT_ACTIONS*, which will automatically generate the most appropriate actions to be undertaken by the SCP. The action generation is based on the computations performed by a special *reward function* implemented by the KnowLang Reasoner. The *KnowLang Reward Function* (KLRF) observes the outcome of the actions to compute the possible successor states of every possible action execution and grants the actions with special reward number considering the current system state (or states, if the current state is a composite state) and goals. KLRF is based on past experience and uses Discrete Time Markov Chains [2] for probability assessment after action executions [9].

Note that when generating actions, the *GENERATE_NEXT_ACTIONS* operator follows a sequential decision-making algorithm where actions are selected to maximize the total reward. This means that the immediate reward of the execution of the first action, of the generated list of actions, might not be the highest one, but the overall reward of executing all the generated actions will be the highest possible one. Moreover, note that, the generated actions are selected from the predefined set of actions (e.g., the implemented cloud actions). The principle of the decision-making algorithm used to select actions is as follows:

1. The average cumulative reward of the reinforcement learning system is calculated.
2. For each policy-action mapping, the KnowLang Reasoner learns the value function, which is relative to the sum of average reward.

3. According to the value function and *Bellman optimality principle*[1], is generated the optimal sequence of actions.

```
//
//==== Cloud Situations =========================================================================
//
CONCEPT_SITUATION HighCPUUsage {
  CHILDREN {}
  PARENTS { SCCloud.Thing..Situation}
  SPEC {
    SITUATION_STATES { SCCloud.Thing..SCP.STATES.OverloadedCPU}
    SITUATION_ACTIONS { SCCloud.Thing..Action.TransferApplication, SCCloud.Thing..Action.SlowDownApplication,
                        SCCloud.Thing..Action. StopApplication }
  }
}
```

As shown, the situation is specified with states and *possible actions*. To consider a situation effective (the system is currently in that situation), its associated states must be respectively effective (evaluated as true). For example, the situation *HighCPUUsage* is effective if the SCP state *OverloadedCPU* is effective. The possible actions define what actions can be undertaken once the system falls in a particular situation. For example, the *HighCPUUsage* situation has three possible actions: *TransferApplication*, *SlowDownApplication*, and *StopApplication*. The following code represents another policy intended to handle the *HighCPUUsage* situation. In this policy, we specified three *MAPPING* sections, which introduce three possible alternative execution paths.

```
CONCEPT_POLICY AIReduceCPUOverhead {
  SPEC {
    POLICY_GOAL { SCCloud.Thing..Self-Optimizing_1 }
    POLICY_SITUATIONS { SCCloud.Thing..HighCPUUsage }
    POLICY_RELATIONS { SCCloud.Thing..Policy_Situation_2 }
    POLICY_ACTIONS { SCCloud.Thing..Action.SlowDownApplication, SCCloud.Thing..Action. StopApplication }
    POLICY_MAPPINGS {
      MAPPING {
        CONDITIONS { SCCloud.Thing..SCP.STATES.Executing }
        DO_ACTIONS { SCCloud.Thing..Action. SlowDownApplication }
        PROBABILITY {0.5}
      }
      MAPPING {
        CONDITIONS { SCCloud.Thing..SCP.STATES.Executing }
        DO_ACTIONS { SCCloud.Thing..Action. StopApplication }
        PROBABILITY {0.4}
      }
      MAPPING {
        CONDITIONS { SCCloud.Thing..SCP.STATES.Executing }
        DO_ACTIONS { GENERATE_NEXT_ACTIONS(SCCloud.Thing..SCP) }
        PROBABILITY {0.1}
      }
    }
  }
}
```

In general, a self-adaptive system has sensors that connect it to the world and eventually help it listen to its internal components. These sensors generate raw data that represent the physical characteristics of the world. The representation of monitoring sensors in KnowLang is handled via the explicit *Metric concept* [9]. In our approach, we assume that cloud sensors are controlled by a software driver (e.g., implemented in C++) where appropriate methods are used to control a sensor and read data from it. By specifying a *Metric concept* we introduce a class of sensors to the KB and by specifying objects, instances of that class, we represent the real sensor. KnowLang allows the specification of four different types of metrics [9]:

---

[1] The Bellman optimality principle: If a given state-action sequence is optimal, and we were to remove the first state and action, the remaining sequence is also optimal (with the second state of the original sequence now acting as initial state).

- *RESOURCE* - measure resources like capacity;
- *QUALITY* - measure qualities like performance, response time, etc.;
- *ENVIRONMENT* - measure environment qualities and resources;
- *ENSEMBLE* - measure complex qualities and resources where the metric might be a function of multiple metrics both of *RESOURCE* and *QUALITY* type.

The following is a specification of metrics mainly used to assist the specification of states in the specification of the SCP concept (see Section 3.1).

```
//Cloud Metrics
CONCEPT_METRIC CPU_Usage {
  SPEC {    METRIC_TYPE { RESOURCE } METRIC_SOURCE { CPU.Usage }
    DATA { DATA_TYPE { Number } VALUE { 0.00 } }
  } }
CONCEPT_METRIC Memory_Usage {
  SPEC {    METRIC_TYPE { RESOURCE } METRIC_SOURCE { Memory.Usage }
    DATA { DATA_TYPE { Number } VALUE { 0.00 } }
  } }
CONCEPT_METRIC Hard_Disk_Usage {
  SPEC {    METRIC_TYPE { RESOURCE } METRIC_SOURCE { HDD.Usage }
    DATA { DATA_TYPE { Number } VALUE { 0.00 } }
  } }
```

4   Conclusion

Formalizing with KnowLang is actually specifying the autonomy requirements captured with ARE. KnowLang is designed as a knowledge representation (KR) language for self-adaptive systems and by using KnwoLang we actually build KR models supporting self-adaptive behavior. Therefore, the formalization of self-adaptive clouds with KnowLang is actually modeling the self-adaptive clouds' behavior, which can be consecutively examined, analyzed, and eventually efficiently tested by using the KnowLang Reasoner. Further, the same and yet verified KR model should be integrated along with the KnowLang Reasoner into the system implementation. Many conventional developers doubt the utility of KR ad reasoning, but our understanding is that this is the only possible way to develop self-adaptive systems. Such systems need to deal with an open set of tasks, which cannot be determined in advance (at least not all of them). This is the big advantage of using KnowLang: the formalized system is modeled to solve complex problems where the operational environment is non-deterministic and the system needs to reason at runtime to find missing answers.

Cloud platforms generally exhibit a number of autonomic features resulting in complex behavior and complex interactions with the operational environment, often leading to a need of self-adaptation. The need of self-adaptation arises when a system needs to cope with changes to ensure realization of its objectives. To properly develop such systems, it is very important to properly handle their self-adaptive behavior. In this paper, we have presented an approach to capturing the requirements for self-adaptive behavior of clouds. We consider that self-adaptive behavior extends upstream the regular goals of a system with special self-managing objectives, also called self-* objectives. Basically, the self-* objectives provide autonomy features in the form of system's ability to automatically discover, diagnose, and cope with various problems. To formalize self-* objectives, the approach relies on the KnowLang language, a formal language dedicated to knowledge representation for self-adaptive systems. A case study has been presented to demonstrate the formalization of Science Clouds, a special class of self-adaptive clouds providing a cloud-scientific platform.

Future work is mainly concerned with further development of the Autonomy Requirements Engineering approach along with full implementation of KnowLang, involving tools and a test bed for autonomy requirements verification and validation.

Acknowledgement. This work was supported by ESTEC ESA (contract No. 4000106016), by the European Union FP7 Integrated Project Autonomic Service-Component Ensembles (ASCENS), and by Science Foundation Ireland grant 03/CE2/I303_1 to Lero-the Irish Software Engineering Research Centre at UL, Ireland.

References

1. ASCENS: ASCENS - Autonomic Service-Component Ensembles. ascens-ist.eu (2014), http://www.ascens-ist.eu/
2. Ewens, W., Grant, G.: Stochastic processes (i): Poison processes and Markov chains. In: Statistical Methods in Bioinformatics, 2nd edn. Springer, New York (2005)
3. Mayer, P., Klarl, A., Hennicker, R., Puviani, M., Tiezzi, F., Pugliese, R., Keznikl, J., Bures, T.: The autonomic cloud: A vision of voluntary, peer-2-peer cloud computing. In: Proceedings of the 3rd Workshop on Challenges for Achieving Self-Awareness in Autonomic Systems, Philadelphia, USA, pp. 1–6 (2013)
4. Vassev, E., Hinchey, M.: Autonomy requirements engineering. In: Proceedings of the 14th IEEE International Conference on Information Reuse and Integration (IRI 2013), pp. 175–184. IEEE Computer Society (2013)
5. Vassev, E., Hinchey, M.: Autonomy requirements engineering: A case study on the Bepi-Colombo mission. In: Proceedings of C* Conference on Computer Science & Software Engineering (C3S2E 2013), pp. 31–41. ACM (2013)
6. Vassev, E., Hinchey, M.: On the autonomy requirements for space missions. In: Proceedings of the 16th IEEE International Symposium on Object/Component/Service-Oriented Real-time Distributed Computing Workshops (ISCORCW 2013). IEEE Computer Society (2013)
7. Vassev, E., Hinchey, M.: Autonomy requirements engineering for self-adaptive science clouds. In: Proceedings of the 28th IEEE International Parallel and Distributed Processing Symposium Workshops (IPDPSW 2014). IEEE Computer Society (2014)
8. Vassev, E., Hinchey, M., Gaudin, B.: Knowledge representation for self-adaptive behavior. In: Proceedings of C* Conference on Computer Science & Software Engineering (C3S2E 2012), pp. 113–117. ACM (2012)
9. Vassev, E., Hinchey, M., Montanari, U., Bicocchi, N., Zambonelli, F., Wirsing, M.: D3.2: Second Report on WP3: The KnowLang Framework for Knowledge Modeling for SCE Systems (2012). ASCENS Deliverable

Towards Performance-Aware Engineering
of Autonomic Component Ensembles

Tomáš Bureš[1,2], Vojtěch Horký[1], Michał Kit[1], Lukáš Marek[1], and Petr Tůma[1]

[1] Faculty of Mathematics and Physics
Charles University in Prague
Prague, Czech Republic
[2] Institute of Computer Science
Academy of Sciences of the Czech Republic
Prague, Czech Republic
{bures,horky,kit,marek,tuma}@d3s.mff.cuni.cz

Abstract. Ensembles of autonomic components are a novel software engineering paradigm for development of open-ended distributed highly dynamic software systems (e.g. smart cyber-physical systems). Recent research centered around the concept of ensemble-based systems resulted in design and development models that aim to systematize and simplify the engineering process of autonomic components and their ensembles. These methods highlight the importance of covering both the functional concepts and the non-functional properties, specifically performance-related aspects of the future systems. In this paper we propose an integration of the emerging techniques for performance assessment and awareness into different stages of the development process. Our goal is to aid both designers and developers of autonomic component ensembles with methods providing performance awareness throughout the entire development life cycle (including runtime).

Keywords: ensemble-based systems, component systems, performance engineering.

1   Introduction

Autonomic component ensembles (ACEs) emerged in the recent years as an abstraction for modeling and constructing open-ended distributed highly dynamic systems (e.g. smart cyber-physical systems as featured by the EU H2020 program). ACEs provide a way of describing dynamic goal-oriented groups of otherwise autonomic components, which combine well the autonomic and cooperative behavior.

ACEs operate in open and partially uncertain environments. This implies that potential interactions of components and their environment are very difficult, often impossible, to fully predict. ACEs also exhibit emergent behavior, which arises from collective actions taken by interacting components.

To cope with the uncertainty and emergent behavior, the software engineering of ACEs typically relies on a dedicated software development process, e.g. Ensemble

T. Margaria and B. Steffen (Eds.): ISoLA 2014, Part I, LNCS 8802, pp. 131–146, 2014.
© Springer-Verlag Berlin Heidelberg 2014

Development Lifecycle [1], which considers design time and run time as two parallel and mutually interacting adaptation loops. The loops integrate development with analysis and monitoring, thus making it possible to discover and reflect the emergent behavior and unanticipated reactions of the environment. The unanticipated behavior (e.g., the occurrence of certain message or reachability of certain state) is subsequently reported back to developers, thus providing input for incremental development.

It is relatively well-understood how to capture functional properties and detect their violations. Moreover, functional properties are (at least partially) addressed by various existing tools that aim to validate their satisfiability. The contrary, however, holds about the performance properties. This is because performance of a system cannot be easily isolated. Performance is highly impacted by resource sharing (e.g. CPU, I/O, network), even between otherwise unrelated and seemingly independent components. Additionally, due to their statistical nature, performance properties are often more complex to express and validate – performance measurements typically involve a complex setup and non-trivial statistical computations over the measured values. Recently, there have emerged helpful mechanisms for assessing performance (e.g. modeling to provide estimates during development, monitoring to provide information during execution), however, as more or less independent and unrelated approaches, they do not provide a comprehensive support being integrated within a development process. This is especially true for engineering ACEs.

In this paper, we strive to fill in this gap in the scope of the ACEs development process. Our goal is to aid both designers and developers of ACEs with methods providing performance awareness throughout the entire development life cycle (including runtime). In particular, we focus on the following three goals: (i) to discuss performance-related issues and objectives of ACEs development process, (ii) to show how the performance objectives can be targeted within the ACEs development process, and (iii) to overview suitable models, techniques and tools that together bring the performance-aware engineering of ACEs.

The structure of the paper is as follows. In Section 2, we elaborate on our running example – a scenario coming from our involvement in the ASCENS EU project. In Section 3, we detail the Ensemble Development Lifecycle, which we extend in Section 4 by performance-awareness (at both design/development time and runtime). We describe how existing tools can be used to address performance awareness in different phases of the development process and exemplify this on the running example. Section 5 surveys the related work, while Section 6 concludes the paper.

2   Case Study

To illustrate a typical representative of a distributed highly-dynamic system and its modeling using ACEs, we consider a scenario of intelligent vehicle navigation, in which vehicles are to efficiently get to given destinations, taking into account the current traffic, road closures, fuel consumption, etc. Vehicles are equipped with a route planning utility that allows a vehicle to autonomously compute the optimal route to its destination. For this purpose, a vehicle is aware of the factors influencing

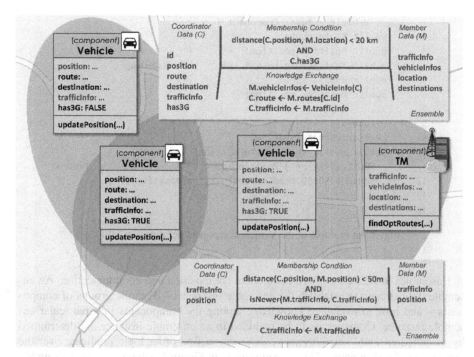

Fig. 1. Modelling scenario with use of DEECo primitives. UML representation of DEECo components together with ensemble description.

the route planning (i.e. traffic situation, fuel state and average fuel consumption, etc.). Such awareness is obtained from the internet (e.g. by 4G/3G based connection) and from the vehicles nearby, by short-range peer-to-peer communication (e.g. based on IEEE 802.15.4). When internet connection is available, a vehicle delegates the route computation to a centralized cloud-hosted service (called Traffic Manager – TM), which balances the traffic on a global level. TM also acts as a primary source of traffic information.

When modeling the case study using ACEs, the vehicles as well as the TM become autonomic components. The autonomic components are dynamically grouped into ensembles (i.e. dynamic goal-oriented groups of mutually cooperating components) to fulfill joint goals. For instance, vehicles that are close to each other group into ensembles to share their awareness about the traffic. Similarly, vehicles form an ensemble with TM in their area if internet connectivity is available.

Because a particular semantics of ACEs can be considered only within a particular component model when it comes to a realization, we exemplify our case-study using the DEECo component model [2]. In DEECo, a component consists of component knowledge, which holds the state of the component and its belief about other components. For instance the knowledge of the vehicle component includes its actual geographical position, the route it needs to follow (computed either locally or remotely by the TM) and the traffic information (see Figure 1). The knowledge is continuously updated by the component processes based on their sensing and internal computation.

```
1.   class Vehicle extends Component {
2.        public Route route;
3.        public Position position;
4.        public TrafficInfo trafficInfo;          Knowledge
5.        public double speed;
6.        public Position position;
7.        ...
8.        @Process
9.        @PeriodicScheduling(250)
10.       public static void updatePosition(
11.          @Out("position") Position p) {         Process
12.          Sensors.SPEED.readCurrentPosition(position);
13.       }
14.   }
```

Fig. 2. An example of the Vehicle component definition in jDEECo

Ensembles in DEECo capture component composition and communication. An ensemble defines how to establish the ensemble instances – dynamic groups of components – and how to exchange knowledge among the components in a particular ensemble instance. Components to be included in an ensemble instance are determined by so called *ensemble membership condition* – a first-order logic predicate over the knowledge of components. This is exemplified in Figure 1, where the upper ensemble groups a TM with vehicles in its sphere of activity, while the lower ensemble groups a vehicle with vehicles in its close vicinity. The communication within an ensemble instance is defined by so called *knowledge exchange function*, which describes how a part of component's knowledge is transformed and stored to the knowledge of another component (see Figure 1). Defined using a relation among a number of components, an ensemble may naturally exist in a system in multiple instances.

Technically, the execution of ACEs is managed by a runtime framework (e.g. JDEE-Co as a runtime framework for DEECo). The runtime framework includes the necessary programming constructs for definition of components and ensembles in a particular programming language and provides the distributed infrastructure for execution of components, formation of ensembles and knowledge exchange within ensembles.

2.1   Performance Considerations

In addition to functional goals (such as vehicle navigation to its destination), ACEs are typically subjects to a number of performance goals. An example of such a high-level goal in our case-study is the time for a navigation utility to plan a suitable route. This high-level goal is further dependent on other (still high-level) goals such as the limits on the route planning time or guarantees on the traffic information propagation delays. When designing for such high-level goals, the developer needs information on multiple performance-relevant properties on lower levels of the design (for example, the route planning time depends on the computing power available in the vehicle computer, and the traffic information propagation delays in the vehicle-to-vehicle networks depend on the information forwarding capacity of each vehicle).

The availability of this performance relevant information varies with the type of the information (e.g., settling time and accuracy of a particular sensor, execution time of a particular method) and the stage of the design. Some information is available very early in the design process, because it is actually a part of the design choices made – for example, we are likely to have a good idea of how reliable the vehicle speed information is because we know what speed sensor we use. Other performance relevant information is more difficult to obtain or guarantee – this may concern for example the frequency and accuracy of GPS position updates, which is strongly influenced by actual signal reception conditions, or the upper bound on the route calculation time, which may depend on the complexity of the map used. Finally, some performance relevant information comes from interactions among the ensemble components, which are especially difficult to predict in an open system.

For the design to progress at all, the developer has to make reasonable assumptions about all the lower level performance properties that contribute to the high-level performance goals. As a particular hallmark of the ensemble development process, relying on wrong assumptions is not necessarily a developer error – in the open environment, some initially reasonable assumptions can turn out to be wrong as the environment continuously evolves. We therefore need a development process that can track the individual performance assumptions between the design and execution phases and, as a matter of course, monitor and reflect on the possible violations of the assumptions.

3   Ensemble Development Lifecycle

The development of ACEs typically follows a dedicated life-cycle model, which in turn provides a concrete frame for supporting performance considerations. In this section, we overview the Ensemble-Development Lifecycle (EDLC), which is one of the primary life-cycle models for ACEs. Taking EDLC as the basis, we then show how it can be extended to address performance-related issues.

3.1   General Model

EDLC is a dedicated lifecycle model for engineering of autonomic component ensembles. EDLC features a "double-wheel" development process (see Figure 3), which combines iterative development (captured by the "first wheel") with two-level adaptation – the autonomous self-adaptation at runtime (captured by the "second wheel") and the developer-controlled adaptation (captured by the feedback loop between the design time and runtime).

Going into more detail, the design part ("first wheel") consists of requirements engineering, modeling/programming and verification/validation. These activities are iteratively executed until a desired product is created. The verification and validation play a very prominent role here. It involves static analysis and simulations, which are employed to predict the large-scale system behavior, accounting for its potentially emergent nature.

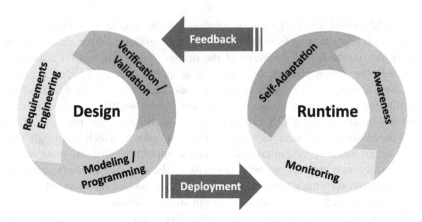

Fig. 3. Ensemble Development Life Cycle

The runtime part ("second wheel") reflects the execution of the system. In contrast to traditional systems, ACEs possess a high degree of self-awareness and self-adaptivity. This is in EDLC embodied by the monitoring, awareness (reasoning) and self-adaptation activities – similar to the MAPE adaptation loops known from autonomic computing [3].

The two wheels of EDLC are connected by deployment of a system and feedback, which brings data collected by monitoring at runtime back to design. The feedback data is used to observe and analyze the behavior of the system and its self-adaptation responses in face of originally unanticipated situations. If the analysis shows that the system was not able to gracefully cope with a particular situation, it is reengineered, analyzed/simulated and again deployed.

Technically, EDLC can be supported by a number of tools – for instance DEECo can be used for modeling/programming, deployment and execution of ACEs. Similarly, DEECo can be also employed for rudimentary support for monitoring, awareness and self-adaptation. The other design activities are covered by IRM [4] / SOTA [5] (for requirements engineering) and by ARGoS [6] / GMC [7] (for verification of functional aspects).

3.2   Performance Perspective

From the performance perspective, the role of the ensemble development process is (1) to collect and deliver available information about performance to developers in relevant situations and (2) to propagate the performance relevant assumptions made during development to the runtime for monitoring and adaptation feedback.

Rather than being acquired en bloc, performance information is collected and improved gradually throughout the development process. In principle, the initial information is limited to guesses about future system performance. This information can be improved along two principal axes:

Isolated computation. As soon as the initial implementation of selected ensemble components becomes available, the performance of these components can be measured in isolation, much in the same way as software components are tested in agile development methodologies. Measurement in isolation requires a test harness that manufactures the input required by the ensemble components. This task is made easier by the fact that the interface of each ensemble component is precisely specified, with communication taking place only through knowledge exchange. The input for testing therefore takes the shape of a snapshot(s) of the knowledge repository, initially prepared by knowledge generators implemented for that purpose [8].

Relying on an artificially generated workload can naturally limit the accuracy or representatives of the performance measurements collected. In the subsequent steps of the development process, this information can be improved by collecting knowledge samples from the executing ensemble. This knowledge can again be fed as input to the components for measurement purposes.

The ultimately authoritative information on individual component performance can be collected by monitoring the deployed ensemble. Thus, the obtained information can be confronted with the estimates and assumptions made in earlier development stages as necessary.

Knowledge exchange. Besides the performance of individual components, the performance relevant behavior of an ensemble is also determined by the interactions between components. These interactions determine both the content and the timing of the input knowledge that the components rely on.

Improving the initial estimates of ensemble performance requires that the development process has progressed enough to provide information on the ensemble communication architecture. Once this architecture is available, estimates on knowledge propagation delays can be made and following ensemble simulations can improve the available performance information.

As in the previous case, the ultimate information on ensemble performance comes from monitoring "live" ensembles once they become available. The entire process of performance information improvement has an iterative character, where each new contribution helps to gradually form the overall ensemble performance picture.

As a major stumbling block, we can eventually end up with too much information – either too much information to collect, with prohibitive measurement costs or disruptive measurement overhead, or too much information to process and accommodate, which can entail significant developer workload. To avoid this particular danger, it is necessary to formally track the process of refining the high-level performance goals into lower level performance assumptions or requirements. We need to monitor and collect performance information only in locations whose performance contributes to a high-level performance goal, and we need to report this performance only when it diverges from the assumptions made during development.

4   Performance-Awareness in EDLC

To bring the performance perspective into engineering of ACEs, we augment EDLC with an extension which addresses performance-related issues as discussed in Section 3.2. Overall, we view the performance-aware engineering as centered around the three principal feedback loops of EDLC (the design one, the runtime one, and the outer one connecting design and runtime). At design time, we introduce four principal activities connected to performance: (D-1) formulating high-level performance goals, (D-2) refining the high-level goals to time constraints on isolated computation and knowledge exchange (as outlined in Section 3.2), (D-3) collecting performance data by isolated benchmarking and simulations, (D-4) providing feedback about predicted performance to development of components and ensembles. At runtime, we (R-1) collect relevant performance indicators (as identified by the high-level and low-level performance goals) and we (R-2) analyze them to detect possible violations of the performance goals. When such a violation happens, (F-1) it is reported back to the design time. The outer feedback loop is additionally used for (F-2) obtaining real-life measurements (e.g. actual network latency, packet drops) to improve the design-time simulations.

This whole process is tool-supported. We use a special computer interpretable logic for capturing performance assumptions in D-1 and D-2; tools for automated performance evaluation, simulations, and analysis for D-3 and for the runtime monitoring and analysis of R-1 and R-2; and an extension to a development IDE (e.g. Eclipse) to provide relevant performance measurements as part of its contextual assistance for D-4. In the following, we overview in more detail the particular methods and tools driving the process described above. Furthermore, we demonstrate their use on our case-study.

4.1   Performance Goals and their Decomposition (D-1, D-2)

High-level performance goals formulation and their further decomposition are the activities that fall into the requirements engineering step of the EDLC. For this task we employ the Invariant Refinement Method (IRM) [4], which has already been used in DEECo for functional goal formulation and decomposition. IRM relies on the top-down approach, where top-level invariants constitute high-level (general) goals of the application and are further decomposed into more specialized (fine-grained) ones, which eventually map into concrete component processes and ensembles. In the context of the EDLC, the refinement of non-functional goals is not much different from the refinement of their functional counterparts and can use IRM as is. Similar to functional goals, performance goals are eventually mapped to component processes or knowledge exchange of the ACEs.

To illustrate the idea behind activities D-1 and D-2, we take a high-level performance goal of not needing more than 30 seconds to provide a suitable route. Following the functional IRM-based decomposition, this goal splits into two alternatives (OR-decomposition) as follows: If the vehicle has no connectivity to the TM, it computes locally the route to its destination, (optionally) relying on the traffic information obtained previously from TM or from other vehicles. Otherwise, the vehicle off-loads route computation to the TM and awaits the results. In this case, the high-level performance goal of vehicle navigation planning time being no longer than 30 seconds decomposes into several time constraints (as shown in Figure 4) that correspond to knowledge exchange (in both directions) and TM's route computation.

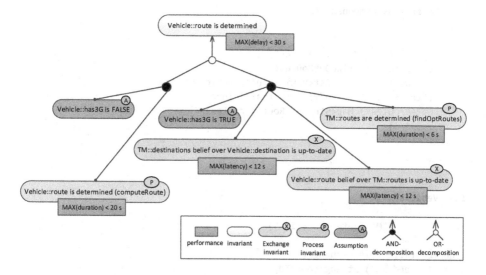

Fig. 4. High-level performance goal decomposition in IRM

4.2 Formalization of Performance Constraints (D-2)

We capture performance goals by Stochastic Performance Logic (SPL) [9], which is a many-sorted first-order logic with well-defined semantics. SPL regards performance as a random variable with probability distribution dependent on a given workload. SPL features performance relational operators, which are based on statistical testing of various statistical measures such as mean, minimum, maximum or an arbitrary quantiles.

We employ SPL as the formal framework for expressing performance goals at design time as exemplified by rectangular boxes in Figure 4 (note that the $<$ operator used in the formulas stands for single-sided statistical testing whether a hypothesis of a negation can be rejected at a given confidence level α). Similarly, we use SPL on the level of the code, where we reflect the performance requirements in the form of annotations (@Performance) – see Figure 5. Tying performance goals to particular methods in the code brings the performance goals to the level where they can be automatically tested.

4.3 Benchmarking of Isolated Computation (D-3)

The SPL-based code annotations can be used at run-time to check that the implementation conforms to the specification and at development time to test the computation performance of components in isolation. Testing in isolation allows getting rough estimates of the performance in situations when an application is not ready to be deployed or when real deployment is too costly to be used for testing.

```
class TM extends Component {
  ...
  @Process
  @Performance("MAX(duration) < 6s")
  public static void findOptRoutes(
    @In("vehicleInfos") List<VehicleInfo> vehicleInfos,
    @In("trafficInfo") TrafficInfo trafficInfo,
    @InOut("routes") Map<String, Route> routes)
  { /* ... */ }
  ...
}

@Ensemble
class VehicleTM {
  ...
  @Performance("MAX(latency) < 12s")
  @KnowledgeExchange
  public static void exchange(
    @In("coord.id") String coordId,
    @In("coord.destination") Position coordDest,
    ...
  )
  { /* ... */ }
}
```

Fig. 5. An example of requirement decomposition

Testing of isolated execution requires a developer (tester) to provide a sample workload. In traditional performance unit testing as described in [9], the tester needs to prepare a workload generator that creates the parameters for the method under test. When testing DEECo components, the tester has to provide artificial knowledge upon which the component can operate. This can be done by providing test-cases that are partitioned in a similar way as in functional black-box and white-box testing. Alternatively, it is possible to use knowledge valuation sampled previously in a real deployment.

The performance testing process itself and the evaluation of the results is driven by SPL tools [10], which take care of all steps necessary for precise and statistically relevant performance measurements. This involves workload preparation, actual measurements preceded by a sufficiently long warm-up, collection of measurement results and their statistical analysis. To improve the relevancy of the measurements, they can be collected on a remote machine, running the actual target hardware, instead of a local, developer's one. SPL tools also allow for regression testing, which makes it possible to detect performance degradation across software versions.

4.4 Benchmarking of Knowledge Exchange (D-3)

Contrary to computational performance, the performance of knowledge exchange has to be established on a system level – at least considering components of an ensemble and other components that use the same shared communication medium.

An important fact is that the performance of the knowledge exchange depends heavily on the particular communication protocols being used. For instance, to date DEECo features two principal knowledge exchange approaches – centralized tuple space [11] and decentralized gossip-based communication [12]. In the former case, every time a process needs to be executed a remote tuple space is queried for the necessary data and the result is stored back immediately after the execution. In the latter case, knowledge is exchanged asynchronously in a best-effort manner. Naturally, the first option brings relatively fast knowledge exchange, which comes at the price of requiring a stable (and reliable) network infrastructure. Gossiping on the other hand seamlessly supports unreliable and continuously changing communication links (e.g. Mobile Ad-hoc NETworks – MANETs), which is carried by the cost of longer (by several orders of magnitude) communication times and weaker consistency of the whole system.

To predict the times for the knowledge exchange, we rely on simulations that take into account the realistic behavior of the network. In particular, in the frame of the DEECo component model, its runtime framework JDEECo supports integration with the OMNet++ network simulator, which is utilized to simulate network contention in static, wireless, mobile and MANET networks. This integration of JDEECo and OM-Net++ makes it possible to gather different statistics (e.g. amount of packets exchanged, amount of drops, and latencies).

An obvious difficulty of the system-level simulation is that it requires a model of the infrastructure nodes (that act as component containers) and their network connectivity. Specifying such a model requires a non-trivial effort. Advantageously, once created, this model can be reused across development increments and possibly even across different ACEs applications. What then remains as an input for the simulation is the deployment plan (i.e. assignment of components to particular infrastructure nodes). Such a deployment plan can be specified in a relatively straightforward way – e.g. by assigning an instance of a particular component to each node of a specific type (e.g. Vehicle).

4.5   Collection and Analysis of Performance Indicators at Runtime (R-1, R-2)

In addition to isolated measurements and simulations at design time, we monitor ACEs also at runtime. This is performed using DiSL [13], which is an instrumentation framework targeted on dynamic analysis of applications. DiSL provides an AOP (Aspect Oriented Programming) inspired domain specific language hosted in Java using annotations, which makes it possible to insert arbitrary instrumentation into an observed application.

In our approach, we instrument component processes marked by the @Performance annotation. DiSL also allows for inside-process instrumentations (e.g. for measuring performance of a particular method or block of statements). Since the instrumentation in DiSL is on-line, meaning it is dynamically applied when the application is loaded, it can be easily switched off when no measurements are required, thus mitigating the runtime overhead. The results from DiSL measurement are stored as an online profile of a component. The online profile can be immediately evaluated by SPL backend and submitted

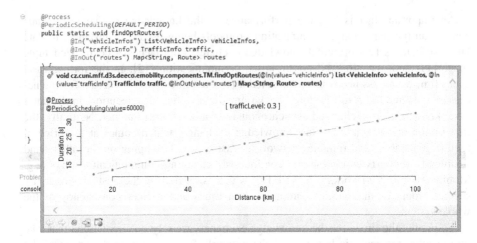

```
@Process
@PeriodicScheduling(DEFAULT_PERIOD)
public static void findOptRoutes(
        @In("vehicleInfos") List<VehicleInfo> vehicleInfos,
        @In("trafficInfo") TrafficInfo traffic,
        @InOut("routes") Map<String, Route> routes
```

Fig. 6. Prospective performance feedback integration into Eclipse IDE

to a component developer if some of the performance requirements are not met (as described in Section 4.6).

4.6   Providing Development feedback (D-4)

We envision that the measurement of computation and knowledge exchange performance should be available to the developer directly in the IDE and similarly to the way results of unit tests are reported and context help is shown in the context assist. This idea is exemplified in Figure 6 – it shows a mock-up of the Eclipse IDE with a context-assist displaying a graph of measured process performance.

Moreover, we envision that the process of providing the results to the IDE should resemble the one applied in continuous integration. In particular, we imagine that the performance measurements are triggered as soon as a particular artifact (component or ensemble) becomes available in a shape allowing for its deployment. This happens asynchronously (most likely on a dedicated server). Although their primary objective is to give a pass/fail answer (according to the specified performance goals), they can be used to determine which performance indicators are of relevance and their detailed statistics can be provided within the IDE.

5   Related Work

Being a relatively young concept, the performance of ACEs has not been so far systematically addressed; in particular, there are no existing works addressing performance in the context of the ACEs development process. Looking at our contribution from a broader perspective, we can identify three main research fields, which are at least partially related to our contribution (though they are not specialized for development of ACEs). These are: performance measurement frameworks used broadly in the context of component-based systems, instrumentation tools for computation time measurements, and approaches for communication latency assessment. We structure the rest of the section along this principal division.

In regard to performance measurement frameworks, in [14] authors present performance measurement framework designed for component systems called TAU. TAU provides a support for two kinds of instrumentation techniques that differ with respect to the flexibility level being traded off for a higher overhead. The later work (described in [15]) extends the TAU framework by performance-oriented regression tests. As a complete framework, TAU delivers a broad range of features, which in the case of the ACEs and the approach proposed in this paper seems to be redundant (introducing unnecessary overhead). The Palladio component model [16] comes with a simulation framework that allows for identification of performance bottlenecks during the design phase of the development process. Being a pure model-based solution, Palladio does not support on-line measurements of a (partially-) developed system, and relies only on individual component performance predictions. This effectively limits its applicability in further stages of the development process (i.e. programming), where more accurate (built on the implementation) estimates are available. An online measurement technique is presented in [17], which describes a method for online measurements of component-based applications. It builds on the Linux Trace Toolkit [18] to capture components performance. In particular, it measures remote invocation overhead (lookup and data marshaling) as well as inter-component communication delays. The measurements are used to predict behavior under different deployment strategies. The proposed solution, however, lacks run-time measurements of an already deployed application and is designed purely for production time analyses.

In terms of execution time measurements, we can distinguish between two common techniques. One is profiling, which periodically observes executed code and based on the acquired stack information creates a statistical execution profile of the observed system. The other technique is instrumentation, which uses probes, injected directly into the observed code, to measure its execution time. Profiling is not precise but has only small impact on the observed system. In contrast, instrumentation provides precise execution times but its high coverage may impose significant overhead. Profiling tools such as HPROF [19] or NetBeans Profiler [20] are in majority accommodating both of these techniques, however they lack the ability to scope the measurement to particular parts of the observed system. For more fine grained measurements (as we presume in our approach) an instrumentation tool is expected to support exact method (or block of code) measurement. Both Perf4J [21] and Xebia tools [22] use annotations to mark methods intended for execution time measurement. Compared to DiSL (which we employ), they lack the ability for more sophisticated measurement logic insertion.

Very often, the measurements may require certain conditions to hold or even perform more complex computation to decide whether to store or discard the measured values. To support such scenarios, the instrumentation framework needs to provide a possibility for an arbitrary instrumentation insertion into the observed code. One of such is the AspectJ framework [23]. It allows one to easily insert any block of code in the instrumented program in order to perform various dynamic analysis task. As it is not primarily designed for performance measurements, it imposes higher overheads than comparable tools. Another examples of instrumentation-based solutions are Sofya [24] and Chord [25], which support creation of custom analysis tools. In our approach, the DiSL framework was selected, as it provides both flexible enough and high-level language for specifying custom instrumentation that is suitable in the context of component process performance analyses. With respect to the approaches for communication cost assessment, these usually build on simulation frameworks that benchmark developed applications against different deployment models. During the simulation process, various statistics are collected, the accuracy of which depends directly on the precision of the model being used. In our method we rely on the OMNet++ network simulator [26], which is a mature product with support for a multitude of network protocols (including wired and wireless IP-based networks, MANETs, etc.). OMNet++ further provides an API for statistical analyses, which makes possible collection of various performance indicators. Naturally, other network simulators exist (e.g. NS-2 and NS-3 [27]) and are used for the same purpose. While our approach incorporates the network simulator, it focuses mostly on the ACEs level of abstraction that allows for reasoning about communication performance at the application level (i.e. it answers questions about the perceived staleness of component knowledge, etc.).

6   Conclusion

In this paper, we have presented an approach for performance-awareness introduction in the development process of autonomic component ensembles. The approach is centered around EDLC, which we have extended by a set of well-defined activities for pinpointing the performance goals, measuring the corresponding performance indicators, and bringing the information about performance to the developer. This allows the developer to have an idea about the expected performance and related interactions already when developing them. Additionally, our approach includes integration with the runtime, which makes it possible to incorporate actual performance of ACEs in a deployment environment and reflect it back to the development. We have demonstrated the core ideas of our approach based on existing tools for monitoring and analyzing performance. To provide for a holistic solution, these tools have to be integrated within a development environment, whose sketch we have also provided. Such an integration and real-life evaluation constitute our future work.

Acknowledgments. This work was partially supported by the EU project ASCENS 257414 and by Charles University institutional funding SVV-2014-260100. The research leading to these results has received funding from the European Union Seventh Framework Programme FP7-PEOPLE-2010-ITN under grant agreement n°264840.

References

[1] Bures, T., De Nicola, R., Gerostathopoulos, I., Hoch, N., Kit, M., Koch, N., Monreale, G.V., Montanari, U., Pugliese, R., Serbedzija, N., Wirsing, M., Zambonelli, F.: A Life Cycle for the Development of Autonomic Systems: The e-Mobility Showcase (2013)

[2] Bures, T., Gerostathopoulos, I., Hnetynka, P., Keznikl, J., Kit, M., Plasil, F.: DEECo – an Ensemble-Based Component System. In: Proc. of CBSE 2013, pp. 81–90 (2013)

[3] IBM, Ed., An Architectural Blueprint for Autonomic Computing (June 2005)

[4] Keznikl, J., Bures, T., Plasil, F., Gerostathopoulos, I., Hnetynka, P., Hoch, N.: Design of Ensemble-Based Component Systems by Invariant Refinement. In: Proc. of CBSE 2013, pp. 91–100 (2013)

[5] Abeywickrama, D.B., Bicocchi, N., Zambonelli, F.: SOTA: Towards a General Model for Self-Adaptive Systems. In: IEEE 21st Int. Workshop Enabling Technologies: Infrastructure for Collaborative Enterprises (WETICE), pp. 48–53 (2012)

[6] ARGoS (2013), http://iridia.ulb.ac.be/argos

[7] GIMPLE Model Checker (2013), http://d3s.mff.cuni.cz/~sery/gmc/

[8] Horký, V., Haas, F., Kotrč, J., Lacina, M., Tůma, P.: Performance Regression Unit Testing: A Case Study. In: Balsamo, M.S., Knottenbelt, W.J., Marin, A. (eds.) EPEW 2013. LNCS, vol. 8168, pp. 149–163. Springer, Heidelberg (2013)

[9] Bulej, L., Bureš, T., Keznikl, J., Koubková, A., Podzimek, A., Tůma, P.: Capturing Performance Assumptions Using Stochastic Performance Logic. In: Proceedings of the 3rd ACM/SPEC Int. Conference on Performance Engineering, pp. 311–322 (2012)

[10] Stochastic Performance Logic (SPL) (2014), http://d3s.mff.cuni.cz/software/spl-java/

[11] Gelernter, D.: Generative communication in Linda. ACM Trans. Program. Lang. Syst. 7(1), 80–112 (1985)

[12] Friedman, R., Gavidia, D., Rodrigues, L., Viana, A.C., Voulgaris, S.: Gossiping on MANETs: the Beauty and the Beast. ACM SIGOPS Oper. Syst. Rev. 41(5), 67–74 (2007)

[13] DiSL Framework (2013), http://disl.ow2.org/xwiki/bin/view/Main/

[14] Shende, S., Malony, A.D., Rasmussen, C., Sottile, M.: A performance interface for component-based applications. In: Proceedings of the Int. Parallel and Distributed Processing Symposium, p. 8 (2003)

[15] De St. Germain, J.D., Morris, A., Parker, S.G., Malony, A.D., Shende, S.: Performance Analysis Integration in the Uintah Software Development Cycle. Int. J. Parallel Program. 31(1), 35–53 (2003)

[16] Becker, S., Koziolek, H., Reussner, R.: The Palladio Component Model for Model-driven Performance Prediction. J. Syst. Softw. 82(1), 3–22 (2009)

[17] Stewart, C., Shen, K.: Performance Modeling and System Management for Multicomponent Online Services. In: Proceedings of the 2nd Conference on Symposium on Networked Systems Design & Implementation, vol. 2, pp. 71–84 (2005)

[18] Yaghmour, K., Dagenais, M.R.: Measuring and Characterizing System Behavior Using Kernel-level Event Logging. In: Proceedings of the Annual Conference on USENIX Annual Technical Conference, p. 2 (2000)

[19] HPROF: A Heap/CPU Profiling Tool (2014), http://docs.oracle.com/javase/7/docs/technotes/samples/hprof.html

[20] NetBeans Profiler (2014), http://profiler.netbeans.org

[21] Perf4J (2014), http://perf4j.codehaus.org

[22] Xebia Tools (2014), http://code.google.com/p/xebia-france

[23] Kiczales, G.: AspectJ(tm): Aspect-Oriented Programming in Java. In: Akşit, M., Mezini, M., Unland, R. (eds.) NODe 2002. LNCS, vol. 2591, p. 1. Springer, Heidelberg (2003)

[24] Kinneer, A., Dwyer, M.B., Rothermel, G.: Sofya: Supporting Rapid Development of Dynamic Program Analyses for Java. In: 29th Int. Conference on Software Engineering - Companion, ICSE 2007, pp. 51–52 (2007)

[25] Chord Group (2014), http://pag.gatech.edu/home

[26] OMNet++ Simulation Framework (2013), http://omnetpp.org

[27] Network Simulatior (2014), http://www.nsnam.org

Self-expression and Dynamic Attribute-Based Ensembles in SCEL

Giacomo Cabri[1], Nicola Capodieci[1], Luca Cesari[2], Rocco De Nicola[3],
Rosario Pugliese[2], Francesco Tiezzi[3], and Franco Zambonelli[1]

[1] Università degli Studi di Modena e Reggio Emilia,
Via Amendola, 2 - 42122 Reggio Emilia, Italy
{giacomo.cabri,nicola.capodieci,franco.zambonelli}@unimore.it
[2] Università degli Studi di Firenze, Viale Morgagni, 65 - 50134 Firenze, Italy
{luca.cesari,rosario.pugliese}@unifi.it
[3] IMT Institute for Advanced Studies Lucca,
Piazza S. Francesco, 19 - 55100, Lucca, Italy
{rocco.denicola,francesco.tiezzi}@imtlucca.it

Abstract. In the field of distributed autonomous computing the current trend is to develop cooperating computational entities enabled with enhanced self-* properties. The expression self-* indicates the possibility of a component inside an ensemble, i.e. a set of collaborative autonomic components, to self organize, heal (repair), optimize and configure with little or no human interaction. We focus on a self-* property called *self-expression*, defined as the ability to deploy run-time changes of the coordination pattern of the observed ensemble; the goal of the ensemble is to achieve adaptivity by meeting functional and non-functional requirements when specific tasks have to be completed. The purpose of this paper is to rigorously present the mechanisms involved whenever a change in the coordination pattern is needed, and the interactions that take place. To this aim, we use SCEL (Software Component Ensemble Language), a formal language for describing autonomic components and their interactions, featuring a highly dynamic and flexible way to form ensembles based on components' attributes.

Keywords: Self-expression, coordination patterns, ensemble computing.

1 Introduction

The current trend in designing distributed systems is to conceive them as ensembles of several, possibly heterogeneous, components. Ensembles are often required to solve complex problems of real life, even situations in which the level of interaction between humans and components of the ensemble is strongly limited or even absent. Therefore, their components usually collaborate with each other in order to achieve a common goal. This calls for further features that increase the self-management capability of the systems, such as self-configuration, self-healing, self-optimization, and self-protection, leading to what is known in literature as self-* properties in autonomic computing [16,31]. The goal is to

T. Margaria and B. Steffen (Eds.): ISoLA 2014, Part I, LNCS 8802, pp. 147–163, 2014.
© Springer-Verlag Berlin Heidelberg 2014

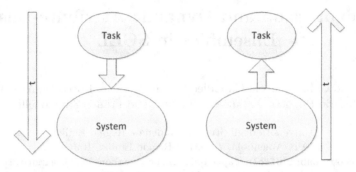

Fig. 1. A two-perspective relationship between task to solve and surrounding system

have self-adaptive ensembles able to promptly react to dynamic changes of the surrounding environment and to optimize their performance when addressing tasks of variable complexity in the presence of dynamic environments. In addition to the previously listed properties, there can be situations in which changes in the components' coordination pattern (as a refactoring of behaviors, roles and interactions among components) can be useful at runtime, especially in open and non-deterministic scenarios. This change should be autonomously made by the ensemble itself by relying on adaptive collaboration of its components. This ability could enable the ensemble to face unexpected and unpredictable situations, often modelled as changes in the environment or fault tolerance issues [26]. Moreover, it could increase performance and robustness of the designed ensemble, because different coordination patterns could require different utilities or qualities for solving a specific task. The dynamic modification of the coordination pattern according to the changes in the external conditions is called *self-expression* [30], meaning that the autonomic system *expresses* itself (i.e., the system still does what is supposed to do) independently of unexpected situations and, to accomplish this, it is capable of modifying its original internal organization.

This paper aims at showing how to *enable* self-expression in a concrete way by exploiting a formal language for defining ensembles. We refer the interested reader to [30,5] for further motivations and details about self-expression.

1.1 More Details on Self-expression

Enhancing adaptivity of an ensemble through self-expression is a problem that can be seen from two different perspectives, as shown in Fig. 1.

A first perspective (left part of Fig. 1) is to think about engineering an ensemble able to solve a specific problem starting from an initial task that can be then subdivided into several sub-tasks to be assigned to ensemble components. For instance, the task "explore a given area" could be split in the sub-tasks "act as a master that proposes sub-areas to explore", "act as a slave for executing the received orders from a master", "act as a peer to negotiate sub-areas to explore", etc. Self-expression can be then represented by a Business Process Logic (BPL) specification that regulates relationships among sub-tasks and how these are assigned to each component. Since each of these sub-tasks is related to how the ensemble will assign roles, behaviors and interaction rules, the BPL specification provides information on how the ensemble will coordinate its components for solving the specified task. BPL specifications are subject to change over time according to the dynamics of the surrounding environment, so to have ensembles whose components will undergo modifications of the sub-tasks assignment and of the way they will coordinate according to the changes in the external conditions.

A second perspective (right part of Fig. 1) is to think about an already existing system that potentially is able to solve a multitude of tasks and for each of these tasks, each component of the system knows different *ways* to collaboratively complete it. For instance, some available tasks could be "area exploration" and "dragging/pushing objects outside the area", while the different ways to accomplish them could be "master-slave", "peer-to-peer" and "swarm". Later on, a request from outside, or a specific contingency, could prepare the system for solving a specific task. Self-expression here is seen as the capability to collaboratively select the fittest way, according to the currently perceived environmental conditions, for solving the selected task. The fittest collaborative effort can be thought of as a coordination pattern that results in an appropriate Quality of Service (QoS). Its selection is a decision that is ideally shared throughout the whole ensemble. As external conditions change over time, the ensemble has to adapt itself by choosing a different way to coordinate.

The modelling and description of the mechanisms for deploying self-expression according to this latter perspective present interesting challenges and are investigated in the rest of the paper by using a formal language specifically designed for defining ensembles.

1.2 Self-expression in a Formal Language for Defining Ensembles

The language SCEL (Software Components Ensemble Language) [10,11] has been introduced to deal with the challenges posed by the design of ensembles of autonomic components. In SCEL, autonomic components are entities with dedicated knowledge repositories and resources that can cooperate while playing different roles. Knowledge repositories also enable components to store and retrieve information about their working environment, and to use it for redirecting and adapting their behavior. Each component is equipped with an *interface*, consisting of a collection of *attributes*, such as provided functionalities, spatial coordinates, group memberships, trust level, response time, etc. Attributes are used by the components to dynamically organize themselves into ensembles.

The way sets of partners are selected for interaction, and thus how ensembles are formed, is one of the main novelties of SCEL. In fact, individual components not only can single out communication partners by using their identities, but they can also select partners by exploiting the attributes in the interfaces of the individual components. Predicates over such attributes are used to specify the targets of communication actions, thus providing a sort of *attribute-based* communication. In this way, the formation rule of ensembles is endogenous to components: members of an ensemble are connected by the interdependency relations defined through predicates. An ensemble is therefore not a rigid fixed network, but rather a highly dynamic structure where components' linkages are dynamically established.

The purpose of this work is to show that SCEL can be conveniently exploited to naturally model ensembles able to deploy self-expression. Indeed, ensembles can be addressed as single entities (by exploiting predicates) and, at the same time, are composed of sub-entities (the ensemble components, which are the actual recipients of ensemble invocations). Our characterization has the additional benefit of fostering dynamic identification of sub-sets of ensembles, since ensembles are highly dynamic structures where components linkages are dynamically established.

The rest of the paper is organized as follows. In Section 2, we recap the SCEL language, while in Section 3 we show how to implement self-expression with it. In Section 4, we present an application of our approach to a case study from the robotics domain. Section 5 discusses more strictly related work. Finally, in Section 6, we draw some conclusions and sketch how our approach can be further extended.

2   SCEL: Software Component Ensemble Language

SCEL is a kernel language for programming autonomic computing systems in terms of Behaviors, Knowledge and Aggregations, according to specific Policies. *Behaviors* describe how computations progress and are modeled as processes executing actions. *Knowledge* is represented through items containing either application data enabling the progress of components' computations, or awareness data providing information about the environment in which the components are running (e.g. monitored data from sensors) or about the status of a component (e.g. its current location). *Aggregations* describe how different entities are brought together to form components and ensembles. In particular, components result from a form of syntax-based aggregation that puts together a knowledge repository, a set of policies and a set of behaviors, by wrapping them in an interface providing a set of *attributes*, i.e. names referring to information stored in the knowledge repository. Components' composition and interaction are implemented by exploiting the attributes exposed in components' interfaces. This form of semantics-based aggregation of components permits defining ensembles, representing social or technical networks of components, and configuring them to dynamically adapt to changes in the environment. Finally, *policies* control and adapt the actions of the different components for guaranteeing accomplishment of specific tasks or satisfaction of specific properties.

The syntax of SCEL is presented in Table 1. There, different syntactic categories are defined that constitute the main ingredients of the language. The basic category is the one defining PROCESSES that are used to build up COMPONENTS that in turn are used to define SYSTEMS. PROCESSES specify the flow of the ACTIONS that can be performed. ACTIONS can have a TARGET to determine the other components that are involved in that action. The rest of this section is devoted to the description of the SCEL's syntactic categories.

Table 1. SCEL syntax (KNOWLEDGE $\mathcal{K}$, POLICIES Π, TEMPLATES T, and ITEMS t are parameters of the language)

SYSTEMS:	S	$::=$	$\mathcal{I}[\mathcal{K}, \Pi, P]$ | $S_1 \parallel S_2$ | $(\nu n)S$
PROCESSES:	P	$::=$	$\mathbf{nil}$ | $a.P$ | $P_1 + P_2$ | $P_1 \| P_2$ | X | $A(\bar{p})$
ACTIONS:	a	$::=$	$\mathbf{get}(T)@c$ | $\mathbf{qry}(T)@c$ | $\mathbf{put}(t)@c$ | $\mathbf{fresh}(n)$
			| $\mathbf{new}(\mathcal{I}, \mathcal{K}, \Pi, P)$
TARGETS:	c	$::=$	n | x | self | $\mathcal{P}$ | p

Systems and components. The key notion is that of *component* $\mathcal{I}[\mathcal{K}, \Pi, P]$, that is graphically depicted in Figure 2 and consists of:

1. An *interface* $\mathcal{I}$ publishing and making available structural and behavioral information about the component itself in the form of attributes. Among them, attribute *id* is mandatory and is bound to the (not necessarily unique) name of the component.
2. A *knowledge repository* $\mathcal{K}$ managing both application data and awareness data, together with a specific handling mechanism providing operations for *adding, retrieving*, and *withdrawing* knowledge items. The knowledge repository of a component stores also the information associated to its interface, which therefore can be dynamically manipulated by means of the operations provided by the knowledge repositories' handling mechanisms.
3. A tuple of *policies* Π regulating the interaction between the different internal parts of the component and the interaction of the component with the others.
4. A *process* P, together with a set of process definitions that can be dynamically activated.

SYSTEMS aggregate COMPONENTS through the *composition* operator $\_ \parallel \_$. It is also possible to restrict the scope of a name, say n, by using the *name restriction* operator $(\nu n)\_$. Thus, in a system of the form $S_1 \parallel (\nu n)S_2$, the effect of the operator is to make name n invisible from within S_1. Essentially, this operator plays a role similar to that of a *begin … end* block in sequential programming and limits visibility of specific names. Additionally, restricted names can be exchanged in communications thus enabling the receiving components to use those "private" names.

Processes. PROCESSES are the active computational units. Each process is built up from the *inert* process $\mathbf{nil}$ via *action prefixing* ($a.P$), *nondeterministic choice* ($P_1 + P_2$), *controlled composition* ($P_1[P_2]$), *process variable* (X), and *parameterized process invocation* ($A(\bar{p})$). We will omit trailing occurrences of $\mathbf{nil}$, writing e.g. a instead of $a.\mathbf{nil}$. The construct $P_1[P_2]$ abstracts the various forms of parallel composition commonly used in process calculi. Process variables can support *higher-order* communication, namely the capability to exchange (the code of) a process, and possibly execute it, by first adding an item containing the process to a knowledge repository and then retrieving/withdrawing this item

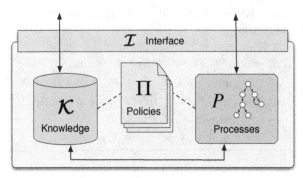

Fig. 2. A SCEL component

while binding the process to a process variable. We assume that A ranges over a set of parameterized *process identifiers* that are used in recursive process definitions. We also assume that each process identifier A has a *single* definition of the form $A(\bar{f}) \triangleq P$ where all free variables in P are contained in $\bar{f}$ and all occurrences of process identifiers in P are within the scope of an action prefixing. $\bar{p}$ and $\bar{f}$ denote lists of actual and formal parameters, respectively.

Actions and targets. Processes can perform five different kinds of ACTIONS. Actions $\mathbf{get}(T)@c$, $\mathbf{qry}(T)@c$ and $\mathbf{put}(t)@c$ are used to manage shared knowledge repositories by withdrawing/retrieving/adding information items from/to the knowledge repository c. These actions exploit templates T as patterns to select knowledge items t in the repositories. They heavily rely on the used knowledge repository and are implemented by invoking the handling operations it provides. Action $\mathbf{fresh}(n)$ introduces a scope restriction for the name n so that this name is guaranteed to be *fresh*, i.e. different from any other name previously used. Action $\mathbf{new}(\mathcal{I}, \mathcal{K}, \Pi, P)$ creates a new component $\mathcal{I}[\mathcal{K}, \Pi, P]$.

Action $\mathbf{get}$ may cause the process executing it to wait for the wanted element if it is not (yet) available in the knowledge repository. Action $\mathbf{qry}$, exactly like $\mathbf{get}$, may suspend the process executing it if the knowledge repository does not (yet) contain or cannot 'produce' the wanted element. The two actions differ for the fact that $\mathbf{get}$ removes the found item from the knowledge repository while $\mathbf{qry}$ leaves the target repository unchanged. Actions $\mathbf{put}$, $\mathbf{fresh}$ and $\mathbf{new}$ are instead immediately executed, provided that their execution is allowed by the policies in force.

Different entities may be used as the target c of an action. Component names are denoted by $n, n', \ldots$, while variables for names are denoted by $x, x', \ldots$. The distinguished variable self can be used by processes to refer to the name of the component hosting them. The target can also be a *predicate* $\mathcal{P}$ or the name p of a predicate, exposed as an attribute in the interface of the component, that may dynamically change. A predicate could be a boolean-valued expression obtained by applying standard boolean operators to the results returned by the evaluation of relations between attributes and expressions. Attribute names occurring in a predicate refer to attributes within the interface of the object components, i.e. components that are target of the communication action.

In actions using a predicate $\mathcal{P}$ to indicate the target (directly or via p), predicates act as 'guards' specifying *all* components that may be affected by the execution of the action, i.e. a component must satisfy $\mathcal{P}$ to be the target of the action. Thus, actions $\mathbf{put}(t)@n$ and $\mathbf{put}(t)@\mathcal{P}$ give rise to two different primitive forms of communication: the former is a *point-to-point* communication, while the latter is a sort of *group-oriented* communication.

The set of components satisfying a given predicate $\mathcal{P}$ used as the target of a communication action can be considered as the *ensemble* with which the process performing the action intends to interact. For example, the names of the components that can be members of an ensemble can be fixed via the predicate $id \in \{n, m, o\}$. When an action has this predicate as target, it will act on all components named n, m or o, if any. Instead, to dynamically characterize the members of an ensemble that are active and have a battery whose level is higher than *low*, by assuming that attributes *active* and *batteryLevel* belong to the interface of any component willing to be part of the ensemble, one can write $active = yes \land batteryLevel > low$.

3   Self-expression in SCEL

In this section, we provide a step-by-step explanation of how a change in the coordination pattern can be obtained in an ensemble of autonomic components described using SCEL. A visual representation of the pattern workflow is shown in Fig. 3, where requests are represented by red arrows (i.e., darker arrows in b/w) and responses by the green arrows (i.e., lighter arrows in b/w). We first present the workflow execution steps performed by the requester, that is a component that requests the execution of a task, and, then, the steps performed by each involved responder.

Changes in the external conditions should trigger a change in the coordination pattern, since once a task has been selected, each different known implementation is likely to result in a different QoS. The QoS may depend on the current conditions of the surrounding environment, therefore for each observable change in the external conditions, a different coordination pattern could have to be selected in order to obtain the desired QoS.

Suppose that one or more components can rely on a table like the one shown in Table 2 in order to select the fittest implementation, once the whole ensemble agreed on the task to solve. Each row of the table can be represented as an item stored in the knowledge repository of the component. Conditions represent all the important features regarding the surrounding environment in which the ensemble is located; for instance, in case of a robot ensemble, everything that can be perceived through sensors. Implementation, identified by an id, is the actual coordination pattern chosen by the whole ensemble among the different patterns of the specified task. The final column relates to the expected QoS.

To sum it up, each important change in the surrounding environment, i.e. each change causing a different set of conditions k_i to be satisfied, triggers a

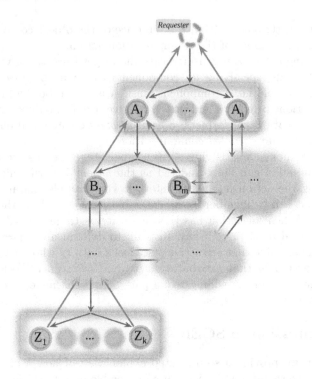

Fig. 3. Workflow of coordination patterns in SCEL

modification of the coordination pattern (i.e., implementation I_i for solving a previously agreed task) to be adopted, so to carry out the specific task with expected quality QoS_i. A single component that is aware that a specific coordination pattern is needed can trigger a dissemination request to all the other components of the ensemble, as we explain in the rest of the section.

3.1 Requester Workflow

We introduce here the steps of the task requester workflow.

Step 1: Task Request. The requester component needs a specific task to be carried out, so by using predicate $\mathcal{P}_r$ it contacts an ensemble of components that could fulfill the task. In order to receive a response, the requester adds its own identifier name (i.e., its component's address) to the request by means of the distinguished variable self, which allows a process to refer to the name of the component hosting it. The requesting action is rendered in SCEL as follows:

$$\textbf{put}(\textit{"taskRequest"},\ \textit{"taskName"},\ QoSconstraints,\ \textsf{self})@\mathcal{P}_r$$

Notably, before sending the request item, variable self will be replaced by the component identifier running the process performing the above **put** action.

Table 2. Example table of Conditions-Implementation-Expected QoS related to a specified task

Conditions	Implementation	Expected QoS
k_1	I_1	QoS_t^1
k_2	I_2	QoS_t^2
k_3	I_3	QoS_t^3
$\vdots$	$\vdots$	$\vdots$

The predicate $\mathcal{P}_r$ can be declared, e.g., as:

$$\mathcal{P}_r \triangleq \text{``taskName''} \in providedTasks$$

where *"taskName"* is the name of the required task and *providedTasks* is an attribute, exposed in the interface of every component, indicating the set of tasks that the component can fulfil.

Step 2: Receipt of proposed implementations. The requester component receives the information about implementations from the contacted components and selects the one that best fits the wanted QoS. Before the selection phase, the component retrieves the proposed implementations from its local repository by means of actions of the form

$$\mathbf{get}(\text{``implementation''}, ?implementationName, ?QoS, ?providers)@\mathsf{self}$$

where variable *implementationName* is bound to the name of a retrieved implementation, *QoS* to the effective QoS of the implementation, and *providers* to the data characterizing the providers of the implementation. The latter information is used to define the predicate $\mathcal{P}_{implementation}$ that will be used to contact the ensemble of components providing the selected implementation.

Step 3: Activation of the selected implementation. By exploiting a table like the one shown in Table 2, the requester selects the fittest implementation according to the currently perceived environmental conditions, the wanted QoS and the information retrieved and elaborated in Step 2. Then, it contacts the selected ensemble by exploiting predicate $\mathcal{P}_{implementation}$. In SCEL, this request can be represented as follows:

$$\mathbf{put}(\text{``executeImplementation''},$$
$$implementationName, arguments)@\mathcal{P}_{implementation}$$

The *arguments* part can be empty if the selected implementation does not need contextual data.

3.2   Responder Workflow

We present now the steps performed by each responder component. The workflow of a responder component is presented in Fig. 4. Each number shows in which

Fig. 4. Steps of a responder component

step the component takes a specific action. Again, the red arrows represent the requests and the green arrows the responses.

Step 1: Task request. Every component reached by a task request can get it by performing the following action:

$$\mathbf{get}(\text{``}taskRequest\text{''}, \ ?taskName, \ ?QoSconstraints, \ ?requester)@\mathsf{self}$$

Then, it checks if the requested task (stored in variable *taskName*) is provided by the component itself. If the component provides the task, the workflow execution can directly go to Step 5; anyhow, this depends on the component's selection criterion. If the component does not provide the task, the execution evolves to Step 2. In case of a 'smart' component, if the requested task is complex the responder component can decide to split it in simpler sub-tasks and handle the search of sub-task implementations.

Step 2: Requests dissemination. The responder component contacts an ensemble of components that, according to its knowledge, provides an implementation for the requested task. This operation is carried out similarly to a task request (see Step 1 in Section 3.1), but in this case it is used a different predicate ($\mathcal{P}_d$). The SCEL action used in this step is the following:

$$\mathbf{put}(\text{``}taskRequest\text{''}, \ taskName, \ QoSconstraints, \ \mathsf{self})@\mathcal{P}_d$$

Step 3: Responses collection. Each component that has disseminated a request collects the responses from the contacted components. Notably, if the component itself provides a solution, this is added to the collected responses. The collection phase is driven by a criterion that depends on the application. For example, some criteria are:

- wait for the first response and go to the next step;
- bounce immediately all the received responses to the requester (that is, Step 4 is skipped);
- wait for k responses and go to the next step;
- wait for responses with a specific QoS value and go to the next step;
- wait for a specific amount of time and go to the next step.

Step 4: Implementation selection. The responder component now selects one or more implementations using some criterion. As in Step 3, the criterion depends on the application. Some examples of criteria are:

- select the first k responses;
- take all the received responses;
- select the best j responses according to a specific parameter;
- select the responses with a specific QoS value.

In order to be selected, an implementation must be accompanied by a set of additional information needed by the receiver to take its decision. Thus, an implementation consists of its name, the associated QoS and the data needed to define the predicate for contacting the partners that provide this particular implementation. This information can be expressed as an item with the following form:

$$(\text{"implementation"},\ implementation\_name,\ QoS\_data,\ providers\_data)$$

Step 5: Response to the requester. After the selection phase, the component will send the results of the selection to the requester, whose identifier was bound to the variable *requester* at Step 1. Thus, for any implementation selected at the previous step, an action of the following form is performed:

put(*"implementation"*,
       implementation_name, *QoS_data*, *providers_data*)@*requester*

4   An Illustrative Example: Multi-robot Exploration Task

In this section we briefly apply our approach to a specific example task. The task is represented by having an ensemble of robots initially randomly distributed in a confined space called *arena*. The robots have to distribute within the arena and start exploring it. The task can be represented as follows:

- id: exploreArena;
- Input: ensemble randomly distributed in an unexplored arena;
- Output: explored arena;
- QoS: minimize the Time-To-Complete ($minTTC$), equally distribute the workload among the robots ($eqDist$).

Regarding the implementations, we can identify three main coordination patterns for executing the task:

- master-slave (id: MS): a robot sends orders about areas to explore to a set of slaves;
- peer-to-peer (id: p2p): robots will ideally subdivide the arena into areas and then negotiate areas to explore;

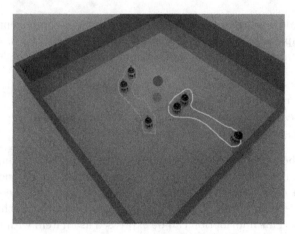

Fig. 5. A small ensemble is randomly distributed in the arena

– swarm (id: SW): all the robots randomly diffuse in the arena and mark areas with digital pheromones. If a robot detects a pheromone, a repulsion effect will take place, causing this latter robot to move to (and, therefore, explore) other areas.

The previous task and its respective different implementations are depicted in Fig. 5, where a small ensemble is randomly distributed in the arena. Different robots *own* different implementations. To own an implementation means that a component has all the processes, in the form of dynamically activable behaviors, that are needed in order to adopt a determined coordination pattern. In the figure, the robots are grouped according to the processes relative to the implementations they own: green for MS, yellow for p2p, and red for SW.

The requester actions are as follows.

Step 1: An external command or a contingency that reaches a single robot enforces the action:

$$\textbf{put}(\textit{``taskRequest''},\ \textit{``exploreArea''},\ minTTC,\ \textsf{self})@\mathcal{P}_r$$

with $\mathcal{P}_r \triangleq \textit{``exploreArea''} \in providedTasks$.

Step 2:

$$\textbf{get}(\textit{``implementation''},\ ?implementationName,\ ?QoS,\ ?providers)@\textsf{self}$$

where variable *implementationName* gets one of the values MS, $p2p$, and SW, QoS indicates if that implementation aims at minimising TTC and/or to equally distribute the workload among the robots and *providers* is bound to the IDs of all the responding robots. These IDs are collected in order to define $\mathcal{P}_{implementation}$.

Step 3: At this point the requester robot knows which robot can execute the *exploreArea* task and according to which implementation; it can then choose the implementation that is likely to satisfy the desired QoS. To make this choice, the robot can ideally rely on a table like the one in Table 3, where

Table 3. *exploreArea* table of defined conditions

Conditions	Implementation	Expected QoS
k'	MS	QoS'
k''	$p2p$	QoS''
k'''	SW	QoS'''

- k': refers to the condition for optimally exploiting a master-slave approach, such as the presence of at least one robot with additional sensing capabilities;
- k'': refers to the conditions in which a peer-to-peer approach is possible, like communication capabilities and easiness to identify areas before negotiation;
- k''': refers to the conditions in which it would be suitable to use a swarm approach for the area exploration task, such as a sufficiently large number of available units.

Depending on how these three patterns are implemented, we can think that a swarm approach will perform better in terms of minimizing exploration time, while a peer-to-peer negotiation could more equally distribute energy consumption among the components. The master-slave approach could minimize Time-To-Complete and distribute the workload more equally, but it is less robust than the other ones because the master constitutes a single point of failure. Now, if we assume that the environmental conditions k' are sensed by the robots, the requester can perform the action

$$\textbf{put}(\text{``executeImplementation''}, MS, \text{``MasterID''})@\mathcal{P}_{implementation}$$

where *MasterID* identifies the robot that will take the role of master (according to some internal logic of the component) and $\mathcal{P}_{implementation}$ potentially involves all the components whose identifiers have been collected in Step 2.

Once an implementation is selected by the requester, all the responding robots will start following that coordination pattern. If a robot does not have the necessary code embedded in its controller, we may think that a code migration process will be executed. Moreover, if every ensemble component is able to communicate with all other components, as in Fig. 5, the responder just executes Steps 1, 4 and 5 as described in Section 3.

5 Related Work

The first definitions of self-* properties can be traced back to the well-known manifestos by IBM in [14] and [16] about autonomic computing. From the point of view of the designer, a fairly complete survey on the efforts of designing autonomic systems with traditional methodologies, mainly coming from standard software engineering methodologies, can be found in [15]. In the design phase, more challenges arise when the observed systems are actually composed of large sets of potentially heterogeneous components. In this case indeed the blueprints for adaptive feedback loops (like IBM's MAPE-K [14]) have to be thought of as distributed, thus problems regarding inter-components coordination could become to light. More recently, [4] shows a complete life cycle for the design and development of ensembles of collaborative autonomic components.

Self-expression, as detailed in Section 1, is an additional instrument for the designer of autonomic distributed systems. However, in previous literature, the term self-expression is used for both describing reconfigurations at level of design patterns [6] and for describing reconfigurations at the level of roles, behaviors and interactions among components [7]. While a summary of possible real world applications for self-expression is presented in [5], a modelling choice that can help us understanding the concept of self-expression is the Holonic paradigm for Multi-Agent Systems (HMAS, [28]). Holons, i.e. self-repeating structures organized in hierarchies, present specific interfaces called capacities. A capacity is defined as a description of a know-how/service and can be associated to different implementations (representing different ways of providing that capacity). In our case, we can think that holons are single components, or subsets of the entire ensemble, and that a coordination pattern is the implementation of a capacity. To each implementation corresponds an organizational level in which behaviors, roles (i.e. specific states inside the same organization) and interactions (i.e. how parts in the same level influence each other) characterize a set of holons.

In the area of distributed artificial intelligence and multiagent systems [32], the idea of dynamically forming ensembles or coalitions of agents – getting together to cooperatively work towards some collective goals – has been extensively analyzed [13,17]. However, the accent of such researches has been mostly at analyzing the different strategies and algorithms for forming the ensembles and for controlling their cooperative behavior, rather than in the actual mechanisms to model and implement ensembles of agents capable of expressing the needed self-adaptive coordination scheme.

For what concerns SCEL, it combines the notion of ensemble with concepts that have emerged from different research fields of Computer Science and Engineering. Indeed, it borrows from software engineering the importance of component-based design and of separation of concerns [20], from multi-agent systems the relevance of knowledge handling and of spatial representation [27,3,29,2,9], from middleware and network architectures the importance of flexibility in communication [22,8,18,25,23], from distributed systems' security the role of policies [24], from actors and process algebras the importance of minimality and formality [1,21]. Summing it up, the main distinctive aspect of SCEL is the actual choice of the specific programming abstractions for autonomic computing and their reconciliation under a single roof with a uniform formal semantics. For a more complete account about SCEL and works related to it, we refer the interested reader to [12].

6   Concluding Remarks

In this paper we have illustrated how to foster the self-adaptive features of an ensemble of autonomic components by describing a previously introduced property called self-expression. More specifically, we have exploited SCEL as a language for properly describing and modeling the mechanisms involved in the run-time changes of coordination patterns. The rigorous grammar and the formal semantics that characterize SCEL provide a valuable instrument for understanding (1) *how* a change in the collaborative structure of the ensemble is performed and (2) *when* a change of the coordination pattern is needed. Regarding (1), we have presented a step-by-step description of inter-component interactions by means of workflows, in which we stressed how different requests that may lead to change of the coordination pattern can be disseminated among different parts of the observed ensemble. Regarding (2), we showed how the selection of the fittest pattern depends both on the current perceived environmental conditions and on the expected QoS: new patterns will have to be selected according to the dynamics of the variations in the external conditions and/or QoS. A simple, yet explicative case study in robotics is demonstrated to further clarify the presented concepts.

We are currently investigating how a component could autonomously extend and modify the table regarding Conditions/Implementations/Expected QoS so to provide more possibilities in terms of adaptivity. We will apply our approach to other case studies, not necessarily in the robotics domain.

We also plan to investigate the use of SCEL components policies to drive and regulate the selection of implementations and coordination patterns according to possibly locally different criteria. Specifically, according to the approach introduced in [19], we plan to use the FACPL language to express policies.

To show the effectiveness of the proposed SCEL-based solution to self-expression and provide a more concrete evidence of its benefits, we intend to implement the approach considered in this work in jRESP [12], a Java runtime environment for developing autonomic and adaptive systems according to the SCEL paradigm. In particular, jRESP provides a simulation environment that enables statistical model-checking, which will allow us to verify qualitative and quantitative properties of SCEL programs.

References

1. Agha, G.A.: ACTORS - a model of concurrent computation in distributed systems. MIT Press series in artificial intelligence. MIT Press (1990)
2. Bellifemine, F.L., Caire, G., Greenwood, D.: Developing Multi-Agent Systems with JADE. Wiley Series in Agent Technology. John Wiley & Sons (2007)
3. Bordini, R.H., Hübner, J.F., Vieira, R.: Jason and the golden fleece of agent-oriented programming. In: Multi-Agent Programming. Multiagent Systems, Artificial Societies, and Simulated Organizations, vol. 15, pp. 3–37. Springer (2005)
4. Bureš, T., De Nicola, R., Gerostathopoulos, I., Hoch, N., Kit, M., Koch, N., Monreale, G., Montanari, U., Pugliese, R., Serbedzija, N., Wirsing, M., Zambonelli, F.: A life cycle for the development of autonomic systems: The e-mobility showcase. In: 3rd Workshop on Challenges for Achieving Self-Awareness in Autonomic Systems. IEEE (2013)

5. Cabri, G., Capodieci, N.: Runtime change of collaboration patterns in autonomic systems: Motivations and perspectives. In: AINA Workshops, pp. 1038–1043. IEEE (2013)
6. Cabri, G., Puviani, M., Zambonelli, F.: Towards a taxonomy of adaptive agent-based collaboration patterns for autonomic service ensembles. In: CTS, pp. 508–515. IEEE (2011)
7. Capodieci, N., Hart, E., Cabri, G.: Designing self-aware adaptive systems: from autonomic computing to cognitive immune networks. In: 3rd Workshop on Challenges for Achieving Self-Awareness in Autonomic Systems. IEEE (2013)
8. Costa, P., Mottola, L., Murphy, A.L., Picco, G.: Tuple Space Middleware for Wireless Networks. In: Middleware for Network Eccentric and Mobile Applications, pp. 245–264. Springer (2009)
9. Dastani, M.: 2APL: A practical agent programming language. Autonomous Agents and Multi-Agent Systems 16(3), 214–248 (2008)
10. De Nicola, R., Ferrari, G., Loreti, M., Pugliese, R.: A language-based approach to autonomic computing. In: Beckert, B., Bonsangue, M.M. (eds.) FMCO 2011. LNCS, vol. 7542, pp. 25–48. Springer, Heidelberg (2012)
11. De Nicola, R., Loreti, M., Pugliese, R., Tiezzi, F.: SCEL: A language for autonomic computing. TR (2013), http://rap.dsi.unifi.it/scel/pdf/SCEL-TR.pdf
12. De Nicola, R., Loreti, M., Pugliese, R., Tiezzi, F.: A formal approach to autonomic systems programming: The SCEL Language. Transactions on Autonomic and Adaptive Systems (to appear, 2014)
13. Durfee, E., Lesser, V., Corkill, D.D.: Trends in cooperative distributed problem solving. IEEE Transactions on Knowledge and Data Engineering 1(1), 63–83 (1989)
14. Horn, P.: Autonomic Computing: IBM's Perspective on the State of Information Technology. Technical Report, October 15 (2001)
15. Huebscher, M.C., McCann, J.A.: A survey of autonomic computing – degrees, models, and applications. ACM Comput. Surv. 40(3), 7:1–7:28 (2008)
16. Kephart, J., Chess, D.: The vision of autonomic computing. Computer 36(1), 41–50 (2003)
17. Klusch, M., Gerber, A.: Dynamic coalition formation among rational agents. IEEE Intelligent Systems 17(3), 42–47 (2002)
18. Mamei, M., Zambonelli, F.: Programming pervasive and mobile computing applications: The TOTA approach. ACM Trans. Softw. Eng. Methodol. 18(4) (2009)
19. Margheri, A., Pugliese, R., Tiezzi, F.: Linguistic abstractions for programming and policing autonomic computing systems. In: UIC/ATC, pp. 404–409. IEEE (2013)
20. McKinley, P., Sadjadi, S., Kasten, E., Cheng, B.H.C.: Composing adaptive software. Computer 37(7), 56–64 (2004)
21. Milner, R.: Communication and concurrency. PHI Series in Computer Science. Prentice Hall (1989)
22. Mottola, L., Picco, G.P.: Logical Neighborhoods: A Programming Abstraction for Wireless Sensor Networks. In: Gibbons, P.B., Abdelzaher, T., Aspnes, J., Rao, R. (eds.) DCOSS 2006. LNCS, vol. 4026, pp. 150–168. Springer, Heidelberg (2006)
23. Mottola, L., Picco, G.P.: Middleware for wireless sensor networks: an outlook. J. Internet Services and Applications 3(1), 31–39 (2012)
24. NIST. A survey of access control models (2009), http://csrc.nist.gov/news_events/privilege-management-workshop/PvM-Model-Survey-Aug26-2009.pdf
25. Nordström, E., Gunningberg, P., Rohner, C.: A search-based network architecture for mobile devices. Uppsala University, TR 2009-003 (2009)

26. Puviani, M., Pinciroli, C., Cabri, G., Leonardi, L., Zambonelli, F.: Is Self-Expression Useful? Evaluation by a Case Study. In: Reddy, S., Jmaiel, M. (eds.) WETICE (AROSA Track), pp. 62–67. IEEE (2013)

27. Rao, A.S.: AgentSpeak(L): BDI Agents Speak Out in a Logical Computable Language. In: Van de Velde, W., Perram, J.W. (eds.) MAAMAW 1996. LNCS, vol. 1038, pp. 42–55. Springer, Heidelberg (1996)

28. Rodriguez, S., Gaud, N., Hilaire, V., Galland, S., Koukam, A.: An analysis and design concept for self-organization in holonic multi-agent systems. In: Brueckner, S.A., Hassas, S., Jelasity, M., Yamins, D. (eds.) ESOA 2006. LNCS (LNAI), vol. 4335, pp. 15–27. Springer, Heidelberg (2007)

29. Winikoff, M.: JACK^{TM} Intelligent Agents: An Industrial Strength Platform. In: Multi-Agent Programming. Multiagent Systems, Artificial Societies, and Simulated Organizations, pp. 175–193. Springer (2005)

30. Zambonelli, F., Bicocchi, N., Cabri, G., Leonardi, L., Puviani, M.: On self-adaptation, self-expression, and self-awareness in autonomic service component ensembles. In: SASO Workshops, pp. 108–113. IEEE (2011)

31. Zambonelli, F., Castelli, G., Ferrari, L., Mamei, M., Rosi, A., Serugendo, G.D.M., Risoldi, M., Tchao, A.-E., Dobson, S., Stevenson, G., Ye, J., Nardini, E., Omicini, A., Montagna, S., Viroli, M., Ferscha, A., Maschek, S., Wally, B.: Self-aware pervasive service ecosystems. Procedia CS 7, 197–199 (2011)

32. Zambonelli, F., Omicini, A.: Challenges and research directions in agent-oriented software engineering. Autonomous Agents and Multi-Agent Systems 9(3), 253–283 (2004)

On Programming and Policing
Autonomic Computing Systems[*]

Michele Loreti[1], Andrea Margheri[1,2], Rosario Pugliese[1], and Francesco Tiezzi[3]

[1] Università degli Studi di Firenze, Viale Morgagni, 65 - 50134 Firenze, Italy
[2] Università di Pisa, Largo Bruno Pontecorvo, 3 - 56127 Pisa, Italy
[3] IMT Advanced Studies Lucca, Piazza S. Francesco, 19 - 55100, Lucca, Italy

Abstract. To tackle the complexity of autonomic computing systems it is crucial to provide methods supporting their systematic and principled development. Using the PSCEL language, autonomic systems can be described in terms of the constituent components and their reciprocal interactions. The computational behaviour of components is defined in a procedural style, by the programming constructs, while the adaptation logic is defined in a declarative style, by the policing constructs. In this paper we introduce a suite of practical software tools for programming and policing autonomic computing systems in PSCEL. Specifically, we integrate a Java-based runtime environment, supporting the execution of programming constructs, with the code corresponding to the policing ones. The integrated, semantic-driven framework also permits simulating and analysing PSCEL programs. Usability and potentialities of the approach are illustrated by means of a robot swarm case study.

Keywords: Autonomic systems, Semantic-driven development tools, Robot swarms.

1 Introduction

Autonomic computing systems [1] are self-managing computing systems, capable of autonomously adapting to unpredictable changes in order to achieve desired behaviours, while hiding at the same time intrinsic complexity to users. Since their first appearance they are becoming more common and integrated with a variety of other heterogeneous and interactive systems. The resulting systems usually include massive numbers of components, featuring complex interactions in open and non-deterministic environments. To enable systematic and principled development of autonomic computing systems it is then crucial to provide high level, linguistic abstractions – capable of describing how the different components are brought together to form the overall system architecture – together with a clear identification of the adaptation logic and an unambiguous account of the semantics.

---

[*] This work has been partially sponsored by the EU project ASCENS (257414) and by the Italian MIUR PRIN project CINA (2010LHT4KM).

T. Margaria and B. Steffen (Eds.): ISoLA 2014, Part I, LNCS 8802, pp. 164–183, 2014.
© Springer-Verlag Berlin Heidelberg 2014

In this paper we introduce some software tools for programming and policing autonomic computing systems in PSCEL (*Policed SCEL*) [2]. This is a language with a formally defined semantics which results from the integration of SCEL and FACPL. SCEL [3] is one of the many languages for programming autonomic computing systems that have been proposed in the literature (see e.g. [4,5,6,7,8]). In SCEL, autonomic systems are programmed in terms of the constituent components and their reciprocal interactions. Components result from the aggregation of knowledge and behaviours, according to some policies. Knowledge acquisition and behaviour manipulation allow components to self-adapt. *Ensembles* of components are dynamically formed and referred to in communication actions by means of predicates over component *attributes*. These latter ones describe components' public features such as identity, functionalities, spatial coordinates, trust level, etc. that may dynamically change. FACPL [9,10] is a simple, yet expressive, language for defining access control, resource usage and adaptation policies. Policy specifications are intuitive and easy to maintain because of their declarative nature, therefore policy languages (see e.g. [11,6,12]) are receiving much attention in many research fields. In FACPL, policies are sets of rules specifying strategies, requirements, constraints, guidelines, etc. about the behaviour of systems and their components.

PSCEL appropriately integrates the linguistic abstractions of the two languages on which it is based. It is thus possible to develop autonomic computing systems in terms of software components capable of adapting their behaviour for reacting to new requirements or environment changes. For example, it is possible to define policies implementing adaptation strategies by exploiting specific actions that are produced at runtime as an effect of policy evaluation and are used to modify the behaviour of components. Moreover, policies can depend on the values of components' attributes (reflecting the status of components and their environment) and can be dynamically replaced as a reaction to system changes. Dynamically changing policies are indeed a powerful means for controlling, in a natural and clear way, the evolution of autonomic systems having a very high degree of dynamism, which in principle would be quite difficult to manage.

According to the *separation of concerns* principle, PSCEL design decouples the functional aspects from the adaptation ones. In fact, the application logic generating the computational behaviour of components is defined in a procedural style, by the programming constructs, while the adaptation logic is defined in a declarative style, by the policing constructs. At run-time, as clarified by the language operational semantics [13] and by the description of the supporting Java runtime environment (see Section 4), the adaptation actions generated by policy evaluation will be executed as part of components' behaviour.

The two languages at the basis of PSCEL come equipped with specific software tools providing development and run-time support to SCEL systems and FACPL policies, separately. In particular, SCEL programs can be executed and simulated in the jRESP environment. This environment provides an API allowing Java programs to use the SCEL linguistic constructs for controlling the computation and interaction of autonomic components, and for defining the architecture of systems and ensembles. jRESP API serves as a guidance to assist programmers in the implementation of autonomic systems, which turns out to be simplified with respect to using 'pure' Java. Finally, jRESP provides specific components that can be used to simulate and analyze SCEL programs. The development and the enforcement of FACPL policies, instead, are supported by an Eclipse IDE and a Java library for the policy evaluation process. Once the desired policies have been written with the IDE, they can be automatically transformed in Java classes according to the rules defining the FACPL's semantics.

The main contribution of this work is the definition of a practical tool suite supporting the development, execution, simulation and analysis of PSCEL programs. This is based on the integration of the Java code resulting from FACPL policies with the jRESP code corresponding to a SCEL system. In the integrated code, FACPL classes are invoked for authorizing interactions among components, while jRESP code is able to modify its workflow for executing the adaptation actions returned by policies evaluation. Usability and potentialities of this approach are illustrated by means of a simple, yet illustrative, case study of autonomic computing borrowed from the robotics domain. We show a complete specification of the case study, together with its simulation and analysis through jRESP.

The rest of the paper is organized as follows. Section 2 briefly reports the syntax of PSCEL. Section 3 presents the PSCEL specification of two scenarios of the robotics case study. Section 4 presents the development tools; it also describes the main features of jRESP and shows how it can be used to execute, as Java code, the PSCEL specification of the scenarios. Section 5 reviews more strictly related work. Finally, Section 6 concludes the paper by touching upon directions for future work.

2   PSCEL Syntax

In this section we review the syntax of PSCEL in two steps, by introducing first the constructs for programming autonomic computing systems and then the constructs for policing their behaviour. We also informally present the semantics of the different constructs (the interested reader is referred to [13] for a formal account of the semantics).

The constructs for programming autonomic computing systems are presented in Table 1. The key notion is that of *component* $\mathcal{I}[\mathcal{K}, \Pi, P]$ that consists of:

– An *interface* $\mathcal{I}$ publishing and making available structural and behavioural information about the component itself in the form of *attributes*, i.e. names acting as references to information stored in the component's repository.
– A *knowledge repository* $\mathcal{K}$ managing component's data.
– A set of *policies* Π regulating the interaction with other components.
– A *process* P, together with a set of process definitions.

It is worth noticing that there is a clear separation of concerns: the normal computational behaviour of a component is defined in the process P, while the adaptation logic is defined in the policies Π. At runtime, the adaptation actions

Table 1. Programming constructs (POLICIES Π are in Table 2)

SYSTEMS:	S	$::=$	$\mathcal{I}[\mathcal{K}, \Pi, P] \mid S_1 \parallel S_2 \mid (\nu n)S$
PROCESSES:	P	$::=$	$\mathbf{nil} \mid a.P \mid P_1 + P_2 \mid P_1 \mid P_2 \mid X \mid A(\bar{p})$
ACTIONS:	a	$::=$	$\mathbf{get}(T)@c \mid \mathbf{qry}(T)@c \mid \mathbf{put}(t)@c \mid \mathbf{fresh}(n)$
		$\mid$	$\mathbf{new}(\mathcal{I}, \mathcal{K}, \Pi, P)$
DESTINATIONS:	c	$::=$	$n \mid x \mid \mathsf{self} \mid \mathcal{P} \mid p$
KNOWLEDGE:	$\mathcal{K}$	$::=$	$\emptyset \mid \langle t \rangle \mid \mathcal{K}_1 \parallel \mathcal{K}_2$
ITEMS:	t	$::=$	$e \mid c \mid P \mid t_1, t_2$
TEMPLATES:	T	$::=$	$e \mid c \mid ?x \mid ?X \mid T_1, T_2$

generated by the policy evaluation will be executed, of course, as part of the component's process.

We describe below the syntactic categories of the language.

SYSTEMS aggregate components through the *composition* operator, as in $S_1 \parallel S_2$. It is also possible to restrict the scope of a name, say n, by using the *name restriction* operator $(\nu n)S$.

PROCESSES are the active computational units. Each process is built up from the *inert* process $\mathbf{nil}$ via *action prefixing* $(a.P)$, *nondeterministic choice* $(P_1 + P_2)$, (interleaved) *parallel composition* $(P_1 \mid P_2)$, *process variable* (X), and *parametrized process invocation* $(A(\bar{p}))$. Process variables can support *higher-order* communication, namely the capability to exchange (the code of) a process, and possibly execute it, by first adding an item containing the process to a knowledge repository and then retrieving/withdrawing this item while binding the process to a process variable. We let A to range over a set of parametrized *process identifiers* that are used in recursive process definitions. We also assume that each process identifier A has a *single* definition of the form $A(\bar{f}) \triangleq P$, with $\bar{p}$ and $\bar{f}$ denoting lists of actual and formal parameters, respectively.

Processes can perform five different types of ACTIONS. Actions $\mathbf{get}(T)@c$, $\mathbf{qry}(T)@c$ and $\mathbf{put}(t)@c$ are used to manage shared knowledge repositories by withdrawing/retrieving/adding information items from/to the knowledge repository identified by c. These actions exploit templates T to select knowledge items t in the repositories. Action $\mathbf{fresh}(n)$ introduces a scope restriction for the name n thus this name is guaranteed to be *fresh*, i.e. different from any other name previously used. Action $\mathbf{new}(\mathcal{I}, \mathcal{K}, \Pi, P)$ creates a new component $\mathcal{I}[\mathcal{K}, \Pi, P]$. Actions $\mathbf{get}$ and $\mathbf{qry}$ may cause the process executing them to wait for the wanted item if it is not (yet) available in the knowledge repository. The two actions differ for the fact that $\mathbf{get}$ removes the found item from the target repository while $\mathbf{qry}$ leaves the repository unchanged. Actions $\mathbf{put}$, $\mathbf{fresh}$ and $\mathbf{new}$ can be instead immediately executed.

Knowledge ITEMS are *tuples*, i.e. sequences of values, while TEMPLATES are sequences of values and variables. KNOWLEDGE repositories are then *tuple spaces*, i.e. (possibly empty) multisets of tuples. Values within tuples can either be destinations c, or processes P or, more generally, can result from the evaluation of some given expression e. We assume that expressions may contain attribute names, *boolean, integer, float* and *string* values and variables, together with the corresponding standard operators. To pick a tuple out from a tuple space by means of a given template, the *pattern-matching* mechanism is used: a tuple matches a template if they have the same number of elements and corresponding elements have matching values or variables; variables match any value of the same type ($?x$ and $?X$ are used to bind variables to values and processes, respectively), and two values match only if they are identical. If more tuples match a given template, one of them is arbitrarily chosen.

Different entities may be used as the DESTINATION c of an action. As a matter of notation, n ranges over component names, while x ranges over variables for names. The distinguished variable **self** can be used by processes to refer to the name of the component hosting them. The destination can also be a *predicate* $\mathcal{P}$ or the name p, exposed as an attribute in the interface of the component, of a predicate that may dynamically change. A predicate is a boolean-valued expression obtained by applying standard operators to relations between components attributes and expressions.

In actions using a predicate $\mathcal{P}$ to indicate the destination (directly or via a name p), predicates act as 'guards' specifying *all* components that may be affected by the execution of the action, i.e. a component must satisfy $\mathcal{P}$ to be the target of the action. Thus, actions **put**(t)@n and **put**(t)@$\mathcal{P}$ give rise to two different primitive forms of communication: the former is a *point-to-point* communication, while the latter is a sort of *group-oriented* communication. The set of components satisfying a given predicate $\mathcal{P}$ used as the destination of a communication action can be considered as the *ensemble* with which the process performing the action intends to interact. For example, to dynamically characterize the members of an ensemble that have the same role, say *landmark*, by assuming that attribute *role* belongs to the interface of any component willing to be part of the ensemble, one can write *role*="*landmark*".

Each action is executed only if it is authorized by the policies in force at the component willing to perform the action. The policies define authorization predicates, to grant or forbid actions, and *obligations*, i.e. actions that should be performed in conjunction with the enforcement of an authorization decision. They correspond to, e.g., updating a log file, sending a message, generating an event, setting an attribute. For example, if an action is forbidden due to unavailable resources, it can be needed to execute some other actions to reconfigure system's resources.

The constructs for policing autonomic computing systems are presented in Table 2. Notationally, symbol ? stands for optional elements, * for (possibly empty) sequences, and + for non-empty sequences. For the sake of readability, whenever an element is missing, we also omit the possibly related keyword; thus, e.g., we simply write (d **target** : τ) in place of rule (d **target** : τ **condition** : **obl** :).

Table 2. Policing constructs

POLICY AUTOMATA:	Π	$::=$	$\langle A, \pi \rangle$
POLICIES:	π	$::=$	$\langle \alpha \ \text{target}:\tau^? \ \text{rules}:r^+ \ \text{obl}:o^* \rangle$
			$\mid \ \{\alpha \ \text{target}:\tau^? \ \text{policies}:\pi^+ \ \text{obl}:o^* \}$
COMBINING ALGORITHMS:	α	$::=$	deny-overrides $\mid$ permit-overrides
			$\mid$ deny-unless-permit $\mid$ permit-unless-deny
			$\mid$ first-applicable $\mid$ only-one-applicable
RULES:	r	$::=$	$(d \ \text{target}:\tau^? \ \text{condition}:be^? \ \text{obl}:o^*)$
DECISIONS:	d	$::=$	permit $\mid$ deny
TARGETS:	τ	$::=$	$f(pv,sn) \mid \tau \wedge \tau \mid \tau \vee \tau$
MATCHING FUNCTIONS:	f	$::=$	equal $\mid$ not-equal $\mid$ greater-than
			$\mid$ less-than $\mid$ greater-than-or-equal
			$\mid$ less-than-or-equal $\mid$ pattern-match
OBLIGATIONS:	o	$::=$	$[d \ s]$
OBLIGATION ACTIONS:	s	$::=$	$\epsilon \mid a.s$

A POLICY AUTOMATON Π explicitly represents the fact that the policies in force at any given component can dynamically change while the component evolves. It is a pair $\langle A, \pi \rangle$, where

- A is an automaton of the form $\langle Policies, Targets, \mathcal{T} \rangle$ where the set of states *Policies* contains all the POLICIES that can be in force at different times, the set of labels *Targets* contains the security relevant events (expressed as TARGETS) that can trigger policy modification and the set of transitions $\mathcal{T} \subseteq (Policies \times Targets \times Policies)$ represents policy replacement.
- $\pi \in Policies$ is the current state of A.

A POLICY is either an atomic policy $\langle \ldots \rangle$ or a set of policies $\{ \ldots \}$. An *atomic policy* (resp. *policy set*) is made of a target, a set of rules (resp. policy/policy sets) combined through one of the combining algorithms, and a set of obligations.

A TARGET indicates the *authorization requests* to which a policy/rule applies. It is either an atomic target or a pair of simpler targets combined using the standard logic operators $\wedge$ and $\vee$. An *atomic target* $f(pv,sn)$ is a triple denoting the application of a matching function f to *policy values pv* from the policy and to policy values from the evaluation context identified by *attribute (structured) names*[1] *sn*. In fact, an attribute name refers to a specific attribute of the request or of the environment, which is available through the evaluation context. In this way, an authorization decision can be based on some characteristics of the request, e.g. subjects' or objects' identity, or of the environment, e.g. presence of charging stations. For example, the target less-than(10%,*subject/batteryLevel*) matches whenever the battery level of the subject component is less than 10%.

---

[1] A structured name has the form *name/name*, where the first name stands for a category name and the second for an attribute name.

Similarly, the structured name *action/action-id* refers to the identifier of the action to be performed (such as **get**, **qry**, **put**, etc.) and, thus, the target equal(**qry**,*action/action-id*) matches whenever such an action is the retrieving one. Instead, for checking the content of the exchanged data in a communication action, via a template T, we can use the target pattern-match(T,*action/item*).

Rules (...) are the basic elements for request evaluation. A RULE defines the tests that must be successfully passed by attributes for returning a positive or negative DECISION — i.e. permit or deny — to the enclosing policy. This decision is returned only if the target is 'applicable', i.e. the request matches the target; otherwise the evaluation of the rule returns not-applicable. Rule applicability can be further refined by the CONDITION expression *be*, which permits more complex calculations than those permitted in target expressions. *be* is a boolean term of the expression language used for defining item or template fields in Table 1, extended with policy values and structured names.

A COMBINING ALGORITHM computes the authorization decision corresponding to a given request by combining a set of rules/policies' evaluation results. PSCEL provides six algorithms but, due to lack of space, here we only present permit-unless-deny, which is used in the case study in Section 3 (the descriptions of the other algorithms is reported in [13]): if any rule/policy in the considered set evaluates to deny, then the result of the combination returned by permit-unless-deny is deny; otherwise, the result of the combination is permit (i.e., not-applicable is never returned).

An OBLIGATION is a sequence (ϵ denotes the empty one) of actions that should be performed in conjunction with the enforcement of an authorization decision. It is returned when the authorization decision for the enclosing element, i.e. rule, policy or policy set, is the same as the one attached to the obligation. An OBLIGATION ACTION is a process action which (with abuse of notation) may also contain structured names that are fulfilled during request evaluation. Thus, fulfilled obligation actions coincide with the (process) actions defined in Table 1. For example, the obligation [deny **put**("direction", $env/station.x, env/station.y$)@self] could be fulfilled, w.r.t. a given request, as follows **put**("direction", 10, 13)@self. It is used to set the robot's direction towards the position $(10, 13)$ corresponding to the location of a charging station perceived in the robot's environment.

3   PSCEL at Work on a Robot Swarm Case Study

In this section, we show the effectiveness of the PSCEL approach by modelling a robot swarm case study [14] defined in the EU project ASCENS [15]. We consider a scenario where a swarm of robots spreads throughout a given area where some kind of disaster has happened. The goal of the robots is to locate and rescue possible victims. As common in swarm robotics, all robots playing the same role execute the same code. According to the separation of concerns principle fostered by PSCEL, this code consists of two parts: *(i)* a process, defining the functional behaviour; and *(ii)* a collection of policies, regulating the interactions among robots and with their environment and generating the (adaptation) actions to react to specific (internal or environmental) conditions. This

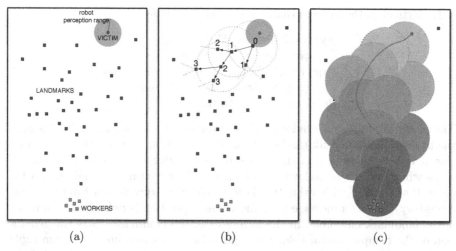

Fig. 1. Scenario 1: (a) scenario setting, (b) computational field creation, (c) computational field usage

combination permits conveniently designing and enacting a collaborative swarm behaviour aiming at achieving the goal of rescuing the victims. We propose two different scenarios of the disaster case study that differ for the capabilities of the robots, mainly due to the availability of the GPS tracking system.

3.1 Scenario 1: Different Types of Robot for Different Roles

The first scenario includes two different kinds of robots: *landmarks* and *workers*. Landmarks randomly explore the area of the disaster looking for victims. When a victim is found, its position is spread among landmarks, which stop to move. In this way, on the basis of the landmarks' positions and the information they receive, it is generated a sort of computational field [16] leading workers to the victim. Workers are the robots devoted to perform the actual rescuing task. They are initially motionless and are activated by informed landmarks. A graphical representation of the scenario, the creation of the computation filed and its use are depicted in Figure 1. For the sake of simplicity, we consider here just one victim and all workers go to rescue him when it is found. The scenario could be accommodated to deal with more victims by organizing landmarks and workers in different teams. We will deal with multiple victims in the next scenario.

This scenario can be modelled in PSCEL as

$$\textsc{Landmark}_1 \parallel \ldots \parallel \textsc{Landmark}_n \parallel \textsc{Worker}_1 \parallel \ldots \parallel \textsc{Worker}_m$$

where $\textsc{Landmark}_i$ and $\textsc{Worker}_j$ are PSCEL components of the form $\mathcal{I}_{L_i}[\mathcal{K}_{L_i}, \Pi_L, P_L]$ and $\mathcal{I}_{W_j}[\mathcal{K}_{W_j}, \Pi_W, P_W]$ modelling the two kinds of robots, respectively. Notably, all landmarks (resp. workers) enforce the same policy Π_L (resp. Π_W) and execute the same process P_L (resp. P_W).

In particular, the process run by a landmark is as follows

$$P_L \triangleq (\mathbf{qry}(\text{"victimPerceived"}, \text{true})@\text{self}.$$
$$\mathbf{put}(\text{"victim"}, \text{self}, 0)@\text{self}$$
$$+ \mathbf{qry}(\text{"victim"}, ?id, ?d)@(role = \text{"landmark"}).$$
$$\mathbf{put}(\text{"victim"}, \text{self}, d + 1\text{"})@\text{self})$$
$$| \ RandomWalk \ | \ IsMoving$$

The landmark follows a random walk to explore the disaster area. To this aim, the process *RandomWalk* randomly selects a direction that is followed until either a wall is hit or a stop signal is sent to the wheels actuator. A landmark stops when one of the following cases holds: *(i)* a victim is found (i.e., a tuple victimPerceived with value true is retrieved via a **qry** action from the local repository), or *(ii)* a message with the victim's position is published by a robot of the landmark ensemble. In the former case, the landmark starts the generation of the computational field, i.e. it publishes in its repository a victim tuple indicating that it is at distance 0 (measured in terms of 'number of hops') from the victim. In the latter case, instead, the robot non-deterministically retrieves a victim tuple from one robot of the landmark ensemble (i.e., the group of robots satisfying the predicate *role = "landmark"*) and locally publishes a victim tuple with the distance increased by one. It is worth noticing that the robots' range of communication is limited and, hence, the accessed ensemble may not contain all landmarks, but just the reachable ones. However, the range of communication is not explicitly specified in the PSCEL code, as well as in the jRESP one. Indeed, this is a physical constraint that will be only defined in the model of the physical scenario used by the jRESP simulation environment (see Section 4.2).

To stop a landmark immediately after the execution of one of the two **qry** actions, we define the following policy

```
⟨ permit-unless-deny
  rules : (permit  target : equal(qry,action/action-id)
                    ∧ (pattern-match(("victim", _, _),action/item)
                       ∨ pattern-match(("victimPerceived", true),action/item))
            obl : [permit put("stop")@self] ) ⟩
```

The policy contains a positive rule, whose only purpose is to return the obligation **put**("stop")@self when one of the **qry** actions is executed. This action requests the wheels actuator to stop the movement.

The *RandomWalk* process calculates the random direction followed by the landmark for exploring the arena. When the proximity sensor signals a possible collision, by means of the tuple ⟨"collision", true⟩, a new random direction is calculated. This behaviour corresponds to the following PSCEL process

$$RandomWalk \triangleq \mathbf{put}(\text{"direction"}, 2\pi\text{rand}())@\text{self}.$$
$$\mathbf{qry}(\text{"collision"}, \text{true})@\text{self}.RandomWalk$$

The process defines only the direction of the motion not the will of moving.

During the movement, in order to check the level of charge of the battery and possibly halting the robot when the battery is low, we need to capture the movement status. This information is represented by the tuple $\langle$ "isMoving"$\rangle$, produced by the wheels sensor, and monitored by the following process

$$IsMoving \triangleq \mathbf{qry}(\text{"isMoving"})@\text{self}.IsMoving$$

The reading of this datum is exploited by the following authorization rule (which must be added to the landmark's policy above)

$$(\text{deny } target : \text{equal}(\mathbf{qry}, action/action\text{-}id)$$
$$\wedge \text{ pattern-match}((\text{"isMoving"}), action/item)$$
$$\wedge \text{ less-than}(10\%, subject/batteryLevel)$$
$$\text{obl} : [\text{deny } \mathbf{put}(\text{"stop"})@\text{self}])$$

to generate a stop action when the battery level is lower than 10%. In such a case, the robot will wait for new batteries and, eventually, restart the exploration.

Finally, the process for the worker is as follows

$$P_W \triangleq \mathbf{qry}(\text{"victim"}, ?id, ?d)@(role=\text{"landmark"}).$$
$$\mathbf{put}(\text{"start"})@\text{self}.$$
$$\mathbf{put}(\text{"direction"}, towards(id))@\text{self}.$$
$$\mathbf{while}(d>0)\{d := d-1.$$
$$\mathbf{qry}(\text{"victim"}, ?id, d)@(role=\text{"landmark"}).$$
$$\mathbf{put}(\text{"direction"}, towards(id))@\text{self})\}.$$
$$\mathbf{qry}(\text{"victimPerceived"}, true)@\text{self}.$$
$$\mathbf{put}(\text{"rescue"})@\text{self}$$

When the information about the discovery of a victim is retrieved by a worker (i.e., a victim tuple is read), the robot starts moving by following the direction indicated by the computational field defined by the landmarks. When the victim is reached, i.e. the tuple with distance 0 is read, the sensor perceives the victim and the worker starts the rescuing procedure.

For the worker process we do not report here any policy. Such policies could add additional actions when the worker is activated under specific conditions, e.g. a camera could be turned on in case there is enough daylight.

3.2   Scenario 2: The Same Type of Robot for Two Different Roles

In the second scenario of the case study, we consider robots with the same characteristics (in particular, all of them are equipped with a GPS tracking system) and capable of playing both the *explorer* and *rescuer* role. Thus, using its GPS, each robot can directly reach a given position (specified by coordinates (x, y)) and avoid the use of the computational field as in the previous scenario. A robot plays the *explorer* role during the exploration of the environment to locate the victim position, and the *rescuer* role when it is moving to reach a victim. Notably, the role changes according to the sensors and data values, e.g. this happens when the robot is close to a victim that needs help.

Therefore, this second scenario is modelled as a set of components (ROBOT$_1$ ‖ ... ‖ ROBOT$_n$), where ROBOT$_i$ has the form $\mathcal{I}_{R_i}[\mathcal{K}_{R_i}, \Pi_R, P_R]$. Each robot initially plays the explorer role and possibly change it when victims are found. The behaviour of a single robot corresponds to the following PSCEL process

$P_R \triangleq$ (**qry**("victimPerceived", true)@self.
　　　　put("victim", $x, y, 3$)@self. **put**("rescue")@self
　　　　$+$ **get**("victim", $?x_v, ?y_v, ?count$)@($role=$"rescuer"). *HelpRescuer*)
　　| *RandomWalk* | *IsMoving*

Besides the processes *RandomWalk* and *IsMoving* still present for managing the movement, the robot recognises the presence of a victim by means of the **qry** action, while it helps other robots for rescuing a victim by means of the **get** action and according to the *HelpRescuer* process definition. When a victim is found, an information about his position (retrieved by the attributes x and y of the robot's interface) and the number of other robots needed for rescuing him (3 robots in our case, but a solution with a varying number can be easily accommodated) is locally published.

The *HelpRescuer* process is defined as follows

HelpRescuer $\triangleq$ **if** ($count > 1$) **then** { **put**("victim", $x_v, y_v, count$-1)@self }.
　　　　put("direction", x_v, y_v)@self.
　　　　qry("position", x_v, y_v)@self. **put**("rescue")@self

This process is triggered by a victim tuple retrieved from the rescuers ensemble (see P_R). The tuple indicates that additional robots (whose number is stored in $count$) are needed at position (x_v, y_v) to rescue a victim. If more than one robot is needed, a new victim tuple is published (with decremented counter). Then, the robot, which became a rescuer, goes towards the victim position and, once reaches him (i.e., the current position coincides with the victim's one), it starts the rescuing procedure. It is worth noticing that, if more victims are in the scenario, different groups of rescuers will be spontaneously organised to rescue them. To avoid that more than one group is formed for the same victim, we assume that the sensor of an explorer used to perceive the victim is configured so that a victim that is already receiving assistance by some rescuers is not detected as a victim.

An explorer changes its role to rescuer when it finds a victim or helps other rescuers. Each role corresponds to a different enforced policy, and the transition triggering the policy change is defined as follows

$$
\begin{array}{c}
(\,\text{equal}(\mathbf{qry}, action/action\text{-}id) \\
\wedge\ \text{pattern-match}((\,\text{"victimPerceived"}, \text{true}), action/item)\,) \\
\vee\ (\,\text{equal}(\mathbf{get}, action/action\text{-}id) \\
\wedge\ \text{pattern-match}((\,\text{"victim"}, \_, \_, \_), action/item)\,)
\end{array}
$$

EXPLORER $\xrightarrow{\hspace{5cm}}$ RESCUER

Thus, the explorer policy change to the rescuer one either when a victimPerceived tuple is read or when a victim tuple is consumed.

The policy enforced in the EXPLORER state is as follows

⟨ permit-unless-deny
   rules : (permit target : equal(**qry**,*action/action-id*)
                         ∧ pattern-match(("victimPerceived" , true),*action/item*))
               obl : [permit **put**("stop")@self.**put**(*role, "rescuer"*)@self])
     (deny target : equal(**qry**,*action/action-id*)
                      ∧ pattern-match(("isMoving"),*action/item*)
                      ∧ less-than(20%,*subject/batteryLevel*)
             obl : [deny **put**("direction" , *env/station.x, env/station.y*)@self])⟩

The first rule stops the robot when a victim is found and changes the interface attribute *role* to *rescuer* by means of the action **put**(*role, "rescuer"*)@self. The second rule monitors the battery level and redirects the robot to the recharging station when the level is low. Notably, with respect to the previous scenario, the battery level is considered low when it is less than 20%, which should ensure enough battery power to allow the explorer to reach the recharging station or to rescue the victim, if he would be found in the meanwhile. We assume that each robot can obtain the position of the charging station, which is retrieved here by means of the interface attributes *env/station.x* and *env/station.y*.

The policy enforced in the RESCUER status is instead as follows

    ⟨ permit-unless-deny
      rules : (permit target : equal(**qry**,*action/action-id*)
                        ∧ pattern-match(("position" , _, _),*action/item*))
           obl : [permit **put**("stop")@self]) ⟩

The policy, as previously, stops the robot when the victim is reached.

4 Deployment and Simulation of PSCEL Programs

jRESP[2] is a Java runtime environment providing a framework for developing autonomic and adaptive systems according to the SCEL paradigm. Specifically, jRESP provides an API that permits using in Java programs the SCEL's linguistic constructs for controlling the computation and interaction of autonomic components, and for defining the architecture of systems and ensembles.

Like SCEL, jRESP has been designed to accommodate alternative instantiations of specific knowledge and policy managers that may change for tailoring to different application domains.

A detailed description of the jRESP architecture and its basic features can be found in [3]. In this section we will briefly present jRESP and its basic elements and the specific classes we have implemented to integrate FACPL in jRESP. The new classes, which specialize the jRESP architecture, have been included in a specific package enabling the execution of PSCEL programs.

Components. PSCEL components are implemented via the class PscelNode. Nodes are executed over virtual machines or physical devices providing access

---

[2] jRESP website: http://jresp.sourceforge.net/.

to input/output devices and network connections. A node aggregates a tuple space, a set of running processes, and a set of FACPL policies. Structural and behavioural information about a node are collected into an *interface* via *attribute collectors*. Nodes interact via *ports* supporting both *point-to-point* and *group-oriented* communications.

Knowledge repository. Since PSCEL specializes the knowledge repositories of SCEL's components as *tuple spaces*, the version of jRESP considered here provides an implementation of the interface Knowledge of PscelNodes. This is the class TupleSpace that defines the methods for withdrawing/retrieving/adding pieces of knowledge from/to repositories. Knowledge items are defined as *tuples*, i.e. sequences of Objects, that can be collected into a knowledge repository. They can be retrieved/withdrawn via pattern-matching through Templates, consisting of a sequence of actual and formal TemplateFields.

External data can be collected into a knowledge repository via *sensors*. Each sensor can be associated to a logical or physical device providing data that can be retrieved by processes and that can be the subject of adaptation. Similarly, *actuators* can be used to send data to an external device or service attached to a node. This approach allows processes to control exogenous devices that identify logical/physical actuators.

The interface associated to a node is computed by exploiting *attribute collectors*. Each such collector is able to inspect the local knowledge and to compute the value of the attributes. This mechanism equips a node with *reflective capabilities* allowing a component to self-project the image of its state on the interface. Indeed, when the local knowledge is updated the involved collectors are *automatically* activated and the node interface is modified accordingly.

Network Infrastructure. Each PscelNode is equipped with a set of ports for interacting with other components. A port is identified by an *address* that can be used to refer to other jRESP components. Indeed, each jRESP node can be addressed via a pair composed of the node name and the address of one of its ports. The abstract class AbstractPort implements the generic behaviour of a port. It implements the communication protocol used by jRESP components to interact with each other. The class AbstractPort also provides the instruments to dispatch messages to components. However, in AbstractPort the methods used for sending messages via a specific communication network/media are abstract. Also the method used to retrieve the address associated to a port is abstract in AbstractPort. The concrete classes defining specific kinds of ports extend AbstractPort to provide concrete implementations of the above outlined abstract methods, so to use different underlying network infrastructures (e.g., Internet, Ad-hoc networks, ...). An additional instance, named VitualPort, is used to *simulate* nodes interaction within a single application without using a specific network infrastructure. Indeed, VirtualPort implements a port where interactions take place through a memory buffer.

Behaviours. Processes are implemented as threads via the abstract class Agent, which provides the methods implementing the PSCEL actions. In fact, they can be used for generating fresh names, for instantiating new components and for withdrawing/retrieving/adding items from/to shared knowledge repositories. The latter methods extend those considered in Knowledge with another parameter identifying either the (possibly remote) node where the target repository is located or the group of nodes whose repositories have to be accessed. As previously mentioned, group-oriented interactions are supported by the communication protocols defined in the node ports and by attribute collectors.

4.1   Integration of FACPL in jRESP

In jRESP policies are used to regulate the interaction between the different internal parts of components and their mutual interactions. Indeed, when a method of an instance of the class Agent is invoked, its execution is delegated to the policy associated to the node where the agent is running. The policy can then control the execution of the action (for instance, by suspending a behaviour when some access rights are missing) and, possibly, define additional *behaviours*. Different kinds of policies can be easily integrated in jRESP by implementing the interface IPolicy. Currently, two implementations of this latter interface are included in jRESP: NodePolicy and PolicyAutomaton. NodePolicy is the policy enforced by default in each node. It always allows any operations, thus directly delegating the execution of each action to the associated node. PolicyAutomaton implements instead a generic POLICY AUTOMATON Π (like those presented in Section 2). In this way, transitions caused by the execution of agent actions can trigger changes of the policies. In particular, a PolicyAutomaton consists of a set of PolicyStates, each of which identifies the possible policies enforced in the node, and of a reference to the current state, which is used to *evaluate* agent actions with respect to the current policies. This automaton can be easily integrated with various policy languages, although here we focus on its integration with FACPL policies.

The full integration of FACPL in jRESP can be now achieved by considering the class FacplPolicyState that, by extending PolicyState, relies on the Java-translated FACPL policies. This Java code is automatically obtained by using the FACPL IDE available for the Eclipse platform from the FACPL website [17].

When a PolicyAutomaton receives a request for the execution of a given action, first of all an AutorisationRequest is created. This is the object identifying the PSCEL action the node wants to perform, thus it provides information about the kind of action performed, its argument, its target and the list of attributes currently published in the node interface. The created AuthorizationRequest is then evaluated with respect to the current policy state via the (abstract) method evaluate(AutorisationRequest r) defined in the class PolicyState. In the class FacplPolicyState this method delegates the authorization to the referred FACPL policy. The method returns an instance of the class AuthorisationResponse, which contains a *decision*, i.e. permit or deny, and a set of *obligations*. The latter ones are rendered as a sequence of Actions that must be performed just after the completion of the requested action. Hence, if the decision is permit, the requested action is completed as soon as the obligations are executed. Instead, if the decision is deny, the requested action cannot be performed. In this case, first the obligations possibly returned along with the decision must be executed, then a new

AutorisationRequest is created and evaluated in order to establish executability of the requested action.

Finally, the evaluation of a request by a PolicyAutomaton can trigger an update of its current state. Indeed, for each state, a sequence of *transitions* are stored in the automaton. These are instances of the class PolicyAutomatonTransition that provides two methods: apply(AutorisationRequest r): boolean and nextState(): PolicyState. A transition is *enabled* if the first method returns true. The next state is then obtained by invoking nextState() on the first enabled transition. If no transition is enabled, the current state is not changed.

In the first scenario of Section 3 the PolicyAutomaton associated to each PscelNode contains only a single state; this is the FacplPolicyState that interacts with the considered Java-translated FACPL policies. Instead, in the second scenario, the PolicyAutomaton consists of two states that enforce *explorer* and *rescuer* behaviour, respectively. The PolicyAutomatonTransition associated in the automaton to the *explorer* state is the following:

```
public class ExplorerToRescuer implements PolicyAutomatonTransition {
    public boolean apply( AutorisationRequest req ) {
        return ( (req.getActionId() == ActionID.QUERY)
          && (new Template(
            new ActualTemplateField( "VICTIM_PERCEIVED" ) ,
            new ActualTemplateField( true ) ).match( req.getItem() )))
        ||((req.getActionId() == ActionID.GET)
          && (new Template(
            new ActualTemplateField( "VICTIM" ) ,
            new FormalTemplateField( Object.class ) ,
            new FormalTemplateField( Object.class ) ,
            new FormalTemplateField( Object.class ) ).match( req.getItem() )));
    }
    public PolicyState nextState() { return new FacplPolicyState( new Policy_Rescuer() ); }
}
```

In the code above, Policy_Rescuer is the Java-translated FACPL policy associated to the policy presented at the end of Section 3.

4.2   Simulating Robots in jRESP

To support analysis of adaptive systems specified in PSCEL, the jRESP environment provides a set of classes that permits simulating jRESP *programs*. These classes enable the execution of *virtual components* over a simulation environment that can control component interactions and collect relevant simulation data. In fact, although in principle jRESP code could be directly executed in real robots (provided that a Java Virtual Machine is running on them and that jRESP's sensors and actuators invoke the API of the corresponding robots' devices), this may not be always possible. Therefore, jRESP also provides simulation facilities.

To set-up the simulation environment in jRESP one has first of all to define a class that provides the machinery to manage the physical data of the scenario. These data include, e.g., robots position, direction and speed. In our case, we consider the class ScenarioArena that, in addition to the above mentioned data, also provides the methods for updating robots position and computing collisions. These methods are periodically executed by the jRESP simulation environment.

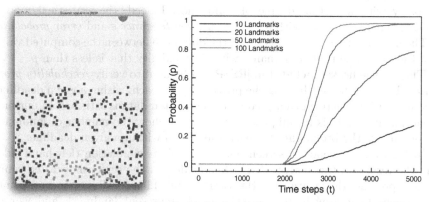

Fig. 2. Simulation and analysis of the first robot swarm scenario in jRESP

For the sake of simplicity, in the simulation, only collisions with the borders of the arena are considered, while collisions among robots are ignored.

For both scenarios, in jRESP we consider a network of PscelNodes each of which identifies a single robot. We assume that each robot/node is equipped with sensors, like *collision* and *victim* detection sensors, which are used to retrieve information about the state of the robot and of its working environment. All the above mentioned sensors are built via the class ScenarioArena and permit to directly access the data associated to the state of the simulated physical environment. Similarly, each instance of PscelNode modelling a robot is equipped with *actuators* used to control robots movement, like *direction* and *stop* actuators. Also these actuators are built via the class ScenarioArena and permit to update the parameters of the simulated physical environment when the corresponding data are received. For instance, when the *RandomWalk* process running at the node corresponding to robot i produces a tuple of the form $\langle$*"direction"*, *dir*$\rangle$, the local direction actuator sets to *dir* the direction of the robot i in the ScenarioArena. This behaviour mimics the fact that in a *real* robot the actuator directly interacts with the wheels controller.

Each PscelNode also executes the agents presented in the previous sections. For instance, the *RandomWalk* process is rendered in jRESP as reported below:

```
public class RandomWalk extends Agent {
    Random r = new Random();
    public RandomWalk() { super("RandomWalk"); }
    @Override
    protected void doRun() throws IOException, InterruptedException{
        while (true) {
            double dir = r.nextDouble()*2*Math.PI;
            put( new Tuple( "direction" , dir) , Self.SELF );
            query( new Template( new ActualTemplateField( "COLLISION" ) ,
                        new ActualTemplateField( true ) ), Self.SELF );
        }
    }
}
```

By relying on the jRESP simulation environment, a prototype framework for *statistical model-checking* has been also developed. A randomized algorithm is used to verify whether the implementation of a system satisfies a specific property with a certain degree of confidence. Indeed, the statistical model-checker is parameterized with respect to a given *tolerance* ε and *error probability* p. The used algorithm guarantees that the difference between the computed value and the exact one is greater than ε with a probability that is less than p.

The model-checker included in jRESP can be used to verify *reachability properties*. These permit evaluating the probability to reach, within a given deadline, a configuration where a given predicate on collected data is satisfied. In our first scenario, this analysis technique is used to study how the number of landmark robots affects the probability to reach the victim within a given deadline.

In Figure 2, we report a screenshot of the robots simulation (left-hand side) and the results of the analysis (right-hand side). In the screenshot, a red semi-circle represents the locations of the victim, while blue (dark grey in b/w print) and green (light grey in b/w print) squares represent landmark and worker robots, respectively. The analysis results are represented as a chart showing the probability of rescuing the victim within a given time according to different numbers of landmark robots (i.e., 10, 20, 50 and 100). Notably, the victim can be rescued only after 2000 time steps and, beyond a certain threshold, increasing the number of robots is not worthy (in fact, the difference in terms of rescuing time between 100 and 50 robots is marginal with respect to the cost of deploying a double number of robots).

5   Related Work

Autonomic computing systems are currently studied within many research communities. To deal with such systems different approaches have been advocated both for programming them, like multi-agent systems, component-based design and context-oriented programming, and for regulating their behavior, mainly through policy languages. Below, we mention the most closely related works.

Multi-agent systems (as e.g. [18,19,4]) pursue the importance of the knowledge representation and how it is handled for choosing adaptive actions. PSCEL, instead, bases the knowledge repository implementation on tuple-spaces, which is a more flexible and lightweight mechanism to, e.g., support adaptive context-aware activities in pervasive computing scenarios.

Component-based design has been indicated as a key approach for adaptive software design [20]. A relevant example in this field is FRACTAL [21], a hierarchical component model that, in addition to standard component-based systems, permits defining systems with a less rigid structure by means of components without completely fixed boundaries. However, communication among components is still defined via connectors and system adaptation is obtained by adding, removing or modifying components and/or connectors. Communication and adaptation in PSCEL, instead, are more flexible, and, hence, more adequate to deal with highly dynamic ensembles.

Another paradigm advocated to program autonomic systems [22] is Context-Oriented Programming (COP) [23]. It exploits ad-hoc linguistic constructs to define context-dependent behavioral variations and their run-time activation.

The most of the literature on COP is devoted to the design and implementation of concrete programming languages (a comparison can be found in [24]). Only few works provide a foundational account, like e.g. [25], focussing on an object-oriented language extended with COP facilities. All these approaches are however quite different from ours, that instead focusses on distribution and attribute-based aggregations and supports a highly dynamic notion of adaptation regulated by policies.

As concerns policy languages, many such languages have been recently developed for managing different aspects of programs' behaviour as, e.g., adaptation and autonomic computing. For example, a policy-based approach to autonomic computing issues has also been proposed by IBM through a simplified policy language [12], which, however, comes without a precise syntax and semantics. [6] introduces PobSAM, a policy-based formalism that combines an actor-based model, for specifying the computational aspects of system elements, and a configuration algebra, for defining autonomic managers that, in response to changes, lead the adaptation of the system configuration according to given adaptation policies. This formalism relies on a predefined notion of policies expressed as Event-Condition-Action (ECA) rules. Adaptation policies are specific ECA rules that change the manager configurations. PSCEL constructs for defining policies, being strictly integrated with a powerful autonomic programming language, is more flexible and expressive permitting not only to produce adaptation actions, but also authorisation controls and resource assignments. Moreover, the full integration of obligation actions with the programming constructs permits a runtime code generation and, hence, enables more flexible adaptation strategies. A policy language for which a number of toolkits have been developed and applied to various autonomous and pervasive systems is Ponder [11]. The language uses two separate types of policies for authorisation and obligation. Policies of the former type have the aim of establishing if an operation can be performed, while those of the latter type basically are ECA rules. Differently from Ponder, and similarly to more recent languages (e.g. XACML), in PSCEL obligations are expressed as part of authorisation policies, thus providing a more uniform specification approach.

Finally, the international standard XACML, which FACPL is inspired to, defines policy specifications in XML format without a formal description of the evaluation process. FACPL instead has a compact and intuitive syntax and is endowed with a formal semantics based on solid mathematical foundations. These features, as well as its supporting software tools, make FACPL easy to learn and use. This motivates our choice of FACPL as policy language to be integrated with the programming constructs provided by SCEL.

6   Conclusion

In this paper we tackled the issue of practically programming and policing autonomic computing systems. To this aim, we propose the use of the formal language PSCEL, which fosters an approach based on the 'separation of concerns' principle. Indeed, on the one hand, the behaviour of autonomic components and their ensembles are programmed through the SCEL constructs. On the other hand, the interactions between components and the adaptation actions to be performed in reaction to changes in their working environment are regulated by means of FACPL policies. From a practical perspective, SCEL specifications can be implemented in Java by relying on the jRESP runtime environment, while FACPL policies can be developed and automatically translated in Java by using a specific tool suite. The main contribution of this paper is the integration of these Java-based tools in order to provide a uniform software framework for the development and execution of PSCEL programs. In order to illustrate how jRESP supports simulation and analysis of autonomic systems specified in PSCEL, we have exploited a simple case study from the robotics domain.

As a future work, we plan to improve the practical applicability of the PSCEL approach by extending the Eclipse-based IDE for FACPL policies with the possibility of defining SCEL specifications. In this way, an autonomic system will be completely specified at high-level of abstraction using PSCEL's constructs and then automatically transformed in a Java application integrating the code corresponding to SCEL behaviours and FACPL policies. Moreover, to assess the potentialities of PSCEL tools, we also plan to consider other application domains and case studies among those developed within the ASCENS project, concerning cooperative e-vehicles and cloud systems.

References

1. Kephart, J.O., Chess, D.M.: The Vision of Autonomic Computing. Computer 36, 41–50 (2003)
2. Margheri, A., Pugliese, R., Tiezzi, F.: Linguistic Abstractions for Programming and Policing Autonomic Computing Systems. In: UIC/ATC, pp. 404–409. IEEE (2013)
3. De Nicola, R., Loreti, M., Pugliese, R., Tiezzi, F.: A formal approach to autonomic systems programming: The SCEL language. ACM TAAS (to appear, 2014)
4. Dastani, M.: 2APL: A practical agent programming language. Autonomous Agents and Multi-Agent Systems 16(3), 214–248 (2008)
5. Ashley-Rollman, M.P., Goldstein, S.C., Lee, P., Mowry, T.C., Pillai, P.: Meld: A declarative approach to programming ensembles. In: IROS, pp. 2794–2800. IEEE (2007)
6. Khakpour, N., Jalili, S., Talcott, C.L., Sirjani, M., Mousavi, M.R.: Formal modeling of evolving self-adaptive systems. Sci. Comput. Program. 78(1), 3–26 (2012)
7. Lanese, I., Bucchiarone, A., Montesi, F.: A framework for rule-based dynamic adaptation. In: Wirsing, M., Hofmann, M., Rauschmayer, A. (eds.) TGC 2010, LNCS, vol. 6084, pp. 284–300. Springer, Heidelberg (2010)
8. Banâtre, J.P., Radenac, Y., Fradet, P.: Chemical Specification of Autonomic Systems. In: IASSE, ISCA, pp. 72–79 (2004)
9. Margheri, A., Masi, M., Pugliese, R., Tiezzi, F.: A Formal Software Engineering Approach to Policy-based Access Control. Technical report, Univ. Firenze (2013), http://rap.dsi.unifi.it/facpl/research/Facpl-TR.pdf
10. Masi, M., Pugliese, R., Tiezzi, F.: Formalisation and implementation of the XACML access control mechanism. In: Barthe, G., Livshits, B., Scandariato, R. (eds.) ESSoS 2012. LNCS, vol. 7159, pp. 60–74. Springer, Heidelberg (2012)

11. Damianou, N., Dulay, N., Lupu, E.C., Sloman, M.: The Ponder Policy Specification Language. In: Sloman, M., Lobo, J., Lupu, E.C. (eds.) POLICY 2001. LNCS, vol. 1995, pp. 18–38. Springer, Heidelberg (2001)
12. IBM: Autonomic Computing Policy Language - ACPL, http://www.ibm.com/developerworks/tivoli/tutorials/ac-spl/
13. Margheri, A., Pugliese, R., Tiezzi, F.: Linguistic Abstractions for Programming and Policing Autonomic Computing Systems. Technical report, Univ. Firenze (2013), http://rap.dsi.unifi.it/scel/pdf/PSCEL-TR.pdf
14. Serbedzija, N., et al.: Integration and simulation report for the Ascens case studies. D7.3 (2013), http://www.pst.ifi.lmu.de/~mayer/papers/2013-11-30_D73.pdf
15. EU project ASCENS: http://www.ascens-ist.eu/
16. Mamei, M., Zambonelli, F., Leonardi, L.: Co-fields: A physically inspired approach to motion coordination. IEEE Pervasive Computing 3(2), 52–61 (2004)
17. FACPL website: http://rap.dsi.unifi.it/facpl
18. Winikoff, M.: Jack^{tm} intelligent agents: An industrial strength platform. In: Multi-Agent Programming, vol. 15, pp. 175–193. Springer (2005)
19. Bellifemine, F.L., Caire, G., Greenwood, D.: Developing Multi-Agent Systems with JADE. Wiley Series in Agent Technology. John Wiley & Sons (2007)
20. McKinley, P., Sadjadi, S., Kasten, E., Cheng, B.H.C.: Composing adaptive software. Computer 37(7), 56–64 (2004)
21. Bruneton, E., Coupaye, T., Leclercq, M., Quéma, V., Stefani, J.B.: The FRACTAL component model and its support in Java. Softw., Pract. Exper. 36(11-12), 1257–1284 (2006)
22. Salvaneschi, G., Ghezzi, C., Pradella, C.: Context-Oriented Programming: A Programming Paradigm for Autonomic Systems. CoRR abs/1105.0069 (2011)
23. Hirschfeld, R., Costanza, P., Nierstrasz, O.: Context-oriented programming. Journal of Object Technology 7(3), 125–151 (2008)
24. Appeltauer, M., Hirschfeld, R., Haupt, M., Lincke, J., Perscheid, M.: A comparison of context-oriented programming languages. In: COP, pp. 6:1–6:6. ACM (2009)
25. Hirschfeld, R., Igarashi, A., Masuhara, H.: ContextFJ: A minimal core calculus for context-oriented programming. In: FOAL, pp. 19–23. ACM (2011)

Rigorous System Design Flow
for Autonomous Systems

Saddek Bensalem, Marius Bozga, Jacques Combaz, and Ahlem Triki

Verimag, France,
{firstname.lastname}@imag.fr

Abstract. We currently lack rigorous approaches for modeling and implementing complex systems. BIP (Behavior, Interaction, Priority) is a component-based framework intended to rigorous system design. It relies on single semantic model for system descriptions all along the design flow. It also includes methods and tools for guaranteeing system correctness to avoid a posteriori verification. Our approach is to check safety properties (e.g. deadlock freedom) at design time using D-Finder verification tool. In addition, source-to-source transformers allow progressive refinement of the application to generate a correct implementation. Our framework was successfully applied in various context including robotics case studies presented here.

1 Introduction

System design is the process leading to a mixed hardware/software system meeting given specifications. It involves the development of application software taking into account features of an execution platform. The latter is defined by its architecture involving a set of processors equipped with hardware-dependent software such as operating systems as well as primitives for coordination of the computation and interaction with the external environment.

System design radically differs from pure software design in that it must take into account not only functional but also extra-functional specifications regarding the use of resources of the execution platform such as time, memory and energy. Meeting extra-functional specifications is essential for the design of embedded systems. It requires evaluation of the impact of design choices on the overall behavior of the system.

We currently lack rigorous techniques for deriving global models of a given system from models of its software and its execution platform. We call rigorous a design flow which allows guaranteeing essential system properties. Most of the existing rigorous design flows privilege a unique programming model together with an associated compilation chain adapted for a given execution model. For example, synchronous system design relies on synchronous programming models and usually targets hardware or sequential implementations on single processors [1]. Alternatively, real-time programming based on scheduling theory for periodic tasks, targets dedicated real-time multitasking platforms [2].

T. Margaria and B. Steffen (Eds.): ISoLA 2014, Part I, LNCS 8802, pp. 184–198, 2014.

We strongly believe that a rigorous design flow should be *model-based*, that is, all the system description should be based on a single semantic model, should be *component-based*, that is, it provides primitives for building composite components as the composition of simpler component, and should rely on tractable theory for guaranteeing *correctness by construction* to avoid as much as possible monolithic a posteriori verification. An instance of rigorous design flow is the BIP approach presented below.

The BIP Desgin Flow. Behavior—Interaction—Priority (BIP) is a component framework intended to rigorous system design. It allows the construction of composite hierarchically structured components from atomic components characterized by their behavior and their interface. Components are composed by layered application of interactions and of priorities. Interactions express synchronization constraints between actions of the composed components while priorities are used to filter amongst possible interactions and to steer system evolution so as to meet performance requirements e.g. to express scheduling policies. Interactions are described in BIP as the combination of two types of protocols: rendez-vous to express strong symmetric synchronization and broadcast to express triggered asymmetric synchronization. The combination of interactions and priorities confers BIP expressiveness not matched by any other existing formalism [3]. It defines a clean and abstract concept of architecture separate from behavior. Architecture in BIP is a first class concept with well-defined semantics that can be analyzed and transformed. BIP relies on rigorous operational semantics that has been implemented by three Execution Engines for centralized, distributed and real-time execution. It is used as a unifying semantic model in a rigorous system design flow. Rigorousness is ensured by two kinds of tools: 1) D-Finder a verification tool for checking safety properties and deadlock-freedom in particular; 2) source-to-source transformers that allow progressive refinement of the application to get a correct implementation.

BIP can be considered as an ADL (Architecture Description Language) or as a coordination language as it focuses on the organization of computation between components. As other existing ADL such as ACME [4] and Darwin [5], BIP uses the concept of connector to express coordination between components. Nonetheless, connectors in BIP are stateless. There is a clear distinction between architecture which involves connectors and priorities and behavior. Another significant difference is that BIP is intended to system modeling as it directly encompasses timing and resource management aspects. It differs from other system modeling formalisms which either seek generality at the detriment of rigorousness, such as SySML [6] and AADL [7] or have a limited scope as they are based on specific models of computation such as Ptolemy [8].

In previous work, we successfully applied the BIP design flow to the robot DALA, an autonomous rover for extraterrestria exploration [9,10,11]. This paper is based on the extension of BIP to time proposed in [12], which was not considered by [9,10,11]. Its contributions[1] are: *(i)* the application of recently developed

---

[1] This work was supported by the European Integrated Project 257414 ASCENS.

verification and validation techniques to autonomous systems case studies, and
(ii) the extension of the method for generation of distributed implementations
proposed in [13] to timed systems. The rest of the paper is organized as follows.
Section 2 provides a formalization of the BIP language and its semantics. Section 3 describes the BIP toolchain consisting mainly of: a compiler, including
backends for the generation of both single-threaded and multi-threaded C++
code, as well as message passing based implementations for their deployment
on distributed platforms, and verification and validation tools for checking the
correctness of the system and its performance. Finally, Section 4 demonstrates
our approach by the application of our tools to various robotics case studies.

2   Basic Semantic Model of BIP

Definition 1 (abstract model). *An abstract model is a timed automaton*
$M = (\mathsf{A}, \mathsf{Q}, \mathsf{X}, \longrightarrow, \mathsf{tpc})$ *such that:*

- A *is a finite set of* actions.
- Q *is a finite set of* control locations
- X *is a finite set of* clocks
- $\longrightarrow$ *is a finite set of labeled transitions. A transition is a tuple* (q, a, g, r, q')
  where $q, q' \in \mathsf{Q}$ *are control locations, a is an action executed by the transition,*
  g a constraint over X *called* guard, *and r is a subset of clocks that are reset*
  by the transition. We write $q \xrightarrow{a,g,r} q'$ *for* $(q, a, g, r, q') \in \longrightarrow$
- tpc *is a function associating to each control location* $q \in \mathsf{Q}$ *a constraint* $\mathsf{tpc}[q]$
  over X *called* time progress condition.

An abstract model describes the platform-independent behavior of the system.
Timing constraints, that is, guards of transitions and time progress conditions
of control locations, are any boolean combination of simple constraints of the
form $x \sim k$, where $x \in \mathsf{X}$ is a clock, $k \in \mathbb{N}$ is a non-negative integer, and $\sim$
is a comparison operator: $\sim \in \{<, \leq, \geq, >\}$. They take into account only user
requirements (e.g. deadlines, periodicity, etc.). The semantics assumes timeless
execution of actions.

Definition 2 (abstract model semantics). *An abstract model* $M =$
$(\mathsf{A}, \mathsf{Q}, \mathsf{X}, \longrightarrow)$ *defines a transition system* TS. *States of* TS *are pairs* (q, v), *where*
q is a control location of M *and* $v : \mathsf{X} \to \mathbb{R}^+$ *is a valuation of the clocks* X *mapping each clock* $x \in \mathsf{X}$ *to its current value* $v(x) \in \mathbb{R}^+$, *where* $\mathbb{R}^+$ *denotes the set*
of non-negative reals.

- Actions. *We have* $(q, v) \xrightarrow{a} (q', v[r \mapsto 0])$ *if* $q \xrightarrow{a,g,r} q'$ *in* M *and both* $g(v)$
  and $\mathsf{tpc}[q'](v[r \mapsto 0])$ *are true, where* $v[r \mapsto 0]$ *denotes the valuation of the*
  clocks such that $v[r \mapsto 0](x) = 0$ *if* $x \in r$, $v[r \mapsto 0](x) = v(x)$ *otherwise.*
- Time steps. *For a waiting time* $\delta \in \mathbb{R}^+$, $\delta > 0$, *we have* $(q, v) \xrightarrow{\delta} (q, v + \delta)$
  if the time progress condition $\mathsf{tpc}[q]$ *allows the system to wait for* δ *at* (q, v),
  that is, if for all $\delta' \in [0, \delta]$, $\mathsf{tpc}[q](v + \delta')$ *is true.*

In an abstract model, clocks are non-negative real variables increasing synchronously. Guards are used to specify for which values of the clocks the actions may take place, and time progress conditions specify whether the system can wait at a given state or needs to execute an action to leave this state. Given an abstract model $M = (\mathsf{A}, \mathsf{Q}, \mathsf{X}, \longrightarrow)$, an *execution sequence* of M from an *initial* state (q_0, v_0) is a maximal sequence actions and time-steps $(q_i, v_i) \xrightarrow{\sigma_i} (q_{i+1}, v_{i+1})$, $\sigma_i \in \mathsf{A} \cup \mathbb{R}^+$, $i \geq 0$.

Example 1. Consider an abstract model $M = (\mathsf{A}, \mathsf{Q}, \{x\}, \longrightarrow)$ with two actions $\mathsf{A} = \{sync_1, p\}$, two states $\mathsf{Q} = \{q^1, q^2\}$, a single clock x, and two transitions $\longrightarrow = \{ (q^1, sync_1, \emptyset, \{x\}, q^2), (q^2, p, [10 \leq x \leq 20]^d, \emptyset, q^1) \}$ (see Figure 1). It can be easily shown that the execution sequences of M from the initial state $(q^2, 0)$ that are an infinite repetition of the sequence $(q^2, 0) \xrightarrow{\delta_1} (q^2, \delta_1) \xrightarrow{p} (q^1, \delta_1) \xrightarrow{\delta_2} (q^1, \delta_1 + \delta_2) \xrightarrow{sync_1} (q^2, 0)$, where $10 \leq \delta_1 \leq 20$.

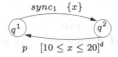

$$sync_1 \quad \{x\}$$

$$p \qquad [10 \leq x \leq 20]^d$$

Fig. 1. Example of abstract model

Definition 3 (composition of abstract models). *Let $M_i = (\mathsf{A}_i, \mathsf{Q}_i, \mathsf{X}_i, \longrightarrow_i, \mathsf{tpc}_i)$, $1 \leq i \leq n$, be a set of abstract models. We assume that their sets of actions and clocks are disjoint, i.e. for all $i \neq j$ we have $\mathsf{A}_i \cap \mathsf{A}_j = \emptyset$ and $\mathsf{X}_i \cap \mathsf{X}_j = \emptyset$. A set of interactions γ is a subset of 2^A, where $\mathsf{A} = \bigcup_{i=1}^n \mathsf{A}_i$, such that any interaction $a \in \gamma$ contains at most one action of each component M_i, that is, $a = \{ a_i \mid i \in I \}$ where $a_i \in \mathsf{A}_i$ and $I \subseteq \{ 1, 2, \ldots, n \}$. The composition of the abstract models M_i, $1 \leq i \leq n$, by using a set of interactions γ, denoted by $\gamma(M_1, \ldots, M_n)$, is the composite abstract model $M = (\gamma, \mathsf{Q}, \mathsf{X}, \longrightarrow_\gamma, \mathsf{tpc})$ such that:*

- $\mathsf{Q} = \mathsf{Q}_1 \times \mathsf{Q}_2 \times \ldots \times \mathsf{Q}_n$
- $\mathsf{X} = \bigcup_{i=1}^n \mathsf{X}_i$
- tpc *is defined by* $\mathsf{tpc}[q_1, \ldots, q_n] = \bigwedge_{i=1}^n \mathsf{tpc}_i[q_i]$
- $\longrightarrow_\gamma$ *is defined by the rules:*

$$\frac{a = \{a_i\}_{i \in I} \in \gamma \qquad g = \bigwedge_{i \in I} g_i \qquad r = \bigcup_{i \in I} r_i \qquad \forall i \in I \,.\, q_i \xrightarrow{a_i, g_i, r_i}_i q_i' \qquad \forall i \notin I \,.\, q_i' = q_i}{(q_1, \ldots, q_n) \xrightarrow{a, g, r}_\gamma (q_1', \ldots, q_n')}$$

A composition $M = \gamma(M_1, \ldots, M_n)$ of abstract models $M_i, 1 \leq i \leq n$ executes interactions $a = \{a_i\}_{i \in I} \in \gamma$ which corresponds to synchronizations of actions a_i of models $M_i, i \in I$. An interaction $a = \{a_i\}_{i \in I} \in \gamma$ is enabled from a state of M if all actions a_i are enabled.

In a composite model $M = \gamma(M_1, \ldots, M_n)$, many interactions can be enabled at the same time introducing a degree of non-determinism in the behavior of M. In order to restrict non-determinism, we introduce priorities that specify which interaction should be executed among the enabled ones. A priority on $M = \gamma\,(M_1,\ldots,M_n)$ is a relation $\pi \subseteq \gamma \times Q \times \gamma$ such that for all q the relation $\pi_q = \{\,(a,a') \mid (a,q,a') \in \pi\,\}$ is a partial order. We write $a\pi_q a'$ for $(a,q,a') \in \pi$ to express the fact that a has weaker priority than a' at state q. That is, if both a and a' are enabled at state q, only the action a' can be executed. Thus, priority $a\pi_q a'$ is applied only when the conjunction of the guards of a and a' is true. Let $q \xrightarrow{a,g,r}_\gamma q'$ and $q \xrightarrow{a',g',r'}_\gamma q''$ be transitions of M. Applying priority $a\pi_q a'$ boils down to transforming the guard g of a into the guard $g_\pi = g \wedge \neg g'$ and leaving the guard g' of a' unchanged.

Henceforth, we denote by $\mathrm{en}_q(a)$ the predicate characterizing the valuations of clocks for which an interaction a is enabled at state q. It is defined by:

$$\mathrm{en}_q(a) = \begin{cases} \text{false} & \text{if } \nexists (q,a,g,r,q') \in \longrightarrow_\gamma \\ \displaystyle\bigvee_{(q,a,g,r,q') \in \longrightarrow_\gamma} g & \text{otherwise.} \end{cases}$$

Definition 4 (priority). *Given a composite model $M = (\gamma, Q, X, \longrightarrow_\gamma)$, the application of a priority π to M defines a new model $\pi M = (\gamma, Q, X, \longrightarrow_\pi)$ such that $\longrightarrow_\pi$ is defined by the rule:*

$$\frac{q \xrightarrow{a,g,r}_\gamma q' \qquad g_\pi = g \wedge \neg \bigvee_{a\pi_q a'} \mathrm{en}_q(a')}{q \xrightarrow{a,g_\pi,r}_\pi q'}$$

Example 2. Consider an abstract model $M = \pi\gamma(M_1, M_2, M_3)$ such that:

- abstract models M_1, M_2, and M_3 are provided by Figure 2,
- interactions $\gamma = \{a_1, a_2, a_3\}$ are defined by $a_1 = \{sync_1, sync_2, sync_3\}$, $a_2 = \{p, q\}$ and $a_3 = \{r, s\}$,
- priority π is such that $a_2\pi_q a_3$ for any control location q of M.

From the initial state $(q_1^1, q_2^1, q_3^1, 0)$, it can be easily shown that the execution sequences of M have the following form: $((q_1^1, q_2^1, q_3^1), 0) \xrightarrow{a_1} ((q_1^2, q_2^2, q_3^2), 0) \xrightarrow{5} ((q_1^2, q_2^2, q_3^2), 5) \xrightarrow{a_3} ((q_1^2, q_2^3, q_3^1), 5) \xrightarrow{\delta_2} ((q_1^2, q_2^3, q_3^1), 5 + \delta_2) \xrightarrow{a_2} ((q_1^1, q_2^1, q_3^1), 5 + \delta_2) \xrightarrow{a_1} ((q_1^2, q_2^2, q_3^2), 0)$, where $5 \leq \delta_2 \leq 15$. Notice that control location err cannot be reached in M_2 due to the application of priority $a_2\pi_q a_3$ for $q = (q_1^2, q_2^2, q_3^2)$.

3   The BIP Toolchain

This section presents the toolchain available with the BIP framework (see Figure 3). It consists in a rich set of tools for modeling, executing and verifying BIP models. The frontend of the toolchain is the parser which takes as input textual representations of BIP models according to the BIP grammar, and builds BIP models which are implemented using the EMF meta-modeling technology. Such models are the input for the rest of the tools, which fall into two main categories.

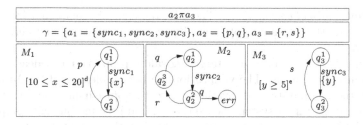

Fig. 2. Example of composition of abstract models with priorities

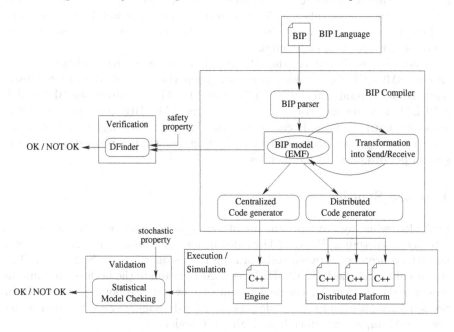

Fig. 3. Overview of the BIP Toolchain

Code generators. The BIP toolchain provides code generators for simulation and/or execution of models on target platforms. The standard code generator produces C++ code that relies on an engine for its execution. The centralized engine directly implements the operational semantics of BIP. It plays the role of the coordinator in selecting and executing synchronizations between the components, taking into account interactions and priorities specified in the input model. It supports both single-threaded and multi-threaded execution modes.

We have also developed a code generator for distributed platforms. It allows the transformation of BIP models into a set of standalone programs communicating through message passing which is implemented using the primitives available on the target platform. Such transformation has been proven correct, that is, it preserves the semantics of the input model.

Verification and validation tools. The BIP toolchain is completed by verification and validation tools for both checking system correctness and performance evaluation.

D-Finder is a verification tool targeting safety properties, e.g. deadlock freedom or mutual exclusion. The verification method implemented by D-Finder is based on the computation of invariants used to approximate the set of reachable states of the target system, hence the method is sound but not complete: it may not be able to prove a property even if it is satisfied by the system. Invariants are computed following the architecture of the system, that is, we generate invariants for components and for interactions. The approach is compositional and can be applied incrementally, allowing to better scale to large systems than traditional verification techniques.

In addition to D-Finder, the BIP toolchain includes the statistical model-checker SMC-BIP for checking stochastic properties expressed as probabilistic bounded linear temporal logic (PBLTL) formulas. Given a stochastic BIP model, a PBLTL formula and confidence parameters, SMC-BIP computes execution sequences until the formula can be proven with the target degree of confidence. Such a tool is particularly suited for evaluating quantitative properties including system performance related metrics.

4   Case Studies

In the following, we illustrate the use of our approach and tools through various robotics case studies. We used D-Finder to formally prove the correctness of a non trivial protocol between collaborating robots, as shown in Section 4.1. The statistical model-checker SMC-BIP was used to evaluate the performance and to fine-tune the strategy for the deployment of a swarm of robots (Section 4.2). In Section 4.3 we used our C++ code generator for deriving correct by construction distributed implementations from high-level models.

4.1   Compositional Verification of Safety Properties

We applied the compositional verification techniques for timed systems presented in [14] to a robotics scenario. It consists of cooperating robots used in a child's bedroom for home automation, automatic cleaning, or child assistance in tidying up. We considered the following types of robots/devices in the room, all capable of wireless communications.

Cleaning Robot. We assume the presence of an autonomous vacuum cleaner (e.g. Roomba) that can cooperate with other types of robots.

Toy Case Robot. The toy case robot—called Ranger—is currently developed in a research project of EPFL [15]. Its goal is to encourage the child to put away the toys in the case. We also assume that this robot has sensors able to detect the presence of the child when he is close enough.

Bed and desk chair. They are equipped with sensors allowing to detect when the child sits on.

Door. The bedroom door is equipped with an electric closing and locking system. A safety mechanism stops any closing procedure if the child tries to enter the bedroom while the door is closing.

Ceiling Camera. A camera located on the ceiling takes pictures at a given period P. They can be analyzed to detect whether the child is in the bedroom. The shape of the child can be tracked in these pictures only if it is not too close to other shapes (i.e. the toy case, on the bed and the chair).

In this scenario we were interested in a safety property stating that the child should not be in the bedroom while the cleaning robot is cleaning. To this end, we designed a protocol in which the cleaning robot (1) checks if child is outside the bedroom by correlating information from all the other robots / devices, (2) if so, closes and locks the door to keep the child outside, and (3) cleans the bedroom. We used formal verification to prove that our protocol satisfies the safety property.

The first thing one can observe in this system is that knowledge—e.g. the presence of the child—is distributed amongst the robots. One major issue for the cleaning robot is to build a consistent view of the status of the child (inside or outside) from local knowledge of the robots, and all this in real-time. We assume continuous sensing of the child for the case, the bed and the chair. On the other hand, pictures are taken only at specific time instants meaning that we have to deal with outdated information for the camera. If the child is not on a picture taken at a given time, then it was either outside, or inside and playing with the case, or on the bed or the chair. If we want to be sure that the child was outside the bedroom at the time the picture was taken, we need to know what was the status of the sensors of the case, the bed and the chair at this time. For this purpose we associate one timer to each sensor and reset it each time the child leaves. We also used a freshness parameter F for controlling the knowledge of the camera: the child is considered outside by the camera if he was not in a picture taken at most F time units ago. In a slightly different way, we used parameter R for the case, the bed and the chair: the child is considered outside by these devices if he was not detected for at least R time units. Notice that if $R \geq F$ we can safely conclude whether the child was outside or inside at the time the last picture was shot from the camera (see Figure 4). We also use R for the door, that is, it is considered closed if it was closed for more than R time units.

We built a BIP model for verifying the principles of the proposed protocol at high level (see Figure 5). If the child is not detected by all the devices (w.r.t. F and R), the cleaning robot starts locking the door since there is a high probability

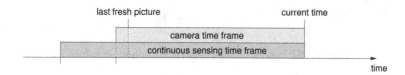

Fig. 4. Freshness parameters F for the camera and R for the other devices

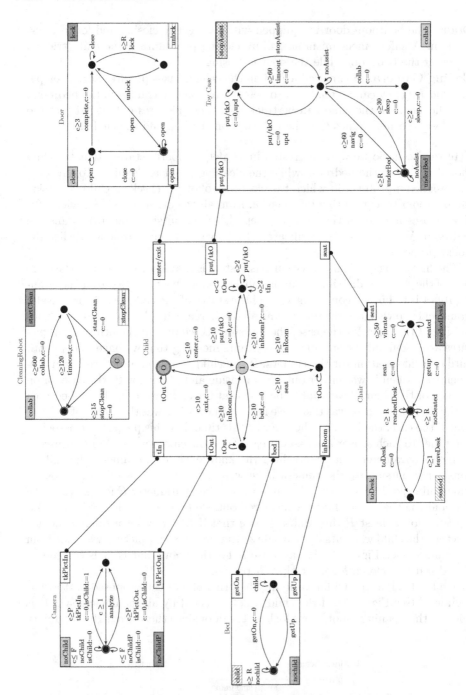

Fig. 5. BIP model of the cooperating robots example

that the child is not in the bedroom at the current time (we are sure that at some instant in the last F time units, the child was not in the bedroom). This is represented by a strong synchronization between ports collab, close and noChild (the yellow ports of Figure 5). Notice that the behavior for parameters F and R is ensured by local conditions based on components clocks. Once executed, the door starts closing, and the case and the chair move towards locations that ease the cleaning robot to operate. Then the cleaning robot starts cleaning only if the child is still not detected by the devices and the door is still closed, considering again parameters F and R. If so, it locks the door and starts cleaning, which is modelled by a strong synchronization between ports startClean, lock, underBed, reachedDesk, noChild, noChildP (the green ports of Figure 5). Otherwise, if the cleaning is not possible for 120 time units, the cleaning robot timeouts and returns to its initial state. Intuitively this protocol is safe (provided $R \geq F$) since the cleaning starts only if the child was outside when the last picture was taken and the door was kept closed since this time. Moreover, during cleaning, the door remains closed by using the locking mechanism.

Using verification technique of [14] we managed to prove formally that the child is not in the bedroom while the robot is cleaning, provided $R \geq F$. More precisely, if the cleaning robot is in control state C, then the child is in state 0 (these control states are in blue in Figure 5). This property is non trivial as it strongly depends on the individual behavior of all the devices and in particular their timings, and it can be tricky to ensure for the system. We did several attempts before we obtained a correct design. For instance, we started with discreted and periodic sensing instead of continuous sensing. The flaw in this design was difficult to detect by simulation as it very rarely led to a violation of the safety property. Verification tools helped us in finding and fixing the problem.

Notice that the model proposed here is far too abstract to be used directly for implementing the devices. It uses primitives such as atomic synchronizations between two or more components (i.e. multi-party interactions) that should be translated into simpler interactions (e.g. messages passing). To get correct-by-construction implementations we could transform the proposed BIP model into a Send/Receive BIP model using techniques developed for generating distributed implementations from BIP, as presented explained in Section 4.3.

4.2   Quantitative Analysis of a Deployment Scenario

We considered a robotics scenario in which a swarm of marXbots [16] should (1) be deployed to find 5 victims (which are other marXbots) distributed all over an arena shown in Figure 6,

and (2) rescue the victims. In this scenario, we assume that the robots cannot use localization mechanisms (e.g. GPS, SLAM, etc.). Instead, during the deployment phase some of the robots stop and become landmarks, i.e., they are used to guide other robots for exploring the arena and rescuing the victims.

We used the statistical model-checking tool SMC-BIP to analyze to the deployment phase only. We first built a BIP model of a single marXbot including a faithful implementation of its sensors. Following the approach implemented in the simulator ARGoS [17], we rely on synchronous discrete time execution with a duration of 10 ms for the time steps. The model of the swarm represents 1500 lines of BIP code along with 1200 lines of external C++ code.

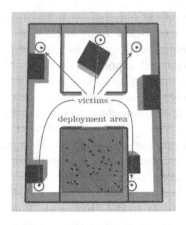

Fig. 6. Arena of the scenario

Single robot behavior. We started by experimenting with several behavioral strategies for a single robot: straight walk, random walk, and random walk improved using the rotating scanner. All includes basic obstacle avoidance so as not to bump into walls and/or other robots. Figure 7 shows examples of simulations obtained for the different strategies, where the path followed by the explorer is represented by the red drawing and the victims are represented by the five small black circles (three at the top and two at bottom of the arena). Using straight walk minimize the distance for travelling from one location to another. However, it resulted in a very poor coverage since the explorer was trapped on the left side of the arena from which it did not escape even after a long time. Random walk led to good coverage but longer delays for finding the first three victims than the ones obtained with straight walk. We improved random walk by using the rotating scanner which allows the explorer to track long distances obstacles and to follow corridors and walls, which is clearly visible on simulations (see Figures 7). All these observations are confirmed by the analysis performed by SMC-BIP with which we computed the expected time for finding the 1st and the 5th considering probability 0.85, provided in Figure 8. Parameters α, β and δ in table of Figure 8 correspond to the target degree of confidence for SMC-BIP. The lower these parameters are, the lower the probability to obtain an incorrect answer is. They are formally defined in [18]. Using SMC-BIP we also managed to show that increasing the number of explorers (we tested for 11, 21, and then 31) tends to reduce the expected delays for finding victims (see Figure 8).

Cooperation between robots. We completed the model by including landmarks behavior and corresponding communications. If a robot become too far away from other landmarks, or if it finds a victim, it stops to establish a new landmark. The goal of these landmarks during the deployment phase is to avoid exploring areas that have been already explored. Landmarking alone reduced drastically the performances, as shown by Figure 8. This can be explained by the fact that landmarking reduces the moving range of the explorers and decreases the number of active robots, sometimes to the point where all robots were stopped (i.e. were landmarks) whereas victims remained to be found. An example of such situation can be observed in Figure 9(a).

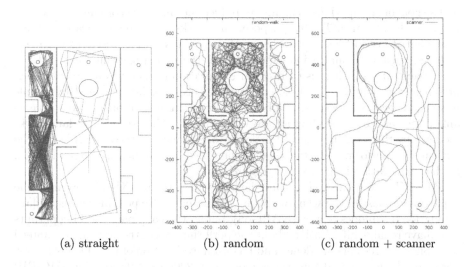

(a) straight   (b) random   (c) random + scanner

Fig. 7. Simulation of a single robot and various moving strategies

strategy:	straight	random	random + scanner			landmark	comm.
number of explorers:	1	1	1	11	21	31	31	31
1st victim ($\alpha=\beta=\delta=0.05$)	343	2996	892	211	188	152	?	375
5th victim ($\alpha=\beta=\delta=0.01$)	timeout	41250	11562	1171	820	742	timeout	1797

Fig. 8. Delays in seconds for finding victims with probability $P=0.85$

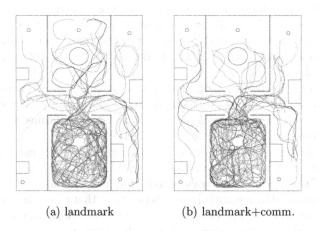

(a) landmark   (b) landmark+comm.

Fig. 9. Simulation of landmarking strategies for 31 explorers

The goal of landmarking is mainly to reduce the time to accomplish the second phase of the scenario. To this purpose, landmarks must communicate with active robots to route them for achieving their goal (exploring, rescuing, etc.). We included basic communication capabilities in the model allowing landmarks to route back robots if there is no need for exploration in their given direction (e.g. presence of a dead end). These communications were implemented by simple binary connectors between the robots. Adding communications allowed acceptable performances for finding all the five victims, while establishing landmarks required by the second phase of the scenario. Simulation traces clearly show the switchbacks performed by the robots when meeting landmarks from which no further exploration is needed (see Figure 9(b)).

SMC-BIP allowed us to fine-tune the behavior of the marXbot to optimize the deployment phase of the scenario. Such fine-tuning is also possible with standard simulation techniques (e.g. with ARGoS), but statistical model-checking permits us to have reliable information about the performances of the swarm, guaranteed by explicit degrees of confidence and based on exploration of possible behaviors. For example, it required sometimes more than 20000 simulations for SMC-BIP to conclude on a single delay value. The BIP model we developed can also be a basis for computing stochastic abstractions and/or for applying verification techniques and tools.

4.3   Collaborating Robots

Our third case study is a robotic application that consists of a set of communicating robots that collaborate to perform a given task. The scenario is described as following: initially, the robots, with blue color, are dispatched in an arena with different positions. They start by exploring the arena in order to find each others. When 3 robots become sufficiently close, they group themselves to form a "V" form and change their color to red. Then, they go towards an object (e.g a ball) which is positioned at the center of the arena, and push it. Finally, the other robots go towards the border of the arena when they "see" the red robots. We assume that the robots are equipped by proximity sensors to detect obstacles (arena's walls and the ball), a camera to detect the robot's colors and a led to change the color.

Our case study is composed of 6 instances of robot. Figure 10 shows the BIP model of a single robot. We used timing constraints and time progress conditions to express timeout when the grouping action cannot be performed within a given amount of time.

The grouping of robots is modeled by a connector that synchronizes group transitions of any 3 robots. The connector enables the interaction between the robots only if they are sufficiently close to each others. As shown in Figure 11 the connector is guarded by a guard on robot's positions that determines if the robots are close to each others. The challenging issue in this application is to come up with distributed implementation that correcly achieves the expected synchronization of three robots. Following [13], instead of writing directly the distributed implementation, we used BIP connectors to express the grouping of three robots

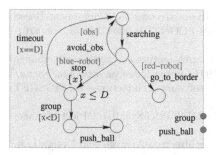

Fig. 10. Model of a single robot.

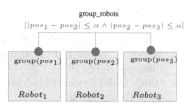

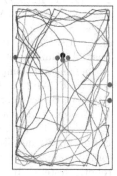

Fig. 11. Synchronization of robots for achieving their grouping.

on high-level models, and were able to generate all the communications needed for its realization at runtime.

In order to make simulations as realistic as possible, we also modeled robot's behavior, such as robot's movement, sensor's reading and camera image processing. Figure 12 presents the simulation results for 6 robots, where the red circles represent the final positions of the robots and the black one represents the ball. It shows that the robots effectively managed to group themselves and push the ball.

Fig. 12. Experimental results for 6 robots.

5   Conclusion

We have presented a rigorous system design flow for timed systems. It is based on the BIP language in which the notion of behavior—expressed a set of components—is clearly separated from the notion of architecture—expressed by interactions and priorities. Correct implementations are obtained by *(i)* checking the design on abstract models using verification tool D-Finder, and *(ii)* refining such models using proven correct source-to-source transformers. In addition, system performances can also be evaluated at design time using statistical model-checker SMC-BIP. In this paper, we showed how this framework was successfully applied to robotics case studies.

As future work, we plan to improve our method for the generation of distributed implementations by considering non perfectly synchronized clocks and disconnected communication networks.

References

1. Halbwachs, N.: Synchronous Programming of Reactive Systems. Kluwer Academic Publishers (1993)
2. Burns, A., Welling, A.: Real-Time Systems and Programming Languages, 3rd edn. Addison-Wesley (2001)

3. Bliudze, S., Sifakis, J.: A Notion of Glue Expressiveness for Component-Based Systems. In: van Breugel, F., Chechik, M. (eds.) CONCUR 2008. LNCS, vol. 5201, pp. 508–522. Springer, Heidelberg (2008)

4. Garlan, D., Monroe, R., Wile, D.: ACME: An architecture description interchange language. In: CASCON 1997, pp. 169–183 (1997), http://www.cs.cmu.edu/~acme/

5. Magee, J., Kramer, J.: Dynamic structure in software architectures. In: SIGSOFT 1996, pp. 3–14 (1996)

6. OMG: OMG Systems Modeling Language SysML (OMG SysML). Object Management Group (2008)

7. Feiler, P.H., Lewis, B., Vestal, S.: The SAE Architecture Analysis and Design Language (AADL) Standard: A basis for model-based architecture-driven embedded systems engineering. In: RTAS Workshop on Model-driven Embedded Systems, pp. 1–10 (2003), http://www.sae.org

8. Eker, J., Janneck, J.W., Lee, E.A., Liu, J., Liu, X., Ludvig, J., Neuendorffer, S., Sachs, S., Xiong, Y.: Taming heterogeneity: The Ptolemy approach. Proceedings of the IEEE 91(1), 127–144 (2003)

9. Basu, A., Gallien, M., Lesire, C., Nguyen, T.H., Bensalem, S., Ingrand, F., Sifakis, J.: Incremental Component-Based Construction and Verification of a Robotic System. In: ECAI 2008. FAIA, vol. 178, pp. 631–635. IOS Press (2008)

10. Basu, A., Bensalem, S., Bozga, M., Combaz, J., Jaber, M., Nguyen, T.-H., Sifakis, J.: Rigorous component-based system design using the bip framework. IEEE Software 28(3), 41–48 (2011)

11. Bensalem, S., de Silva, L., Griesmayer, A., Ingrand, F., Legay, A., Yan, R.: A formal approach for incremental construction with an application to autonomous robotic systems. In: Apel, S., Jackson, E. (eds.) SC 2011. LNCS, vol. 6708, pp. 116–132. Springer, Heidelberg (2011)

12. Abdellatif, T., Combaz, J., Sifakis, J.: Model-based implementation of real-time applications. In: Carloni, L.P., Tripakis, S. (eds.) EMSOFT, pp. 229–238. ACM (2010)

13. Bonakdarpour, B., Bozga, M., Jaber, M., Quilbeuf, J., Sifakis, J.: From high-level component-based models to distributed implementations. In: EMSOFT (2010)

14. Aştefănoaei, L., Ben Rayana, S., Bensalem, S., Bozga, M., Combaz, J.: Compositional invariant generation for timed systems. In: Ábrahám, E., Havelund, K. (eds.) TACAS 2014 (ETAPS). LNCS, vol. 8413, pp. 263–278. Springer, Heidelberg (2014)

15. Intelligent robots for improving the quality of life, http://www.nccr-robotics.ch

16. Bonani, M., Longchamp, V., Magnenat, S., Rétornaz, P., Burnier, D., Roulet, G., Vaussard, F., Bleuler, H., Mondada, F.: The MarXbot, a Miniature Mobile Robot Opening new Perspectives for the Collective-robotic Research. In: International Conference on Intelligent Robots and Systems (IROS), 2010 IEEE/RSJ. IEEE International Conference on Intelligent Robots and Systems, pp. 4187–4193. IEEE Press (2010)

17. Pinciroli, C., Trianni, V., O'Grady, R., Pini, G., Brutschy, A., Brambilla, M., Mathews, N., Ferrante, E., Caro, G.D., Ducatelle, F., Birattari, M., Gambardella, L.M., Dorigo, M.: Argos: a modular, parallel, multi-engine simulator for multi-robot systems. Swarm Intelligence 6(4), 271–295 (2012)

18. Bensalem, S., Bozga, M., Delahaye, B., Jegourel, C., Legay, A., Nouri, A.: Statistical model checking qoS properties of systems with SBIP. In: Margaria, T., Steffen, B. (eds.) ISoLA 2012, Part I. LNCS, vol. 7609, pp. 327–341. Springer, Heidelberg (2012)

Learning Models for Verification and Testing — Special Track at ISoLA 2014 Track Introduction

Falk Howar[1] and Bernhard Steffen[2]

[1] Carnegie Mellon University, Moffett Field, CA, USA
[2] TU Dortmund, Germany

Specifications play an important role in modern-day software engineering research. Formal specifications, e.g., are the basis for automated verification and testing techniques. In spite of their potentially great positive impact, formal specifications are notoriously hard to come by in practice. One reason seems to be that writing precise formal specifications is not an easy task for most of us. As a consequence, e.g., many software systems in use today lack adequate specifications or make use of un/under-specified components. Moreover, in many practical contexts, revision cycle times are often extremely short, which makes the maintenance of formal specifications unrealistic. At the same time, component-based design and short development cycles necessitate extensive testing and verification effort. Problems of this kind are inherent in systems that continuously undergo change as the ones specifically addresses in [16].

Learning-based approaches have been proposed to overcome this situation by automatically 'mining' formal specifications. Promising results have been obtained here using active automata learning technology in verification [15,7] and testing [9,2], and there seems to be a high potential to exploit also other learning techniques [10]. At the same time, active automata learning has been extended to support the inference of program structures [12,6] (it was first introduced for regular languages).

This track aims at bringing together practitioners and researchers in order to explore the practical impact and challenges associated with automated generation and maintenance of formal specifications using learning-based methods. The track continues a series of special tracks focused on the application of automata learning techniques in testing and verification at ISoLA conferences [8,14]. This year's special track has three contributions, focusing on evaluating latest advances in automata learning tools, on the connection between learning and testing, and on using inferred models for the verification of GUI applications.

The first contribution *"Algorithms for Inferring Register Automata — A comparison of existing approaches"* by Fides Aarts, Falk Howar, Harco Kuppens, and Frits Vaandrager [3] (in this volume) presents a repository for benchmarks for active automata learning approaches and evaluates two recent approaches and tools for learning automata with parameterized labels, registers and guards (so-called Register Automata or Scalarset Mealy Machines) on these benchmarks. Register automata extend regular languages and finite state acceptors with data parameters, registers for storing data values and guarded transitions. Such languages and

T. Margaria and B. Steffen (Eds.): ISoLA 2014, Part I, LNCS 8802, pp. 199–201, 2014.
© Springer-Verlag Berlin Heidelberg 2014

models have proven useful for representing (relatively) simple infinite-state systems, where data is passed around but no or only a limited set of operations are allowed on data values, e.g., protocols, and data structures. The presented repository collects a number of models ranging from actual industrial case-studies to manually created and parameterized benchmarks that can be scaled in complexity. The authors compare two recent approaches for inferring register automata (presented in [11,1]) that have been developed independently using these benchmarks.

The second contribution *"Active Learning of Nondeterministic Systems from an ioco Perspective"* by Michele Volpato, and Jan Tretmans [17] (in this volume) explores the connections between test-based modeling and model-based testing. In particular, the authors investigate links between active automata learning and the ioco conformance theory. The authors present an active learning algorithm for non-deterministic labeled transition systems, inferring the so-called suspension automaton representation of a labeled transition system. The authors base their work on the popular L^* algorithm for inferring regular languages [4], which is based on an observation table for storing all information during learning. The paper introduces additional conditions on this observation table. These conditions exploit the structure of *valid* suspension automata and their languages and help reducing the number of tests to be executed on a system under learning.

The third contribution *"Verification of GUI Applications: a Black-Box Approach"* by Stephan Arlt, Evren Ermis, Sergio Feo-Arenis, and Andreas Podelski [5] (in this volume) presents a novel approach to verifying GUI applications: The implementation of the user interface, which oftentimes contains code that would be hard to verify and maybe is not even available as source-code, is replaced by a lean driver program that can simulates the user-interface by sending sequences of events to the underlying application. The (event-driven) application together with the lean driver is then amenable to verification as a first series of experiments shows. The driver program is generated from a model of the (regular) language of events that can be emitted by the user interface. This model, in turn, is inferred using a dynamic analysis (presented in [13]). The work shows nicely how inferred models can be used to aid the verification of reactive systems.

References

1. Aarts, F., Heidarian, F., Kuppens, H., Olsen, P., Vaandrager, F.: Automata learning through counterexample guided abstraction refinement. In: Giannakopoulou, D., Méry, D. (eds.) FM 2012. LNCS, vol. 7436, pp. 10–27. Springer, Heidelberg (2012)
2. Aarts, F., Kuppens, H., Tretmans, G.J., Vaandrager, F.W., Verwer, S.: Learning and testing the bounded retransmission protocol. In: Heinz, J., de la Higuera, C., Oates, T. (eds.) Proceedings 11th International Conference on Grammatical Inference (ICGI 2012), September 5-8. JMLR Workshop and Conference Proceedings, vol. 21, pp. 4–18. University of Maryland, College Park (2012)
3. Aarts, F., Howar, F., Kuppens, H., Vaandrager, F.: Algorithms for inferring register automata: A comparison of existing approaches. In: Margaria, T., Steffen, B. (eds.) ISoLA 2014, Part I. LNCS, vol. 8802, pp. 202–219. Springer, Heidelberg (2014)

4. Angluin, D.: Learning regular sets from queries and counterexamples. Inf. Comput. 75(2), 87–106 (1987)
5. Arlt, S., Ermis, E., Feo-Arenis, S., Podelski, A.: Verification of GUI applications: A black-box approach. In: Margaria, T., Steffen, B. (eds.) ISoLA 2014. LNCS, vol. 8802, pp. 236–252. Springer, Heidelberg (2014)
6. Cassel, S., Howar, F., Jonsson, B., Steffen, B.: Learning extended finite state machines. In: SEFM, pp. 250–264 (2014)
7. Cobleigh, J.M., Giannakopoulou, D., Păsăreanu, C.S.: Learning assumptions for compositional verification. In: Garavel, H., Hatcliff, J. (eds.) TACAS 2003. LNCS, vol. 2619, pp. 331–346. Springer, Heidelberg (2003)
8. Giannakopoulou, D., Păsăreanu, C.S.: Learning techniques for software verification and validation – special track at iSoLA 2010. In: Margaria, T., Steffen, B. (eds.) ISoLA 2010, Part I. LNCS, vol. 6415, pp. 640–642. Springer, Heidelberg (2010)
9. Hagerer, A., Hungar, H.: Model generation by moderated regular extrapolation. In: Kutsche, R.-D., Weber, H. (eds.) FASE 2002. LNCS, vol. 2306, pp. 80–95. Springer, Heidelberg (2002)
10. Hähnle, R., Knoop, J., Margaria, T., Schreiner, D., Steffen, B. (eds.): ISoLA 2011 Workshops 2011. CCIS, vol. 336. Springer, Heidelberg (2012)
11. Howar, F., Steffen, B., Jonsson, B., Cassel, S.: Inferring canonical register automata. In: Kuncak, V., Rybalchenko, A. (eds.) VMCAI 2012. LNCS, vol. 7148, pp. 251–266. Springer, Heidelberg (2012)
12. Isberner, M., Howar, F., Steffen, B.: Learning register automata: from languages to program structures. Machine Learning 96(1-2), 65–98 (2014)
13. Memon, A., Banerjee, I., Nagarajan, A.: Gui ripping: Reverse engineering of graphical user interfaces for testing. In: Proceedings of the 10th Working Conference on Reverse Engineering, WCRE 2003, p. 260. IEEE Computer Society, Washington, DC (2003)
14. Păsăreanu, C.S., Bobaru, M.: Learning techniques for software verification and validation. In: Margaria, T., Steffen, B. (eds.) ISoLA 2012, Part I. LNCS, vol. 7609, pp. 505–507. Springer, Heidelberg (2012)
15. Peled, D., Vardi, M.Y., Yannakakis, M.: Black Box Checking. Journal of Automata, Languages, and Combinatorics 7(2), 225–246 (2002)
16. Steffen, B.: LNCS transaction on foundations for mastering change: Preliminary manifesto. In: Margaria, T., Steffen, B. (eds.) ISoLA 2014. LNCS, vol. 8802, pp. 514–517. Springer, Heidelberg (2014)
17. Volpato, M., Tretmans, J.: Active learning of nondeterministic systems from an ioco perspective. In: Margaria, T., Steffen, B. (eds.) ISoLA 2014. LNCS, vol. 8802, pp. 220–235. Springer, Heidelberg (2014)

Algorithms for Inferring Register Automata
A Comparison of Existing Approaches*

Fides Aarts[1], Falk Howar[2], Harco Kuppens[1], and Frits Vaandrager[1]

[1] Institute for Computing and Information Sciences, Radboud University Nijmegen
P.O. Box 9010, 6500 GL Nijmegen, The Netherlands
[2] Carnegie Mellon University, Moffett Field, CA, USA

Abstract. In recent years, two different approaches for learning register automata have been developed: as part of the LearnLib tool algorithms have been implemented that are based on the Nerode congruence for register automata, whereas the Tomte tool implements algorithms that use counterexample-guided abstraction refinement to automatically construct appropriate mappers. In this paper, we compare the LearnLib and Tomte approaches on a newly defined set of benchmarks and highlight their differences and respective strengths.

1 Introduction

Model-driven engineering (MDE) is attracting a lot of attention since it appears to be a software development methodology that can control the increasing complexity of computer-based systems. In the MDE approach, the main objects of the software system being developed are represented at a higher level of abstraction using models. Model checking and automata learning are two core techniques in MDE. In model checking [15] one explores the state space of a given state transition model, whereas in automata learning [32,20] the goal is to obtain such a model through interaction with a software component by providing inputs and observing outputs. Both techniques face a combinatorial blow up of the state-space, commonly known as the state explosion problem. In order to find new techniques to combat this problem, it makes sense to follow a cyclic research methodology in which tools are applied to challenging applications, the experience gained during this work is used to generate new theory and algorithms, which in turn are used to further improve the tools. Consistent application of this methodology for 25 years has led to a situation in which model checking is applied routinely to industrial problems [18]. Work on the use of automata learning in MDE started much later [30] and has not yet reached the same maturity level yet, but in recent years there has been tremendous progress.

* The work of Aarts, Kuppens and Vaandrager was supported by STW project 11763 ITALIA: Integrating Testing And Learning of Interface Automata.

T. Margaria and B. Steffen (Eds.): ISoLA 2014, Part I, LNCS 8802, pp. 202–219, 2014.
© Springer-Verlag Berlin Heidelberg 2014

We have seen, for instance, several convincing applications of automata learning in the area of security and network protocols. Cho et al. [14] successfully used automata learning to infer models of communication protocols used by botnets. Automata learning was used for fingerprinting of EMV banking cards by Aarts et al. [8]. It also revealed a security vulnerability in a smartcard reader for internet banking that was previously discovered by manual analysis, and confirmed the absence of this flaw in an updated version of this device [13]. Fiterau et al. [16] used automata learning to demonstrate that both Linux and Windows violate the TCP protocol standard. Using a similar approach, Tijssen [33] showed that implementations of the Secure Shell (SSH) protocol violate the standard. In [31] automata learning is used to infer properties of a network router, and for testing the security of a web-application (the Mantis bug-tracker). The first application of learning in testing was presented in 2002 in [19]: the authors use generated models for testing a telephony system.

In many of these applications, an intermediate component or mapper is placed in between the implementation and the learning tool. This mapper takes care of abstracting (in a history dependent manner) the large set of (parametrized) actions of the implementation into a small set of abstract actions that can be handled by automate learning algorithms for finite state systems [10,32]. The fact that these mappers need to be constructed manually is unsatisfactory. A major theoretical challenge therefore is to lift learning algorithms for finite state systems to richer classes of models involving data. A recent breakthrough has been the definition of a Nerode congruence for the class of register automata [11] and the resulting generalization of learning algorithms to this class [23,22,2,1]. Register automata are a type of extended finite state machines in which one can test for equality of data parameters, but no operations on data are allowed. This notion of a scalarset data type originates from model checking, where it has been used for symmetry reduction [24] (hence register automata are called scalarset Mealy machines in [2,1]). The results on register automata have been generalized to even larger classes of models in [12], where the guards can be arithmetic constraints and inequalities.

In recent years, two different approaches for learning register automata have been developed. As part of the LearnLib tool algorithms have been implemented that are based on the Nerode congruence [23,22], whereas the Tomte tool implements algorithms that use counterexample-guided abstraction refinement to automatically construct an appropriate mapper [2,1]. The goal of this paper is to compare these two approaches. To this end we have developed an open exchange format for automata, and set up a repository with benchmarks[1], which will also allow to compare other tools and approaches in the future.

The rest of this paper is organized as follows. Section 2 recalls basic definitions of Mealy machines, register automata, and automata learning. Sections 3 and 4 present an overview of the approaches implemented by the Tomte and LearnLib tools. Finally, Section 5 presents and discusses the experimental evaluation of both tools.

---

[1] http://www.github.org/learnlib/raxml

2 Learning Register Automata

In this section, we recall the definition of register automata, their semantics in terms of Mealy machines, and the assumed learning model. *Register automata*, also known as *scalarset Mealy machines*, are an extension of Mealy machines with data. No operations are allowed on data and the only predicate symbol that may be used is equality.

Register Automata. We assume universes $\mathcal{V}$ of *variables* and $\mathcal{P}$ of *parameters*, with $\mathcal{V} \cap \mathcal{P} = \emptyset$. A *valuation* for a set $X \subseteq \mathcal{V} \cup \mathcal{P}$ is a partial function ξ from X to a set $\mathcal{D}$ of *data values*. We write $\mathsf{Val}(X)$ for the set of valuations for X. We also assume a set C of *constants*, disjoint from $\mathcal{V} \cup \mathcal{P}$, and a function $\gamma : C \to \mathcal{D}$ that assigns a value to each constant. We write $\mathcal{T} = \mathcal{V} \cup \mathcal{P} \cup C$ and refer to elements of $\mathcal{T}$ as *terms*.

A *guard* g is a Boolean combination of expressions of the form $t = t'$, where $t, t' \in \mathcal{T}$. We write $\mathcal{G}$ for the set of guards. If ξ is a valuation for X and g is a guard with variables and parameters from X, then we write $\xi \models g$ to denote that ξ satisfies g.

We assume a set E of *event primitives* and a function $\mathsf{arity} : E \to \mathbb{N}$ that assigns to each event primitive an arity. An *event term* for ε is an expression $\varepsilon(t_1, \ldots, t_n)$ where $t_1, \ldots, t_n \in \mathcal{T}$ and $n = \mathsf{arity}(\varepsilon)$. We write $\mathcal{ET}$ for the set of event terms.

Definition 1. *A register automaton (RA) is a tuple* $\mathcal{S} = \langle E_I, E_O, V, L, l_0, \Gamma \rangle$, *where*

- $E_I, E_O \subseteq E$ *are disjoint sets of event primitives,*
- $V \subseteq \mathcal{V}$ *is a finite set of state variables,*
- L *is a finite set of locations,*
- $l_0 \in L$ *is the initial location,*
- $\Gamma \subseteq L \times \mathcal{ET} \times \mathcal{G} \times (V \to \mathcal{T}) \times \mathcal{ET} \times L$ *is a finite set of transitions. For each transition* $\langle l, \varepsilon_I(p_1, \ldots, p_k), g, \varrho, \varepsilon_O(u_1, \ldots, u_n), l' \rangle \in \Gamma$, *we refer to* l *as the* source, g *as the* guard, ϱ *as the* update, *and* l' *as the* target. *We require* $\varepsilon_I \in E_I$, $p_1, \ldots, p_k$ *pairwise different parameters in* $\mathcal{P}$, $\varepsilon_O \in E_O$, *and* g, $\varrho(v)$, *for any* $v \in V$, *and* $\varepsilon_O(u_1, \ldots, u_n)$ *only contain terms from* $V \cup \{p_1, \ldots, p_k\} \cup C$.

Example 1. As a running example of a register automaton we use a FIFO-set with a capacity of two, similar to the one presented in [22]. A FIFO-set corresponds to a queue in which only different values can be stored, see Figure 1. There are a Push(p) input that tries to insert a value in the set and a Pop() input that tries to retrieve a value from the set. The output in response to a Push(p) input is OK if p could be added successfully or NOK if p is already an element of the set or if the set is full. The output in response to a Pop() input is Out(x), where x is the first value that has been added to the set and not been returned, or NOK if the set is empty.

The semantics of a register automaton can be defined in terms of Mealy machines.

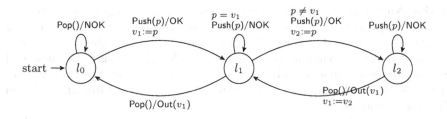

Fig. 1. FIFO-set with a capacity of 2 modeled as a register automaton

Definition 2. *A Mealy machine is a tuple* $\mathcal{M} = \langle I, O, Q, q_0, \rightarrow \rangle$, *where* I, O, *and* Q *are nonempty sets of input symbols, output symbols, and states, respectively,* $q_0 \in Q$ *is the initial state, and* $\rightarrow \subseteq Q \times I \times O \times Q$ *is the transition relation. We write* $q \xrightarrow{i/o} q'$ *if* $(q, i, o, q') \in \rightarrow$, *and* $q \xrightarrow{i/o}$ *if there exists a* q' *such that* $q \xrightarrow{i/o} q'$. *Mealy machines are assumed to be* input enabled: *for each state* q *and input* i, *there exists an output* o *such that* $q \xrightarrow{i/o}$. *A Mealy machine is* deterministic *if for each state* q *and input symbol* i *there is exactly one output symbol* o *and exactly one state* q' *such that* $q \xrightarrow{i/o} q'$.

The transition relation is extended to finite sequences by defining $\overset{u/s}{\Rightarrow}$ to be the least relation that satisfies, $q \overset{\epsilon/\epsilon}{\Rightarrow} q$, and for $u \in I^*$, $s \in O^*$, $i \in I$, and $o \in O$, $q \xrightarrow{i/o} q'$ and $q' \overset{u/s}{\Rightarrow} q''$ implies $q \overset{i\,u/o\,s}{\Rightarrow} q''$. Here ϵ denotes the empty sequence.

The semantics of a register automaton is a Mealy machine. The states of this Mealy machine are pairs of a location l and a valuation ξ of the state variables. A transition may fire if its guard, which may contain both state variables and parameters of the input action, evaluates to true. Then a new valuation of the state variables is computed using the update part of the transition. This new valuation, together with the values of the input parameters, also determines the values of the output parameters.

Definition 3 (Semantics RA). *The semantics of an event primitive* $\varepsilon \in E$ *is the set* $[\![\varepsilon]\!] = \{\varepsilon(d_1, \ldots, d_{\mathsf{arity}(\varepsilon)}) \mid d_i \in \mathcal{D}, 1 \leq i \leq \mathsf{arity}(\varepsilon)\}$. *The semantics of a set of event primitives is defined by pointwise extension.*

Let $\mathcal{S} = \langle E_I, E_O, V, L, l_0, \Gamma \rangle$ *be a RA. The semantics of* $\mathcal{S}$, *denoted* $[\![\mathcal{S}]\!]$, *is the Mealy machine* $\langle I, O, Q, q_0, \rightarrow \rangle$, *where* $I = [\![E_I]\!]$, $O = [\![E_O]\!]$, $Q = L \times \mathsf{Val}(V)$, $q_0 = (l_0, \xi_0)$, *with* $\xi_0(v)$ *undefined for all* v, *and* $\rightarrow \subseteq Q \times I \times O \times Q$ *is given by the rule*

$$\frac{\langle l, \varepsilon_I(p_1, \ldots, p_k), g, \varrho, \varepsilon_O(u_1, \ldots, u_n), l' \rangle \in \Gamma \quad \forall i \leq k, \iota(p_i) = d_i \quad \xi \cup \iota \models g \quad \xi' = (\xi \cup \gamma \cup \iota) \circ \varrho \quad \forall i \leq n, (\xi \cup \gamma \cup \iota)(u_i) = d_i'}{(l, \xi) \xrightarrow{\varepsilon_I(d_1, \ldots, d_k)/\varepsilon_O(d_1', \ldots, d_n')} (l', \xi')}$$

We call a RA $\mathcal{S}$ deterministic if its semantics $[\![\mathcal{S}]\!]$ is deterministic.

Active Automata Learning. Active automata learning algorithms have originally been presented for inferring finite state acceptors for unknown regular languages [10]. Since then these algorithms have become popular with the testing and verification communities for inferring models of systems in an automated fashion. Active automata learning has been extended to many classes of systems, including Mealy Machines [29], I/O-Automata [7], Timed Automata [17], and Register Automata.

While the details change for concrete classes of systems, all of these algorithms follow basically the same pattern. They model the learning process as a game between a learner and a teacher. The learner has to infer an unknown concept with the help of the teacher. The learner can ask three types of queries to the teacher:

Output Queries (or membership queries) ask for the expected output for a concrete sequence of inputs. In practice, output queries can be realized as simple tests.

Reset queries prompt the teacher to reset its current state to the initial state and are typically asked in turn with a sequence of output queries.

Equivalence Queries check whether a conjectured model produced by the learner is correct. In case the model is not correct, the teacher provides a counterexample, a trace exposing a difference between the conjecture and the expected behavior of the system to be learned. Equivalence queries are approximated through testing in black-box scenarios.

A learning algorithm will use these three kinds of queries and produce a sequence of models converging towards the correct one. We skip further details here and refer the interested reader to [32,25] for an introduction to active automata learning.

3   Tomte

Tomte implements the approach to inferring Register Mealy Machines presented in [2,1]. Figure 2 presents the overall architecture of the Tomte tool. At the right we see the *System Under Learning (SUL)*, an implementation whose behavior can be described by an (unknown) deterministic register automaton. We send parametrized input symbols to the SUL via port 3 and receive parametrized output symbols via port 4. Via port 3 we can also reset the SUL. At the left we see the *learner*, which is a tool for learning regular Mealy machines. In our current implementation we use LearnLib, but any other tool for learning Mealy machines can be used instead. The learner sends output queries and test sequences (as approximation of equivalence queries) via port 1 and receives the resulting outputs via port 6. In between the learner and the teacher we place two auxiliary components, a mapper and a lookahead oracle, which take care of mapping the large set of concrete symbols of the SUL to a small set of abstract symbols that can be handled by the learner. Whereas the lookahead oracle annotates events with information about the future behavior of the SUL, the mapper computes

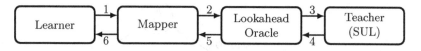

Fig. 2. Architecture of Tomte

an abstraction for each event based on information about the past. The behavior of the two components is thus reminiscent of the prophecy and history variables of Abadi & Lamport [9].

3.1   Lookahead Oracle

The *lookahead oracle* is a component that stores traces of the SUL in a so-called *observation tree*. The observation tree can be used as a cache for repeated queries on the SUL. However, the main task of the lookahead oracle is to annotate each node in the observation tree with a set of *memorable values*. Intuitively, a parameter value d is memorable if it has an impact on the future behavior of the SUL: either d occurs in a future output, or a future output depends on the equality of d and a future input.

Definition 4. *Let S be a register automaton with $[\![S]\!] = \langle I, O, Q, q_0, \rightarrow \rangle$. Suppose $q_0 \overset{u/s}{\Rightarrow} q$ and d is a parameter value that occurs in u and that is not denoted by any constant ($\forall c \in C : \gamma(c) \neq d$). Then d is* memorable *after u iff there exists a witness transition $q \overset{v/t}{\Rightarrow}$, such that either d occurs in output t but not in input v, or d occurs in input v and if we replace all occurrences of d in v with a fresh value f then the output changes, i.e., $q \overset{v[f/d]/t'}{\Rightarrow}$ with $t' \neq t[f/d]$.*

In our running example of Figure 1, the set of memorable values after input sequence $u = \mathsf{Push}(0)\ \mathsf{Push}(1)\ \mathsf{Push}(2)$ is $\{0, 1\}$. Values 0 and 1 are memorable, because the suffix $v = \mathsf{Pop}()\ \mathsf{Pop}()$ triggers outputs $\mathsf{Out}(0)\ \mathsf{Out}(1)$. Value 2 is not memorable since the future behavior of the FIFO-set does not depend on it. Figure 3 shows an observation tree for our FIFO-set example. Whenever a new node is added to the tree, the oracle computes a set of memorable values for it. To this end, the oracle maintains a set of *lookahead traces*, i.e., sequences of (symbolic) inputs. Instances of each these traces are run in each new node to compute memorable values. At any point in time, the set of computed values is a subset of the set of memorable values of a node. The observation tree of Figure 3 is not lookahead complete since (for instance) memorable value 1 of node N_6 is neither part of the memorable values of the predecessor node N_3 nor has it been inserted via the incoming $\mathsf{Pop}()$ input. Whenever we detect such an incompleteness, we add a new lookahead trace (in this case $\mathsf{Pop}()\ \mathsf{Pop}()$) and restart the entire learning process with the updated set of lookahead traces to retrieve a lookahead-complete observation tree.

When the oracle receives an input symbol from the mapper via port 2 this is just forwarded to the SUL via port 3. When the lookahead oracle receives a

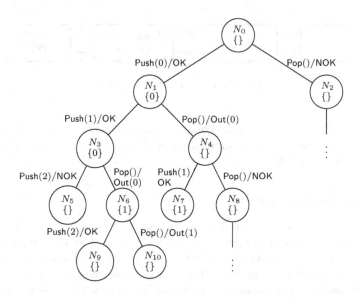

Fig. 3. Observation tree of the FIFO-set

concrete output symbol o from the SUL via port 4 (see Figure 2), it forwards a pair consisting of o and a valuation ξ to the mapper via port 5. The valuation ξ assigns to each variable in a given set of variables X either a value that is memorable in the node after o, or the undefined value $\bot$. (The set X grows dynamically: its size is equal to the largest set of memorable values in the observation tree.)

3.2   Mapper

Following the theory elaborated in [3,4], the mapper component transforms the concrete inputs and outputs from the lookahead oracle into abstract inputs in a history dependent manner. The mapper remembers the most recent valuation from the variables in X that it has received from the lookahead oracle. The mapper is parametrized by a function $F : P \to 2^{X \cup C \cup P}$. The abstraction does not record the actual value of an input parameter, but only whether or not this value is equal to one of the variables, constants or parameters in $F(p)$. Thus the domain of the abstract parameter p is the set $F(p) \cup \{\bot\}$. Initially, $F(p) = \emptyset$ for all parameters p. Using a counterexample-guided abstraction approach, the sets $F(p)$ are subsequently extended. Upon receipt of a concrete output action (o, ξ) from the lookahead oracle via port 5, the mapper component forgets the actual value of parameters in o and only records whether a value is equal to one of the variables, constants or parameters in $V \cup C \cup P$. The valuation ξ is abstracted to an update function that specifies how ξ can be computed from the mapper state and the parameters of the preceding input. The abstract output pair is then send to the learner via port 6, When the mapper receives an abstract input from the learner via port 1, it computes a corresponding concrete input and forwards it to the lookahead oracle via port 2. During learning the abstract parameter value $\perp$ is always concretized as a fresh value.

As a result of interaction with the mapper, the learner succeeds to construct the abstract hypothesis shown in Figure 4. (We refer to [1] for a discussion of how a concrete register automaton can be obtained from an abstract hypothesis.)

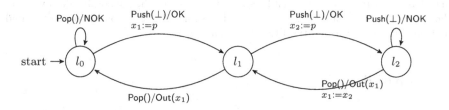

Fig. 4. First hypothesis of the FIFO-set

3.3 Counterexample Analysis

This hypothesis does not check if the same value is inserted twice since the mapper only uses fresh values in the output queries. During hypothesis verification the mapper selects random values from a small range for every abstract parameter value $\perp$. In this way it will find a concrete counterexample input trace, e.g. Pop() Push(9) Pop() Push(3) Push(3), for which the SUL produces a NOK output and the hypothesis generates an OK. In order to simplify the analysis, Tomte first tries to reduce the length of the counterexample. Long sequences of inputs typically lead to loops when you run them in the hypothesis. Tomte eliminates these loops and checks if the result is still a counterexample. Removing cycles from the concrete counterexample results in the reduced counterexample Push(3) Push(3). To determine if it is a counterexample for the learner, we convert the reduced concrete counterexample into a fresh trace Push(1) Push(2) and run it on the SUL via the lookahead oracle. The concrete outputs returned by the SUL are OK OK. Since, after abstraction, the outputs of the fresh trace are also produced by the abstract hypothesis, Tomte needs to refine the input abstraction.

By careful analysis of the counterexample, Tomte discovers that apparently it is relevant whether or not parameter p is equal to variable x_1. Therefore, the set $F(p)$ is extended to $\{x_1\}$. Consequently, the alphabet of the learner is extended with a new input symbol Push(x_1) and a corresponding lookahead trace is added to the lookahead oracle. Again, the entire learning process is restarted from scratch. The next hypothesis learned is equivalent to the model in Figure 1 and the learning algorithm stops.

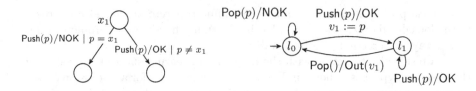

Fig. 5. Left: SDT for concrete prefix Push(1)/OK and abstract suffix Push(p). The SDT has one register at the initial location at the top for the memorable data value of the prefix and two guarded transitions for the suffix. Right: Second hypothesis found by LearnLib when learning the FIFO-set from Fig. 1.

4 LearnLib

LearnLib implements the approach to inferring Register Automata and Register Mealy Machines presented in [23,22]. In the recent past, LearnLib has been generalized to learning systems, where the guards can be simple arithmetic constraints and inequalities [12]. The conceptual basis for this extension was a reformulation of the original algorithms. Technical basis of the implementation in LearnLib are so-called symbolic decision trees (SDTs), which can be used to summarize the results of many tests using a concise symbolic representation — similar to execution trees obtained by symbolic execution [26]. While we evaluate the version of LearnLib that infers Register Mealy Machines, we provide an overview of the central ideas of inferring Register Automata with LearnLib in the more intuitive terms of our more recent work. However, the description we give here is faithful to the work of [22].

Symbolic Decision Trees. Active automata learning algorithms usually rely on the Nerode relation [28] for identifying the states and transitions of a learned automaton. Two words lead to the same state if their residual languages coincide. When extending LearnLib to Register Automata, the basic idea of the approach was to formulate a Nerode-like congruence for RAs, which would serve to determine locations, transitions, and registers of the inferred automaton.

The central observation for such a relation is that it is not sufficient anymore to consider only concrete words and data values. Take for example the FIFO-set from Fig. 1. While after prefixes Push(1)/OK and Push(2)/OK the concrete input Push(1) will lead to different outputs (NOK and OK, respectively), we still want both prefixes to lead to the same location in a learned automaton. Using the classic Nerode relation, we would introduce a location for every concrete prefix Push(d) with $d \in \mathcal{D}$.

We mitigate this problem by treating the relevant (so-called *memorable*) data values of a prefix in a symbolic fashion: We introduce abstract suffixes (sequences of actions with symbolic data parameters) and corresponding symbolic decision trees (SDT)s. Formally, SDTs can be understood as (partial) Register Automata where L and Γ form a tree rooted at l_0. Fig. 5 (left) shows an SDT for the concrete prefix $push(1)$/OK and the abstract suffix Push(p) (with symbolic data

Prefixes	SDTs for Pop()	Memorables
(l_0) $\qquad\qquad\qquad\qquad \lambda$	$\bigcirc\!\longrightarrow\!\bigcirc$ Pop()/NOK	
(l_1) $\qquad\qquad\qquad$ Push(1)/OK	$\underset{x_1}{\bigcirc\!\longrightarrow\!\bigcirc}$ Pop()/Out(x_1)	$x_1 = 1$
Push(1)/OK Push(2)/OK	$\underset{x_1}{\bigcirc\!\longrightarrow\!\bigcirc}$ Pop()/Out(x_1)	$x_1 = 1$
$\cdots$	$\cdots$	

Fig. 6. Observation table for hypothesis in the right of Fig. 5. Rows are labeled by concrete prefixes. The only column is for the abstract suffix Pop(). The second and third prefix lead to the same location. To the right, rows are labeled by initial values (from prefixes) for registers of SDTs.

value p). The tree encodes the relation of the data value of the prefix symbolically for all p through a register at the root location (x_1) and using guarded transitions. The SDT for $push(2)/OK$ would look identical. Except it would store the concrete value 2 in x_1.

Symbolic decision trees can be constructed from output queries and reset queries in two steps. First, we create test cases for all possible equalities between data values in a prefix and a suffix. In the case of the above example there would only be two tests, Push(1) Push(2) and Push(1) Push(1). However, in general constructing an SDT requires exponentially many (in the number of parameters of the suffix) reset queries and output queries. In a second step, we describe all tests and results symbolically in a detailed tree and merge compatible paths of the trees until only the relevant guards remain.

Conjectures. As noted before, active learning algorithms usually maintain two sets of words: a prefix-closed set of words that covers all transitions of an inferred automaton and a set of suffixes, identifying the states reached by prefixes. We follow this pattern and use sequences with concrete data values as prefixes, and SDTs for abstract suffixes to identify locations, and registers: Symbolic decision trees provide a basis for formulating a congruence on the set of data words [11]. Additionally, SDTs provide information about the data values of a prefix that have to be stored by an automaton (the ones referred to by the initial registers of an SDT).

Fig. 6 shows an observation table, storing the information obtained from output queries during learning. Rows are labeled with prefixes, the only column with SDTs is for the abstract suffix Pop(). In the right-most column we show which memorable values have to be stored to obtain the SDTs. From an observation table we can generate a hypothesis once certain consistency requirements are met (cf. [23]). In this particular case, the model shown in the right of Fig. 5 can be generated from the observation table: Prefixes in the upper part of the table identify locations (the SDTs for these rows are unique). All prefixes (except the empty word λ) correspond to transitions. The only word shown from the lower part of the table, e.g., corresponds to the Push()-loop at l_1. The initial registers of the decision trees are used to obtain the assignments of the Register Automaton; the assignment $v_1 := p$ on the transition from l_0 to l_1 is derived from the SDT and memorable values in the second row of the table.

The sets of prefixes and suffixes are extended when the consistency requirements on the table are violated or when a counterexample is processed.

Counterexamples. Counterexamples exhibit a difference between the current hypothesis of the learning algorithm and the observable behavior of the system under learning. They contain information about how and where a hypothesis is not valid. Counterexamples can show that two prefixes that currently lead to the same location are not equivalent (under the assumed relabeling of registers). In some cases this leads to a new location. They can also show that the hypothesis is missing a guarded transition, or that it is missing a register. The main challenges when analyzing counterexamples are (a) identifying the exact location of the hypothesis which has to be split, or extended by a new register or transition, and (b) deciding which of the three cases applies.

In order to find the exact location, we exchange prefixes of the counterexample by corresponding words from the set of prefixes from the upper part of the observation table (i.e., words that were used to represent the location reached by the prefix). For an exchanged prefix we check if the SDT for the remaining abstract (!) suffix of the counterexample contains a counterexample. If this is the case, we can use the replaced prefix, which corresponds to a fix location in the hypothesis.

Replacing prefixes is continued until we either find that one of the constructed SDTs (i) has an initial guard that is not present in the hypothesis, or (ii) has an initial register that is not identified by the observation table, or (iii) until at some point the SDT for the replaced prefix and remaining abstract suffix does not contain a counterexample anymore. In the first and second case, we extend the table with a new prefix or suffix, respectively. The third case indicates that two prefixes lead to different states (one SDT contains a counterexample while the next one does not). In this case we also add a suffix to the table. The technical details are, of course, a little bit more intricate than discussed here. In-depth discussions can be found in [23,12].

We limit ourselves to a small example for case (ii) here. The intermediate hypothesis shown in the right of Fig. 5 for the FIFO-set from Fig. 1 is missing (among other things) the Push(p)-transition from l_1 that is guarded by $p = v_1$. This is because initially LearnLib adds only words without new equalities to the observation table. The counterexample Push(1)/OK Push(1)/NOK would reveal the missing transition: The SDT for prefix Push(1)/OK and suffix Push(p) is shown in Fig. 5. It has two guarded initial transitions. Adding the word Push(1)/OK Push(1)/NOK to the observation table will refine the hypothesis accordingly. Please note, that while in this small example the word we add to the set of prefixes coincides with the counterexample, this is not the case usually.

Table 1. Benchmarks.

Name	Inputs/ Outputs	Registers	Con- stants	States	Tran- sitions	Source
Biometric passport	9/2	0	3	5	48	[1,2,6]
Session initiation protocol	4/7	2	0	10	48	[1,2,4]
Alternating bit protocol sender	3/3	1	2	7	27	[1,2]
Alternating bit protocol receiver	2/3	0	2	4	10	[1,2]
Alternating bit protocol channel	3/3	2	0	2	6	[1,2]
Login procedure	3/2	2	0	3	10	[1,2,23]
River crossing puzzle	1/4	0	4	9	45	[1,2]
Palindrome/repnumber checker	5/2	0	0	1	10	[1,2]
Queue/stack(n)	2/3	n	0	$n+1$	$2n+2$	[1,22,25]
FIFO-set(n)	2/3	n	0	$n+1$	$3n+1$	[1,22]

Discussion. Since the approach taken by LearnLib is based on an extended Nerode relation, it comes with nice guarantees: for a perfect equivalence oracle, the learning algorithm will terminate with the smallest (in terms of locations and number of registers) correct Register Automaton of a given form. The number of transitions may not be minimal since LearnLib uses multiple transitions for encoding disjunctions. Also, the introduction of SDTs and abstract suffixes has proven to be a powerful conceptual framework that scales beyond simple register automata.

The guarantees and conceptual power, however, come at a price. Computing SDTs from tests is expensive. It requires to exhaustively explore all possible equalities between data values in a prefix and a suffix. Especially, long counterexamples, which in turn may lead to long suffixes, can incur many tests quickly as the evaluation shows (cf. Section 5).

5 Comparison and Evaluation

The LearnLib tool [27] and the Tomte tool [2,1] implement quite similar algorithms for fully automatically inferring large or infinite-state systems. Therefore, it is worthwhile to examine the differences between both tools in more detail. Both tools have been developed independently of each other, but by mutual agreement a standardized XML format has been introduced, which is supported by both tools. This did not affect the framework or inner workings of the tools. They still reveal a number of differences, which will be evaluated and discussed in the remainder of this section.

We evaluate the tools on the benchmarks shown in Table 1. The table specifies the complexity of the different benchmarks in terms of the size of the input and output alphabet as well as the number of registers, constants, Mealy machine states, and Mealy machine transitions. The source column lists work, where these benchmarks have been used previously in the context of automata learning.

Table 2. Results for experiments with random testing

	Learnlib						Tomte					
	learn res	learn inp	test res	test inp	ana res	ana inp	learn res	learn inp	test res	test inp	ana res	ana inp
Alternating bit protocol sender												
avg	452	2368	1217	23872	40551	405577	465	2459	3	26	7	15
stddev	453	2781	973	19424	125904	1258919	0	2	2	28	4	11
Alternating bit protocol receiver												
avg	6077	102788	17	278	72	1420	271	1168	6	68	19	56
stddev	13184	245291	9	176	57	2813	1	0	4	67	4	13
Biometric passport												
avg	914	8517	4209	83761	365	7768	8769	43371	660	13164	55	287
stddev	614	12089	2271	45568	112	4334	5	35	492	9839	7	56
Alternating bit protocol channel												
avg	52	252	2	13	29	173	67	210	0	0	0	0
stddev	29	235	2	9	12	115	0	0	0	0	0	0
Login procedure												
avg	2968	34922	21	366	21	82	3769	19586	117	2072	53	230
stddev	7959	102706	19	396	8	73	0	0	136	2564	19	81
Palindrome/repnumber checker												
avg	5	5	59	1079	2050	8032	8366	24713	249	4502	80	139
stddev	0	0	28	599	6225	24909	4	9	129	2464	14	27
Session initiation protocol												
avg	92324	1962160	129	2486	106868	1178964	6195	39754	236	4535	256	1568
stddev	137990	4078104	127	2579	336225	3696587	1103	7857	210	4251	94	626
River crossing puzzle												
avg	unable to learn						2078	14121	112	2089	100	621
stddev							73	674	56	1174	23	244

The upper part of the table contains models that have been inferred from actual systems, the middle part refers to systems we have modeled ourselves, and the lower part comprises manually written specifications of data structures with a capacity of n.

We performed experiments with two different types of equivalence oracles. The first (realistic but imperfect) oracle uses random test case generation. Both tools implement a random walk over the hypothesis that will generate at most 10,000 runs per equivalence query. Every run has a maximum length of 100 inputs, and is ended with a probability of 5% after every input. This produces an exponential distribution on the length of runs (cut off at length 100). Data values of new inputs are instantiated using values from the prefix and a fresh value with equal probability. Additionally, we have performed experiments with a perfect equivalence oracle, providing shortest counterexamples. In realistic applications of our tools, such an oracle does not exist since we do not have access to a model of the SUL, but since we have models of all our benchmarks, a perfect equivalence oracle can be implemented simply using an equivalence algorithm for Mealy machines. The two equivalence oracles reflect different usage scenarios: While Tomte is geared towards testing and has been used very successfully in testing (e.g., [5]), LearnLib was designed and used to provide guarantees up to some depth in exhaustive exploration [12] (similar to interface generation in a white-box scenario [21]).

For the experiments we used the perfect equivalence oracle in order to determine when to stop learning. We have run each experiment ten times with

Table 3. Results for experiments with a perfect equivalence oracle

	Learnlib				Tomte			
	learn res	learn inp	ana res	ana inp	learn res	learn inp	ana res	ana inp
Alternating bit protocol sender								
avg	181	794	7412	131082	465	2461	5	8
stddev	0	0	0	0	0	0	0	0
Alternating bit protocol receiver								
avg	240	856	14	32	272	1168	21	62
stddev	0	0	0	0	0	0	0	0
Biometric passport								
avg	474	1944	88	471	8764	43347	37	168
stddev	0	0	0	0	0	0	0	0
Alternating bit protocol channel								
avg	13	25	7	13	67	210	0	0
stddev	0	0	0	0	0	0	0	0
Login procedure								
avg	273	991	5	10	3771	19586	139	644
stddev	0	0	0	0	0	0	0	0
Palindrome/repnumber checker								
avg	5	5	52	52	8370	24719	88	150
stddev	0	0	0	0	0	0	0	0
Session initiation protocol								
avg	621	2585	39	139	5460	33002	101	467
stddev	0	0	0	0	0	0	0	0
River crossing puzzle								
avg	7344	48990	41	184	2042	13791	47	225
stddev	0	0	0	0	0	0	0	0

different seeds. For every experiment we have measured the following data and determined its average over the ten runs together with the standard deviation:

- **learn res**: total number of reset queries sent to SUL during learning
- **learn inp**: total number of output queries sent to SUL during learning
- **test res**: total number of reset queries sent to SUL during equivalence testing
- **test inp**: total number of concrete input symbols sent to SUL during equivalence testing (without last test, where no counterexample has been found)
- **ana res**: total number of reset queries sent to SUL during counterexample analysis
- **ana inp**: total number of concrete input symbols sent to SUL during counterexample analysis

We also measured the time of our experiments, but we do not mention these numbers in our learning statistics as in our opinion the other measures are more relevant. Also, due to space limitations, we present only a selection of results in this paper. The complete set of benchmarks and the complete results can be found online[2].

Series 1. First, we have employed both tools to execute the benchmarks in the upper and middle part of Table 1. The learning results with a random walk and perfect equivalence oracle (shortest counterexamples) are displayed in Tables 2 and 3, respectively.

---

[2] http://www.github.org/learnlib/raxml

In our analysis we are mainly interested in the total number of concrete input symbols sent to the SUL during learning and counterexample analysis as comparing test algorithms is a separate object of investigation. Therefore, we tried to implement the equivalence test in both tools as similar as possible. The results show that in the majority of experiments Tomte outperforms LearnLib if a random test case generator is used, see Table 2. However, with a proper equivalence test it is the very reverse: In most cases, LearnLib outperforms Tomte, see Table 3.

The reason for the performance difference is due to the length of the counterexamples found, which are typically longer when a random walk over the hypothesis is performed. As already mentioned in Section 3, Tomte first reduces the length of the counterexample by eliminating irrelevant loops, which in combination with a simpler counterexample analysis lead to less inputs sent to the SUL, compare **ana inp** for LearnLib and Tomte in Table 2. To measure the effect of the counterexample reduction, we have repeated the experiments above with the Tomte tool, without executing the loop elimination algorithm. They show that in our experiments the loop elimination algorithm reduces the length of the counterexample on average by more than 60%, which again reduces the inputs sent to the SUL during counterexample analysis significantly, i.e. on average by more than 90%.

Series 2. In a second series of experiments, we have applied both tools to learn models of the data structures from the lower part of Table 1. Table 4 shows the results for inferring models of a FIFO-set of capacity n (a FIFO-set with capacity 2 is depicted in Figure 1). We have gradually scaled up the capacity of the FIFO-set to test the limits of both tools. Using the test setup of the previous experiments (at most $10,000$ runs per equivalence query, maximum length of 100 inputs, and reset probability of 5%), we quickly reach the boundaries of both tools. The reset probability of 5% after every input leads to relatively short test traces, such that guards deep in the data structure cannot be found with random testing.

We thus have changed the test setup for Tomte: the columns for Tomte in Table 4 show the results for $1,000$ test traces of length $1,000$ with reset probability of 0%. For LearnLib, Table 4 shows the results with a reset probability of 5%. Tomte is able to successfully learn the FIFO-set with up to 30 elements, whereas LearnLib can only infer models up to size 7. For the smaller models, LearnLib outperforms Tomte, but the costs of finding and analyzing counterexamples quickly explode, as does the number of queries during learning from adding new suffixes to the observation table.

The figures indicate that Tomte consistently needs fewer counterexamples than LearnLib: it spends fewer resets on finding counterexamples. Since both tools implement the same random test algorithm for finding counterexamples, this suggests that Tomte uses fewer counterexamples. Another series of experiments for which we do not show the detailed results in this paper confirms this pattern. We have used both tools for inferring models of a queue and a stack of size n. In this series, Tomte does not need any counterexamples for learning

Table 4. Results for learning the FIFO-set with LearnLib (resetProbability=0.05 maxSize=100 maxNumTraces=10000) and Tomte (resetProbability=0 maxSize=1000 maxNumTraces=1000)

	Learnlib						Tomte					
	learn res	learn inp	test res	test inp	ana res	ana inp	learn res	learn inp	test res	test inp	ana res	ana inp
FIFO-set(1)												
avg	12	22	1	3	4	9	23	66	0	0	0	0
stddev	3	6	0	2	2	7	0	0	0	0	0	0
FIFO-set(2)												
avg	44	136	4	20	12	44	99	423	1	20	6	17
stddev	11	49	2	14	9	44	0	2	0	25	1	5
FIFO-set(3)												
avg	114	463	12	135	41	410	257	1396	4	562	19	88
stddev	19	115	4	84	27	499	0	6	1	897	5	37
FIFO-set(4)												
avg	250	1234	26	387	94	1294	568	3727	6	1190	47	315
stddev	72	426	9	179	53	1515	5	30	2	1767	31	284
FIFO-set(5)												
avg	761	5522	74	1231	210	3056	1104	8443	9	2158	80	705
stddev	589	5380	46	782	39	951	5	31	1	1098	40	507
FIFO-set(6)												
avg	855	6066	174	3053	378	7275	1955	17049	9	631	103	932
stddev	283	2689	47	949	100	3086	7	62	0	469	30	418
FIFO-set(7)												
avg	66392	1097470	394	7229	634	13530	3215	31487	13	2392	132	1284
stddev	195580	3310472	147	2803	66	2397	7	70	1	1370	44	616
FIFO-set(10)												
avg	unable to learn						10760	139708	23	7526	446	7029
stddev							22	277	8	7317	210	4918
FIFO-set(20)												
avg	unable to learn						129628	3056149	94	63422	4169	106467
stddev							54	1138	31	30834	565	14495
FIFO-set(30)												
avg	unable to learn						591668	20206862	761	718060	15714	620479
stddev							72	2112	319	319098	1427	232984

the correct models (of up to size 40), while LearnLib behaves very similar to the series with the FIFO-set. The reason for Tomte needing fewer counterexamples is the lookahead oracle that finds new registers without counterexamples. In LearnLib, on the other hand, all progress is driven by counterexamples. With a perfect equivalence oracle this is an advantage. For counterexamples of random length, on the other hand, the overhead of the lookahead oracle is quickly amortized through the queries saved by using fewer counterexamples.

Summary. Using the standardized format and the variety of benchmarks that we have collected makes it easy to compare different algorithms in more detail, e.g. with respect to their limits and the exact number of queries asked for learning and counterexample analysis. In addition, this allows us to compare the two approaches presented in this paper also to other related approaches. This will provide an insight into the strengths and weaknesses of different techniques and enable us to learn from each other. We believe there is still a lot of room for improvement in both tools.

References

1. Aarts, F.: Tomte: Bridging the Gap between Active Learning and Real-World Systems. PhD thesis, Radboud University Nijmegen (October 2014)
2. Aarts, F., Heidarian, F., Kuppens, H., Olsen, P., Vaandrager, F.: Automata learning through counterexample guided abstraction refinement. In: Giannakopoulou, D., Méry, D. (eds.) FM 2012. LNCS, vol. 7436, pp. 10–27. Springer, Heidelberg (2012)
3. Aarts, F., Jonsson, B., Uijen, J.: Generating models of infinite-state communication protocols using regular inference with abstraction. In: Petrenko, A., Simão, A., Maldonado, J.C. (eds.) ICTSS 2010. LNCS, vol. 6435, pp. 188–204. Springer, Heidelberg (2010)
4. Aarts, F., Jonsson, B., Uijen, J., Vaandrager, F.W.: Generating models of infinite-state communication protocols using regular inference with abstraction. In: Formal Methods in System Design (to appear, 2014)
5. Aarts, F., Kuppens, H., Tretmans, G.J., Vaandrager, F.W., Verwer, S.: Learning and testing the bounded retransmission protocol. In: Heinz, J., de la Higuera, C., Oates, T. (eds.) Proceedings 11th International Conference on Grammatical Inference (ICGI 2012), University of Maryland, College Park, USA, September 5-8. JMLR Workshop and Conference Proceedings, vol. 21, pp. 4–18 (2012)
6. Aarts, F., Schmaltz, J., Vaandrager, F.: Inference and abstraction of the biometric passport. In: Margaria, T., Steffen, B. (eds.) ISoLA 2010, Part I. LNCS, vol. 6415, pp. 673–686. Springer, Heidelberg (2010)
7. Aarts, F., Vaandrager, F.: Learning I/O automata. In: Gastin, P., Laroussinie, F. (eds.) CONCUR 2010. LNCS, vol. 6269, pp. 71–85. Springer, Heidelberg (2010)
8. Aarts, F., Ruiter, J.D., Poll, E.: Formal models of bank cards for free. In: IEEE International Conference on Software Testing Verification and Validation Workshop, pp. 461–468. IEEE Computer Society, Los Alamitos (2013)
9. Abadi, M., Lamport, L.: The existence of refinement mappings. Theoretical Computer Science 82(2), 253–284 (1991)
10. Angluin, D.: Learning regular sets from queries and counterexamples. Inf. Comput. 75(2), 87–106 (1987)
11. Cassel, S., Howar, F., Jonsson, B., Merten, M., Steffen, B.: A succinct canonical register automaton model. In: Bultan, T., Hsiung, P.-A. (eds.) ATVA 2011. LNCS, vol. 6996, pp. 366–380. Springer, Heidelberg (2011)
12. Cassel, S., Howar, F., Jonsson, B., Steffen, B.: Learning Extended Finite State Machines. In: Giannakopoulou, D., Salaün, G. (eds.) SEFM 2014. LNCS, vol. 8702, pp. 250–264. Springer, Heidelberg (2014)
13. Chalupar, G., Peherstorfer, S., Poll, E., de Ruiter, J.: Automated reverse engineering using Lego. In: Proceedings 8th USENIX Workshop on Offensive Technologies (WOOT 2014), San Diego, California, IEEE Computer Society, Los Alamitos (2014)
14. Cho, C.Y., Babic, D., Shin, E.C.R., Song, D.: Inference and analysis of formal models of botnet command and control protocols. In: Al-Shaer, E., Keromytis, A.D., Shmatikov, V. (eds.) ACM Conference on Computer and Communications Security, pp. 426–439. ACM (2010)
15. Clarke, E.M., Grumberg, O., Peled, D.: Model Checking. MIT Press, Cambridge (1999)
16. Fiterău-Broştean, P., Janssen, R., Vaandrager, F.: Learning fragments of the TCP network protocol. In: Lang, F., Flammini, F. (eds.) FMICS 2014. LNCS, vol. 8718, pp. 78–93. Springer, Heidelberg (2014)

17. Grinchtein, O., Jonsson, B., Pettersson, P.: Inference of event-recording automata using timed decision trees. In: Baier, C., Hermanns, H. (eds.) CONCUR 2006. LNCS, vol. 4137, pp. 435–449. Springer, Heidelberg (2006)
18. Grumberg, O., Veith, H. (eds.): 25 Years of Model Checking. LNCS, vol. 5000. Springer, Heidelberg (2008)
19. Hagerer, A., Hungar, H.: Model generation by moderated regular extrapolation. In: Kutsche, R.-D., Weber, H. (eds.) FASE 2002. LNCS, vol. 2306, pp. 80–95. Springer, Heidelberg (2002)
20. de la Higuera, C.: Grammatical Inference: Learning Automata and Grammars. Cambridge University Press (April 2010)
21. Howar, F., Giannakopoulou, D., Rakamaric, Z.: Hybrid learning: interface generation through static, dynamic, and symbolic analysis. In: Proc. of ISSTA 2013, pp. 268–279. ACM (2013)
22. Howar, F., Isberner, M., Steffen, B., Bauer, O., Jonsson, B.: Inferring Semantic Interfaces of Data Structures. In: Margaria, T., Steffen, B. (eds.) ISoLA 2012, Part I. LNCS, vol. 7609, pp. 554–571. Springer, Heidelberg (2012)
23. Howar, F., Steffen, B., Jonsson, B., Cassel, S.: Inferring canonical register automata. In: Kuncak, V., Rybalchenko, A. (eds.) VMCAI 2012. LNCS, vol. 7148, pp. 251–266. Springer, Heidelberg (2012)
24. Ip, C.N., Dill, D.L.: Better verification through symmetry. Formal Methods in System Design 9(1/2), 41–75 (1996)
25. Isberner, M., Howar, F., Steffen, B.: Learning register automata: from languages to program structures. Machine Learning 96(1-2), 65–98 (2014)
26. King, J.C.: Symbolic execution and program testing. Commun. ACM 19(7), 385–394 (1976)
27. Merten, M., Steffen, B., Howar, F., Margaria, T.: Next generation learnLib. In: Abdulla, P.A., Leino, K.R.M. (eds.) TACAS 2011. LNCS, vol. 6605, pp. 220–223. Springer, Heidelberg (2011)
28. Nerode, A.: Linear automaton transformations. Proceedings of the American Mathematical Society 9(4), 541–544 (1958)
29. Niese, O.: An Integrated Approach to Testing Complex Systems. PhD thesis, University of Dortmund (2003)
30. Peled, D., Vardi, M.Y., Yannakakis, M.: Black box checking. In: Wu, J., Chanson, S.T., Gao, Q. (eds.) Proceedings FORTE. IFIP Conference Proceedings, vol. 156, pp. 225–240. Kluwer (1999)
31. Raffelt, H., Merten, M., Steffen, B., Margaria, T.: Dynamic testing via automata learning. STTT 11(4), 307–324 (2009)
32. Steffen, B., Howar, F., Merten, M.: Introduction to active automata learning from a practical perspective. In: Bernardo, M., Issarny, V. (eds.) SFM 2011. LNCS, vol. 6659, pp. 256–296. Springer, Heidelberg (2011)
33. Tijssen, M.: Automatic Modeling of SSH Implementations with State Machine Learning Algorithms. Bachelor thesis, ICIS, Radboud University Nijmegen (June 2014)

Active Learning of Nondeterministic Systems from an ioco Perspective*

Michele Volpato[1] and Jan Tretmans[1,2]

[1] Institute for Computing and Information Sciences
Radboud Universiteit Nijmegen, Nijmegen, The Netherlands
{m.volpato,tretmans}@cs.ru.nl
[2] TNO - Embedded Systems Innovation
Eindhoven, The Netherlands

Abstract. Model-based testing allows the creation of test cases from a model of the system under test. Often, such models are difficult to obtain, or even not available. Automata learning helps in inferring the model of a system by observing its behaviour. The model can be employed for many purposes, such as testing other implementations, regression testing, or model checking. We present an algorithm for active learning of nondeterministic, input-enabled, labelled transition systems, based on the well known Angluin's L^* algorithm. Under some assumptions, for dealing with nondeterminism, input-enabledness and equivalence checking, we prove that the algorithm produces a model whose behaviour is equivalent to the one under learning. We define new properties for the structure used in the algorithm, derived from the semantics of labelled transition systems. Such properties help the learning, by avoiding to query the system under learning when it is not necessary.

1 Introduction

The field of model-based testing has grown and has made much progress in the last years. Model-based testing automates the creation of test cases, and often even their execution, by deriving them from a model [16]. This solves the laborious task of writing tests manually. It also requires the presence of formal models representing the system under test, which are often unavailable. *Automata learning* helps in the construction of such models, reducing the gap between theory and practice of model-based testing. If the system can be queried about its own behaviour, e.g., we can provide an input of our choice in order to observe the possible outputs, we talk about *active learning*. A well known algorithm for active learning of deterministic finite automata (DFA) is Angluin's L^* algorithm [3]. Variations of L^* have been used for learning related formalisms, such as deterministic finite state machines (DFSM) in the form of Mealy machines [11],

---

* This research is supported by the Dutch Technology Foundation STW, which is part of the Netherlands Organisation for Scientific Research (NWO), and which is partly funded by the Ministry of Economic Affairs.

Proofs available at http://www.italia.cs.ru.nl/publications/

T. Margaria and B. Steffen (Eds.): ISoLA 2014, Part I, LNCS 8802, pp. 220–235, 2014.
© Springer-Verlag Berlin Heidelberg 2014

or their nondeterministic versions (NFSM) [6]. Unfortunately, not much work has been done in active learning of nondeterministic systems such as *labelled transition systems*, a formalism widely used in model-based testing of reactive systems. The **ioco** framework [15], for example, addresses the theory of model-based testing of systems behaving like a labelled transition system.

In this paper we extend Angluin's L* to active learning of nondeterministic input/output labelled transition systems. Our approach uses concepts belonging to the **ioco** framework, such as *quiescence*, i. e., the absence of output, the *outset*, i. e., the set of observable outputs (or quiescence) from a given state, and the *suspension automaton*, i. e., the deterministic automaton obtained by making quiescence explicit and then determinizing the result. Three assumptions are considered in this paper: (i) the *testing assumption* [15], i. e., the system under learning (SUL) behaves as an input-enabled labelled transition system, (ii) the *equivalence exhaustiveness*, that implies that we are capable to exhaustively check the equivalence of our conjecture with respect to the SUL, and (iii) the *all weather conditions* [8], that states the ability of, eventually, obtaining all the observable outputs of a state, even if nondeterminism is present. The second assumption suggests that, theoretically, we cannot replace the equivalence check with a testing tool. In practice, it is common to test for equivalence until a certain depth, inferring that the conjecture is "similar enough" to the SUL. Given the last assumption, we are able to obtain the set of all possible outputs after a given sequence of actions. This is strong for real nondeterministic systems. However it is needed for a proper functioning of the active learning algorithm. As future work, a relaxation of it is under consideration, with the possibility of using a relation weaker than equivalence.

In L*-style algorithms, an *observation table* is filled and extended during the learning. If the observation table satisfies two properties, called *closedness* and *consistency*, then a model can be constructed and, based on its equivalence to the SUL, the learning can either stop or continue with more information. We show how some properties of labelled transition systems make the learning easier. In fact, given those properties, some entries of the observation table can be inferred either from other, already filled, entries, or even from the properties themselves. Furthermore, in situations where normally we would try to determine if the current learned conjecture is equivalent to the SUL, which is usually a hard task, we can directly improve the conjecture by looking only at the observation table. More specifically, the contributions of the paper are the following: (i) an algorithm for active learning of labelled transition systems, using concepts from the **ioco** framework, (ii) the adaptation of the structures used in classical L* to learning labelled transition systems, (iii) the definition of a new property, called *quiescence reducibility*, from [18], that must be fulfilled by the observation table in addition to *closedness* and *consistency*.

Related Work. Besides the already mentioned original L* algorithm, other work has been done in active learning in the last years. In [9], [4] and [11] active learning of Mealy machines is widely addressed, leading to a tool, LEARNLIB [14], that performs well in practice. In [7] the approach is extended to structures with data, called *register Mealy machines*. Independently, work has also been done, in the same direction, in [1], resulting in a tool called TOMTE, which adds an abstraction layer on top of LEARNLIB. In [2], a link is presented between *i/o automata*, labelled transition systems and Mealy machine. The authors show that, by using a transducer, i/o automata that are deterministic and *output determined*, i.e., each state has at most one outgoing output transition, can be learned using any tool capable of learning Mealy machines. As in this paper, they apply L* to reactive systems, where there is a distinction between inputs and outputs. Such systems, however, are all deterministic, which is not the case for labelled transition systems.

Active learning of a subclass of NFSM, called *observable* NFSM (ONFSM), is studied in [6] and [10]. The behaviour of a system belonging to this class is comparable to the one of a labelled transition system, except for the strict alternation between inputs and outputs. All previously mentioned techniques produce a deterministic version of the system under learning. In [5], the authors develop an algorithm for learning *residual FSA*, a nondeterministc representation of DFAs. The work in [18] gives an approximation-based algorithm and a set of heuristics, for inferring a model using **ioco**-based testing. Some of the contributions of this paper rely on the suspension automaton, which is one of the results in [18]. A combination of the techniques exposed in that paper and the ones we present here is likely to be considered for future work.

2   Preliminaries

Labelled Transition Systems. An (input/output) labelled transition system [15] is a 5-tuple $\langle Q, L_I, L_U, \rightarrow, q_0 \rangle$, where Q is a set of states, L_I and L_U are two disjoint sets of input and output labels, respectively, $\rightarrow$ is the transition relation and $q_0 \in Q$ is the initial state. We use the name of the labelled transition system and its initial state interchangeably. A special label τ is used to mark internal unobservable transitions. We indicate $(q, \lambda, q') \in \rightarrow$ as $q \xrightarrow{\lambda} q'$ and we say that q enables λ. The union of L_I and L_U is shortened in L. The class of all labelled transition systems over L_I and L_U is denoted by $\mathcal{LTS}(L_I, L_U)$. Let q, q' be states of a labelled transition system in $\mathcal{LTS}(L_I, L_U)$ and ϵ be the empty sequence, we define $q \xRightarrow{\epsilon} q' \iff q = q'$ or $q \xrightarrow{\tau} \ldots \xrightarrow{\tau} q'$. Given a label λ, we define $q \xRightarrow{\lambda} q'$ as $q \xRightarrow{\epsilon} p \xrightarrow{\lambda} p' \xRightarrow{\epsilon} q'$ and extend $\Rightarrow$ for sequences of labels in the usual way. The set of traces enabled in a state q is $traces(q) = \{\sigma \in L^* \mid \exists q' . q \xRightarrow{\sigma} q'\}$. We denote the set of states that are reachable from a given state q via a trace σ as $(q \text{ after } \sigma) = \{q' \mid q \xRightarrow{\sigma} q'\}$ and by extension, given a set of states P: $P \text{ after } \sigma = \bigcup\{q \text{ after } \sigma \mid q \in P\}$.

A state q is called quiescent if $\forall \lambda \in L_U \cup \{\tau\} : q \xnrightarrow{\lambda} q'$ for all $q' \in Q$, i.e., q does not enable any output or internal action. Let $\delta \notin L_I \cup L_U$, L_δ is defined as $L \cup \{\delta\}$ and $\langle Q, L_I, L_U \cup \{\delta\}, \rightarrow_\delta, q_0 \rangle$ is the labelled transition system $\langle Q, L_I, L_U, \rightarrow, q_0 \rangle$ to which we add a δ-loop transition $q \xrightarrow{\delta} q$ to all quiescent states. The set of suspension traces accepted by a state q is $Straces(q) = \{\sigma \in L_\delta^* \mid \exists q' . q \xRightarrow{\sigma} q'\}$.

We denote the set of outputs, including quiescence, that are enabled by a set of states P as $out(P) = \{\lambda \in L_U \cup \{\delta\} \mid \exists q \in P, q' \in Q : q \stackrel{\lambda}{\Rightarrow} q'\}$. In an input-enabled labelled transition system all states enable all inputs, we denote the class of all input-enabled labelled transition systems over L_I and L_U as $\mathcal{IOTS}(L_I, L_U)$ and its elements are called *input-ouput transition systems*.

From this point forward, we write $\sigma_1 \cdot \sigma_2$ or just $\sigma_1 \sigma_2$ to denote the concatenation of sequences σ_1 and σ_2. We also use $S \cdot A$, where S is a set of traces and A a set of labels, to indicate the set of traces obtained by extending each element of S with each label in A. We usually indicate a single label with λ and a trace with σ. From now on, we consider only finite settings, even if not explicitly stated.

Active Learning of Deterministic Finite Automata. In the setting of *active learning*, Angluin's L* [3] is a well known, efficient algorithm that infers a DFA for a regular language. The algorithm assumes the existence of a *teacher* which is able to reply to two kinds of questions: *membership* queries and *equivalence* queries. With a membership query the algorithm checks if a particular trace over the alphabet is accepted by the language and it stores the answers in a table, called an *observation table*. The observation table maintains a prefix closed set of traces S, representing the states of the DFA and a suffix closed set of traces E, used to distinguish such states. A set containing the one label extensions of S is also stored. Membership queries are asked until the observation table satisfies two properties, *closedness* and *consistency*, that allow the algorithm to conjecture a unique, minimal DFA which is consistent with the observation table. Now the algorithm poses an equivalence query, asking the teacher if the language accepted by the DFA is the one under learning. The teacher can reply affirmatively, and then the learning is finished, or it can provide a counterexample that distinguishes the DFA from the language. The algorithm, then, uses the counterexample to extend S and E, resulting in asking more membership queries and improving the guess with the successive equivalence query. The observation table will, eventually, produce the correct conjecture, that is isomorphic to the minimal DFA accepting the target language. The approach that we present in this paper follows the one described in this section, except for the counterexample handling, which maintains consistency in the table, and for an additional property that the table must fulfill, before asking an equivalence query.

In the next sections we claim that, while learning a labelled transition system, the result of some membership queries can be inferred without asking the query to the teacher. This is due to some properties of labelled transition systems. Given a labelled transition system q: (1) the set of traces $traces(q)$ is prefix-closed, (2) $out(q \text{ after } \sigma) \neq \emptyset \iff \sigma \in traces(q)$. Other properties are explained, later, in Definition 1.

3   Towards Learning of Labelled Transition Systems

The observation table presented in this paper has some differences with respect to the observation table used for Angluin's L*. Given the input-output nature of the system, it is logical to include outputs in the entries, as for learning Mealy machines [14]. Moreover, nondeterminism makes the use of multiple outputs in the table a natural choice, as for ONFSM [10]. For instance, in Figure 1a the system can observe the sequence of inputs aa and then the output x, ending in two different states, one of them enables y (right branch), the other one enables x (left branch). However, differently from ONFSM, the presence of possible multiple inputs and outputs in sequence, e. g. the trace $aaxx$ in Figure 1a, implies the use of outputs also in S and E.

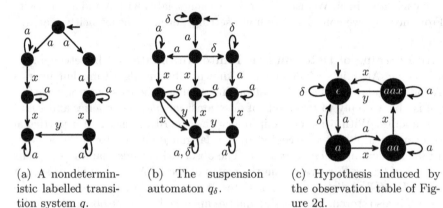

(a) A nondeterministic labelled transition system q.

(b) The suspension automaton q_δ.

(c) Hypothesis induced by the observation table of Figure 2d.

Fig. 1. Labelled transition systems used as examples in the paper

Equivalence of Labelled Transition Systems. In general, an equivalence query asks if a conjecture, or hypothesis, that the algorithm is able to produce from an observation table is equivalent to the SUL. In model-based testing, labelled transition systems are widely used, and previous work in the field suggests the use of suspension-trace equivalence [18,16]. We can employ such a relation if we assume *equivalence exhaustiveness*, i. e., the teacher is always able to answer correctly to the equivalence query, in a finite amount of time. Given that, in practice, answering an equivalence query can be complex [13], instead of using a strong trace equivalence, a conformance relation, such as **ioco** [15], can also be used. Therefore, two labelled transition systems q_1 and q_1 are (suspension-trace) equivalent if and only if they have the same set of suspension traces, i. e., $Straces(q_1) = Straces(q_2)$. We use $[q]_\delta$ to denote the equivalence class of all labelled transition systems equivalent to q, i. e., all labelled transition systems having the same set of suspension traces of q.

3.1   Valid Suspension Automata

In the context of model-based testing, a suspension automaton is a deterministic labelled transition system that can be used to describe the behaviour of a more general labelled transition system to which δ transitions have been added. This notion was first introduced in [15], acting as basis for the derivation of test cases for checking the conformance of an *implementation* with respect to a *specification*. Given a labelled transition system q, we obtain a suspension automaton q_δ by making quiescence explicit, i.e., by adding δ loops to quiescent states, and then determinizing the result. It is trivial that the set of traces accepted by q_δ is equivalent to the set of suspension traces of q. Figure 1b depicts the suspension automaton obtained from the labelled transition system of Figure 1a. We extend the use of $[\bullet]_\delta$ to suspension automata: $[q_\delta]_\delta$ represents the equivalence class of all labelled transition systems whose set of suspension traces is equivalent to the set of traces accepted by q_δ.

Not all deterministic labelled transition systems, over a given alphabet containing δ, are good candidates for being the suspension automaton of some labelled transition systems. In [18] some properties are given to determine when a deterministic labelled transition system is a valid suspension automaton, i.e., there exists at least one labelled transition system belonging to its suspension-trace equivalence class. These properties are exhibited in the following definition.

Definition 1. *A valid suspension automaton is a labelled transition system* $\langle Q, L_I, L_U \cup \{\delta\}, \rightarrow, q_0\rangle$ *that is: (i) non-blocking, i.e.,* $\forall q \in Q, \exists \lambda \in L_U \cup \{\delta\} . q \xrightarrow{\lambda};$ *(ii) quiescent reducible, i.e.,* $\forall q \in Q, \forall \sigma \in L_\delta^* . \delta \cdot \sigma \in traces(q) \Rightarrow \sigma \in traces(q);$ *(iii) anomaly-free, i.e.,* $\forall q \in Q, \forall \lambda \in L_U . \delta \cdot \lambda \notin traces(q);$ *(iv) stable, i.e.,* $\forall q, q', q'' \in Q . q \xrightarrow{\delta} q' \xrightarrow{\delta} q'' \Rightarrow traces(q') = traces(q'').$

In [15] is provided a constructive definition of suspension automata, showing that for each labelled transition system there exists a (valid) suspension automaton accepting the same suspension traces. Theorem 1 proves the converse.

Theorem 1. *Let* $q_\delta \in \mathcal{LTS}(L_I, L_U \cup \{\delta\})$ *be a valid suspension automaton. Then, there exists a labelled transition system* $q \in \mathcal{LTS}(L_I, L_U)$ *such that* $Straces(q) = traces(q_\delta)$.

In the rest of the paper we will present an algorithm that, given a system that behaves as an input-ouput transition system q, learns a valid suspension automaton q_δ such that $q \in [q_\delta]_\delta$.

4   Improving Queries and Observation Tables

In the context of active black box learning, where one tries to learn an unknown system by providing inputs and observing outputs, the learner should always be able to try an input, independently from the state of the system. For this reason we consider the system under learning as an input-ouput transition system. The assumption that the system, indeed, behaves as an input enabled input-ouput transition system, is known as the *testing assumption* [15].

Membership and Equivalence Queries. In any L^*-style learning algorithm, the teacher must be able to reply to two types of queries: *membership queries* and *equivalence queries*. A membership query, in the form of a trace σ, is used to obtain the set of outputs, $out(\text{SUL after } \sigma)$. For this reason, the teacher must be able to reply with all output actions (including quiescence) that are observable after executing the trace σ. The *all weather condition* [8] ensures that the teacher provides the entire set of outputs with one single query. Not all membership queries, however, bring new information. In fact the behaviour of labelled transition systems makes certain that, for some membership queries, the reply can be inferred from the observation table. For instance, $out(\text{SUL after } \sigma \cdot \lambda)$, where σ ends with δ and $\lambda \in L_U$, is the empty set, for any SUL, because of Definition 1.(iii). Moreover, this is also the case, if we already know that λ does not belong to the result of the query σ, see Property (2) in Section 2. Finally, testing a trace containing sequences of δ is the same as testing the trace obtained by reducing all such sequences to a single δ, Definition 1.(iv).

An equivalence query confirms the equivalence of the current conjecture to the SUL. If they are not equivalent, the teacher provides a counterexample, i. e., a trace c such that $out(\text{SUL after } c) \neq out(\text{conjecture after } c)$. The idea is that the counterexample contains a suffix that distinguishes two states that are currently represented by the same state in our conjecture. In practice it is not easy for the teacher to reply to an equivalence query.

Observation Tables. In our approach, the observation table is composed of a non-empty, finite, prefix-closed set $S \subsetneq L_\delta^*$, a non-empty, finite, suffix-closed set $E \subsetneq L_\delta^*$, and a function T which maps traces in $((S \cup S \cdot L_\delta) \cdot E)$ to a subset of $(L_U \cup \{\delta\})$. We use s and e to identify elements of S and E, respectively. The function T provides a set containing the last, observable, outputs, i. e., $T(s \cdot e) = out(\text{SUL after } s \cdot e)$. We refer to an observation table as (S, E, T). The observation table is viewed as a matrix. Its rows are indexed by elements of S and their extensions with one label (elements of $(S \cdot L_\delta)$), while columns are elements of E. The entry for row s (resp. row $s\lambda$) and column e is given by $T(s \cdot e)$ (resp. $T(s\lambda \cdot e)$). Given an observation table (S, E, T) and a trace $s \in (S \cup S \cdot L_\delta)$, $row(s)$ denotes the function f from E to $2^{(L_U \cup \{\delta\})}$ defined by $f(e) = T(s \cdot e)$. In Figure 2 are given (the matrix views of) some observation tables. Note the absence of some elements from the part of the tables representing $(S \cdot L_\delta)$. For instance, in Table 2a is missing the row indexed by x (one letter extension of ϵ). We avoid to indicate such a row, because, being $x \notin out(\text{SUL after } \epsilon)$, $T(x \cdot \epsilon) = \emptyset$, and given the prefix-closedness of $traces(\text{SUL})$, the entire row is filled with empty sets. In Table 2b, instead, a is not present in the bottom part, i. e., $(S \cdot L_\delta)$, because that row is already present in the top part (S), and by not showing it again, we avoid redundancy. Furthermore, note that for each observation table and prefix s, $T(s\delta \cdot \epsilon) \subseteq \{\delta\}$, because after observing quiescence in any labelled transition system (under learning), another output cannot be observed [17].

Closed and Consistent Tables. A table is *closed* if, for each $s_1 \in (S \cdot L_\delta)$, if $T(s_1 \cdot \epsilon) \neq \emptyset$, then there exists an $s_2 \in S$ such that $row(s_1) = row(s_2)$. A trace $s \in S$ for which $T(s \cdot \epsilon) = \emptyset$ is not considered because it represents a trace s extended with an output not in $out($SUL **after** $s)$. Due to the prefix-closedness of the set of traces, the entire row would be filled with empty sets, expressing, semantically, a non-accepting sink state. In such case, we say that $row(\sigma)$ is *undefined*. A table is *consistent* if, for each $s_1, s_2 \in S$ such that $row(s_1) = row(s_2)$, for each $\lambda \in L_\delta$, $row(s_1 \lambda) = row(s_2 \lambda)$. From a closed and consistent table it is possible to build an input-ouput transition system $\langle Q', L_I, L_U \cup \{\delta\}, T', q_0' \rangle$, by using Algorithm 1. We call it the *hypothesis induced by the observation table* and denote it as $\mathcal{H}$.

Algorithm 1. Construct Hypothesis $\mathcal{H}$

Input: A closed and consistent observation table (S, E, T).
Output: A labelled transition system $\mathcal{H} = \langle Q, L_I, L_U \cup \{\delta\}, \rightarrow, q_0 \rangle$.

1: $Q = \{row(s) \mid s \in S\}$
2: $q_0 = row(\epsilon)$
3: **for each** $row(s) \in Q$ **do**
4:     **for each** $\lambda \in L_I$ **do**
5:         add $row(s) \xrightarrow{\lambda} row(s \cdot \lambda)$
6:     **for each** $\lambda \in (L_U \cup \{\delta\})$ **do**
7:         **if** $\lambda \in T(s, \epsilon)$ **then**
8:             add $row(s) \xrightarrow{\lambda} row(s \cdot \lambda)$

A state $row(s)$ of $\mathcal{H}$ is represented by an element s of S. An outgoing transition, labelled with λ, is added accordingly to $row(s\lambda)$, i. e., the transition labelled with λ leaving $row(s)$ will reach the state $row(s\lambda)$, if it is defined.

Note that $\mathcal{H}$ is deterministic and that it is a well defined labelled transition system, in fact, being S non-empty and prefix closed, it contains ϵ, thus Q and q_ϵ are well defined. Let us consider two elements s_1 and s_2 belonging to S, such that $row(s_1) = row(s_2)$. Consistency implies that, for all $\lambda \in L_\delta$ either $row(s_1 \lambda) = row(s_2 \lambda)$ or none of them are defined. Closedness implies that, if $row(s_1 \lambda)$ and $row(s_2 \lambda)$ are defined, there exists $s \in S$ such that $row(s) = row(s_1 \lambda) = row(s_2 \lambda)$. Furthermore, since E is non-empty and suffix closed, it contains ϵ, thus $T(s_1 \cdot \epsilon) = T(s_2 \cdot \epsilon)$. The transition function $\rightarrow$ is then well defined.

Example 1. Consider the observation table (S, E, T) of Figure 2d. It is closed, thus we can construct an hypothesis. Figure 1c is the result of running Algorithm 1 on (S, E, T). Each state is labelled with the related trace of S. The initial state is the one labelled with ϵ (Line 2 of Algorithm 1). Then, for each state, a transition is added for all the inputs (Lines 4 to 5) and for all the outputs that are enabled in that state (Lines 6 to 8).

The correctness of Algorithm 1 is given by Theorem 2 and Theorem 3. We follow a proving path similar to the one in [9].

Theorem 2. *If an observation table (S, E, T) is closed and consistent, S is prefix closed and E is suffix closed, then the hypothesis $\mathcal{H}$, obtained by running Algorithm 1 on it, is compatible with the function T, i.e., $\forall s \in (S \cup S \cdot L_\delta), \forall e \in E \,.\, out(\mathcal{H} \textbf{ after } s \cdot e) = T(s \cdot e)$.*

Theorem 3. *Let (S, E, T) be a closed and consistent observation table such that S is prefix closed and E is suffix closed, and let $\mathcal{H} = \langle Q, L_I, L_U \cup \{\delta\}, \rightarrow, q_0 \rangle$ be the input-ouput transition system induced by (S, E, T). For any deterministic input-ouput transition system $\mathcal{H}' = \langle Q', L_I, L_U \cup \{\delta\}, \rightarrow', q_0' \rangle$ compatible with T, $|Q'| \geq |Q|$.*

An observation table that is not closed has some elements of $(S \cdot L_\delta)$ for which there exists no element of S with the same row function. To close such table, we add a representative of each of those elements to S and, then, we update the function T accordingly to SUL (see Algorithm 2).

Algorithm 2. Close (S, E, T)

Input: An observation table (S, E, T).
Output: A closed observation table.

1: **while** $\exists s_1 \in (S \cdot L_\delta)$ such that $T(s_1 \cdot \epsilon) \neq \emptyset$ and $\forall s \in S, row(s_1) \neq row(s)$ **do**
2:     $S \leftarrow S \cup \{s_1\}$
3:     Complete (S, E, T) by asking membership queries
4: **return** the updated observation table (S, E, T)

Note that prefix closedness of S and consistency of the table are preserved. After having added an element to S, the set $(S \cdot L_\delta)$ is extended with new elements. Some rows indexed by new elements are empty, thus we need to ask membership queries to fill them. We denote this action as *completing* T (Line 3).

Example 2. Let us consider the labelled transition system q of Figure 1a and an observation table (S, E, T) where $S = E = \{\epsilon\}$. Figure 2a represents such a table, after completing T accordingly to q. Such a table is not closed, because of $row(a)$ not being represented in S. Thus we add a to S and then we ask membership queries obtaining Table 2b. Table 2b is not yet closed, after two more attempts we, finally, obtain a closed table (Table 2d).

Counterexample Analysis. In the original L^* algorithm, when a counterexample is found, all its prefixes are added to S. This could lead to an inconsistent observation table. In [11], a different approach is proposed: by adding a proper suffix of the counterexample to E, the learning can continue, without adding any element to S, avoiding possible inconsistencies in the observation table.

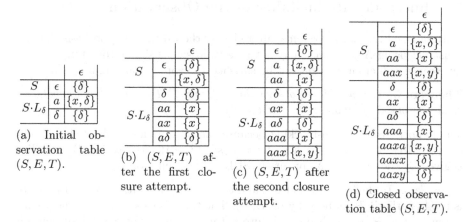

(a) Initial observation table (S, E, T).

(b) (S, E, T) after the first closure attempt.

(c) (S, E, T) after the second closure attempt.

(d) Closed observation table (S, E, T).

Fig. 2. Three attempts of closing an observation table

We adapt the approach used in [12] for Mealy machines, inspired by [11], to labelled transition systems: given a counterexample we decompose it into $s \cdot v$, where s is the longest element in $(S \cdot L_\delta)$. A counterexample distinguishes the hypothesis from the system under learning, i.e., it contains a suffix that distinguishes two (or more) states that are equivalent in the hypothesis. For this reason we add the suffix closure of v to the set of suffixes E. This approach is known to preserve consistency in the observation table, so that checking for consistency is not necessary. After completing T with membership queries, two (or more) rows that were equivalent will differ in the entry related to such suffix. The difference in those rows makes the table not closed. This is explained

---

Algorithm 3. Analyse counterexample c

Input: An observation table (S, E, T) and a counterexample c.
Output: A suffix-closed set E'.

1: Decompose c in $s \cdot v$ where
   s is the longest prefix of c such that $s \in (S \cup S \cdot L_\delta)$
2: **return** $\{v' \in L_\delta^* \mid v' \text{ is a suffix of } v\}$

---

formally in Theorem 4.

Theorem 4. *The observation table obtained by adding the result of Algorithm 3, executed on a closed and consistent observation table (S, E, T) and a counterexample c, to the set of suffixes E is not closed.*

Thus, the analysis of a counterexample, and the subsequent table closure, always ends in adding (at least) a state to the induced hypothesis.

5   Quiescence Reducibility of the Observation Table

With labelled transition systems, after closing the table, the hypothesis that we construct using Algorithm 1 may not be a valid suspension automaton, because quiescence reducibility might not be satisfied (Theorem 5 and Example 3).

Theorem 5. *Given a closed observation table* (S, E, T), *the induced hypothesis* $\mathcal{H}$ *is non-blocking, anomaly-free and stable.*

The hypothesis $\mathcal{H}$ is non-blocking because the observation table is closed, and anomaly-free because for each prefix s, $T(s\delta\cdot\epsilon) \subseteq \{\delta\}$ (see Section 4). Stability is given by the fact that δ appears in SUL only as self-loops.

Example 3. Table 2d shows a closed and consistent observation table.. Figure 1c is the hypothesis $\mathcal{H}$ induced by (S, E, T). The table is closed (and trivially consistent), thus $\mathcal{H}$ is a well defined automaton, but it is not a valid suspension automaton, i.e., there is no labelled transition system in $\mathcal{LTS}(\{a\}, \{x, y\})$ that is suspension-trace equivalent to $\mathcal{H}$. This is due to the state $row(a)$: the trace $\delta a\delta$ is accepted by that state, while $a\delta$ is not. Thus $\mathcal{H}$ is not *quiescence reducible*.

By checking quiescence reducibility for the hypothesis induced by a closed table, we can improve our guess, i.e., ˙construct a better hypothesis. In fact, if the hypothesis is not quiescence reducible, then there is one (or more) state that needs to be split. We can identify this state directly in the table, without asking any membership or equivalence query; if the hypothesis is not quiescence reducible, then we find a suffix-closed set to be added to E which makes the table not closed. This property of the suspension automaton can be seen as a new property of the observation table, that must be fulfilled before an equivalence query is asked. Quiescence reducibility of a suspension automaton implies a *simulation* relation between a state and the one reached from it by observing a δ transition, i.e., trace inclusion, given the deterministic behaviour.

Algorithm 4 checks if the hypothesis induced by a given table (S, E, T) is quiescence reducible. It checks that each state that enables δ simulates the state that is reachable by observing δ. The list of state pairs that still need to be checked for simulation contains also the information on how a pair of states has been reached from the initial one (Line 3). This trace is needed for constructing the counterexample from which we obtain new elements that must be added to E. Once a pair of states that are trivially not in simulation relation is found, i.e., a pair $\langle s_1, s_2 \rangle$ such that $out(\text{SUL after } s_1)$ does not include $out(\text{SUL after } s_2)$ (Line 8), we found the element that added to E will make the table not closed. With this approach we split one of the states that have been encountered while constructing the counterexample. This is similar to the counterexample analysis described in Section 4. Note that in checking quiescence reducibility, if the algorithm finds that the simulation does not hold for a pair of states $row(s)$ and $row(s\delta)$, then it returns a set of suffixes built from a trace σ that, appended to either s or $s\delta$ or both is, indeed, a counterexample, i.e., $out(\mathcal{H} \text{ after } s\sigma) \neq out(\text{SUL after } s\sigma)$ or $out(\mathcal{H} \text{ after } s\delta\sigma) \neq out(\text{SUL after } s\delta\sigma)$. Thus the same result of Theorem 4 applies. For those states that do not enable any output, i.e., those $row(s)$ for

---

Algorithm 4. Check for *quiescence reducibility*

Input: An observation table (S, E, T).
Output: A set of suffixes E'.

1: **for each** $s_1 \in S$. $\{\delta\} \subsetneq T(s_1 \cdot \epsilon)$ **do**
2:     $s_2 \leftarrow s \in S$. $row(s) = row(s_1 \delta)$
3:     $wait \leftarrow \{\langle s_1, s_2, \epsilon \rangle\}$ {*list of state pairs to be checked associated with the sequence of labels needed to reach them from the first pair*}
4:     $past \leftarrow \emptyset$ {*list of checked pairs*}
5:     **while** $wait \neq \emptyset$ **do**
6:        Pick $\langle s_1, s_2, \sigma \rangle \in wait$
7:        **for each** $\lambda \in T(s_2 \cdot \epsilon) \cup L_I$ **do**
8:           **if** $\lambda \notin T(s_1 \cdot \epsilon) \cup L_I$ **then**
9:              **return** $\{\sigma' \in L_\delta^* \mid \sigma' \text{ is a suffix of } \sigma\}$
10:          **else**
11:             $s_1' \leftarrow s \in S$. $row(s) = row(s_1 \lambda)$
12:             $s_2' \leftarrow s \in S$. $row(s) = row(s_2 \lambda)$
13:             **if** $\langle s_1', s_2' \rangle \notin past \wedge s_1' \neq s_2'$ **then**
14:                $wait \leftarrow wait \cup \{\langle s_1', s_2', \sigma\lambda \rangle\}$
15:          $wait \leftarrow wait \setminus \{\langle s_1, s_2, \sigma \rangle\}$
16:          $past \leftarrow past \cup \{\langle s_1, s_2 \rangle\}$
17: **return** $\emptyset$ {*no counterexample has been found*}

---

which $T(s \cdot \epsilon) = \{\delta\}$, the simulation check is not needed, because, for each of those states, $row(s\delta) = row(s)$.

Example 4. Consider the hypothesis of Figure 1c, which is induced by the observation table represented by Table 2d. The only interesting state for checking quiescence reducibility is $row(a)$. So we want to check if $row(a)$ simulates $row(a\delta) = row(\epsilon)$ (Line 2). At Line 6 $\langle a, \epsilon, \epsilon \rangle$ is chosen (it is the only element in $wait$), and given that $T(a \cdot \epsilon) = \{x, \delta\} \supseteq \{\delta\} = T(a\delta \cdot \epsilon)$ the *if* clause at Line 8 is never satisfied. Thus the algorithm tries to update $wait$ with $\langle aa, a, a \rangle$, for $\lambda = a$. If $\lambda = \delta$ the algorithm does not add any pair of states to $wait$ because $row(a\delta) = row(\delta) = row(epsilon)$. The algorithm has finished with the pair of states $\langle a, \epsilon \rangle$ and it picks another element from $wait$: $\langle aa, a, a \rangle$. In this case $T(aa \cdot \epsilon) = \{x\} \not\supseteq \{x, \delta\} = T(a \cdot \epsilon)$, thus $row(a)$ does not simulate $row(\epsilon)$, and a is the trace that, observed after those two states, proves it. Finally the algorithm returns the set $\{a\}$ containing such distinguish suffix.

Theoretically, checking for quiescence reducibility is not necessary. In fact, if the hypothesis is not valid, it is not equivalent to the SUL. Thus an equivalence query will eventually be able to spot the inequality, providing a counterexample, possibly the same we discover with Algorithm 4. However, equivalence query is, in practice, more expensive, in time, than performing an analytic checking on the table. In a real system, if it is large enough, spotting the inequality with an equivalence query could take a large amount of time [13].

6   Learning Input-Output Transition Systems

The algorithm for learning input-ouput transition systems is an adaptation from Angluin's L*, with the use of the algorithms already described previously in the paper. The only difference in the main algorithm is the added quiescence reducibility check at Line 6 which also implies the addition of the *repeat* loop for closing the table.

Algorithm 5. Learn the input-ouput transition system SUL

Input: The set of input labels L_I
Output: A valid suspension automaton $\mathcal{H}$ s.t. SUL $\in [\mathcal{H}]_\delta$.

  // Initialize (S, E, T)
 1: $S = E = \{\epsilon\}$
 2: Complete (S, E, T) by asking membership queries
  // Start learning
 3: **loop**
 4:     **repeat**
 5:         Close (S, E, T) using Algorithm 2
 6:         Check quiescence reducibility with Algorithm 4 on (S, E, T), obtaining a suffix-closed set E'
 7:         $E \leftarrow E \cup E'$
 8:         Complete (S, E, T) by asking membership queries
 9:     **until** $E' = \emptyset$
10:     Construct the hypothesis $\mathcal{H}$ using Algorithm 1 on (S, E, T)
11:     Ask an equivalence query for $\mathcal{H}$
12:     **if** a counterexample c is found **then**
13:         Analyse counterexample c using Algorithm 3 on (S, E, T) obtaining a suffix-closed set E'
14:         $E \leftarrow E \cup E'$
15:         Complete (S, E, T) by asking membership queries
16:     **else**
17:         **return** $\mathcal{H}$

Example 5. Let us run Algorithm 5 on the labelled transition system q of Figure 1a. First the observation table is closed (Line 5 obtaining the observation table of Table 2d. Then quiescence reducibility is checked at Line 6, see Example 3, and a is added to E. The table is then updated (Line 8), obtaining Table 3a. This table is not closed, we close it obtaining Table 3b. Now the table is closed again and the induced hypothesis is quiescence reducible. Thus we ask an equivalence query at Line 11. Let assume that the teacher replies with the counterexample axx, because $out(\text{SUL after } axx) = \{\delta\} \neq \{x, y\} = out(\mathcal{H} \text{ after } axx)$. By analysing the counterexample with Algorithm 3 we obtain the set $\{x\}$, thus we add x to E resulting in updating the observation table to the one of Table 4a. Note that Table 4a does not show the row for $a\delta\delta$, because, given Definition 1.(iv), $row(a\delta\delta)$ is always equal to $row(a\delta)$. After some closing steps the

		ϵ	a
S	ϵ	$\{\delta\}$	$\{x,\delta\}$
	a	$\{x,\delta\}$	$\{x\}$
	aa	$\{x\}$	$\{x\}$
	aax	$\{x,y\}$	$\{x,y\}$
$S \cdot L_\delta$	δ	$\{\delta\}$	$\{x,\delta\}$
	ax	$\{x\}$	$\{x\}$
	$a\delta$	$\{\delta\}$	$\{x\}$
	aaa	$\{x\}$	$\{x\}$
	$aaxa$	$\{x,y\}$	$\{x,y\}$
	$aaxx$	$\{\delta\}$	$\{\delta\}$
	$aaxy$	$\{\delta\}$	$\{\delta\}$

(a) Observation table after adding a to E.

		ϵ	a
S	ϵ	$\{\delta\}$	$\{x,\delta\}$
	a	$\{x,\delta\}$	$\{x\}$
	aa	$\{x\}$	$\{x\}$
	aax	$\{x,y\}$	$\{x,y\}$
	$a\delta$	$\{\delta\}$	$\{x\}$
	$aaxy$	$\{\delta\}$	$\{\delta\}$
$S \cdot L_\delta$	δ	$\{\delta\}$	$\{x,\delta\}$
	ax	$\{x\}$	$\{x\}$
	aaa	$\{x\}$	$\{x\}$
	$aaxa$	$\{x,y\}$	$\{x,y\}$
	$aaxx$	$\{\delta\}$	$\{\delta\}$
	$a\delta a$	$\{x\}$	$\{x\}$
	$aaxya$	$\{\delta\}$	$\{\delta\}$
	$aaxy\delta$	$\{\delta\}$	$\{\delta\}$

(b) Closed observation table.

Fig. 3. The closure of an observation table after the addition of a suffix

		ϵ	a	x
S	ϵ	$\{\delta\}$	$\{x,\delta\}$	$\emptyset$
	a	$\{x,\delta\}$	$\{x\}$	$\{x\}$
	aa	$\{x\}$	$\{x\}$	$\{x,y\}$
	aax	$\{x,y\}$	$\{x,y\}$	$\{\delta\}$
	$a\delta$	$\{\delta\}$	$\{x\}$	$\emptyset$
	$aaxy$	$\{\delta\}$	$\{\delta\}$	$\emptyset$
$S \cdot L_\delta$	δ	$\{\delta\}$	$\{x,\delta\}$	$\emptyset$
	ax	$\{x\}$	$\{x\}$	$\{\delta\}$
	aaa	$\{x\}$	$\{x\}$	$\{x,y\}$
	$aaxa$	$\{x,y\}$	$\{x,y\}$	$\{\delta\}$
	$aaxx$	$\{\delta\}$	$\{\delta\}$	$\emptyset$
	$a\delta a$	$\{x\}$	$\{x\}$	$\{y\}$
	$aaxya$	$\{\delta\}$	$\{\delta\}$	$\emptyset$
	$aaxy\delta$	$\{\delta\}$	$\{\delta\}$	$\emptyset$

(a) Adding x to E.

		ϵ	a	x
S	ϵ	$\{\delta\}$	$\{x,\delta\}$	$\emptyset$
	a	$\{x,\delta\}$	$\{x\}$	$\{x\}$
	aa	$\{x\}$	$\{x\}$	$\{x,y\}$
	aax	$\{x,y\}$	$\{x,y\}$	$\{\delta\}$
	$a\delta$	$\{\delta\}$	$\{x\}$	$\emptyset$
	$aaxy$	$\{\delta\}$	$\{\delta\}$	$\emptyset$
	ax	$\{x\}$	$\{x\}$	$\{\delta\}$
	$a\delta a$	$\{x\}$	$\{x\}$	$\{y\}$
	$a\delta ax$	$\{y\}$	$\{y\}$	$\emptyset$
$S \cdot L_\delta$	...	...	...	...

(b) Closed observation table.

Fig. 4. The construction of the final observation table

final table is produced (Table 4b). Part of the table is hidden for the sake of presentation. The hypothesis induced by that table is the one of Figure 1b, which is the suspension automaton of q, and the algorithm terminates.

Note that Algorithm 5 does not check for consistency in the table. The only action that adds elements to S is the closure of the table. The algorithm starts with a single element in S, i.e., ϵ, and table closure preserves consistency. Thus consistency is always satisfied. Algorithm 5 always terminates with a correct suspension automaton:

Theorem 6. *Given a finite input-ouput transition system SUL, running Algorithm 5 on SUL will terminate with a valid suspension automaton $\mathcal{H}$ whose set of accepted traces is equivalent to the set of suspension traces of SUL, i. e., $SUL \in [\mathcal{H}]_\delta$.*

7   Conclusions

In this paper we have applied L^*-style active learning to nondeterministic input/output labelled transition systems. The problems arising from the structure of labelled transition systems, such as the nondeterminism and the possibility to observe multiple inputs or outputs in sequence, have been addressed by modifying the observation table. Properties of the conjecture inferred from a closed table have been studied, and a new property has been described. This new property, quiescence reducibility, must be fulfilled by the observation table. Validating this new property, by acting on the observation table, leads to new states being added without the need of an equivalence query. We gave an algorithm that works on the modified observation table, checking also for the newly defined property. It is our belief that this paper can be the starting point for research leading to an efficient implementation of L^* for reactive systems behaving as labelled transition systems.

Future Work The results of this paper, are based on three assumptions: (i) the *testing assumption*, (ii) the *equivalence exhaustiveness*, and (iii) the *all weather conditions*. As future work, a study should be considered on the relaxation of the last two assumptions. Especially, obtaining the entire output set in one query is not feasible in practice. As a result, having less observations leads to construct an hypothesis which might be nonequivalent to the SUL. In this case, a different relation should be considered. An investigation might be done on **ioco** being a proper relation for this purpose. For the same reason, the table might be incomplete, making the construction of a valid hypothesis impossible, thus closedness and consistency might need to be redefined, as well. Another generalization of the problem can be addressed by dropping the input-completeness of the system under learning. In that setting, a different version of **ioco**, called **wioco** [17], could be helpful, given that it deals with non input-enabled implementations. Finally, an implementation of the algorithm is also to be considered.

References

1. Aarts, F., Heidarian, F., Kuppens, H., Olsen, P., Vaandrager, F.: Automata learning through counterexample guided abstraction refinement. In: Giannakopoulou, D., Méry, D. (eds.) FM 2012. LNCS, vol. 7436, pp. 10–27. Springer, Heidelberg (2012)
2. Aarts, F., Vaandrager, F.: Learning I/O automata. In: Gastin, P., Laroussinie, F. (eds.) CONCUR 2010. LNCS, vol. 6269, pp. 71–85. Springer, Heidelberg (2010)
3. Angluin, D.: Learning regular sets from queries and counterexamples. Information and Computation 75(2), 87–106 (1987)

4. Berg, T., Grinchtein, O., Jonsson, B., Leucker, M., Raffelt, H., Steffen, B.: On the correspondence between conformance testing and regular inference. In: Cerioli, M. (ed.) FASE 2005. LNCS, vol. 3442, pp. 175–189. Springer, Heidelberg (2005)
5. Bollig, B., Habermehl, P., Kern, C., Leucker, M.: Angluin-style learning of NFA, IJCAI 2009, pp. 1004–1009. Morgan Kaufmann Publishers Inc. (2009)
6. El-Fakih, K., Groz, R., Irfan, M.N., Shahbaz, M.: Learning finite state models of observable nondeterministic systems in a testing context. In: ICTSS 2010, pp. 97–102 (2010)
7. Howar, F., Isberner, M., Steffen, B., Bauer, O., Jonsson, B.: Inferring semantic interfaces of data structures. In: Margaria, T., Steffen, B. (eds.) ISoLA 2012, Part I. LNCS, vol. 7609, pp. 554–571. Springer, Heidelberg (2012)
8. Milner, R.: A Calculus of Communication Systems. LNCS, vol. 92. Springer, Heidelberg (1980)
9. Niese, O.: An integrated approach to testing complex systems. Ph.D. thesis, University of Dortmund (2003)
10. Pacharoen, W., Toshiaki, A., Bhattarakosol, P., Surarerks, A.: Active Learning of Non-deterministic Finite State Machines. In: Mathematical Problems in Engineering 2013, p. 11 (2013)
11. Rivest, R., Schapire, R.: Inference of finite automata using homing sequences. In: Hanson, S.J., Rivest, R.L., Remmele, W. (eds.) MIT-Siemens 1993. LNCS, vol. 661, pp. 51–73. Springer, Heidelberg (1993)
12. Shahbaz, M., Groz, R.: Inferring mealy machines. In: Cavalcanti, A., Dams, D.R. (eds.) FM 2009. LNCS, vol. 5850, pp. 207–222. Springer, Heidelberg (2009)
13. Smeenk, W.: Applying Automata Learning to Complex Industrial Software. Radboud University Nijmegen, master's thesis (2012)
14. Steffen, B., Howar, F., Merten, M.: Introduction to active automata learning from a practical perspective. In: Bernardo, M., Issarny, V. (eds.) SFM 2011. LNCS, vol. 6659, pp. 256–296. Springer, Heidelberg (2011)
15. Tretmans, J.: Test Generation with Inputs, Outputs and Repetitive Quiescence. Software-Concepts and Tools 3, 103–120 (1996)
16. Tretmans, J.: Model-based testing and some steps towards test-based modelling. In: Bernardo, M., Issarny, V. (eds.) SFM 2011. LNCS, vol. 6659, pp. 297–326. Springer, Heidelberg (2011)
17. Volpato, M., Tretmans, J.: Towards quality of model-based testing in the ioco framework. In: Proceedings of the 2013 International Workshop on Joining AcadeMiA and Industry Contributions to Testing Automation, JAMAICA 2013, pp. 41–46. ACM, New York (2013)
18. Willemse, T.A.C.: Heuristics for ioco-based test-based modelling. In: Brim, L., Haverkort, B.R., Leucker, M., van de Pol, J. (eds.) FMICS 2006 and PDMC 2006. LNCS, vol. 4346, pp. 132–147. Springer, Heidelberg (2007)

Verification of GUI Applications: A Black-Box Approach

Stephan Arlt, Evren Ermis, Sergio Feo-Arenis, and Andreas Podelski

University of Freiburg, Freiburg, Germany

Abstract. In this paper, we propose to base the verification of a GUI application on a reference model used in *black-box testing*. The reference model is a formal model for the behavior of the GUI application. It is derived by dynamic analysis (hence "black-box"). Thus, it can be used to account for the graphical interface even when the GUI toolkit is not amenable to formal analysis or its source code is not available. We have implemented our approach; a preliminary case study indicates its feasibility in principle.

> *"All models are wrong, but some are useful."*
> George E. P. Box

1 Introduction

A long line of research has lead to advanced testing methods for GUI applications [1,2,14,18,20], but so far there has been only little work on the verification of GUI applications [10,13,24]. Technically, a GUI application is a system where we can distinguish two layers: (1) the actual program which is written by the application programmer (it consists of a set of functions, the *event handlers*, one for each *event*) and (2) the GUI toolkit which accommodates the (graphical) interaction between the user and the program (it translates each user-triggered event to the call of the corresponding event handler).

Often the source code of the GUI toolkit is not amenable to formal analysis (it may not even be available). This is an issue for verification since the graphical interface determines the space of possible sequences of events. For example, an event may lead to opening a window and thus enable another event (which, say, can now be triggered via a button in the window). The space of possible sequences of events corresponds to the space of possible sequences of function calls and thus to the execution space of the GUI application.

In this paper, we propose a new approach to verification that allows one to resolve this issue. Our solution is to base the verification on the model of reference for *black-box testing*. In black-box testing, a model for the space of executable sequences of events is derived by a dynamic analysis. The dynamic analysis executes the GUI application in a systematic fashion (an example is the *GUI Ripper* of [21]) and ignores the source code (hence "black-box"). The purpose of this *black-box model* is to define a space of sequences of events that is

T. Margaria and B. Steffen (Eds.): ISoLA 2014, Part I, LNCS 8802, pp. 236–252, 2014.

useful for the selection of ('executable') test cases. The black-box model defines an infinite execution space and the set of selected test cases must be finite. Thus, (in Dijkstra's words [9]) the test can never prove the absence of a bug in the execution space defined by the black-box model. The new approach to verification can.

We present a verification method that proves the absence of a class of runtime errors (formalized as the safety of **assert** statements) in the execution space defined by the black-box model. I.e., the method verifies the correctness of the GUI application with respect to a particular formal semantics, namely the one that is defined by the black-box model.

The input to the verification method consists of (1) the event handler program and (2) the black-box model. The first step of the method consists of a semantics-preserving translation of the black-box model into a *driver program*. The driver program simulates the user interaction by non-determinism but restricts the choice of events in such a way that their order in each possible sequence conforms to the black-box model. The second step of the method is to construct a new program which is composed of the event handler program (which, as mentioned above, defines the event handler functions) and the driver program (which calls the event handler functions in the order of the simulated events). The third step of the method consists of applying a program verification tool (e.g., the software model checker AUTOMIZER [15]) to the new program.

We have implemented the verification method in a prototypical infrastructure; a preliminary case study indicates its feasibility in principle. Many design choices are open, however, and there are several directions in which one can explore the practical potential of the approach. This is not the focus of this paper. The focus in this paper is to introduce the approach of black-box verification for GUI applications and to define its formal foundation.

Roadmap. The next section uses an example to illustrate the overall approach. Section 3 introduces a formal setting for verification and in particular it defines the black-box semantics of a GUI application and the corresponding notion of correctness. This sets the stage for the black-box approach to verification. Section 4 instantiates the approach and introduces a verification method which is based on a particular version of a black-box model (the *EFG*). Section 5 presents the case study for the implementation of the verification method in a rather prototypical infrastructure. Section 6 discusses limitations and extensions of our approach, and Section 7 presents related work. Section 8 is the conclusion section.

2 Example

In this section we illustrate the application of our approach on an example of a GUI application. The example application depicted in the screenshot in Figure 1 consists of a `MainWindow` and a `Dialog`. The `MainWindow` contains two buttons which can fire the events e_1 and e_2. The `Dialog` contains one button which can fire event e_3.

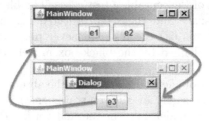

Fig. 1. An example of a GUI application. The arrows between the two screenshots indicate the transition between two views: Clicking the button for event e_2 leads to the Dialog; i.e., the buttons for the events e_1 and e_2 are no longer enabled. Clicking the button for event e_3 closes the Dialog and leads back to the first view; i.e., the buttons for the events e_1 and e_2 are enabled again.

```
1   class MainWindow extends JFrame {
2     File file;
3
4     void e1() {
5       file = null;
6     }
7
8     void e2() {
9       file = new File();
10      // assert(null != file);
11      file.open();
12
13      Dialog dialog = new Dialog(this);
14      // assert(null != dialog);
15      dialog.setVisible(true);
16    }
17
18    class Dialog extends JDialog {
19      void e3() {
20        // assert(null != file);
21        file.write(42);
22        file.close();
23
24        this.setVisible(false);
25      }
26    }
27  }
```

Fig. 2. A code snippet of the event handler program of our example application. The event handler e_1 assigns the value *null* to the field file (line 5). The event handler e_2 opens a file (line 9-11) and displays the dialog (line 13-15). The event handler e_3 writes something to the file (line 20-22), closes it, and hides the dialog (line 24).

We show the event handler program (which, as mentioned above, is written by the application programmer and which contains the event handler function for each of the three events) in Figure 2.

In the example application, the correctness of executions is specified with the help of **assert** statements. Each assertion expresses that the access to a variable is well-defined (here: that the variable is not **null**; see line 10, line 14, and line 20 in Figure 2). In our implementation, we exploit the fact that such **assert** statements are inserted automatically by the translation to the Boogie code; see [4]. The execution is correct (or: *safe*) if the specified assertion holds whenever the **assert** statement is executed.

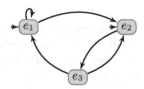

Fig. 3. A black-box model (an Event Flow Graph (EFG)) for the example application. Note that event e_3 can follow only after e_2. A path in the EFG encodes a sequence of user interactions. The marking of initial nodes encodes that a user interaction can start with e_1 and e_2, but not with e_3.

Figure 3 shows the black-box model that is derived automatically by the *GUI Ripper* presented in [21] (which is essentially a systematic way to execute the GUI application). Here, a set of sequences of events is represented by an *Event Flow Graph*, short EFG (which is used to generate test cases in [20]). Each node in this directed graph corresponds to one of the three events e_1, e_2, and e_3. An edge between two events states that the corresponding events can be executed consecutively. The idea is that a path in the EFG encodes a possible history of user interactions, i.e., an executable sequence of events. The marking of e_1 and e_2 as initial nodes encodes how a user interaction can start. The EFG is equivalent to a finite automaton (over the alphabet of events) which has essentially three states, one for each event; each state records the letter read by the transition leading to the state. As an aside, to discuss a (perhaps non-trivial) engineering issue, we can apply the tool *Gazoo* [1,2] and the tool *Joogie* [3] in order to extract the event handlers (first in Java bytecode [17], then in Boogie [4]).

In the first step of our verification method, we translate the EFG into a *driver program* (not shown). In the second step, we construct a new program which composes the driver program and the event handlers. The new program is shown in Figure 4. The program starts with the block **START**, which provides a **goto** statement, which in turn allows the non-deterministic choice of the blocks **e1** and **e2**. The blocks that can be chosen within the block **START** conform to the initial events that can be chosen from the EFG. In this program, each event handler is encoded as a set of blocks. For example, the event handler for event

e_1 is encoded in block e1, the one for event e_2 in block e2 etc.. The last block of each event handler contains a goto statement, which allows a non-deterministic choice of possible succeeding events according to the EFG. Finally, the block EXIT is responsible for closing the GUI application.

The third step of our verification method is to apply the software model checker AUTOMIZER in [15] to the program in Figure 4, which returns that the program is SAFE.

In the example, it is easy to see that all executions according to the black-box semantics specified by the EFG are safe. We note that the variable file is set to null in (the event handler for) event e_1 and accessed in event e_3. However, as specified by the EFG, it is not possible to have event e_3 follow directly after event e_1.

Discussion. The following two points concern the relationship between the set of event sequences that are executable in the GUI application (i.e., the system for which we build a formal model using the EFG) and the set of event sequences that is defined by the EFG; see Figure 5.

(1) The correctness statement produced by the verification method does not extend to executions outside of the black-box semantics specified by the EFG. The edges in the EFG arise from sample executions; it is possible that an edge is missing because the construction of the EFG by the GUI Ripper misses a crucial sample execution. In this case, there exists an event sequence in the set obtained by the set-theoretic difference blue\gray of the sets in Figure 5.

(2) The motivation for the construction of the EFG in black-box testing is to optimize the selection of test cases, i.e., to avoid the selection of (*too many*) event sequences that are not executable (e.g., because the button for an event is not enabled). Nevertheless, in general not every event sequence in the black-box model is executable (to optimize the scalability of the construction of the black-box model, only binary dependencies between the order of events are recorded); i.e., there may exist event sequences in the set obtained by the set-theoretic difference gray\blue of the sets in Figure 5. In other words, the black-box semantics is an abstraction (a conservative approximation) of the set of executions that are the target of the black-box test (i.e., of the intersection gray ∩ blue).

For verification, it does not matter whether the event sequence is executable or not *as long as the corresponding execution is correct* (a principle which is exploited in all abstraction-based verification methods). As always in abstraction-based verification, the abstraction must not be too coarse, which here means that non-executable event sequences may correspond to unsafe executions. For example, if we took the trivial EFG (a totally connected graph), the verification for the corresponding black-box semantics would not succeed (take any event sequence where event e_3 follows directly after event e_1, which leads to the violation of the assertion in the event handler for e_3).

```
1   procedure GUI_Application () modifies ... {
2     START:
3       // do initialization
4       ...
5       goto e1, e2;
6
7     // handler of event 1
8     e1:
9       $file := $null;
10      goto e1, e2, EXIT;
11
12    // handler of event 2
13    e2:
14      // open file
15      call $file := File$File$ctor ();
16      assert($file != $null);
17      call void$File$open ($file);
18
19      // open dialog
20      call void$Dialog$setVisible (true);
21      goto e3, EXIT;
22
23    // handler of event 3
24    e3:
25      // write to file and close it
26      assert($file != $null);
27      call void$File$write ($file, 42);
28      call $file := void$File$close ($file);
29
30      // close dialog
31      call void$Dialog$setVisible (false);
32      goto e1, e2;
33
34    EXIT:
35      return;
36  }
```

Fig. 4. A code snippet of the Boogie program constructed in Step 2 of our verification method. The program is composed from the driver program (obtained by translating the EFG in Figure 3) and the event handler program of the GUI application in Figure 1. The procedure GUI_Application defines a set of blocks for the event handlers e1, e2, and e3. The event handler e1 assigns the value null to variable file (line 9). The event handler e2 opens a file (line 14-17) and displays the dialog (line 19-20). The event handler e3 writes something to the file (line 25-28) and closes it afterwards. Finally, the event handler e3 hides the dialog (line 30-31).

GUI application   EFG

Fig. 5. Venn diagram illustrating the relationship between the (blue) set of event sequences that are executable in the GUI application (i.e., the system for which we build a formal model using the EFG) and the (gray) set of event sequences that is defined by the EFG. The two sets that are obtained by set-theoretic difference (i.e., blue\gray and gray\blue) are generally non-empty.

3   Black-Box Semantics

We assume given a set of *events* E. The event handler program $\mathcal{P}$ consists of definitions of functions,

$$\mathcal{P} = \{f_e \mid e \in E\}$$

where f_e is an *event handler* function for each event e in E.

An execution of a GUI application is a sequence of calls of event handler functions. Each sequence starts with the call of an *initialization function* f_{init} which we associate with a dummy event e_{init} (i.e., $f_{\text{init}} = f_{e_{\text{init}}}$). Note that the dummy event must not be confused with *initial events*, i.e., events with which a user interaction can start (and which are singled out by the EFG).

We assume that the definitions of the event handler functions come with a correctness specification (e.g., an annotation of the code with **assert** statements as in Boogie [4]) and that it is well-defined when a sequence of calls of functions of $\mathcal{P}$ is correct (e.g., when the execution of all its **assert** statements is *safe*).

The intuition is that the sequence of function calls stems from a sequence of interactions of a user with the GUI application. Each function call is triggered by an event (whenever the user initiates an event, e.g., by clicking a button). Thus, an execution corresponds to a sequence of events. Which event sequences are possible depends on the GUI toolkit.

In our formal setting, we model the behavior of the GUI toolkit by a set L of *event sequences*, i.e., L is a formal language over the alphabet of events.

$$L \subseteq E^{\star}$$

We assume that the language L is defined by a *black-box model* which is usually represented by some variant of finite automata [5,20,26]. In principle, the language L can be defined by the GUI toolkit itself. In this case, the definition is constructive only if the source code is available, and L will be not regular in general, and perhaps not even effectively representable.

We model the GUI application as a *closed system*. I.e., we simulate the user interaction by non-determinism and restrict the non-deterministic choice of events in each sequence in such a way that their order conforms to the black-box model (i.e., the sequence is a word in the language L). Formally, the event handler program $\mathcal{P}$ and the black-box model defining the language of event sequences L determine the semantics for the GUI application.

Definition 1 (Black-box semantics, correctness of a GUI application).
We assume that a GUI application is given by the event handler program $\mathcal{P} = \{f_e \mid e \in E\}$ which defines a set of event handler functions, and a black-box model which defines the language of event sequences L. The black-box semantics *of the GUI application is the set of all executions corresponding to a sequence of calls of event handler functions, i.e., a sequence of the form $f_{e_0}, f_{e_1}, \ldots, f_{e_n}$ where f_{e_0} is the initialization function and the sequence of events $e_1, \ldots, e_n$ forms a word in the language L.*

$$[\![\, \mathcal{P} \,]\!]_L = \{f_{e_0}, f_{e_1}, \ldots, f_{e_n} \mid f_{e_0} = f_{\mathsf{init}}, \; e_1 \ldots e_n \in L\}$$

The GUI application is correct *if each execution in the black-box semantics is correct.*

4   Verification Method

We now instantiate our approach and define a verification method where the black-box model, i.e., the set of event sequences L, is given by an event flow graph (EFG). An overview of the steps involved is shown in Figure 6.

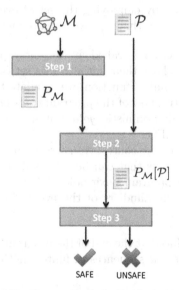

Fig. 6. Overview of our verification method. In the first step, a black-box model $\mathcal{M}$ is translated into the *driver program* $P_\mathcal{M}$. The second step composes the new program $P_\mathcal{M}[\mathcal{P}]$ by using the driver program $P_\mathcal{M}$ and the event handler program $\mathcal{P}$. In the third step, a program verification tool is applied to the new program.

The verification method takes as input an event handler program $\mathcal{P}$ (which defines functions) and an event flow graph $\mathcal{M}$. The EFG $\mathcal{M}$ can be created automatically [21]. An event flow graph [20] is a black-box model in the form of a directed graph

$$\mathcal{M} = (E, E_0, \delta),$$

where E is the set of events, $E_0 \subseteq E$ is the set of initial events and $\delta \subseteq E \times E$ is the event flow relation. An edge $(e, e') \in \delta$ between two events $e, e' \in E$ states that the event e' can be executed after the event e. If there is no edge between events e, e' then event e' cannot be executed after event e.

An EFG model $\mathcal{M}$ defines a formal language over the alphabet of events, $L(\mathcal{M})$, which is defined as the set of sequences of events which label a path in the EFG starting with an initial node. Thus, $L(\mathcal{M})$ is the set of sequences of the form $\sigma = e_0, e_1, \ldots, e_n$ where $e_0, \ldots, e_n \in E$ and $e_0 \in E_0$, the edge (e_i, e_{i+1}) is in the event flow relation δ for all indices $1 \leq i < n$.

We now present the verification method. The method establishes the correctness of an application defined by program $\mathcal{P}$ with respect to an event flow graph $\mathcal{M}$. By Definition 1, the correctness means that all sequences in $[\![\mathcal{P}]\!]_{L(\mathcal{M})}$ are correct.

The verification method consists of three steps.

(1) In the first step of our method, we construct a driver program $P_{\mathcal{M}}$ which simulates the message loop by employing the set of event handlers E and the EFG $\mathcal{M}$. For that, we perform the steps we already indicated in Section 2:

(a) The initialization function is called at the entry point to make sure the application's variables have their initial values set correctly.
(b) Immediately after the initial function, we simulate the message loop of the GUI toolkit. The control flow of the program transfers non-deterministically (by means of a non deterministic *goto* statement) to the handlers of the initial nodes e in the EFG.
(c) At the end of each call, the control transfers again non-deterministically to the handlers of the events that can be executed subsequently as indicated by the EFG or to the program's exit point. That is, the targets of the jump after calling f_{e_i} are the handlers of the events in the set $\{e_i \mid (e, e_i) \in \delta\} \cup \{EFG\_Exit\}$.

The exit label is introduced at the end of the program. The jump to that label is necessary to simulate event sequences of finite length in the case of a cyclic EFG.

(2) In the second step, we use the driver program $P_{\mathcal{M}}$ and the event handler definitions provided in the input program $\mathcal{P}$ to compose the verification program $P_{\mathcal{M}}[\mathcal{P}]$. The code of the event handlers is introduced into the driver program. Note that in contrast to what is shown in the example in Figure 4 (where the functions are inlined), we here phrase the program construction in terms of function calls.

To better illustrate the program transformation, the control flow graph of the program generated for the example in Section 2 is shown in Figure 7, a simplified version of the source code is shown in Figure 4. Note the similarity of the control flow graph of the generated program and the original EFG (see Figure 3).

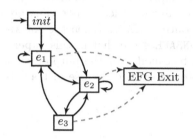

Fig. 7. Control flow graph of the program generated for the example of Section 2. The nodes correspond to the function calls for the initialization function and the event handlers.

An execution of $P_{\mathcal{M}}[\mathcal{P}]$ is a sequence of function calls where the functions are the event handlers which are defined in $\mathcal{P}$. We are thus in a situation analogous to Definition 1 and we can define the semantics $[\![\, P_{\mathcal{M}}[\mathcal{P}]\,]\!]$ as the set of sequences of function calls.

The soundness of our verification method can now be phrased in terms of the black-box semantics and the semantics of the program $P_{\mathcal{M}}[\mathcal{P}]$, as stated in the theorem below.

Theorem 1 (Soundness of black-box verification method). *Given an EFG $\mathcal{M}$, the black-box semantics of the GUI application coincides with the semantics of the program constructed in Step 2 of the verification method. I.e.,*

$$[\![\, \mathcal{P}\,]\!]_{L(\mathcal{M})} = [\![\, P_{\mathcal{M}}[\mathcal{P}]\,]\!]$$

The theorem holds essentially by the construction of $P_{\mathcal{M}}$. To give more details, let $\ell = f_{e_0}, \ldots, f_{e_n}$ be a function call sequence in $[\![\, \mathcal{P}\,]\!]_{L(\mathcal{M})}$. By the construction of $P_{\mathcal{M}}$, step (a), $f_{e_0} = f_{e_{\mathsf{init}}}$ is the function called at the entry point of the program. Functions called immediately after initialization are the handlers of initial events. This is ensured by step (b) of the program construction. By step (c), every pair of functions $(f_{e_i}, f_{e_{i+1}})$ for $1 \leq i < n$ corresponds to the edge of the EFG (e_i, e_{i+1}). Thus, ℓ is an execution of $P_{\mathcal{M}}$.

Finally, let $\ell = f_{e_0}, f_{e_1}, \ldots, f_{e_n}$ be a function call sequence not in $[\![\, \mathcal{P}\,]\!]_{L(\mathcal{M})}$. We distinguish three cases:

- The first function call f_{e_0} is not the initialization function. This contradicts step (a) of the construction.
- The following function call f_{e_1} is not the handler of an initial event, i.e. $e_1 \notin E_0$. This contradicts step (b).

– There exists some position i, with $1 \leq i < n$, such that (e_i, e_{i+1}) is not an edge of the EFG. This contradicts step (c).

Thus, ℓ is not an execution of $P_{\mathcal{M}}$.

(3) In the third step, we apply a software model checker to the program $P_{\mathcal{M}}[\mathcal{P}]$ obtained in Step 2 to determine whether all assertions are safe. If this is the case, our verification method outputs SAFE. When the software model checker finds a violation, we output UNSAFE. Note that in this paper, we concentrate on the verification of the black box model for the purpose of proving correctness. We leave it to future work to investigate the use of black-box verification for bug finding.

5   Case Study

5.1   Implementation

We have implemented and integrated the translation of a black-box model and the translation of an event handler program into *Joogie* [3]. As input, Joogie accepts an Event Flow Graph as the black-box model, and a Java program (e.g., a JAR archive) as the event handler program. The implementation is available for download at joogie.org.

For simplicity, and without loss of generality, we considered only events whose handlers change the program state without considering user inputs such as, e.g., string values in text boxes or choices of radio buttons. Those events that read user inputs can be trivially replaced by a family of events where there is one for every possible input value, at the cost of an increased program size. Alternatively, the scope of the verification can be reduced by introducing restricted input ranges as assumptions in the translation to Boogie code, at the cost of providing a verification result applicable only to the input ranges specified.

Furthermore, the implementation makes use of inlining the event handlers (as opposed to issuing function calls) to avoid the problem of inferring function contracts and enable the use of a modular static analyzer. In our setting, we apply the model checker AUTOMIZER [15]. However, our approach is not restricted by the use of a specific software model checker.

5.2   Results

We apply our prototype implementation to the example presented in Section 2, and to a suite of benchmarks from the *Community Event-based Testing (COMET)*. The benchmarks contain GUI applications (written in Java) and a corresponding black-box model respectively (here, an Event Flow Graph)[1]. These benchmarks have been used in several studies on GUI testing (e.g., [16,19]). All experiments are run on a workstation with 4 GHz CPU, 8 GB RAM. The focus of this study is to evaluate, whether our approach is technically feasible.

---

[1] Available for download at comet.unl.edu

The results of our experiments are summarized in Table 1. We report the number of events, the time needed for the model checking and the final result of the benchmark. The time required for the translation of the original Java application is approximately one second for all benchmarks.

Table 1. The results of the case study. We report the name of the benchmark; the number of events in the black-box model; the duration (in seconds) of the model checking; and finally the result of the model checking.

Benchmark	Events	Time (s)	Result
Our example	3	0,268	SAFE
COMET repair-2-cons	3	0,606	SAFE
COMET repair-2-excl	3	0,558	SAFE
COMET repair-3-cons	4	0,789	SAFE
COMET repair-3-excl	5	1,005	SAFE
COMET repair-cmpd	5	0,968	SAFE

For all benchmarks, our approach correctly proved the corresponding Event Flow Graphs as SAFE. The time needed ranges from 0.2 to 1.0 seconds. Both the result of the benchmark as well as the time needed indicate, that our approach is technically feasible in principle.

We must leave the verification of fully-fledged GUI applications to future work. The reason is the prototypical nature of our implementation. Some language features used by the open-source applications are not yet supported by our infrastructure.

The current implementation assumes calls to external library functions (including those in the GUI toolkit) to be side-effect free and to correctly handle all exceptions caused. Thus, finding an assertion violation in $P_\mathcal{M}[\mathcal{P}]$ points either to a real bug in the original program $\mathcal{P}$ or to a false alarm caused by our assumptions on the semantics of library function calls.

The handling of external function calls would need to extend the analysis in order to check whether the calls issued from $\mathcal{P}$ do not cause errors by violating the library contracts and by considering any modifications in the state of $\mathcal{P}$ caused indirectly, e.g., through call-backs or the modification of global state variables.

6   Discussion

In this section we discuss the creation of the black-box model and a possible extension of our approach to enable model learning.

6.1   Black-Box Model

As shown in Section 4, the verification method presented in this paper is sound with respect to the event sequences represented by the provided EFG. That is, when the verification reports SAFE, it is guaranteed that none of the sequences analyzed violate the specifications.

However, our approach is based on the model of reference for black-box testing. The black-box model represents the space of executable event sequences and is derived by a dynamic analysis called *GUI Ripper* [21] which ignores the source code. The GUI Ripper constructs an event flow graph (the black-box model) by executing the GUI application. For completeness we describe it briefly: The execution of the GUI application explores the hierarchical structure of the GUI using depth-first search. For each widget found during the execution, say a button OK, the GUI Ripper triggers the assigned event, i.e., a button click. By recording the history of triggered events, the GUI Ripper detects the event flow and stores it in the EFG. Since the GUI Ripper represents a dynamic analysis (i.e., the GUI application is executed in order to extract events) using depth-first search, there exist two major limitations:

First, the GUI Ripper cannot guarantee that all event sequences in the resulting black-box model are executable. That is, a path in the EFG (forming an event sequence) might not be executable, since its events are only pair-wise executable. Note that there is empirical evidence that even long event sequences obtained from an EFG can run without failures [28]. However, the EFG represents an approximation of the actual event-flow of the GUI application.

The second limitation of the GUI Ripper is that it cannot guarantee to find all widgets of the GUI application. For instance, the application itself might be faulty, e.g., a new window opens in the background and the GUI Ripper misses it. Furthermore, whether a widget is visible or hidden during the dynamic analysis may depend on the environment (e.g., user settings). These problems tend to be of technical nature and their severity might differ depending on the platform used.

To summarize, the dynamic analysis is neither sound nor complete as it may either miss events available in the GUI application or construct a model that contains non-executable event sequences.

6.2   Model Learning

Due to the nature of our verification approach, spurious counterexamples can be output. That is, the model checker may output UNSAFE for event sequences that are not executable. A model learning refinement step may be added to our approach to enable those sequences to be excluded automatically. Other authors propose analogous approaches [8,25,27].

The violating sequence output by the model checker can be replayed on the GUI application to determine whether it is executable. An event sequence is a path in the input EFG. If it is not executable, the graph can be modified to ensure that the sequence is no longer contained in a refined EFG. In order to achieve this goal, we first convert both the EFG and the non-executable event sequence into non-deterministic finite automata, which allows us to apply regular languages operations on these automata. In particular, the non-executable event sequence is encoded as an accepting word of the EFG automaton. We construct the complement of the accepting word and intersect it with the EFG automaton. The result is a refined EFG automaton which does not accept the non-executable event sequence. Finally, we convert the refined EFG automaton back into an EFG and restart the verification using it as input. A detailed elaboration of the learning step is the subject of future work.

7 Related Work

To precede the summary of our comparison with related work, our work is the first to investigate the definition of a formal semantics based on a black-box model and the verification of a GUI application with respect to a black-box semantics.

An approach which comes closest to our work is [22,23] which incorporates planning from the domain of artificial intelligence to generate test cases for GUI applications. The input to the planning system is a set of operators (namely, the event handlers), an initial state, and a goal state of the GUI application. The planning system outputs a sequence of operators that lead from the initial state to the goal state. However, in this approach a test engineer has to manually define the preconditions and effects of each operator. Our approach extends this idea as follows: First, we propose an automatic translation of the operators of a GUI application into a Boogie program. Second, the static analysis of our approach can be replaced by other techniques.

The work in [6] presents a general approach to specify user interactions in GUI applications from a design perspective. This technique allows the analysis of user interactions using model checking, and the synthesis of user interactions to executable GUI applications. Since the work in [6] presents a high-level approach, it obviates the efforts of extracting models, e.g., from the source code of an existing application. In our case, we focus on supporting a test engineer which usually deals with executable GUI applications instead of abstract models. Hence, the translation of an existing application into a verifiable program presents one of the main technical contribution of this paper. In particular, our approach allows the analysis of an executable GUI application, e.g., even in the phase of *release-to-manufacturing* within a software release life cycle.

An approach which identifies useful abstractions of existing GUI applications is presented in [10]. Those abstractions are based on structural features of GUI applications, e.g., the enabledness of a button (enabled or disabled) using a boolean value, or the current value of slider control using an integer value. First, the abstractions are inferred manually from a GUI application. Then, the abstractions are used to build a model which is checked by SMV [7]. In order to overcome the manual identification abstractions, the work in [11] focuses on the automatic analysis of interaction orderings with model checking. In the work [11] the model is inferred via analyzing the code statically. The static analysis is tailored to a specific GUI toolkit, namely Java Swing. Our approach uses a dynamic approach: a model (the EFG) is created during the execution of the GUI application. Since GUI code is written in many ways, a static analysis technique must be tailored to comprehend the behavior of each GUI toolkit. The use of a black-box model is justified by the reasonable trade-off between applicability and precision of a black-box model. Furthermore, the EFG is a black-box model which works independently from a currently used GUI toolkit.

The work in [1] (with shared co-authors) presents a lightweight static analysis, which generates all event sequences that are at the same time executable and justifiably relevant. First, the approach infers a model which expresses dependencies of events of the GUI application. Second, event sequences of bounded length are generated from this dependency model. Third, an event flow graph is incorporated in order to convert event sequences from the dependency model into executable event sequences. The work presented in this paper represents a logical next step in the line of that work: it uses an advanced static analysis which is able to reason about properties of a GUI application, instead of generating all event sequences that might violate a specific property.

8   Conclusion

We have presented a novel approach to the verification of GUI applications, an approach that deals with the setting where one of its layers, the GUI toolkit, is not amenable to static analysis or is not available at all. We have shown that one can define a formal semantics even in this setting, namely by basing the formal semantics on a black-box model which accounts for the behavior of the graphical user interface.

A disclaimer is in order. Our approach is not compatible with the goal of *pervasive* verification. We use a formal model (the black-box model) that is constructed with the help of a dynamic analysis, i.e., with a systematically chosen but nevertheless finite and thus incomplete set of sample executions. Our method is rather comparable with the verification of models that are constructed manually. As every formal method, our method can give a guarantee only as far as the model is concerned, and every model can account only for some part of the system. The difference with the manually constructed model (and a bit of an unorthodoxy) lies in the fact that the black-box model is constructed automatically with a technique that stems from a notoriously incomplete method (namely testing).

We have implemented the verification method in a prototypical infrastructure; a preliminary case study indicates its feasibility in principle. Many design choices are open, however, and there are several directions in which one can explore the practical potential of the approach.

An interesting potential for our verification method may lie in its use to *complete* a test; i.e., its success tells the tester that she can stop testing (at least for the specified runtime error, and at least among the test cases that can be selected from the derived black-box model). Additionally, the analysis of GUI programs could be extended by automatically deriving and integrating specifications for external libraries whose code is not necessarily available.

We also see an interesting potential of our verification method for bug finding (an incorrect execution in the black-box semantics may correspond to a bug). We must leave the exploration of this direction to future work.

Other applications are also subject of further investigation: The idea of generating a driver program to encode non-determinism is also useful for verification tasks in areas such as interrupt-driven programming or data structure and library invariants [12]. Here, as in our work, a model of the behavior of external users or components can be useful to move from strenuous testing towards formal verification.

References

1. Arlt, S., Podelski, A., Bertolini, C., Schaef, M., Banerjee, I., Memon, A.M.: Lightweight Static Analysis for GUI Testing. In: ISSRE, pp. 301–310 (2012)
2. Arlt, S., Podelski, A., Wehrle, M.: Reducing GUI Test Suites via Program Slicing. In: ISSTA, pp. 270–281 (2014)
3. Arlt, S., Schäf, M.: Joogie: Infeasible Code Detection for Java. In: Madhusudan, P., Seshia, S.A. (eds.) CAV 2012. LNCS, vol. 7358, pp. 767–773. Springer, Heidelberg (2012)
4. Barnett, M., Chang, B.-Y.E., DeLine, R., Jacobs, B., M. Leino, K.R.: Boogie: A Modular Reusable Verifier for Object-Oriented Programs. In: de Boer, F.S., Bonsangue, M.M., Graf, S., de Roever, W.-P. (eds.) FMCO 2005. LNCS, vol. 4111, pp. 364–387. Springer, Heidelberg (2006)
5. Belli, F.: Finite-State Testing and Analysis of Graphical User Interfaces. In: ISSRE, pp. 34–43 (2001)
6. Berstel, J., Crespi-Reghizzi, S., Roussel, G., Pietro, P.S.: A Scalable Formal Method for Design and Automatic Checking of User Interfaces. In: ICSE, pp. 453–462 (2001)
7. Clarke, E.M., Grumberg, O., Long, D.E.: Model Checking and Abstraction. In: POPL, pp. 342–354 (1992)
8. Cobleigh, J.M., Giannakopoulou, D., Păsăreanu, C.S.: Learning Assumptions for Compositional Verification. In: Garavel, H., Hatcliff, J. (eds.) TACAS 2003. LNCS, vol. 2619, pp. 331–346. Springer, Heidelberg (2003)
9. Dijkstra, E.W.: Notes on Structured Programming. Circulated privately (April 1970)
10. Dwyer, M.B., Carr, V., Hines, L.: Model Checking Graphical User Interfaces Using Abstractions. In: ESEC / SIGSOFT FSE, pp. 244–261 (1997)
11. Dwyer, M.B., Tkachuk, O., Visser, W.: Analyzing Interaction Orderings with Model Checking. In: ASE, pp. 154–163 (2004)
12. Feo-Arenis, S.: Evaluation of a Data Structure Invariant Generation Technique. Master's thesis, University of Freiburg (March 2010)
13. Ganov, S., Killmar, C., Khurshid, S., Perry, D.E.: Event Listener Analysis and Symbolic Execution for Testing GUI Applications. In: Breitman, K., Cavalcanti, A. (eds.) ICFEM 2009. LNCS, vol. 5885, pp. 69–87. Springer, Heidelberg (2009)
14. Gross, F., Fraser, G., Zeller, A.: Search-based system testing: high coverage, no false alarms. In: ISSTA, pp. 67–77 (2012)
15. Heizmann, M., Christ, J., Dietsch, D., Ermis, E., Hoenicke, J., Lindenmann, M., Nutz, A., Schilling, C., Podelski, A.: Ultimate Automizer with SMTInterpol. In: Piterman, N., Smolka, S.A. (eds.) TACAS 2013 (ETAPS 2013). LNCS, vol. 7795, pp. 641–643. Springer, Heidelberg (2013)

16. Huang, S., Cohen, M.B., Memon, A.M.: Repairing GUI Test Suites Using a Genetic Algorithm. In: ICST, Paris, France (April 2010)
17. Lindholm, T., Yellin, F.: Java Virtual Machine Specification, 2nd edn. Addison-Wesley Longman Publishing Co., Inc., Boston (1999)
18. Mariani, L., Pezzè, M., Riganelli, O., Santoro, M.: AutoBlackTest: Automatic Black-Box Testing of Interactive Applications. In: ICST, pp. 81–90 (2012)
19. McMaster, S., Memon, A.M.: Call-Stack Coverage for GUI Test-Suite Reduction. IEEE Trans. Softw. Eng. (2008)
20. Memon, A.M.: An event-flow model of GUI-based applications for testing. Softw. Test., Verif. Reliab. 17(3), 137–157 (2007)
21. Memon, A.M., Banerjee, I., Nagarajan, A.: GUI Ripping: Reverse Engineering of Graphical User Interfaces for Testing. In: WCRE, pp. 260–269 (2003)
22. Memon, A.M., Pollack, M.E., Soffa, M.L.: Using a Goal-Driven Approach to Generate Test Cases for GUIs. In: ICSE, pp. 257–266 (1999)
23. Memon, A.M., Pollack, M.E., Soffa, M.L.: Hierarchical GUI Test Case Generation Using Automated Planning. IEEE Trans. Software Eng. 27(2), 144–155 (2001)
24. Paiva, A.C.R., Faria, J.C.P., Mendes, P.M.C.: Reverse Engineered Formal Models for GUI Testing. In: Leue, S., Merino, P. (eds.) FMICS 2007. LNCS, vol. 4916, pp. 218–233. Springer, Heidelberg (2008)
25. Raffelt, H., Merten, M., Steffen, B., Margaria, T.: Dynamic testing via automata learning. STTT 11(4), 307–324 (2009)
26. White, L.J., Almezen, H.: Generating Test Cases for GUI Responsibilities Using Complete Interaction Sequences. In: ISSRE, pp. 110–123 (2000)
27. Windmüller, S., Neubauer, J., Steffen, B., Howar, F., Bauer, O.: Active continuous quality control. In: CBSE, pp. 111–120 (2013)
28. Yuan, X., Cohen, M.B., Memon, A.M.: Covering array sampling of input event sequences for automated gui testing. In: ASE, pp. 405–408 (2007)

Fomal Methods and Analyses
in Software Product Line Engineering
(Track Summary)

Ina Schaefer[1] and Maurice H. ter Beek[2]

[1] Technical University of Braunschweig, Germany
[2] ISTI–CNR, Pisa, Italy

1 Motivation

Software product line engineering (SPLE) [5,11] aims to develop a family of software-intensive systems via systematic, large-scale reuse in order to reduce time-to-market and costs and to increase the quality of individual products. In order to achieve these goals, formal methods offer promising analysis techniques, which are best applied throughout the product-line lifecycle so as to maximize their overall efficiency and effectiveness.

While some analysis approaches (e.g. for feature modeling and variant management) and formal methods and automated verification techniques and tools (e.g. CSPs, SAT solvers, model checkers and formal semantics of variability models) have already been applied to SPLE (cf. [12,3,13] and the references therein), a considerable potential still appears to be unexploited. In fact, despite the work that we just mentioned, the respective communities (SPLE, formal methods and analysis tools) are only loosely connected.

2 Goals

This track brings together researchers and practitioners interested in raising the efficiency and effectiveness of SPLE by applying formal methods and innovative analysis techniques. Participants review the state-of-the-art and practice in their respective fields, identify further promising application areas, report practical requirements and constraints from real-world product lines, discuss drawbacks and complements of the various approaches, or present recent emerging ideas and results. The two long-term objectives of the FMSPLE workshop series are:

1. to raise awareness and to find a common understanding of practical challenges and existing solution approaches in the different communities working on formal methods and analyses techniques for SPLE, and
2. to create a broader community interested in formal methods and analysis techniques for SPLs in order to keep SPLE research and tools up-to-date with the latest technologies and with practical challenges.

T. Margaria and B. Steffen (Eds.): ISoLA 2014, Part I, LNCS 8802, pp. 253–256, 2014.
© Springer-Verlag Berlin Heidelberg 2014

While in the previous four years, FMSPLE has successfully been held as a work-shop affiliated with the international Software Product Line Conference (SPLC), its 5th edition is held as a track at ISoLA in order to facilitate discussions with other application domains of formal methods, verification and validation. Its 6th edition will be held as a workshop at ETAPS 2015. Because of the highly inter-active format of ISoLA tracks, locating FMSPLE as a track at ISoLA offers an excellent opportunity for exchanging results and experiences of applying formal methods and analysis techniques between SPLE and other application domains.

3   Contributions

The contributions of this track are separated into two parts. The first part con-sists of formal modeling approaches for variable software. The second part consid-ers formal analysis, testing and verification techniques for variant-rich software systems and SPLs.

Part 1: Formal Modeling. Iosif-Lazar et al. [9] present a core calculus for separate variability modeling. The approach is inspired from the Common Vari-ability Language (CVL), but aims at unifying other variability modeling ap-proaches such as Delta Modeling and Orthogonal Variability Modeling (OVM). The introduced language, Featherweight VML, contains a single kind of varia-tion point to define transformations of software artifacts in object models. Its semantics comprehensively formalizes variant derivation, encompassing feature models, variation points, implementation artifacts and transformations.

Collet [6] focuses on the modeling and management of multiple and com-plex feature models. This paper reports on the development and evolution of the FAMILIAR domain-specific language (for FeAture Model scrIpt Language for manIpulation and Automatic Reasoning) and toolset. The author presents the FAMILIAR language and discusses its various applications with advantages and drawbacks. Furthermore, he identifies challenges for feature modeling and management in the near future.

Damiani et al. [7] present a programming language approach for SPLs that builds on their existing work on delta-oriented programming and trait-based implementation of SPLs. In this approach, program modifications are expressed by delta modules which rely on the trait composition mechanism. This smooth integration of the modularity mechanisms provided by delta modules and traits constitutes a new approach for programming SPLs which is particularly well suited for evolving SPLs.

Broch Johnsen et al. [4] focus on deployment variability in virtualized product lines. Their approach is based on the ABS language which supports deployment models with a separation of concerns between execution cost and server capacity. This allows the model-based assessment of deployment choices on a product's quality of service. In this paper, the authors combine deployment models with the delta-oriented variability modeling to capture deployment choices as features when designing a family of products.

Part 2: Formal Analysis, Testing and Verification. Lochau et al. [10] propose a delta-oriented extension to the process calculus CCS, called DeltaCCS, that allows for modular reasoning about behavioral variability. In DeltaCCS, modular change directives, i.e. deltas, are applied to core processes in order to alter term rewriting semantics. Variability-aware congruences capture the preservation of behavioral properties defined by the modal μ-calculus between different CCS variants. A DeltaCCS model checker allows to efficiently verify the members of a family of process variants.

Devroey et al. [8] focus on coverage criteria for model-based testing of SPLs based on Featured Transition Systems (FTS). FTSs constitute a family-based representation of SPLs extending labeled transition systems such that transitions are moreover tagged with a feature. The authors define several FTS-aware structural testing coverage criteria and combine these with usage-based testing for configurable websites.

Ter Beek et al. [2] apply variability analyses on a small bike-sharing product line. To this aim, they adopt a chain of existing feature modeling and variability analysis tools (including S.P.L.O.T., FeatureIDE, Clafer, ClaferMOO and VMC) to specify a discrete feature model, non-functional quantitative properties and a behavioral model, and to perform a quantitative evaluation of the attributes of products and model checking over value-passing modal specifications.

Ter Beek and De Vink [1] present a proof-of-concept of a feature-oriented modular verification technique for analyzing the behavior of SPLs with the mCRL2 toolset. The behavioral model of a SPL is modularized into components, based on feature-driven borders, with interfaces that allow a driver process to glue them back together on the fly. This is a powerful abstraction technique that eases the model checking task, since it allows mCRL2 to concentrate on the relevant components (features) for a specific property, and moreover allows the result to be reused in other settings.

References

1. ter Beek, M.H., de Vink, E.P.: Towards Modular Verification of Software Product Lines with mCRL2. In: Margaria, T., Steffen, B. (eds.) ISoLA 2014. LNCS, vol. 8802, pp. 368–385. Springer, Heidelberg (2014)
2. ter Beek, M.H., Fantechi, A., Gnesi, S.: Challenges in Modelling and Analyzing Quantitative Aspects of Bike-Sharing Systems. In: Margaria, T., Steffen, B. (eds.) ISoLA 2014. LNCS, vol. 8802, pp. 351–367. Springer, Heidelberg (2014)
3. Borba, P., Cohen, M.B., Legay, A., Wąsowski, A.: Analysis, Test and Verification in The Presence of Variability (Dagstuhl Seminar 13091). Dagstuhl Reports 3(2), 144–170 (2013)
4. Johnsen, E.B., Schlatte, R., Tapia Tarifa, S.L.: Deployment Variability in Delta-Oriented Models. In: Margaria, T., Steffen, B. (eds.) ISoLA 2014, Part I. LNCS, vol. 8802, pp. 304–319. Springer, Heidelberg (2014)
5. Clements, P., Northrop, L.: Software Product Lines: Practices and Patterns. Addison Wesley, Longman (2001)
6. Collet, P.: Domain Specific Languages for Managing Feature Models: Advances and Challenges. In: Margaria, T., Steffen, B. (eds.) ISoLA 2014, Part I. LNCS, vol. 8802, pp. 273–288. Springer, Heidelberg (2014)

7. Damiani, F., Schaefer, I., Schuster, S., Winkelmann, T.: Delta-Trait Programming of Software Product Lines. In: Margaria, T., Steffen, B. (eds.) ISoLA 2014, Part I. LNCS, vol. 8802, pp. 289–303. Springer, Heidelberg (2014)
8. Devroey, X., Perrouin, G., Legay, A., Cordy, M., Schobbens, P.-Y., Heymans, P.: Coverage Criteria for Behavioural Testing of Software Product Lines. In: Margaria, T., Steffen, B. (eds.) ISoLA 2014, Part I. LNCS, vol. 8802, pp. 336–350. Springer, Heidelberg (2014)
9. Iosif-Lazăr, A.F., Schaefer, I., Wąsowski, A.: A Core Language for Separate Variability Modeling. In: Margaria, T., Steffen, B. (eds.) ISoLA 2014, Part I. LNCS, vol. 8802, pp. 257–272. Springer, Heidelberg (2014)
10. Lochau, M., Mennicke, S., Baller, H., Ribbeck, L.: DeltaCCS: A Core Calculus for Behavioral Change. In: Margaria, T., Steffen, B. (eds.) ISoLA 2014, Part I. LNCS, vol. 8802, pp. 320–335. Springer, Heidelberg (2014)
11. Pohl, K., Böckle, G., van der Linden, F.: Software Product Line Engineering: Foundations, Principles, and Techniques. Springer, Heidelberg (2005)
12. Schaefer, I., Rabiser, R., Clarke, D., Bettini, L., Benavides, D., Botterweck, G., Pathak, A., Trujilol, S., Villela, K.: Software Diversity: State of the Art and Perspectives. STTT 14(5), 477–495 (2012)
13. Thüm, T., Apel, S., Kästner, C., Schaefer, I., Saake, G.: A Classification and Survey of Analysis Strategies for Software Product Lines. ACM Comput. Surv. 47(1), 1–6 (2014)

A Core Language for Separate Variability Modeling*

Alexandru F. Iosif-Lazăr[1], Ina Schaefer[2], and Andrzej Wąsowski[1]

[1] IT University of Copenhagen
{afla,wasowski}@itu.dk
[2] Technische Universität Braunschweig
i.schaefer@tu-braunschweig.de

Abstract. Separate variability modeling adds variability to a modeling language without requiring modifications of the language or the supporting tools. We define a core language for separate variability modeling using a single kind of variation point to define transformations of software artifacts in object models. Our language, Featherweight VML, has several distinctive features. Its architecture and operations are inspired by the recently proposed Common Variability Language (CVL). Its semantics is considerably simpler than that of CVL, while remaining confluent (unlike CVL). We simplify complex hierarchical dependencies between variation points via copying and flattening. Thus, we reduce a model with intricate dependencies to a flat executable model transformation consisting of simple unconditional local variation points. The core semantics is extremely concise: it boils down to two operational rules, which makes it suitable to serve as a specification for implementations of trustworthy variant derivation. Featherweight VML offers insights in the execution of other variability modeling languages such as the Orthogonal Variability Model and Delta Modeling. To the best of our knowledge, this is the first attempt to comprehensively formalize variant derivation, encompassing feature models, variation points, implementation artifacts and transformations.

1 Introduction

Model-driven development [30] of software products exploits rich system models to represent the product architecture. When several products share a common set of core assets they can be developed as a software product line [9]. Modeling the product line architecture as a single *base model* facilitates the *derivation* of new *product variants* by reusing artifacts from existing ones. Variability models describe how the artifacts can be selected and recombined into new products.

Problem space modeling is performed by using feature models [21] (or alternatives such as decision models [28]) to describe how the characteristics of the products vary in a product line. Individual products are described by selecting a

---

* Supported by ARTEMIS JU under grant agreement n° 295397 and by Danish Agency for Science, Technology and Innovation.

T. Margaria and B. Steffen (Eds.): ISoLA 2014, Part I, LNCS 8802, pp. 257–272, 2014.
© Springer-Verlag Berlin Heidelberg 2014

set of features or resolving the decisions thus creating a particular configuration. Dependencies between features and decisions are often specified to determine which configurations are valid. Both feature and decision models have been studied extensively, including from the formal perspective [29], and their meaning is now widely accepted both in research and practice.

Solution space modeling means specifying which artifacts from the base model implement the product characteristics. It also specifies the method through which new products can be derived. Annotative Variability Modeling [11] uses annotations to mark the involvement of specific artifacts in the various aspects/characteristics. Product derivation is done by selecting only the artifacts with the desired annotations based on a configuration. Feature-Oriented Programming (FOP) [25] uses features to wrap the artifacts and describes a compositional approach to deriving new products. Other approaches [13] involve model transformations where artifacts can be both removed and added to existing models. All these approaches have been studied from a practical perspective, but they lack a formal understanding.

Software variability leads to great diversity which impacts all phases of software development, from requirements analysis, over system design and implementation, up to quality assurance and system analysis [27]. Separate variability models are independent of the language in which the base model is developed so they can be reused to some extent to handle a system's variability at multiple development phases. The *Orthogonal Variability Model* (OVM) [24], *Delta Modeling* [26] and the *Common Variability Language* (CVL) [10] are examples of separate variability modeling languages. While these languages have greatly advanced variability modeling and SPL development, their not so strict specifications have left room for confusion when implementing derivation tools.

Our objectives are (i) to understand the execution semantics used by the aforementioned languages and determine the core requirements for separate variability modeling, and (ii) to provide the formal specification of a language that could be used in the development of a trustworthy product variant derivation tool. Trustworthy product variant derivation is essential to the development of safety critical embedded systems in domains such as automotive or industrial automation [3,19]. Industrial standards such as IEC 61508 mandate the use of state of the art tools and quality assurance techniques. So far, the industry certifies individual products, or even avoids introducing any variability into safety critical parts of the systems[1]. Our goal is to facilitate the development of such systems and to enable usable certification strategies for product line tools.

Contributions presented in this paper are:

- A core language for separate variability modeling, Featherweight VML, along with an abstract semantics, which is as expressive and versatile as other existing variability modeling languages.
- A formal specification of semantics for features with cardinalities [14] and complex dependencies in the solution space model by copying and flattening the variability model.

---

[1] Personal communication with partners in ARTEMIS projects.

- A copying semantics for executing the model transformations defined in the solution space. We define *two* simple rules for determining which model elements are part of the desired product variant. Compared to in-place model transformations, a copying semantics can more easily be implemented in declarative rule-based model transformation languages and it is easier to reason about using theorem provers.
- A confluence result for our semantics: while other approaches suggest an implementation by in-place transformations (which makes the transformation order critical) our rules always produce the same result, independently of the order in which they are applied. This opens for new opportunities to implement product variant derivation tools using graph transformations.

The paper proceeds as follows. Section 2 provides an analysis of different variability modeling languages in order to determine the core requirements. Section 3 introduces a minimal representation of object-oriented models. Sections 4 and 5 describe the formal syntax and semantics of Featherweight VML. We discuss the advantages and limitations of Featherweight VML and also the related work in Sec. 6 and we conclude in Sec. 7.

2   Core Requirements

In order to develop a versatile foundation for variability modeling, we compare CVL, Delta Modeling and OVM. We aim to find similarities in the way these languages represent the problem and solution spaces and the execution of variability models. The results helps us setting a foundation for defining the semantics of Featherweight VML.

2.1   Overview of Variability Modeling Languages

The *Orthogonal Variability Model* (OVM) [24] is designed to handle variability between products. It leaves aside the common parts. It uses *variation points* to specify which characteristics can vary (e.g. color) and *variants* to specify how they vary (e.g. red, blue etc.). Dependency relations between the variation points and variants limit the set of valid configurations. All artifacts are contained in a single model. Both variation points and variants are mapped directly to these artifacts so the solution space does not involve complex transformations. When a configuration is selected (the desired variants are selected for each variation point) the model is executed by extracting only the artifacts that the configuration refers to.

In *Delta Modeling* [26], a product line is represented by a core module and a set of delta modules. The core module provides an implementation of a valid product that can be developed with well-established single application engineering techniques. Delta modules specify changes to be applied to the core module to implement further products by adding, modifying and removing artifacts. Delta Modeling can use any problem space model representation. Each delta module has an application condition which the configuration must respect in order for the delta to be executed. Delta Modeling can be applied to textual languages, such as the HATS Abstract Behavioral Specification Language [6], or graphical modeling languages, such as Matlab/Simulink [16].

The *Common Variability Language* (CVL) [10] is an industrial attempt to create a generic language that facilitates separate variability modeling for models specified in any MOF-based language [22]. It handles problem space modeling through a *variability specification* tree. The variability specifications are specialized features that can be resolved in particular ways: choices require a yes/no resolution; variables require a value for a specific artifact; classifiers represent features that can be instantiated multiple times in a configuration (similar to features with cardinalities [14]). CVL uses a constraint language to specify constraints over the variability specification tree. Configurations are represented as *resolution models*. CVL models the solution space by starting from a base model on which a wide range of transformations called *variation points*[1] is applied.

2.2 Comparative Analysis

Modeling the problem space and the configurations is done for all three variability modeling languages using some form of feature models or decision models. OVM is closely related to decision modeling where each variation point is a decision. CVL's variability specification tree is an enhanced feature model with cardinalities [14]. Delta modeling accepts any form of problem space model. Featherweight VML handles the problem space using feature trees by allowing abstract features with no implementation [31]. Also, by employing a constraint language we can define any kind of dependencies between features or decisions.

Modeling the solution space is done in multiple ways. OVM uses an annotative approach to mark which artifacts are implementing specific decisions. Delta modeling uses a transformational approach to add, remove and modify artifacts from the model. A delta module's effects can span over the implementation of multiple features so it is not restricted by the structure of a feature tree. CVL variation points, especially the fragment substitution, can define complex transformations. However, they are directly bound to variability specifications so they are constrained by the tree structure. Featherweight VML models the solution space by using fragment substitutions exclusively. The other CVL variation points, delta modules and of the OVM annotative technique can be encoded as syntactic sugar using fragment substitutions.

Product derivation requires a clear understanding of how to execute a variability model given a specific configuration. CVL defines how each kind of variation point is executed. The variation points are partially ordered by the resolution tree structure. However, execution is not confluent as two variation points at the same level can have conflicting effects resulting in different variants depending on the order. OVM uses a projection on the model artifacts referenced by the selected variants. Delta Modeling executes each delta module by adding, modify-

---

[1] CVL and OVM variation points are different concepts.

ing and removing elements as specified by the modules. The modules also specify a partial order using special clauses. The execution can be made confluent by adding conflict resolving deltas for any pair of conflicting deltas [7].

Orthogonality of variability modeling is the degree to which variability is modeled as a separate concern [12]. CVL defines a clear distinction between the problem space modeling (via a variability specification tree), and solution space modeling (via variation points). The variability model is completely separate from the artifacts. OVM design is based on orthogonality. The artifacts can be anything from requirements to model elements or code fragments. Delta Modeling can be applied to any language, textual and graphical alike. Delta modules can use references to artifacts in a separate model to specify what is added, removed and modified. Featherweight VML borrows the layered architecture of CVL as it is general enough to be used with OVM and Delta Modeling.

3   Abstract Model Representation

Featherweight VML is designed to specify variability in models defined using MOF-based metamodels, consisting of objects and relationships between them. We represent models as multi-graphs of attribute-less, untyped objects connected by directed links. We write $\mathbb{O}$ (respectively $\mathbb{L}$) to denote the infinite universe of all objects (resp. links). Both objects and links are discrete identifiable entities. The links are equipped with endpoint mappings indicating source and target objects: src l and tgt l, both total functions of type $\mathbb{L} \to \mathbb{O}$. We assume that the universe of links is complete, in the sense that it contains infinitely many links with unique identities between any two objects in $\mathbb{O}$.

Fig. 1. A fragment

Definition 1. *A model m is a pair of sets of finitely many objects and finitely many links, $m = (m_{\mathsf{Obj}}, m_{\mathsf{Lnk}}), m_{\mathsf{Obj}} \subseteq \mathbb{O}, m_{\mathsf{Lnk}} \subseteq \mathbb{L}$. A model fragment is a subset of objects and links of a model, so syntactically it is also a pair $f = (f_{\mathsf{Obj}}, f_{\mathsf{Lnk}})$.*

Models represent products or other complete systems. Model fragments represent components or incomplete pieces of models.

We say that a model (or a fragment) m is *closed under links* if for each link $l \in m_{\mathsf{Lnk}}$ its endpoints are contained in the model, so src l, tgt $l \in m_{\mathsf{Obj}}$. Figure 1 illustrates a closed model fragment $r_1 = (\{o_1, o_2, o_3\}, \{l_1, l_2, l_3\})$. For the remainder of the paper we lift set operators to fragment operators, e.g. $f_1 \dot{\subseteq} f_2$ means $f_{1\mathsf{Obj}} \subseteq f_{2\mathsf{Obj}} \wedge f_{1\mathsf{Lnk}} \subseteq f_{2\mathsf{Lnk}}$.

4   The Fragment Substitution Variation Point

We introduce the formal definition of Featherweight VML in two steps: first we explain the execution of fragment substitutions, then we define the entire variability model relating feature models and fragment substitutions.

4.1   Syntax of the Fragment Substitution

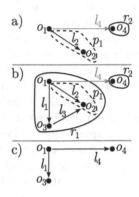

Fragment r_1 introduced in Fig. 1 represents a component that can be customized by replacing o_2 with a new object, o_4. In Fig. 2a we define a *placement* fragment, p_1 (enclosed by a dashed line), containing the elements that must be removed from r_1. We also define a new *replacement* fragment, r_2 (enclosed by a solid line), containing the elements that must be added. Finally, we create a new link, l_4 (represented by a gray arrow), that binds r_2 to the rest of the model. The placement and replacement fragments, p_1 and r_2, together with the new link, l_4, constitute a fragment substitution. Figure 2b shows how the fragment substitution interacts with r_1. After execution we obtain the result shown in Fig. 2c. The link l_3

Fig. 2. a) A fragment substitution. b) Fragment interaction. c) The execution result.

was removed even though it was not part of the placement fragment, in order to avoid dangling links.

Definition 2. *A fragment substitution fs is a triple (p, r, b) where p is a placement fragment containing all the elements that must be removed, r is the replacement fragment and b is a set of new links called a* binding. *The placement and replacement fragments are disjoint, $p \mathbin{\hat{\cap}} r = (\emptyset, \emptyset)$.*

Most variability modeling languages mark a model fragment to be copied by default and form the common base of any product variant (the core module in Delta Modeling or the base model in CVL). In order to keep the number of concepts low, in Featherweight VML we use fragment substitutions to represent both the common base and the subsequent changes applied to it. The example in Fig. 3a,b,c,d illustrates a set of fragment substitutions. We assume that we start from an empty model and fs_1 has only a replacement fragment which introduces the common base. The remaining substitutions perform further customization: fs_2 and fs_3 are removing the elements of p_1 and attach two other fragments, r_2 and r_3. The substitution fs_4 attaches a new fragment so its binding links have endpoints in r_3. Figure 3e represents the interactions between all fragment substitutions in a single model. Figure 3f represents the substitutions with the Featherweight VML abstract syntax and Fig. 3g shows the final result.

Definition 3. *The* boundary *of a fragment substitution $fs = (p, r, b)$ is the set of all endpoints of binding links that are not part of the replacement fragment:*
boundary$fs = \{o \mid o = \mathsf{src}\, l \vee o = \mathsf{tgt}\, l, l \in b\} \setminus r_{\mathsf{Obj}}$.

We require that for any fragment substitution $fs = (p, r, b)$, the boundary links are not incident with placement objects, boundary$fs \cap p_{\mathsf{Obj}} = \emptyset$. All such links would be removed as dangling since their endpoints belonging to a placement would be removed.

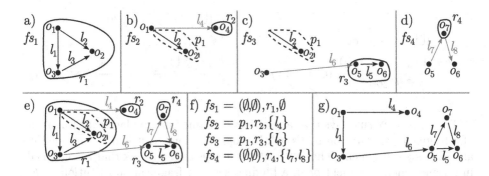

Fig. 3. a,b,c,d) A set of fragment substitutions. e) Interactions between fragment substitutions. f) Syntactic representation. g) The execution result.

In Fig. 3 we have boundary $fs_2 = \{o_1\}$, boundary $fs_3 = \{o_3\}$ and boundary $fs_4 = \{o_5, o_6\}$. In Sec. 5 we will need to identify all artifacts that a fragment substitution affects outside of its own replacement fragment. These are the artifacts in the placement fragment and the boundary objects used by the binding links.

Definition 4. *Given a fragment substitution $fs = (p, r, b)$, the closure of the placement fragment p, written $\lceil p \rceil_{fs}$, is defined as all objects of p plus the boundary of the fragment substitution; the set of links remains unchanged:* $\lceil p \rceil_{fs} = (p_{Obj} \cup$ boundary $fs, p_{Lnk})$.

In Fig. 3, $\lceil p \rceil_{fs_2} = (\{o_1, o_2\}, \{l_2\})$, $\lceil p \rceil_{fs_3} = (\{o_2, o_3\}, \{l_2\})$ and $\lceil p \rceil_{fs_4} = (\{o_5, o_6\}, \emptyset)$. Substitutions fs_2 and fs_3 have different placement closures even if they refer the same placement fragment. This is because the binding links differ.

4.2 Execution Semantics of the Fragment Substitution

The example in Fig.3 gave the intuition of the fragment substitution execution process. Instead of performing in-place changes to the model, we propose a copying semantics, meaning that we decide for each object/link whether it should be part of the product variant and we copy only those for which we decide positively.

Given a set of fragment substitutions, Fs, we will copy all replacement fragments and all binding links. However, we know that what is contained by placement fragments should be removed and replaced so we will not copy these elements. We will not copy links that are incident with placement fragments either. The result $[\![Fs]\!]$ of executing a set of fragment substitutions Fs is called a product variant model; it is a pair of sets of objects/links. The following rules precisely describe which objects and links are copied in $[\![Fs]\!]$:

$$o \in (\bigcup_{(\_,r,\_) \in Fs} r_{\mathsf{Obj}})$$
$$\frac{o \notin (\bigcup_{(p,\_,\_) \in Fs} p_{\mathsf{Obj}})}{o \in [\![Fs]\!]_{\mathsf{Obj}}} \text{ (OBJ-COPY)}$$

$$l \in (\bigcup_{(\_,r,b) \in Fs} r_{\mathsf{Lnk}} \cup b)$$
$$l \notin (\bigcup_{(p,\_,\_) \in Fs} p_{\mathsf{Lnk}})$$
$$\frac{\mathsf{src}\, l, \mathsf{tgt}\, l \notin \bigcup_{(p,\_,\_) \in Fs} p_{\mathsf{Obj}}}{l \in [\![Fs]\!]_{\mathsf{Lnk}}} \text{ (LNK-COPY)}$$

The OBJ-COPY rule says that any object contained in a replacement fragment of a fragment substitution in Fs will be copied as long as it is not contained in any placement fragment. The LNK-COPY rule says that any link that is contained in a replacement fragment or in a binding set of a fragment substitution in Fs will be copied as long as the link or its endpoints are not contained in any placement fragment. The rules are applied exhaustively for all objects and links in all fragments and bindings in the set of fragment substitutions. The complete input model is illustrated in Fig. 3e. Even though individual fragments do not have to be closed, the complete input model may be closed. Lemma 1 ensures that applying the rules to a closed input model results in a product variant model without any dangling links.

Lemma 1. *Given a set of fragment substitutions Fs such that the union of all placement, replacement fragments and bindings is a closed graph, the product variant model $[\![Fs]\!]$ is closed under links.*

Proof. (Sketch) By assumption, the union of all objects and links is a closed graph, so for every link that might be copied, the graph also contains its endpoints. Then we notice that premise of (LNK-COPY) is that neither the source or the target of the link being copied are contained in a placement fragment. Thus it is guaranteed that for any link that is being copied, both link ends will also be copied.

Lemma 2. *Given a set of fragment substitutions, there exists a unique product variant model created by the above rules.*

The lemma holds by construction: objects and links are deterministically selected from a finite set. It follows from the above lemma that the execution of fragment substitution sets is order independent (in other words the semantics is *confluent*), which opens for various implementation strategies.

5   The Variability Model

We have shown how to execute a set of fragment substitutions, Fs, to obtain a product variant model. In a normal scenario, we would like Fs to describe multiple variants and to be able to select only those fragment substitutions that describe a specific product variant before executing them. We would also like to be able to execute a fragment substitution multiple times and to use a configuration to specify how many copies of the replacement fragment to include in the product variant.

Figure 4a illustrates a variability model where each fragment substitution, $fs_{1..4}$, is mapped to a feature, $ft_{1..4}$, from a feature tree. Each feature displays a cardinality constraint for how many instances are allowed for that feature under a single parent. In Fig. 4b the features are instantiated

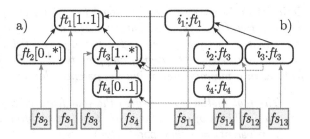

Fig. 4. a) A variability model. b) A configuration and a flattened set of fragment substitutions.

in a configuration tree. The root feature has one root instance, feature ft_2 is not instantiated and ft_3 is instantiated twice, meaning that its fragment substitutions should be executed twice. Feature ft_4 is only instantiated as a child of i_2.

Section 4.2 does not handle multiple execution of fragment substitutions. Instead we will show how to flatten the model and the chosen configuration in a set of fragment substitutions that contains as many copies of each fragment substitution as there are instances of its feature. Flattening the model in out example would result in a set containing two copies of fs_3, but no copies for fs_2.

5.1   Syntax of the Variability Model

A feature model defines all characteristics that can be activated in a product variant. Some characteristics may occur multiple times in a product variant (e.g. the number of USB ports on a computer). For this reason, a *feature* in Featherweight VML is similar to a type that can be instantiated multiple times in the product variant so our features have cardinality [14].

Definition 5. *A* feature model *is a rooted directed tree of features, $Fm = (Ft, ft_0, \mathsf{parent})$, where Ft is a set of features, $\mathsf{parent} \subseteq Ft \times Ft$ is a connected acyclic parent relation with no sharing (a tree), and $ft_0 \in Ft$ is the root of the tree. We write $\mathsf{parent}\, ft_2 = ft_1$, if feature ft_1 is a parent node of ft_2 in Fm.*

Each feature ft has an associated cardinality constraint $\mathsf{card}\, ft = (\mathsf{min}\, ft, \mathsf{max}\, ft)$, where $\mathsf{min}\, ft, \mathsf{max}\, ft \in \mathbb{N} \cup \{*\}$, $\mathsf{min}\, ft \leq \mathsf{max}\, ft$ (the symbol $*$ is considered greater than any natural).

A set of fragment substitutions and the feature model that controls which combinations of fragment substitutions can be executed together constitute a complete variability model.

Definition 6. *A* variability model *is a triple, $(Fs, Fm, \mathsf{mapping})$, where Fs is a set of fragment substitutions, $Fm = (Ft, ft_0, \mathsf{parent})$ is a feature model and $\mathsf{mapping} : Fs \to Fm$ maps each fragment substitution to a feature.*

A configuration represents a combination of features that are active in a product variant.

Definition 7. *Given a feature model $Fm = (Ft, ft_0, \mathsf{parent})$, a configuration is a rooted tree $Cfg = (I, i_0, \mathsf{parent}, ty)$, where I is a finite set of instances, $i_0 \in I$ is the root of the tree, $\mathsf{parent} \subseteq I \times I$ is a connected acyclic parent relation with no sharing (a tree). The typing mapping $ty : I \to Fm$ maps every instance to its feature, in a manner preserving the parent relations:*

  i. *The root instance is typed by the root feature: $ty\, i_0 = ft_0$,*
  ii. *The children of an instance are typed by children of its type: for instances i, j, if $\mathsf{parent}\, i = j$ then $\mathsf{parent}(ty\, i) = ty\, j$.*
  iii. *The feature cardinality constraints are satisfied, so for each instance $j \in I$ and feature $ft \in Ft$, if $\mathsf{parent}\, ft = ty\, j$ then*

$$\mathit{min}\, ft \le |\{i \in I \mid \mathsf{parent}\, i = j \text{ and } ty\, i = ft\}| \le \mathit{max}\, ft$$

Before moving on to the execution semantics we give a set of well-formedness constraints that guarantee that the flattening of variability models produces unique sets of fragment substitutions that can be executed with the rules introduced in Sec. 4.

C 1 *The $\mathsf{mapping}$ of fragment substitutions to features is injective. Any two fragment substitutions, $fs_i = (p_i, r_i, b_i)$ and $fs_j = (p_j, r_j, b_j)$, that should be mapped to the same feature can be merged into a single fragment substitution, $fs_n = (p_i \dot{\cup} p_j, r_i \dot{\cup} r_j, b_i \cup b_j)$.*

C 1 helps simplifying the following constraints and the semantics. It does not limit the expressive power of Featherweight VML. If fs_i and fs_j should anyway be mapped to the same feature then they should be executed together for each instance of that feature. Thus, requiring that they should be combined into one fragment substitution does not change their effect.

It is not required that every feature has a substitution mapped to it. The inverse $\mathsf{mapping}^{-1} : Ft \to [Fs \cup \{\bot\}]$ returns the fragment substitution mapped to a feature or $\bot$ if such a fragment substitution does not exist.

C 2 *All replacement fragments are closed under links. This constraint enforces that for any link cloned during flattening, its endpoints are also cloned and all the clones will be consistent with the original fragment.*

Figure 5 illustrates the replacement fragment problem fixed by constraint 2. Assume we have two replacement fragments r_1 and r_2 such that a link form r_2 has an endpoint

Fig. 5. The replacement fragment problem

in r_1. Each fragment is used in a fragment substitution and each substitution is mapped to a different feature. If we instantiate r_1 two times and r_2 three times then there is no clear intuition about which of the new objects should be used as endpoints for the new links. In fact, we could even instantiate the links, but not their endpoints.

C 3 *For any fragment substitution $fs_i = (p_i, r_i, b_i) \in Fs$ for which the placement closure $\lceil p \rceil_{fs_i} \neq (\emptyset, \emptyset)$, we say that fs_i applies to fs_j and we write $fs_i \sqsubset fs_j$ if there exists one and only one $fs_j = (p_j, r_j, b_j) \in Fs$ such that $\lceil p \rceil_{fs_i} \dot{\subseteq} r_j$.*

C 4 *The structure enforced by the application, $\sqsubset$, of fragment substitutions is consistent with the classifier tree: if $fs_i \sqsubset fs_j$ then $mapping\, fs_j \in parent^*(mapping\, fs_i)$, so if one fragment substitution applies to another, then it is mapped to a feature in the subtree rooted by the feature of the other. Function $parent^*$ is the reflexive transitive closure of $parent$.*

5.2   Execution Semantics of the Variability Model

In Fig. 6 we recall the fragment substitutions of Fig. 4. On the left side we have the detailed contents of the initial four fragment substitutions. On the right side we have the flattened set. The configuration does not contain an instance for ft_2 so fs_2 is not

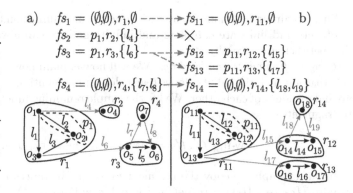

a) $fs_1 = (\emptyset, \emptyset), r_1, \emptyset$ - - - - ►$fs_{11} = (\emptyset, \emptyset), r_{11}, \emptyset$ b)
$fs_2 = p_1, r_2, \{l_4\}$ - - - - ►✗
$fs_3 = p_1, r_3, \{l_6\}$ - - - ►$fs_{12} = p_{11}, r_{12}, \{l_{15}\}$
                               ►$fs_{13} = p_{11}, r_{13}, \{l_{17}\}$
$fs_4 = (\emptyset, \emptyset), r_4, \{l_7, l_8\}$ ►$fs_{14} = (\emptyset, \emptyset), r_{14}, \{l_{18}, l_{19}\}$

Fig. 6. Illustration of the flattening process: a) before, b) after

copied. The substitution fs_3 must be executed two times – once for the instance i_2 and once for i_3. Since the semantics presented in Sec. 4.2 only execute each substitution once, we flatten the model by computing how many times each fragment substitution should be executed and cloning it the appropriate amount of times (carefully updating references).

Preliminaries: Copying and renaming basic entities. Given a variability model, $(Fs, Fm, mapping)$, we use the sets O and L to reference all artifacts contained in this model, $O = \bigcup_{(p,r,b) \in Fs}[p_{\mathsf{Obj}} \cup r_{\mathsf{Obj}}]$ and $L = \bigcup_{(p,r,b) \in Fs}[p_{\mathsf{Lnk}} \cup r_{\mathsf{Lnk}} \cup b]$.

Given a configuration $Cfg = (I, i_0, \mathsf{parent}, ty)$ we use the set I of instances as an index for renaming artifacts. Since the product variant model may end up containing several copies of the same artifacts, we will need to create fresh objects and links, and then be able to refer to them unambiguously. We model this using two injective functions new-obj and new-lnk that create new objects/links for any given feature instance.

$$\mathsf{new\text{-}obj} : I \times O \to \mathbb{O} \setminus O \qquad \mathsf{new\text{-}lnk} : (I \times I) \times L \to \mathbb{L} \setminus L$$

We write the first argument in all renaming functions as an index to make the notation more lightweight. Intuitively, the first argument represents an ordinal index of the copy, whereas the second argument is the entity being copied.

We require that the two functions map to an isomorphic graph structure, so they are injective and for every pair of feature instances i, j (possibly but not necessarily, $i = j$) and any link l we have that: $\mathsf{src}\,(\mathsf{new\text{-}lnk}_{i,j}l) = \mathsf{new\text{-}obj}_i(\mathsf{src}\,l)$ and $\mathsf{tgt}\,(\mathsf{new\text{-}lnk}_{i,j}l) = \mathsf{new\text{-}obj}_j(\mathsf{tgt}\,l)$.

For every instance-object pair we get a different new object, which was not in O. Similarly, for every instance pair (i,j) and a link we get a link connecting copies of the objects related with $\mathsf{new\text{-}obj}_i$ and $\mathsf{new\text{-}obj}_j$.

We lift the two functions to rename (create) entire sets of objects and links:

$$\mathsf{new\text{-}Obj} : I \times 2^O \to 2^{O\backslash O}, \text{ where } \mathsf{new\text{-}Obj}_i O' = \{\mathsf{new\text{-}obj}_i o \mid o \in O'\} \text{ and}$$

$$\mathsf{new\text{-}Lnk} : (I \times I) \times 2^L \to 2^{L\backslash L}, \text{ where } \mathsf{new\text{-}Lnk}_{i,j} L' = \{\mathsf{new\text{-}lnk}_{i,j} l \mid l \in L'\}.$$

Such renaming functions always exist due to our assumption that the universes of objects and links are complete and infinite and we can always obtain a new link between any two objects.

Copying fragments and bindings. We will now explain how to copy a fragment substitution such that all its clones (each clone implementing a different instance) are independent of each other. We lift the simple renaming functions shown above to fragments:

$$\mathsf{new\text{-}frg}_i(O', L') = (\mathsf{new\text{-}Obj}_i O', \mathsf{new\text{-}Lnk}_{i,i} L').$$

In our example we copy the fragment r_3 for the instances i_2 and i_3:
$\mathsf{new\text{-}frg}_2(\{o_5, o_6\}, \{l_5\}) = (\mathsf{new\text{-}Obj}_2\{o_5, o_6\}, \mathsf{new\text{-}Lnk}_{2,2}\{l_5\}) = (\{o_{14}, o_{15}\}, \{l_{14}\})$,
$\mathsf{new\text{-}frg}_3(\{o_5, o_6\}, \{l_5\}) = (\mathsf{new\text{-}Obj}_3\{o_5, o_6\}, \mathsf{new\text{-}Lnk}_{3,3}\{l_5\}) = (\{o_{16}, o_{17}\}, \{l_{16}\})$.

Renaming bindings is more complex—the endpoints may be renamed differently, according to which fragment they belong to. We formalize binding renaming to take as parameter two disjoint sets of objects. We apply i-renaming if an endpoint is in the first set, and j renaming if the endpoint is in the other set:

$$\mathsf{new\text{-}bdg}_{i,j}(O_1, O_2, L) = \{\mathsf{new\text{-}lnk}_{\mathsf{ns}(\mathsf{src}\,l),\mathsf{ns}(\mathsf{tgt}\,l)} l \mid l \in L\},$$

where ns is a function mapping object to name spaces (instances), depending to which replacement they belong; $\mathsf{ns}\,o$ returns i if $o \in O_1$ and it returns j if $o \in O_2$. In our example we want to copy the binding links l_7 and l_8. The ns function allows us to copy the source of l_7 and target of l_8 with the appropriate instance i_2: $\mathsf{new\text{-}bdg}_{4,2}(\{o_7\}, \{o_5, o_6\}, \{l_7, l_8\}) = \{\mathsf{new\text{-}lnk}_{2,4}l_7, \mathsf{new\text{-}lnk}_{4,2}l_8\} = \{l_{18}, l_{19}\}$.

Finally, we lift the renaming functions to entire fragment substitutions:

$$\mathsf{new\text{-}fs}_{i,j}(p, r, b)\, O_j = \left(\mathsf{new\text{-}frg}_j p, \mathsf{new\text{-}frg}_i r, \mathsf{new\text{-}bdg}_{i,j}\,(r_{\mathsf{Obj}}, O_j, b)\right).$$

Intuitively, if objects are in set O_j then they should be renamed using the j-indexed renaming functions. It they are in the replacement of the fragment substitution then the i-indexed renaming functions apply. The set O_j will be provided in the semantics according to the context, and it should always be disjoint from objects of the replacement r_{Obj}.

In our example copying fs_3 for i_2 is done by copying p_1 for i_1, r_3 for i_2 and the binding link has its source copied for i_1 and its target for i_2:

$\text{new-fs}_{2,1}(p_1, r_3, \{l_6\}) \, r_1 = \left(\text{new-frg}_1 p_1, \text{new-frg}_2 r_3, \text{new-bdg}_{2,1}\left(\{o_5, o_6\}, r_1, \{l_6\}\right)\right).$

Flattening variability models and configurations. By constraint 1 we know that there can be only one fragment substitution mapped to any feature, but it is not required that every feature has a substitution mapped to it. Each feature can be instantiated multiple times in which case the fragment substitution mapped to it (if it exists) is executed multiple times (once per instance). We compute how many times each substitution should be executed and clone it the appropriate amount of times (carefully updating references). This will produce a flat set of fragment substitutions that can be executed using the rules of Sec. 4.2.

The flattening of a variability model M with respect to a configuration *Cfg* is a set of fragment substitutions, denoted below as $[\![M, Cfg]\!]$. Flattening moves all the necessary information from the feature model and from the realization model to the new set of fragment substitutions. After this, the features and their instances can be disregarded.

Given a variability model $M = (Fs, Fm, \text{mapping})$ and a configuration *Cfg*, $\text{mapping}^{-1}(\text{ty}\, i)$ returns the fragment substitution that has to be executed in the context of an instance i or $\bot$ if there is no such substitution.

There are three cases to consider when flattening the model. In the first case, instances of features that have no substitutions mapped to them are ignored by the semantics. In the second case, instances of features that have substitutions with empty placement closures such that they do not apply to any other substitution are copied with the following rule:

$$\frac{i \in Cfg \quad \text{mapping}^{-1}(\text{ty}\, i) = fs_i \quad \lceil p \rceil_{fs_i} = (\emptyset, \emptyset)}{\text{new-fs}_{i,\_} \; fs_i \; \emptyset \in [\![M, Cfg]\!]} \; (\text{COPY-INDEP})$$

Since the placement fragment is empty and the binding links endpoints can only be objects of the replacement fragment itself, binding links can be appropriately cloned by using just the instance i, by new-fs.

In the third case, instances of features that have substitutions which apply to other substitutions are copied with the following rule:

$$\frac{i, j \in Cfg \quad \text{mapping}^{-1}(\text{ty}\, i) = fs_i \quad \text{mapping}^{-1}(\text{ty}\, j) = fs_j \quad fs_i \sqsubset fs_j}{\text{new-fs}_{i,j} \; fs_i \; r_j \in [\![M, Cfg]\!]} \frac{fs_i = (p_i, r_i, b_i) \quad fs_j = (\_, r_j, \_) \quad j \in \text{parent}^* i}{} \; (\text{COPY})$$

The intended meaning of COPY is that we copy the replacement fragment using the instance i, the placement with the instance j and the binding links with a combination of the two. We use r_j, the replacement fragment of fs_j to state that a binding link endpoint can either be in the r_i or r_j. By constraint 1 we know that for any pair of instances i and j, $\text{mapping}^{-1}(\text{ty}\, i)$ and $\text{mapping}^{-1}(\text{ty}\, j)$ are uniquely determined (if they exist), thus the rule can be applied deterministically.

In our example we know that $i_2, i_1 \in Cfg$, $\text{mapping}^{-1}(\text{ty}\, i_2) = fs_3$ and $\text{mapping}^{-1}(\text{ty}\, i_1) = fs_1$, $fs_3 \sqsubset fs_1$ and $i_1 \in \text{parent}^* i_2$, therefore we copy fs_3 in the flattened set: $\text{new-fs}_{2,1}(p_1, r_3, \{l_6\}) \, r_1 \in [\![M, Cfg]\!]$.

Lemma 3. *For a well-formed variability model M and a valid configuration Cfg, the above rules define a unique well-formed variability realization model* $[\![M, Cfg]\!]$.

The well-formedness of outputs follows from isomorphism of all renaming operations (all functions are injective and preserve links)—all non-overlapping conditions of well-formedness are thus transferred from the input variability realization model.

Theorem 1. *Given a well-formed variability model M and a valid configuration Cfg the result of executing the model is unique, and given by* $[\![M, Cfg]\!]$, *and consequently the above formulation of the semantics is confluent.*

The well-formedness constraints (C 1,2,3,4) ensure that the flattening input set of fragment substitutions form a closed union of fragments. Lemma 3 ensures that the output of the flattening is a unique set of substitutions forming a closed union of fragments. Lemma 3 ensures that copying process results in a closed product variant model and Lemma 2 ensures that the result is unique regardless of the ordering of the input objects and links.

6   Discussion and Related Work

Featherweight VML is closely related to CVL as it is able to express CVL models with great accuracy. Most CVL variability specifications can be reduced to features with cardinalities and the variation points are all specific cases of the fragment substitution. Featherweight VML can be seen as a generalization of OVM. We can use abstract features to group variation points together, giving OVM a tree structure while retaining the same meaning. Delta modules are almost identical to fragment substitutions. The only difference is that a delta module is guarded by an application condition over a set of features while Featherweight VML fragment substitutions are each mapped to a single feature. In order to express a Delta model without adding extra concepts we would have to change Featherweight VML's mapping function to a more general expression.

So far, most work on variability was dedicated to analyzing feature models [2,29]. Recent work has provided valuable insight such as formalizing feature models represented in a textual language [8] or even providing full proofs in the PVS proof assistant [20]. However, the formalization is limited to feature models and do not touch on the subject of executing realization models. Czarnecki et al. [1] show how to model the three layers of variability modeling within the single Clafer syntax. This is the closest that comes to modeling solution space, however no actual link to implementation artifacts is considered, just a Boolean abstraction of dependency. Such a formalization cannot directly be used as a specification of correctness for a product variant derivation tool.

Other works consider analyzing variability models as a whole, including checking for consistency (for instance [4,5,15,17,18]). All these methods assume correctness of the product variant derivation implementation. In this work we make the first step to allow fulfilling this assumption by setting the foundation of analyzing the implementation of variability realization tools.

A crucial feature of our semantics is that it is confluent. We achieve this by identifying sufficient conditions for confluence, and adopting copying style for definition of semantics, to minimize dependencies between executions of individual variation points. Oldevik et al. [23] take a dual route and attempt to detect lack of confluence. As such they belong well to the group of works that are more interested in ensuring that models are correct than that the model manipulation tools are correct.

7 Conclusion

We proposed a formal definition of Featherweight VML, a compact variability modeling language, which retains the expressiveness of the CVL on which it is based, but in the same time it has much simpler syntax and semantics. To our best knowledge this is the first attempt to fully formalize an entire variability model. This is the first necessary step towards producing variability modeling and product derivation tools for which the whole execution can be formally verified (and certified for usage in production of safety critical software). Featherweight VML relates to CVL, OVM and Delta Modeling. Our semantics processes the model in an order-agnostic manner. It is the first confluent formalization of a CVL-like language. The copying semantics can be implemented in declarative rule-based model transformation languages more easily and it is easier to reason about it using theorem provers.

References

1. Bąk, K., Czarnecki, K., Wąsowski, A.: Feature and meta-models in Clafer: Mixed, specialized, and coupled. In: Malloy, B., Staab, S., van den Brand, M. (eds.) SLE 2010. LNCS, vol. 6563, pp. 102–122. Springer, Heidelberg (2011)
2. Benavides, D., Cortés, A.R., Trinidad, P., Segura, S.: A survey on the automated analyses of feature models. In: JISBD, pp. 367–376 (2006)
3. Berger, T., Rublack, R., Nair, D., Atlee, J.M., Becker, M., Czarnecki, K., Wasowski, A.: A survey of variability modeling in industrial practice. In: VaMoS, p. 7 (2013)
4. Berger, T., She, S., Lotufo, R., Czarnecki, K., Wąsowski, A.: Feature-to-code mapping in two large product lines. In: Bosch, J., Lee, J. (eds.) SPLC 2010. LNCS, vol. 6287, pp. 498–499. Springer, Heidelberg (2010)
5. Bodden, E., Tolêdo, T., Ribeiro, M., Brabrand, C., Borba, P., Mezini, M.: Spl^{lift}: statically analyzing software product lines in minutes instead of years. In: PLDI, pp. 355–364 (2013)
6. Clarke, D., Diakov, N., Hähnle, R., Johnsen, E.B., Schaefer, I., Schäfer, J., Schlatte, R., Wong, P.Y.H.: Modeling Spatial and Temporal Variability with the HATS Abstract Behavioral Modeling Language. In: Bernardo, M., Issarny, V. (eds.) SFM 2011. LNCS, vol. 6659, pp. 417–457. Springer, Heidelberg (2011)
7. Clarke, D., Helvensteijn, M., Schaefer, I.: Abstract delta modeling. In: Visser, E., Järvi, J. (eds.) GPCE, pp. 13–22. ACM (2010)
8. Classen, A., Boucher, Q., Heymans, P.: A text-based approach to feature modelling: syntax and semantics of TVL. Sci. Comput. Program. 76(12), 1130–1143 (2011)
9. Clements, P., Northrop, L.M.: Software Product Lines: Practices and Patterns. Addison-Wesley (2002)

10. CVL Joint Submission Team. Common Variability Language (CVL). OMG Revised Submission (2012)
11. Czarnecki, K., Antkiewicz, M.: Mapping features to models: A template approach based on superimposed variants. In: Glück, R., Lowry, M. (eds.) GPCE 2005. LNCS, vol. 3676, pp. 422–437. Springer, Heidelberg (2005)
12. Czarnecki, K., Grünbacher, P., Rabiser, R., Schmid, K., Wasowski, A.: Cool features and tough decisions: A comparison of variability modeling approaches. In: VaMoS, pp. 173–182 (2012)
13. Czarnecki, K., Helsen, S.: Feature-based survey of model transformation approaches. IBM Systems Journal 45(3), 621–646 (2006)
14. Czarnecki, K., Helsen, S., Eisenecker, U.W.: Formalizing cardinality-based feature models and their specialization. Software Process: Improvement and Practice 10(1), 7–29 (2005)
15. Czarnecki, K., Pietroszek, K.: Verifying feature-based model templates against well-formedness ocl constraints. In: GPCE 2006, pp. 211–220. ACM (2006)
16. Haber, A., Kolassa, C., Manhart, P., Nazari, P.M.S., Rumpe, B., Schaefer, I.: First-class variability modeling in matlab/simulink. In: VaMoS, p. 4 (2013)
17. Haugen, Ø.: Cvl: common variability language or chaos, vanity and limitations. In: VaMoS, p. 1 (2013)
18. Heidenreich, F., Kopcsek, J., Wende, C.: Featuremapper: mapping features to models. In: ICSE Companion, pp. 943–944 (2008)
19. Hutchinson, J., Rouncefield, M., Whittle, J.: Model-driven engineering practices in industry. In: ICSE, pp. 633–642 (2011)
20. Janota, M., Kiniry, J.: Reasoning about feature models in higher-order logic. In: SPLC, pp. 13–22 (2007)
21. Kang, K.C., Cohen, S.G., Hess, J.A., Novak, W.E., Peterson, A.S.: Feature-Oriented Domain Analysis (FODA) Feasibility Study. Technical report, CMU SEI (November 1990)
22. Object Management Group. Meta Object Facility (MOF) Core Specification Version 2.0 (2006)
23. Oldevik, J., Haugen, Ø., Møller-Pedersen, B.: Confluence in domain-independent product line transformations. In: Chechik, M., Wirsing, M. (eds.) FASE 2009. LNCS, vol. 5503, pp. 34–48. Springer, Heidelberg (2009)
24. Pohl, K., Böckle, G., van der Linden, F.J.: Software Product Line Engineering: Foundations, Principles and Techniques. Sprinter (2005)
25. Prehofer, C.: Feature-oriented programming: A new way of object composition. Concurrency and Computation: Practice and Experience 13(6), 465–501 (2001)
26. Schaefer, I., Bettini, L., Bono, V., Damiani, F., Tanzarella, N.: Delta-oriented programming of software product lines. In: Bosch, J., Lee, J. (eds.) SPLC 2010. LNCS, vol. 6287, pp. 77–91. Springer, Heidelberg (2010)
27. Schaefer, I., Rabiser, R., Clarke, D., Bettini, L., Benavides, D., Botterweck, G., Pathak, A., Trujillo, S., Villela, K.: Software diversity: state of the art and perspectives. STTT 14(5), 477–495 (2012)
28. Schmid, K., Rabiser, R., Grünbacher, P.: A comparison of decision modeling approaches in product lines. In: VaMoS, pp. 119–126 (2011)
29. Schobbens, P.-Y., Heymans, P., Trigaux, J.-C., Bontemps, Y.: Generic semantics of feature diagrams. Computer Networks 51(2), 456–479 (2007)
30. Stahl, T., Voelter, M.: Model-Driven Software Development. John Wiley & Sons (2004)
31. Thüm, T., Kästner, C., Erdweg, S., Siegmund, N.: Abstract features in feature modeling. In: SPLC, pp. 191–200 (2011)

Domain Specific Languages for Managing Feature Models: Advances and Challenges

Univ. Nice Sophia Antipolis, CNRS, I3S, UMR 7271, 06900 Sophia Antipolis, France
Philippe.Collet@unice.fr

Abstract. Managing multiple and complex feature models is a tedious
and error-prone activity in software product line engineering. Despite
many advances in formal methods and analysis techniques, the supporting tools and APIs are not easily usable together, nor unified. In this
paper, we report on the development and evolution of the FAMILIAR
Domain-Specific Language (DSL). Its toolset is dedicated to the large
scale management of feature models through a good support for separating concerns, composing feature models and scripting manipulations. We
overview various applications of FAMILIAR and discuss both advantages
and identified drawbacks. We then devise salient challenges to improve
such DSL support in the near future.

1 Introduction

Following a *Software Product Line* SPL paradigm offers benefits such as shortened time-to-market, economies of scale and increased quality by reducing defect
rates [1,2]. This paradigm basically relies on a factoring process, identifying common artifacts and managing what varies among them. These artifacts typically
range from product descriptions (documentations, tabular data), requirements
to models, programs and even tests. Modeling variability and managing the resulting models is a critical activity within the SPL paradigm. To deal with it,
a widely used approach is to organize variability around features, which are
domain abstractions relevant to stakeholders, typically being increments in program functionality [3]. Inside a SPL, a *Feature Model* (FM) is used to describe,
through a compact AND-OR graph with propositional constraints, all identified
features and their valid combinations [4–6]. Developments around formal semantics, analysis and reasoning techniques, as well as tool support [3–5,7] currently
make FM a *de facto* standard for managing variability.

All these advances also led to a wider usage of variability models. As one
can use FM to model variability of very different kinds of concerns [3], the
inherent complexity of the relations between these concerns has to be handled.
With FM of hundreds to thousands of features, understanding the organization
of variabilities and their complex relation rules is getting harder and harder.
Reports also showed that the maintenance of a single large FM is not really
feasible as some analysis techniques reach their limits, and is also not advisable
as the resulting FM would be too complex to be understandable [8–13].

T. Margaria and B. Steffen (Eds.): ISoLA 2014, Part I, LNCS 8802, pp. 273–288, 2014.
© Springer-Verlag Berlin Heidelberg 2014

Tackling these issues, our research team initiated in previous work [14–18] the foundations for applying the principle of *Separation of Concerns* (SoC) to feature modeling on a large scale. Composition operators for FMs were first developed [15,16]. They notably preserve semantic properties expressed in terms of configuration sets of the composed FMs. They are complemented by a slicing operator, which produces a projection of an FM [14], and a differencing operator between FMs [18].

At that time, these operators could have been implemented using or extending one of the several Java APIs that were available (FaMa [19], FeatureIDE [20], SPLAR [21], etc.), as they provide some operations using different kinds of solvers (BDD, CSP, SAT). But with the aim to provide a better support when dealing with several feature models at the same time, we decided to build a *Domain-Specific Language* (DSL) that would provide both reasoning operations and new compositions, while focusing only on the domain concepts, i.e., feature models, features and configurations. This DSL, named FAMILIAR (for FeAture Model scrIpt Language for manIpulation and Automatic Reasoning) [22], also provides support for importing and exporting FMs, as well as for writing parameterized scripts. The language has been used in various case studies [23–25], ranging from forward to reverse engineering, with different domains and varied stakeholders. It has also evolved with extended merging techniques [26], better reverse engineering mechanisms [27], but also an additional Java API and a new implementation as an internal DSL in Scala.

In this paper, we take a step back from the development of the FAMILIAR ecosystem. After summarizing its main features, of which details can be found in references mentioned above, our contributions consist in:

- Discussing observed benefits in different case studies, while determining several recurring drawbacks. They mainly concern the fine-grained bridging with analysis and reasoning tools, the connection to other artifacts and the maintenance of the DSL itself.
- Identifying several challenges that this DSL centric approach is currently facing, from mechanisms and scope issues to the facilitation of different usages.

2   Background

2.1   Feature Modeling

The FODA method [8] first introduced the notions of feature models (FMs) together with a graphical representation through feature diagrams. An FM is structured around a *hierarchy* of features, getting into increasing detail with sub-levels, and different variability mechanisms related to feature decomposition and inter-feature constraints. In the hierarchy, the subfeatures of a feature can be *optional* or *mandatory* or can form *Xor* or *Or*-groups. Propositional constraints, typically implies or excludes rules, can be specified to express more complex dependencies between features wherever in the hierarchy.

The expressiveness of feature modeling also comes from the fact that an FM defines a set of valid feature configurations. During the configuration phase, features are selected and some rules ensure the validity of a configuration (e.g. automatic parent selection, satisfied constraints) [8]. A configuration of an FM g is defined as a set of selected features. $[[g]]$ denotes the set of valid configurations of the FM g, being a set of sets of features.

FMs and propositional logic have been semantically related [5]. The set of configurations of an FM can be described by a propositional formula defined over a set of Boolean variables, in which each variable corresponds to a feature. Translating FMs into logic representations typically enables automated analysis [7].

2.2 Domain-Specific Languages

A DSL is a computer language of limited expressiveness focused on a particular domain [28]. Contrary to general purpose languages, which are aimed at handling most problems in software development, a DSL can only handle one specific aspect of a system. It is usually a small, simple and focused language [29].

In different technical domains (Unix, databases with SQL, etc.), DSLs have been used for a very long time. With their strong relation with model-driven engineering techniques, they are now getting more attention with usages in different areas related to software, being business-oriented or still technical. DSLs bring value as they can facilitate both communication with domain experts [30, 31] and programming activities in comparison with a basic Application Programming Interface (API).

But designing a DSL is not an easy task and many design trade-offs, from the scope of the language to its implementation and future maintenance, are to be made [28, 30]. These languages can take the form of plain *external* DSLs, with their own custom syntax, parser and processing engine, which make a domain-specific tooling, or the form of better crafted APIs, known as *fluent* APIs, or even moving towards embedded or *internal* DSLs built on top of a host language. Numerous advances towards language workbenches [32] have been made to support the development of external DSLs. Conversely, recent advances in language design allow for easier embedding with host languages being extensible in very flexible ways [33].

3 The FAMILIAR Ecosystem

As discussed in the introduction, the FAMILIAR language was created to provide an appropriate support for the FM composition operators (see Section 3.4) that enable the large scale management of FMs following separation of concerns principles. When studying numerous examples and different case studies in which these composition operators were going to be applied [15], we observed that manipulating several FMs requires to describe and replay sequences of operations on them. We thus focused the development towards a textual language, FAMILIAR, which can define such operations in executable scripts. The DSL functionalities comprise FM authoring and accessing operations, main reasoning operations, and the (de-)composition mechanisms. As the developed FM merging operations are restricted to propositional FMs (no feature attributes or other extensions), we also aligned the DSL on operations at the same level. Finally we decided to build an external DSL to restrict the possible manipulations to the envisioned set, and to facilitate learning and usage for different kinds of users.

FAMILIAR is available at http://familiar-project.github.io, with associated documentation. The reader can also refer to [22] for a presentation of FAMILIAR and to [14] for a summary of operators, more illustrations of their usage. For the sake of brevity, we do not here discuss all related work. Basically, FAMILIAR composition operators for FMs such as merging were original as they handle each operation at the semantic level (reasoning on configuration sets, see Section 3.4). The FAMILIAR language itself differs from other textual languages for feature modeling, such as Clafer [34] or TVL [35], by its capabilities to write scripts that handle several FMs at the same time.

We now overview the main constructs and data types of the FAMILIAR *external* DSL. Tool support and variants of FAMILIAR through a Java API or as a Scala based internal DSL are discussed at the end of this section.

3.1 Language Basics

FAMILIAR is a typed language that supports primitive and complex types. New types cannot be created, as the various provided types aim at supporting manipulation of FMs through a reduced but expressive set of elements. Complex types are domain-specific (*Feature Model, Configuration, Feature, Constraint*, etc.) or generic *Set*. Primitive types are quite common, with *String* (feature names are strings), *Boolean, Enum, Integer* and *Real*.

Operators are defined for each type, and runtime type checking is performed by the FAMILIAR interpreter. For example, the operator **counting** acts on a *Feature Model* and returns an *Integer* value. Basic arithmetic, logical, set and string operators are also provided. User-defined *variables* are also provided. In the listing below, line 1 defines a variable of type *Feature Model*. Accessors are provided for observing the content of a variable. A classical **if then else** and a loop control structure (i.e., **foreach**) complement the constructs.

```
1 mi1 = FM ( MI: Mod [Anon];  Mod: (PET | CT) ;)
2 n = counting mi1 // n is an integer
3 f1 = parent PET // f1 refers feature 'Mod' in mi1
4 f2 = root mi1 // f2 refers feature 'MI' in mi1
5 fs = children f1 // feature set {'PET','CT'} in mi1
```

3.2 Modularization

Identifiers in FAMILIAR refer to a variable identifier or to a feature in an FM. Inside one FM, feature names are supposed to be unique. The language relies on namespaces to allow disambiguation of variables having the same name.

A namespace is associated to each FM variable so that the name of such a variable followed by "." can be used to refer to a feature name, if needed.

Furthermore FAMILIAR provides modularization mechanisms that allow for the creation and use of multiple *scripts* in a single SPL project, supporting reusability of scripts. Namespaces are also used to logically group related variables of a script, making the development more modular. The listing below illustrates the reuse of existing scripts. Line 1 shows how to run a script contained in the file *fooScript1* from the current script. The namespace *script_declaration* is an abstract container providing context for all the variables of the script *fooScript1*. Then, in line 2, we access to the set of all variables of *script_declaration* using a classical wildcard pattern.

```
1 run "fooScript1" into script_declaration
2 varset = script_declaration.*
3 export varset
```

Also, a script can be parameterized using a list of **parameters**, a parameter recording a variable and, optionally, the type expected. Parameterized scripts are typically used to develop reusable analysis procedures for FMs and configurations. Apart from this reuse, we also found that FAMILIAR can also be used as a target language, by generating scripts handling specific tasks in SPL toolchain (checking compatibility through merging, building catalogs of descriptions). All applications discussed in Section 4 have used a combination of generated scripts and developer written ones.

3.3 Operators

For importing and exporting FMs, different FM formats are supported, including FeatureIDE, S2T2, SPLOT, subsets of TVL and FaMa. A concise notation, largely inspired from FeatureIDE [20] and the feature-model-synthesis project, is also provided. The listing below covers the main syntactic elements. In line 1, the variable *fm0* represents a FM in which MI is the root feature. Mod and Anon are child-features of MI: Mod is mandatory and Anon is optional. PET and CT are child-features of Mod and form a Xor-group. Sx and Sy are child-features of PET and form an Or-group. A cross-tree constraint is shown in line 4, as PET **excludes** Anon.

```
1 fm0 = FM ( MI: Mod [Anon];
2          Mod: (PET | CT) ;) // Xor-group
3                    PET : (Sx|Sy)+ ; // Or-group
4          PET excludes Anon ; // constraint )
```

FAMILIAR also allows to create FM configurations, and then **select, deselect**, or **unselect** a feature. Each of these configuration manipulation operations returns true if the feature does exist and if the choices conform to the FM constraints. Based on well-known applications of solvers (BDD and SAT), several operators support reasoning about FMs and their configurations. **isValid** checks whether a configuration is consistent according to its FM. Applied to a FM,

isValid determines its *satisfiability*. Besides the **isComplete** operation checks whether all features of a configuration have been chosen, i.e., selected or deselected.

The integration objective of FAMILIAR is also shown by functionalities to compare FMs. Based on the algorithm and terminology used in [6], the **compare** operation determines whether an FM is a refactoring, a generalization, a specialization or an arbitrary edit of another FM. Results from the differentiation computation between two FMs [18] are also provided through a **diff** operation.

3.4   Decomposition and Composition

The main objective of FAMILIAR is to support large-scale combinations of FMs, through decomposition and composition operations. The key feature of the main composition operations (merge, slice, diff) is that they rely on a clear semantics based on the represented configuration sets. Moreover, defining the operations through the propositional logic counterpart of the FMs allows to automatically take into account cross-tree constraints, which cannot be easily handled by syntactic techniques.

Regarding decomposition, a first basic mechanism is to **extract** a sub-tree of an FM, including cross-tree constraints involving features of the subtree. This operator is purely syntactical as it ignores cross-tree constraints that involve features not present in the sub-tree. The *semantic* counterpart of **extract** is the **slice** operator that returns a partial view of an FM according to a criterion of interest (a set of features). The semantics of the operation is based on the *projected* set of configurations of the selected features. This set is represented as its propositional logic formula and automatically takes into account cross-tree constraints. The projection is done through some logic reasoning and the result of the **slice** is a FM reconstructed from the projected set. The reader can refer to [14, 17] for formal definition and implementation details.

Two forms of composition, aggregate and merge, are supported by the FAMILIAR language. The **aggregate** operator is intended to be used when separated FMs do not have features in common, i.e., features with the same name. The operator supports cross-tree constraints, written in propositional logic, over the set of features so that the different FMs can be inter-related. The input FMs are simply put under a synthetic root as mandatory children and the propositional constraints are added to the resulting FM.

On the other hand, **merge** operators are dedicated to the composition of FMs with similar features. In this case, the operators can be used to merge the overlapping parts of the input FMs in a new FM. Variants of the merge operators defer on the production mode, e.g., merging in intersection mode computes a FM corresponding to the set of common configurations of the input FMs. Consequently the semantics of the **merge** operator variants mainly relies on the configuration sets of the input FMs (cf. Table 1). Different applications of these merge variants are mentioned in Section 4.

The default implementation of this operator computes the resulting propositional formula [16] and restores as much as possible the parent-child relationships

Table 1. Main merge variants in FAMILIAR

Mode	Semantic properties	Mathematical notation	FAMILIAR notation
Intersection	$[\![FM_1]\!] \cap [\![FM_2]\!] \cap \ldots$ $\cap [\![FM_n]\!] = [\![FM_r]\!]$	$FM_1 \oplus_\cap FM_2 \oplus_\cap \ldots$ $\oplus_\cap FM_n = FM_r$	fmr = **merge intersection** { fm1 fm2 ... fmn}
Union	$[\![FM_1]\!] \cup [\![FM_2]\!] \cup \ldots$ $\cup [\![FM_n]\!] = [\![FM_r]\!]$	$FM_1 \oplus_{\cup_s} FM_2 \oplus_{\cup_s} \ldots$ $\oplus_{\cup_s} FM_n = FM_r$	fmr = **merge union** { fm1 fm2 ... fmn}
Diff	$\{x \in [\![FM_1]\!] \mid x \notin [\![FM_2]\!]\}$ $= [\![FM_r]\!]$	$FM_1 \setminus FM_2 = FM_r$	fmr = **merge diff** { fm1 fm2 }

of the input FMs in the merged FM. To do so, it relies on the synthesis algorithm from [36] to build back a hierarchy. Recently, new forms of composition have been explored with differences in the expressed configurations and the ontological semantics [26]. Two new implementations have been devised and implemented, one relying on the slice operator, the other one using a local synthesis approach. This provides a range of merging variants that have different impacts on the resulting quality of the FM, the capacity to reason on it or to compose it.

3.5   Tool Support

The first version of FAMILIAR was developed in Java using Xtext[1], a framework for the development of external DSLs. Xtext facilities were used to provide a FAMILIAR script parser, an Eclipse text editor and a stand-alone console. They are all connected to the FAMILIAR kernel that deals with the main manipulated concepts (feature model, configuration, etc.), but also with transformations from feature models to the different internal and external representations (cf. Figure 1). To foster interoperability, different languages and framework format are supported through import/export methods (FeatureIDE, S2T2, SPLOT). Some of them (TVL, FaMa) are going beyond propositional FMs with feature attributes or non-boolean constructs. They are then only partially supported. This support enables FAMILIAR outputs to be processed by third party tools. For example, a connection with the graphical editor and configurator of the FeatureIDE framework [20] allows us to synchronize graphical edits and interactive FAMILIAR commands.

One of the goals was to make some existing analysis techniques available in FAMILIAR, focusing on the most important ones when several FMs have to be manipulated or composed. Consequently some FAMILIAR internal code is directly reusing or adapting several implementations, notably feature model synthesis [36] for hierarchy reconstruction of FMs, FeatureIDE [20] code for FM comparison, SPLAR for different analysis operations [21]. To perform over propositional formulas, the kernel follows a lazy strategy to compute the formulas only when needed. It relies on SAT4J for SAT solving and JavaBDD for BDDs. As they expose different advantages and drawbacks, these techniques can be switched with

---

[1] http://www.eclipse.org/Xtext/

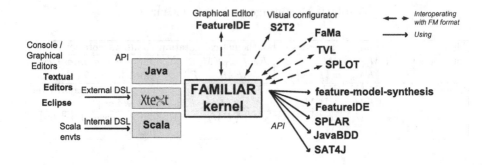

Fig. 1. Current stable FAMILIAR ecosystem

an annotation in FAMILIAR in many operators (except merge, which is implemented only with BDDs). A default implementation is also set for each operator. More details can be found in [22].

While FAMILIAR was more and more used in different applications and case studies (see next section), the source code was made open and available on github, so that the toolset can be jointly managed by three research teams, namely the Triskell team (INRIA - IRISA - University of Rennes 1), the MODALIS team (I3S laboratory - Université Nice Sophia Antipolis - CNRS) and at Colorado State University. Different extensions were then developed. The console has been extended with an interactive graphical editor, so that feature models can be directly edited or configured in sync with a text console. As FAMILIAR was also integrated in many applicative toolchains, we finally develop a Java API from the kernel to facilitate these integration tasks. Finally, we recently explored the internal DSL way to provide integration capabilities with a syntax closer to the original FAMILIAR language. We thus developed an internal DSL on top of the Scala[2] language, which provides a flexible syntax and supports mechanisms such as implicit type conversions, call-by-name parameters and mixin classes. Ongoing work notably comprise development for bridging with a CSP library and providing a web console.

4   Applications

We now report on our experience in applying FAMILIAR in various case studies, classifying them in forward and reverse engineering scenarios. They all deal with large and multiple FMs, as well as complex relationships between FMs and assets at different levels (various concerns on the same artifact, different abstraction levels, representation of different SPLs).

4.1   Forward Engineering

Scientific Workflow: Multiple Compositions. FAMILIAR was first used to support a tooled process for assisting medical imaging experts in the error-prone

---

[2] http://www.scala-lang.org

activity of constructing scientific workflows [24]. These workflows are built from many highly customizable software services (e.g., intensity correction, segmentation), which encapsulate code from different suppliers. Separated FMs are then used to describe the variability of the different artifacts, i.e., services and workflow, with several functional and non-functional concerns, (e.g., input/ouput port, image type, used algorithm).

From a built catalog (using the merge union operator on separate descriptions of services), the workflow design process is facilitated at each step, with the capability to choose from different competing services, connect the select one in the workflow. Through automated reasoning, configuration choices and constraints on and between services are checked (using the merge intersection operator) and propagated among the workflow (using generated scripts), ensuring an overall consistent composition.

Video-Surveillance: End-to-End Multi-level Variability. FAMILIAR has also been used on a different kind of workflow, with a more stable architecture but with more variability concerns at different levels [23]. The aim was to tame the complexity of the configuration process of a video-surveillance software pipeline. Each step was also considered as an SPL so that the variability (components, algorithms, parameters, tasks) of the underlying software platform was represented together with the variability of the hardware parts (e.g., camera capabilities). The application requirement variability was then separately captured in a domain FM, aggregating information on many context elements (e.g., lighting conditions) and expected tasks (e.g., intrusion detection). The two resulting FMs are finally related by constraints (using the aggregate operator).

Salient properties can then be checked (using parameterized scripts), such as reachability, i.e., for each high-level configuration of the domain, there exists at least one valid configuration in the software platform. The organization of the variability also allows for step-wise specialization at both levels and automatic propagation in all FMs, drastically reducing the configuration process. The remaining variability is kept at runtime to make the application self-adaptive, handling for example day/night switches.

Digital Signage: Multiple Product Lines. More recently, FAMILIAR has started to be used in the heart of an industrial-strength digital signage system developed by a start-up company and organized as a Multiple Software Product Line (MSPL) [37]. The information broadcast relies on an innovative web architecture allowing for easy aggregation of information sources and highly customizable rendering on multiple displays. Each element in the information flow is handled by a subsystem SPL represented by an FM, and a domain metamodel relates all SPLs and keeps a set of constraints between the FMs.

In this context, FAMILIAR is used for the variability definition (using merge union on all descriptions of the product instances), but also to compute the relationships between the FMs (generating appropriate scripts). As the model instance of the MSPL varies at configuration time (e.g., when a new source is added), the number of configurations also evolves. In this context, appropriate

FAMILIAR scrips allow for automatic propagation and consistency checking so that at any time, the final user is ensured to manipulate a consistent product under configuration.

Benefits. These applications illustrate different benefits of using FAMILIAR. In all of them, repositories of FMs are built and organized as reusable FAMILIAR scripts merging FMs that document some artifacts. Querying the repository is also supported by FAMILIAR with merge and slice operators. In the scientific workflow case, another DSL was designed to map services with their variability definition, and FAMILIAR was then used as an embedded language.

Generally, a Model-Driven Engineering (MDE) approach is used together with FAMILIAR and scripts are generated by the SPL toolchain to automatize some checking or propagation (e.g. at service connection, at configuration time, when the model evolves, etc.). Depending on the complexity of this coupling, the FAMILIAR Java API is more or less used in conjunction with the external DSL. Another benefit is the capability to implement more efficiently interesting properties such as realisability or usefulness when several FMs are inter-related [9,14].

Drawbacks. In the first two applications, the variability reasoning relies on **ad hoc bridges** or model-to-text transformations. The complete semantics of the solution is thus scattered through the SPL tool chain. Moreover, as there is no simple mechanism to compose external DSLs, embedding FAMILIAR in another DSL is implemented through some hacks in the Xtext back-end. Consequently very few code parts can be reused if one needs to embed FAMILIAR in another context. This is partly solved in the MSPL approach as a model drives the variability part, but still the connection semantics between the metamodel and the variability models could have been better captured.

As for the usage of FAMILIAR during execution, the adaptive part of the video-surveillance system calling the interpreter led to **performance issues at runtime**. Integrating the variability-based adaptation logic in the application engine was also very hard and it seems that a internal DSL approach would have largely simplified this task. Furthermore even at configuration time, the only means to change the implementation of the most complex operators is through a simple parameter. An average FAMILIAR user will have not enough knowledge to make the appropriate choices, especially if a script involves several operations.

Another **lack of flexibility** also appeared when we had to compute some metrics on FMs that were not present in the original DSL definition. Some of them were available in the Java API while they were needed in the DSL itself. On the other hand, implementing them in the Scala-based flavor of FAMILIAR was very fast and they were directly available in the extended language.

4.2 Reverse Engineering

Plugin-Based Systems: Software Architecture. FAMILIAR was also used to reverse engineer a variability model representing a software architecture with plugins [25]. This was applied on several successive versions of the implemented systems.

Each time, the architectural FM was obtained by extracting variability information from both the architecture and the plugin dependencies. This creates an over-approximation of the variability, which is fixed by a slice operation made on the pure architectural part of the FM [25]. Moreover, this extracted FM was compared with another FM representing the intention of the software architect. Using several steps, scripted in FAMILIAR, the two views were reconciled to form a stable FM, which was then used to follow the evolution of the different versions.

Product Descriptions: Tabular Data. We also explored the semiautomatic extraction of variability models from one of the most used descriptions of products, that is tabular data defining product features. A front-end enables one to give some directives on how to interpret variability and how to build the hierarchy of the resulting FM.

From the extraction tool, several FAMILIAR scripts are generated, leading to one FM per product, and all FMs are then merged in union mode to obtain an exact representation of the variability. From the first application on several public product matrices [38], this technique was applied and adapted in different contexts, such as web configurators [39] or competing visualization APIs for dashboards [40]. It is also used in the digital signage MSPL evoked in the previous section, so to populate it from different input SPLs.

Benefits. These extraction applications show again some benefits in coupling reusable parts with generated scripts in FAMILIAR. As parts of the extraction procedures have to be *ad hoc* to be adapted to the input data, the simple syntax of the external DSL was a clear advantage so to easily generate FMs. As more cases were studied, the need for a more finely parameterized operation to build a FM hierarchy arose and it was integrated in the DSL [27]. The experiment on software architecture was also the opportunity to make a software architect use the DSL to discover *hidden* features.

Drawbacks. In the extraction scenarios **ad hoc bridges** are again present. As FAMILIAR was designed to move away from a general purpose programming language, it offers only basic control structures and nothing to handle the input data. Again, the absence of a clear interface of what could or should be produced from the analyzed input to produce the resulting FM is hampering reuse between extraction chains.

Similarly the previously identified **lack of flexibility** is also characterized by the required evolution on the *ksynthesis* operator, which drives the FM hierarchy building. A first change was thus made on the whole external DSL chain, but as many different techniques are currently experimented on this hot topic of variability extraction, a more flexible evolution process is clearly needed.

5   Challenges Ahead

The development of the FAMILIAR DSL started with composition of several FMs as the main requirement. The experience built-up through its usage in different domains, life-cycle stages and with different stakeholders clearly show that the DSL is meeting this requirement. On the other hand, we identify here the main challenges that must be tackled to provide a better support to a larger variability engineering community.

Managing More Explicit Mechanisms. Several mechanisms inside FAMILIAR should be made more explicit and more configurable. A first obvious location in the DSL architecture is the management of reasoning back-ends. Handling the variability of back-ends is already done in some variability tool sets [19, 41]. For example FaMa [19] manages the different analyses and reasoners with a feature model capturing functional capabilities and a few non-functional properties. The challenge for FAMILIAR is to go beyond such organization, so that new solvers can be easily integrated (CSP and SMT solvers are the primary targets) and that both functional and non-functional properties can be captured and inter-related into feature models. This would also better organize the heuristics of used algorithms, like in the SPLAR Java API [21]. In addition, results from performance comparison between solvers for feature modeling operations [42] may serve as starting point.

The description of the other challenges will also show that a systematic and uniform approach should be followed to master all configurable properties in FAMILIAR, that is, not only for reasoning back-ends. The recent implementation of some variants of the merge operation is an example [26], but this is actually the case in the kernel of the DSL and in all its interaction points (extraction of variability, internal representation, relations to other models).

Extending the Scope of the DSL. The second challenge is related to the advances that were made thanks to FM composition. In all the applications, FAMILIAR was an appropriate engine to deal with variability in conjunction with many different software artifacts, but the connection with these artifacts was quite often cumbersome in terms of software engineering. The move towards an internal DSL in Scala should partially solve this issue, but exploring how to facilitate the management of relationships between feature models and the whole model-driven engineering steps seems an interesting track to follow.

First this should allow to make advances in the relation between the semantics of artifact composition and the semantics of FM composition. In our recent experience on the MSPL of digital signage systems, we used a combination of metamodels and feature models that seems to be related of what is available in Clafer [34]. Still Clafer is focused on understanding domain models, whereas we completely define and implement the MSPL toolchain down to the code generation level. Different extensions of feature models should be introduced in the DSL, but this should be especially organized in terms of operations and inter-relations between the extensions. This point is related to the previous challenge, as each extension of feature models is likely to need a fine-tuned usage of the available reasoning back-ends.

Extending the FAMILIAR scope is also needed to facilitate variability manipulation on a larger scale, especially in (semi-)automatically extraction scenarios. Currently, there is some lazy strategy implemented to reduce the transformation to propositional logic, but the available internal representations should be extended so to handle cases where only a feature set is desirable or feasible, for example when very large feature models are split and their hierarchy partially flattened [43]. The ideal functionality would handle a continuum of representations, from feature sets to feature models and the different representations needed by different reasoning approaches.

Facilitating Different Usages. The last challenge consists in providing the appropriate customised variants of the DSL for the different users and tasks that would be then facilitated. With an extended scope and more explicit mechanisms, different scenarios must be envisaged. Extraction processes should be supported with recurring patterns being provided in the DSL. The highly functional flavor of programming provided in Scala should enable to design a small but powerful toolkit for this purpose. Conversely the different mappings between feature models and other models, the associated realization techniques, as well as the transformation processes to different back-ends should be abstracted and organized in the same way.

Besides, one *usage* not to be neglected is the visualization and comprehension of these large and inter-related feature models. The current FAMILIAR implementation relies on interoperability formats, so that other visualization tools, such as S2T2 can be used. If different usages are supported, appropriate visualizations has to be envisaged and relationships between the DSL and third-parties toolkits should be supported as well.

Finally, these different specific parts should cleverly rely on the different internal representations discussed in the previous challenge. This, together with an efficient runtime interpreter in Scala, would be also very useful to provide a scalable variability support when the DSL is heavily exploited at runtime.

6   Conclusion

The FAMILIAR language was first developed to manipulate and compose feature models in the large, relying on formal underpinnings and bridging some existing APIs. Separation of concerns and reasoning facilities are made available through an external DSL, which has been evolved with an additional Java API and recently, an Scala based internal implementation.

We have reported several applications of the FAMILIAR toolset, ranging from semi-automatic extraction of feature models from product descriptions or software architectures, to more forward engineering cases, with scientific workflow, video-surveillance software, and digital signage systems organized in multiple software product lines. Based on these varied experiences, we summarized obtained benefits, but especially focused on identified drawbacks: *ad hoc* integration in toolchains or applications, lack of flexibility, or performance issues during heavily runtime usage. We then devised three inter-related challenges to improve such DSL support, i.e. *i)* managing more explicit mechanisms, both internally in the used algorithms and externally when dealing with reasoning back-ends, *ii)* extending the scope of the DSL to better support extraction procedures and downstream engineering stages, and *iii)* facilitating different usages through appropriate DSL extensions.

Ongoing work aims at tackling these challenges. First steps consist in exploring how Scala facilities can help in easily integrating variability in the FAMILIAR architecture, so that other needed functionalities can be nicely and efficiently provided. We notably plan to bridge an extended version of FAMILIAR with the SIGMA family of DSLs for manipulating EMF models [44], which is also implemented in Scala. We expect to partly cover some functionalities provided by implementations of the CVL variability standard [45], but with a more lightweight and decoupled approach. Being able to easily integrate a small service provided by the FAMILIAR DSL in any toolchain is kept as a prime requirement.

Acknowledgments. The author would like to thank all the people that have worked on developing FAMILIAR (http://familiar-project.github.io), and especially Mathieu Acher, Philippe Lahire and Robert B. France, who were at the roots of it.

References

1. Pohl, K., Böckle, G., van der Linden, F.J.: Software Product Line Engineering: Foundations, Principles and Techniques. Springer (2005)
2. Clements, P., Northrop, L.M.: Software Product Lines: Practices and Patterns. Addison-Wesley Professional (2001)
3. Apel, S., Kästner, C.: An overview of feature-oriented software development. Journal of Object Technology (JOT) 8(5), 49–84 (2009)
4. Schobbens, P.Y., Heymans, P., Trigaux, J.C., Bontemps, Y.: Generic semantics of feature diagrams. Comput. Netw. 51(2), 456–479 (2007)
5. Czarnecki, K., Wasowski, A.: Feature diagrams and logics: There and back again. In: SPLC 2007, pp. 23–34. IEEE (2007)
6. Thüm, T., Batory, D., Kästner, C.: Reasoning about edits to feature models. In: ICSE 2009, pp. 254–264. ACM (2009)
7. Benavides, D., Segura, S., Ruiz-Cortes, A.: Automated Analysis of Feature Models 20 years Later: a Literature Review. Information Systems 35(6) (2010)
8. Kang, K., Kim, S., Lee, J., Kim, K., Shin, E., Huh, M.: Form: A feature-oriented reuse method with domain-specific reference architectures. Annals of Software Engineering 5(1), 143–168 (1998)
9. Metzger, A., Pohl, K., Heymans, P., Schobbens, P.Y., Saval, G.: Disambiguating the documentation of variability in software product lines: A separation of concerns, formalization and automated analysis. In: RE 2007, pp. 243–253 (2007)
10. Dhungana, D., Grünbacher, P., Rabiser, R., Neumayer, T.: Structuring the modeling space and supporting evolution in software product line engineering. Journal of Systems and Software 83(7), 1108–1122 (2010)
11. Abo Zaid, L., Kleinermann, F., De Troyer, O.: Feature assembly: A new feature modeling technique. In: Parsons, J., Saeki, M., Shoval, P., Woo, C., Wand, Y. (eds.) ER 2010. LNCS, vol. 6412, pp. 233–246. Springer, Heidelberg (2010)

12. Dhungana, D., Seichter, D., Botterweck, G., Rabiser, R., Gruenbacher, P., Benavides, D., Galindo, J.A.: Configuration of multi product lines by bridging heterogeneous variability modeling approaches. In: SPLC 2011. IEEE (2011)
13. Hubaux, A., Tun, T.T., Heymans, P.: Separation of concerns in feature diagram languages: A systematic survey. ACM Computing Surveys (2012)
14. Acher, M., Collet, P., Lahire, P., France, R.: Separation of Concerns in Feature Modeling: Support and Applications. In: AOSD 2012, ACM (2012)
15. Acher, M., Collet, P., Lahire, P., France, R.: Composing Feature Models. In: van den Brand, M., Gašević, D., Gray, J. (eds.) SLE 2009. LNCS, vol. 5969, pp. 62–81. Springer, Heidelberg (2010)
16. Acher, M., Collet, P., Lahire, P., France, R.: Comparing approaches to implement feature model composition. In: Kühne, T., Selic, B., Gervais, M.-P., Terrier, F. (eds.) ECMFA 2010. LNCS, vol. 6138, pp. 3–19. Springer, Heidelberg (2010)
17. Acher, M., Collet, P., Lahire, P., France, R.: Slicing Feature Models. In: Proc. of ASE 2011 (short paper). ACM (2011)
18. Acher, M., Heymans, P., Collet, P., Quinton, C., Lahire, P., Merle, P.: Feature Model Differences. In: Ralyté, J., Franch, X., Brinkkemper, S., Wrycza, S. (eds.) CAiSE 2012. LNCS, vol. 7328, pp. 629–645. Springer, Heidelberg (2012)
19. Trinidad, P., Benavides, D., Ruiz-Cortes, A., Segura, S., Jimenez, A.: FAMA framework. In: Int'l Software Product Line Conference (SPLC 2008), Limerick, Ireland, pp. 359–359 (2008)
20. Thüm, T., Kästner, C., Benduhn, F., Meinicke, J., Saake, G., Leich, T.: FeatureIDE: An extensible framework for feature-oriented software development. Science of Computer Programming (SCP) (2012)
21. Mendonca, M., Branco, M., Cowan, D.: S.p.l.o.t.: software product lines online tools. In: OOPSLA 2009 (companion). ACM Press, New York (2009)
22. Acher, M., Collet, P., Lahire, P., France, R.: Familiar: A domain-specific language for large scale management of feature models. Science of Computer Programming (SCP) Special issue on programming languages 78(6), 657–681 (2013)
23. Acher, M., Collet, P., Lahire, P., Moisan, S., Rigault, J.P.: Modeling variability from requirements to runtime. In: ICECCS 2011, pp. 77–86. IEEE (2011)
24. Acher, M., Collet, P., Lahire, P., Gaignard, A., France, R., Montagnat, J.: Composing multiple variability artifacts to assemble coherent workflows. Software Quality Journal (Special issue on Quality Engineering for SPLs) (2011)
25. Acher, M., Cleve, A., Collet, P., Merle, P., Duchien, L., Lahire, P.: Extraction and Evolution of Architectural Variability Models in Plugin-based Systems. Software & Systems Modeling (SoSyM), 27 (July, 2013)
26. Acher, M., Combemale, B., Collet, P., Barais, O., Lahire, P., France, R.B.: Composing Your Compositions of Variability Models. In: Moreira, A., Schätz, B., Gray, J., Vallecillo, A., Clarke, P. (eds.) MODELS 2013. LNCS, vol. 8107, pp. 352–369. Springer, Heidelberg (2013)
27. Acher, M., Heymans, P., Cleve, A., Hainaut, J.L., Baudry, B.: Support for reverse engineering and maintaining feature models. In: VaMoS 2013, ACM (2013)
28. Fowler, M.: Domain Specific Languages. Addison-Wesley Professional (2010)
29. Hermans, F., Pinzger, M., van Deursen, A.: Domain-Specific Languages in Practice: A User Study on the Success Factors. In: Schürr, A., Selic, B. (eds.) MODELS 2009. LNCS, vol. 5795, pp. 423–437. Springer, Heidelberg (2009)
30. Mernik, M., Heering, J., Sloane, A.M.: When and how to develop domain-specific languages. ACM Comput. Surv. 37(4), 316–344 (2005)
31. Kosar, T., Mernik, M., Carver, J.: Program comprehension of domain-specific and general-purpose languages: comparison using a family of experiments. Empirical Software Engineering 17(3), 276–304 (2012)

32. Erdweg, S., et al.: The state of the art in language workbenches. In: Erwig, M., Paige, R.F., Van Wyk, E. (eds.) SLE 2013. LNCS, vol. 8225, pp. 197–217. Springer, Heidelberg (2013), http://dx.doi.org/10.1007/978-3-319-02654-1_11

33. Chafi, H., DeVito, Z., Moors, A., Rompf, T., Sujeeth, A.K., Hanrahan, P., Odersky, M., Olukotun, K.: Language virtualization for heterogeneous parallel computing. In: Proceedings of the ACM International Conference on Object Oriented Programming systems Languages and Applications, OOPSLA 2010. ACM (October 2010)

34. Bąk, K., Czarnecki, K., Wąsowski, A.: Feature and meta-models in clafer: Mixed, specialized, and coupled. In: Malloy, B., Staab, S., van den Brand, M. (eds.) SLE 2010. LNCS, vol. 6563, pp. 102–122. Springer, Heidelberg (2011)

35. Classen, A., Boucher, Q., Heymans, P.: A text-based approach to feature modelling: Syntax and semantics of TVL. Science of Computer Programming, Special Issue on Software Evolution, Adaptability and Variability 76(12), 1130–1143 (2011)

36. Andersen, N., Czarnecki, K., She, S., Wasowski, A.: Efficient synthesis of feature models. In: Proceedings of SPLC 2012, pp. 97–106. ACM Press (2012)

37. Urli, S., Mosser, S., Blay-Fornarino, M., Collet, P.: How to Exploit Domain Knowledge in Multiple Software Product Lines? In: Fourth International Workshop on Product LinE Approaches in Software Engineering at ICSE 2013 (PLEASE 2013), p. 4. ACM, San Francisco (2013)

38. Acher, M., Cleve, A., Perrouin, G., Heymans, P., Vanbeneden, C., Collet, P., Lahire, P.: On extracting feature models from product descriptions. In: VaMoS 2012, pp. 45–54. ACM Press, New York (2012)

39. Abbasi, E.K., Acher, M., Heymans, P., Cleve, A.: Reverse Engineering Web Configurators. In: 17th European Conference on Software Maintenance and Reengineering (CSMR). IEEE, Antwerp (2014)

40. Logre, I., Mosser, S., Collet, P., Riveill, M.: Sensor Data Visualisation: A Composition-Based Approach to Support Domain Variability. In: Cabot, J., Rubin, J. (eds.) ECMFA 2014. LNCS, vol. 8569, pp. 101–116. Springer, Heidelberg (2014)

41. Cordy, M., Classen, A., Heymans, P., Schobbens, P.Y., Legay, A.: Provelines: A product line of verifiers for software product lines. In: Proceedings of the 17th International Software Product Line Conference Co-located Workshops, SPLC 2013 Workshops, pp. 141–146. ACM, New York (2013)

42. Pohl, R., Lauenroth, K., Pohl, K.: A performance comparison of contemporary algorithmic approaches for automated analysis operations on feature models. In: Proceedings of the 2011 26th IEEE/ACM International Conference on Automated Software Engineering. ASE 2011, pp. 313–322. IEEE Computer Society, Washington, DC (2011)

43. Dintzner, N., Van Deursen, A., Pinzger, M.: Extracting feature model changes from the linux kernel using fmdiff. In: Proceedings of the Eighth International Workshop on Variability Modelling of Software-Intensive Systems. VaMoS 2014, pp. 22:1–22:22. ACM, New York (2014)

44. Křikava, F., Collet, P., France, R.: Manipulating Models Using Internal Domain-Specific Languages. In: Symposium on Applied Computing (SAC), Programming Languages Track(SAC), Short paper. ACM, Gyeongju (2014)

45. Haugen, O., Wąsowski, A., Czarnecki, K.: Cvl: Common variability language. In: Proceedings of the 17th International Software Product Line Conference, SPLC 2013, pp. 277–277. ACM, New York (2013)

Delta-Trait Programming of Software Product Lines*

Ferruccio Damiani[1], Ina Schaefer[2], Sven Schuster[2], and Tim Winkelmann[2]

[1] Università di Torino, Dipartimento di Informatica, 10149 Torino, Italy
ferruccio.damiani@unito.it
[2] Technische Universität Braunschweig, Germany
{i.schaefer,s.schuster,t.winkelmann}@tu-braunschweig.de

Abstract. Delta-oriented programming (DOP) is a flexible approach for implementing software product lines (SPLs). DOP SPLs are implemented by a set of
delta modules encapsulating changes to class-based object-oriented programs.
A particular product in a DOP SPL is generated by applying to the empty program the modifications contained in the delta modules associated to the selected
product features. Traits are pure units of behavior, designed to support flexible
fine-grained reuse and to provide an effective means to counter the limitations
of class-based inheritance. A trait is a set of methods which is independent from
any class hierarchy and can be flexibly used to build other traits or classes by
means of a suite of composition operations. In this paper, we present an approach
for programming SPLs of trait-based programs where the program modifications
expressed by delta modules are formulated by exploiting the trait composition
mechanism. This smooth integration of the modularity mechanisms provided by
delta modules and traits results in a new approach for programming SPLs, *delta-
trait programming (DTP)*, which is particularly well suited for evolving SPLs.

1 Introduction

A *software product line (SPL)* is a set of software systems with well-defined commonality and variability [13,29]. SPL engineering aims at developing these systems by
managed reuse. Products of an SPL are commonly described in terms of *features* [20],
where a feature is a unit of product functionality. Feature-based product variability has
to be captured in the product line artifacts that are reused to realize the single products.
On the implementation level, reuse mechanisms for product implementations have to
be flexible enough to express the desired product variability [34].

Today, many product implementations of SPLs are carried out within the object-
oriented paradigm. Although class-based inheritance in object-oriented languages provides means for code reuse with static guarantees, the rigid structure of class-based
inheritance puts limitations on the effective modeling of product variability and on the
reuse of code [27,17]. *Feature-oriented programming (FOP)* [5,2,16,1] allows to flexibly implement product lines within the object-oriented paradigm by class refinement.
In FOP, a product implementation for a particular feature configuration is obtained by
composing *feature modules* for the respective features. A feature module contains class

---

* Work partially supported by MIUR (proj. CINA), Ateneo/CSP (proj. SALT), Deutsche
Forschungsgemeinschaft (grant SCHA1635/2-1), and ICT COST Action IC1201 BETTY.

T. Margaria and B. Steffen (Eds.): ISoLA 2014, Part I, LNCS 8802, pp. 289–303, 2014.

definitions and class refinements. A class refinement can modify an existing class by adding new fields/methods, by wrapping code around existing methods or by changing the superclass. *Delta-oriented programming (DOP)* [31,33,32,9] extends FOP by the possibility to remove code from an existing product (see [33] for a straightforward embedding of FOP into DOP). In DOP, a product implementation is obtained by applying modifications specified in *delta modules* to existing products. Using FOP/DOP for implementing SPLs results in a scenario where class-based inheritance is the mechanism for *intra-product code reuse* (i.e., for reusing code within single products) and FOP/DOP class refinement/modification is the mechanism for *inter-product code reuse* (i.e., for reusing code across different products). Since class-based inheritance does not support low coupling [27,17], FOP/DOP class refinement/modification do not mix well with class-based inheritance and, as a matter of fact, little or no intra-product code reuse is realized via class-based inheritance in many FOP/DOP SPL implementations [36].

In object-oriented languages with class-based inheritance, classes have two competing roles: (i) generators of objects and (ii) units of reuse. To counter this, traits are introduced as pure units of behavior, designed for flexible, fine-grained reuse [35,17]. A trait contains a set of methods, which is independent from any class hierarchy. Thus, the common methods of a set of classes can be factored into a trait. The distinctive characteristic of traits is that they can be composed in an arbitrary order and that the resulting composite unit (which can be a class or another trait) has complete control over the conflicts that may arise in the composition and must solve these conflicts explicitly. Since their first formulation [35,17], various formulations of traits in a JAVA-like setting can be found in the literature (see, e.g., [38,28,30,12,25,11,8,7]).

In this paper, we present delta-oriented programming for software product lines of trait-based programs. In the proposed approach, delta modules and traits work synergically together for modeling program variability by flexibly supporting both inter- and intra-product code reuse. In particular, the program modifications expressed by delta modules are formulated by exploiting the trait composition mechanism. This smooth integration of delta modules and traits results in a new approach for programming SPLs, that we call *delta-trait programming (DTP)*. As in DOP, intra-product code reuse is rarely achieved by class-based inheritance, but it could be realized by using design patterns in the implementation of the core products [37]. However, when the SPL evolves the patterns used in core products might not be suitable for supporting intra-product code reuse in the new products. So, either we accept to have code duplications in the code of the new products, or we refactor the whole code base which is both undesirable. To mitigate this problem, DTP offers trait-based intra-product code reuse. As *unanticipated SPL evolution* (i.e., evolution involving changes for which developers have not prepared in the original design of the SPL) scenarios become more common in long-living software systems, DTP is a promising approach to alleviate the arising problems.

The paper is organized as follows. Section 2 introduces pure trait-based programming. Section 3 discusses the main design choices made during the development of DTP. Section 4 introduces DTP by a small case study. Section 5 illustrates how DTP supports proactive, reactive and extractive SPL development and is particularly well suited for evolving SPLs. Section 6 discusses related work. Section 7 concludes the paper by outlining some directions for further work.

2   Pure Trait-Based Programming

Pure trait-based programming [12,11,7,10,7] aims at supporting low coupling and at maximizing the opportunities of reuse. It completely separates the competing roles of object generators and units of code reuse, and the competing roles of types and units of code reuse. Namely, trait names are not types and class-based inheritance is ruled out.

In this section, we summarize TRAITJ, a pure trait-based programming language (based on [10]), which highlights the specific characteristics of pure trait-based programming.

The syntax of TRAITJ is given in Figure 1, where we use the overbar notation for sequences (as in [19]) and where the big square brackets '[' and ']' denote an optional element of the syntax. A program consists of interface declarations, trait declarations, and class declarations. The syntax of interface declarations ID, method headers H, field declarations F, method declarations M, field initializations FI and class constructors K is similar as in JAVA (without considering, e.g., visibility modifies and checked exception declarations).

A *trait declaration* associates a name to a *trait expression*. We say that a trait declaration is: *basic* (or *flat*) if its body consists of a basic trait expression $\{\overline{TM}\}$, *composite* (or *non-flat*) otherwise. A *basic trait expressions* $\{\overline{TM}\}$ declares a set of provided methods together with their required fields and required methods. *Provided methods* are the methods defined in the trait, which will be included in any class using the trait. *Required fields* and *required methods* are fields and abstract methods which are assumed to be available in any class using the trait. The provided/required methods and the required fields of a trait can be directly accessed in the body of the provided methods of the trait. For instance, the following trait declaration

ID	::=	**interface** I [**extends** Ī] { H̄; }	*interface*
H	::=	S m (S̄ x̄) | **void** m (S̄ x̄)	*method header*
S	::=	I | **boolean** | **int** | ···	*type*
TD	::=	**trait** T **is** TE	*trait*
TE	::=	{TM̄} | T | TE + TE | T[TA]	*trait expression*
TM	::=	F; | H; | M	*trait member*
TA	::=	**exclude** m | m **aliasAs** m	*trait alteration*
		| m **renameTo** m | f **renameTo** f	
F	::=	S f	*field*
M	::=	H { ··· }	*method*
CD	::=	**class** C **implements** Ī **by** TE { FĪ; K̄ }	*class*
FI	::=	F | F = ···	*field initialization*
K	::=	C(S̄ x̄){ ··· }	*constructor*

Fig. 1. TRAITJ syntax (I ∈ interface names, T ∈ trait names, C ∈ class names, m ∈ method names, f ∈ field names, x ∈ variables names)

```
trait T1 is {  int y;   int getX();   int getY() { return this.y; }   void setY(int value) { this.y = value; }
                String toString() { return "(" + this.getX() + "," + this.getY() + ")"; } }
```

associates the name T1 to a basic trait expression which provides the methods getY, setY and toString and requires the field y and the method getX.

The type system checks that each field/method requirement declared in a basic trait is *used* by some method m provided by the basic trait (that is, the required method/field is selected on **this** in the body of m).

Traits are building blocks that can be used to compose classes and other traits by means of a suite of trait composition operations. In the following, we illustrate the semantics of trait composition by associating to each composite trait declaration a flat trait declaration with the same semantics. This way of specifying the semantics of traits, called *flattening* [35,17,28], is quite common in the literature on traits.

The *symmetric sum* operation, +, merges two traits to form a new trait. The summed traits must be disjoint (i.e., they must not provide identically named methods) and consistent (i.e., required fields with the same name and required/provided methods with the same name must have the same type). For instance, given the trait declaration

```
trait T2 is { int x;    int getX() { return this.x; }    void setX(int value) { this.x = value; } }
```

the composite trait declaration **trait** TPoint **is** T1 + T2 is equivalent to the flat trait declaration

```
trait TPoint is { int x;    int y;    int getX() { return this.x; }    int getY() { return this.y; }
                  void setX(int value) { this.x = value; }    void setY(int value) { this.y = value; }
                  String toString() { return "(" + this.getX() + "," + this.getY() + ")"; } }
```

The operation **exclude** forms a new trait by removing a method from an existing trait. For instance, the composite trait declaration **trait** T3 **is** T1[exclude toString] is equivalent to the flat trait declaration

```
trait T3 is { int y;    int getY() { return this.y; }    void setY(int value) { this.y = value; } }
```

(where the method requirement **int** getX() from T1 has been automatically dropped, since getX is not used by the provided methods of T3), and the composite trait declaration **trait** T4 **is** T1[exclude getY, exclude setY] is equivalent to the flat trait declaration

```
trait T4 is { int getX();    int getY();    String toString(){return "("+this.getX()+","+this.getY()+")";} }
```

(where the field requirement **int** y from T1 has been automatically dropped, while the excluded method getY has been changed into a requirement since it is used by the provided methods of toString).

The operation **aliasAs** forms a new trait by adding a copy of an existing method with a different name. When a recursive method is aliased, the recursive invocations in the body of the new method are not renamed. For instance, given the trait declaration

```
trait T5 is
{ int x;    void resetX(){if (this.x<0){this.x=−x; this.resetX();} else if (this.x>0){this.x−−; this.resetX();}} }
```

the composite trait declaration **trait** T6 **is** T5[resetX aliasAs resetXaux] is equivalent to the flat trait declaration

```
trait T6 is {
    int x;
    void resetX() { if (this.x < 0){this.x=−x; this.resetX();} else if (this.x > 0){this.x−−; this.resetX();} }
    void resetXaux() { if (this.x < 0){this.x=−x; this.resetX();} else if (this.x > 0){this.x−−; this.resetX();} }
}
```

The operation **renameTo** creates a new trait by renaming all the occurrences of a required field name or of a required/provided method name from an existing trait. For instance, the composite trait declaration **trait** T7 **is** T1[y renameTo x, getY renameTo getX, setY renameTo setX] is equivalent to the flat trait declaration

```
trait T7 is { int x;    int getX() { return this.x; }    void setX(int value) { this.x = value; }
              String toString() { return "(" + this.getX() + "," + this.getX() + ")"; } }
```

Since traits do not introduce any state, a class assembled from traits has to declare and initialize the fields required by its constituent traits (non-explicitly initialized fields ar implicitly initialized, as in JAVA). For instance, the class declaration

```
interface IPoint  {  int getX();  int getX();  void setX(int value);  void setY(int value);  String toString();  }
interface IColor  {  void setColor(String name);  String toString();  }
interface IColoredPoint extends IPoint, IColor  { }
```

Listing 1: Interfaces IPoint, IColor and IColoredPoint

```
class CPoint implements IPoint by TPoint
  {  int x = 0;     int y;     CPoint() { }     CPoint(int x, int y) { this.x = x; this.y = y; }  }
```

defines a generator of objects of type IPoint (the interface IPoint is defined at the top of Listing 1) with two constructors. The class, which is built by using the trait TPoint (defined above in Section "Trait sum"), has the same semantics of the JAVA class obtained by removing the clause "**by** TPoint" from the class header and inserting in the class body the code of the methods provided by TPoint.

The following example shows the flexibility of traits. A trait TColor introduced for building a class CColor:

```
trait TColor
  {  String name;     void setColor(String name){this.name = name;}     String toString(){return this.name;}  }
class CColor implements IColor by TColor { String name = ""; }
```

(the interface IColor is defined in Listing 1) can be straightforwardly reused for building a class CColoredPoint:

```
trait TColoredPoint is TPoint[toString renameTo pointToString]+TColor[toString renameTo colorToString]+{
  { String pointToString();     String colorToString();
    String toString() { return this.pointToString() + ":" + this.colorToString(); }  }
class CColoredPoint implements IColoredPoint by TColoredPoint { int x=0;   int y=0;   String name=""; }
```

(the interface IColoredPoint is defined in Listing 1) supporting the same kind of reuse provided by multiple class-based inheritance.

Pure trait-based programming targets a scenario where a trait, which was developed for a particular purpose, may later be adapted and reused in a completely different context. For instance, trait TPoint introduced for defining a point in a plane can be reused to define a counter:

```
interface ICounter {  int getValue();     void setValue(int value);     String toString();  }
trait TCountert is TPoint[exclude setY,  exclude getY,  exclude toString,
                      x renameTo n,  getX renameTo getValue,  setX renameTo setValue] +
  { int n;     String toString() { return n; }     void increment() { n++; }  }
class CCounter implements ICounter by TCounter { int n = 0; }
```

3   Design Choices for DTP

In this section, we discuss the main design choices made during the development of DTP. We choose a *pure* trait-based programming language as the language for writing the products of the SPL because pure trait-based programming has been developed in order to maximize the opportunities of reuse. In particular, we consider TRAITJ since, in previous work [10], it has been used to directly implement SPLs.

We approached the challenge of designing a suitable notion of delta module for trait-based programs by exploring the possibility to adapt DOP delta modules. A DOP delta module is a container of modification operations to a JAVA program. The modifications may add, remove or modify interfaces and classes. Modifying an interface means changing the super interfaces, or adding or removing methods. Modifying a class means: *(i)* changing the super class; *(ii)* adding or removing fields; and/or *(iii)* adding, removing or modifying methods. The method-modification operation can either replace the method body by another implementation, or wrap the existing method using the **original** construct (similar to the **Super** construct in AHEAD [5])—the call **original**($\cdots$) expresses a call to the method with the same name before the modifications and is bound at the time the product is generated. Since TRAITJ interfaces are literally JAVA interfaces, the DOP delta operations for adding, removing or modifying an interface can be straightforwardly adopted for defining delta modules for trait-based programs. Also the operations of adding or removing classes and traits do not pose design challenges and can be straightforwardly defined.

The main challenge is to define suitable delta operations for expressing modifications to traits. As a first attempt, we have tried to adapt to traits the class-modification operations provided by DOP (see above), thus defining delta operations for modifying the body TE of a trait definition **trait** T **is** TE by: *(i)* replacing the used traits (i.e., the trait names occurring in TE) by arbitrary trait expressions; *(ii)* adding or removing field requirements and method requirements; and/or *(iii)* adding, removing or modifying (possibly using the **original** construct) methods. However, through some experiments, we realized that such delta operations are quite complex to use and that the delta operation on methods (point *(iii)* above) is less flexible than the TRAITJ composition operations, which include also method/field renaming.

Thus, we realized that a flexible trait-modification operation can be expressed by replacing the body of the trait with a new trait expressions. The new trait expression may contain occurrences of the **TOriginal** keyword, which refers to the trait with the same name before the modification and is bound at the time the product is generated. In this way, a smooth integration of the modularity mechanisms provided by delta modification operations (modeling inter-product code reuse) and by trait composition operations (modeling intra-product code reuse) is achieved.

4   Delta-Trait Programming

In order to illustrate the main concepts of delta-trait programming, we use a case study of a simple product line of data structures for sequences, that we call the Sequences PL.

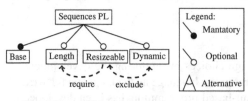

Figure 2 depicts the feature model of the Sequences PL as a feature diagram. The Sequences PL has five products. Each product provides a stack and a queue data structure. The base product (implementing only the Base feature) provides a fixed capacity stack and queue implementing the

Fig. 2. Feature Model for the Sequences PL

empty/full tests and the canonical insertion/extraction operations. The other products offer additional functionalities: an operation for getting the number of existing elements in a stack/queue (feature Length), and in mutual exclusion either operations for changing the capacity of a stack/queue (feature Resizeable) or for the automatic management of the capacity (feature Dynamic). Since it would not be sensible to change the capacity of a stack/queue without knowing the number of contained elements, the feature Resizeable requires the feature Length.

The syntax of DELTATRAITJ is given in Figure 3. Delta modules are containers of modification operations to programs. In the context of trait-based programs, delta operations may add, remove or modify interfaces, traits or classes. Modifying an interface means changing the super interfaces, or adding or removing methods. Modifying a trait means replacing its body or wrapping the existing trait body by means of the **TOriginal** construct. Modifying a class means changing the implemented interfaces, or replacing/wrapping the trait expression providing the methods, or adding/removing/modifying field initializations, or adding/removing/modifying constructors.

DD ::= **delta** D { $\overline{DO}$ }		*delta module*
DO ::= IO | TO | CO		*delta operation*
IO ::= ID | **remove** I |		*interface operation*
modify interface I [**extends** $\overline{I}$] { $\overline{HO}$; }		
HO ::= H | **remove** m		*header operation*
TO ::= TD | **remove** T | **modify** TD		*trait operaton*
CO ::= CD | **remove** C |		*class operations*
modify class C [**implements** $\overline{I}$] [**by** TE] { $\overline{FO}$; $\overline{KO}$ }		
FO ::= FI | **remove** f | **modify** FI		*field operation*
KO ::= K | **remove** C($\overline{S}$ $\overline{x}$) | **modify** K		*constructor op.*

Fig. 3. DELTATRAITJ delta modules syntax (D ∈ delta module names and ID, H, TD, TE, CD, FI, K, m, f, x are defined in Fig. 1). The body TE of the trait definition TD specified by a trait-modify operation **modify** TD may contain occurrences of the **TOriginal** keyword, which denotes the original version of the trait. The body {···} of the constructor definition K specified by a constructor-modify operation **modify** K may start with **COriginal**(···), which represents a call to the original version of the constructor.

Modifying a constructor means replacing its body or wrapping the existing constructor body by means of the **COriginal** construct.

A delta-trait product line (similar to a delta-oriented product line) consists of a *code base* (containing the delta modules) and a *product line declaration*. The code in Listings 2 and 3 is a code base for the Sequences PL. The product line declaration creates the connection to the product line variability specified in terms of product features. Listing 4 shows a product line declaration for the Sequences PL. The product line declaration: *(i)* Lists the product features. *(ii)* Describes the set of *valid* feature configurations. In the examples, the valid feature configurations are represented by a propositional formula over the set of features. We refer to [4] for a discussion on other possible representations. *(iii)* Describes the possible application orders of the delta modules by defining a total order on the sets of a partition of the delta modules. Delta modules in the same set can be applied in any order, while the order of the sets must be respected. The ordering allows the programmer to enforce semantic requires-relations that are necessary for the applicability of the delta modules. In Listing 4, the ordering is represented by writing an ordered list of the delta module sets after the keyword **deltas** {...}. *(iv)* A delta module name can have an application condition to evaluate for which feature configurations the delta module has to be included in the code of the corresponding product. In Listing 4, the application condition is represented by a propositional constraint over the set of features, given by **when** clauses. Since only feature configurations that are valid according to the feature model are used for product generation, the application conditions are understood as a conjunction with the formula describing the set of valid feature configurations. In Listing 4, the delta modules DBase, DLength, DResizeable and DDynamic are associated to the features Base, Length, Resizeable and Dynamic, respectively. Moreover, in order to realize the feature Resizeable, both the delta modules DResizeable and DResisazableOrDynamic must be applied. In order to realize the feature Dynamic, both the delta modules DResizeableOrDynamic and DDynamic must be applied.

A product is *valid* if it corresponds to a valid feature configuration. The generation of a product for a given feature configuration consists of two steps (that can be performed automatically): *(i)* find the selected delta modules (that is, the delta modules with a satisfied application condition); and *(ii)* apply them to the empty program in any linear ordering that respects the total order on the partition of the delta modules. A delta module is applicable to a program if: *(i)* each interface/trait/class to be added does not exist; *(ii)* each interface/trait/class to be removed or modified exists; *(iii)* each interface-modify operation is such that each method to be removed exists and each method to be added does not exist; and *(iv)* each class-modify operation is such that each field to be removed exists and each field to be added does not exist. During the product generation, the selected delta modules must be applicable in the given order (otherwise the product generation fails). In particular, the first delta module (which is applied to the empty product) must contain only additions. I.e., its body must be a TRAITJ program.

Listing 2 illustrates the DBase delta module that, when applied to the empty product, generates the product with the feature Base. Applying the delta module DBase is mandatory for all feature configurations. It creates the classes for the basic data structures Stack and Queue. The functionality of the data structures are described in the interfaces IStack and IQueue with the methods pop, push and enqueue, dequeue. Both interfaces are extending the interface ISequence which describes the functionality to check the status of a sequence. The trait TSequence implements the functionality of the interface ISequence with an array of objects (for storing the elements of the sequence) and an integer field (for storing the number of elements currently in the sequence). The traits TStack and TQueue implement the interfaces IStack and IQueue and extend the trait TSequence. The data structures are instantiated in the two classes CStack and CQueue which use the implementation of the according traits and the description of the interfaces.

The delta module DLength for the Length feature (in Listing 3) modifies the interface ISequence to add the method getLength and adds the implementation of the method to the trait TSequence. The depending traits and classes will be automatically updated by these modifications. The delta module DResizeableOrDynamic (Listing 3) contains the commonality of the related features Resizeable and Dynamic. It implements the method resize which can be used to increase the capacity of the data structures. The delta module DResizeable for the Resizeable feature (Listing 3) extends the interface ISequence with the two methods resize and getCapacity. In this module only the getCapacity method is implemented which returns the capacity of the data structure. The delta module DDynamic implements the Dynamic feature (Listing 3) which automatically coordinates the size of the data structures. When the feature Dynamic is selected, the operation for test-

```
delta DBase {

interface ISequence {
  boolean isEmpty();
  boolean isFull();
}

interface IStack extends ISequence {
  void push(Object e);
  Object pop();
}

interface IQueue extends ISequence {
  void enqueue(Object e);
  Object dequeue();
}

trait TSequence is {
  int length;
  Object[] elements;
  boolean isEmpty() { return (this.length == 0); }
  boolean isFull()
    { return (this.length == this.elements.length); }
}

trait TStack is TSequence + {
  int length;
  Object[] elements;
  boolean isFull(); //required Methods
  boolean isEmpty(); //required Methods
  void push(Object o) {
    if (this.isFull()) throw new IllegalStateException();
    this.elements[this.length] = o;
    this.length++;
  }
  Object pop() {
    if (this.isEmpty()) throw new IllegalStateException();
    this.length--;
    Object o = this.elements[this.length];
    this.elements[this.length] = null;
    return o;
  }
}

trait TQueue is TSequence + {
  int length;
  Object[] elements;
  int first;
  boolean isFull(); //required Methods
  boolean isEmpty(); //required Methods
  void enqueue(Object o) {
    if (this.isFull()) throw new IllegalStateException();
    this.elements[(this.first + this.length)
                  % this.elements.length] = o;
    this.length++;
  }
  Object dequeue() {
    if (this.length == 0)
      throw new IllegalStateException();
    this.length--;
    Object o = this.elements[this.first];
    this.first=(this.first + 1) % this.elements.length;
    return o;
  }
}

class CStack implements IStack by TStack {
  Object[] elements;
  int length = 0;
  CStack(int capacity)
    { this.elements = new Object[capacity]; }
}

class CQueue implements IQueue by TQueue {
  Object[] elements;
  int length = 0;
  int first = 0;
  CQueue(int capacity)
    { this.elements = new Object[capacity]; }
}

} // end of DBase
}
```

Listing 2: Delta module DBase

ing whether a stack/queue is full (that is present in all the other products, including the base product) is not present. Therefore, the delta module DDynamic removes the method isFull from the interface ISequence. Then it creates a new trait TDynamic which implements new methods for the insertion and extraction of objects in the data structure. The traits for the stack and the queue are then combined with the trait TDynamic in which the original insertion and extraction methods are renamed to fit the required methods of the trait TDynamic. The methods of trait TDynamic are renamed to fit the description from the interfaces IStack or IQueue. Additionally, the classes for the stack and queue data structure are extended with a new field for the minimal capacity of the data structures. In order to realize the feature Resizeable both delta modules DResisazableOrDynamic and DResizeable must be applied, and in order to realize the feature Dynamic both the delta modules DDynamic and DResizeableOrDynamic must be applied.

```
delta DLength {
 modify interface ISequence { int getLength(); }
 modify trait TSequence is TOriginal + {
  int length;
  int getLength() { return this.length; }
 }
}

delta DResizeableOrDynamic {
 trait TResize is {
  Object[] elements;
  int length;
  void resizeAndCopy(int newCapacity, int from) {
   if (this.length > newCapacity)
    throw new IllegalStateException();
   Object[] newElements = new Object[newCapacity];
   for (int i = 0; i <= this.length − 1; i++) {
    newElements[i] = this.elements[(from + i)
                    % this.elements.length];
   }
   this.elements = newElements;
  }
 }
 modify trait TStack is TOriginal + TResize + {
  void resizeAndCopy(int newCapacity, int from);
  void resize(int newCapacity)
   { this.resizeAndCopy(newCapacity,0); }
 }
 modify trait TQueue is TOriginal + TResize + {
  int first;
  void resizeAndCopy(int newCapacity, int from);
  void resize(int newCapacity) {
   this.resizeAndCopy(newCapacity,this.first);
   this.first = 0;
  }
 }
}

delta DResizeable {
 modify interface ISequence {
  void resize(int newCapacity);
  int getCapacity();
 }
 modify trait TSequence is TOriginal + {
  int getCapacity() { return this.elements.length; }
 }
}
```

```
delta DDynamic {
 modify interface ISequence{remove boolean isFull();}
 trait TDynamic is {
  Object[] elements;
  int length;
  int minCapacity;
  boolean isFull();
  void resize(int cap);
  void originalInsert(Object o);
  Object originalExtract();
  void insert(Object o) {
   if (this.isFull()) {
    resize(this.elements.length * 2);
   }
   this.originalInsert(o);
  }
  Object extract() {
   if ((this.length <= this.elements.length / 2)
    && (this.elements.length!=this.minCapacity)){
    resize(this.elements.length / 2);
   }
   return this.originalExtract();
  }
 }
 modify trait TStack is
  TOriginal[push renameTo originalInsert,
          pop renameTo originalExtract] +
  TDynamic[insert renameTo push,
          extract renameTo pop]
 modify trait TQueue is
  TOriginal[enqueue renameTo originalInsert,
          dequeue renameTo originalExtract] +
  TDynamic[insert renameTo enqueue,
          extract renameTo dequeue]
 modify class CStack {
  int minCapacity;
  CStack(int capacity) {
   COriginal(capacity);
   this.minCapacity = capacity;
  }
 }
 modify class CQueue {
  int minCapacity;
  CQueue(int capacity) {
   COriginal(capacity);
   this.minCapacity = capacity;
  }
 }
}
```

Listing 3: Delta modules DLength, DResizeableOrDynamic, DResizeable and DDynamic

```
features Base, Length, Resizeable, Dynamic configurations Base
& (Resizeable −> Length) & (!(Resizeable & Dynamic)) deltas
 { DBase }
 { DLength when Length }
 { DResizeableOrDynamic when (Resizeable | Dynamic)}
 { DResizeable when Resizeable }
 { DDynamic when Dynamic }
```

Listing 4: Declaration of the Sequences PL

5   Development and Evolution of Delta-Trait Product Lines

As an example of unanticipated SPL evolution, consider the case of evolving the Sequences PL by adding three products that additionally contain the feature Peekable. This feature creates a product that, in addition to the classes CStack and CQueue, contains the classes CPeekableStack and CPeekableQueue. These new classes provide a method Object peek(int i) for returning the value of the i-th element of a sequence. Figure 4 depicts the feature model of the evolved Sequence PL. In order to be able to safely peek the elements of a sequence, it is useful to know the length of the sequence. Therefore, the feature Peekable requires feature Length.

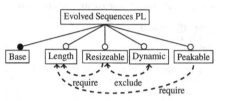

Fig. 4. Feature model for the evolved Sequences PL

The declaration of the evolved Sequences PL is shown in Listing 5. The delta module DPeekable for implementing the feature Peekable is shown in Listing 6. In the application order, the delta module DPeekable is included in the first set of the partition (together with the DBase delta module). Indeed, DPeekable can be safely moved to any other set of the partition, since it does not modify or remove existing interfaces/traits/classes and, thus, it does not interfere with the other delta modules.

The delta module DPeekable adds three new interfaces (IPeekableSequence, IPeekableStack and IPeekableQueue), three new traits (TPeekable, TPeekableStack and TPeekableQueue), and two new classes (CPeekableStack and CPeekableQueue). The last two interfaces IPeekableStack and IPeekableQueue extend the first interface by adding the methods to add and remove an element of the respective data structure. The methods for removing an element (pop and dequeue) no longer return that element. The trait TPeekable provides the implementation of the method peek of the IPeekableSequence interface. The new traits for the peekable data structures are based on the trait TPeekable and the corresponding trait from Listing 2 (TStack and TQueue, respectively)—this straightforward intra-product code reuse would not be possible in DOP, which relies on class-based inheritance for intra-product code reuse. Note that, in the products with feature Peekable, the classes CPeekableStack and CPeekableQueue (which use the trait TPeekableStack and TPeekableQueue, respectively) coexists with the classes CStack and CQueue (which use the trait TStack and TQueue, respectively).

```
features Base, Length, Resizeable, Dynamic, Peekable
configurations Base & (Resizeable -> Length) & (Peekable -> Length) & (!(Resizeable & Dynamic))
deltas
    { DBase}
    { DLength when Length, DPeekable when Peekable }
    { DResizeableOrDynamic when (Resizeable | Dynamic)}
    { DResizeable when Resizeable }
    { DDynamic when Dynamic }
```

Listing 5: Declaration of the evolved Sequences PL

```
delta DPeekable {
interface IPeekableSequence extends ISequence {
    Object peek(int i);
}
interface IPeekableStack extends IPeekableSequence {
    void push(Object e);    void pop();
}
interface IPeekableQueue extends IPeekableSequence {
    void enqueue(Object e);    void dequeue();
}
trait TPeekable is {
    int length;    Object[] elements;    int first;
    Object peek(int i) {
        if (i >= this.length)
            throw new IllegalArgumentException();
        return this.elements[(this.first + i)
                        % this.elements.length];
    }
}
trait TPeekableStack is
    TStack[pop renameTo topPop] +
    TPeekable + { void pop() { topPop(); } }
}

trait TPeekableQueue is
    TQueue[dequeue renameTo frontDequeue] +
    TPeekable + {
    void dequeue() { frontDequeue(); }
}
class CPeekableStack implements IPeekableStack
                        by TPeekableStack {
    Object[] elements;
    int length = 0;
    int first = 0;
    CPeekableStack(int capacity)
        { this.elements = new Object[capacity]; }
}
class CPeekableQueue implements IPeekableQueue
                        by TPeekableQueue {
    Object[] elements;
    int length = 0;
    int first = 0;
    CPeekableQueue(int capacity)
        { this.elements = new Object[capacity]; }
}
} // end of DPeakable
```

Listing 6: Delta module `DPeekable`

As we can see in this example, DTP seems well suited for evolving SPLs, since the developer is allowed to flexibly reuse already existing code both within single products and across different products. Proactive SPL development [23] prescribes to analyze beforehand the set of products to be supported and to plan and develop in advance all reusable artifacts. The Sequence PL case study presented in Section 4 can be seen as an example of proactive product line development, since the feature model defining the scope of the product line is first introduced and then the delta modules and the product line declaration for implementing the products are developed. When applying proactive development, a high upfront investment is required to define the scope of the of the product line and to develop reusable artifacts. Therefore, in order to reduce the adoption barrier Krueger [23] proposed reactive and extractive SPL development. In reactive SPL development, an initial product line that comprises only a basic set of products is created. Then, the initial SPL is evolved in order to deal with changing requirements. The evolved Sequence PL case study presented above can be seen as an example of reactive product line development.

In extractive SPL development, the engineering process starts with a set of existing legacy application that are turned into a product line. For instance, a product line described by the feature diagram in Fig. 4 could be developed from 5 legacy products corresponding to the feature configurations {Base, Length, Resizeable}, {Base, Dynamic}, {Base, Length, Peekable}, {Base, Length, Resizeable, Peekable}, and {Base, Length, Dynamic, Peekable}. Traits have been designed for factoring common methods of a set classes. In [6], a tool is presented for identifying the methods in a JAVA class hierarchy that could be good candidates to be refactored in traits. The tool is an adaptation of the SMALLTALK analysis tool of [24] to a JAVA setting. Since DTP smoothly integrates delta modules and traits mechanisms, it represents a promising approach for extractive SPL development starting from a set of legacy JAVA applications.

6   Related Work

Schaefer et. al. [34] mention three approaches to support variability and code reuse on the implementation level. The first is the annotative approach which marks the source code in relation to the features of the product line. A prominent instances are conditional compilation, frames [3] and CIDE [21]. The second is the compositional approach where product implementations are built by composing code fragments. Prominent examples of the compositional approach are traits [35,17], FOP [5,2,16,1] and aspect-oriented programming (AOP) [22]—see also the evaluation presented in [26]. Transformational implementation techniques constitute the third approach which can be considered as an extension of the second and offer more flexible, modular implementation possibilities. Delta-oriented programming [31,33,32,9] is an instance of transformational programming. In this paper, we presented DTP, a novel approach to implement SPL variability by smoothly integrating the modularization mechanisms provided by delta modules and traits, which overcomes some of the limitations of DOP w.r.t. intra-product code reuse.

A comparison of DOP and FOP can be found in [33], and a comparison of DOP and AOP can be found in [9]. Some related work on traits has been quoted in Sect.s 1-2. Recently [10], we have investigated the use of pure trait-based programming to directly implement SPLs. The main difference between the trait-only approach and DTP/DOP/FOP is that, in the former: *(i)* the artifact base consists of a well-formed program consisting of the interfaces, traits and classes of all the products; and *(ii)* in order to generate a product is enough to select a subset of these artifacts. In [10], it is shown that the trait composition operations provided by TRAITJ are not enough in order to flexibly modeling inter-product variability alone. To overcome this limitation, a trait parameterization mechanism is proposed. A parametric trait is a trait parameterized by interface names and class names. It can be applied to interface names and class names to generate traits that can be composed to build other (possibly parametric) traits or classes. The trait-only approach looks appealing because the code base has a simpler structure and product generation is straightforward (cf. points *(i)* and *(ii)* above). But, the modeling of inter-product variability (which relies both on trait parameterization and on trait composition operations) might be less evident. In the trait-only approach the sole mechanism for reusing interface definition code is interface extension, which is less flexible than the interface-modify operation supported by DTP and DOP. In DTP, inter-product variability is modeled by delta-modules. The trait parameterization mechanism in the underlying trait language would provide additional flexibility.

7   Conclusion

We presented DTP, a novel approach to implement SPL variability by smoothly integrating the modularization mechanisms provided by delta modules and traits, and realized it in the programming language DELTATRAITJ (which is currently under development) and compared it with DOP by case studies. DTP overcomes some of the limitations of DOP w.r.t. intra-product code reuse and represents a flexible approach for implementing evolving SPLs (cf. Sect. 5). As unanticipated SPL evolution scenarios become more common in long-living software systems, DTP is a promising approach for decreasing maintenance and development effort in the life cycle of these software systems on the implementation level supporting evolution at coarser levels of abstraction, e.g., the architecture level. In previous work, we have developed type systems for trait-based languages [12,10,8] and for DOP [9]. We are currently developing a type system for DTP. We have also developed compositional proof systems for the verification of pure traits [14] and for the verification of DOP SPLs of JAVA programs [18,15]. In future work, we would like to investigate compositional proof systems for DTP.

References

1. Apel, S., Kästner, C., Grösslinger, A., Lengauer, C.: Type safety for feature-oriented product lines. Automated Software Engineering 17(3), 251–300 (2010)
2. Apel, S., Kästner, C., Lengauer, C.: Feature Featherweight Java: A Calculus for Feature-Oriented Programming and Stepwise Refinement. In: Proc. of GPCE 2008, pp. 101–112. ACM (2008)
3. Bassett, P.G.: Framing software reuse: lessons from the real world. Prentice-Hall, Inc., Upper Saddle River (1997)
4. Batory, D.: Feature Models, Grammars, and Propositional Formulas. In: Obbink, H., Pohl, K. (eds.) SPLC 2005. LNCS, vol. 3714, pp. 7–20. Springer, Heidelberg (2005)
5. Batory, D., Sarvela, J.N., Rauschmayer, A.: Scaling step-wise refinement. In: Proc. of ICSE 2003, pp. 187–197. IEEE (2003)
6. Bettini, L., Bono, V., Naddeo, M.: A trait based re-engineering technique for Java hierarchies. In: Proc. of PPPJ, pp. 149–158. ACM (2008)
7. Bettini, L., Damiani, F.: Pure trait-based programming on the java platform. In: Proc. of PPPJ 2013, pp. 67–78. ACM, New York (2013)
8. Bettini, L., Damiani, F., Geilmann, K., Schäfer, J.: Combining traits with boxes and ownership types in a Java-like setting. Science of Computer Programming 78(2), 218–247 (2013)
9. Bettini, L., Damiani, F., Schaefer, I.: Compositional type checking of delta-oriented software product lines. Acta Informatica 50(2), 77–122 (2013)
10. Bettini, L., Damiani, F., Schaefer, I.: Implementing type-safe software product lines using parametric traits. Science of Computer Programming (2013), http://dx.doi.org/10.1016/j.scico.2013.07.016
11. Bettini, L., Damiani, F., Schaefer, I., Strocco, F.: TraitRecordJ: A programming language with traits and records. Science of Computer Programming 78(5), 521–541 (2013)
12. Bono, V., Damiani, F., Giachino, E.: On Traits and Types in a Java-like setting. In: Ausiello, G., Karhumäki, J., Mauri, G., Ong, L. (eds.) TCS 2008. IFIP, vol. 273, pp. 367–382. Springer, Heidelberg (2008)
13. Clements, P., Northrop, L.: Software Product Lines: Practices and Patterns. Addison Wesley Longman (2001)
14. Damiani, F., Dovland, J., Johnsen, E.B., Schaefer, I.: Verifying traits: An incremental proof system for fine-grained reuse. Formal Aspects of Computing 26(4), 761–793 (2014)
15. Damiani, F., Owe, O., Dovland, J., Schaefer, I., Johnsen, E.B., Yu, I.C.: A transformational proof system for delta-oriented programming. In: Proc. of SPLC, vol. 2, pp. 53–60. ACM (2012)

16. Delaware, B., Cook, W.R., Batory, D.: A Machine-Checked Model of Safe Composition. In: Proc. of FOAL, pp. 31–35. ACM (2009)
17. Ducasse, S., Nierstrasz, O., Schärli, N., Wuyts, R., Black, A.: Traits: A mechanism for fine-grained reuse. ACM TOPLAS 28(2), 331–388 (2006)
18. Hähnle, R., Schaefer, I.: A Liskov Principle for Delta-Oriented Programming. In: Margaria, T., Steffen, B. (eds.) ISoLA 2012, Part I. LNCS, vol. 7609, pp. 32–46. Springer, Heidelberg (2012)
19. Igarashi, A., Pierce, B., Wadler, P.: Featherweight Java: A minimal core calculus for Java and GJ. ACM TOPLAS 23(3), 396–450 (2001)
20. Kang, K.C., Cohen, S.G., Hess, J.A., Novak, W.E., Peterson, A.S.: Feature-Oriented Domain Analysis (FODA) Feasibility Study. Technical report, Carnegie Mellon Software Engineering Institute (1990)
21. Kastner, C., Apel, S.: Type-checking software product lines - a formal approach. In: Proc. of ASE 2008, pp. 258–267. IEEE (2008)
22. Kiczales, G., Hilsdale, E., Hugunin, J., Kersten, M., Palm, J., Griswold, W.G.: An Overview of AspectJ. In: Lindskov Knudsen, J. (ed.) ECOOP 2001. LNCS, vol. 2072, pp. 327–354. Springer, Heidelberg (2001)
23. Krueger, C.: Eliminating the Adoption Barrier. IEEE Software 19(4), 29–31 (2002)
24. Lienhard, A., Ducasse, S., Arévalo, G.: Identifying traits with formal concept analysis. In: Proc. ASE 2005, pp. 66–75. IEEE Computer Society (2005)
25. Liquori, L., Spiwack, A.: Extending feathertrait java with interfaces. Theor. Comput. Sci. 398(1-3), 243–260 (2008)
26. Lopez-Herrejon, R.E., Batory, D., Cook, W.: Evaluating support for features in advanced modularization technologies. In: Gao, X.-X. (ed.) ECOOP 2005. LNCS, vol. 3586, pp. 169–194. Springer, Heidelberg (2005)
27. Mikhajlov, L., Sekerinski, E.: A Study of the Fragile Base Class Problem. In: Jul, E. (ed.) ECOOP 1998. LNCS, vol. 1445, pp. 355–382. Springer, Heidelberg (1998)
28. Nierstrasz, O., Ducasse, S., Schärli, N.: Flattening traits. JOT 5(4), 129–148 (2006) www.jot.fm
29. Pohl, K., Böckle, G., van der Linden, F.: Software Product Line Engineering - Foundations, Principles, and Techniques. Springer (2005)
30. Reppy, J., Turon, A.: Metaprogramming with traits. In: Ernst, E. (ed.) ECOOP 2007. LNCS, vol. 4609, pp. 373–398. Springer, Heidelberg (2007)
31. Schaefer, I., Bettini, L., Bono, V., Damiani, F., Tanzarella, N.: Delta-oriented programming of software product lines. In: Bosch, J., Lee, J. (eds.) SPLC 2010. LNCS, vol. 6287, pp. 77–91. Springer, Heidelberg (2010)
32. Schaefer, I., Bettini, L., Damiani, F.: Compositional type-checking of delta-oriented programming. In: Proc. of AOSD 2011, pp. 43–56. ACM (2011)
33. Schaefer, I., Damiani, F.: Pure Delta-oriented Programming. In: Proc. of FOSD 2010, pp. 49–56. ACM (2010)
34. Schaefer, I., Rabiser, R., Clarke, D., Bettini, L., Benavides, D., Botterweck, G., Pathak, A., Trujillo, S., Villela, K.: Software diversity: state of the art and perspectives. International Journal on Software Tools for Technology Transfer 14(5), 477–495 (2012)
35. Schärli, N., Ducasse, S., Nierstrasz, O., Black, A.P.: Traits: Composable units of behavior. In: Cardelli, L. (ed.) ECOOP 2003. LNCS, vol. 2743, pp. 248–274. Springer, Heidelberg (2003)
36. Schuster, S.: Design Patterns in Feature-Oriented Programming. Bachelor's thesis, TU Braunschweig (2012)
37. Schuster, S., Schulze, S.: Object-oriented design in feature-oriented programming. In: Proc. of FOSD 2012, pp. 25–28. ACM (2012)
38. Smith, C., Drossopoulou, S.: Chai: Traits for Java-like languages. In: Gao, X.-X. (ed.) ECOOP 2005. LNCS, vol. 3586, pp. 453–478. Springer, Heidelberg (2005)

Deployment Variability
in Delta-Oriented Models*

Einar Broch Johnsen, Rudolf Schlatte, and S. Lizeth Tapia Tarifa

Department of Informatics, University of Oslo, Norway
{einarj,rudi,sltarifa}@ifi.uio.no

Abstract. Software engineering increasingly emphasizes variability by
developing families of products for a range of application contexts or user
requirements. ABS is a modeling language which supports variability in
the formal modeling of software by using feature selection to transform
a delta-oriented base model into a concrete product model. ABS also
supports deployment models, with a separation of concerns between execution cost and server capacity. This allows the model-based assessment
of deployment choices on a product's quality of service. This paper combines deployment models with the variability concepts of ABS, to model
deployment choices as features when designing a family of products.

1 Introduction

Variability is prevalent in modern software in order to satisfy a range of application contexts or user requirements [34]. A software product line (SPL) realizes
this variability through a family of product variants (e.g., [29]). A specific product is obtained by selecting features from a feature model [36]; these models
typically focus on the functionality and software quality attributes of different
features and products. To express variability in system *design*, features typically
take the form of architectural models, behavioral models, and test suites [35].
Architectural variability [16] focuses on the presence of component variants,
and can be described using, e.g., the Variability Modeling Language [27], UML
stereotypes [14], or (hierarchical) component models such as Koala [37]. In Delta
modeling [10,30,31], a set of deltas specifies modifications to a core product. Δ-
MontiArch applies delta modeling to architectural description [15]; a delta can
add or remove components, ports, and connections between components.

Whereas architectural models describe the *logical* organization of a system
in terms of components and their connections, we are interested in the *physical*
organization of software units on physical or virtual machines; we call this physical organization the *deployment architecture*. Varying deployment architectures
will perform the same computations, but with different cost and/or time spent.
Thus, a deployment architecture comprises specifications of execution costs and
available resources.

---

* Partly funded by the EU project FP7-610582 ENVISAGE: Engineering Virtualized
Services (http://www.envisage-project.eu).

T. Margaria and B. Steffen (Eds.): ISoLA 2014, Part I, LNCS 8802, pp. 304–319, 2014.

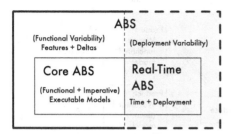

Fig. 1. ABS language extension

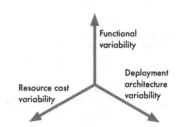

Fig. 2. The SPL variability space with deployment variability

This paper integrates deployment variability in SPL models such that different targeted deployment architectures may be taken into account early in the design of the SPL. We aim at a reasonable orthogonality between functional and deployment variability in the SPL model. The starting point for this work is the abstract behavioral specification language ABS, which adds support for variability to models in the kernel modeling language Core ABS [20]. ABS is *object-oriented* to be easy to use for software developers; it is *executable* to support code generation and (timed) validation of models; and it has a *formal semantics* which enables the static analysis of models (e.g., the worst-case resource consumption can be derived for a model). ABS is particularly suitable for our objective because (1) ABS supports SPL modeling based on deltas [9,11], and (2) ABS supports the modeling of deployment decisions based on the modeling concept of *deployment components* [23] in Real-Time ABS [7]. Real-Time ABS leverages resources and their dynamic management to the abstraction level of software models. Fig. 1 shows how functional variability modeling in ABS and time and deployment models in Real-Time ABS both extend Core ABS. Although these extensions of ABS coexist, they have so far never been combined. The purpose of this paper is to combine these two extensions in order to model deployment variability, corresponding to the dotted area in Fig. 1.

Our approach to deployment variability for SPL models makes a separation of concerns between cost and capacity which introduces two new variation points in the variability space of ABS feature models (depicted in Fig. 2):

- **Resource cost variability**: These features determine the costs associated with executing the SPL's logical artifacts; and
- **Deployment architecture variability**: These features determine how the logical artifacts are deployed on locations with different execution capacities.

The main contribution of the paper is an integration of delta models with deployment architectures in ABS. This integration allows orthogonality between functional and deployment variability, such that features expressing functionality, resource cost and deployment variability are kept in different trees in the ABS feature models. The integration is illustrated by variability patterns for MapReduce [12], a programming model for highly parallelizable programs. Furthermore, this integration allows ABS tools to be used to analyze functional

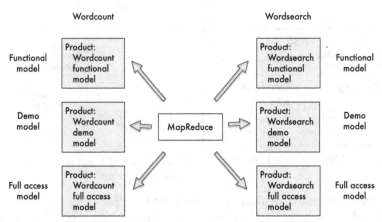

Fig. 3. A family of products sharing an underlying MapReduce structure

features with respect to deployment architecture during the early design stage of SPLs.

Paper overview. Sect. 2 motivates our work by an example of deployment variability. Sect. 3 presents modeling in the abstract behavioral specification language ABS and Sect. 4 delta modeling and its realization in ABS. Sect. 5 combines delta-oriented variability with deployment modeling, and discusses how to extend a feature model with deployment variability. Sect. 6 revisits the example, Sect. 7 discusses related work, and Sect. 8 concludes the paper.

2   Motivating Example

MapReduce [12] is a programming pattern for processing large data sets in two stages; first the *Map* stage separates parallelizable jobs on distinct subsets of data to produce intermediate results, then the *Reduce* stage merges the intermediate data into a final result. The initial and intermediate data are on the form of key/value pairs, and the final result is a list of values per key. MapReduce does not specify the computations done by the two stages or the distribution of workloads across machines, making it a good abstract base model for SPLs.

Our example uses MapReduce to model product variants of a range of services which inspect a set of documents. Individual products may implement, e.g., Wordcount, which counts the occurrences of words in the given documents, and Wordsearch, which searches for documents in which a given word occurs. For simplicity, we assume that a service either provides the Wordcount or the Wordsearch feature. The services are implemented on a cluster of computers, using MapReduce.

To attract clients to the word count and word search services, freely available demo versions offer the same functionality as the full versions, albeit with a lower quality of service. When the services are deployed, the demo versions will run

on a few machines, whereas the full versions have access to the full power of
the cluster. Our model has three versions of each service: the purely functional
model, the model with full access to the cluster, and a model with restricted
access to the cluster. This product family (see Fig. 3) is a running example in
the paper.

3   Behavioral and Deployment Modeling in ABS

The abstract behavioral specification language ABS targets the executable design of distributed object-oriented systems. It has a formally defined kernel called
Core ABS [20]. ABS is based on concurrent object groups (COGs), akin to concurrent objects [8,21], Actors [1], and Erlang processes [5]. COGs support interleaved concurrency based on guarded commands. ABS has a functional and an
imperative layer, combined with a Java-like syntax. Real-Time ABS [7] extends
Core ABS models with (dense) time; in this paper we do not specify execution
time directly but rather *observe* time by measurements of the executing model.

ABS has a *functional layer* with algebraic data types such as the empty type
Unit, booleans Bool, integers Int; parametric data types such as sets Set<A> and
maps Map<A, B> (for type parameters A and B); and functions over values of
these data types, with support for pattern matching. The modeler can define
additional types to succinctly express data structures of the problem domain.

The *imperative layer* of ABS describes side-effectful computation, concurrency, communication and synchronization. ABS objects are *active* in the sense
that their run method, if defined, gets called upon creation. Communication
and synchronization are decoupled: Communication is based on asynchronous
method calls. After executing f=o!m(e), which assigns the call to a *future variable* f, the caller proceeds execution *without blocking* while m(e) executes in the
context of o. Two operations on future variables control synchronization in ABS.
First, the statement **await** f? *suspends the active process* unless a return value
from the call associated with f has arrived, allowing other processes in the same
COG to execute. Second, the return value is retrieved by the expression f.**get**,
which *blocks all execution in the COG* until the return value is available. Inside
a COG, Core ABS also supports standard synchronous method calls o.m(e).

A COG can have at most one active process, executing in one of the objects
of the COG. Scheduling is cooperative via **await** g statements, which suspend
the current process until g (a condition over object or future variable state)
becomes true. The remaining statements of ABS (assignment, object creation,
conditionals and loops) are designed to be familiar to a Java programmer.

Deployment Modeling. One purpose of describing deployment in a modeling language is to differentiate execution time based on *where* the execution
takes place, i.e., the model should express how the execution time varies with
the available *capacity* of the chosen deployment architecture. For this purpose,
Real-Time ABS extends Core ABS with primitives to describe *deployment architectures* which express how distributed systems are mapped on physical and/or

virtual media with many locations. Real-Time ABS lifts deployment architectures to the abstraction level of the modeling language, where the physical or virtual media are represented by *deployment components* [22].

A *deployment component* is part of the model's deployment architecture, on which a number of COGs are deployed. Deployment components are first-class citizens and they support a number of methods for load monitoring and load balancing purposes (cf. [22]). Each deployment component has an *execution capacity*, which is the amount of resources available per accounting period. By default, all objects execute in a default (root) environment with unrestricted capacity. Other deployment components with restricted capacities may be created to capture different deployment architectures. COGs are created on the same deployment component as their creator by default; a different deployment component may be selected by an optional *deployment annotation* [DC: dc] to object creation, for a deployment component dc.

The available resource capacity of a deployment component determines the amount of computation which may occur in the objects deployed on that deployment component. Objects allocated to the deployment component compete for the shared resources in order to execute, and they may execute until the deployment component runs out of resources or they are otherwise blocked. For the case of CPU resources, the resources of the deployment component define its capacity inside an accounting period, after which the resources are renewed.

The resource consumption of executing statements in the Real-Time ABS model is expressed by means of adding a *cost annotation* [Cost: e] to any statement. It is the responsibility of the modeler to specify appropriate resource costs. A behavioral model may be gradually transformed to provide more realistic resource-sensitive behavior by inserting more fine-grained cost annotations. The automated static analysis tool COSTABS [2] can compute a worst-case approximation of resource consumption, based on static analysis techniques. However, the modeler may also want to capture *normative* constraints on resource consumption, such as resource limitations, at an abstract level; these can be made explicit in the model during the very early stages of the system design. To this end, cost annotations may be used by the modeler to abstractly represent the cost of some computation which is not fully specified in the model.

4   Delta-Oriented Variability in ABS

This section describes how SPLs are modeled in ABS. ABS includes a delta-oriented framework for variability [9,11]. Fig. 4 depicts a delta-oriented variability model where a feature model F with orthogonal variability [18] is represented as two trees that hierarchically structure the set of features of this model. Sets of features from the feature model F are linked to sets of delta modifications from the delta model Δ, which apply to the common base model P to produce different product line configurations C, C' and C', and finally a specific product ρ is extracted from the product line configuration C.

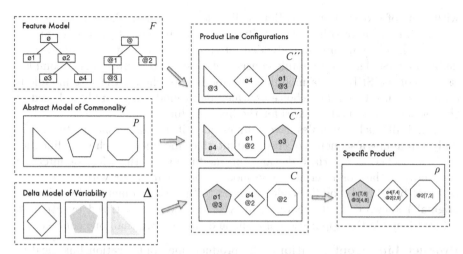

Fig. 4. A graphical representation of a Delta-Oriented variability model

Feature Model. A feature model in ABS is represented textually as a forest of nested features where each tree structures the hierarchical dependencies between related features, and each feature in a tree may have a collection of Boolean or integer attributes. The ABS feature model can also express other cross-tree dependencies, such as mandatory and optional sub-features, and mutually exclusive features. The **group** keyword is used to specify the sub-features of a feature; the **oneof** keyword means that exactly one of the sub-features must be selected in the created product line, the range of values associated to an attribute specify the values in which an attribute can be instantiated when an specify product is generated. For the full details, we refer the reader to [9, 11].

Example 1. In the functional feature model of the MapReduce example from Section 2, a tree with a root Calculations offers two alternative and mutually exclusive features that can be selected to express that a specific product supports counting words or searching for words.

```
root Calculations { group oneof { Wordcount, Wordsearch }}
```

In addition ABS allows a feature model with multiple roots (hence, multiple trees) to describe orthogonal variability [18], which is useful for expressing unrelated functional and other features (e.g., features related to quality of service).

Delta Model. The concept of delta modeling was introduced by Schaefer et al. [6, 31–33] as a modeling and programming language approach for SPLs. This approach aims at automatically generating software products for a given valid collection of features, providing flexible and modular techniques to build different products that share functionality or code. In delta-oriented programming, application conditions over the set of features and their attributes, are associated with units of program modifications called delta modules. These delta modules may add, remove, or otherwise modify code. The implementation of an SPL in delta-oriented programming is divided into a common core module and a set of delta modules. The core module consists of classes that implement a complete product of the SPL. Delta modules describe how to change the core module to obtain new products. The choice of which delta modules to apply is based on the selection of desired features for the final product.

Technically, delta modules have a unique identifier, a list of parameters, and a body containing a sequence of class and interface modifiers. Such a modification can add a class or interface declaration, modify an existing class or interface, or remove a class or interface. The modifications can occur within a class or interface body, and modifier code can refer to the original method by using the **original**() keyword. Delta modules in ABS can be parametrized by attribute values to enable the application of a single delta in more than one context.

Product Line Configuration. The product line configuration links feature models with delta modules to provide a complete specification of the variability in an ABS product line. A product line configuration consists of the set of features of the product line and a set of delta clauses. Each delta clause names a delta module and specifies the conditions required for its application, called application conditions. A partial ordering on delta modules constrains the order in which delta modules can be applied to the core module.

Specific Product. A product selection clause generates a specific product from an ABS product line. It states which features are to be included in the product and specifies concrete values for their attributes. A product selection is checked against the feature model for validity. The product selection clause is used by the product line configuration to guide the application of the delta modules during the generation of the final product.

Generated Final Product. Given a Core ABS program P, a set of delta modules Δ, a product line configuration C, and a feature model F (as depicted in Fig. 4), the final product ρ, which will be a Core ABS program, is derived as follows: First check that the selection of features for ρ satisfies the constraints imposed by the feature model F; then select the delta modules from Δ with a valid application condition with respect to ρ; and finally apply the delta modules to the core program P in some order respecting the partial order described in C, replacing delta parameters in the code with the literal values supplied by the feature.

5   Deployment Variability in ABS

Feature models usually describe functional variability in a software product line. This section discusses lifting deployment variability to ABS feature models and its interaction with functional variability. Our approach aims to establish orthogonality between the functional and deployment aspects in an SPL model in order to maintain multiple axes of variability (see Fig. 2). The further separation of concerns between cost and capacity in the deployment models of ABS is reflected in the feature models as well.

Thus, variability in a deployment-aware SPL comprises these variation points in the feature models:

Functional Variability: These features determine the functional behavior of a product and are used as in standard SPL engineering.

Resource Cost Variability: These features describe the choice of how the incurred resource cost is estimated during execution of the model. The basic feature is the *no cost* feature, typically selected for functional analysis of the SPL model. Other cost models are fixed-cost for selected jobs (similar to costs in a basic queuing network or simulation model; see, e.g., [19]), and data-sensitive costs. These can be either measured, real cost for selected jobs or worst-case approximations (which may depend on data flow as well as control flow). All of these can be expressed via cost annotations.

Deployment Architecture Variability: These features determine how the logical artifacts of the model are mapped to a specific deployment architecture, which determines the execution capacity of the different locations on which the logical artefacts execute. The basic feature is the *undeployed* feature which does not impose any capacity restrictions on the execution. This feature is typically selected together with *no cost* during functional analysis and testing. When analyzing non-functional properties, features describe how selected parts of the logical architecture are deployed on deployment components with restricted capacity, either statically or (for virtualized deployment) dynamically.

Example 2. We extend the feature model of Example 1 with a Resources tree for resource costs, and a Deployments tree for deployment architecture. The Resources root has the basic feature NoCost, the feature FixedCost for a basic data-independent cost model specified in the attribute cost, the feature WorstcaseCost for a worst-case cost model in terms of the size of the input files, and MeasuredCost for using the actual incurred cost measured during execution of the model. The Deployments root has three alternative features related to the number of available machines in the physical deployment architecture; the capacity of each machine is specified by the attribute capacity.

```
root Resources {
    group oneof {
        NoCost,
        FixedCost { Int cost in [ 0 .. 10000 ] ; },
        WorstcaseCost,
        MeasuredCost
    }
}
root Deployments {
    group oneof {
        NoDeploymentScenario,
        UnlimitedMachines { Int capacity in [ 0 .. 10000 ] ; },
        LimitedMachines { Int capacity in [ 0 .. 10000 ] ; Int machinelimit in [ 0 .. 100 ] ; }
    }
}
```

```
// These definitions to be changed in delta modifications
type InKeyType = String; // filename
type InValueType = List<String>; // file contents
type OutKeyType = String; // word
type OutValueType = Int; // count

interface MapReduce {
  List<Pair<OutKeyType, List<OutValueType>>>
      mapReduce(List<Pair<InKeyType, InValueType>> docs); // invoked by client
  Unit finished(Worker w); // invoked by workers when finished with 1 task
}

interface IMap { // invoked by MapReduce controller
  List<Pair<OutKeyType, OutValueType>>
    invokeMap(InKeyType key, InValueType value);
}

interface IReduce { // invoked by MapReduce controller
  List<OutValueType>
    invokeReduce(OutKeyType key, List<OutValueType> value);
}

interface Worker extends IMap, IReduce { }
```

Fig. 5. Interfaces of the base model of the MapReduce example in ABS

6   Example: Product Variability in the MapReduce Example

This section describes the implementation of a generic MapReduce framework in ABS and its adaptation to different products as described in Section 2. It will become apparent that a product that is implemented according to best practices for object-oriented software (i.e., decomposing functionality, methods implementing one task only, and the careful definition of datatypes) also makes the product well-suited as a base product for a software product line.

6.1   Commonalities in the ABS Base Product

Fig. 5 shows the interfaces for the main MapReduce object and for the Worker objects which will carry out the computations in parallel. The computation is started by calling the mapReduce method with a list of *(key, value)* pairs. The main object will then create a number of worker objects, call invokeMap on these objects, gather and collate the results of the mapping phase, call invokeReduce on the workers and collate and return the final result.

The base product in our example implements a word count function (computing word occurrences over a list of files), without a resource or deployment model. Worker objects are reused from a pool, but there is no bound on the number of workers created. Workers add themselves back to the pool by calling finished.

Figure 6 shows part of the worker implementation of the base product (i.e., a Wordcount product without any cost model). The invokeReduce method sets up the result, calls a private method reduce which emits intermediate results using the method emitReduceResult. The reduce method in Fig. 6 is equivalent to the

```
class Worker(MapReduce master) implements Worker {
  List<OutValueType> reduceResults = Nil;

  List<OutValueType> invokeReduce(OutKeyType key, List<OutValueType> value) {
    reduceResults = Nil;
    this.reduce(key, value);
    List<OutValueType> result = reduceResults;
    reduceResults = Nil;
    master!finished(this);
    return result;
  }

  Unit emitReduceResult(OutValueType value) {
    reduceResults = Cons(value, reduceResults);
  }

  // variation point for functional model
  Unit reduce(OutKeyType key, List<OutValueType> value) {
    OutValueType result = 0;
    ... // sum up value list into result variable ...
    this.emitReduceResult(result);
  }
}
```

Fig. 6. The reduce part of the Wordcount example in the Worker class

one shown in the original MapReduce paper [12]. The mapping functions of the worker objects are implemented in the same way.

6.2 Variability in the ABS Product Line

To change the functional feature of the model from computing word counts to computing word search, some parts of the model need to be altered via delta application. The same applies when varying the deployment and cost model, as explained in Section 5. These variation points turn out to be orthogonal and can be modified independently of each other.

In the example, the methods to be modified by deltas are not public; i.e., they are not part of the published interface of the classes comprising the base model. This appears to be a recurring pattern: public methods like invokeReduce of Fig. 6 interact with the outside world, gather and decompose data for computation and returning. If the modeler factors out computation into private methods with only one single task to perform (like reduce in Fig. 6), these methods can be cleanly replaced in deltas, without imposing constraints on the implementation. This suggests that clean object-oriented code will in general be likely to be amenable to delta-oriented modification.

Functional Variability. The following delta shows a delta fragment that modifies the functionality of the base model:

```
delta DOccurrences;
modifies type OutValueType = String; // Change the method signatures
modifies class Worker {
  modifies Unit map(InKeyType key, InValueType value) {
    ... // change non-public map method to compute occurrences
  }
```

```
  modifies Unit reduce(OutKeyType key, List<OutValueType> value) {
    ... // change non−public reduce method to compute occurrences
  }
}
```

By modifying the type synonyms InKeyType, InValueType, OutKeyType and OutValueType from the base model, we can change the data types and method signatures of the model without having to change any code in the MapReduce class. Modifying the methods map and reduce of the Worker class changes the computation performed by the product. The new map and reduce methods use emitMapResult and emitReduceResult as in the base model; hence they do not need to care about invocation or return value handling protocols.

Resource Cost Variability. Costs are incurred during (and because of) computational activity. This means that cost model and functional model are related. However, the two aspects can be decoupled
   cleanly via the **original**() call, which we use to associate the given cost with the original code. Care must be taken in the productline definition to ensure that any deltas incurring costs are applied *after* deltas modifying functionality; otherwise, the cost association would be overwritten.

```
delta DFixedCost (Int cost);
modifies class Worker {
  modifies Unit emitMapResult(OutKeyType key, OutValueType value) {
    [Cost: cost] original(key, value);
  }
  modifies Unit emitReduceResult(OutValueType value) {
    [Cost: cost] original(value);
  }
}
```

This FixedCost delta assigns a cost (given as a delta attribute) to each computation of an intermediate result; the feature attribute is passed in as a delta parameter. In general, costs are introduced into MapReduce by wrapping the methods invokeMap and invokeReduce for assigning costs to starting a computation step, and by modifying emitMapresult and emitReduceresult for assigning costs to the production of a result. Figure 6 shows where these methods are invoked.

An alternative approach to adding resource costs via hooks is to use the ABS **original**() call, wrapping the original map, emitMapresult etc. methods with costs. This approach makes the functional model simpler, but leads to a more complicated product line configuration since the correct order of delta application must be specified in that case.

Deployment Architecture Variability. Deployment architecture, i.e., decisions on how many workers to create and how many resources to supply them with, is implemented in the MapReduce class. As mentioned, this class manages a pool of Worker instances which is by default of unbounded size. To change this behavior, the modeler implements a delta that overrides a method getWorker (and also the method finished of the MapReduce implementation in case the new getWorker method does not use the resource pool of the base model). The capacity and number of deployment components can be adjusted via delta parameters:

```
productline MapReduceSPL;

features
    Wordcount, Wordsearch,                              // Functional features
    NoCost, FixedCost, WorstCaseCost, MeasuredCost,     // Resource cost features
    NoDeploymentScenario, UnlimitedMachines, LimitedMachines;  // Deployment architectures

delta DOccurrences when Wordsearch;
delta DFixedCost(Cost.cost) after DOccurrences when Cost;
delta DUnboundedDeployment(UnlimitedMachines.capacity) when UnlimitedMachines;
delta DBoundedDeployment(LimitedMachines.capacity, LimitedMachines.machinelimit)
    when LimitedMachines;
...
```

Fig. 7. Product line configuration for the MapReduce example in ABS

```
product WordcountModel (Wordcount, NoCost, NoDeploymentScenario);
product WordcountFull (Wordcount, Cost{cost=10}, UnlimitedMachines{capacity=20});
product WordcountDemo (Wordcount, Cost{cost=10},
    LimitedMachines{capacity=20, machinelimit=2});

product WordsearchModel (Wordsearch, NoCost, NoDeploymentScenario);
product WordsearchFull (Wordsearch, Cost{cost=10}, UnlimitedMachines{capacity=20});
product WordsearchDemo (Wordsearch, Cost{cost=10},
    LimitedMachines{capacity=20, machinelimit=2});
```

Fig. 8. Specifying Products for the MapReduce example in ABS

```
delta DBoundedDeployment (Int capacity, Int maxWorkers);
modifies class MapReduce {
    ... // adjust behavior of resource pool and capacities of created deployment components
}
```

The product line configuration. The feature model presented in Section 5 extends the model of Section 2 with resource cost variability, resulting in 14 different products. Fig. 7 shows part of the product line configuration and Fig. 8 shows the specification of some of the derivable products.

In the deployment components of the deployment architecture features, capacity is defined by the amount of resource costs that can be processed per accounting period (in terms of the dense time semantics of execution in Real-Time ABS). When the base model is extended with features for deployment architecture and resource cost, the *load* on the individual deployment components, defined as the actual incurred cost per accounting period, can be recorded and visualized.

We illustrate how deployment variability for products can be validated using the simulation tool of ABS, by comparing the performance of two different deployments of the Wordcount product, varying the number of available machines between 5 (the "Demo" version) and 20 (the "Full" version), but keeping the cost model, input data and computation model constant. The graphs in Fig. 9 shows the total load of all machines over simulated time for the two products. The figure shows two typical instances of a typical MapReduce workload; first, the map processes execute until they are finished, then the reduce processes execute.

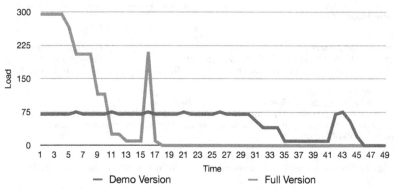

Fig. 9. Varying deployment model, constant cost and functional model

The start of the reduce phase can be observed in the graph of Fig. 9 as the second spike in processing activity. It can be seen that the demo version takes over twice as much simulated time to complete its execution, while the full version completes its execution earlier by incurring a load that is higher than for the demo version (while still decreasing as the map processes terminate).

Similar qualitative investigations can be performed regarding the influence of varying cost models (e.g., worst-case vs. average cost) and more involved deployment strategies.

7   Related Work

The inherent compositionality of the concurrency model considered in this paper allows objects to be naturally distributed on different locations, because only an object's local state is needed to execute its methods. In previous work [4, 22, 23], the authors have introduced *deployment components* as a modeling concept to captures restricted resources shared between a group of concurrent objects, and shown how components with parametric resources may be used to capture a model's behavior for different assumptions about the available resources. The formal details of this approach are given in [23]; two larger case studies on virtualized systems deployed on the cloud are presented in [3, 24]. Our approach to deployment modeling would be a natural fit for resource-sensitive deployment in other Actor-based approaches, e.g., [5, 17].

Deployment variability is not considered in the recent software diversity survey [35], but it has been studied in the context of feature models. For example, a feature model that captures the architectural and technological variability of multilayer applications is described in [13] together with an associated model-driven development process. In contrast our paper considers a much simpler feature model, but it is integrated in a full SPL framework and explicitly linked to executable models which can be compared by tool-based analysis. Without considering variability, a platform ontology and modeling framework based on description logic is proposed by [38], which can be used to automatically configure various reusable concrete platforms that can be later be integrated with a platform-independent model using the Model Driven Architecture approach. We follow a similar approach based on the extending a purely functional model with deployment features, but our framework is based on simpler concepts which does not introduce the overhead of description logic. In the context of QoS variability, [25] study a modeling and analysis framework for testing the QoS of an orchestration before deployment to determine realistic Service Level Agreement contracts; their analysis uses probabilistic model of QoS. Our work similarly allows the model-based comparison of QoS variability, but focuses on deployment architecture and processing capacity rather than orchestration.

The MapReduce programming pattern which is the basis for the example of this paper, has been formalized and studied from different perspectives. [39] develop a CSP model of MapReduce, with a focus on the correctness of the communication between the processes. [26] develops a rigorous description of MapReduce using Haskell, resulting in an executable specification of MapReduce. [28] formalizes an abstract model of MapReduce using the proof assistant Coq, and use this formalization to verify JML annotations of MapReduce applications. However, none of these works focus on deployment strategies or relate MapReduce to deployment variability in SPLs.

8   Conclusion

Software today is increasingly often developed as a range of products for devices with restricted resource capacity or for virtualized utility computing. For an SPL targeting such platforms, the deployment of different products in the range should also be considered as a variation point in the SPL.

This paper integrates explicit resource restricted deployment scenarios into a formal modeling language for SPL engineering. This integration is based on delta models to systematize the derivation of product variants, and demonstrated in the ABS modeling language. The proposed integration emphasizes orthogonality between functional features, resource cost features, and deployment architecture features, to facilitate finding the best match between functional features and a target deployment architecture for a specific product. The supported analysis allows the validation of deployment decisions for specific products in the SPL, which may entail a refinement of the feature model. Resource cost variability can be exploited to compare product performance under different cost models such as fixed cost, measured simulation cost, and worst-case cost.

The approach is demonstrated on an example using the MapReduce programming pattern as its common base product, and used to compare the performance of full versions to restricted demo versions of product variants. A restriction of our work is the concrete semantics which makes it difficult to reason about whole product lines, requiring a per-product approach to validation. This could be lifted by using a symbolic semantics and applying symbolic execution techniques to analyze the deployment sensitive SPL models, allowing the analysis to be lifted from concrete deployment architectures for specific products to a more generalized analysis.

References

1. Agha, G.A.: ACTORS: A Model of Concurrent Computations in Distributed Systems. The MIT Press (1986)
2. Albert, E., Arenas, P., Genaim, S., Gómez-Zamalloa, M., Puebla, G.: COSTABS: A cost and termination analyzer for ABS. In: PEPM 2012, pp. 151–154. ACM (2012)
3. Albert, E., de Boer, F.S., Hähnle, R., Johnsen, E.B., Schlatte, R., Tapia Tarifa, S.L., Wong, P.Y.H.: Formal modeling and analysis of resource management for cloud architectures. an industrial case study using Real-Time ABS. J. of Service-Oriented Computing and Applications (to appear, 2014)
4. Albert, E., Genaim, S., Gómez-Zamalloa, M., Johnsen, E.B., Schlatte, R., Tarifa, S.L.T.: Simulating concurrent behaviors with worst-case cost bounds. In: Butler, M., Schulte, W. (eds.) FM 2011. LNCS, vol. 6664, pp. 353–368. Springer, Heidelberg (2011)
5. Armstrong, J.: Programming Erlang: Software for a Concurrent World. Pragmatic Bookshelf (2007)
6. Bettini, L., Damiani, F., Schaefer, I.: Compositional type checking of delta-oriented software product lines. Acta Inf. 50(2), 77–122 (2013)
7. Bjørk, J., de Boer, F.S., Johnsen, E.B., Schlatte, R., Tapia Tarifa, S.L.: User-defined schedulers for real-time concurrent objects. Innovations in Systems and Software Engineering 9(1), 29–43 (2013)
8. Caromel, D., Henrio, L.: A Theory of Distributed Object. Springer (2005)
9. Clarke, D., Diakov, N., Hähnle, R., Johnsen, E.B., Schaefer, I., Schäfer, J., Schlatte, R., Wong, P.Y.H.: Modeling spatial and temporal variability with the HATS abstract behavioral modeling language. In: Bernardo, M., Issarny, V. (eds.) SFM 2011. LNCS, vol. 6659, pp. 417–457. Springer, Heidelberg (2011)
10. Clarke, D., Helvensteijn, M., Schaefer, I.: Abstract delta modeling. In: GPCE 2010, pp. 13–22. ACM (2010)
11. Clarke, D., Muschevici, R., Proença, J., Schaefer, I., Schlatte, R.: Variability modelling in the ABS language. In: Aichernig, B.K., de Boer, F.S., Bonsangue, M.M. (eds.) FMCO 2010. LNCS, vol. 6957, pp. 204–224. Springer, Heidelberg (2011)
12. Dean, J., Ghemawat, S.: MapReduce: Simplified data processing on large clusters. In: OSDI 2004, pp. 137–150. USENIX (2004)
13. Garcia-Alonso, J., Olmeda, J.B., Murillo, J.M.: Architectural variability management in multi-layer web applications through feature models. In: FOSD 2012, pp. 29–36. ACM (2012)
14. Gomaa, H.: Designing Software Product Lines with UML. Addison-Wesley (2005)
15. Haber, A., Kutz, T., Rendel, H., Rumpe, B., Schaefer, I.: Delta-oriented architectural variability using Monticore. In: European Conference on Software Architecture (ECSA 2011), Companion, Workshop on Software Architecture Variability (SAVA), p. 6. ACM (2011)
16. Haber, A., Rendel, H., Rumpe, B., Schaefer, I., van der Linden, F.: Hierarchical variability modeling for software architectures. In: SPLC, pp. 150–159. IEEE (2011)
17. Haller, P., Odersky, M.: Scala actors: Unifying thread-based and event-based programming. Theoretical Computer Science 410(2-3), 202–220 (2009)
18. Hendrickson, S.A., van der Hoek, A.: Modeling product line architectures through change sets and relationships. In: ICSE 2007, pp. 189–198. IEEE (2007)
19. Jain, R.: The Art of Computer Systems Performance Analysis. Wiley (1991)
20. Johnsen, E.B., Hähnle, R., Schäfer, J., Schlatte, R., Steffen, M.: ABS: A core language for abstract behavioral specification. In: Aichernig, B.K., de Boer, F.S., Bonsangue, M.M. (eds.) FMCO 2010. LNCS, vol. 6957, pp. 142–164. Springer, Heidelberg (2011)

21. Johnsen, E.B., Owe, O.: An asynchronous communication model for distributed concurrent objects. Software and Systems Modeling 6(1), 35–58 (2007)
22. Johnsen, E.B., Owe, O., Schlatte, R., Tapia Tarifa, S.L.: Dynamic resource reallocation between deployment components. In: Dong, J.S., Zhu, H. (eds.) ICFEM 2010. LNCS, vol. 6447, pp. 646–661. Springer, Heidelberg (2010)
23. Broch Johnsen, E., Owe, O., Schlatte, R., Tapia Tarifa, S.L.: Validating timed models of deployment components with parametric concurrency. In: Beckert, B., Marché, C. (eds.) FoVeOOS 2010. LNCS, vol. 6528, pp. 46–60. Springer, Heidelberg (2011)
24. Johnsen, E.B., Schlatte, R., Tapia Tarifa, S.L.: Modeling resource-aware virtualized applications for the cloud in Real-Time ABS. In: Aoki, T., Taguchi, K. (eds.) ICFEM 2012. LNCS, vol. 7635, pp. 71–86. Springer, Heidelberg (2012)
25. Kattepur, A., Sen, S., Baudry, B., Benveniste, A., Jard, C.: Variability modeling and QoS analysis of web services orchestrations. In: ICWS, pp. 99–106. IEEE (2010)
26. Lämmel, R.: Google's MapReduce programming model - revisited. Sci. Comput. Program. 70(1), 1–30 (2008)
27. Loughran, N., Sánchez, P., Garcia, A., Fuentes, L.: Language support for managing variability in architectural models. In: Pautasso, C., Tanter, É. (eds.) SC 2008. LNCS, vol. 4954, pp. 36–51. Springer, Heidelberg (2008)
28. Ono, K., Hirai, Y., Tanabe, Y., Noda, N., Hagiya, M.: Using Coq in specification and program extraction of Hadoop MapReduce applications. In: Barthe, G., Pardo, A., Schneider, G. (eds.) SEFM 2011. LNCS, vol. 7041, pp. 350–365. Springer, Heidelberg (2011)
29. Pohl, K., Böckle, G., van der Linden, F.J.: Software Product Line Engineering: Foundations, Principles and Techniques. Springer (2005)
30. Schaefer, I.: Variability modelling for model-driven development of software product lines. In: VaMoS 2010, ICB-Res. Rep. 37, pp. 85–92. Univ. Duisburg-Essen (2010)
31. Schaefer, I., Bettini, L., Bono, V., Damiani, F., Tanzarella, N.: Delta-oriented Programming of Software Product Lines. In: Bosch, J., Lee, J. (eds.) SPLC 2010. LNCS, vol. 6287, pp. 77–91. Springer, Heidelberg (2010)
32. Schaefer, I., Bettini, L., Damiani, F.: Compositional type-checking for delta-oriented programming. In: AOSD 2011, pp. 43–56. ACM (2011)
33. Schaefer, I., Damiani, F.: Pure delta-oriented programming. In: FOSD 2010, pp. 49–56. ACM (2010)
34. Schaefer, I., Hähnle, R.: Formal methods in software product line engineering. IEEE Computer 44(2), 82–85 (2011)
35. Schaefer, I., Rabiser, R., Clarke, D., Bettini, L., Benavides, D., Botterweck, G., Pathak, A., Trujillo, S., Villela, K.: Software diversity: state of the art and perspectives. Software Tools for Technology Transfer (STTT) 14(5), 477–495 (2012)
36. Schobbens, P.-Y., Heymans, P., Trigaux, J.-C.: Feature diagrams: A survey and a formal semantics. In: Intl. Conf. on Requirements Engineering (RE2006), pp. 136–145. IEEE (2006)
37. van Ommering, R.C., van der Linden, F., Kramer, J., Magee, J.: The Koala component model for consumer electronics software. IEEE Computer 33(3), 78–85 (2000)
38. Wagelaar, D., Jonckers, V.: Explicit platform models for MDA. In: Briand, L.C., Williams, C. (eds.) MoDELS 2005. LNCS, vol. 3713, pp. 367–381. Springer, Heidelberg (2005)
39. Yang, F., Su, W., Zhu, H., Li, Q.: Formalizing MapReduce with CSP. In: Intl. Conf. on Engineering of Computer-Based Systems, pp. 358–367. IEEE (2010)

DeltaCCS:
A Core Calculus for Behavioral Change

Malte Lochau[1], Stephan Mennicke[2], Hauke Baller[2], and Lars Ribbeck[2]

[1] TU Darmstadt, Germany
malte.lochau@es.tu-darmstadt.de
[2] TU Braunschweig, Germany
{s.mennicke,h.baller,l.ribbeck}@tu-bs.de

Abstract. Concepts for enriching formal languages with variability capabilities aim at comprehensive specifications and efficient development of families of similar software variants as propagated, e.g., by the software product line paradigm. However, recent approaches are usually limited to purely structural variability, e.g., by adapting choice operator semantics for variant selection. Those approaches lack (1) a modular separation of common and variable parts and/or (2) a rigorous formalization of semantical impacts of structural variations. To overcome those deficiencies, we propose a delta-oriented extension to Milner's process calculus CCS, called DeltaCCS, that allows for modular reasoning about behavioral variability. In DeltaCCS, modular change directives are applied to core processes by altering term rewriting semantics in a determined way. We define variability-aware CCS congruences for a modular reasoning on the preservation of behavioral properties defined by the Modal μ-Calculus after changing CCS specifications. We implemented a DeltaCCS model checker to efficiently verify the members of a family of process variants.

Keywords: Variability Modeling, Operational Semantics, Model Checking.

1 Introduction

Inherent diversity becomes more and more prevalent nowadays in software systems, e.g., due to the ever-growing number of configuration parameters, runtime adaptation capabilities etc. Software product line engineering constitutes a promising paradigm for efficiently developing families of similar software *variants* upon a common core platform [10]. The common and variable *features* provided by the different product family members correspond to variable product characteristics during product line development and product derivation apparent in all development phases and abstraction levels. This concept allows for a fine-grained reuse of feature artifacts among the different variants. Thus, enhancing modeling and programming languages with explicit *variability* capabilities constitute a key technology for efficiently engineering a product line. To benefit from those concepts also during quality assurance, the reasoning required, e.g., to verify

T. Margaria and B. Steffen (Eds.): ISoLA 2014, Part I, LNCS 8802, pp. 320–335, 2014.
© Springer-Verlag Berlin Heidelberg 2014

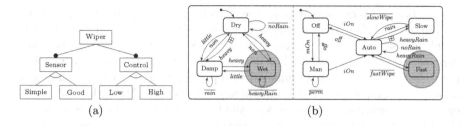

Fig. 1. Feature Model (a) and State Machine for Wiper Control System (b)

correctness properties for a complete product line should also be performed in a variability-aware manner. Accordingly, various attempts appeared in the literature to define core calculi for capturing the essence of variability in a formal way [1,2,6,7,12,15,16,18,19,21,22]. However, most of those approaches have at least one of the following two major drawbacks:

1. A so-called 150% specification of the complete product line is required comprising all variants [13]. Therefore, variability is usually emulated by adapting existing and/or adding new language constructs, e. g., selection/projection [7], (guarded) choice [18,15,21], and modal refinement [16,19,2]. Those representations become intractable for large-scale product lines.
2. They focus on structural/syntactical variability rather than the behavioral impact of variations [1,13,15,6]. This obstructs a systematic propagation of behavioral properties established for some variant to other variants.

To illustrate the challenges imposed by inherent variability, consider the sample state machine model in Fig. 1(b) denoting one variant of a *wiper control system* product line (cf. [18]) serving as our running example. The *sensor* subsystem on the left continuously detects the amount of rain and the *control* subsystem on the right adapts the wiper speed, accordingly, when running in automatic mode. In addition, the manual mode enables permanent wiping. The *feature model* in Fig. 1(a) defines the possible variants of the wiper control system product line. The control system is either configured as variant *High* as shown in Fig. 1(b), or it is *Low* thus omitting the state *Fast*. Similarly, the sensor system is either equipped with a *Good* sensor (Fig. 1(b)), or it is a *Simple* one thus omitting state *Wet*, whereas the transition between state *Dry* and *Damp* is added to properly handle *heavy* rain. The system is intended to perform *fast* wiping whenever receiving the input *heavy*, if the control subsystem is in state *Auto* after receiving input *iOn* and not yet receiving input *off*. This *temporal* property holds for the variant in Fig. 1(b), whereas changes imposed by the variant using the simple sensor obstructs this property as the control system awaits the input *heavyRain* which is not provided by the simple sensor. Verifying those properties for every variant anew is expensive and inefficient due to the high number of possible configurations and the inherent similarities among the variants.

To tackle this challenge, we propose the core calculus DeltaCCS to reason about the semantic impacts of variability by means of change operations applied to behavioral specifications. We enhance Milner's process calculus CCS [24] with a modular variability concept that is inspired by the principles of delta modeling [6]. We separate core processes from change directives altering the term rewriting semantics for the core in a determined way. In contrast to recent 150% approaches, variability is not emulated by a priori *resolution* of variation points within a 150% model, e. g., by an adapted choice rule [18,21,15], but rather by *changing* the rewriting of processes on-the-fly by overriding the CCS recursion rule. This way, arbitrary structural variations of core processes are rigorously propagated onto the semantic level. This allows for a modular reasoning on the preservation of behavioral properties defined by the Modal μ-Calculus after changing CCS specifications thus constituting a formal characterization of behavioral change in terms of variability-aware congruences on CCS process terms. Thereupon, we present a model checker implementation that allows for applying an efficient, incremental verification strategy to delta-oriented product lines.

This paper is organized as follows. In Sect. 2 we review the basics of CCS being enhanced to DeltaCCS in Sect. 3. A formalization of behavioral change impact with respect to properties expressed by the Modal μ-Calculus is given in Sect. 4 by means of variability-aware congruences for DeltaCCS. Our DeltaCCS model checker implementation and corresponding experimental results are presented in Sect. 5. In Sect. 6 we discuss related work and Sect. 7 concludes.

2   Preliminaries

We first revisit the foundations of CCS [24]. In CCS, system behavior is specified by a set of *process* definitions. A process is able to perform predefined sequences of atomic *actions*. The overall system behavior results from concurrent process composition communicating via synchronization over common actions.

By $\mathcal{N}$ we refer to a global set of names denoting (visible) actions of CCS process definitions. We reserve the name τ, i. e., $\tau \notin \mathcal{N}$ for internal actions as usual. Action names $a \in \mathcal{N}$ used in CCS processes represent *directed* communication primitives, i. e., either a *receiving action* a, or its complementary $\bar{a}$ representing a *sending action*. We denote the set of all actions over names $\mathcal{N}$ by $\mathsf{Act} = \{a, \bar{a} \,|\, a \in \mathcal{N}\}$. A *CCS process definition* follows the grammar

$$P ::= \alpha.P \mid \textstyle\sum_{i \in I} P_i \mid P \,|\, P \mid X$$

with $\alpha \in \mathsf{Act}$, index set I, and process constants $X \in \mathcal{K}$ referring to CCS processes P' by $X \stackrel{Def}{=} P'$. The *prefix process* $\alpha.P$ first performs action α and then behaves as process P. The *generalized sum process* $\sum_{i \in I} P_i$ proceeds by choosing among one of the processes P_i ($i \in I$), where the *binary choice* operator $+$ constitutes a special case with $|I| = 2$. Accordingly, the *nil process* $\mathbf{0}$ that terminates without performing any action is obtained by $I = \emptyset$. In the *parallel composition* $P \,|\, Q$, both processes P and Q may precede concurrently, as well as in cooperation by synchronizing over complementary names α, $\bar{\alpha}$ resulting in an internal, i. e., unobservable τ action. Process constants X refer to process definition P', i. e., whenever X occurs in some process P, it proceeds by behaving as process

$$\text{(pre)} \; \frac{}{\alpha.P \xrightarrow{\alpha} P} \qquad \text{(rec)} \; \frac{P \xrightarrow{\alpha} P' \quad K \overset{Def}{=} P}{K \xrightarrow{\alpha} P'} \qquad \text{(choice)} \; \frac{P_j \xrightarrow{\alpha} P'_j \quad j \in I}{\sum_{i \in I} P_i \xrightarrow{\alpha} P'_j}$$

$$\text{(par-1)} \; \frac{P \xrightarrow{\alpha} P'}{P \mid Q \xrightarrow{\alpha} P' \mid Q} \qquad \text{(par-2)} \; \frac{Q \xrightarrow{\alpha} Q'}{P \mid Q \xrightarrow{\alpha} P \mid Q'} \qquad \text{(comm)} \; \frac{P \xrightarrow{\alpha} P' \quad Q \xrightarrow{\bar{\alpha}} Q'}{P \mid Q \xrightarrow{\tau} P' \mid Q'}$$

Fig. 2. SOS Rules for CCS Step Semantics

P' thus permitting *recursive* process definitions. Processes of the form $X \overset{Def}{=} X$ are prohibited by convention. The set of CCS processes defined over predefined sets of actions Act and process constants $\mathcal{K}$ is denoted by $\mathcal{P}(\mathsf{Act}, \mathcal{K})$. Note that we omitted the relabeling and hiding operator of CCS as the following concepts are canonically adoptable to those constructs.

The operational semantics of a CCS process $P \in \mathcal{P}(\mathsf{Act}, \mathcal{K})$ defines a *labeled transition system* (LTS) $[\![P]\!]_{\mathsf{CCS}} = (\mathcal{P}(\mathsf{Act}, \mathcal{K}), \longrightarrow, P)$ whose *traces* represent valid action sequences of the specified system. The set of states is identified with CCS processes. Transitions are labeled over actions $\mathsf{Act} \cup \{\tau\}$, i.e.,

$$\longrightarrow \subseteq \mathcal{P}(\mathsf{Act}, \mathcal{K}) \times (\mathsf{Act} \cup \{\tau\}) \times \mathcal{P}(\mathsf{Act}, \mathcal{K}),$$

and the initial state refers to process P. The transition relation is defined as the least relation satisfying the rules in Fig. 2 with α ranging over Act and τ.

3   DeltaCCS

We now introduce the concept of *deltas* into CCS to represent predefined changes of process definitions at both syntactical and semantical level.

3.1   Syntax of DeltaCCS

Delta modeling is a comprehensive approach for extending arbitrary languages with capabilities to specify variable parts of a given *core* model [6]. For this, (syntactical) *change* operations (*deltas*) are applied to predefined variation points. The delta approach propagates (1) a separation of the core from the deltas definitions and (2) deltas to constitute modular encapsulations of basic, yet language-specific change directives applicable at any level of granularity.

Adopting delta modeling to CCS to reason about the semantic impacts of syntactic variations is appealing due to the close relationship between process terms and their operational semantics by means of process term rewriting rules. Assume CCS process $P_c \in \mathcal{P}(\mathsf{Act}, \mathcal{K})$ to represent the core behavior of a variable system. Therein, process constants $K \in \mathcal{K}$ implicitly impose arbitrary decompositions of P_c into sub-processes, e.g., referring to syntactical entities of a high-level modeling language after being translated into CCS. As an example, consider the translation of the state machine in Fig. 1(b) into the CCS process in Fig. 3(b). For each state machine state, a dedicated process constant is introduced whose process definition constitutes a choice over the outgoing transitions of that state.

Thus, names K occurring in core process P_c correspond to basic model entities potentially being subject to *structural* change operations and, therefore, serving as well-defined variation points for delta applications on CCS terms.

For instance, the state machine deltas for changing the sensor subsystem from variant *Good* to variant *Simple* (cf. Fig. 1(b)) are depicted in Fig. 3(a), where elements marked with "+" are added and those marked "-" are deleted from the core. The corresponding CCS deltas δ_1–δ_4 are shown in Fig. 3(c), e. g., δ_1 removes the transition that switches from *Dry* to *Wet* when observing heavy rain by altering definition of constant *Damp* to *Damp'*. Thus, a *CCS delta* consists of a process constant $K \overset{Def}{=} P$ to be changed by a process constant $K' \overset{Def}{=} P'$ substituting K. Depending on the similarities between P and P', the delta constitutes either an *add*, *remove*, or *modify* operation [6] (cf. Fig. 3(b)). Similar to 150% approaches for encoding variability, those different kinds of deltas arise from tradeoffs between (1) granularity of process decomposition into process names and (2) repetitions of process terms within delta definitions [15].

Besides the occurrence of constants K to be substituted in a CCS term, the applicability of a delta is often further restricted by stating an *application condition* ϕ, e. g., a condition over feature parameters in a feature model (cf. Fig. 1(a)) related to that particular delta. For instance, the application condition for δ_1 in our example requires the feature *Simple*. In the following, we abstract from the concrete representation and evaluation mechanism for application conditions ϕ but rather assume an abstract domain Φ with $\phi \in \Phi$. Summarizing, a *DeltaCCS* specification consists of a core process P_c and a collection of CCS deltas.

Definition 1 (DeltaCCS Specification). *A CCS Delta is a triple* $(K, \phi, K') \in \mathcal{K} \times \Phi \times \mathcal{K}$. *A DeltaCCS Specification is a pair* (P_c, Δ) *with* $P_c \in \mathcal{P}(\mathsf{Act}, \mathcal{K})$ *and* Δ *a finite set of CCS deltas.*

According to [18], we assume any process constant K appearing in a DeltaCCS specification, i. e., within the core process and/or within CCS deltas to be contained in $\mathcal{K}$. The set of all CCS deltas operating on process constants $\mathcal{K}$ is denoted as $\Delta(\mathcal{K}, \Phi) = \mathcal{K} \times \Phi \times \mathcal{K}$. The (syntactic) application of a CCS delta $\delta = (K, \phi, K')$ to a CCS process P substitutes any occurrence of K in P by K'.

Definition 2 (CCS Delta Application). *CCS Delta Application is defined by the function apply* : $\mathcal{P}(\mathsf{Act}, \mathcal{K}) \times \Delta(\mathcal{K}, \Phi) \to \mathcal{P}(\mathsf{Act}, \mathcal{K})$ *such that in* $P' = apply(P, \delta)$ *with* $\delta = (K, \phi, K')$, *every occurrence of* K *in* P *is substituted by* K'.

We write $\delta(P) := apply(P, \delta)$ for short. To generalize the notion of delta applications to sets $\Delta' \subseteq \Delta(\mathcal{K}, \Phi)$ of CCS deltas, we define

$$\Delta'(P) := \{\delta_{i_1}(\ldots \delta_{i_n}(P)\ldots) \,|\, |\Delta'| = n \wedge k \neq \ell \Rightarrow \delta_{i_k} \neq \delta_{i_\ell}\},$$

where $P \in \mathcal{P}(\mathsf{Act}, \mathcal{K})$, i. e., yielding the set of process definitions obtained from all possible permutations of delta applications. In case of $|\Delta'(P)| = 1$, the resulting process is *independent* of the ordering of delta applications.

The delta application considered so far performs *direct* applications, i. e., only those process names K literally occurring in process term P are substituted. However, due to the recursive nature of CCS term definitions, a delta application may require preceding process constant substitutions and even other delta

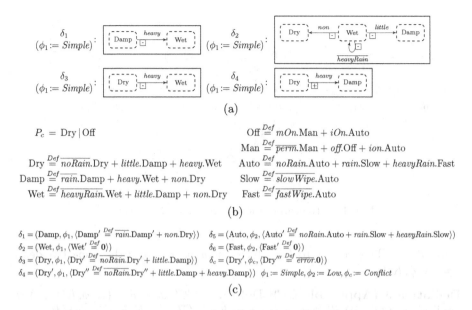

(a)

$P_c = \text{Dry} \mid \text{Off}$

$\text{Dry} \stackrel{Def}{=} \overline{noRain}.\text{Dry} + little.\text{Damp} + heavy.\text{Wet}$
$\text{Damp} \stackrel{Def}{=} \overline{rain}.\text{Damp} + heavy.\text{Wet} + non.\text{Dry}$
$\text{Wet} \stackrel{Def}{=} \overline{heavyRain}.\text{Wet} + little.\text{Damp} + non.\text{Dry}$

$\text{Off} \stackrel{Def}{=} mOn.\text{Man} + iOn.\text{Auto}$
$\text{Man} \stackrel{Def}{=} \overline{perm}.\text{Man} + off.\text{Off} + ion.\text{Auto}$
$\text{Auto} \stackrel{Def}{=} noRain.\text{Auto} + rain.\text{Slow} + heavyRain.\text{Fast}$
$\text{Slow} \stackrel{Def}{=} \overline{slowWipe}.\text{Auto}$
$\text{Fast} \stackrel{Def}{=} \overline{fastWipe}.\text{Auto}$

(b)

$\delta_1 = (\text{Damp}, \phi_1, \langle \text{Damp}' \stackrel{Def}{=} \overline{rain}.\text{Damp}' + non.\text{Dry}\rangle)$ $\delta_5 = (\text{Auto}, \phi_2, \langle \text{Auto}' \stackrel{Def}{=} noRain.\text{Auto} + rain.\text{Slow} + heavyRain.\text{Slow}\rangle)$
$\delta_2 = (\text{Wet}, \phi_1, \langle \text{Wet}' \stackrel{Def}{=} 0\rangle)$ $\delta_6 = (\text{Fast}, \phi_2, \langle \text{Fast}' \stackrel{Def}{=} 0\rangle)$
$\delta_3 = (\text{Dry}, \phi_1, \langle \text{Dry}' \stackrel{Def}{=} \overline{noRain}.\text{Dry} + little.\text{Damp}\rangle)$ $\delta_c = (\text{Dry}', \phi_c, \langle \text{Dry}''' \stackrel{Def}{=} \overline{error}.0\rangle)$
$\delta_4 = (\text{Dry}', \phi_1, \langle \text{Dry}'' \stackrel{Def}{=} \overline{noRain}.\text{Dry}'' + little.\text{Damp} + heavy.\text{Damp}\rangle)$ $\phi_1 := Simple, \phi_2 := Low, \phi_c := Conflict$

(c)

Fig. 3. State Machine Deltas for Variant *Simple* (a), CCS Specification for Variant *Good/High* (b), CCS Deltas and Conflicting Delta δ_c (c)

applications on P to eventually become applicable. For instance, δ_1 in Fig. 3(c) is not directly applicable to P_c but requires a preceding rewriting of constant *Dry* via the recursion rule. Similarly, applicability of delta δ_4 requires the constant *Dry'* and, therefore, a preceding application of δ_3.

To reason about well-formedness properties of DeltaCCS specifications, we employ a *dependency graph* (cf. [18]) to make explicit (syntactical) interdependencies between process definitions and CCS deltas. The dependency graph comprises for each constant $K \in \mathcal{K}$, $K \stackrel{Def}{=} P$, the respective syntax tree of process term P with K as its root node. Each node of the dependency graph is identified with some syntactical CCS element where constants K occurring as inner nodes refer to the respective syntax tree of those constants. Figure 4 shows an extract of the dependency graph for our running example, where gray nodes refer to process constants of the core process and white nodes refer to process constants introduced by CCS deltas. Two types of edges between nodes referring to process constants emerge: (1) (unlabeled) *recursion*-edges leading from inner process constant nodes to the respective process root node and (2) (labeled) *delta*-edges leading from process constant root nodes to that process constant root node substituting the constant in a CCS delta.

We denote the dependency graph of a DeltaCCS specification (P_c, Δ) by $Dep(P_c, \Delta) = (\mathcal{V}, \mathcal{E})$ comprising a set of nodes $\mathcal{V}$ and a set of edges $\mathcal{E}$. A path $(v_1, \ldots, v_n) \in \mathcal{V}^+$ in $Dep(P_c, \Delta)$ is a finite sequence of nodes such that $(v_i, v_{i+1}) \in \mathcal{E}$ $(0 < i < n)$. A path p starting from node P_c and reaching a

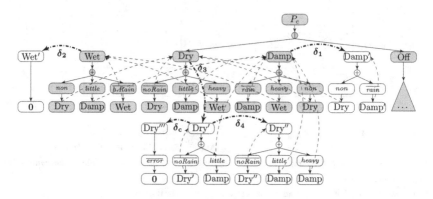

Fig. 4. Extract from the Sample Dependency Graph

delta-edge leading from K to K' induces the *applicability* of the respective delta $\delta = (K, \phi, K')$.

Definition 3 (Applicable CCS Delta). *A CCS delta* $\delta = (K, \phi, K') \in \Delta$ *is applicable in* (P_c, Δ) *iff there exists a path* $p = (P_c, \ldots, K, K')$ *in* $Dep(P_c, \Delta)$.

A delta δ is *directly applicable* if no other *delta*-edge precedes the *delta*-edge of δ in a path p. In our running example, $\delta_1, \delta_2, \delta_3$ are directly applicable, whereas the application of δ_4 requires a preceding application of δ_3. We assume every CCS delta in a given DeltaCCS specification to be applicable in the following which, e.g., holds for the example in Fig. 4. A special kind of interdependency among CCS deltas arises if the applicability of a delta *always* requires the previous application of another delta. For instance, δ_4 in our running example is *dependent* on δ_3. We introduce a respective *dependency relation* $\prec$ on a set of CCS deltas.

Definition 4 (CCS Delta Dependency). *Let* (P_c, Δ) *be a DeltaCCS specification,* $\delta_i = (K_i, \phi_i, K_i') \in \Delta$ *(i = 1, 2), and* $Dep(P_c, \Delta) = (V, \mathcal{E})$.

$\delta_1 \prec \delta_2 :\Leftrightarrow$ *for all paths* $p = (P_c, \ldots, K_2, K_2') : p = (P_c, \ldots, K_1, K_1', \ldots, K_2, K_2')$.

Requiring applicability of CCS deltas prevents from cyclic delta dependencies thus inducing the following property.

Lemma 1. *The reflexive closure of* $\prec$ *is a partial order.*

In our example, $\delta_3 \prec \delta_4$ holds as all paths leading to δ_4 pass δ_3. Otherwise, if two deltas are unrelated under $\prec$, they are either in *conflict*, i.e., the resulting process variant depends on their application order, or they are *independent* [6]. First, consider two distinct deltas to substitute the same constant K. The results of their applications on K differ as, otherwise, both CCS deltas would be equal. Hence, those deltas have a *direct conflict*. Two CCS deltas unrelated under $\prec$ that are not in a direct conflict may be also conflicting by indirectly influencing each other, or they are independent, otherwise. CCS deltas $\delta_i = (K_i, \phi_i, K_i')$ $(i = 1, 2)$ are *independent* if (1) they have no direct conflict and (2) if they may occur in arbitrary application order, then any order (eventually) yields the same results, i. e., for all pairs of paths $(P_c, \ldots, K_i, K_i' \ldots, K_j, K_j')$ and $(P_c, \ldots, K_j, K_j' \ldots, K_i, K_i')$ there exists some node $v \in \mathcal{V}$ such that both paths commute in v. If two CCS deltas are neither dependent, nor independent, they are in conflict.

Definition 5 (CCS Delta Conflict). *Let (P_c, Δ) be a DeltaCCS specification and $\delta_i = (K_i, \phi_i, K_i') \in \Delta$ (i = 1, 2) with $\delta_1 \not\prec \delta_2$ and $\delta_2 \not\prec \delta_1$. δ_1 and δ_2 are in conflict iff δ_1 and δ_2 are not independent.*

In Fig. 4, δ_1 and δ_2 are independent whereas δ_4 and δ_c have a (direct) conflict.

Due to its purely syntactic nature, the introduced notion of conflict is efficiently verifiable on the basis of the dependency graph. However, actual occurrences of conflicts further depend on the application conditions as well as the (semantic) reachability of the respective process constants substituted by the conflicting deltas. In addition, further purely semantic conflicts might arise among deltas altering concurrent, but interacting sub-processes. Hence, a variability-aware semantics for DeltaCCS is defined.

3.2 Operational Semantics of DeltaCCS

We first describe the derivation of the operational semantics for a particular process variant defined by a subset of CCS deltas. Thereupon, we present an extension of CCS semantics for applying deltas on-the-fly to obtain a closed semantic characterization of all derivable process variants.

Given a DeltaCCS specification (P_c, Δ), the operational semantics of the core process P_c is defined by the LTS $[\![P_c]\!]_{\mathsf{CCS}} = (\mathcal{P}(\mathsf{Act}, \mathcal{K}), \longrightarrow, P_c)$ as usual. For deriving LTS semantics of a process variant defined by a subset $\Delta' \subseteq \Delta$ of CCS deltas, the SOS rule application for the construction of the transition relation is to be interleaved with a consecutive application of Δ'.

Definition 6 (DeltaCCS Variant Semantics). *Let (P_c, Δ) be a DeltaCCS specification. The LTS $[\![(P_c, \Delta)]\!]_{\mathsf{CCS}}^{\Delta'} = (\mathcal{P}(\mathsf{Act}, \mathcal{K}), \longrightarrow_{\Delta'}, P)$ for $P \in \Delta'(P_c)$ defines the semantics of the process variant for $\Delta' \subseteq \Delta$ where*

$$\longrightarrow_{\Delta'} \subseteq (\mathcal{P}(\mathsf{Act}, \mathcal{K}) \times (\mathsf{Act} \cup \{\tau\}) \times \mathcal{P}(\mathsf{Act}, \mathcal{K}))$$

is the least relation satisfying the rule (dstep) $\dfrac{P \xrightarrow{\alpha} P' \quad P'' \in \Delta'(P')}{P \xrightarrow{\alpha}_{\Delta'} P''}$.

In rule (dstep), the premise $P \xrightarrow{\alpha} P'$ refers to the CCS transition derivation via $[\![\cdot]\!]_{\mathsf{CCS}}$ as usual. If Δ' is not conflict-free, $\Delta'(P')$ yields more than one process and the resulting LTS contains (non-deterministic) choices among all possible delta application orderings.

Deriving LTS semantics for every subset $\Delta' \subseteq \Delta$ is usually impracticable due to the high number of possible variants. Instead, we propose an alternative semantic characterization of DeltaCCS specifications by means of a variability-aware operational step semantics applying deltas on-the-fly during transition derivation. Therefore, LTS states are enriched by subsets $\Sigma \subseteq \Delta$ comprising those CCS deltas applied prior to reaching that state and, therefore, to be re-applied in subsequent steps. An additional rule is introduced for applying deltas

$$\text{(delta)} \frac{(K',\Sigma) \xrightarrow{\alpha} (P,\Sigma') \quad \delta = (K,\phi,K') \in \Delta}{(K,\Sigma) \xrightarrow{\alpha} (P,\Sigma' \cup \{\delta\})}$$

$$\text{(drec)} \frac{(P,\Sigma) \xrightarrow{\alpha} (P',\Sigma') \quad K \overset{Def}{=} P \quad \Sigma \cap (\{K\} \times \Phi \times \mathcal{K}) = \emptyset}{(K,\Sigma) \xrightarrow{\alpha} (P',\Sigma')}$$

$$\text{(dpref)} \frac{}{(a.P,\Sigma) \xrightarrow{\alpha} (P,\Sigma)}$$

$$\text{(dchoice)} \frac{(P_j,\Sigma) \xrightarrow{\alpha} (P'_j,\Sigma') \quad j \in I}{(\sum_{i \in I} P_i,\Sigma) \xrightarrow{\alpha} (P'_j,\Sigma')}$$

$$\text{(dpar-1)} \frac{(P,\Sigma) \xrightarrow{\alpha} (P',\Sigma')}{(P \,|\, Q,\Sigma) \xrightarrow{\alpha} (P' \,|\, Q,\Sigma')}$$

$$\text{(dpar-2)} \frac{(Q,\Sigma) \xrightarrow{\alpha} (Q',\Sigma')}{(P \,|\, Q,\Sigma) \xrightarrow{\alpha} (P \,|\, Q',\Sigma')}$$

$$\text{(dcomm)} \frac{(P,\Sigma) \xrightarrow{\alpha} (P',\Sigma') \quad (Q,\Sigma) \xrightarrow{\overline{\alpha}} (Q',\Sigma'') \quad compatible(\Sigma',\Sigma'')}{(P \,|\, Q,\Sigma) \xrightarrow{\tau} (P' \,|\, Q',\Sigma' \cup \Sigma'')}$$

Fig. 5. SOS Rules for Variability-Aware DeltaCCS Step Semantics

on process constants. This rule overrides the original recursion rule such that (1) applications of those deltas already applied previously are enforced and (2) further non-conflicting deltas may by applied. Apart from the enhanced recursion rule, the original SOS rules of CCS (cf. Fig. 2) are only slightly adapted to preserve the CCS delta sets collected up to this point. The resulting LTS thus includes every possible variant semantics.

Definition 7 (DeltaCCS Semantics). *Let* (P_c,Δ) *be a DeltaCCS specification. The LTS* $[\![(P_c,\Delta)]\!]_\Delta = (\mathcal{P}(\mathsf{Act},\mathcal{K}) \times \Delta(\mathcal{K},\Phi), \longrightarrow, (P_c,\emptyset))$ *defines the semantics of* (P_c,Δ) *where*

$$\longrightarrow \subseteq (\mathcal{P}(\mathsf{Act},\mathcal{K}) \times \Delta(\mathcal{K},\Phi)) \times (\mathsf{Act} \cup \{\tau\}) \times (\mathcal{P}(\mathsf{Act},\mathcal{K}) \times \Delta(\mathcal{K},\Phi))$$

is the least relation satisfying the rules in Fig. 5.

The predicate *compatible* ensures consistent delta applications in processes P and Q in case of parallel composition $P|Q$. Direct conflicts between delta applications in P and Q shall be resolved using an appropriate set of application conditions.

For instance, reaching state $(\mathrm{Dry}, \{\delta_1,\delta_2\})$ of our running example after some arbitrary steps, the next possible steps are either

$$\cdots \xrightarrow{heavy} (\mathrm{Wet},\Sigma), \quad \cdots \xrightarrow{little} (\mathrm{Damp},\Sigma), \text{ and } \cdots \xrightarrow{\overline{noRain}} (\mathrm{Dry},\Sigma)$$

for $\Sigma = \{\delta_1,\delta_2\}$, i.e., similar to the core behavior, or

$$\cdots \xrightarrow{little} (\mathrm{Damp},\Sigma') \text{ and } \cdots \xrightarrow{\overline{noRain}} (\mathrm{Dry},\Sigma')$$

for $\Sigma' = \{\delta_1,\delta_2,\delta_3\}$, i.e., when applying δ_3 to remove handling of heavy rain.

For correctness, we require the enhanced DeltaCCS semantics to be bisimilar to each process variant semantics. For a conflict-free subset $\Delta' \subseteq \Delta$ of a DeltaCCS specification (P_c,Δ), we require $[\![(P_c,\Delta')]\!]_\Delta$ with initial state (P_c,Δ') to be bisimilar to $[\![P_c]\!]_{\mathsf{CCS}}^{\Delta'}$, denoted by $\simeq$.

Theorem 1 (Correctness). *Let* (P_c,Δ) *be a DeltaCCS specification,* $\Delta' \subseteq \Delta$ *conflict-free,* $[\![(P_c,\Delta')]\!]_\Delta = (Q_1, \longrightarrow, q_1)$ *and* $[\![P_c]\!]_{\mathsf{CCS}}^{\Delta'} = (Q_2, \longrightarrow_{\Delta'}, q_2)$. *Then for* $q_1' = (P_c,\Delta') \in Q_1$ *it holds that* $q_1' \simeq q_2$.

The proof follows from the fact that rule delta emulates a replacement of a process constant by delta application, making available the steps of changed processes. Thus, when a process variant (Def. 6) reaches a changed constant K', then the DeltaCCS semantics (Def. 7) may apply a CCS delta to K, simulating steps of K'. As Δ' is conflict-free, the DeltaCCS semantics always performs steps of K' (and only K'), which is why the variant semantics also simulates the DeltaCCS semantics. All other cases follow from each CCS rule being canonically extended to CCS delta sets. The necessary bisimulation relation is therefore $\mathcal{S} = \{(P_c, (P_c, \Delta))\} \cup \{(P', (P, \Delta')) \mid P' \in \Delta'(P)\}$. If Δ' is not conflict-free, then the variant semantics is simulated by the DeltaCCS semantics, i.e., $q_1' \sqsubseteq q_2$ with $\mathcal{S}$ being the corresponding simulation relation. Allowing process variants to be derived for conflicting subsets $\Delta' \subseteq \Delta$ imposes non-deterministic variation point resolution. This can be avoided, e.g., by providing conflict-resolving, i.e., mutually excluding application conditions for conflicting deltas [15]. However, in addition to those syntactically detectable conflicts, further semantical conflicts might arise. Consider process $P = (K_1 | K_2) \setminus \{\overline{a}\}^1$ with $K_1 \stackrel{Def}{=} a.K_1'$ and $K_2 \stackrel{Def}{=} \overline{a}.K_2'$ and two deltas $\delta_1 = (K_1, \phi_1, K_1'')$ with $K_1'' \stackrel{Def}{=} b.K_1'$ and $\delta_2 = (K_2', \phi_2, K_2'')$. Although δ_1 and δ_2 are applicable and (syntactically) independent, applying δ_1 prior to δ_2 causes δ_2 to become inapplicable.

In the next section, we use the Modal μ-calculus to formalize behavioral properties of CCS specifications and to reason about the semantical impact of delta applications concerning those properties in a concise way.

4   Formalizing Behavioral Change with DeltaCCS

Process languages like CCS allow for rigorous specifications of system behaviors by means of alternating sequences of states and transitions with corresponding action occurrences as permitted by the underlying LTS semantics. CCS specifications P, therefore, serve as a basis for the formal verification of correctness properties φ imposed for P, denoted as $P \models \varphi$. Properties φ of CCS processes usually comprise (1) particular LTS states to satisfy atomic propositions $(p, q, r, \ldots)$ and/or to be able to perform α-labeled transitions, $\alpha \in \mathsf{Act}$, as well as (2) global safety (always) and liveness (eventually) properties to hold for the entire LTS [25]. For our example to be correct, we require that $fastWipe$ is performed whenever $heavy$ rain occurs and automatic mode is selected. Here, we consider a restricted version of the Modal μ-Calculus as proposed in [4] to express properties φ.

Definition 8 (Modal μ-Calculus). *A modal μ-calculus formula is an expression following the form $\nu Z.\psi \wedge [\alpha]Z$ or $\mu Z.\psi \vee \langle\alpha\rangle Z$ where*

$$\psi ::= \mathit{tt} \mid \mathit{ff} \mid q \mid \neg q \mid Z \mid \psi \wedge \psi \mid \psi \vee \psi \mid \langle\alpha\rangle\psi \mid [\alpha]\psi$$

---

[1] Here, the output action $\overline{a}$ is restricted by the $\setminus\{\overline{a}\}$ construct, i.e., $\overline{a}$ is not visible beyond P, especially not in the LTS of P. In this paper, we left out the restriction operator of CCS for compactness reasons.

where $q \in \mathcal{P}$, $\alpha \in \mathsf{Act}$ *and* $Z \in \mathsf{Var}$. *Let* $P \in \mathcal{P}(\mathsf{Act}, \mathcal{K})$ *and* φ *a formula. Given an evaluation of atomic propositions* $\mathcal{I}_\mathcal{P} : \mathcal{P} \to 2^{\mathcal{P}(\mathsf{Act}, \mathcal{K})}$ *and an evaluation of variables* $\mathcal{I}_\mathsf{Var} : \mathsf{Var} \to 2^{\mathcal{P}(\mathsf{Act}, \mathcal{K})}$, $P \models \varphi$ *iff* $P \in \|\varphi\|_{\mathcal{I}_\mathsf{Var}}^{\mathcal{I}_\mathcal{P}}$ *(cf. Fig. 6).*

Set $\mathcal{P}$ contains atomic propositions, ranged over by $p, q, r, \ldots$ and set Var contains variable names, ranged over by X, Y, Z. Besides Boolean constants tt (true), ff (false) and standard logical connectives $\wedge, \vee, \neg$, the modal operators $[\alpha]$ meaning 'for all α-transitions' and $\langle \alpha \rangle$ meaning 'there exists an α-transition' are supported. Both are evaluated locally, e.g., process P satisfies $[\alpha]\varphi$ if for every P', $P \xrightarrow{\alpha} P'$ implies that P' satisfies φ. In addition, the modal μ-calculus provides constructs for largest ($\nu Z.\varphi(Z)$) and least ($\mu Z.\varphi(Z)$) fixpoints. Bradfield and Stirling describe the former as 'looping' (always) and the latter as 'finite looping' (eventually) [4]. Thus, the μ-calculus supports temporal properties in combination with propositions on action labels, i.e., progress, e.g., $\nu Z.\varphi \wedge [\alpha]Z$ means that φ holds along every α-path [4]. Here, we restrict our considerations to safety properties as usual and liveness properties of the form $\mu Z.\varphi \vee \langle \alpha \rangle Z$, i.e., within φ no further fixpoint operator occurs. We define the modal μ-calculus in *positive normal form*, i.e., negation ($\neg$) only occurs in front of atomic propositions. This ensures necessary fixpoint properties on variables $Z \in \mathsf{Var}$ and is no limitation, as for every μ-calculus formula, an equivalent μ-calculus formula in positive normal form exists [4]. A formula φ is evaluated to its characteristic set $\|\varphi\|$ containing all processes satisfying φ, i.e., $P \models \varphi$ iff $P \in \|\varphi\|$. Function $\| \cdot \|$ is parameterized over function $\mathcal{I}_\mathsf{Var}$ assigning variables to sets of processes, and function $\mathcal{I}_\mathcal{P}$ assigning to $p \in \mathcal{P}$ sets of processes for which p holds. The evaluation equations for function $\| \cdot \|$ are given in Fig. 6, where we consider *weak* modal operators allowing arbitrary τ-steps before and after an α-action occurs.

The aforementioned correctness property for our running example is expressible in modal μ-calculus as

$$\varphi := \mu Z. \langle heavy \rangle \langle\!\langle \overline{fastWipe} \rangle\!\rangle \mathsf{tt} \vee \langle - \rangle Z.$$

Note that $\langle\!\langle \alpha \rangle\!\rangle$ allows arbitrarily many τ-steps before and after α, and that $\langle - \rangle$ is short for 'every action'. For the core process (cf. Fig. 3(b)) we have $P_c \models \varphi$, whereas for variant P resulting from applying the set of CCS deltas in Fig. 3(c), φ does not hold. Thus, verifying φ to hold for a complete DeltaCCS specification (P_c, Δ) requires to evaluate φ on the LTS semantics $[\![P_c]\!]_{\mathsf{CCS}}^{\Delta'}$ of every possible subset $\Delta' \subseteq \Delta$. Alternatively, the LTS semantics $[\![(P_c, \Delta)]\!]_\Delta$ including the behaviors of all derivable variants may be used to evaluate φ for all subsets Δ' at once. This strategy is similar to recent variability-aware verification approaches based on 150% specifications [18,8,2]. However, both approaches poorly scale as (a) the set of possible process variants grows exponentially with the number of deltas, and (b) the LTS $[\![(P_c, \Delta)]\!]_\Delta$ contains the disjunction of each LTS variant.

Therefore, we propose a novel strategy, i.e., a delta-oriented incremental approach for variability-aware behavioral verification. Starting with some process P and establishing $P \models \varphi$, verifying φ also on variant P' solely requires to re-evaluate φ on those sub-processes of P' (potentially) affected by the differences between P and P', expressed as CCS deltas. If CCS delta δ does not affect the behavior of P, then $\delta(P)$ is said to be congruent to P, denoted as $P \equiv \delta(P)$.

$$\|q\|_{\mathcal{I}_\mathcal{P}}^{\mathcal{I}_{Var}} = \mathcal{I}_\mathcal{P}(q) \qquad\qquad \|[\alpha]\varphi\|_{\mathcal{I}_\mathcal{P}}^{\mathcal{I}_{Var}} = \left\{ P \mid \forall P' : P \xrightarrow{\alpha} P' \Rightarrow P' \in \|\varphi\|_{\mathcal{I}_\mathcal{P}}^{\mathcal{I}_{Var}} \right\}$$

$$\|\neg q\|_{\mathcal{I}_\mathcal{P}}^{\mathcal{I}_{Var}} = \mathcal{P}(Act, \mathcal{K}) \setminus \mathcal{I}_\mathcal{P}(q) \qquad \|\langle\alpha\rangle\varphi\|_{\mathcal{I}_\mathcal{P}}^{\mathcal{I}_{Var}} = \left\{ P \mid \exists P' : P \xrightarrow{\alpha} P' \wedge P' \in \|\varphi\|_{\mathcal{I}_\mathcal{P}}^{\mathcal{I}_{Var}} \right\}$$

$$\|Z\|_{\mathcal{I}_\mathcal{P}}^{\mathcal{I}_{Var}} = \mathcal{I}_{Var}(Z)$$

$$\|\varphi_1 \wedge \varphi_2\|_{\mathcal{I}_\mathcal{P}}^{\mathcal{I}_{Var}} = \|\varphi_1\|_{\mathcal{I}_\mathcal{P}}^{\mathcal{I}_{Var}} \cap \|\varphi_2\|_{\mathcal{I}_\mathcal{P}}^{\mathcal{I}_{Var}} \qquad \|\nu Z.\varphi\|_{\mathcal{I}_\mathcal{P}}^{\mathcal{I}_{Var}} = \bigcup \left\{ \Pi \subseteq \mathcal{P}(Act,\mathcal{K}) \mid \Pi \subseteq \|\varphi\|_{\mathcal{I}_\mathcal{P}}^{\mathcal{I}_{Var}[Z:=\Pi]} \right\}$$

$$\|\varphi_1 \vee \varphi_2\|_{\mathcal{I}_\mathcal{P}}^{\mathcal{I}_{Var}} = \|\varphi_1\|_{\mathcal{I}_\mathcal{P}}^{\mathcal{I}_{Var}} \cup \|\varphi_2\|_{\mathcal{I}_\mathcal{P}}^{\mathcal{I}_{Var}} \qquad \|\mu Z.\varphi\|_{\mathcal{I}_\mathcal{P}}^{\mathcal{I}_{Var}} = \bigcap \left\{ \Pi \subseteq \mathcal{P}(Act,\mathcal{K}) \mid \Pi \supseteq \|\varphi\|_{\mathcal{I}_\mathcal{P}}^{\mathcal{I}_{Var}[Z:=\Pi]} \right\}$$

Fig. 6. Evaluation Equations for the Modal μ-calculus

Proposition 1. *Let* $\delta = (K, \phi, K') \in \Delta(\mathcal{K}, \Phi)$ *and* $P, Q, P' \in \mathcal{P}(Act, \mathcal{K})$.

$$\delta(\alpha.P) \equiv \alpha.\delta(P) \tag{1}$$

$$\delta(P + Q) \equiv \delta(P) + \delta(Q) \tag{2}$$

$$\delta(P \mid Q) \equiv \delta(P) \mid Q \text{ if } \delta(Q) \equiv Q \tag{3}$$

$$\delta(X) \equiv \delta(P') \text{ if } K \neq X \text{ and } X \stackrel{Def}{=} P' \tag{4}$$

$$\delta(P) \equiv P \text{ if } \delta \text{ is not applicable in } P \tag{5}$$

Proofs follow from the congruence on plain CCS terms [24] and the definition of delta applications. Further relations are deducible, e. g., $\delta(\mathbf{0}) \equiv \mathbf{0}$. Those delta-aware congruences allow for a consecutive, property-preserving transformation of processes $\delta(P)$ in a way such that sub-processes of P actually changed by δ are explicitly localized. However, variant derivation usually requires subsets $\Delta' \subseteq \Delta$ of multiple deltas. Thus, potential dependencies among different deltas are to be taken into account.

Lemma 2. *Let* $\delta_1 = (K_1, \phi_1, K_1') \in \Delta(\mathcal{K}, \Phi)$, $\delta_2 = (K_2, \phi_2, K_2') \in \Delta(\mathcal{K}, \Phi)$ *and* $P \in \mathcal{P}(Act, \mathcal{K})$. *Then* $\delta_1(\delta_2(P)) \equiv \delta_2(\delta_1(P))$ *iff* δ_1 *and* δ_2 *are independent.*

For instance, δ_1 and δ_3 in our example are independent and, therefore, applicable in any order to P_c. Both deltas are not applicable to sub-process *Off* but only to sub-process *Dry*. Therein, δ_1 is applicable to sub-process *Damp* whereas δ_3 directly applies to *Dry* without affecting the applicability of δ_1. Considering the dependent deltas δ_3 and δ_4 and applying δ_3 to *Dry* first, it produces *Dry'* on which δ_4 then applies afterwards. Otherwise, if δ_4 is considered first, it is not applicable as *Dry'* is not yet produced. Based on those DeltaCCS congruence notions, the evaluation of properties φ is consecutively decomposable according to the following correspondences.

Proposition 2. *Let* $P, Q, R \in \mathcal{P}(Act, \mathcal{K})$ *and* φ *a* μ-*calculus formula.*

$$P \models \varphi \wedge P \equiv Q \ \Rightarrow \ Q \models \varphi \tag{6}$$

$$P \models \varphi \wedge Q \models \varphi \ \Rightarrow \ P + Q \models \varphi \tag{7}$$

$$P \mid R \models \varphi \wedge P \equiv Q \ \Rightarrow \ Q \mid R \models \varphi \tag{8}$$

Proofs follow from (1) $P \simeq P'$ iff P and P' satisfy the same set of μ-calculus formulae [4] and (2) $P \equiv P'$ implies $P \simeq P'$ [24]. Hence, the (re-)evaluation of

Table 1. Experimental Results for Delta-aware Model Checking

	#	Deltas	Core	p. size	i. size	Deadlock-Freedom i. result	Deadlock-Freedom p. result	Home State i. result	Home State recheck?	Home State p. result
Sensor	1.1	–	–	21	–	–	✓	–	–	✓
	1.2	δ_2	1.1	15	1	✗	implied	✓	no	implied
	1.3	δ_2, δ_1	1.1	13	5	✗	implied	✓	no	implied
	1.4	$\delta_2, \delta_1, \delta_3$	1.1	10	10	✓	implied	✓	no	implied
Control	2.1	–	–	23	–	–	✓	–	–	✓
	2.2	δ_5	2.1	21	9	✓	implied	✗	yes	✓
	2.3	δ_6	2.1	22	1	✗	implied	✓	no	implied
	2.4	δ_5, δ_6	2.1	21	9	✓	implied	✗	yes	✓
	2.5	δ_5, δ_6	2.2	21	0	implied	implied	implied	no	implied

a property φ established for a process P after applying a delta δ is only required for those sub-processes of $\delta(P)$ affected by δ.

Theorem 2. *Let* $\delta = (K, \phi, K') \in \Delta(\mathcal{K}, \Phi)$ *and* $P \in \mathcal{P}(\mathsf{Act}, \mathcal{K})$. *If* $\delta(P) \equiv P$ *and* $P \models \varphi$ *then* $\delta(P) \models \varphi$.

For (pure) safety properties, this is obviously sound. For liveness properties, a positive result obtained from a changed sub-process directly yields a positive result for the entire process variant. In case of negative results, however, local evaluation is not sufficient thus the entire variant has to be re-analyzed.

When applying the deltas to generate variant *Simple* of the wiper example, the sensor subsystem is changed. Based on Eq. (8) the system has to be re-evaluated. The sample liveness property given in this section is violated by the simple wiper example. Other properties, e. g., deadlock-freedom or home states, may be decided component-wise and, therefore, re-evaluation can be decomposed to smaller sub-terms, or even neglected for unaffected sub-processes. For instance, changes induced by δ_5 still allow infinite looping between states *Off* and *Auto* satisfying $\varphi' := \nu Z.[iOn]\langle off \rangle Z$, which can be checked locally for both sub-processes, i. e., without re-checking their parallel composition.

5   Implementation and Experiments

We implemented DeltaCCS on top of the MAUDE framework[2]. MAUDE allows developing arbitrary languages with formalized semantics by means of term rewriting logic [9]. We extended the existing CCS implementation [26] to support CCS deltas. The rewriting rules for the DeltaCCS semantic adopt the principles of conditional rewriting according to the original CCS implementation. We further adopted the *successor* operator on CCS processes to compute the dependency graph for a given DeltaCCS specification. Our MAUDE module enables for applicability analysis on a given DeltaCCS specification. We currently apply the

---

[2] https://www.tu-braunschweig.de/ips/staff/mennicke/tools/deltaccs

model checker MCRL2 [3] for our incremental analysis approach. We analyzed our wiper system example for the liveness property described in the previous section. As already mentioned, applying delta-aware congruence has no immediate effect on the analysis. Instead, we analyzed the components for sensor and control individually for (a) deadlock-freedom and (b) home states (cf. Table 1). Each row in the table represents a sub-variant defined by CCS deltas. The sizes refer to the number of nodes in the syntax trees of the process variants (p. size) and of the processes due to delta-aware congruence (i. size). For deadlock-freedom, *i. results* imply *p. results*, whereas home state properties (potentially) require a re-check of the complete variant if the check of the point of change fails. Please note that *i. sizes* are usually less than half of the according *p. sizes*. For variant 2.4, every property of variant 2.2 is preserved due to Theorem 2.

6   Related Work

Various approaches for a formal reasoning about variability can be found in the recent literature. We discuss the relation to our approach concerning (1) the way variability is specified and (2) the aspects of variability being investigated.

Concerning (1), most formalisms rely on a so-called 150% specification of a variable system. Fischbein et al. were the first to use modal specifications to represent variability by means of modal *refinement* [16]. Thereupon, Larsen et al. [19] and Asirelli et al. [2] applied modal transition systems as basis for behavioral modeling and model checking of product lines.

In contrast, Gruler et al. and Leucker et al. [18,21], as well as Erwig and Walkingshaw [15] express variability in terms of (guarded) *choice* applied at well-defined variation points. Gnesi and Petrocchi [17] present *CL4SPL*, another process algebraic interpretation of product lines, defining variation points via contexts, one possible interpretation of application conditions in DeltaCCS. FLAN by ter Beek et al. [3] adds feature handling mechanisms via an adaptable constraint store with which the process interacts. In addition, FLAN includes dynamic variation points by explicit *installation/removel* of features. Third, for *parametric* variability, *annotations* are attached to variable elements, e. g., transitions [7,12], defining selection conditions for a particular variant [13]. In contrast, less approaches represent variability in a modular way by separating a common from variable system parts. Those modular representations *decompose* systems into artifacts to assemble product variants either on the basis of compatibility notions of module interfaces [1,22,20], or by means of a well-defined composition operator [1]. Other approaches define *transformation rules* to change a core representation into a variant. Besides the delta approach [6], also the $\mathcal{E}$-calculus [5] uses this concept.

Concerning (2), we distinguish formalisms to reason about structural aspects and behavioral impacts of variability. Calculi for structural variability usually investigate criteria for syntactical well-formedness preservation after applying a

---

[3] http://www.mcrl2.org/

particular variability mechanism, i. e., choice [15], composition [1] and transformation [6] of variable artifacts. Calculi for behavioral reasoning mainly focus on adapting model checking techniques to families of systems on the basis of a 150% specification [18,21,7,12,11,19,2]. In contrast, modular approaches to variability-aware model checking mainly rely on rich artifact interfaces [20,22] rather than rigorous change impact analysis as in our approach.

Summarizing, the most related approaches are the $\mathcal{E}$-calculus [5] and PL-CCS [21] both also being built on top of CCS. However, both do not deal with the propagation of (syntactical) changes onto the semantical level, but rather enrich plain CCS by additional operators to express variability. Thereupon, the $\mathcal{E}$-calculus focuses on decidability issues of model checking for different classes of process changes rather than defining novel strategies for a variability-aware model checking, whereas PL-CCS relies on a 150% specification as usual.

7   Conclusions and Future Work

We presented the novel core calculus DeltaCCS for variability modeling to reason about behavioral change in a formal way. We also presented a sample implementation of an incremental model checker for delta-oriented specifications that makes use of the change impact analysis capabilities provided by DeltaCCS. As a future work, we plan to investigate enhancements to the core calculus concerning advanced language constructs, e. g., actions on (typed) variables, as well as different kinds of application conditions including dynamic deltas [14]. Besides state machines, we plan to define further translations of high-level delta-oriented modeling languages as well as programming languages into DeltaCCS and, thereupon, to conduct further evaluations of the approach. Besides reasoning about behavioral change for efficient verification of variable systems, we mainly want to apply the DeltaCCS model checker as incremental model-based test generation tool for software product lines as proposed in our previous work [23].

References

1. Apel, S., Hutchins, D.: A Calculus for Uniform Feature Composition. TOPLAS 32, 1–33 (2008)
2. Asirelli, P., ter Beek, M.H., Fantechi, A., Gnesi, S.: A Model-Checking Tool for Families of Services. In: Bruni, R., Dingel, J. (eds.) FMOODS/FORTE 2011. LNCS, vol. 6722, pp. 44–58. Springer, Heidelberg (2011)
3. ter Beek, M.H., Lafuente, A.L., Petrocchi, M.: Combining declarative and procedural views in the specification and analysis of product families. In: SPLC 2013 Workshops, pp. 10–17. ACM, New York (2013)
4. Bradfield, J., Stirling, C.: Modal mu-Calculi. In: Handbook of Modal Logic, pp. 1–30 (2007)
5. Bravetti, M., Giusto, C.D., Pérez, J.A., Zavattaro, G.: Adaptable Processes. LMCS 8(4) (2012)
6. Clarke, D., Helvensteijn, M., Schaefer, I.: Abstract Delta Modeling. SIGPLAN Notices 46(2), 13–22 (2010)

7. Classen, A., Heymans, P., Schobbens, P.Y., Legay, A.: Symbolic Model Checking of Software Product Lines. In: ICSE 2011, pp. 321–330 (2011)
8. Classen, A., Heymans, P., Schobbens, P.Y., Legay, A., Raskin, J.F.: Model Checking Lots of Systems: Efficient Verification of Temporal Properties in Software Product Lines. In: ICSE 2010 (2010)
9. Clavel, M., Durán, F., Eker, S., Lincoln, P., Martí-Oliet, N., Meseguer, J., Talcott, C.: All About Maude - A High-Performance Logical Framework. LNCS, vol. 4350. Springer, Heidelberg (2007)
10. Clements, P., Northrop, L.: Software Product Lines: Practices and Patterns. Addison-Wesley Longman Publishing Co., Inc. (2001)
11. Cordy, M., Classen, A., Heymans, P., Schobbens, P.Y., Legay, A.: Provelines: A product line of verifiers for software product lines. In: SPLC 2013 Workshops, pp. 141–146. ACM, New York (2013)
12. Cordy, M., Classen, A., Schobbens, P.Y., Heymans, P., Legay, A.: Simulation-Based Abstractions for Software Product-Line Model Checking. In: ICSE 2012 (2012)
13. Czarnecki, K., Antkiewicz, M.: Mapping Features to Models: A Template Approach Based on Superimposed Variants. In: Glück, R., Lowry, M. (eds.) GPCE 2005. LNCS, vol. 3676, pp. 422–437. Springer, Heidelberg (2005)
14. Damiani, F., Padovani, L., Schaefer, I.: A Formal Foundation for Dynamic Delta-oriented Software Product Lines. In: GPCE 2012 (2012)
15. Erwig, M., Walkingshaw, E.: The Choice Calculus: A Representation for Software Variation. ACM TOSEM (2011)
16. Fischbein, D., Uchitel, S., Braberman, V.A.: A Foundation for Behavioural Conformance in Software Product Line Architectures. In: ISSTA 2006, pp. 39–48 (2006)
17. Gnesi, S., Petrocchi, M.: Towards an executable algebra for product lines. In: SPLC 2014, SPLC 2012, pp. 66–73. ACM, New York (2012)
18. Gruler, A., Leucker, M., Scheidemann, K.: Modeling and Model Checking Software Product Lines. In: Barthe, G., de Boer, F.S. (eds.) FMOODS 2008. LNCS, vol. 5051, pp. 113–131. Springer, Heidelberg (2008)
19. Larsen, K.G., Nyman, U., Wąsowski, A.: Modal I/O Automata for Interface and Product Line Theories. In: De Nicola, R. (ed.) ESOP 2007. LNCS, vol. 4421, pp. 64–79. Springer, Heidelberg (2007)
20. Lauenroth, K., Pohl, K., Toehning, S.: Model Checking of Domain Artifacts in Product Line Engineering. In: ASE 2009, pp. 269–280 (2009)
21. Leucker, M., Thoma, D.: A Formal Approach to Software Product Families. In: Margaria, T., Steffen, B. (eds.) ISoLA 2012, Part I. LNCS, vol. 7609, pp. 131–145. Springer, Heidelberg (2012)
22. Li, H.C., Krishnamurthi, S., Fisler, K.: Interfaces for Modular Feature Verification. In: ASE 2002, pp. 195–204 (2002)
23. Lochau, M., Schaefer, I., Kamischke, J., Lity, S.: Incremental Model-based Testing of Delta-oriented Software Product Lines. In: TAP 2012 (2012)
24. Milner, R.: A Calculus of Communicating Systems. Springer, New York (1982)
25. Stirling, C.: An introduction to modal and temporal logics for CCS. Concurrency: Theory, Language, and Architecture (1991)
26. Verdejo, A., Martí-Oliet, N.: Implementing CCS in Maude 2. ENTCS 71, 282–300 (2004)

Coverage Criteria for Behavioural Testing of Software Product Lines

Xavier Devroey[1], Gilles Perrouin[1,*], Axel Legay[2], Maxime Cordy[1,**],
Pierre-Yves Schobbens[1], and Patrick Heymans[1]

[1] PReCISE Research Center, Faculty of Computer Science,
University of Namur, Belgium
{xavier.devroey,maxime.cordy,gilles.perrouin,pierre-yves.schobbens,
patrick.heymans}@unamur.be
[2] INRIA Rennes Bretagne Atlantique, France
axel.legay@inria.fr

Abstract. Featured Transition Systems (FTS) is a mathematical structure to represent the behaviour of software product line in a concise way. The combination of the well-known transition systems approach to formal behavioural modelling with feature expressions was pivotal to the design of efficient verification approaches. Such approaches indeed avoid to consider products' behaviour independently, leading to often exponential savings. Building on this successful structure, we lay the foundations of model-based testing approach to SPLs. We define several FTS-aware coverage criteria and report on our experience combining FTS with usage-based testing for configurable websites.

Keywords: Coverage Criteria, Model Based Testing, Software Product Line Engineering.

1 Introduction

A *Software Product Line* (SPL) "is a set of software-intensive systems that share a common, managed set of features satisfying the specific needs of a particular market segment or mission and that are developed from a common set of core assets in a prescribed way" [8]. Features are thus the key to the discrimination of SPL members by showing their commonalities and differences. Such features are commonly organized in a *Feature Model* (FM) [18] which represents all the possible products of the SPL by expressing relationships and constraints between such features.

As for any software engineering paradigm, providing efficient Quality Assurance (QA) (e.g. model-checking and testing) techniques is essential to SPL engineering success. Devising an approach to SPLs QA requires to deal with the well-known *combinatorial explosion* problem as the number of products to consider for validation is growing exponentially with the number of features. In the

---

* FNRS Postdoctoral Researcher.
** FNRS Research Fellow.

T. Margaria and B. Steffen (Eds.): ISoLA 2014, Part I, LNCS 8802, pp. 336–350, 2014.
© Springer-Verlag Berlin Heidelberg 2014

worst case, no more than 270 features are needed to derive as many products as there are atoms in the universe. Industry reports dealing regularly with thousands of features in their product lines [14,2] and the Linux kernel model is now roughly composed of 8,000 features. Thus, combinatorial explosion poses both theoretical and practical challenges for SPL QA. Depending on the QA approach (model checking or testing) and abstraction level (model, code) several strategies have been designed, which can be positioned on various edges of the product-line analysis cube [26]. Our research strives to provide generic solutions at the model level, both for verification and testing. In [7,5,6], we have proposed model-checking algorithms for *Featured Transition Systems* (FTSs), a variability-aware extension of transition systems. Contrary to enumerating approaches that would visit the state space of each product, our algorithms exploit the structure of the FTS in order to explore common behaviours only once. All those model-checking results have been implemented in ProVeLines,[10] that is a product line of model checkers for FTS.

Automated model-based testing [29] and shared execution [20] are established testing methods that allows test reuse across a set of software. They can thus be used to reduce the SPL testing effort. Even so, the problem remains entire as these methods still need to cover all the products. To address this issue, we previously developed ideas based on sampling and prioritization principles [25,16]. Typical methods in this area define a coverage criterion on an FM (e.g. all the valid couples of features must occur in at least one tested product [25,9]) and extract configurations of interest to be validated. *Combinatorial interaction testing* allows drastic reduction of the configuration space from billions to few dozens or hundreds of products. It is possible to prioritize extracted configurations using coverage metrics or by assigning weights to features [16,17], eventually leading multi-objective SPL testing [16]. This actually helps testers to scope more finely and flexibly relevant products to test than a covering criteria alone. Yet, assigning meaningful weights is cumbersome in the absence of additional information regarding their behaviour.

In line with our preliminary vision [11], we believe that FTS are also suitable to establish a model-based testing framework for SPLs enabling both family-based and product-based strategies and benefiting from the experience gained by the model-checking community. In this paper, we are currently concerned with the definition of various coverage criteria to support FTS-based testing. We adapt existing concepts and structural coverage criteria known for transition systems to the FTS formalism. We then report on our previous experience [12] defining a *usage-based* [31] coverage approach, based on the extraction of Discrete Time Markov Chain (DTMC) from an Apache log of an online course management system. Behaviours of interests (selected according to a given probability interval) in the DTMC are then run on an FTS (assumed to be provided by SPL designers), enabling the projection of associated products and features related to those behaviours and test case generation.

Section 2 provides the background to FTS-based modelling and verification, required to define what FTS-based testing is as well as structural and usage

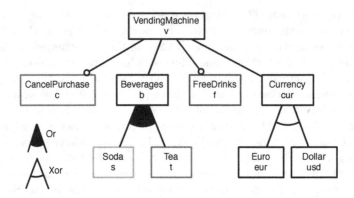

Fig. 1. Soda Vending Machine Feature Diagram [5]

coverage criteria in section 3. Section 5 concludes the paper and outlines future directions.

2   FTSs: Background

A key concern in SPL modeling is how to represent variability. To achieve this purpose, SPL engineers usually reason in terms of features. Relations and constraints between features are usually represented in a Feature Diagram (FD) [18]. For example, Fig. 1 presents the FD of a soda vending machine [6]. A common semantics associated to a FD d (noted $[\![d]\!]$) is the set of all the valid products allowed by d.

Different formalisms may be used to model the behaviour of a system. To allow the explicit mapping from feature to SPL behaviour, Featured Transition Systems (FTS) [6] were proposed. FTSs are Transition Systems (TSs) where each transition is labelled with a feature expression (i.e., a boolean expression over features of the SPL), specifying which products can execute the transition. Thus it is possible to determine products that are the cause of a violation or a failed test.

Definition 1 (Featured Transition System (FTS)). *Formally, an FTS is a tuple $(S, Act, trans, i, d, \gamma)$, where*

- *S is a set of states;*
- *Act a set of actions;*
- *$trans \subseteq S \times Act \times S$ is the transition relation (with $(s_1, \alpha, s_2) \in trans$ sometimes noted $s_1 \xrightarrow{\alpha} s_2$);*
- *$i \in S$ is the initial state;*
- *d is a FD; and $\gamma : trans \rightarrow [\![d]\!] \rightarrow \{\top, \bot\}$ is a total function labelling each transition with a boolean expression over the features, which specifies the products that can execute the transition.*

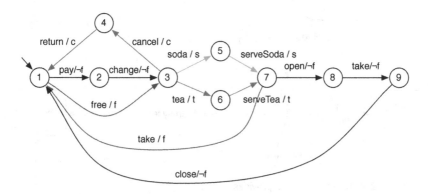

Fig. 2. Soda Vending Machine FTS [5]

Additionally, we consider the *projection* of an FTS onto a product $p \in [\![d]\!]$ noted $fts_{|p}$, the syntactical transformation of removing all transitions labelled with features not in p, thus resulting in the TS representing the behaviour of this particular product (see [6]). For instance: $\neg f$ in Fig. 2 indicates that only products that have not the *free* feature may fire the *pay, change, open, take* and *close* transitions. Thus, only those transitions will appear in their respective projections.

We define the semantics of an FTS as a function that associates each valid product with its set of finite and infinite traces, i.e. all the sequences of actions starting from the initial state available, satisfying the transition relation and such that its transitions are available to that product. According to this definition, an FTS is indeed a behavioural model of a whole SPL. Fig. 2 presents the FTS modeling a vending machine SPL. Without loss of generality, we consider FTSs in which the only allowed loops go through the initial state. This is useful to deal with finite traces in practice [12].

For instance, transition ③ $\xrightarrow{pay/\neg f}$ ④ is labelled with the feature expression c. This means that only the products that do have the feature *Cancel* (c) are able to execute the transition. Other works on modeling software product lines can be found, e.g., in [15,13].

3   SPL Behavioural Testing Using FTSs

Fig. 3 presents the classical testing process in a Model-Based Testing approach for single systems [29]. First, the test engineer builds a test model of the System Under Test (SUT) from its requirements. Then, according to some selection criteria, an abstract test suite (i.e., set of abstract test cases) is automatically generated. For instance, if using Transitions Systems in order to model the behaviour of a SUT, abstract test cases will represent sequences of abstract actions

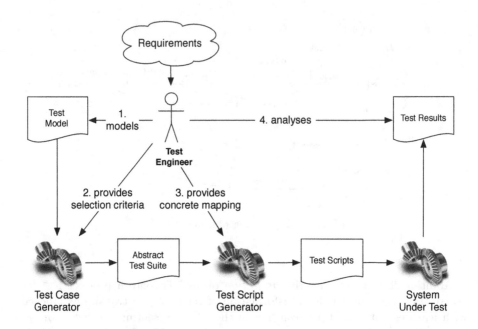

Fig. 3. Model-Based Testing general approach [29]

that should be executed on the SUT [28]. The abstract test cases are concretized using a mapping provided by the test engineer in order to match actions (with input values) of the system before being executed on the SUT. This execution may be manual or automated depending on the formalism of the concrete test cases (e.g., textual description of the operations to perform, automated scripts, etc.). Finally, the results of the tests executions are analysed by the test engineer.

In order to efficiently test SPLs, we propose to adopt FTSs as the formalism to represent SPLs behaviour as the test model of a MBT approach. In [11], we sketched a Quality Assessment (QA) framework with FTSs as the shared behavioural model representation for SPLs. As illustrated in figure 4, FTSs serve as input for QA activities (roughly decomposed in Model-Checking and Testing). Other processing oriented models (e.g., Markov Chain [12], LTL formula [6]) may be joined to the FTS for specific QA activities (e.g., test case prioritization [12]). FTS and computation oriented models are not meant to be used by QA engineer. They are the results of a model to model transformation from abstracted representations of the Feature Diagram (FD), SPL behaviour, formula and/or coverage criteria used by the QA activities. The framework will offer a language (with abstraction and composition mechanisms), *State Diagram Variability Analysis (SDVA)* based on UML state machines to model the behaviour of the SPL. Once the input models are transformed into a FTS and processing oriented models, they can be used to perform model-checking and/or

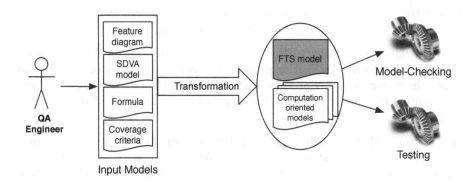

Fig. 4. Framework overview

testing activities (e.g., test case generation). By using a common representation (i.e., FTSs), we believe that the testing community may benefits from the last advances made in model-checking SPLs [6]. In [12] we present a first step in this direction by combining statistical testing techniques with FTSs in order to prioritize product testing.

3.1 Transition Systems MBT Applied to FTSs

In order to select relevant test cases, proper coverage criteria have to be defined at the SPL level. A coverage criteria is an adequacy measure to qualify if a test objective is reached when executing a test suite on a SUT. In classical MBT approaches, when working with state-transitions models (e.g., TS), most commonly used selection criteria are structural criteria: state, transition, transition-pair and path coverage [22,29]. The state/transition coverage criteria specifies that when executing a test suite on the SUT, all the states /transitions (resp.) of the test model are visited/fired (resp.) at least once. The transition-pair coverage specifies that for each state, all the ingoing-outgoing transitions pairs are fired at least once. The path coverage criteria specifies that each path in the test model has to be executed at least once. In the following, we define the notion of test case for a FTS, transpose the classical structural criteria, discuss some observations and redefine the test case selection problem for FTSs.

Abstract Test Case and Test Suite. An abstract test case corresponds to a finite trace (i.e., finite sequence of actions) in the FTS.

Definition 2 (Abstract Test Case). *Let* $fts = (S, Act, trans, i, d, \gamma)$ *be an FTS, let* $atc = (\alpha_1, \ldots, \alpha_n)$ *where* $\alpha_1, \ldots, \alpha_n \in Act$ *be a finite sequence of actions. The abstract test case* atc *is valid iff :*

$$fts \stackrel{(\alpha_1, \ldots, \alpha_n)}{\Longrightarrow}$$

Where $fts \overset{(\alpha_1,...,\alpha_n)}{\Longrightarrow}$ is equivalent to $i \overset{(\alpha_1,...,\alpha_n)}{\Longrightarrow}$, meaning that there exists a state $s_k \in S$ with sequence of transitions labelled $(\alpha_1,...,\alpha_n)$ from i to s_k.

This definition is similar to classical test case definitions for TS test models [22]. However, for an FTS, it is possible to extract sequences of actions that cannot be executed by any product of the SPL (e.g., the related transitions contains mutually exclusive features). This leads us to the definition of an executable abstract test case:

Definition 3 (Executable Abstract Test Case). *Let $fts = (S, Act, trans, i, d, \gamma)$ be an FTS, let $atc = (\alpha_1,...,\alpha_n)$ where $\alpha_1,...,\alpha_n \in Act$ represents a sequence of actions in fts be an abstract test case. An abstract test case atc is executable if it can be executed by at least one product of the product line:*

$$\exists p \in [\![d]\!] : fts_{|p} \overset{(\alpha_1,...,\alpha_n)}{\Longrightarrow}$$

Where $fts_{|p} \overset{(\alpha_1,...,\alpha_n)}{\Longrightarrow}$ is equivalent to $i \overset{(\alpha_1,...,\alpha_n)}{\Longrightarrow}$, meaning that there exists a state $s_k \in S$ with sequence of transitions labelled $(\alpha_1,...,\alpha_n)$ from i to s_k in the projection of the FTS onto p.

We make a difference between abstract test case and *executable* abstract test case. Contrary to executable abstract test case, an abstract test case has not to be necessary executable by at least one product of the SPL. Since the FTS is a model of the behaviour of the SPL, it may be interesting to use abstract test cases which may not (according to the model) be executed by any product in order to do mutation testing (by mutating feature expressions), security testing (to detect undesired behaviours), etc. If this abstract test case can be executed on a concrete implementation, it reveals a modelling issue or an implementation error. Similarly:

Definition 4 (Executable Abstract Test Suite). *An abstract test suite is a (possibly empty) finite set of abstract test cases. An executable abstract test suite is an abstract test suite that contains only executable abstract test cases.*

An "empty" abstract test suite has no practical value, but it can be the result of a too restrictive or inconsistent selection process. However, we keep this liberal definition to support the definition of selection procedures in the general case.

3.2 Coverage Criteria

In order to efficiently select abstract test cases, the test engineer has to provide selection criteria [29]. We redefine hereafter classical structural selection criteria as a function that, for a given FTS and an executable abstract test suite, returns a value between 0 and 1 specifying the coverage degree of the executable abstract test suite over the FTS (0 meaning no coverage and 1 the maximal coverage). As for TS [29], we consider only coverage criteria for states reachable from the initial state (a state s_i is reachable iff $\exists p \in [\![d]\!] \wedge \exists \alpha_1,...,\alpha_n \in Act$ such as $fts_{|p} \overset{(\alpha_1,...,\alpha_n)}{\Longrightarrow} s_i$). Formally :

Definition 5 (Coverage Criterion). *A coverage criterion is a function cov that associates an FTS and an abstract test suite over this FTS to a real value in* $[0, 1]$

Classical structural coverage criteria are defined as follow, we illustrate each coverage criteria with test suites satisfying the criteria for the Soda Vending Machine FTS [5] defined in figure 2 :

Definition 6 (State/All-States Coverage). *The state coverage criterion relates to the ratio between the states visited by the test cases pertaining to the abstract test suite and all the states of the FTS. When the value of the function equals to 1, the abstract test suite satisfies* **all-states coverage**.

The all-states coverage criteria is the weakest structural coverage criteria, it specifies that when executing the test suite, each state has to be visited at least once. On the Soda Vending Machine, an all-states covering abstract test suite may be:

$$\{(pay, change, soda, serveSoda, open, take, close)$$
$$(free, tea, serveTea, take); (free, cancel, return)\}$$

Definition 7 (Transition/All-Transitions Coverage). *Transition coverage relates to the ratio between transitions covered when running abstract test cases on the FTS and the total number of transitions of the FTS that are executable by at least one valid product. When this ratio equals to 1, then the abstract test suite satisfies* **all-transitions** *coverage.*

The all-transitions coverage specifies that, ideally, each transition is fired at least once when executing the abstract test suite on the FTS. In this case, a satisfying abstract test suite for a coverage of 1 on the Soda Vending Machine may be the same as the one defined for the all-state coverage.

Definition 8 (Transition-Pairs/All-Transition-Pairs Coverage). *The transition-pairs coverage considers adjacent transitions successively entering and leaving a given state. As for transition coverage, only pairs that are executable by at least one product are considered in the ratio. When the coverage function reaches the value of 1, then the abstract test suite covers* **all-transition-pairs**.

The all-transition-pairs coverage specifies that for each state, each couple of entering/leaving transition has to be fired at least once. On the soda vending machine, an abstract test suite with a all-transitions-pairs coverage of 1 may be:

$$\{(pay, change, soda, serveSoda, open, take, close); (pay, changecancel, return);$$
$$(pay, change, tea, serveTea, open, take, close); (free, soda, serveSoda, take);$$
$$(free, tea, serveTea, take); (free, cancel, return)\}$$

Definition 9 (Path/All-Paths Coverage). *Path coverage takes into account executable paths, that is sequence of actions* $(\alpha_1, \ldots, \alpha_n)$ *from i to i such that*

$\exists p \in [\![d]\!] : fts_{|p} \overset{(\alpha_1,...,\alpha_n)}{\Longrightarrow} i$. *If the coverage function value computing the ratio between executable paths covered by the test cases runs on the FTS and total executable paths in the FTS is* 1, **all-paths** *coverage has been reached.*

The all-path coverage specifies that each executable path in the FTS should be followed at least once when executing the abstract test suite on it. On the soda vending machine, it gives an executable abstract test suite equal to the one defined for all-transitions-pair coverage.

3.3   Test Case Product Selection

Once the test cases are selected, they have to be concretized (step 3 in Fig. 3) in order to (i) get the implementation of the products on which the concrete test cases will be executed and (ii) get the concrete actions to perform with the adequate input values for each test case. This last point may be done using existing concretization techniques once the products are selected [22,29]. For (i), the implementations able to execute a given abstract test case atc in a FTS corresponds to all the products (i.e., valid configurations) of the FD ($[\![d]\!]$) that satisfy all the feature expressions associated to the transitions fired in the FTS when executing atc :

Definition 10 (Abstract Test Case Product Selection). *Given a FTS* $fts = (S, Act, trans, i, d, \gamma)$ *and an abstract test case* $atc = (\alpha_1, \ldots, \alpha_n)$ *with* $(\alpha_1, \ldots, \alpha_n) \in Act$, *the set of products able to execute* atc *is defined as:*

$$prod(fts, atc) = \{p \in [\![d]\!] \mid fts_{|p} \overset{(\alpha_1,...,\alpha_n)}{\Longrightarrow}\}$$

It corresponds to all the products able to execute the sequence of actions in the abstract test case.

Similarly, for an abstract test suite, we have:

Definition 11 (Abstract Test Suite Product Selection). *Given a FTS* $fts = (S, Act, trans, i, d, \gamma)$ *and an abstract test suite* $ats = \{atc_1, \ldots, atc_n\}$, *the set of products able/needed to execute* ats:

$$prods(fts, ats) = \bigcup_{k=1}^{n} prod(fts, atc_i)$$

Since the main interest in SPL testing is to reduce the number of products to test, we also define the minimal set of products needed to execute an abstract test suite.

Definition 12 (P-Minimal Abstract Test Suite Product Selection). *Let* fts *be an FTS and* ats *be an abstract test suite. A minimal set of products needed to execute* ats *over* fts *is a minimal subset* $pMinProd(fts, ats)$ *of* $prods(fts, ats)$ *such that* $\forall atc \in ats : \exists p \in pMinProd(fts, ats)$ *such that* $fts_{|p} \overset{atc}{\Longrightarrow}$

Test Case Minimality. Since FTSs represents all the TSs of all the possible products of the SPL, it is possible that some coverage criteria may not be completely achieved ($\forall atc : cov(fts, ats) < 1$). For instance, some states may not be reachable during the execution of any valid product behaviour. From the definitions here above, we derive the following properties :

Property 1 (Minimal Test Suite). An executable abstract test suite *ats* over a given FTS $fts = (S, Act, trans, i, d, \gamma)$ is minimal w.r.t. a coverage criteria *cov* iff $\nexists ats'$ such that ats' is executable and $\#ats' < \#ats$ and $cov(ats', fts) \geq cov(ats, fts)$. In other words, an executable abstract test suite is minimal if there exists no smaller executable abstract test suite with a better coverage.

Property 2 (P-Minimal Test Suite). An executable abstract test suite *ats* over a given FTS $fts = (S, Act, trans, i, d, \gamma)$ is product-minimal (p-minimal) regarding a coverage criteria *cov* iff $\nexists ats'$ such as ats' is executable and $(cov(ats', fts) \geq cov(ats, fts)) \wedge (\# pMinProd(ats', fts) < \# pMinProd(ats, fts))$. A p-minimal executable abstract test suite for a given coverage criteria over an FTS represents the minimal set of executable abstract test cases (with the best coverage) such as the number of products needed to execute all of them is minimal.

For instance, the abstract test suite $\{(pay, change, soda, serveSoda, open, take, close); (free, tea, serveTea, take); (free, cancel, return)\}$ is minimal for the all-states-coverage criteria but not p-minimal since it needs at least two different products (i.e., *free* and *not free* machines) to be executed on the FTS in Fig. 1. A p-minimal abstract test suite satisfying the all-paths coverage could be: $\{(pay, change, soda, serveSoda, open, take, close); (pay, change, tea, serveTea, open, take, close); (pay, change, cancel, return)\}$. Which only needs one product to execute the abstract test suite.

When designing an abstract test suite using a coverage criteria, the most interesting product to select in order to execute this abstract test suite is the one who will achieve the best coverage using this abstract test suite. We define here the p-coverage as the coverage reached by the execution of an executable abstract test suite for a given product and p-coverage upper bound as the product which will be able to execute the subset of an abstract test suite with the best coverage.

Definition 13 (P-Coverage). *Let ats be an abstract test suite over fts, a given FTS, and a covering criteria cov(ats, fts). Given a product $p \in prod(ats, fts)$ and $ats_p \subseteq ats$ the set of all abstract test cases of ats executable by p. The p-coverage is the coverage reached when executing ats_p :*

$$p - coverage = cov(fts, ats_p).$$

Equipped with this notion of product coverage by a subset of the test suites, we may look for the product(s) that optimize(s) a given coverage function.

Definition 14 (P-Coverage Upper Bound). *Given an executable abstract test suite ats over a given FTS $fts = (S, Act, trans, i, d, \gamma)$ and a covering criteria cov(ats, fts). Given a product $p \in prod(ats, fts)$ and $ats_p \subseteq ats$*

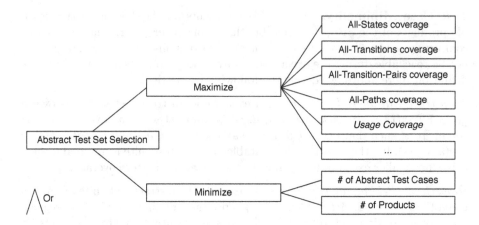

Fig. 5. Abstract Test Suite Selection problem

the abstract test suite executable by p. The product p will be the p-cov upper bound iff $\nexists ats'_p \subset ats$ executable by $p' \in prod(ats, fts)$ such as $cov(ats'_p, fts) > cov(ats_p, fts)$.

For instance, the p-all-transition-pairs upper bounds products are :

- $\{VendingMachine, CancelPurchase, Beverage, Soda, Tea, Currency, Euro\}$
- $\{VendingMachine, CancelPurchase, Beverage, Soda, Tea, Currency, Dollar\}$

Each one with a all-transition-pairs coverage of 68.75%. It means that concretizing the abstract test suite derived to achieve a all-transition-pairs coverage using one of those products and executing the concretized test cases on the selected product will achieve a all-transition-pairs coverage of 68.75% for the *behaviour of the SPL*.

3.4   SPL Test Case Selection

As illustrated in Fig. 5, the abstract test case selection problem may be formulated as an optimisation problem. In its most simple expression, the considered selection criteria has to be maximised and either the size of the executable abstract test suite (minimal test suite) or the number of product needed to execute the test suite (p-minimal test suite) has to be minimized. Of course, in reality we expect more complex situations where a finer grained objective function will be designed. For instance by adding weights to features in the FD [16] and/or transitions [1] in the FTS and try to minimize the total cost of the test suite.

Adding weight to transitions is a classical approach developed in statistical testing where weight (between 0 and 1) represents the probability of a transition

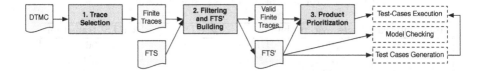

Fig. 6. Test-Case Prioritization process [12]

to be fired. In our previous work [12], we apply this idea to product lines in order to prioritize behaviours and products to test. In the following section, we define one more additional coverage criteria: the *Usage Coverage*, specifying that the selected abstract test suite should cover the most or least common behaviours of the SPL.

3.5   Usage Coverage Criteria

In [12], FTSs are combined to a Deterministic Timed Markov Chain (DTMC) in order to select and prioritize SPL behaviours to assess. The result of the process is a FTS' representing a subset of the original FTS that has to be assessed (using testing and/or model checking) in priority. The complete process is presented in figure 6. First, traces are selected in the DTMC according to their probability to happen (step 1), e.g., probability between a lower and upper bound, most probable traces, etc. A trace represents a sequence of actions in the DTMC. Since the DTMC does not have any notion of features (which allows us to use existing statistical testing tools like MeTeLo [1]), the selected traces have to be filtered using the FTS to ensure they can be performed by at least one valid product (step 2). By pruning the FTS and keeping only transitions fired when executing selected traces, we get a FTS', representing a (priority) subset of the original FTS. Optionally, in step 3, valid traces, and FTS' are used to generate valid configurations (i.e., products) which have to be tested in priority. We assessed the feasibility of this process on an existing system (see section 4 of [12]), the local Claroline instance at the University of Namur (an online course management system) using a 5Go Apache access log to build the DTMC, a FTS with 107 states and 11236 transitions and a feature digram with 44 features. In this first version, we run a depth first search algorithm 4 times in order to get behaviours with probability between $[10^{-4}; 1]$, $[10^{-5}; 1]$, $[10^{-6}; 1]$ and $[10^{-7}; 1]$. The average probabilities of the traces selected in the DTMC and the size of the generated FTS' are presented in Tab. 1.

We intend to combine the usage coverage criteria with other structural coverage criteria in order to asses the behaviour of a SPL. The classical scenario we imagine would be:

1. The test engineer select the lowest or highest probable usage of the system based on a DTMC and build a FTS' (using [12]), prioritized subset of the

Table 1. Claroline Feasability Assessment Results [12]

Proba. interval	Traces avg. proba.	σ	# FTS' states	# FTS' transitions
$[10^{-4}; 1]$	$2,06E^{-3}$	$1,39E^{-2}$	16	66
$[10^{-5}; 1]$	$3,36E^{-4}$	$5,46E^{-3}$	36	224
$[10^{-6}; 1]$	$5,26E^{-5}$	$2,12E^{-3}$	50	442
$[10^{-7}; 1]$	$8,10E^{-6}$	$8,18E^{-4}$	69	844

original FTS. We did not make any assumption on how the usage model is build. In the experiment presented in [12], the usage model was obtain from actual usage of the system using an Apache log. It could also be done manually by a system expert who will tag the transitions in the DTMC with probabilities based on its own knowledge of the system [27].

2. The test engineer select a minimal or p-minimal (executable or not) abstract test suite in the FTS' using a structural coverage criteria.
3. The test engineer concretize this abstract test suite and execute it on one product of the SPL.

4   Related Work

Other strategies to perform SPLs testing have been proposed. One of those considers incremental testing in the SPL context [30,24,21]. For example, Lochau et al. [21] proposed a model-based approach that shifts from one product to another by applying "deltas" to statemachine models. These deltas enable automatic reuse/adaptation of test model and derivation of retest obligations. Oster et al. [24] extend combinatorial interaction testing with the possibility to specify a predefined set of products in the configuration suite to be tested. There are also approaches focused on the SPL code by building variability-aware interpreters for various languages [19]. Based on symbolic execution techniques such interpreters are able to run a very large set of products with respect to one given test case [23]. In [4], Cichos et al. use the notion of 150% test model (i.e., a test model of the behaviour of a product line) and test goal to derive test cases for a product line but do not redefine coverage criteria at the SPL level. In [3], Beohar et al. propose to adapt the *ioco* framework proposed by Tretmans [28] to FTSs. Contrary to this approach, we do not seek exhaustive testing of an implementation but rather to select relevant abstract test cases based on the criteria provided by the test engineer.

5   Conclusion and Perspectives

In this paper, we have established the preliminary foundations to support SPL testing using FTS by defining dedicated testing concepts and providing several coverage criteria to support test generation. Next steps naturally include the design of strategies that realize the extraction of behaviours based on such criteria. Experience and optimisation realised for model-checking algorithms will be key to the design of efficient and scalable FTS traversals. We also plan to devise an FTS-aware random test generation strategy (e.g. systematically producing random executable abstract test cases). Finally, we also plan to combine such criteria with each other and with test case selection based on temporal properties. Our approach will be integrated with the ProVeLines family of SPL model-checkers [10].

References

1. ALL4TEC: MaTeLo, http://www.all4tec.net/index.php/en/model-based-testing (last visit January 31, 2014)
2. Astesana, J.M., Cosserat, L., Fargier, H.: Constraint-based vehicle configuration: A case study. In: 2010 22nd IEEE International Conference on Tools with Artificial Intelligence (ICTAI), vol. 1, pp. 68–75 (October 2010)
3. Beohar, H., Mousavi, M.R.: Spinal Test Suites for Software Product Lines. ArXiv e-prints (2014)
4. Cichos, H., Oster, S., Lochau, M., Schürr, A.: Model-based Coverage-driven Test Suite Generation for Software Product Lines. In: Whittle, J., Clark, T., Kühne, T. (eds.) MODELS 2011. LNCS, vol. 6981, pp. 425–439. Springer, Heidelberg (2011)
5. Classen, A.: Modelling and Model Checking Variability-Intensive Systems. Ph.D. thesis, PReCISE Research Center, Faculty of Computer Science, University of Namur, FUNDP (2011)
6. Classen, A., Cordy, M., Schobbens, P.Y., Heymans, P., Legay, A., Raskin, J.F.: Featured Transition Systems: Foundations for Verifying Variability-Intensive Systems and their Application to LTL Model Checking. TSE PP(99), 1–22 (2013)
7. Classen, A., Heymans, P., Schobbens, P.Y., Legay, A., Raskin, J.F.: Model checking lots of systems: efficient verification of temporal properties in software product lines. In: ICSE 2010, pp. 335–344. ACM (2010)
8. Clements, P., Northrop, L.: Software Product Lines: Practices and Patterns. Addison Wesley, Reading (2001)
9. Cohen, M., Dwyer, M., Shi, J.: Interaction testing of highly-configurable systems in the presence of constraints. In: ISSTA 2007, pp. 129–139 (2007)
10. Cordy, M., Classen, A., Heymans, P., Schobbens, P.Y., Legay, A.: Provelines: A product-line of verifiers for software product lines. In: SPLC 2013 Workshops, pp. 141–146. ACM (2013)
11. Devroey, X., Cordy, M., Perrouin, G., Kang, E.-Y., Schobbens, P.-Y., Heymans, P., Legay, A., Baudry, B.: A vision for behavioural model-driven validation of software product lines. In: Margaria, T., Steffen, B. (eds.) ISoLA 2012, Part I. LNCS, vol. 7609, pp. 208–222. Springer, Heidelberg (2012)
12. Devroey, X., Perrouin, G., Cordy, M., Schobbens, P.Y., Legay, A., Heymans, P.: Towards statistical prioritization for software product lines testing. In: VaMoS 2014, pp. 10:1–10:7. ACM (2013)
13. Fantechi, A., Gnesi, S.: Formal modeling for product families engineering. In: SPLC 2008, pp. 193–202 (2008)
14. Flores, R., Krueger, C., Clements, P.: Mega-scale product line engineering at general motors. In: SPLC 2012, pp. 259–268. ACM (2012)
15. Gruler, A., Leucker, M., Scheidemann, K.: Modeling and model checking software product lines. In: Barthe, G., de Boer, F.S. (eds.) FMOODS 2008. LNCS, vol. 5051, pp. 113–131. Springer, Heidelberg (2008)

16. Henard, C., Papadakis, M., Perrouin, G., Klein, J., Traon, Y.L.: Multi-objective test generation for software product lines. In: SPLC 2013, pp. 62–71. ACM (2013)

17. Johansen, M.F., Haugen, Ø., Fleurey, F., Eldegard, A.G., Syversen, T.: Generating better partial covering arrays by modeling weights on sub-product lines. In: France, R.B., Kazmeier, J., Breu, R., Atkinson, C. (eds.) MODELS 2012. LNCS, vol. 7590, pp. 269–284. Springer, Heidelberg (2012)

18. Kang, K.C., Cohen, S.G., Hess, J.A., Novak, W.E., Spencer Peterson, A.: Feature-Oriented domain analysis (FODA) feasibility study. Tech. rep., Soft. Eng. Inst., Carnegie Mellon Univ. (1990)

19. Kästner, C., von Rhein, A., Erdweg, S., Pusch, J., Apel, S., Rendel, T., Ostermann, K.: Toward variability-aware testing. In: FOSD 2012, pp. 1–8. ACM (2012)

20. Kim, C.H.P., Khurshid, S., Batory, D.S.: Shared execution for efficiently testing product lines. In: ISSRE 2012, pp. 221–230 (2012)

21. Lochau, M., Schaefer, I., Kamischke, J., Lity, S.: Incremental model-based testing of delta-oriented software product lines. In: Brucker, A.D., Julliand, J. (eds.) TAP 2012. LNCS, vol. 7305, pp. 67–82. Springer, Heidelberg (2012)

22. Mathur, A.P.: Foundations of software testing. Pearson Education (2008)

23. Nguyen, H.V., Kästner, C., Nguyen, T.N.: Exploring variability-aware execution for testing plugin-based web applications. In: ICSE 2014. IEEE (2014)

24. Oster, S., Markert, F., Ritter, P.: Automated incremental pairwise testing of software product lines. In: Bosch, J., Lee, J. (eds.) SPLC 2010. LNCS, vol. 6287, pp. 196–210. Springer, Heidelberg (2010)

25. Perrouin, G., Oster, S., Sen, S., Klein, J., Baudry, B., Traon, Y.L.: Pairwise testing for software product lines: comparison of two approaches. Software Quality Journal 20(3-4), 605–643 (2012)

26. von Rhein, A., Apel, S., Kästner, C., Thüm, T., Schaefer, I.: The pla model: On the combination of product-line analyses. In: VaMoS 2013, p. 14. ACM (2013)

27. Samih, H.: Relating Variability Modeling and Model-Based Testing for Software Product Lines Testing. In: Weise, C., Nielsen, B. (eds.) Proceedings of the ICTSS 2012 Ph.D. Workshop, pp. 18–22. Aalborg University, Department of Computer Science, Aalborg, Denmark (2012)

28. Tretmans, J.: Model based testing with labelled transition systems. In: Hierons, R.M., Bowen, J.P., Harman, M. (eds.) FORTEST. LNCS, vol. 4949, pp. 1–38. Springer, Heidelberg (2008)

29. Utting, M., Legeard, B.: Practical Model-Based Testing: A Tools Approach. Morgan Kaufmann (2007)

30. Uzuncaova, E., Khurshid, S., Batory, D.: Incremental test generation for software product lines. IEEE Transactions on Software Engineering 36(3), 309–322 (2010)

31. Whittaker, J.A., Thomason, M.G.: A markov chain model for statistical software testing. TSE 20(10), 812–824 (1994)

Challenges in Modelling and Analyzing Quantitative Aspects of Bike-Sharing Systems[*]

Maurice H. ter Beek[1], Alessandro Fantechi[1,2], and Stefania Gnesi[1]

[1] ISTI–CNR, Via G. Moruzzi 1, Pisa, Italy
{terbeek,gnesi}@isti.cnr.it
[2] DINFO, Università di Firenze, Via S. Marta 3, Firenze, Italy
alessandro.fantechi@unifi.it

Abstract. Bike-sharing systems are becoming popular not only as a sustainable means of transportation in the urban environment, but also as a challenging case study that presents interesting run-time optimization problems. As a side-study within a research project aimed at quantitative analysis that used such a case study, we have observed how the deployed systems enjoy a wide variety of different features. We have therefore applied variability analysis to define a family of bike-sharing systems, and we have sought support in available tools. We have so established a tool chain that includes (academic) tools that provide different functionalities regarding the analysis of software product lines, from feature modelling to product derivation and from quantitative evaluation of the attributes of products to model checking value-passing modal specifications. The tool chain is currently experimented inside the mentioned project as a complement to more sophisticated product-based analysis techniques.

1 Introduction

Bike-sharing systems (BSS) are becoming popular not only as a sustainable means of smart transportation in the urban environment, but also as a challenging case study that presents interesting run-time optimization problems.

A case study of the EU project QUANTICOL (http://www.quanticol.eu) concerns the quantitative analysis of BSS seen as collective adaptive systems (CAS). The design of CAS must be supported by a powerful and well-founded framework for quantitative modelling and analysis. CAS consist of a large number of spatially distributed entities, which may be competing for shared resources even when collaborating to reach common goals. The nature of CAS, together with the importance of the societal goals they address, mean that it is imperative to carry out thorough analyses of their design and to investigate all aspects of their behaviour before they are put into operation. In this context it is important to realize that the design and behaviour of the individual entities from which a CAS is composed, may exhibit variability not only in the kind of features but also in the quantitative characteristics of features themselves.

[*] Research partly supported by the EU FP7-ICT FET-Proactive project QUANTI-COL (600708) and by the Italian MIUR project CINA (PRIN 2010LHT4KM).

T. Margaria and B. Steffen (Eds.): ISoLA 2014, Part I, LNCS 8802, pp. 351–367, 2014.
© Springer-Verlag Berlin Heidelberg 2014

Starting from the BSS case study identified in QUANTICOL, we sought to apply variability analyses on a small bike-sharing product line. For this purpose, we modelled a family of BSS, covering the specification of a discrete feature model [21], the specification of several non-functional quantitative properties, and behavioural specifications. To specify and analyze this family of BSS, we chose to adopt existing feature modelling and analysis tools rather than to build yet another tool. Looking for academic, freely available tools, we realized that no single tool was ready to fully satisfy our expectations. This led to the conclusion that the best option was the synergic use of the tool chain in Fig. 1, including S.P.L.O.T. [23], FeatureIDE [28], Clafer [15] and ClaferMOO [25], and VMC [12].

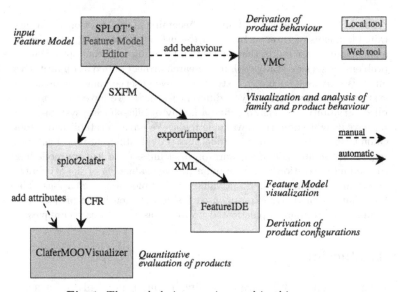

Fig. 1. The tool chain experimented in this paper

This tool chain includes academic tools that provide different functionalities regarding the analysis of software product lines, from feature modelling to product derivation and from quantitative evaluation of the attributes of products to model checking value-passing modal specifications.

We first specified a feature model of a BSS in S.P.L.O.T., which is a de facto standard for sharing feature models publicly that also allows to edit, debug, analyze, and configure feature models, after which this model was imported in FeatureIDE [28] for visualization in the FODA syntax [21,13] and automatic code generation in the future. The model was then imported in Clafer and, after the manual addition of feature attributes and global quantitative constraints over these attributes, ClaferMOOVisualizer was used for quantitative analyses and multi-objective optimization of the resulting attributed feature model. Finally, we manually specified several behavioural models of BSS in the recent extension of VMC that can handle data through value passing, allowing the automatic generation of one, some, or all valid product behaviours and the simulation, visualization, and verification of either the full product line or a set of its valid products by properties expressed in a value-passing action-based branching-time modal temporal logic. The tool chain is currently further experimented to complement more sophisticated product-based analysis techniques in QUANTICOL.

As far as we know, there was no study available concerning the possible different realizations of a BSS starting from its description as a product line and then using methods and tools developed in the field of software product lines to

1. analyze the set of admissible products by inspecting the possible variability;
2. take into account the different attributes that may be used to measure, e.g., the development cost of the derivable products or the customer satisfaction;
3. verify satefy and liveness (e.g., availabiliy) properties of a behavioural model.

The paper is organized as follows. In §2 we introduce the bike-sharing case study. In §3 we show how to model the BSS with SPLOT and how to import it into FeatureIDE. In §4 we instead show how to import this model in Clafer, after which we extend it with attributes and evaluate it with ClaferMOOVisualizer. Finally, in §5, we consider a concrete BSS and model and analyze its behaviour with VMC. Our conclusions from this experience are presented in §6, followed by a list of future work in §7. The complete specifications of all models used in the case study presented in this paper are available in [9] and online at URL: http://milner.inf.ed.ac.uk/wiki/files/yOR2Q6q/TRQC072014pdf.html.

2   BSS: Bike-Sharing Systems

An increasing number of cities of varying size are adopting fully automated public bike-sharing systems (BSS) as a green urban mode of transportation [24]. The concept is simple (a user arrives at a station, pays for a bike, uses it for a while and returns it to a station) and their benefits multiple, including the reduction of vehicular traffic (congestion), pollution, and energy consumption.

The current third generation technology-based BSS have almost nothing (but the bikes) in common with the first generation free BSS introduced in Amsterdam nearly half a century ago. *Vélib'*, the well-known and highly successful BSS of the city of Paris, currently consists of over 20,000 bikes and some 1,800 stations. There are now similar BSS in more than 500 cities worldwide. The largest BSS can be found in China with upto 90,000 bikes and over 2,000 stations, one every 100 meters. Fourth generation BSS are already being developed. These include movable and solar-powered stations, electric bikes and smartphone real-time availability applications [24].

In the context of QUANTICOL we are collaborating with "PisaMo S.p.A. azienda per la mobilità pisana", an in-house public mobility company of the Municipality of Pisa. They recently introduced the public BSS *CicloPi* in the city of Pisa, which currently consists of roughly 140 bikes and 14 stations.

More in detail, a BSS consists of parking stations distributed over a city, typically in close proximity to other public transportation hubs such as subway and tram stations. (Subscribed) users may rent an available bike and drop it off at any station in the city. To improve the efficiency and the user satisfaction of BSS, the load between the different stations may be balanced, e.g., by using incentive schemes that may change the behaviour of users but also by efficient (dynamic) redistribution of bikes between stations.

3 Modelling a BSS: From S.P.L.O.T. to FeatureIDE

To develop an initial feature model we performed a requirements elicitation in the form of text mining a set of documents from the literature describing current BSS (mainly [24]) and the specific BSS of Pisa [20,26]. This allowed us to extract the main features of BSS and to identify their commonalities and variabilities. This led to bikes equipped with an optional localization feature (RFID or GPS) and an optional antithieves feature (which requires GPS though), parking stations with a capacity that is either fixed permanent or fixed portable or flexible, optional maintenance and redistribution of bikes, and – finally – an optional incentive scheme based on rewards. Obviously we could have taken many more features of BSS into account, but we believe that the chosen ones represent a sufficient starting point for this exploratory study.

The feature model representation in Fig. 2 was created with S.P.L.O.T.'s feature model editor, which is an online application developed by Marcílio Mendonça and others at the University of Waterloo [23]. Software Product Lines Online Tools is actually a web portal which integrates a number of research tools. S.P.L.O.T. allows to edit, debug, analyze, configure, share and download feature models. In particular, it allows to save models online to consult them later or to export them in the SXFM format.[1] It does not allow code generation, nor does it provide a way to render feature models in the graphical FODA syntax [21,13]. The main reason for which we nevertheless opted for S.P.L.O.T. as the first tool in the chain is that it is a de facto standard for sharing feature models publicly (its feature model repository currently has nearly 400 entries).

A tool that does allow to directly generate code (Java or C++) as well as a graphical representation in the FODA syntax, starting from a feature model, is FeatureIDE [28], which is an Eclipse plug-in developed mainly at the University of Magdeburg. FeatureIDE actually supports the full lifecycle of a software product line, from domain engineering to feature-oriented software development. However, it operates on feature models in an XML format. To nevertheless be able to use FeatureIDE to work with feature models created with S.P.L.O.T. (or directly with one of the feature models in its repository), it thus becomes necessary to translate the SXFM format. To this aim, FeatureIDE has a feature that automatically converts SXFM files into the desired XML format.

Using FeatureIDE's visualization functionalities we subsequently obtained the graphical representation of this feature model depicted in Fig. 3 (with an implicit conjunction among the 5 constraints). From this model, FeatureIDE allows the user to generate one of the 60,840 valid configurations (i.e., products).

---

[1] Simple XML Feature Model, a concise textual format to denote feature models.

Feature Diagram

- ⊟ 🏛 Bikesharing
  - ⊟ ○ Status
    - ⊟ ⋏ [1..*]
      - ▫ RTInfoWeb
      - ▫ AllBikesNow
  - ⊟ ● Bike
    - ⊟ ○ Localization
      - ⊟ ⋏ [1..*]
        - ▫ GPS
        - ▫ RFID
    - ○ Antithieves
  - ⊟ ● DockingStation
    - ⊟ ⋏ [1..1]
      - ▫ Fixed
      - ▫ FixedPortable
      - ▫ Flexible
    - ○ Maintenance
  - ⊟ ○ Redistribution
    - ○ Reward
  - ⊞ ● Users

Cross-Tree Constraints

- 🔲 (¬AllBikesNow ∨ GPS)
- 🔲 (GPS ∨ ¬Antithieves)
- 🔲 (Keycard ∨ ¬KeycardDispenser)
- 🔲 (¬Keycard ∨ KeycardReader)
- 🔲 (¬Keycard ∨ KeycardDispenser)

Click to create a constraint

Feature Information Table

Id:
Name:
Description:
Type:
#Children:
Tree level:

Update Feature Model

Feature Model Statistics

#Features	29
#Mandatory	5
#Optional	10
#XOR groups	1
#OR groups	4
#Grouped	13
#Cross-Tree Constraints (CTC)	5
CTCR (%)	0.21
#CTC distinct vars	6
CTC clause density	0.83

Feature Model Analysis

✔	Consistency	Consistent
✔	Dead Features	None
✔	Core Features	6 feature(s)
✔	Valid Configurations	60,840

Fig. 2. The BSS feature model in S.P.L.O.T., not showing the Users' subfeatures

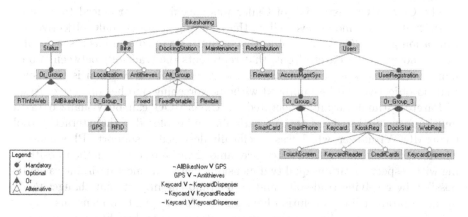

Fig. 3. The complete BSS Feature Model in FeatureIDE

4   Adding Attributes to the BSS: From S.P.L.O.T. to ClaferMOOVisualizer

Until now we considered ordinary feature models, i.e., feature diagrams modelling the hierarchical parent-child relationships between a set of features as a rooted tree and possibly some additional cross-tree constraints. As outlined in the introduction, in the context of QUANTICOL we are specifically interested in quantitative analyses of BSS, meaning that we consider the behaviour of the components of a BSS to exhibit variability not only in the kind of features they possess, but also in the quantitative (non-functional) characteristics of their features. To achieve this, we manually add attributes and quantitative constraints among attributes and features to the BSS specification and perform quantitative analyses, i.e., we perform modelling and analysis of attributed feature models [13]. Neither S.P.L.O.T. nor FeatureIDE currently cater for attributed feature models, but FeatureIDE is being extended to support quality attributes [28].

Clafer, a lightweight textual modelling language for software (product lines) developed jointly at the University of Waterloo and the IT University of Copenhagen, does allow attributed feature modelling [15]. Moreover, splot2clafer, a small tool written in Java, automatically translates files from S.P.L.O.T.'s SXFM format into the CFR format of Clafer.

In Clafer, each feature can have an associated attribute and quality constraints can be specified either globally or within the context of a feature. Think, e.g., of associating a cost to each feature and a global constraint that only allows products (feature configurations) whose total costs remain within a predefined threshold value. This is an example of a single optimization objective, but usually there can be more than one attribute associated to a feature, leading to multiple optimization objectives. It suffices to imagine that each feature also has a value for user satisfaction associated to it and while the objective might be to minimize the cost of a product it might at the same time be desirable to maximize user satisfaction.

The ClaferMOO extension of Clafer was specifically introduced to support attributed feature models as well as the resulting complex multi-objective optimization goals [25]. A multi-objective optimization problem has a set of solutions, known as the Pareto front, that represents the trade-offs between two or more conflicting objectives. Intuitively, a Pareto-optimal solution is thus such that no objective can be improved without worsening another objective. A set of Pareto-optimal variants generated by ClaferMOO can be visualized (as a multi-dimensional space of optimal variants) and explored in the interactive tool ClaferMOOVisualizer, which was specifically designed to support SPL scenarios. The tool can help understand differences among variants, establish their positioning with respect to various quality dimensions, select the most desirable variants, possibly by resolving trade-offs, and understand the impact that changes made during a product line's evolution have on a variant's quality dimensions.

The outcome of evaluating the various options (costs, benefits, etc.) in a systematic way can help finding the right BSS for a particular city, i.e., providing concrete answers to questions like:

- How many and what kind of bikes to buy?
- How many and what kind of stations to buy, and where to place them?
- Which features (antitheft, maintenance, smart services, etc.) to include?
- Include or exclude the (dynamic) redistribution of bikes?
- Set incentives for users to return bikes to less popular stations (e.g., uphill)?
- How much should the users pay and according to which charging policy?

We thus decided to annotate the features of the BSS with attributes and to define global quantitative constraints over these attributes. For now we limited ourselves to the cost and customer satisfaction and, in specific cases, capacity and security. Consequently, these constraints aim to minimize the total cost of a configuration and at the same time maximize customer satisfaction, capacity, and security of a BSS. We obtained realistic numbers for cost and security from documents from companies selling BSS (obtained from PisaMo) and kept their ratio in the model. The values for customer satisfaction instead stem from discussions with PisaMo. The specification (in Clafer's CFR format) of the resulting attributed feature model, excluding the Users (sub)features because Clafer-MOOVisualizer currently runs out of memory in case of too large models, is:

```
// BBS+.cfr
abstract Feature
  customersat : integer
  cost : integer

abstract SecurityFeature : Feature
  security : integer

abstract CapacityFeature : Feature
  capacity : integer

abstract Bikesharing
  or Status : Feature ?
    [ customersat = 0 ]
    [ cost = 0 ]
    RTInfoWeb : Feature
      [ customersat = 10 ]
      [ cost = 5 ]
    AllBikesNow : Feature
      [ customersat = 20 ]
      [ cost = 10 ]
  Bike : SecurityFeature
    [ customersat = 0 ]
    [ cost = 0 ]
    [ security = 0 ]
    or Localization : SecurityFeature ?
      [ customersat = 0 ]
      [ cost = 0 ]
      [ security = 0 ]
      RFID : SecurityFeature
        [ customersat = 10 ]
        [ cost = 10 ]
        [ security = 1 ]
      GPS : SecurityFeature
        [ customersat = 15 ]
        [ cost = 15 ]
        [ security = 2 ]
      Antithieves : SecurityFeature ?
        [ customersat = 5 ]
        [ cost = 7 ]
        [ security = 4 ]

xor DockingStation : CapacityFeature
  [ customersat = 0 ]
  [ cost = 0 ]
  Fixed : CapacityFeature
    [ customersat = 17 ]
    [ cost = 30 ]
    [ capacity = 10]
  FixedPortable: CapacityFeature
    [ customersat = 20 ]
    [ cost = 35 ]
    [ capacity = 10]
  Flexible: CapacityFeature
    [ customersat = 23 ]
    [ cost = 40 ]
    [ capacity = 20]
Maintenance : Feature ?
  [ customersat = 15 ]
  [ cost = 10 ]
Redistribution : Feature ?
  [ customersat = 15 ]
  [ cost = 10 ]
  Reward : Feature ?
    [ customersat = 5 ]
    [ cost = 10 ]
[ Antithieves => GPS ]
[ AllBikesNow => GPS ]

total_customersat : integer =
  sum Feature.customersat
total_cost : integer =
  sum Feature.cost
total_security : integer =
  sum SecurityFeature.security
total_capacity : integer =
  sum CapacityFeature.capacity

Mybike : Bikesharing
<< max Mybike.total_customersat >>
<< min Mybike.total_cost >>
<< max Mybike.total_security >>
<< max Mybike.total_capacity >>
```

By default, features are mandatory, but appended by '?' they become optional. Their hierarchy is represented by indentation. Parent features of an (exclusive) or group of subfeatures are preceeded by or (xor). Cross-tree constraints can be written as first-order logic formulae. Attributes are listed under the features, after which optimization objectives can be set to maximize or minimize their sums (or possibly other arithmetic operations on integers).

Figure 4 depicts the result of optimizing this specification with ClaferMOO-Visualizer. After running for over an hour, it generated a feature and quality matrix over four quality dimensions with 106 optimal variants (53 are visible) out of the 360 valid configurations of the feature model without the Users subtree. The feature model is in the first column, followed by sums of attributes. The numbered columns represent variants, indicating presence (green 'tick') or absence (red crossed circle) of optional features, followed by the variants' numeric quality values (summing attributes). This allows to spot common or rare features. It is also possible to filter variants by selecting features that should be present in all or none of the variants without recalculating the Pareto front. We see, e.g., that variant 51 offers maximal security and capacity at a high cost and with a high customer satisfaction. If this is too expensive, then variant 52 offers the same capacity, near-optimal security, and still a reasonable customer satisfaction at a more affordable cost. The variants are also depicted in a graph as bubbles in at most four quality dimensions (x-axis, y-axis, size, colour). This view can be narrowed down by setting specific quality ranges. The tool can also sort or compare variants (fixing features in advance), list commonalities and differences, do trade-off analysis (e.g., with preconfigured variants), etc.

5   Adding Behaviour and Value-Passing to the BSS: VMC

In recent years, we have laid the basis for the use of modal specifications and temporal logics to specify and analyze behavioural variability in SPL, by developing the modelling and verification environment presented in [2,3,4], which has been implemented in the variability model checker VMC [10,12] that is freely usable online (http://fmt.isti.cnr.it/vmc/v6.0). VMC is a model checker for product lines modelled as modal transition systems (MTS) [1] with additional variability constraints, but with no specific reference to feature models. This is one of the differences[2] with the successful approaches based on featured transition systems (FTS) [17,16], in which transitions are labelled with actions *and* features and an encoding of the feature model *is* included (basically, the set of features and the set of valid products in terms of their features).

VMC offers the automatic generation of one, some, or all valid product behaviours of a product line and the simulation, visualization, and verification of either the full product line or a set of its valid products. VMC's explicit-state on-the-fly model-checking algorithm allows the verification of properties expressed in so-called variability-ACTL interpreted over MTS. It moreover offers the possibility to inspect the (interactive) explanations of a verification result.

---

[2] The commonalities and differences between these two approaches are discussed in [3].

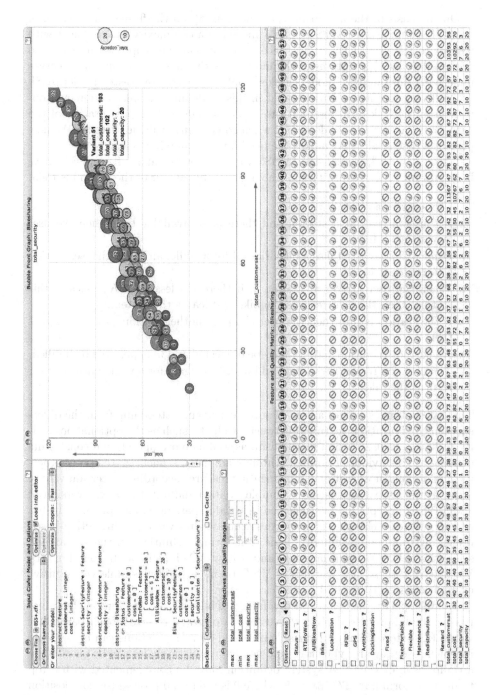

Fig. 4. The BSS Feature Model in ClaferMOOVisualizer, corresponding to the BSS+.cfr specification, i.e., excluding the Users features and their subfeatures

On the basis of the algorithms presented in [8], on-the-fly model checking of v-ACTL formulas over MTS can be achieved in a complexity that is linear with respect to the size of the state space. It is beyond the scope of this paper to present detailed descriptions of the model-checking algorithms and architecture underlying this family of model checkers, but we refer the interested reader to [8].

Until very recently, a critical point in this modelling and verification environment was the lack of a possibility to model an adequate representation of the data that may need to be described when considering realistic systems. We now present a case study that makes the need for data handling clear.

Inspired by [19], we consider a BSS with N stations and a fleet of M bikes. Each station i has a capacity K_i. The dynamic behaviour of the system is then:

1. Users arrive at station i.
2. If a user arrives at a station and there is no available bike, then the user leaves the system.
3. Otherwise, the user takes a bike, rides it for a while, and then chooses station j to return it to.
4. When the user arrives at station j, if there are less than K_j bikes in this station, then the user returns the bike and leaves the system.
5. If the station is full, then the user chooses another station, say k, and goes there.
6. A bike redistribution activity *may* be requested and *may* possibly be fulfilled.
7. The user can repeat these steps, riding a bike again for a while until the user returns the bike.

This list contains a mix of a kind of static constraints stemming from the differences in configuration (features) between products, such as the optional possibility to have a redistribution mechanism, as well as more operational constraints defining the behaviour of products through admitted sequences (temporal orderings) of actions or operations implementing features according to certain values.

As a first step towards more complex data handling, the latest version of VMC (v6.0) accepts models specified in a value-passing modal process algebra and allows model checking of properties expressed in a value-passing action-based branching-time modal temporal logic. The formal definitions of the syntax and semantics of VMC's input language and of its v-ACTL logic can be found in [11]. We illustrate these new features of VMC by means of two simple yet intuitive examples from [11] inspired by the case study.

We first specify the behaviour of a family of bike-sharing stations in the value-passing modal process algebra. Processes can pass and receive integer parameter values (and store them in a variable preceded by a '?'), actions can be optional in which case they are typed may, and nondeterministic choice can be guarded by a comparison of values. A system definition must be complemented with a top term of the form net SYSTEM = P, where P is the initial process (or composition of processes). The below specification accounts for the possibility of having a dynamic redistribution scheme as an optional feature of the BSS. Without loss of generality, we assume a bike-sharing station with 2 as its maximum capacity.

```
Station(X) = request.StationBikeRequested(X)
StationBikeRequested(Y) =
  [Y<1] ( nobike.Station(Y) + redistribute(may).Station(Y+2) ) +
  [Y>0] givebike.Station(Y-1)
```

```
net BSS = Station(2)
```

From this specification of a family of bike-sharing stations, VMC generates the
MTS in Fig. 5(a) and derives its possible product behaviours in Figs. 5(b)-5(c).

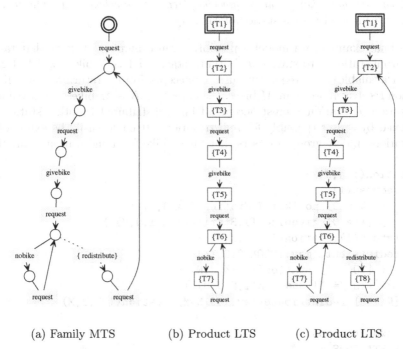

(a) Family MTS   (b) Product LTS   (c) Product LTS

Fig. 5. (a)-(c) A family MTS and two product LTS generated by VMC

To consider also the behaviour of a user whose bike request can result in either
a bike, no bike, or a redistribution, we can specify the following BSS family:

```
User = request.(givebike.User + nobike.User + redistribute.User)
```

```
net BSS = Station(2) /request,givebike,nobike,redistribute/ User
```

Due to the simplistic user behaviour and the synchronous parallel composition[3]
of Station(2) and User on all possible actions, this specification actually results
in the same family behaviour (MTS) and product behaviours (LTS) as in Fig. 5.

---

[3] The parallel composition operator is parametrized by the actions /.../ to synchronize.

To illustrate what kind of variability analyses can be performed, we present a few properties expressed in v-ACTL, and the result of model checking them with VMC against the example BSS depicted in Fig. 5:[4]

Eventually it must occur that no more bike is available: $EF^{\square}\{nobike\}$ *true*. This formula is true (due to $F^{\square}$ only must actions may occur before *nobike*).

It is always the case that eventually it must occur that no bike is available: $AG\,EF^{\square}\{nobike\}$ *true*. Also this formula is true.

It is possible for the user to request and receive a bike for three times in a row: $\langle request \rangle\,\langle givebike \rangle\,\langle request \rangle\,\langle givebike \rangle\,\langle request \rangle\,\langle givebike \rangle$ *true*. This formula is of course false for a station of capacity 2.

As a final example, we model a possibly infinite number of users that take a bike from station I to station J. Initially, station I has N bikes, which it gives (when available) to a requesting user or accepts from a returning user. If the station receives more than M bikes, the exceeding $N - M$ bikes are distributed to station J. Station I must accept all bikes distributed by other stations or returned by a user (possibly for redistribution). It could easily be extended to N stations and K groups of users that take a bike from one station to another.

```
Station(I,N,J,M) =
  request(I).
    ( [N = 0] nobike(I).Station(I,N,J,M) +
      [N > 0] givebike(I).Station(I,N-1,J,M) ) +
  return(I).Station(I,N+1,J,M) +
  redistribute(may,?FROM,?TO,?K).
    ( [TO = I] Station(I,N+K,J,M) +
      [TO /= I] Station(I,N,J,M) ) +
  [N > M] redistribute(may,I,J,N-M).Station(I,M,J,M)

-- two stations:
net STATIONS =
  Station(s1,2,s2,2) /redistribute/ Station(s2,2,s1,2)

Users(I,J) =
  request(I).
    ( givebike(I).return(J).Users(I,J) +
      nobike(I).Users(I,J) )

-- one or two groups of users
net USERS = Users(s1,s2) -- // Users(s2,s1)

net BSS = STATIONS /request,givebike,nobike,return/ USERS
```

---

[4] In VMC, $[]^{\square}$, μ, ν and $F^{\square}$ need to be written as []#, min, max and F#, respectively.

Note that the two stations only synchronize on redistribution, which is an optional may action with parameter values to distribute $N - M$ bikes from station I to J. From this specification of a family of bike-sharing stations, VMC generates the MTS with 18 states depicted in Fig. 6 in case there is only one user group (i.e., net USERS = Users(s1,s2)); in case of two user groups (i.e., net USERS = Users(s1,s2) // Users(s2,s1)) it has 224 states.[5]

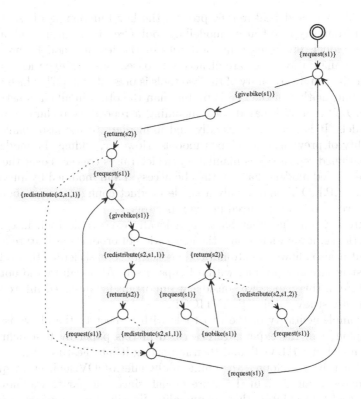

Fig. 6. A family MTS of a BSS with 2 stations and 1 group of users generated by VMC

We model checked the following properties expressed in v-ACTL with VMC, now against the example family of BSS with one user group depicted in Fig. 6:

Eventually it must occur that station 1 has no bikes: $EF^{\square} \{nobike(s1)\}$ *true.* This formula is true (cf. the path of only must actions leading to *nobike(s1)*).

Eventually it may occur that station 2 has no more bikes: $EF \{nobike(s2)\}$ *true.* This formula however is false.

---

[5] In VMC, text or code can be commented out by prefixing it with --.

For all products, if redistribution is implemented, then it is always the case that eventually station 1 must give a bike:[6] $(\neg\, EF^{\square}\, \{redistribute(*,s1,*)\}\ true) \lor$ $(AG\, EF^{\square}\, \{givebike(s1)\}\ true)$. This formula is true for all products (LTS) of the family (MTS in Fig. 6).

6   Conclusions

Both S.P.L.O.T. and FeatureIDE provide the key functioning of what can be expected from a typical feature modelling tool: Creating, editing and analyzing a feature model, providing some statistics of the feature model, and deriving product configurations. A careful account, based on user experiences, of the commonalities and variability of the two tools is presented in [27], which confirms the fact that neither of the two is better than the other in all circumstances.

S.P.L.O.T. is a Web-based tool, including a repository of hundreds of feature models. It is quite user friendly and immediate to use also thanks to the availability of previously developed models. However, adding the model to the aforementioned repository is mandatory, which raises concerns over the privacy of the developed models that can thus be accessed and modified by anyone. Furthermore, S.P.L.O.T. allows only a single product configuration to be created, which however cannot be saved in the repository.

FeatureIDE, on the other hand, is a locally executable tool, integrated in Eclipse. Hence, it allows not only the generation of products as feature combinations, but it also allows to automatically generate code skeletons that reflect the feature structure of a product within Eclipse itself. Although we did not exploit this feature in this paper, we consider it important for intended future work on the BSS case study within QUANTICOL.

The complementarity of the two tools with respect to the above issues has been exploited in the experience described in this paper by first defining the feature model in S.P.L.O.T. and then importing it into FeatureIDE.

Subsequently, we adopted the online tool ClaferMOOVisualizer for quantitative analyses of an attributed feature model, since – as far as we know – it is the only tool that exhibits this functionality. Specific tooling exists to interface with S.P.L.O.T., and this was an important reason for maintaining a copy of the feature model in S.P.L.O.T. Unfortunately, we had to reduce the Clafer specification of an attributed feature model of the BSS by leaving out the entire Users feature and its subfeatures. The reason is that ClaferMOOVisualizer currently runs out of memory in case of too large models.

Finally, we moved from the analysis of structural aspects of BSS to that of behavioural aspects by considering possible behaviours of BSS by manually defining process-algebraic models of both the users and the docking stations and verifying some illustrative properties with the Web-based model checking tool VMC. More specifically, we used the most recent value-passing extension of the aforementioned modelling and verification environment.

---

[6] Note how '*' can be used as a 'don't care' symbol for parameter values.

Our overall experience with the tools was influenced by the fact that all of them are academic tools that at times present some minor problems: S.P.L.O.T., FeatureIDE, and VMC showed more maturity in this respect, while the online version of ClaferMOOVisualizer still manifests some instability.

Obviously, a single standard format for feature models and the use of locally running versions of the tools would increase the synergy between the tools. For now, however, the exploited tool chain was sufficient for our aim of a preliminary modelling and analysis of a bike-sharing product line.

7 Future Work

In the context of planned future work on the BSS case study within QUANTI-COL, we are currently studying a further, more general, parametric extension of the above environment as well as the addition of a quantitative dimension to the behavioural model. For the latter aim, we are considering an extension to weighted MTS [5]. For the former aim, on the other hand, we plan to borrow ideas from parametric MTS [14] and from the way in which the parametrized processes and data handling features of the formal specification language mCRL2 [18] (http://www.mcrl2.org) have been exploited for SPL in [7,6,22].

Actually there exists specific 'quantitative' behaviour (e.g., finding another docking station if the initially chosen station is found full) that might lower or raise user satisfaction, based on the success rate, thus impacting the attributes in the feature model. It remains a challenge for the future to try to capture also such a scenario in our approach.

Acknowledgments. We thank Marco Bertini from PisaMo S.p.A. for generously sharing with us his knowledge on BSS in general and *CicloPi* in particular. We thank Franco Mazzanti, who is the developer of VMC, for helping us with §5. Finally, we thank the reviewers for their useful comments.

References

1. Antonik, A., Huth, M., Larsen, K.G., Nyman, U., Wąsowski, A.: 20 Years of Modal and Mixed Specifications. Bulletin of the EATCS 95, 94–129 (2008)
2. Asirelli, P., ter Beek, M.H., Fantechi, A., Gnesi, S.: A Logical Framework to Deal with Variability. In: Méry, D., Merz, S. (eds.) IFM 2010. LNCS, vol. 6396, pp. 43–58. Springer, Heidelberg (2010)
3. Asirelli, P., ter Beek, M.H., Fantechi, A., Gnesi, S.: Formal Description of Variability in Product Families. In: de Almeida, E.S., Kishi, T., Schwanninger, C., John, I., Schmid, K. (eds.) Proceedings of the 15th International Software Product Lines Conference (SPLC 2011), pp. 130–139. IEEE (2011)
4. Asirelli, P., ter Beek, M.H., Fantechi, A., Gnesi, S.: A Compositional Framework to Derive Product Line Behavioural Descriptions. In: Margaria, T., Steffen, B. (eds.) ISoLA 2012, Part I. LNCS, vol. 7609, pp. 146–161. Springer, Heidelberg (2012)

5. Bauer, S.S., Fahrenberg, U., Juhl, L., Larsen, K.G., Legay, A., Thrane, C.R.: Weighted modal transition systems. Formal Methods in System Design 42(2), 193–220 (2013)

6. ter Beek, M.H., de Vink, E.P.: Towards Modular Verification of Software Product Lines with mCRL2. In: Margaria, T., Steffen, B. (eds.) ISoLA 2014, Part I. LNCS, vol. 8802, pp. 368–385. Springer, Heidelberg (2014)

7. ter Beek, M.H., de Vink, E.P.: Using mCRL2 for the analysis of software product lines. In: Proceedings of the 2nd FME Workshop on Formal Methods in Software Engineering (FormaliSE 2014). IEEE (2014)

8. ter Beek, M.H., Fantechi, A., Gnesi, S., Mazzanti, F.: A state/event-based model-checking approach for the analysis of abstract system properties. Science of Computer Programming 76(2), 119–135 (2011)

9. ter Beek, M.H., Fantechi, A., Gnesi, S., Mazzanti, F.: A collection of models of a bike-sharing case study. Technical Report TR-QC-07-2014, QUANTICOL (May 2014), http://milner.inf.ed.ac.uk/wiki/files/yOR2Q6q/TRQC072014pdf.html

10. ter Beek, M.H., Gnesi, S., Mazzanti, F.: Demonstration of a model checker for the analysis of product variability. In: Proceedings of the 16th International Software Product Line Conference (SPLC 2012), vol. 2, pp. 242–245. ACM (2012)

11. ter Beek, M.H., Gnesi, S., Mazzanti, F.: Model Checking Value-Passing Modal Specifications. In: Perspectives of System Informatics - Revised selected papers of the 9th International Andrei Ershov Memorial Conference (PSI 2014). LNCS. Springer (2014)

12. ter Beek, M.H., Mazzanti, F., Sulova, A.: VMC: A Tool for Product Variability Analysis. In: Giannakopoulou, D., Méry, D. (eds.) FM 2012. LNCS, vol. 7436, pp. 450–454. Springer, Heidelberg (2012)

13. Benavides, D., Segura, S., Ruiz-Cortés, A.: Automated Analysis of Feature Models 20 Years Later: A Literature Review. Information Systems 35(6) (2010)

14. Beneš, N., Křetínský, J., Larsen, K.G., Møller, M.H., Srba, J.: Parametric Modal Transition Systems. In: Bultan, T., Hsiung, P.-A. (eds.) ATVA 2011. LNCS, vol. 6996, pp. 275–289. Springer, Heidelberg (2011)

15. Bąk, K., Czarnecki, K., Wąsowski, A.: Feature and Meta-Models in Clafer: Mixed, Specialized, and Coupled. In: Malloy, B., Staab, S., van den Brand, M. (eds.) SLE 2010. LNCS, vol. 6563, pp. 102–122. Springer, Heidelberg (2011)

16. Classen, A., Cordy, M., Heymans, P., Legay, A., Schobbens, P.-Y.: Formal semantics, modular specification, and symbolic verification of product-line behaviour. Science of Computer Programming 80(B), 416–439 (2014)

17. Classen, A., Cordy, M., Schobbens, P.-Y., Heymans, P., Legay, A., Raskin, J.-F.: Featured Transition Systems: Foundations for Verifying Variability-Intensive Systems and Their Application to LTL Model Checking. IEEE Transactions on Software Engineering 39(8), 1069–1089 (2013)

18. Cranen, S., Groote, J.F., Keiren, J.J.A., Stappers, F.P.M., de Vink, E.P., Wesselink, W., Willemse, T.A.C.: An Overview of the mCRL2 Toolset and Its Recent Advances. In: Piterman, N., Smolka, S.A. (eds.) TACAS 2013 (ETAPS 2013). LNCS, vol. 7795, pp. 199–213. Springer, Heidelberg (2013)

19. Fricker, C., Gast, N.: Incentives and Redistribution in Bike-Sharing Systems with Stations of Finite Capacity. arXiv:1201.1178v3 [nlin.AO] (September 2013)

20. Gianfrotta, L., Topazzini, S.: Progettare Servizi Pubblici: Elaborazione di un Modello per lo Sviluppo di Nuovi Servizi e sua Applicazione al caso Bike Sharing di Pisa. Master's thesis, Università di Pisa (2013) (in Italian)

21. Kang, K.C., Cohen, S.G., Hess, J.A., Novak, W.E., Peterson, A.S.: Feature-Oriented Domain Analysis (FODA) Feasibility Study. Technical Report CMU/SEI-90-TR-21, Carnegie Mellon University (November 1990)
22. Lochau, M., Mennicke, S., Baller, H., Ribbeck, L.: DeltaCCS: A Core Calculus for Behavioral Change. In: Margaria, T., Steffen, B. (eds.) ISoLA 2014, Part I. LNCS, vol. 8802, pp. 320–335. Springer, Heidelberg (2014)
23. Mendonça, M., Branco, M., Cowan, D.D.: S.P.L.O.T.: software product lines online tools. In: Arora, S., Leavens, G.T. (eds.) Companion Proceedings of the 24th Conference on Object-Oriented Programming, Systems, Languages, and Applications (OOPSLA 2009), pp. 761–762. ACM (2009)
24. Midgley, P.: Bicycle-Sharing Schemes: Enhancing Sustainable Mobility in Urban Areas. Background Paper CSD19/2011/BP8, Commission on Sustainable Development, United Nations Department of Economic and Social Affairs (May 2011)
25. Murashkin, A., Antkiewicz, M., Rayside, D., Czarnecki, K.: Visualization and exploration of optimal variants in product line engineering. In: Kishi, T., Jarzabek, S., Gnesi, S. (eds.) Proceedings of the 17th International Software Product Line Conference (SPLC 2013), pp. 111–115. ACM (2013)
26. Niccolai, C., Zanzi, E.: Progettare i servizi: Creazione di un modello di validità generale e applicazione al servizio di Bike Sharing a Pisa. Master's thesis, Università di Pisa (2013) (in Italian)
27. Pereira, J.A., Souza, C., Figueiredo, E., Abílio, R., Vale, G., Costa, H.A.X.: Software Variability Management: An Exploratory Study with Two Feature Modeling Tools. In: Proceedings of the 7th Brazilian Symposium on Software Components, Architectures and Reuse (SBCARS 2013), pp. 20–29. IEEE (2013)
28. Thüm, T., Kästner, C., Benduhn, F., Meinicke, J., Saake, G., Leich, T.: FeatureIDE: An extensible framework for feature-oriented software development. Science of Computer Programming 79, 70–85 (2014)

Towards Modular Verification
of Software Product Lines with mCRL2*

Maurice H. ter Beek[1] and Erik P. de Vink[2,3]

[1] ISTI–CNR, Pisa, Italy
`maurice.terbeek@isti.cnr.it`
[2] Eindhoven University of Technology, Eindhoven, The Netherlands
[3] CWI, Amsterdam, The Netherlands
`evink@win.tue.nl`

Abstract. We introduce by means of an example a modular verification technique for analyzing the behavior of software product lines using the mCRL2 toolset. Based on feature-driven borders, we divide a behavioral model of a product line into a set of separate components with interfaces and a driver process to coordinate them. Abstracting from irrelevant components, we verify properties over a smaller behavioral model, which not only simplifies the model checking task but also makes the result amenable for reuse. This is a fundamental step forward for the approach to scale up to industrial-size product lines.

1 Introduction

Modular or compositional verification by means of model checking has been widely studied as a way to cope with the state space explosion phenomenon (see, e.g., [1,23] or the survey papers in [16]). Traditionally, the idea is to exploit the native modular structure of a design to decompose system properties into properties over system modules or components. In practice, it turns out that this is far from trivial, mainly due to the difficulty to (de)compose properties. A major reason for this difficulty is the misalignment between behavioral properties and the modular design structures that tend to reflect conceptual rather than behavioral borders. Hence, for modular verification to be successful, it is important that a design can be decomposed into components that align well with the properties under consideration. Fisler and Krishnamurthi were the first to notice that this characteristic is inherent to software product lines or feature-oriented system designs, since most properties of interest concern features and system modules or components, and naturally decompose around features [19,27,28]. In line with their findings, in this paper we present a feature-oriented modular approach to the verification of software product lines with mCRL2.

In [5] we showed how the formal specification language mCRL2 and toolset can be exploited to model and analyze software product lines. In particular, we

---

* Research partly supported by the EU FP7-ICT FET-Proactive project QUANTI-COL (600708) and by the Italian MIUR project CINA (PRIN 2010LHT4KM).

T. Margaria and B. Steffen (Eds.): ISoLA 2014, Part I, LNCS 8802, pp. 368–385, 2014.
© Springer-Verlag Berlin Heidelberg 2014

presented a basic example to illustrate the use of mCRL2's parametrized data language to model and select valid product configurations, in the presence of feature attributes and quantitative constraints, and to model and check the behavior of valid products. This is in line with the analysis recommendations from [3] to "adopt and extend state-of-the-art analysis tools" and to "examine[s] only valid product variants". We also hinted at the use of model reduction. In this paper, we concretize this. Using the example from [5], we show how its behavioral model can be modularized (in a feature-oriented fashion) into components, with interfaces that allow a driver process to glue them back together on the fly. This is a powerful abstraction technique that allows mCRL2 to concentrate on the relevant components (features) for the specific property under scrutiny, and in accordance with the modeling recommendation from [3] to "support (feature) modularity" in order "to visualize and (manually or automatically) analyze feature combinations corresponding to products of the product line".

Formal methods and analysis tools are gaining popularity in software product line engineering, as can be witnessed from the successful FMSPLE workshop series affiliated with the last four editions of SPLC. While initial approaches focused on their use in proving structural properties, recently a lively community of researchers is verifying behavioral properties in the presence of variability [9]. Given the rise of software product line engineering in embedded, distributed and safety-critical systems, it is important to provide a means of quality assurance. The work closest to ours are the process-algebraic approaches of [26,6] and, originating from [18], the transition system-based approaches of [25,2,12]. However, a product line's variability is exponential in the number of features. So, a major challenge is to make the proposed techniques (more) scalable, in particular by mitigating the input problem with the help of abstraction. Since mCRL2 is highly optimized and comes with powerful behavioral abstraction techniques, it fosters the hope that scalable verification of product lines is not an utopy.

The goal of this paper is to contribute towards making the variability analysis approach introduced in [5] scale to industrial-size product lines. In that approach, a product line is modeled as an mCRL2 process consisting of two (sequential) parts. The first part concerns feature selection and its output are consistent and complete product configurations; the second part captures product behavior. By keeping the two parts together, model checking can be treated on the system as a whole without restricting to a specific product a priori. This way, also feature interaction is reflected in product behavior as the execution of an action depends on the presence or absence of the corresponding feature.

The focus of the present paper is on the second part of an mCRL2 specification of a product family, which models product behavior. Based on feature-driven borders, we divide the behavioral mCRL2 model into a set of separate components with interfaces in the form of exit and (re-)entry transitions, and we define an additional driver process that coordinates them into exhibiting the same behavior as before. As a result, we can concentrate property verification on part of the state space, by considering a specific (set of) components only, abstracting from the other components, i.e. the environment.

Overall the approach with mCRL2 runs as follows. An attributed feature model and a labeled transition system (LTS) are represented by a 'sequential' composition of a selection process Sel and a parametrized product behavior process Beh. Next, the Beh process is refactored into a driver process Driver in parallel with a number of components depending on disjoint sets of features. When verifying a specific property for a component $Comp_0$, an abstraction of the irrelevant components $Comp_1, \dots, Comp_n$ is formulated, called Stub. If it is the case that the specification Sel; (Driver $\parallel$ $Comp_0$ $\parallel$ Stub) is branching bisimilar to the specification Sel; (Driver $\parallel$ $Comp_0$ $\parallel$ $Comp_1$ $\parallel$ $\dots$ $\parallel$ $Comp_n$) the property holds for the latter specification exactly when the property holds for the former. However, the state space of the abstracted process is significantly smaller in general.

The technique is implemented in our mCRL2 model by creating a 'stub' to replace the environment, creating a smaller model that is branching bisimilar [20] with the original one, hence enjoying the same behavioral properties. In programming, stubs are used as placeholders for unknown implementations whose interfaces *are* known. Such stubs contain just enough code to allow them to be compiled and connected with the rest of the program. In our approach, a stub makes use of the interface of the selected component(s) to simulate the transition sequences from every possible output (exit transition) of the component to each reachable input ((re-)entry transition) for the component. This makes it possible to abstract from other, irrelevant components and thus verify local properties over a smaller behavioral model. This not only simplifies the model checking, in the sense that standard algorithms suffice and limited computing power is required, but it moreover allows the result to be reused for other verifications. Under conditions, as long as the interface with the chosen component remains unaltered, and the complete environment and stub are equivalent processes (i.c. branching bisimilar), the property of the component verified already remains valid. In this sense the obtained result can be reused in a subsequent but different setting. We believe this to be an important step towards scaling the approach to industrial-size product lines.

In this paper, we present our ideas on the basis of a toy example, but we have started to work on a larger industrial case study that we hope to present in the near future. The contribution of this paper is a proof-of-concept for feature-based modular verification of software product lines using the mCRL2 toolset. To this end, Section 2 introduces the type of feature models we use and the coffee machine product line we use as a running example. Section 3 provides the background on mCRL2 necessary to understand Sections 4 and 5, where our approach to modular verification is illustrated by applying it to our example product line. Section 6 discusses related work, while Section 7 closes the paper with concluding remarks and ideas for future work.

2   A Product Line as Running Example

Our running example is an extension of the family of coffee machines from [2] and a slight adaptation of the one in [5]. It has the following list of requirements:

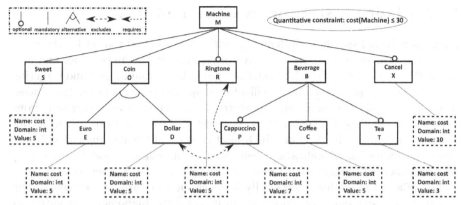

Fig. 1. Attributed feature model of family of coffee machines (with shorthand names)

- To start operation, money must be inserted: either one euro, exclusively for European products, or one dollar, exclusively for Canadian products.
- Optionally, input of money can be canceled via a cancel button, after which the machine returns the inserted coin.
- Once the machine contains money, the user may indicate whether (s)he wants sugar, by pressing one of two buttons, after which (s)he can select a beverage.
- The choice of beverage (coffee, tea, cappuccino) varies, but all products must offer coffee while only European products may offer cappuccino.
- Optionally, a ringtone may be rung after delivering a beverage. However, a ringtone must be rung by all products that offer cappuccino.
- After the beverage is taken, the machine returns idle.

In this paper, we reserve the term *feature diagram* for an and/or-hierarchy of features of a product line, regulating their presence in products, whereas we speak of a *feature model* when a feature diagram is also equipped with *cross-tree constraints*. Finally, by adding (non-functional) attributes to features and quantitative constraints we obtain an *attributed feature model* [8].

Figure 1 depicts the attributed feature model of our example product line, with root feature M and the set *Feature* consisting of the 10 non-trivial features $S, O, R, B, X, E, D, P, C$, and T. As usual, we identify a product from the product line with a non-empty subset of *Feature* united with the root feature. The cost function $cost: Feature \rightarrow \mathbb{N}$, associated to the attribute $cost$, extends to products straightforwardly: $cost(product) = \sum\{ cost(feature) \mid feature \in product \}$.

Our particular example only involves binary cross-tree constraints, non-interacting feature-wise quantifiable attributes and a single optimization objective. However, more general and complex constraints, properties and objectives can be treated as well [8,37]. The feature diagram, i.e. ignoring the cross-tree constraints, gives rise to 2^5 valid products out of the $2^{10} - 1$ possible non-empty sets of non-trivial features. The feature model reduces this number to 20, while the number is further reduced to 16 valid products if the attributed feature model is considered (e.g. $cost(\{M, S, O, R, B, X, E, C, T\}) = 33$ exceeds the limit of 30).

3   Analyzing System Behavior with mCRL2

mCRL2 is a formal specification language with an associated toolset for the modeling and verification of distributed and/or concurrent system behavior and protocols [22]. For about a decade, mCRL2 is actively being maintained and targeting industrial-size applications. Its specification language originates from the process algebra ACP [4]. The user can use abstract datatypes to parametrize actions and has maximal access to artifacts constructed during analysis, allowing tailored manipulation. To this aim, the toolset consists of a wide range of tools and supports simulation, visualization, behavioral reduction and model checking, as well as dedicated optimization techniques and back-ends to other tools.

The mCRL2 toolset has successfully been applied in various settings, among which the massive data collection system used for the high-energy experiments conducted at the large hadron collider of CERN [35] and the FlexRay communication protocol used in the automotive industry to equip car components with a reliable, high-bandwidth communication channel [13]. The toolset is open source and the associated boost license allows free use for any purpose. Its binaries and lots of further documentation can be downloaded from www.mcrl2.org.

We will not use the full expressivity of mCRL2 in our approach here. Relatively simple structured models suffice, which extends the range of the toolset.

A simple example is the LTS in Fig. 2 (left), which can be modeled by the mCRL2 process Foo, with integer st as a state parameter and actions a to e:

```
proc Foo(st:Int) =
  ( st==0 ) -> ( b.Foo(1) + a.Foo(2) ) +
  ( st==1 ) -> ( c.Foo(3) ) +
  ( st==2 ) -> ( b.Foo(1) + b.Foo(3) + a.Foo(4) ) +
  ...
```

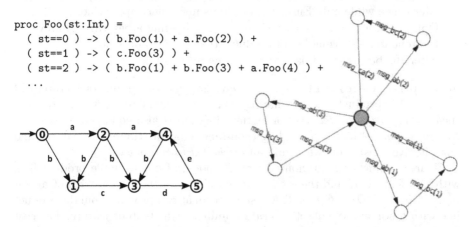

Fig. 2. LTS of Foo process (left) and three communicating mCRL2 processes (right)

Another construction that is typical for the specification of parallel processes in mCRL2 is the combined use of the communication and encapsulation operator. Consider the following three processes:

```
proc A = ( send_a(1) + send_a(2) + send_a(3) ) .
            sum n:Int . receive_a(n) . A;
proc B = sum n:Int . receive_b(n) . send_b(n) . B;
proc C = sum n:Int . receive_c(n) . send_c(n) . C;
```

Thus, process A starts sending value 1, 2, or 3. Next it is willing to receive any integer value n and then starts all over again. Note that the summation over integers should be interpreted as an infinite non-deterministic choice. Processes B and C are similar, but they first receive a value n, send it out, and start again.

To enforce matching of actions, e.g. to arrange for A sending to B, B sending to C, and C sending to A, we make use of a communication function. The function states which actions combine into other actions, e.g. send_a and receive_b may combine into the action msg_ab, similar to a synchronization of actions a and $\bar{a}$ yielding τ in CCS [32]. In mCRL2, for successful synchronization it is required that the parameters of the actions, if any, are the same. In our case the net result is communication: a receive action with a parameter bound by a summation gets instantiated by the parameter value of the sending action. On top of this, to constrain the interaction of processes and to prune the state space, we forbid unmatched actions by explicitly listing which actions are allowed to happen, excluding actions that are supposed to resolve into another. Note that in mCRL2 synchronization is multi-party, hence not restricted to handshaking as in CCS.

For the above three processes we may have:

```
allow( { msg_ab, msg_bc, msg_ca },
  comm( { send_a | receive_b -> msg_ab,
          send_b | receive_c -> msg_bc,
          send_c | receive_a -> msg_ca },
        A || B || C ));
```

The resulting state space of these three communicating processes is depicted in Fig. 2 (right). We see that only the allowed actions msg_ab, msg_bc, and msg_ca occur, hence no occurrences of unmatched send and receive actions. Also, in the three cycles the same parameter value is mentioned, viz. either 1, 2, or 3; the infinite sums of the processes B and C have been resolved.

A system property can be expressed as a formula in a variant of the modal μ-calculus [21]. Subsequently, the property can be verified against a mCRL2 specification of the system using the model checking facilities of the toolset. Here are some properties that hold for the Foo process above:

- [true*]<true>true: absence of deadlock, i.e. after any sequence of actions, an action can be done.
- [true*.b.true*.a] false: after any sequence where the action b precedes the action a, *false* will hold. As the latter never holds, the formula can be reformulated: no a-action is possible after a b-action has happened.
- mu Y.(<d>true || [true] Y): a least-fixed-point construction. Always, after a finite amount of steps, a d-action can be done (or deadlock occurs earlier). The smallest set of states Y that can do a d-action or cannot step outside of Y, can be computed by iteration: Start from the empty set $Y_0 = \varnothing$. Then include state 3 which can do d, yielding $Y_1 = \{3\}$. Then add states 1 and 4 since their single step leads to Y_1, yielding $Y_2 = \{1, 3, 4\}$. Then include

2 and 5 since all their steps lead to Y_2, yielding $Y_3 = \{1,2,3,4,5\}$. The next step adds 0 and yields the fixed point $Y_4 = \{0,1,2,3,4,5\}$. Since the initial state $0 \in Y_4$, the formula holds.

- mu Y.((nu Z.(<d.e> Z)) || [true] Y): a nesting of a least-fixed-point and a greatest-fixed-point construction. Always, after a finite amount of steps, an infinite repetition of d and e is possible.

The modal μ-calculus, a.k.a. the 'Logic of Everything', is renowned to be highly expressive and to subsume temporal logics like LTL and (A)CTL [17,10,14]. The model-checking approaches of [12,6] are based on LTL, that of [26] on the multi-valued modal μ-calculus, and those of [25,2] on (A)CTL. Only the approach of [6] is implemented, viz. in the Maude toolset (maude.cs.uiuc.edu). The appeal of the modal μ-calculus variant in mCRL2 exploited here is the possibility to quantify over data. Moreover, well-chosen hiding of actions and minimization with respect to one of the process equivalences offered by the mCRL2 toolset (e.g. trace equivalence, weak and branching bisimulation [32,20]) allow to narrow the state space and to focus on specific behavioral aspects. The latter technique can significantly reduce a state space with millions of states to a state space of a few dozens, making visual inspection feasible.

4   Modeling of the Running Example

To model the product family underlying our example in mCRL2 we follow the approach set out in [5]. We will have two main processes: a feature selection process and a process (actually a combination of a number of component processes together with a driver process) representing an actual product of the family.

First, a valid feature set is selected by the three-stage non-deterministic process Sel. The resolution of the non-determinacy leads to a product configuration which is checked for its consistency with global constraints. First, a breadth-first traversal of the feature model selects features, taking 'mandatority' and possible local constraints, like m-out-of-n selection, into account. Second, cross-tree constraints are checked and violating configurations result in a transition to an error state. In our example we have two such constraints: the mutual exclusion of Dollar vs. Cappuccino, and the required inclusion of Ringtone in the presence of Cappuccino. Finally, attribute constraints are checked. For the example it is required for the selected features not to exceed a cost limit of 30. Also here, violating configurations are forced to transit to an error state.

Configurations that have passed through all three stages successfully are genuine sets of features complying to all requirements as expressed by the attributed feature model. These configurations are passed as an argument to the process that represents the corresponding product. An excerpt of the process Sel is depicted next.

```
proc Sel(st:Int,fs:FSet) =
  %% feature selection
  ( st == 0 ) -> ( ( M in fs ) -> ( setS . Sel(1, ins(S,fs) ) ) ) +
  ( st == 1 ) -> ( ( M in fs ) -> ( setO . Sel(2, ins(O,fs) ) ) ) +
  ( st == 2 ) -> ( ( M in fs ) -> (
      tau  . Sel(3, fs ) +  setR . Sel(3, ins(R,fs) ) ) ) +
  ...
  ( st == 5 ) -> ( ( O in fs ) -> (
      setD . Sel(6, ins(D,fs) ) +  setE . Sel(6, ins(E,fs) ) ) ) +
  ...
  %% cross-tree constraints
  ( st == 8 ) -> ( ( ( D in fs ) && ( P in fs ) ) ->
      dollar_cappo_fault( fs ) . Sel(801,fs) <> skip . Sel(9,fs) ) +
  ...
  %% attribute constraints
  ( st == 10 ) -> ( ( tcost(fs) <= 30 ) ->
      attr_ok . cost( tcost(fs) ) . put_config(fs) <>
        attr_fault( fs , tcost(fs) ) . Sel(1001,fs) ) +
  ...
```

The full mCRL2 specification is available from http://www.win.tue.nl/~evink/research/mCRL2.

The selection process Sel has two parameters: a local state st represented by an integer, and a feature set fs represented as a sorted list of features without duplicates. As we will see later, the selection process starts with the root feature Machine, abbreviated as M, chosen. Thus initially we have Sel(0,[M]). In state 0 of the Sel process, since M in fs holds, the mandatory feature Sweet is added to the current feature set; Sel continues in state 1 and feature set ins(S,fs). Similarly, in state 1 the mandatory coin feature is included. In state 2, the optional ringtone feature is handled, which may or may not be selected, leading to a non-deterministic choice between tau.Sel(3,fs) and setR.Sel(3,ins(R,fs). In the former option the Sel parameters remain unchanged, in the latter the R-feature is added to the current feature set. In the same vein, but slightly different, is the 1-out-of-2 selection of the dollar or the euro feature. Here either choice leads to an update of the current feature set.

As outcome of the first stage of the Sel process a feature set fs is selected that is consistent with the local feature requirements (mandatory, optional, alternative, etc.). Next cross-tree constraints are checked for fs. For example, the mutual exclusion of Dollar vs. Cappuccino is captured by the test in state 8 of Sel. If both the D and the P feature are present in fs the constraint is violated and control is transferred to the error state 801. Otherwise the process continues checking for the next cross-tree constraint. Finally, in the third stage of Sel, attribute constraints are checked, in the case of the example the costs should not be higher than 30. If it is too high, Sel moves to a specific error state. If it is sufficiently low, i.e. tcost(fs) <= 30, the attribute is marked as OK, the costs are outputted, and moreover, via the action put_config(fs), the eligible feature set is passed on to the product process modeling actual behavior.

The potential behavior of our example is shown by the LTS in Fig. 3 (left), which is the one from [2] with simplified money insertion. In line with [12,6], transitions are assumed to be tagged with a feature (not made explicit here for readability). An action can only occur in a product if the corresponding feature is selected for the product, i.e. the feature set that configures the product needs to be checked for the presence of a feature for feature-dependent actions to occur.

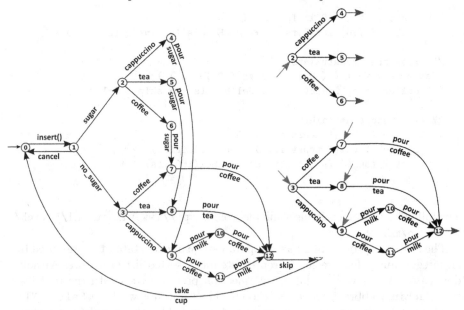

Fig. 3. LTS modeling family behavior (left) and its beverage component (right)

From starting state 0, a coin (either a dollar or a euro) can be inserted. Control then moves to state 1. There, either the user cancels the interaction with the machine, and control returns to state 0, or chooses for sugar or no sugar, and control moves to state 2 or 3, respectively. The user chooses one of the available drinks, a choice of coffee, tea or cappuccino, and control reaches state 6 or 7, 5 or 8, 4 or 9, depending on the choices made. Then the necessary ingredients are added, control moves to state 7, 8, or 9 if sugar was added, and subsequently to state 12 after the drink has been poured. Note that a cappuccino request leads to an interleaving of pouring coffee and milk. Next, control moves to state 13, ringing or not according to the feature set. Then the user can take her/his cup and control returns to state 0.

In our mCRL2 encoding, a product as given by an eligible feature set fs is represented by a parallel composition of six component processes, one for each of the features Sweet, Coin, Ringtone, Beverage, Cancel and one for the root feature Machine. After being woken up by the selection process, the process belonging to the product with feature set fs as configuration is given by a system of seven parallel processes

$$\text{Driver(0) || Sweet(fs) || Coin(fs) ||}$$
$$\text{Ringtone(fs) || Beverage(fs) || Cancel(fs) || Machine} \qquad (1)$$

We underline that, although not explicitly mentioned, the selection process Sel is always part of the mCRL2 specifcations considered below. By taking feature selection and coupled product behavior as a whole, verification can be done at the family level, rather than for each product or subset of products separately. See [5] for more detail.

In order to enforce the proper control flow the component processes are put in parallel with a driver process Driver. The Coin process, e.g., is given by

```
proc Coin(fs:FSet) =
  cmp_start(0) . (
  ( D in fs ) -> insert(dollar) . raise(1) . Coin() +
  ( E in fs ) -> insert(euro) . raise(1) . Coin() ) +
  cmp_start(1) .  cancel . raise(0) . Coin() ;
```

On a drv_start(0) request of the driver, the Coin component can execute the matching cmp_start(0) action upon which either the action insert(dollar) or the action insert(euro) follows. As the preceding feature selection process has enforced that exactly one of the two features D and E is included in the product feature set fs, exactly one of the two actions can be taken. After executing either of them, the Coin process raises that the driver should proceed in state 1. The action raise(1) of Coin is matched by the action catch(1) of Driver.

The driver process is relatively simple. It proclaims the current state of the product via a drv_start(st) action, allowing any component with an active transition in state st to perform an action. Next it catches the new state number st', raised by the component, and the driving starts anew from that state:

```
proc Driver(st:Int) =
  drv_start(st) . sum st':Int . catch(st') . Driver(st') ;
```

Now, in state 1 three actions are possible: a cancel from the Cancel process, or a sugar action or a no_sugar action from the Sweet process, partly defined by

```
proc Sweet(fs:FSet) =
  cmp_start(1) . ( S in fs ) -> sugar . raise(2) . Sweet() +
  cmp_start(1) . ( S in fs ) -> no_sugar . raise(3) . Sweet() +
  ...
```

The non-determinacy in state 1 reflects the user's choice. (S)he can press a button to cancel the interaction with the coffee machine or opt for sugar or no sugar. However, the action cancel will only be offered if the feature set fs of the product actually holds the X. This explains the guarding by the check for X in fs of the cmp_start(1) action of Cancel in

```
proc Cancel(fs:FSet) =
  ( X in fs ) -> cmp_start(1) . cancel . raise(0) . Cancel() ;
```

5   Analysis of the Running Example

To illustrate our approach to feature-oriented modular verification we focus on the beverage component. Its isolated sub-LTS is depicted in Fig. 3 (right). Note that the transitions belonging to other components do not appear in this representation. However, next to the component's behavior the interface to the environment is given, as mediated through the driver. It can receive requests from the driver on its unlabeled incoming (re-)entry transitions (red), while it can provide input to the driver via its unlabeled outgoing exit transitions (blue).

An obvious requirement for the beverage component to hold is that coffee is delivered at least when coffee is asked for. We may express this by the formula

$$[\text{ true* . coffee . (!pour\_coffee)* . take\_cup }] \text{ false}$$

However, this does not guarantee that a `pour_coffee` will take place, rather that a `take_cup` is avoided. Another disadvantage of the formula is that the action `take_cup` does not belong to the beverage component but to the machine component instead. This can be remedied using a minimal fixed point construction. This is reflected by the modal μ-calculus formula

$$[\text{ true*.coffee }](\text{ mu } X. \text{ [!pour\_coffee] } X) \tag{2}$$

i.e., after a `coffee` action a `pour_coffee` action happens within a finite number of steps. Thus, a coffee request is answered by the pouring of coffee eventually. To ensure that the `pour_coffee` action matches the occurrences of the `coffee` action mentioned, we can forbid that the beverage component is left:

$$[\text{true*.coffee}](\text{mu} X. ([\text{!pour\_coffee}] X \text{ \&\& } [\text{event(12)}] \text{ false}))$$

i.e., after a coffee request coffee will be poured eventually and this happens before the beverage component is exited. Note that the mCRL2 toolset supports modal μ-calculus with data.

If control enters the beverage component via the **no_sugar** entrance state 3, clearly property (2) holds. After the `coffee` request of the transition from state 3 to state 7 there is no other action than the `pour_coffee` action of the transition from state 7 to state 12, as control may enter at state 7, but may not leave. This is all different when control enters the beverage component via the **sugar** entrance state 2. Then a coffee request issued by the transition from state 2 to state 6 relies on the environment, in particular the sweet component, for a transition (or sequence of transitions as far as the beverage component is concerned) leading to state 7 so that the `pour_coffee` action becomes enabled.

In fact, as the actions `coffee` and `pour_coffee` belong to the beverage component, it suffices that the environment caters for (i) a transfer from state 4 to state 9, (ii) a transfer from state 5 to state 8, and (iii) a transfer from state 6 to state 7. Additionally, the environment is expected to allow a return to states 2 and 3 after the beverage component is left via state 12.

To model this in mCRL2 we introduce a process `BeverageStub`, a stub for the behavior of the environment of the `Beverage` component, given by

```
proc BeverageStub =
  cmp_start(0)  . other . ( raise(2) + raise(3) ) . BeverageStub +
  cmp_start(4)  . other . raise(9) . BeverageStub +
  cmp_start(5)  . other . raise(8) . BeverageStub +
  cmp_start(6)  . other . raise(7) . BeverageStub +
  cmp_start(12) . other . ( raise(2) + raise(3) ) . BeverageStub ;
```

With BeverageStub in place, rather than considering the 7-process system used previously, i.e. the driver and the six component processes in equation (1), we can now deal with three processes only:

$$\text{Driver(0) || Beverage(fs) || BeverageStub} \qquad (3)$$

Note the summand with the cmp_start(0) action of BeverageStub to be able to pick up the simulation of the environment right from the start. Also, the stub process does not have a feature set as an argument. This is in line with the intuition that it is not for the beverage component to make specific assumptions on the configuration of the environment nor on its behavior, beyond the entering and exiting of control regarding the beverage component itself. Rephrased more technically, the 7-process system of the driver and all six components is branching bisimilar to the 3-process system of the driver, beverage component and its stub. Therefore, modal μ-formulas in the CTL*-fragment without the next operator [15], like the one of (2), equally hold for the two systems.

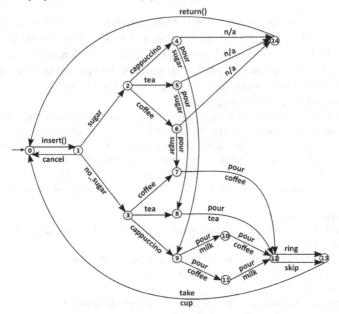

Fig. 4. LTS modeling alternative family behavior

Next we modify the sweet component according to the LTS in Fig. 4. Now, as an improved service, whenever the machine is out of sugar, it returns the inserted money instead of delivering the chosen beverage (without sugar). Apart from an adaptation of the Sweet process to accommodate the 'not-available' action n/a from states 4, 5, and 6 to the new state 14, the Cancel process is extended to return the inserted money via the return transition from state 14 back to state 0.

Because of the transition to the new state 14, from the point of view of the beverage component, the flow of control may unexpectedly be diverted. A request for coffee with sugar, i.e. the action coffee leaving state 2, may be followed by the action n/a leading away from further handling by the beverage component. Thus no action pour_coffee is performed (in case the n/a is always taken at that point). So, counterintuitively, while the sweet and cancel component have changed, a basic requirement for the beverage component becomes violated.

The crucial point we want to underline is that no model checking is needed for the designer to be warned. The full 7-process system (1), with the 'improved' sweet and cancel component, is no longer branching bisimilar to the smaller 3-process system (3) that includes the beverage stub. The ltscompare tool in the mCRL2 toolset, which can decide e.g. on the branching-bisimilarity of two systems, finds this quickly. Thus, a simple check suffices to alert the designer that a property of the component that was valid previously, may not hold anymore.

If this new behavior to deal with the lack of sugar is to be maintained, the coffee vs. pour_coffee requirement needs to be weakened. One may propose

```
[ true*.coffee ]( mu X. ([ !( pour_coffee || return ) ] X ))
```

i.e., a coffee request is answered by either pouring the coffee or a refund. As the action return does not belong to the action set of the Beverage process, the system to be model checked needs to comprise the Cancel process as well, possibly combined with an adapted stub process to replace the other four components. However, from a scalability perspective it is less attractive to deal with specific combinations of components.

Reconsidering the very idea of isolating the beverage component, we need to make the distinction between the 'acceptable' action pour_sugar and the 'non-acceptable' action n/a visible in the stub process. We introduce for the process BeverageStub2 below the action escape to represent behavior that may/will affect the behavior of the beverage component, besides the indifferent action other that was used earlier. The code for BeverageStub2 reads as follows.

```
proc BeverageStub2 =
  cmp_start(0) .  other . ( raise(2) + raise(3) ) . BeverageStub2 +
  cmp_start(4) .(
    escape . ( raise(2) + raise(3) ) . BeverageStub2 +
    other . raise(9) . BeverageStub2 ) +
  cmp_start(5) . (
    escape . ( raise(2) + raise(3) ) . BeverageStub2 +
    other . raise(8) . BeverageStub2 ) +
  cmp_start(6) . (
    escape . ( raise(2) + raise(3) ) . BeverageStub2 +
    other . raise(7) . BeverageStub2 ) +
  cmp_start(12) . other . ( raise(2) + raise(3) ) . BeverageStub2;
```

E.g., the stub captures that in state 6, right after the request for coffee, control either 'escapes' from the neighborhood of the beverage component and may return via the entrance state 2 or 3, or control remains in the vicinity of the component, having 'other' activity but picking up the beverage thread in state 7. With the BeverageStub2 in place, the enhanced 7-process system and adapted 3-process system can again be shown to be branching bisimilar.

6 Related Work

In this section, we continue the discussion of related work on the compositional verification of software product lines (SPL) initiated in the introduction. In [29], improving part of the pioneering work of [19,27,28] mentioned already, an incremental compositional model checking approach for SPL is presented. It uses variation point obligations expressed in CTL to guarantee that the (sequential) feature-based composition satisfies a property if and only if the added features satisfy the relevant variation point obligations. Whenever possible, verification results are reused in an incremental fashion within the product being composed, which reduces the overall verification effort, but the approach does not aim to reuse properties of behavioral feature models across different products.

In [36], an existing compositional verification technique for safety properties of flow-graph behavior of general-purpose programs is adapted to programs from the SPL domain, that are organized according to a hierarchical variability model defining variation points and interfaces. This compositional approach scales well, but it is not feature-based and limited to control-flow behavior, for which it can express properties in a fragment of the modal μ-calculus.

In [33], feature Petri nets are introduced as a modular (feature- and interface-based) behavioral modeling formalism. A few correctness criteria, based on bisimulation, for the preservation of properties in composed models are given. This is a promising approach that deserves further study, as does the precise relationship with our approach, apart from the fact that model checking is not addressed nor the question for the reuse of verification results.

In [31], for each feature of an SPL two finite state machines with variability (implemented by guarded variables on transitions) are built, one for the requirements and one for the design level, after which their conformance can be checked in a compositional, feature-based fashion. The prototype tool SPLEnD makes use of the SPIN model checker (spinroot.com) to implement such conformance checking. Reuse of verification results is not considered.

Recent work on delta-oriented SPL analysis using mCRL2 is reported in [30].

Some of the other behavioral variability models mentioned in the introduction come with a special-purpose tool for SPL model checking. SNIP [11] is a model checker for product lines modeled as featured transition systems [12] specified in a language based on that of SPIN. The tool VMC [7] (fmt.isti.cnr.it/vmc) is a model checker for product lines modeled as modal transition systems with additional variability constraints [2] specified in a modal process algebra. Neither of these currently make use of modular or compositional verification.

7   Discussion and Future Work

We have presented a proof-of-concept of a feature-oriented modular verification technique for analyzing the behavior of SPL with mCRL2. We use branching bisimulation techniques to isolate the behavior of a specific feature (set) by abstracting from the environment. This eases the model checking and allows the result to be reused in other settings; if adapted behavior leads to an environment that is branching bisimilar, say, to the stub used, then a verified property is also valid in the new situation. mCRL2 is a toolset that has already shown its merits in dealing with huge state spaces consisting of billions of states. Although at present stubs are crafted manually, we believe that scalable verification of SPL can successfully be achieved with mCRL2 along the lines of the modular verification strategy illustrated in this paper. A demonstration of this is left for future work.

Our approach thus differs from modular or compositional verification in the classic sense of (re)composing smaller verification results on modules or components to derive properties of the composed system. It remains to investigate whether we could apply compositional model checking under sequential composition as defined in [24] to our feature-oriented modularization of behavioral SPL models. Likewise it remains to study whether a notion like modular validity (a property holds over a module if it holds over any system that includes that module [34]) can be effectively used in our setting.

Another challenge for our feature-oriented modular verification approach stems from the fact that, ideally, we want to be able to handle dynamic feature-based composition. If a feature is added, then on the one hand we want to prove that properties of the system continue to hold, while on the other hand we want to verify new properties that the new system should now satisfy. This is complicated by the well-known fact that features may interact. We have seen this problem arise in our running example when we modeled the 'improved' service signaling the lack of sugar in a coffee machine.

This brings us to concrete future work on our running example. If we consider the notion of a neighborhood of a component, then we can distinguish (re-)entry points, exit points, and interrupt points. The latter come in these three flavors:

Type 1 like `pour_sugar` of the `other` or `continue` type; other components do their business, but control is picked up again by the component at hand.

Type 2 like `n/a` of the `escape` or `break` type; another component takes over control and control re-enters the component at a re-entry point rather than continuing its thread.

Type 3 (not encountered in the above discussion) of the `diverge` type; another component takes over control and the component itself is never visited again.

We may claim that with these three corresponding types of actions (`continue`, `break`, and `diverge`) a sufficiently rich class of stubs can be constructed that can simulate the environment. Checking a component property would then mean:

1. Verify the property for the 3-process system of driver, component, and stub.

2. Check branching bisimilarity for the 3-process system and the complete all-process system.

Finally, we need to identify which class of properties exactly fits within our approach. Evidently, further work is to be done on larger examples and convincing case studies to support our claims.

References

1. Abadi, M., Lamport, L.: Conjoining Specifications. ACM Transactions on Programming Languages and Systems 17(3), 507–534 (1995)
2. Asirelli, P., ter Beek, M.H., Fantechi, A., Gnesi, S.: Formal Description of Variability in Product Families. In: Proc. SPLC 2011, pp. 130–139. IEEE (2011)
3. Atlee, J.M., Beidu, S., Day, N.A., Faghih, F., Shaker, P.: Recommendations for Improving the Usability of Formal Methods for Product Lines. In: Proc. FormaliSE 2013, pp. 43–49. IEEE (2013)
4. Baeten, J.C.M., Basten, T., Reniers, M.A.: Process Algebra: Equational Theories of Communicating Processes. Cambridge University Press (2010)
5. ter Beek, M.H., de Vink, E.P.: Using mCRL2 for the analysis of software product lines. In: Proc. FormaliSE 2014, pp. 31–37. IEEE (2014)
6. ter Beek, M.H., Lluch-Lafuente, A., Petrocchi, M.: Combining declarative and procedural views in the specification and analysis of product families. In: Proc. SPLC 2013, vol. 2, pp. 10–17. ACM (2013)
7. ter Beek, M.H., Mazzanti, F., Sulova, A.: VMC: A Tool for Product Variability Analysis. In: Giannakopoulou, D., Méry, D. (eds.) FM 2012. LNCS, vol. 7436, pp. 450–454. Springer, Heidelberg (2012)
8. Benavides, D., Segura, S., Ruiz-Cortés, A.: Automated Analysis of Feature Models 20 Years Later: A Literature Review. Information Systems 35(6) (2010)
9. Borba, P., Cohen, M.B., Legay, A., Wąsowski, A.: Analysis, Test and Verification in The Presence of Variability (Dagstuhl Seminar 13091). Dagstuhl Reports 3(2), 144–170 (2013)
10. Bradfield, J.C., Stirling, C.: Modal μ-calculi. In: Blackburn, P., van Benthem, J.F.A.K., Wolter, F. (eds.) Handbook of Modal Logic. Studies in Logic and Practical Reasoning, vol. 3, pp. 721–756. Elsevier (2007)
11. Classen, A., Cordy, M., Heymans, P., Legay, A., Schobbens, P.-Y.: Model checking software product lines with SNIP. International Journal on Software Tools for Technology Transfer 14(5), 589–612 (2012)
12. Classen, A., Cordy, M., Schobbens, P.-Y., Heymans, P., Legay, A., Raskin, J.-F.: Featured Transition Systems: Foundations for Verifying Variability-Intensive Systems and Their Application to LTL Model Checking. IEEE Transactions on Software Engineering 39(8), 1069–1089 (2013)
13. Cranen, S.: Model Checking the FlexRay Startup Phase. In: Stoelinga, M., Pinger, R. (eds.) FMICS 2012. LNCS, vol. 7437, pp. 131–145. Springer, Heidelberg (2012)
14. De Nicola, R., Vaandrager, F.: Action versus State based Logics for Transition Systems. In: Guessarian, I. (ed.) LITP 1990. LNCS, vol. 469, pp. 407–419. Springer, Heidelberg (1990)
15. De Nicola, R., Vaandrager, F.W.: Three logics for branching bisimulation. Journal of the ACM 42(2), 458–487 (1995)

16. de Roever, W.-P., Langmaack, H., Pnueli, A. (eds.): COMPOS 1997. LNCS, vol. 1536. Springer, Heidelberg (1998)
17. Emerson, E.A.: Model Checking and the Mu-calculus. In: Immerman, N., Kolaitis, P.G. (eds.) Proc. of DIMACS Workshop on Descriptive Complexity and Finite Models. DIMACS Series in Discrete Mathematics and Theoretical Computer Science, vol. 31, pp. 185–214. AMS (1996)
18. Fischbein, D., Uchitel, S., Braberman, V.A.: A foundation for behavioural conformance in software product line architectures. In: Hierons, R.M., Muccini, H. (eds.) Proc. ROSATEA 2006, pp. 39–48. ACM (2006)
19. Fisler, K., Krishnamurthi, S.: Modular Verification of Collaboration-Based Software Designs. In: Proc. FSEC/FSE 2001, Vienna, pp. 152–163. ACM (2001)
20. van Glabbeek, R.J., Weijland, W.P.: Branching Time and Abstraction in Bisimulation Semantics. Journal of the ACM 43(3), 555–600 (1996)
21. Groote, J.F., Mateescu, R.: Verification of Temporal Properties of Processes in a Setting with Data. In: Haeberer, A.M. (ed.) AMAST 1998. LNCS, vol. 1548, pp. 74–90. Springer, Heidelberg (1998)
22. Groote, J.F., Mathijssen, A., Reniers, M.A., Usenko, Y.S., van Weerdenburg, M.J.: Analysis of Distributed Systems with mCRL2. In: Alexander, M., Gardner, W. (eds.) Process Algebra for Parallel and Distributed Processing, pp. 99–128. Chapman & Hall (2009)
23. Grumberg, O., Long, D.E.: Model Checking and Modular Verification. ACM Transactions on Programming Languages and Systems 16(3), 843–871 (1994)
24. Laster, K., Grumberg, O.: Modular Model Checking of Software. In: Steffen, B. (ed.) TACAS 1998. LNCS, vol. 1384, pp. 20–35. Springer, Heidelberg (1998)
25. Lauenroth, K., Pohl, K., Töhning, S.: Model Checking of Domain Artifacts in Product Line Engineering. In: Proc. ASE 2009, pp. 269–280. IEEE (2009)
26. Leucker, M., Thoma, D.: A Formal Approach to Software Product Families. In: Margaria, T., Steffen, B. (eds.) ISoLA 2012, Part I. LNCS, vol. 7609, pp. 131–145. Springer, Heidelberg (2012)
27. Li, H.C., Fisler, K., Adsul, B.: The Influence of Software Module Systems on Modular Verification. In: Bošnački, D., Leue, S. (eds.) SPIN 2002. LNCS, vol. 2318, pp. 60–78. Springer, Heidelberg (2002)
28. Li, H.C., Krishnamurthi, S., Fisler, K.: Interfaces for Modular Feature Verification. In: Proc. ASE 2002, Edinburgh, pp. 195–204. IEEE (2002)
29. Liu, J., Basu, S., Lutz, R.R.: Compositional model checking of software product lines using variation point obligations. Automated Software Engineering 18(1), 39–76 (2011)
30. Lochau, M., Mennicke, S., Baller, H., Ribbeck, L.: DeltaCCS: A Core Calculus for Behavioral Change. In: Margaria, T., Steffen, B. (eds.) ISoLA 2014, Part I. LNCS, vol. 8802, pp. 320–335. Springer, Heidelberg (2014)
31. Millo, J.-V., Ramesh, S., Krishna, S.N., Narwane, G.K.: Compositional Verification of Software Product Lines. In: Johnsen, E.B., Petre, L. (eds.) IFM 2013. LNCS, vol. 7940, pp. 109–123. Springer, Heidelberg (2013)
32. Milner, R.: Communication and Concurrency. Prentice Hall (1989)
33. Muschevici, R., Proença, J., Clarke, D.: Modular Modelling of Software Product Lines with Feature Nets. In: Barthe, G., Pardo, A., Schneider, G. (eds.) SEFM 2011. LNCS, vol. 7041, pp. 318–333. Springer, Heidelberg (2011)
34. Pnueli, A.: In Transition from Global to Modular Temporal Reasoning about Programs. In: Apt, K.R. (ed.) Logics and Models of Concurrent Systems, pp. 123–144. Springer, Heidelberg (1985)

35. Remenska, D., Willemse, T.A.C., Verstoep, K., Fokkink, W., Templon, J., Bal, H.E.: Using Model Checking to Analyze the System Behavior of the LHC Production Grid. In: Proc. CCGrid 2012, pp. 335–343. IEEE (2012)
36. Schaefer, I., Gurov, D., Soleimanifard, S.: Compositional Algorithmic Verification of Software Product Lines. In: Aichernig, B.K., de Boer, F.S., Bonsangue, M.M. (eds.) FMCO 2010. LNCS, vol. 6957, pp. 184–203. Springer, Heidelberg (2011)
37. Siegmund, N., Rosenmüller, M., Kuhlemann, M., Kästner, C., Apel, S., Saake, G.: SPL Conqueror: Toward optimization of non-functional properties in software product lines. Software Quality Journal 20(3-4), 487–517 (2012)

Model-Based Code-Generators and Compilers - Track Introduction

Uwe Aßmann[1], Jens Knoop[2], and Wolf Zimmermann[3]

[1] Institut für Software- und Multimediatechnik
TU Dresden, Dresden, Germany
uwe.assmann@tu-dresden.at
[2] Institut für Computersprachen
TU Wien, Vienna, Austria
jens.knoop@tuwien.ac.at
[3] Institut für Informatik
Martin-Luther-Universität Halle-Wittenberg, Halle (Saale), Germany
wolf.zimmermann@informatik.uni-halle.de

1 Motivation and Goals

In the last years, model-based software development received more and more attraction [8,22]. Often, models are expressed in a formal language - often a domain specific language (short: DSL) [7,17,24] -, and implementations are derived by model-based code generators [12]. There are toolboxes for defining domain-specific languages and generating compilers for them such as the Eclipse Modeling Framework (short: EMF) [10,23]. DSLs are defined by a Meta-Model [14] and their compilation is by model-transformations [4,13,16,21]. From these specifications, code generators can be generated. In addition, the toolboxes often generate editors, debuggers and embeddings in programming environments such as Eclipse [5]. Meta models are frequently denoted by a graphical notation analogous to UML class diagrams or by context-free grammars. Consistency constraints are then specified by OCL [20] or similar languages. Often, the generated code is manually improved. Therefore, some research focuses on the consistency between models and their implementations.

Compilers nearly perform the same task as model-based code generators: a program in a high-level programming language is translated into an equivalent program in machine language or another high-level programming language (cross-compiler) [1]. In this sense, a code-generator for a DSL that generates e.g. C-Code is a cross-compiler. However, the technology used for the implementation of compilers is rather different. For textual languages, the first step is in both cases a parser that generates an abstract syntax tree. Then consistency constraints (e.g. typing rules) are being analyzed and the abstract syntax tree is transformed in an intermediate representation. Finally, the target code is generated from this intermediate representation. Optimizations might be applied at all these steps. For compilers there are also toolboxes available that allow to generate compilers from specifications such as Eli [6,9]: context-free grammars for the concrete syntax and the abstract syntax, a mapping from

T. Margaria and B. Steffen (Eds.): ISoLA 2014, Part I, LNCS 8802, pp. 386–390, 2014.

concrete to abstract syntax, e.g. attribute grammars for specifying consistency constraints, tree transformations for specifying the generation of intermediate code, and bottom-up rewrite systems for specifying code selection. The technology is well-established and there is no need to manually improve generated code. However, there is little work on generating syntax-directed editors, debuggers or embeddings in programming environments.

The goal of the model-based code-generators and compilers track was to bring together people from both disciplines, and to enfoster discussions between them. In particular, contributions discussing both aspects, compilers and model-based code-generators were sought addressing topics such as type systems for DSLs and their implementation, editor generation using classical compiler technology, formal semantics of DSLs, correctness of model transformations and program transformations, case studies comparing model-based code generation and compilation. Together, the papers in this track address and investigate these topics from different angles and perspectives and highlight important research questions in these fields and up-to-date responses to them.

2 Contributions

The track consisted of six contributed papers. Their contributions are highlighted below.

The paper of Berg and Zimmermann [2] presents an approach supporting a current industrial design process for developing pumps. At the core of this approach is a DSL for pumps that is based on models, metamodels and attribute grammars for constraint checking. This way, the new approach allows to automatically detect inconsistencies in the requirements and specifications of newly designed pumps, which is impossible in the mostly informal underlying original design process. This is not only an interesting application of compiler technology to model-based DSL construction, it is also an important step towards formalizing the underlying industrially used design process of pumps.

The paper by Birken [3] proposes the construction of code generators for DSLs by utilizing the second Futamura projection and partially evaluating an interpreter of the DSL. The approach is demonstrated by implementing a partial evaluator for the widely used DSL toolset Xtext/Xtend. It is illustrated by the construction of C code generators for a DSL for microcontroller programming. Going beyond this concrete application, the overall approach might serve as a blue-line print for other DSL projects in industry and academia.

In their paper, Jörges and Steffen [11] introduce a semantics-based testing approach for model-based code generators. The approach works by extracting execution traces from the model using classical test case generation approaches, which are then compared with the generated code. An important feature of the Genesys code generator framework the approach is implemented in is that models, code generators, and tests are all specified using the same formalism.

Besides simplifying the usage of the system for application engineers, this enables a kind of higher-order proceeding called multi-meta level testing where code generators are themselves input to the testing procedure. The generation of test cases for the code generator enabled this way introduces another dimension of the approach.

Lepper and Trancón y Widemann [15] argue that metaprogramming with classical compiler technology is similar to model-based code generation and differences between compilation and model-based code generation mostly superficial that can be resolved on the level of metaprogramming. This is substantiated by discussing an important aspect of the generation of complex data model implementations in Java, where concerns of both compiler theory and model-based development apply. This is the rewriting of data models in object-oriented style, based on the visitor pattern, with support for reference graphs and nested collection-valued fields. Building on a compiler constructor's viewpoint, the discussion reveals enlightening analogies to model-based technology.

The paper of Motika, Smyth, and von Hanxleden [18] presents an approach for compiling a variant of statecharts called SCCharts to C or VHDL. The compilation process is interactive and proceeds by a series of model-to-model transformations, where the intermediate results can be improved and optimized by the compiler user. This is in contrast to more classical model-based approaches where only the finally resulting code might be manually optimized. The focus of the presentation lies on the compilation process and the tool environment provided by the current prototype implementation. The usage of the tools is illustrated by a case study from an industrial background.

In their paper, Naujokat, Traonouez, Isberner, Steffen, and Legay [19] propose a domain-specific language for code generators which simplifies the specification of code generators. The power of the approach is demonstrated by its application to generate graphical interfaces for different kinds of state transition systems like (probabilistic) timed automata used by widely applied model-checkers like UPPAAL, SPIN, and others. The approach has been implemented within the CINCO meta tooling suite. The examples of the case study demonstrate how the subtle semantic differences of model-checking tools and state transition systems can be compensated and dealt with by the new domain-specific code generation approach.

In spite of the diversity of themes addressed in the papers of this track, there is one theme in common to all of them: mastering technical change. This is the title of this volume of the ISoLA 2014 conference proceedings. In fact, model-based code generation approaches and compiler technology have a lot to offer to master technical change by providing convenient tools and methods that can fast, easily and reliably be adapted to accommodate changing or newly upcoming requirements and demands. The papers in this track illustrate this impressively.

References

1. Aho, A.V., Lam, M.S., Sethi, R., Ullman, J.D.: Compilers: Principles, Techniques, and Tools, 2nd edn. Addison-Wesley (2007)
2. Berg, C., Zimmermann, W.: DSL implementation for model-based development of pumps. In: Margaria, T., Steffen, B. (eds.) ISoLA 2014, Part I. LNCS, vol. 8802, pp. 391–406. Springer, Heidelberg (2014)
3. Birken, K.: Building Code Generators for DSLs Using a Partial Evaluator for the Xtend Language. In: Margaria, T., Steffen, B. (eds.) ISoLA 2014, Part I. LNCS, vol. 8802, pp. 407–424. Springer, Heidelberg (2014)
4. Czarnecki, K., Helsen, S.: Feature-based Survey of Model Transformation Approaches. IBM Systems Journal, special issue on Model-Driven Software Development 45(3), 621–646 (2006)
5. Eclipse, https://www.eclipse.org/ (Online. Last accessed July 25, 2014)
6. Eli, http://eli-project.sourceforge.net/ (Online. Last accessed July 25, 2014)
7. Fowler, M.: Domain-Specific Languages. Addison-Wesley (2011)
8. France, R., Rumpe, B.: Model-driven Development of Complex Software: A Research Roadmap. In: Proceedings 2007 Future of Software Engineering (FOSE 2007), pp. 37–54. IEEE Computer Society (2007)
9. Gray, R.W., Heuring, V.P., Levi, S.P., Sloane, A.M., Waite, W.M.: Eli: A Complete, Flexible Compiler Construction System. Communications of the ACM 35(2), 121–131 (1992)
10. Gronback, R.C.: Eclipse Modeling Project: A Domain-Specific Language (DSL) Toolkit. Addison-Wesley, Boston (2009)
11. Jörges, S., Steffen, B.: Back-To-Back Testing Of Model-Based Code Generators. In: Margaria, T., Steffen, B. (eds.) ISoLA 2014, Part I. LNCS, vol. 8802, pp. 425–444. Springer, Heidelberg (2014)
12. Kelly, S., Tolvanen, J.P.: Domain-Specific Modeling: Enabling Full Code Generation. John Wiley & Sons (2008)
13. Kleppe, A.: Software Language Engineering: Creating Domain-Specific Languages Using Metamodels. Addison-Wesley (2008)
14. Kühne, T.: Matters of (Meta-)Modeling. Software and System Modeling 5(4), 369–385 (2006)
15. Lepper, M., Widemann, B.T.y.: Rewriting Object Models With Cycles and Nested Collections: A Model-Based Metaprogramming Problem. In: Margaria, T., Steffen, B. (eds.) ISoLA 2014, Part I. LNCS, vol. 8802, pp. 445–460. Springer, Heidelberg (2014)
16. Mens, T., Van Gorp, P.: A Taxonomy of Model Transformation. Electronic Notes in Theoretical Computer Science 152, 125–142 (2006)
17. Mernik, M., Heering, J., Sloane, A.M.: When and How to Develop Domain-Specific Languages. ACM Computing Surveys 37(4), 316–344 (2005)
18. Motika, C., Smyth, S., von Hanxleden, R.: Compiling SCCharts — A Case-Study on Interactive Model-Based Compilation. In: Margaria, T., Steffen, B. (eds.) ISoLA 2014, Part I. LNCS, vol. 8802, pp. 461–480. Springer, Heidelberg (2014)
19. Naujokat, S., Traonouez, L.-M., Isberner, M., Steffen, B., Legay, A.: Domain-Specific Code Generator Modeling: A Case Study for Multi-Faceted Concurrent Systems. In: Margaria, T., Steffen, B. (eds.) ISoLA 2014, Part I. LNCS, vol. 8802, pp. 481–498. Springer, Heidelberg (2014)
20. OCL, http://www.omg.org/spec/OCL/ (Online. Last accessed July 25, 2014)

21. Sendall, S., Kozaczynski, W.: Model Transformation – the Heart and Soul of Model-Driven Software Development. IEEE Software 20(5), 42–45 (2003)
22. Stahl, T., Völter, M., Bettin, J., Haase, A., Helsen, S.: Model-driven Software Development – Technology, Engineering, Management. John Wiley & Sons (2006)
23. Steinberg, D., Budinsky, F., Paternostro, M., Merks, E.: EMF: Eclipse Modeling Framework, 2nd edn. Addison-Wesley, Boston (2008)
24. Völter, M., Benz, S.: Dietrich, C., Engelmann, B., Helander, M., Kats, L., Visser, E., Wachsmuth, G.: DSL Engineering – Designing, Implementing and Using Domain-Specific Languages. dslbook.org (2013)

DSL Implementation for Model-Based Development of Pumps*

Christian Berg and Wolf Zimmermann

Institut für Informatik
Martin-Luther-Universität Halle-Wittenberg, Halle (Saale), Germany
{christian.berg,wolf.zimmermann}@informatik.uni-halle.de

Abstract. Domain-specific languages with a formal static semantics allow the early discovery of (domain-specific) inconsistencies. Using attribute grammars we show how such inconsistencies can be found in the pump domain. We compare some analyses using attribute grammars with analyses done in OCL w.r.t. performance and the quality of error messages.

1 Introduction

Roughly half of the energy consumption in industrial processes (or applications) is due to pumps. Pumps are therefore the main consumer of energy [20]. Tailoring pumps to the industrial process lessens the energy consumption, but also results in a large product variability.

Even though a pump has various properties influencing its behaviour, a client, such as the operator of a facility, is mainly interested in the pressure and flow generated by a pump. Hence, tailoring a pump to an industrial process starts with a single requirement: "pressure x and flow y for process z". Up to thousands of requirements may follow from this requirement (and can be traced back to it). Based on these requirements the necessary functions (i.e. mappings from inputs to outputs) are specified and then later transformed into an architecture. This process is influenced by the structured analysis design method. After deciding which craft shall implement certain functions the function is implemented using systems programming or hardware synthesis. Figure 1 illustrates this process using a DSL.

The complexity of pumps and the complexity of the process combined with the need to mass-produce single units causes various problems such as over- and underspecification or inconsistencies along the process steps. An example for the latter is not using a specified function in any architecture while this function is the only one refining a requirement.

Domain-specific languages (DSLs) help in reducing the complexity and length of development time [19]. Another benefit of DSLs is to enable domain experts to specify problems using their own vocabulary while not needing a formal training in general purpose languages such as Java or C. A DSL having a formal

---

* BMBF (16M3202D).

T. Margaria and B. Steffen (Eds.): ISoLA 2014, Part I, LNCS 8802, pp. 391–406, 2014.
© Springer-Verlag Berlin Heidelberg 2014

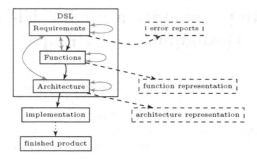

Fig. 1. Graphical Overview of Process and Language Integration for Pump Development; possible inconsistencies arising from (mutual) influences in grey; (iterative) process steps in black; compiler-generated documents dashed

static semantics is of additional benefit: inconsistencies, e.g. over-specification and underspecification, can be found earlier. Giving a formal static semantics to a programming or domain-specific language can be done using traditional compiler methods [1] or using OCL in model-based environments [12]. This paper presents a DSL for the specification of pumps, currently named PDL (Section 2) and a formal static semantics (using compiler-based methods) for finding inconsistencies in the pump domain (Section 3). A comparison of methods from compiler construction with model-based methods using OCL for the specification of the static semantics is given in Section 4. A review of other domain-specific languages applicable in the pump domain and similar model-based works for the specification of a formal semantics of domain-specific languages (Section 5) as well as a short summary and open questions (Section 6) conclude this paper.

2   Pumps, Process, Problems and Examples

Pumps consist of mechanical parts, hardware (i.e. computers), software as well as electric parts (e.g. frequency converter), thus similar problems and research challenges as in the automotive or avionics domain are applicable. Research challenges from an automotive perspective are given in [23]. In contrast to cars, where software control mechanisms are utilized for at least 30 years now [3], control software for pumps is comparatively young, thus less experience with software development and its integration with other components exists in the pump domain. Additionally, pumps are expected to work with little to no service for decades, while cars are expected to only run with regular service for a shorter timespan.

Remark 1. For an easier presentation variability management and the consideration of non-functional requirements (e.g. color) as well as "meta-requirements" (norms and standards) are omitted.

Typically the pump development process is started by a client requesting a non-existent pump. This is usually done by giving a statement similar to the one in the introduction, e.g. "a pump having a pressure of 10 bar and a flow of 400 m³ per hour for the cooling in a steel processing plant". The product development process thus begins with the following requirement:

```
rq "SteelCooling Pump p10f400"
```

Successively this requirement is filled with necessary meta-data, such as the responsible person for implementing this requirement (*owner*), its id in the change request management (*bugid*) and its status. Subsequently, additional requirements, such as the need for a control software or housing, need to be added as well as an actual specification of every requirement. A simplified result of these "first steps" (meta-data omitted) is shown in Listing 1, which specifies the "SteelCooling Pump p10f400" to be the product under consideration. A requirement may depend on other requirements. The keyword require indicates a dependency relation.

The requirements of the example have certain problems:

- "Protection", for protecting the pump and motor from (possibly thermal) damage, is never specified but is required for the pump to "exist",
- the requirements "Housing", to house the control board, and "ControlBoard" (the actual control board) are interdependent and
- the requirement "Switchflow" is never used.

A graphical representation of the requirements hierarchy of Listing 1 is given in Figure 2.

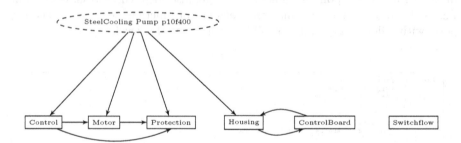

Fig. 2. Graphical Representation of the Requirements Hierarchy of Listing 1

After fixing the above problems and adding (much) more requirements, the input and output behaviour of the pump is refined in terms of functions. A possible specification of such a function for the thermical protection can be seen in Listing 2. Listing 2 also contains type information of the in- and outports as well as timing constraints an implementation has to comply with (due to the industrial application). Using guard expressions the output may be specified in terms of the inputs (and possibly current state information).

Problems during this level of the development process might be missing reasons for the specification of a function (i.e. no requirements for this function) or

```
1   rt rq "SteelCooling Pump p10f400"
2
3   rq "SteelCooling Pump p10f400" {
4     require [rq Motor, rq Control, rq Protection, rq Housing]
5     spec {The pump shall provide pressure X and flow Y for the industrial process
6           z. }
7   }
8
9   rq Motor          { require rq Protection }
10  rq Control        { require [rq Protection, rq Motor] }
11  rq Constrolboard  { require rq Housing }
12  rq Housing        { require rq Controlboard }
13  rq SwitchFlow
```

Listing 1. Simple Requirements Example, root requirement specified using **rt**

using inports as outports or vice versa. Additionally, typing errors always cause quite severe problems in later levels, such as using temperature when actually something else is measured.

It is quite common to consider a pump itself an input-output system: it transforms pressure and flow into another pressure and flow. Hence, the structured analysis and design technique and its derivations for realtime systems (in the following SAs) are recommended in [20] as the formalism to use in the pump domain. Figure 3 shows a compiler-generated image inspired by architecture context diagrams and domain-specific conventions[1]. This also differs from the automotive and avionics domains where UML and derived techniques are widely used.

Before actually implementing a requirement, the architecture of the system is described, i.e. the use-relation of functions and the data- and control-flow and the design alternatives. A resulting architecture specification in PDL can be seen in Listing 3, a corresponding generated image, also inspired by SAs, is given in Figure 4. Missing functions and erroneous use of functions, e.g. by connecting ports with different types, are possible problems at this level.

```
1   fun motorProtect {
2     provides rq Protection
3     in current : Temperature
4     in maximum : Temperature
5
6     out motorProtect : Maybe<Alarm> =
7       | current > maximum := Alarm motorProtect
8       | otherwise := Nothing
9
10    out motorState : Temperature =
11      | current > maximum := stopped
12      | otherwise := motorState
13
14    timings {
15      constant on motorState for 1000 ms
16      change on motorState within 50 ms
17    }
18  }
```

Listing 2. Functions providing the "Protection" requirement using thermal values

Summary: requirements should be acyclic, should not use undefined requirements and each should be used. Similarly, a function should be well-typed and

---

[1] e.g. controls and mechanisms are left out because these should be identical for most products.

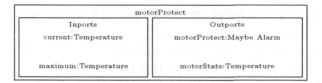

Fig. 3. Graphical Representation of the Function given in Listing 2 generated by our compiler; Representation inspired by structured analysis techniques and domain-specific conventions

```
1  arch motorProtect {
2    require [fun alarmShow, fun motorStateChange]
3    refine fun motorProtect
4    motorProtect.motorProtect -> alarmShow.alarm
5    motorProtect.motorState -> motorStateChange.wish
6    Environment User -> motorProtect.maximum
7    Environment Env -> motorProtect.current
8  }
```

Listing 3. Architectural refinement of the "Protection" function

only be specified when a requirement implies such a function. Furthermore, every port of a function must either be connected to the environment or to another function and the architecture must not use functions without one or more implemented requirements. Hence, inconsistencies may arise in a horizontal, such as cyclic requirements, as well as a vertical manner, such as the use of unrequired functions in an architecture.

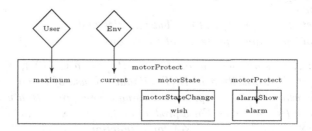

Fig. 4. Graphical Representation of the Architecture Specification of Listing 3 generated by our compiler; representation inspired by structured analysis techniques and domain-specific conventions

3   Language Semantics Using Compiler Methods

We now continue to present the analyses for the problems in Section 2. The tool eli [8] is used to implement lexing, parsing and analyses (as well as output generation). The basis for a variety of formal languages are context-free grammars:

Definition 1. *A **context-free grammar** is a tuple* $G \triangleq (T, N, P, S)$ *with*

- T *being a finite set of terminal symbols,*
- N *being a finite set of non-terminal symbols,*
- $P \subseteq N \times (T \cup N)^*$ *a set of production rules and*
- $S \in N$ *being a distinguished start symbol.*

Notation: *If the language of* G *specifies a correct sequence of terminal symbols we call* G concrete *syntax, if* G *specifies tree construction operations we call* G abstract *syntax. Productions may be given in EBNF or BNF.*

Definition 2. *For a context-free grammar* $G \triangleq (T, N, P, S)$ *and* $X \in N$ *and* $u, v \in (N \cup T)^*$, $Y \in (N \cup T)$, Y *is called **derived** or a **derivation** from* X *iff there is a production* $p \in P$ *with* $p = X ::= uYv$, *written* $X \Rightarrow uYv$. $\stackrel{*}{\Rightarrow}$ *is the reflexive, transitive closure of a derivation.*

Context-free grammars can be extended such that a formal specification for preconditions, postconditions and invariants can be given, which can also be interpreted as the static semantics of a language. We use one class of attribute grammars, ordered attribute grammars [13], to implement such conditions. Attribute grammars were introduced by Knuth in [16] and since then have been classified, limited, extended, and used in various contexts.

Definition 3. *An **attribute grammar** is a tuple* $AG = (G, A, R, C)$ *with*

- *an abstract syntax* $G \triangleq (T, N, P, S)$,
- $A \triangleq \uplus_{X \in (T \cup N)} A(X)$ *being a finite set of attributes (for every symbol* X *of the grammar,*
- *a finite set* $R \triangleq \uplus_{p \in P} R(p)$ *of attribution rules and*
- $C \triangleq \uplus_{p \in P} C(p)$ *being a finite set of conditions.*

Notation: $X.a$ *is an abbrevation for an attribute* $a \in A(X)$, $X \in (T \cup N)$. *Productions* $p \in P$ *are written in BNF without the use of* $\langle$ *and* $\rangle$ *to represent non-terminals while choice is represented using a new production with the same left-hand symbol (instead of* $|$*). For a production* $X_0 ::= X_1 \cdots X_n$ *an attribution has the form* $X_i.a \leftarrow f(X_j, \ldots, X_k)$ *for a function* f, $i, j, k \in [0, n]$. *If* f *is a constant function or the identity function we omit* f. *If a function is commonly used as an infix operator, such as a set operation, we also use this common notation. A condition for a production* p *is written as* $\varphi(X_j, \ldots, X_k)$ *for a predicate* φ. *If we need to distinguish the same symbol in a single production we consecutively number this symbol beginning by 1.*

An example for an attribute grammar definition is given in Listing 4. Using the keyword **rule** a production is indicated for which the attributions following the keyword **attr** shall be evaluated. We declare conditions using the keyword **cond**, followed by the actual condition; the part after $\rightarrow$ causes the error message (indicated by the keyword **error**) to be displayed if the condition evaluates to false.

In order to check that the requirements hierarchy is actually a hierarchy and not some arbitrary graph we construct a dependency graph:

```
1   rule  Description  ::=  ReqDefs RootSpec
2   attr  ReqDefs.rootsIn  ←  ∅
3         RootSpec.rootsIn  ←  ReqDefs.rootsOut
4   cond  |RootSpec.rootsOut| = 1 → {error "wrong number of roots" |RootSpec.rootsOut|}
```

Listing 4. Example of an attribute grammar definition

Definition 4. *A quadruple* $Dep \triangleq (G, DefRqs, UseRqs, r)$ *with*

- *DefRqs being the set of* defined *requirements*
- *UseRqs being the set of* used *requirements*
- $G \triangleq (V, E)$ *is a directed graph where* $V \triangleq DefRqs \cup UseRqs$ *and* $E \subseteq DefRqs \times UseRqs$,
- *a root node* $r \in V$

is called **dependency graph.** *A dependency graph is* **complete** *iff*

- $UseRqs \subseteq DefRqs$
- $r \in DefRqs$

DefRqs and UseRqs are the sets of defined and used requirements, respectively.

A dependency graph can be constructed from the abstract syntax of PDL.

As mentioned in the last paragraph of Sect. 2 undefined requirements are a part of possible inconsistencies. We omit a presentation of this part, because this resembles traditional name analysis – a problem having standard solutions available in most tools, a work describing the standard solution using eli is given in [14].

Definition 5. *A complete dependency graph* $Dep \triangleq (G, DefRqs, UseRqs, r)$ *is called* **bound** *iff for all* $v \in V$ *there is a path from* r *to* v.

Definition 6. *A complete dependency graph* $Dep \triangleq (G, DefRqs, UseRqs, r)$ *is called* **acyclic** *iff* G *is acyclic.*

Definition 5 is used to ensure that there are no unused requirements.

Having set the stage w.r.t. requirements we now require some additions to attribute grammars to make the attributions more convenient and less verbose. In [9,6] and [26] similar definitions have been used to simplify the specification of attribute grammar rules.

Definition 7. *Let* $AG \triangleq (\mathsf{G}, A, R, C)$ *be an attribute grammar with abstract syntax* $\mathsf{G} \triangleq (T, N, P, S)$ *and arbitrary productions* $p, p_1, p_2 \in P$. *Let* $\mathsf{X}_i, \mathsf{Y}_j \in (N \cup T)$ *for* $i \in [1, n]$ *and* $j \in [1, m]$ *and* $\mathsf{X}_0, \mathsf{Y}_0 \in N$ *and some* $k \in \mathbb{N}$. *Furthermore, let*

$$p_1 \triangleq \mathsf{X}_0 ::= \mathsf{X}_1 \ldots \mathsf{X}_n$$

$$p_2 \triangleq \mathsf{Y}_0 ::= \mathsf{Y}_1 \ldots \mathsf{Y}_m$$

$$p \triangleq \mathsf{X}_i ::= \mathsf{X}_{i_1} \ldots \mathsf{X}_{i_{l-1}} \mathsf{X}_{i_l} \mathsf{X}_{i_{l+1}} \ldots \mathsf{X}_{i_k} \qquad with \ \mathsf{X}_{i_l} \triangleq \mathsf{Y}_0$$

then the following **common patterns** *exist:*

Propagation. *An attribute in an upper context can be propagated to lower contexts. For any non-terminal* $X \in N$ *with* $X \overset{*}{\Rightarrow} uYv$, *and all* $Y \in (N \cup T)$, $u, v \in (N \cup T)^*$; *the attribute* **propagage** $X.a$ **as** b *declares the attribute* a *of* X *to be available in any symbol* Y *as* $Y.b$. *For* $X \Rightarrow X_j$, $j \in [1, n]$ *and the above production* p_1 *with* $X_0 \triangleq X$

```
1   rule X::= X₁ ... Xᵢ ... Xₙ
2   propagate X.a as b
```

is equivalent to

```
1     rule X ::= X₁ ... Xᵢ ... Xₙ
2     attr X₁.b ← X.a
:
i+1        Xᵢ.b ← X.a
:
n+1        Xₙ.b ← X.a
```

The attribute b *must be a new attribute.*

Contribution: *For all productions* p_1, p_2, p *as above the attribute grammar definition*

```
1   rule X::= X₁ ... Xᵢ ... Xₙ              rule Xᵢ ::= Xᵢ₁ ... Xᵢₗ₋₁ Y Xᵢₗ₊₁ ... Xᵢₖ
2   rule Y::= Y₁ ... Yₘ
3
4   contribution b of Y to chain X.a using (e, f)
```

is equivalent to

```
1        rule X₀ ::= X₁ ... Xₙ
2        attr X₁.aIn ← e(X₀, X₁, ..., Xₙ)
3             X₂.aIn ← X₁.aOut
:
n+1           Xₙ.aIn ← Xₙ₋₁.aOut
n+2           X₀.aOut ← Xₙ.aOut
n+3      rule Xᵢ ::= Xᵢ₁ ... Xᵢₗ₋₁ Y Xᵢₗ₊₁ ... Xᵢₖ
n+4      attr Xᵢ₁.aIn ← Xᵢ.aIn
n+5           Xᵢ₂.aIn ← Xᵢ₁.aOut
:
n+l+3         Xᵢₗ.aIn ← Xᵢₗ₋₁.aOut
n+l+4         Xᵢₗ₊₁.aIn ← f̄(Y.aOut, Y.b)
:
n+k+3         Xᵢₖ.aIn ← Xᵢₖ₋₁.aOut
n+k+4         Xᵢ.aOut ← Xᵢₖ.aOut
n+k+5    rule Y::= Y₁ ... Yₘ
n+k+6    attr Y₁.aIn ← Y.aIn
n+k+7         Y₂.aIn ← Y₁.aOut
:
n+k+m+6       Y.aOut ← Yₘ.aOut
```

where **aIn** *and* **aOut** *are new attributes used for distinguishing the attribute* a. *The keyword* **chain** *is included as a reminder that the attributes could be evaluated in a depth-first left-right manner.*

Notation: *There is a predefined attribute* **sym** $\in A(X)$ *for every* $X \in T$, *which allows accessing the terminal symbol. If for a non-terminal* $Y \in N$ *only productions of the form* $Y ::= V$ *exist,* $V \in (N \cup T)$, *then the attribute rules for* $Y.a$ *will be omitted iff* $a \in (A(V) \cup A(Y))$ *and for every production the attribution has the form*

```
1   rule Y ::= V
2   attr Y.a ← V.a
```

Figure 5 gives the abstract syntax for all parts of PDL.

⟨*Description*⟩	::=	((⟨*ReqDef*⟩ | ⟨*RootSpec*⟩ | ⟨*FunctDef*⟩ | ⟨*ArchDef*⟩))*
⟨*ReqDef*⟩	::=	⟨*RqDefId*⟩ ⟨*RqUse*⟩*
⟨*RqDefId*⟩	::=	⟨*ID*⟩
⟨*FunctDef*⟩	::=	⟨*FunDefId*⟩ ((⟨*FunInport*⟩ | ⟨*FunOutport*⟩))*
⟨*FunInport*⟩	::=	⟨*InportDefId*⟩ ⟨*Typename*⟩
⟨*FunOutport*⟩	::=	⟨*OutportDefId*⟩ ⟨*Typename*⟩ ⟨*FunGuard*⟩*
⟨*FunGuard*⟩	::=	⟨*FunExpression*⟩ ⟨*FunExpression*⟩
⟨*FunExpression*⟩	::=	⟨*FunExpression*⟩ operator ⟨*InportRef*⟩
⟨*ArchitectureDefinition*⟩	::=	⟨*ArchDefId*⟩ ⟨*ArchConnection*⟩*
⟨*ArchConnection*⟩	::=	⟨*FunRef*⟩ ⟨*PortRef*⟩ ⟨*FunRef*⟩ ⟨*PortRef*⟩
⟨*ID*⟩	::=	string | identifier

Fig. 5. Abstract Syntax of PDL; * ≙ finite closure; non-terminals nt in ⟨nt⟩; except for ⟨*RqDefId*⟩ productions to ⟨*ID*⟩ omitted

Listing 5 gives the attribute grammar rules for the abstract syntax (Fig. 5). Finite closure and grouping have been replaced with appropriate non-terminals (**Decls** and **Decl**; **Funports** and **Funport**). Definition 7 has been used extensively. Without Definition 7 the definition of the attribute grammar would be much larger, an excerpt can be seen in Listing 6 (p. 401).

Listing 5 uses only very simple semantic functions for accessing tuples, which correspond to a definition table in a real implementation. Constraints involving different levels of the development process are shown from line 48 onward. Similar constraints considering requirements and functions corresponding to name analysis have been implemented using attribute grammars (not shown in Listing 5).

As mentioned in remark 1 the presentation of variability management, especially parts which would require a selection of the architecture to be used for the implementation, have been omitted.

4   Requirements Hierarchy Checking Using OCLinEcore

In [2] we showed how to check the requirements hierarchy using the OCLinEcore implementation of the Object Constraint Language (OCL) and compared this with the part of PDL having a corresponding task. An introduction to OCL can be found in [24], a historical perspective of OCL is given in [22]. OCL can be used as a technique for the specification of the semantics of domain-specific languages[12,10,22] and is often used together with models or meta-models.

Definition 8. *A **model** abstracts from a system, a product or properties. A **meta-model** is a model, which defines the concrete and abstract syntax as well as the semantics of a modelling language. An **Object** is an instance of a model and needs to conform to the model, which means it must comply with the syntax and semantics of the model.*

```
1   contribution edge of RqUse to chain Description.edges using (∅, ∪)
2   contribution sym of RootSpec to chain Description.roots using (∅, ∪)
3   contribution sym of RqDefId to chain Description.rqdefs using (∅, ∪)
4   contribution port of Funport to chain FunctDef.ports using (∅, ∪)
5   contribution fun of FunctDef to chain Description.funs using (∅, ∪)
6   propagate Description.funsOut as funsEnv
7   propagate Description.rqdefsOut as rqenv
8   propagate ReqDef.sym as defsym
9   propagate FunctDef.portsOut as fports
10
11  rule RqDefId ::= ID
12  cond RqDefId.sym ∉ RqDefId.rqdefsIn → {error "already defined " RqDefId.sym}
13
14  rule ReqDef ::= RqDefId RqUses
15  attr ReqDef.sym ← RqDefId.sym
16
17  rule RqUse ::= ID
18  attr RqUse.edge ← (RqUse.defsym, RqUse.sym)
19  cond RqUse.sym ∈ RqUse.rqenv → {error "undefined reference " RqUse.sym}
20
21  rule RootSpec ::= ID
22  cond RootSpec.sym ∈ RootSpec.rqenv → {error "root not defined " RootSpec.sym}
23
24  rule Description ::= Decls
25  attr Description.Dep ← ((Description.rqdefsOut, Description.edgesOut),
26                          toElem(Description.rootsOut))
27  cond |Description.roots| = 1 → {error "root number " Description.rootsOut}
28       acyclic(Description.Dep) → {error "cycles " cyclesOf(Description.Dep)}
29       bound(Description.Dep) → {error "unreachable " unusedOf(Description.Dep)}
30
31  rule FunctDef ::= FunDefId FunPorts
32  attr FunctDef.fun ← (FunDefId.sym, FunctDef.portsOut)
33
34  rule FunInport ::= InPortDefId Typename
35  attr FunInport.port ← (In, InPortDefId.sym, Typename.sym)
36
37  rule FunOutport ::= OutportDefId Typename Guards
38  attr FunOutport.port ← (Out, OutportDefId.sym, Typename.sym)
39
40  rule FunExpression₁ ::= FunExpression₂ operator InportRef
41  cond kindOf(InportRef.sym, FunExpression₁.fports) = In
42            → {error "not an inport " InportRef.sym }
43  rule ArchConnection ::= FunRef₁ PortRef₁ FunRef₂ PortRef₂
44  attr ArchConnection.funL ← getFunction (FunRef₁.sym, ArchConnection.funsEnv))
45       ArchConnection.funR ← getFunction (FunRef₂.sym, ArchConnection.funsEnv))
46       ArchConnection.portsL ← portsOf (ArchConnection.funL)
47       ArchConnection.portsR ← portsOf (ArchConnection.funR)
48  cond kindOf(getPort(PortRef₁.sym, ArchConnection.portsL)) = Out
49            → {error "not an outport " PortRef₁.sym }
50       kindOf(getPort(PortRef₂.sym, ArchConnection.portsR)) = In
51            → {error "not an outport " PortRef₂.sym }
52       typeOf(getPort(PortRef₁.sym, ArchConnection.portsL)) =
53           typeOf(getPort(PortRef₂.sym, ArchConnection.portsR))
54            → {error "types dont match " PortRef₁.sym PortRef₂.sym }
```

Listing 5. Concise attribute grammar rules to check PDL for all inconsistencies listed in Section 2

Class diagrams can be used to visualize models and meta-models. Figure 6 shows a meta-model to represent the requirements hierarchy.

Remark 2. We use a more complex meta-model than, for instance, [18] to enable engineers to edit the model exchange files with a standard text editor.

```
 1   rule RqDefId ::= ID
 2   attr RqDefId.sym ← ID.sym
 3        ID.edgesIn ← RqDefId.edgesIn
 4        RqDefId.edgesOut ← ID.edgesOut
 :                                              :
99   rule Decls₁ ::= Decls₂ Decl
100  attr Decls₂.rqdefsIn ← Decls₁.rqdefsIn
101       Decl.rqdefsIn ← Decls₂.rqdefsOut
102       Decls₁.rqdefsOut ← Decl.rqdefsOut
103       Decl.rqenv ← Decls₁.rqenv
 :                                              :
518  rule ArchConnection ::= FunRef₁ PortRef₁ FunRef₂ PortRef₂
519  attr ArchConnection.funL ← getFunction (FunRef₁.sym, ArchConnection.funsEnv))
520       ArchConnection.funR ← getFunction (FunRef₂.sym, ArchConnection.funsEnv))
521       ArchConnection.portsL ← portsOf (ArchConnection.funL)
522       ArchConnection.portsR ← portsOf (ArchConnection.funR)
523       FunRef₁.edgesIn ← ArchConnection.edgesIn
524       ArchConnection.edgesOut ← PortRef₂.edgesOut
525       PortRef₁.edgesIn ← FunRef₁.edgesOut
526       FunRef₂.edgesIn ← PortRef₁.edgesOut
527       PortRef₂.edgesIn ← FunRef₂.edgesOut
 :                                              :
551  cond kindOf(getPort(PortRef₁.sym, ArchConnection.portsL)) = Out
552       → {error "not an outport " PortRef₁.sym }
553       kindOf(getPort(PortRef₂.sym, ArchConnection.portsR)) = In
554       → {error "not an outport " PortRef₂.sym }
555       typeOf(getPort(PortRef₁.sym, ArchConnection.portsL)) =
556          typeOf(getPort(PortRef₂.sym, ArchConnection.portsR))
557          → {error "types dont match " PortRef₁.sym PortRef₂.sym }
```

Listing 6. Excerpt of applying used conventions and Definition 7 to Listing 5; for the given rules not all attributions are shown

OCL is a language to specify pre- and postconditions as well as invariants for a context and thus is similar to attribute grammars. A difference is that OCL is a side-effect free language and every expression *should* evaluate to either true or false. Listing 7 shows the checks using OCL. Checking the requirements hierarchy uses standard solutions found in [4].

Instead of using OCL, a language implementation could use model transformations for checking the formal static semantics. The downside is the possible loss of information due to non-reversible transformations.

The following discussion summarizes the results from [2]. For each row in Table 1 the mean of 1000 executions per implementation are given in seconds. Hundreds up to thousands of requirements with different properties such as connectivity (density) of the hierarchy as well as the presence and abscence of cycles were used. The number of requirements resembles our reference data, which contained products with a few hundred as well as thousands of requirements.

In [2], it can be seen that most of the runtime in the OCLinEcore version is spent in checking if the requirements hierarchy is acyclic, which is due to the usage of the `closure`-operation.

The listings in Figure 7 show the error outputs for our version as well as the OCLinEcore version. Our version precisely states which requirements cause cycles as well as which requirements are not used, whereas the version using OCLinEcore just states that a constraint is not satisfied.

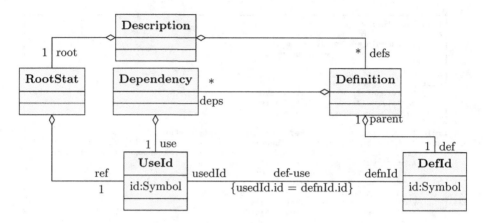

Fig. 6. Class diagram for the presentation of a meta-modell to describe a requirements hierarchy; classes correspond to nodes of the abstract syntax

Table 1. Runtimes of the different tools for checking the consistency of the Requirements Hierarchy

Requirements	Density (%)	Unreachable (%)	Cyclic?	OCLinEcore	Compiler-based
100	3	10	no	3.42 s	< 0.01 s
1000	4	2	no	5.08 s	0.01 s
1000	4	2	yes	3.61 s	0.07 s
2000	5	0	yes	3.80 s	0.04 s
2000	6	10	no	17.60 s	0.08 s
2000	10	0	no	35.10 s	0.17 s
5000	10	10	no	403 s	1.10 s
5000	10	0	yes	Out of Memory	13.95 s
10000	2	4	yes	Out of Memory	17.58 s
10000	2	4	no	> 600 s	1.48 s

5   Related Work

Various works[5,7,18] consider the modeling of requirements but do not consider an integration on the semantic level. The semantic integration of requirements with architecture specifications is content of [7]. The generation of traces for requirements and architecture specifications is discussed and model-checking is used to ensure that the architecture correctly implements functional requirements. Thus, [7] has a wider scope than our work but on the other hand requires more time to give a result (caused by the usage of model-checking).

The use of OCL as a specification technology for language semantics is advocated in [15]. [22] gives a general overview of the history and usage of OCL and also mentions OCL being in use as a specification technology for language

```
1  context Description:
2    inv bound:
3      let rootdef  = root.ref.defnId.parent,
4          rootdeps = rootdef->closure(getdefs())
5      in rootdeps->union(rootdef->asSet())->includesAll(defs)
6    inv acyclic: defs->forAll(c | c->closure(getdefs())->excludes(c.def));
7
8  context Definition:
9    def getdefs() = deps.use.defnId.parent
10
11 context UseId:
12   inv defuse: UseId.allInstances()->forAll(x | def-use(x,x))
13
14 context DefId:
15   inv names: DefId.allInstances()->forAll(x |
16                  DefId.allInstances()->forAll(y |
17                      def-use(x,y) implies x.id = y.id))
```

Listing 7. OCLinEcore variant to check the requirements hierarchy for possible problems using the meta-model of Figure 6; closure computes the transitive hull; let generates names

```
"pump.rq", 1:1 ERROR: Found a cyclic component, Path:
"pump.rq", 1:1 ERROR: etc1 -> "Pump XYZ"
"pump.rq", 68:4 INFO:    Definition of: etc1
"pump.rq", 38:4 INFO:    Definition of: "Pump XYZ"
"pump.rq", 1:1 ERROR: "Pump XYZ" -> Motor
"pump.rq", 38:4 INFO:    Definition of: "Pump XYZ"
"pump.rq", 48:4 INFO:    Definition of: Motor
"pump.rq", 1:1 ERROR: Motor -> etc1
"pump.rq", 48:4 INFO:    Definition of: Motor
"pump.rq", 68:4 INFO:    Definition of: etc1
"pump.rq", 77:4 ERROR: Unreachable: additional2
"pump.rq", 76:4 ERROR: Unreachable: additional1
```

```
ERROR: Diagnosis of Description{file:pump.xml#/}
ERROR: The 'bound' constraint is violated on
       'Description{file:pump.xml#/}'
ERROR: The 'acyclic' constraint is violated on
       'Description{file:pump.xml#/}'
```

(a) Compiler output (eli-based)   (b) OCLinEcore output

Fig. 7. Error output for requirements example

semantics. In [10] Dingel and Solberg report on how to embed OCL in model-based tools, such that model instances can be checked for conformance.

There is a wide variety of architecture description languages (ADLs). The π-ADL family (amongst others [21,17]) uses the μ-calculus as a formal foundation and allows for architectural refinement as well as the specification of behavioural properties. Thus, the π-ADL family is richer than PDL but not geared towards the pump domain.

In [25] Schmittwilken et.al. easily transformed OCL manually in attribute grammars. To the best of our knowledge we are not aware of a completely automatic transformation.

6   Conclusions

Using examples gathered from interviews we have given an overview of the pump development process and which inconsistencies may arise. We introduced a DSL for the development of pumps called PDL. We have shown how a formal static semantics supports the discovery of such inconsistencies. The formal static semantics of PDL was implemented by attribute grammars. We compared our implementation with a similar implementation using OCLinEcore for analyzing the requirements hierarchy.

Methods from compiler construction enable the generation and visualization of various details of pump descriptions. Using simple (syntactical) extensions to "basic" attribute grammars we have shown that concise attribute grammar specifications are possible. Attribute grammars enabled better error messages as well as the generation of a faster "compiler" for the requirements level of PDL.

Faster processing of semantic constraints and richer languages may be beneficial in a model-based environment when using compiler-based methods. In the context of pump development the benefits of using compiler-based methods are the semantic integration of different development levels (i.e. requirement, function and architecture specification) and the integration with model-based tools. Even a bidirectional generation approach for this integration comes into reach using compiler-based methods.

The `closure`-operation in OCL has a high level of abstraction. However, it causes a much longer runtime in the OCLinEcore implementation. It remains open if other implementations of OCL, such as Dresden OCL [11], are better suited for such a comparison and thus may give better results. An evaluation with Dresden OCL and Query-View-Transformation is in the works as well as the integration of PDL in the well known development environment Eclipse. So far we used existing products to check for inconsistencies and found various underspecified requirements as well as small cycles and erroneous use of functions. We plan to evaluate PDL by using it to develop a complete product (vs. using excerpts of existing ones and converting those).

Acknowledgements. We would like to thank the BMBF for supporting this work under project number 16M3202D.

References

1. Aho, A.V., Lam, M.S., Sethi, R., Ullman, J.D.: Compilers: Principles, Techniques, and Tools. Addison-Wesley (2007)

2. Berg, C., Zimmermann, W.: Evaluierung von Möglichkeiten zur Implementierung von Semantischen Analysen für Domänenspezifische Sprachen. In: Software Engineering (Workshops), pp. 111–128 (2014)

3. Broy, M.: Challenges in Automotive Software Engineering. In: Proceedings of the 28th International Conference on Software Engineering, pp. 33–42. ACM (2006)

4. Costal, D., Gómez, C., Queralt, A., Raventós, R., Teniente, E.: Facilitating the definition of general constraints in UML. In: Wang, J., Whittle, J., Harel, D., Reggio, G. (eds.) MoDELS 2006. LNCS, vol. 4199, pp. 260–274. Springer, Heidelberg (2006)

5. Dermeval, D., Castro, J., Silva, C., Pimentel, J., Bittencourt, I.I., Brito, P., Elias, E., Tenório, T., Pedro, A.: On the Use of Metamodeling for Relating Requirements and Architectural Design Decisions. In: Proceedings of the 28th Annual ACM Symposium on Applied Computing, SAC 2013, pp. 1278–1283. ACM (2013)

6. Ekman, T., Hedin, G.: Rewritable reference attributed grammars. In: Odersky, M. (ed.) ECOOP 2004. LNCS, vol. 3086, pp. 147–171. Springer, Heidelberg (2004)
7. Goknil, A., Kurtev, I., van den Berg, K.: Tool Support for Generation and Validation of Traces between Requirements and Architecture. In: Proceedings of the 6th ECMFA Traceability Workshop, ECMFA-TW 2010, pp. 39–46. ACM (2010)
8. Gray, R.W., Levi, S.P., Heuring, V.P., Sloane, A.M., Waite, W.M.: Eli: A Complete, Flexible Compiler Construction System. Communications of the ACM 35(2), 121–130 (1992)
9. Hedin, G.: Reference Attributed Grammars. Informatica (Slovenia) 24(3), 301–317 (2000)
10. Heidenreich, F., Johannes, J., Karol, S., Seifert, M., Thiele, M., Wende, C., Wilke, C.: Integrating OCL and textual modelling languages. In: Dingel, J., Solberg, A. (eds.) MODELS 2010. LNCS, vol. 6627, pp. 349–363. Springer, Heidelberg (2011)
11. Hussmann, H., Demuth, B., Finger, F.: Modular architecture for a toolset supporting OCL. In: Evans, A., Caskurlu, B., Selic, B. (eds.) UML 2000. LNCS, vol. 1939, pp. 278–293. Springer, Heidelberg (2000)
12. Jézéquel, J.-M., Barais, O., Fleurey, F.: Model driven language engineering with kermeta. In: Fernandes, J.M., Lämmel, R., Visser, J., Saraiva, J. (eds.) GTTSE. LNCS, vol. 6491, pp. 201–221. Springer, Heidelberg (2011)
13. Kastens, U.: Ordered Attributed Grammars. Acta Informatica 13(3), 229–256 (1980)
14. Kastens, U., Waite, W.M.: An abstract data type for name analysis. Acta Informatica 28(6), 539–558 (1991)
15. Caskurlu, B., Evans, A.: UML Semantics FAQ. In: Yu, H.-J., Demeyer, S. (eds.) ECOOP 1999 Workshops. LNCS, vol. 1743, pp. 33–56. Springer, Heidelberg (1999)
16. Knuth, D.E.: Semantics of Context-Free Languages. Mathematical systems theory 2(2), 127–145 (1968)
17. Mateescu, R., Oquendo, F.: π-aal: An Architecture Analysis Language for Formally Specifying and Verifying Structural and Behavioural Properties of Software Architectures. ACM SIGSOFT Software Engineering Notes 31(2), 1–19 (2006)
18. Mellegård, N., Staron, M.: A Domain Specific Modelling Language for Specifying and Visualizing Requirements. In: The First International Workshop on Domain Engineering, DE@CAiSE, Amsterdam (2009)
19. Mernik, M., Heering, J., Sloane, A.M.: When and How to Develop Domain-Specific Languages. ACM Comput. Surv. 37(4), 316–344 (2005)
20. Oesterle, M., Leidig, F. (eds.): Methodisch sichere, schnelle Produktionsanläufe in der Mechatronik (MESSPRO) - Band 2 der Reihe "Schneller Produktionsanlauf in der Wertschöpfungskette". VDMA-Verlag, Frankfurt (2007)
21. Oquendo, F.: π-arl: An Architecture Refinement Language for Formally Modelling the Stepwise Refinement of Software Architectures. ACM SIGSOFT Software Engineering Notes 29(5), 1–20 (2004)
22. Pandey, R.K.: Object Constraint Language (OCL): Past, Present and Future. SIGSOFT Softw. Eng. Notes 36(1), 1–4 (2011)
23. Pretschner, A., Broy, M., Kruger, I.H., Stauner, T.: Software Engineering for Automotive Systems: A Roadmap. In: 2007 Future of Software Engineering, pp. 55–71. IEEE Computer Society (2007)
24. Richters, M., Gogolla, M.: OCL: Syntax, Semantics, and Tools. In: Clark, A., Warmer, J. (eds.) Object Modeling with the OCL. LNCS, vol. 2263, pp. 42–68. Springer, Heidelberg (2002)

25. Schmittwilken, J., Saatkamp, J., Forstner, W., Kolbe, T.H., Plumer, L.: A Semantic Model of Stairs in Building Collars. Photogrammetrie, Fernerkundung, Geoinformation 2007(6), 415 (2007)
26. Vogt, H.H., Swierstra, S.D., Kuiper, M.F.: Higher Order Attribute Grammars. In: Proceedings of the ACM SIGPLAN 1989 Conference on Programming Language Design and Implementation, PLDI 1989, pp. 131–145. ACM (1989)

Building Code Generators for DSLs Using a Partial Evaluator for the Xtend Language

Klaus Birken

itemis AG, Stuttgart, Germany
`klaus.birken@itemis.de`

Abstract. For several years now, domain-specific languages (DSLs) are a mainstream tool for establishing model-based development environments in real-world projects. Typical back-end tools for external DSLs are interpreters and code generators.

Partial evaluation is a well-known technique for program specialization, with the use case of specializing interpreters to target programs. However, the automatic generation of code generators from a DSL's interpreter is by no means ubiquitous in industrial DSL projects. In this paper, we show how interpreters for a DSL can be used as a basis for automatic generation of efficient target code. This is possible by implementing a partial evaluator for the mainstream DSL toolset Xtext/Xtend.

Keywords: partial evaluation, program specialization, interpreters, code generation, domain-specific languages, Xtext, Xtend.

1 Introduction

Building Domain-Specific Languages. Since the rise of supporting frameworks and language workbenches, domain-specific languages (DSLs) are a mainstream tool for raising the abstraction level in software development environments. There are two basic approaches of designing DSLs, each with its benefits and drawbacks:

- *internal* DSLs are embedded in a host language, using its infrastructure
- *external* DSLs have their own, independent syntax (often implemented by a parser).

Ideally, the semantics of a DSL should be defined independently of its implementation. However, in industrial projects the semantics of a DSL is often defined implicitly by either implementing an *interpreter*, or a *code generator* (or: compiler). The former executes models (aka programs) of the DSL on a concrete target platform. The latter generates code in a target language. These two ways of defining the semantics of a DSL are closely connected, as both provide a mapping from the DSL's abstraction level to some more concrete level of an underlying (executable) machine. However, in practice this relation is rarely exploited. In

T. Margaria and B. Steffen (Eds.): ISoLA 2014, Part I, LNCS 8802, pp. 407–424, 2014.

Listing 1. An Xtend function and its specialized version ($e = 5$).

```
1  class Power {
2    def int power (int b, int e) {
3      if (e==0) 1
4      else if (e%2==0) { val y = power(b, e/2); y * y }
5      else b * power(b, e-1)
6    }
7  }
8
9  class Power_e_5 {
10   def int power(int b)     { b * power_0(b) }
11   def int power_0(int b)   { val y = power_1(b); y * y }
12   def int power_1(int b)   { val y = power_2(b); y * y }
13   def int power_2(int b)   { b * 1 }
14 }
```

a typical industry environment, it is often the case that several code generators and an interpreter are developed manually and independently, at various points in a project's life cycle. Thus, the semantics of the DSL is not guaranteed to be consistent across the various downstream tools, which might lead to subtle errors.

In this paper, it will be shown how manually implemented interpreters for DSLs can be transformed into code generators automatically by applying *partial evaluation* [7]. This approach offers a variety of benefits:

Consistency. Only the interpreter defines the semantics of the DSL. It is guaranteed by design that the derived code generators are consistent with the semantics defined by the interpreter (assuming the partial evaluator is correct).

Abstraction. The interpreter doesn't have to care about platform-specific details.

Testing. The interpreter can be used as an effective way of validating the DSL itself and its models. This includes static analysis as well as unit and regression testing.

Portability. The DSL can be used for various target environments/languages. The last step of the transformation from an interpreter to a code generator is a mapping to a specific platform, which can be adapted to new target environments.

Performance. The code generators can be optimized for a given target platform. E.g., the interpreter will be implemented in a convenient language, whereas the code generator will produce C code for an embedded system.

Product-Line Support. The solution provides support for variability specialization. The DSL and its interpreter may offer flexible configuration options, supporting a set of possible DSL semantics and resulting code generators. Each concrete code generator can be derived using a specific configuration during the specialization.

Partial Evaluation. The transformation is realized by using *partial evaluation*, which is a well-known method for program specialization [7]. Given the source code of a program and fixed values for some of its parameters, partial evaluation computes a specialized program. Listing 1 shows an Xtend program with a recursive method **power(b,e)** computing the power function b^e. Starting from line 9, the result of specializing this method for **e** = 5 is listed. The results of running the specialized program on a set of values for the remaining parameters (**b** in listing 1) will be the same as running the original program. Thus, the execution of a partial evaluator will be a combination of

- partly interpreting the input program, using the fixed input data to execute the program at specialization time (e.g., computing the condition **e%2==0** in line 4), and
- partly generating code, where *dynamic* input data (unknown at specialization time) defers the execution of the code to runtime.

Throughout the paper, we are using the notation introduced in [7] in order to define program execution. Example:

$$o = [\![p]\!]_L \ [i, \ j]$$

The execution of program **p** in language **L** on inputs **i** and **j** produces the output **o**. If the language indication **L** is omitted, the Xtend language is used by default. Now the basic principle of partial evaluation can be formally defined as

$$[\![p]\!] \ [s, \ d] = [\![[\![xmix]\!] \ [p, \ s]]\!] \ d$$

where **xmix** is the partial evaluator, **p** is the source program, **s** (static) denotes fixed value parameters and **d** the remaining dynamic parameters [7, section 1.1.2].

In order to create a code generator from a DSL's interpreter, the partial evaluator will be used to specialize the interpreter. Partial evaluation of an interpreter with respect to an input DSL model (a program) produces a target program. As the target program's language is still the same as the interpreter's, a source-to-source postprocessing step will be applied which transforms the specialized program into the target language (e.g., Xtend to C).

In 1971, Futamura pointed out that a self-applicable partial evaluator can specialize itself with respect to an interpreter, resulting in a compiler (Futamura's second projection [3]). For a given input program, the resulting compiler produces the same target program as the specialization of the interpreter with respect to this input program. We will specialize the interpreter including the postprocessor, which produces a code generator from DSL models (input programs) to programs in the final target language.

This partial evaluation technique has been implemented fully in the 1990s and meanwhile has been applied and investigated in various research projects (see section 5). However, partial evaluation is only rarely applied as a production tool in today's mainstream DSL projects. This paper remedies this by showing how partial evaluation can be applied in a state-of-the-art DSL tool. Thus, we have chosen the *Xtext* toolbox [14] for building external DSLs and the *Xtend* language [13] for building a self-applicable partial evaluator and DSL interpreters. The combination of Xtext and Xtend on top of the Eclipse tool platform is a practically relevant, mainstream toolset being used in various industry projects (e.g., in the Automotive domain).

Overview. The remainder of the paper is structured as follows: In section 2, the tool environment for building external DSLs will be introduced. Section 3 describes the self-applicable partial evaluation algorithm implemented for Xtend. A full-fledged example of applying the partial evaluation scheme is shown in section 4. It will be explained how microcontroller C code can be automatically generated from an example DSL without implementing a code generator. The paper ends with a short discussion of related work and a conclusion section.

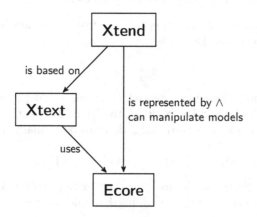

Fig. 1. The relationship of Xtext, Xtend and Ecore

2   The DSL Tool Environment

Domain-Specific Languages with Xtext.   Xtext [14] is a well-established tool for building parser-based external DSLs. It is available as an open-source project on top of the Eclipse IDE and has an active community. Xtext is being used for a wide range of applications in research and industry.

In order to build a DSL with Xtext, a formal grammar has to be defined. Listing 3 shows an example grammar. The language for definition of the grammar is an EBNF-like DSL which itself has been developed with Xtext. From this concrete syntax of the DSL, Xtext generates a metamodel representing the abstract syntax tree (AST). The metamodel format is *Ecore*, which is defined by the *Eclipse Modeling Framework* (EMF, see [11]). From the Ecore-model, a Java-API is generated which allows to access the model programmatically. A DSL-specific, ANTLR-based parser which is also generated by Xtext is able to read textual DSL models and create an AST representation in memory. Xtext also generates a serializer for the opposite direction.

For each DSL, Xtext also provides a user interface with a full-featured editor (with content assist, syntax highlighting, validation) and other extensions of the Eclipse IDE. Xtext offers a default implementation for scoping, linking and validation for the DSL (see [12] or the Xtext documentation for details).

The Xtend Language. The most common development tasks related to DSLs are the implementation of generators and interpreters, as well as model transformations. Each of these tasks requires programmatic access to the DSL's models (AST); for implementing the generator a template mechanism is also useful.

The Xtend programming language [13] has been developed with these tasks in mind. Xtend is statically typed and object-oriented; it is not a JVM language, but is directly transformed into Java. Thus, it is completely and bidirectionally interoperable with Java.

Xtend provides a rich set of language features supporting the above DSL-related tasks:

- no distinction between expressions and statements (everything is an expression)
- extension methods for enhancing closed types (e.g., model elements)
- closures (aka lambda expressions)
- type-based switch statements
- polymorphic method invocation
- template expressions (rich strings)

Due to this rich feature set, Xtend is a powerful language for implementing generators, interpreters and model transformations. The Java API of the DSL's Ecore model can be traversed and manipulated conveniently. Why is Xtend also well-suited for partial evaluation? Figure 1 shows the relationship of Xtext, Xtend and Ecore/EMF. Xtext DSLs represent their AST as Ecore model. The Xtend language itself has been built using Xtext. Thus, each Xtend program is represented as an Ecore model. As described above, Xtend's language features are especially designed for programmatically accessing Ecore models. Therefore, Xtend programs can easily manipulate Xtend programs represented by Ecore models. Earlier languages with this property are Lisp and Prolog, which have been a primary target for partial evaluation implementations in the past.

As both Xtend programs and Xtext-based DSL programs are represented as models, we will use the terms *program* and *model* interchangeably throughout this paper.

3   Partial Evaluation of Xtend Programs

3.1   Challenges

Building a partial evaluator for the complete feature set of the Xtend language offers a variety of implementation challenges.

- Xtend has imperative, object-oriented and functional aspects (see section 2). Existing research on partial evaluation is focusing mainly on functional languages, and is restricted to one (or rarely two) of these aspects. Therefore, the implementation can learn from previous work, but the combination of features is new territory.
- Xtend offers an extended set of syntactic features for member function calls. E.g., the implicit variable it which can be omitted from function calls, or the first argument of an extension method which can be written as a syntactic receiver:

```
"hello".toFirstUpper
    // calls StringExtensions.toFirstUpper("hello")
```

The combination of these syntactic features complicates the implementation of the specializer.
- Xtend provides dispatch-methods, which offer polymorphic dispatching based on the methods' first parameters. This language feature requires particular attention during specialization. If the first argument is fixed at specialization time, polymorphic dispatching will be resolved in the resulting code.

3.2   Partial Evaluator Implementation

A partial evaluation algorithm distinguishes *static* and *dynamic* parameters and expressions in the source program. The values of static parameters and expressions (or more general: model elements) are known at specialization time or can be computed during the specialization. Dynamic model elements are not known at specialization time and can only be computed at runtime. The classification in static vs. dynamic is called *binding time*. *Offline* partial evaluators compute the binding times as a preliminary step, which is called *binding time analysis* (BTA). *Online* partial evaluators compute the binding time during the actual specialization step.

We chose to implement a classical offline partial evaluator, leading to the following sequence of steps:

1. Binding Time Analysis.   In the first step, the binding times for member function arguments, class fields and local variables are computed. A fixpoint iteration based on abstract interpretation according to [7, chapter 5.2] is applied here. In order to support BTA for local and class variables including side effects, we extended this approach by applying a similar notion of *well-annotatedness* as described in [7, chapter 11.5].

In the current implementation, the BTA computes *monovariant* binding times. I.e., for the parameters of each function exactly one set of binding times is computed. We will extend this to a *polyvariant* binding time computation, where a function might have multiple sets of binding times for its parameters. This allows the specializer to compute more efficient and specific residual code.

2. Annotation. Based on the BTA results, every element of the input program's AST is annotated with its actual binding time. This is again a fixpoint iteration over the elements of the AST.

3. Specialization. The actual specialization is implemented as a depth-first traversal over the input program's AST. Based on the annotations from step 2, each language construct of Xtend is either evaluated (the static case) or reduced to a simpler expression. Child expressions are handled recursively. For this step, it helps that Xtend doesn't distinguish between statements and expressions.

For function calls with at least one static parameter, one program point for each unique set of static parameter values is generated. In order to avoid duplicating program points, a proper `equals`-operator has to be provided for each involved class. In the example of listing 1, the generated function calls in the specialized class correspond to static parameter values as follows:

$$
\begin{array}{ll}
\texttt{power(b)} & \Leftrightarrow \quad e = 5 \\
\texttt{power\_0(b)} & \Leftrightarrow \quad e = 4 \\
\texttt{power\_1(b)} & \Leftrightarrow \quad e = 2 \\
\texttt{power\_2(b)} & \Leftrightarrow \quad e = 1
\end{array}
$$

4. Postprocessing. Here the AST of the residual program is cleaned up. For example, this includes the removal of intermediate blocks, constant propagation or inlining of trivial function calls. In listing 1, we omitted this step in order to emphasize the result of the previous steps.

Listing 2 shows the specialization function for `if/else`-constructs. Similar specialization functions are available for all other Xtend language concepts (e.g., variable declarations, for- and while-loops, constructors, arithmetic expressions). Each function in the specializer either evaluates the original expression (if it has been classified as static by BTA), or reduces the original expression as far as possible (if it has been classified as dynamic). The information about the actual binding time (static vs. dynamic) is provided by the annotator. In the example, this information is evaluated and used in line 3 (listing 2).

If the `if`-condition is static, it can be computed at specialization time (line 5). Depending on the boolean value of the condition, either the `then`-branch (line 7) or the `else`-branch (lines 9-14) is executed. If the binding time is dynamic, lines 17-22 are executed. Here, a clone of the `if`-expression is constructed with

Listing 2. One example function of the partial evaluator implemented in Xtend: Specialization of if/else-expressions.

```
 1    def dispatch XExpression reduce (XIfExpression orig, ParamFix vs, IContext context) {
 2      val cond = orig.^if.reduce(vs, context)
 3      if (orig.^if.isStatic) {
 4        // if-condition is static, evaluate and continue with one of the branches
 5        val result = cond.evaluate(context)
 6        if (result.asBoolean) {
 7          orig.then.reduce(vs, context, orig.isStatic)
 8        } else {
 9          if (orig.^else != null)
10            orig.^else.reduce(vs, context, orig.isStatic)
11          else {
12            // no else-branch, return empty block
13            xbaseFactory.createXBlockExpression
14          }
15        }
16      } else {
17        // if-condition is dynamic, hence whole if-expression is dynamic
18        val reduced = xbaseFactory.createXIfExpression
19        reduced.^if = cond.ensureDynamic(orig.^if)
20        reduced.then = orig.then.reduce(vs, context, false)
21        reduced.^else = orig.^else?.reduce(vs, context, false)
22        reduced
23      }
24    }
```

all subexpressions from the original **if**-expression reduced as far as possible. The condition and the corresponding branch will be evaluated only at runtime.

3.3   Specialization Example

Due to the amount of features of the Xtend language it would take a large set of examples to demonstrate all intricacies of the partial evaluation algorithm. We implemented several hundred test cases in order to cover all language features supported by the specializer. We refer to [7] for an overview of partial evaluation of imperative, functional and C-like language features. Some previous work according specialization of object-oriented languages is discussed in detail in [10] and [9].

In order to explain the basic operation of the implemented specializer, we already introduced the simple example from listing 1. It shows an example Xtend class with a recursive function **power(b,e)**. Starting in line 9, the output of the partial evaluation algorithm for $e = 5$ is shown. The static parameter **e** has been discarded. The recursive function calls in the original code have been unrolled by the specializer. A straightforward postprocessing step could inline the trivial function calls in the specialized class **Power_e_5**, resulting in the expression

$$b * ((b * b) * (b * b))$$

We omitted this step here to show the plain output of the specializer.

4 Application: Code Generation for Embedded Systems

In this section we will apply the partial evaluation scheme described in the previous section in order to generate C code for an embedded target from an interpreter. The roadmap for this section is as follows:

1. We use Xtext to build a small, state-machine-based DSL for programming microcontrollers (MCL).
2. A (simple) example program in MCL is defined.
3. The semantics of MCL is defined by implementing an MCL interpreter written in Xtend.
4. The partial evaluator is applied to specialize the interpreter for the example MCL program.
5. The resulting Xtend target program is mapped to the final Arduino C code by a postprocessor.

Listing 3. The Xtext grammar for the MCL language.

```
1  Program:      'program' '(' config+=CfgParam* ')'
2                     decls+=Decl* fsm=FSM;
3  CfgParam:     name=ID;
4
5  Decl:         DigitalIn | DigitalOut;
6  DigitalIn:    'in' name=ID '(' pin=INT ')';
7  DigitalOut:   'out' name=ID '(' pin=INT ')'
8                     ':=' initial=Const;
9
10 FSM:          'fsm' '{' states+=State+ '}';
11 State:        'state' name=ID '{' transitions+=Transition* '}';
12 Transition:   'on' '(' left=Expr '==' right=Expr ')'
13                     '->' to=[State] (action=Block)?;
14
15 Cmd:          SetOutput | IfThen | Block;
16 Block:        '{' commands+=Cmd* '}';
17 SetOutput:    out=[DigitalOut] ':=' expr=Expr ';';
18 IfThen:       'if' '(' cond=Expr ')'
19                     then=Cmd
20                     (=>'else' else=Cmd)?;
21
22 Expr:         ReadInput | Const | CfgValue;
23 ReadInput:    input=[DigitalIn];
24 Const:        value=INT;
25 CfgValue:     '@' ref=[CfgParam];
```

4.1 An Example DSL for Programming Microcontrollers

We are building an example DSL for the embedded systems domain. MCL (short for: MicroControllerLanguage) allows to develop software for microcontrollers using a state machine paradigm. Listing 3 shows the Xtext grammar for MCL. Xtext will convert each parser rule into a corresponding class for the Ecore model. Thus, each parser rule represents a domain concept:

DigitalIn, DigitalOut. General-purpose IO pins on the embedded hardware.

FSM, State, Transition. The top-level finite state machine. It supports equalities as trigger conditions and action codes on transition execution.

Cmd, Block, SetOutput, IfThen. Control structures for the action codes.

Expr, ReadInput, Const. Expression language. The constants will be restricted to the domain $\{0, 1\}$ by validation.

CfgParam, CfgValue. These are configuration parameters which are not visible in the final target program, but will be interpreted during specialization. This is a basic realization of product line specialization.

We deliberately restricted MCL to some core concepts. Extending the language with further hardware abstractions (analog inputs, ...), additional control structures or library calls is straightforward.

Listing 4. An example program in MCL language.

```
1  program (z)
2
3  in a(2)
4  in b(3)
5
6  out led1(13) := 0
7
8  fsm {
9    state s1 {
10     on (a==1) -> s2  { led1 := b; }
11   }
12   state s2 {
13     on (a==0) -> s1  { led1 := @z; }
14   }
15 }
```

4.2 An Example Program in MCL

A simple example MCL program is shown in listing 4. The state machine from this example is additionally depicted in figure 2. In the example, two digital inputs a and b are defined for the hardware pins 2 and 3, respectively. A digital output led1 is defined representing an LED connected to pin 13. The LED is initially turned off. The state machine sets the LED depending on the inputs a and b.

Note that during transition from $s2 \rightarrow s1$, the LED is set according to configuration parameter z. This is a simple, but effective product line approach: The resulting target program will be a configuration-specific refinement of the example MCL. The configuration domain consists of the configurations $\{\{z = 0\}, \{z = 1\}\}$. In a real-world scenario, the possible configurations will be derived from a feature model.

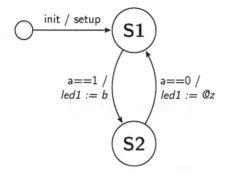

Fig. 2. The statemachine for the example MCL program

4.3   The MCL Interpreter

The semantics of MCL is defined by an interpreter implemented in Xtend. Listing 5 shows the core parts of the interpreter. According to the typical structure of a microcontroller program, the interpreter has two entry points: `executeSetup` (being called once at program startup, for initialization tasks) and `executeLoop` (the main loop body, being called repeatedly until the system terminates).

The arguments of both entry points represent different kinds of input data:

Program pgm: The input program (in MCL).
Params cfg: The configuration parameters for the MCL program.
IDevice d: The platform abstraction interface. This is an Xtend implementation of hardware abstractions and library calls on the microcontroller.

The private functions `handleState`, `execCmd` and `eval` do the actual interpretation of state behavior, control structures and expressions, respectively.

Optimization for Bounded Static Variation.   Depending on properties of the partial evaluator, naïve interpreter implementations can lead to clumsy residual code. E.g., this applies when arguments or variables are of *bounded static variation*. In method `executeLoop` of our example interpreter, the current state has to be selected from the list of states represented by the expression `pgm.fsm.states`. The variable `current` is classified as dynamic by BTA, because it depends on input data which is unknown at specialization time.

Listing 6 shows a straightforward implementation of method `executeLoop` which selects the current state by the expression `get(current-1)` in line 6. This would lead to result state `ss` being also classified as dynamic, although the set of states is limited and known at specialization time. This classification would severely limit the amount of code which can be executed at specialization time.

Fortunately, there is a pattern for refactoring the interpreter's code which allows the binding time analysis to classify `ss` as static. We applied the pattern in listing 5, see lines 13-21. As the index variable `is` depends only on expressions

Listing 5. The MCL interpreter implemented in Xtend (excerpts).

```
1  class MCLInterpreter {
2    var current = 0
3
4    def executeSetup(Program pgm, Params cfg, IDevice d) {
5      for(o : pgm.decls.filter(typeof(DigitalOut))) {
6        val v = o.initial.eval(cfg, o)
7        d.digitalOut(o.pin, v)
8      }
9      current = 1  // set initial state
10   }
11
12   def executeLoop(Program pgm, Params cfg, IDevice d) {
13     var is = 0
14     var next = 0
15     while (is < pgm.fsm.states.size) {
16       if (is+1 == current) {
17         val ss = pgm.fsm.states.get(is)
18         next = ss.handleState(cfg, d)
19       }
20       is = is + 1
21     }
22     if (next!=0) current = next
23   }
24
25   def private handleState(State s, Params cfg, IDevice d) {
26     // handle triggered outgoing transition
27     [...]
28   }
29
30   def private void execCmd(Cmd cmd, Params cfg, IDevice d) {
31     switch(cmd) {
32       SetOutput: {
33         val v = cmd.expr.eval(cfg, d)
34         d.digitalOut(cmd.out.pin, v)
35       }
36       [...]
37     }
38   }
39
40   def private int eval(Expr expr, Params cfg, IDevice d) {
41     switch (expr) {
42       ReadInput: d.digitalIn(expr.input.pin)
43       Constant:  expr.value
44       CfgValue:  cfg.get(expr.ref.name)
45     }
46   }
47
48   [...]
49 }
```

Listing 6. A version of `executeLoop` from the MCL interpreter which is not suited for partial evaluation.

```
 1  class MCLInterpreter {
 2
 3    [...]
 4
 5    def executeLoop(Program pgm, Params cfg, IDevice d) {
 6      val ss = pgm.fsm.states.get(current-1)
 7      val next = ss.handleState(cfg, d)
 8      if (next!=0) current = next
 9    }
10
11    [...]
12  }
```

classified as static, it will itself be of static binding time. The specializer is then able to unroll the body of the `while`-loop for each state of the finite state machine and will specialize each case in turn. This pattern is so well-known in the specialization domain that it is labeled "The Trick". See [6] for a detailed explanation and further hints on designing interpreters which are well-suited for specialization.

4.4 Xtend Code Generation by Specialization

Next we will generate an Xtend version of the target program by applying the partial evaluator:

$$\mathsf{T} = [\![\mathsf{xmix}]\!]~[\mathsf{int},~[\mathsf{M},~\mathsf{cfg}]]$$

where `int` is the MCL interpreter, `M` is the input MCL program with a set of configuration parameters `cfg`, and `T` is the resulting target program (in Xtend). The example input program `M` is listed fully in listing 4, the resulting specialized Xtend program `T` in listing 7. The input configuration `cfg` has been fixed as $\{z = 0\}$, which leads to the constant value 0 in line 33 of the resulting program.

As expected, the target program `T` is a mix of the original MCL program `M` (e.g., lines 5, 21f, 32f) and the infrastructure of the interpreter itself (e.g., the handling of the `current` variable). The constants 2, 3 and 13 defined as I/O pins in input program `M` show up as constants in the resulting program `T`, e.g., 13 in lines 5, 22 and 33. The program is listed exactly as output by the specializer, a postprocessing step could do some syntactic optimizations like removing constant if-conditions or inlining function calls.

4.5 Transformation to C Code

As a final step the Xtend target program from listing 7 is translated into a C program which can be readily compiled and executed on an Arduino target. This is expressed by the equation

420   K. Birken

Listing 7. The target program (in Xtend), which is a specialized interpreter.

```
1  class MCLInterpreter_ssd {
2    var current = 0
3
4    def executeSetup (IDevice d) {
5      d.digitalOut(13, 0)
6      current = 1
7    }
8
9    def executeLoop (IDevice d) {
10     var next = 0
11     switch (current) {
12       case 1: next = handleState_0(d)
13       case 2: next = handleState_1(d)
14     }
15     if (next!=0) current = next
16   }
17
18   def private handleState_0 (IDevice d) {
19     var found = 0
20     if (found == 0) {
21       if (d.digitalIn(2) == 1) {
22         d.digitalOut(13, d.digitalIn(3))
23         found = 2
24       }
25     }
26     found
27   }
28
29   def private handleState_1 (IDevice d) {
30     var found = 0
31     if (found == 0) {
32       if (d.digitalIn(2) == 0) {
33         d.digitalOut(13, 0)
34         found = 1
35       }
36     }
37     found
38   }
39 }
```

$$C = [\![cmap]\!] \ [T, \ m]$$

where cmap is an Xtend program which maps from Xtend to C, T is the specialization residual from the previous section, m is a platform- (e.g, Arduino-) specific mapping table and C is the resulting C code.

Basically, cmap executes a generic 1:1 mapping of Xtend language constructs to C language constructs, which is configured by mapping rules m. Examples for the mappings:

Type	Xtend source	C target
class	"MCLInterpreter_ssd"	put each class in separate C module
function	"executeLoop()"	"loop()"
visibility	"private" function	"static" function

Note that the target program T in listing 7 still has references to the target platform abstraction interface IDevice d. This is needed because the Xtend program T needs access to the platform API. In the resulting C program, these references are replaced by direct C library calls or preprocessor macros, guided by rules defined as target-specific mappings m.

Listing 8 shows the final program after the mapping and some minor clean-up steps. It is a matter of efficiency and readability how much inlining is applied.

Listing 8. The translated program in Arduino C.

```
 1  int current = 0;
 2
 3  void setup()
 4  {
 5    pinMode(13, OUTPUT); digitalWrite(13, 0);
 6    current = 1;
 7  }
 8
 9  void loop()
10  {
11    int next = 0;
12    switch (current) {
13      case 1: next = handleState_0(); break;
14      case 2: next = handleState_1(); break;
15    }
16    if (next!=0) current = next;
17  }
18
19
20  static int handleState_0()
21  {
22    int found = 0;
23    if (digitalRead(2) == 1)  { digitalWrite(13, digitalRead(3)); found = 2; }
24    return found;
25  }
26
27  static int handleState_1()
28  {
29    int found = 0;
30    if (digitalRead(2) == 0)  { digitalWrite(13, 0); found = 1; }
31    return found;
32  }
```

4.6   Generating a Code Generator by Self-Application

Putting all steps together, the final C target code is generated from an MCL program without implementing a code generator. Instead, a generic Xtend partial evaluator is used in order to specialize a generic MCL interpreter; the resulting target code is transformed into a final C program by a generic Xtend-to-C-mapper.

By taking advantage of Futamura's second projection [3], we can now automatically derive a self-contained code generator (in Xtend language) from the basic ingredients. First, a compiler comp has to be generated by self-applying the partial evaluator. The specializer is specialized for the MCL interpreter as follows:

$$comp = [\![xmix]\!] \, [xmix, int]$$

This compiler will transform MCL source programs into Xtend target programs without further need for the specializer. Second, we can combine the compiler and the Xtend-to-C-mapper into a common tool:

$$C = [\![cmap]\!] \, [[\![comp]\!] \, [M, cfg], m]$$

The result is a code generator with takes the MCL source program M, the product line configuration cfg and the platform mapping m as inputs and produces the final C program for the Arduino microcontroller.

5   Related Work

Partial evaluation is available for more than 20 years, although not well-established in today's day-to-day work with DSLs. The book of Jones et al. offers a thorough introduction to the topic [7]. Depending on the style of the language which should be tackled with partial evaluation, there is a different set of problems which have to be solved. The initial partial evaluation work was focused on functional and logic programming languages. Lateron, imperative languages have been treated. A good introduction of how to specialize a subset of C is given in [7, chapter 11].

Around 2000, major work of partial evaluation for object-oriented languages has been done. A detailed description of how a subset of Java can be specialized is given in [10] and [9].

It is interesting that these approaches are not available and used in today's mainstream work with DSLs. This paper builds on the previous results, extends and combines them and puts them into a state-of-the-art application context.

There are some approaches of improving (online) partial evaluation by combining it with other static analysis schemes. In [2], it is described how online partial evaluation can be improved by intermixing it with Symbolic Execution.

In the domain of internal DSLs, there is also ongoing research on *staging*, which has the same goals and similar techniques as partial evaluation. A current, promising approach for staging internal DSLs embedded in Scala is described in [8].

For the generation of a code generator from an interpreter, an alternative to the application of Futamura's second projection is the usage of a *compiler generator*. This compiler generator (often labelled cogen) can either be derived by another self-application of the specializer (Futamura's third projection)

$$cogen = [\![xmix]\!] \, [xmix, xmix]$$

or written manually. In some recent contributions, Glück showed how cogen can be computed by a bootstrapping approach [4], which can be regarded as an application of Futamura's fourth projection [5].

6   Conclusion and Future Work

In this work, we have shown how efficient, platform-specific code can be generated out of DSL programs without the need for implementing a code generator. The technique we used is specialization of an interpreter for the DSL by partial evaluation. All involved tools (partial evaluator, interpreter, mapper to target language) are generic and have been implemented in the Xtend language. By exploiting Futamura's second projection, a standalone code generator from DSL programs to platform code (in a different implementation language) can be generated.

This approach ensures that the DSL semantics defined by the interpreter is adhered to also by the code generators. A product line concept can be embedded into the scheme easily.

Future work will be guided towards three directions:

Partial Evaluator Improvement. We will add special features to the partial evaluators to improve the resulting code and take even more burden from the DSL developer. This includes polyvariant BTA, call-graph analysis to improve the handling of non-local side-effects of recursive functions and data flow analysis to take dead static variables into account. This will also improve the results of self-applying the evaluator.

Bigger Examples. The examples shown in the paper will be extended on several dimensions: We will add more expressivity to the used DSLs and increase the DSL models which are subject to the code generators.

Other Domains. Finally, we want to apply the technique to other domains, e.g., to the development of Automotive software (e.g., DSLs for on-board diagnostics [1]).

Acknowledgments. Part of this work was performed as a 4 + 1-project at itemis AG, where employees are granted one day each week to work on research or open-source projects. Thanks for this inspiring possibility! The author would also like to thank Markus Völter, Tijs van der Storm and the anonymous reviewers for their constructive feedback and insightful comments about this work.

References

[1] Birken, K.: Abstract execution for event-driven systems – an application from automotive/Infotainment development. In: Margaria, T., Steffen, B. (eds.) ISoLA 2012, Part II. LNCS, vol. 7610, pp. 173–186. Springer, Heidelberg (2012)

[2] Bubel, R., Hähnle, R., Ji, R.: Program specialization via a software verification tool. In: Aichernig, B.K., de Boer, F.S., Bonsangue, M.M. (eds.) Formal Methods for Components and Objects. LNCS, vol. 6957, pp. 80–101. Springer, Heidelberg (2011)

[3] Futamura, Y.: Partial Evaluation of Computation Process – An Approach to a Compiler-Compiler. Systems, Computers, Controls 2(5), 45–50 (1971)

[4] Glück, R.: Bootstrapping compiler generators from partial evaluators. In: Clarke, E., Virbitskaite, I., Voronkov, A. (eds.) PSI 2011. LNCS, vol. 7162, pp. 125–141. Springer, Heidelberg (2012)

[5] Glück, R.: Is there a fourth Futamura projection? In: Puebla, G., Vidal, G. (eds.) PEPM, pp. 51–60. ACM (2009) ISBN: 978-1- 60558-327-3

[6] Jones, N.D.: What Not to Do When Writing an Interpreter for Specialisation. In: Danvy, O., Thiemann, P., Glück, R. (eds.) Dagstuhl Seminar 1996. LNCS, vol. 1110, pp. 216–237. Springer, Heidelberg (1996)

[7] Jones, N.D., Gomard, C.K., Sestoft, P.: Partial Evaluation and Automatic Program Generation. Prentice-Hall, Inc., Upper Saddle River (1993) ISBN: 0-13-020249-5

[8] Rompf, T., Odersky, M.: Lightweight modular staging: a pragmatic approach to runtime code generation and compiled DSLs. Commun. ACM 55(6), 121–130 (2012)

[9] Schultz, U.P., Lawall, J.L., Consel, C.: Automatic Program Specialization for Java. ACM Trans. Program. Lang. Syst. 25(4), 452–499 (2003), http://doi.acm.org/10.1145/778559.778561, DOI: 10.1145/778559.778561, ISSN: 0164-0925

[10] Schultz, U.P.: Partial evaluation for class-based object-oriented languages. In: Danvy, O., Filinski, A. (eds.) PADO 2001. LNCS, vol. 2053, pp. 173–197. Springer, Heidelberg (2001)

[11] Steinberg, D., et al.: EMF: Eclipse Modeling Framework 2.0. 2nd. Addison-Wesley Professional (2009) ISBN: 0321331885

[12] Voelter, M., et al.: DSL Engineering - Designing. Implementing and Using Domain-Specific Languages, 1–558 (2013) dslbook.org, ISBN: 978-1-4812-1858-0

[13] Xtend Language homepage, http://www.xtend-lang.org

[14] Xtext homepage, http://www.eclipse.org/Xtext/

Back-To-Back Testing of Model-Based Code Generators

Sven Jörges and Bernhard Steffen

Chair of Programming Systems, Technische Universität Dortmund, Germany
sven.joerges@tu-dortmund.de,
bernhard.steffen@cs.tu-dortmund.de

Abstract. In this paper, we present the testing approach of the Genesys code generator framework. The employed approach is based on back-to-back-testing, which tests the translation performed by a code generator from a semantic perspective rather than just checking for syntactic correctness of the generation result. We describe the basic testing framework and show that it scales in three dimensions: parameterized tests, testing across multiple target platforms and testing on multiple meta-levels.

In particular, the latter is only possible due to the fact that Genesys code generators are constructed as models. Furthermore, in order to facilitate simplicity, Genesys consistently employs one single notation for all artifacts involved in this testing approach: Test data, test cases, the code generators under test, and even the testing framework itself are all modeled using the same graphical modeling language.

1 Introduction

Code generators are an important part of model-driven approaches to software engineering. They revert the abstraction that is immanent in models, and translate them to code that runs on a particular target platform[1]. Code generators are ubiquitous in Integrated Development Environments (IDEs) and language workbenches, and thus they belong to the standard repertoire of software engineers.

Due to this central role, the requirements imposed on a code generator's reliability are high. A defective code generator generates defective software artifacts: The consequences range from uncompilable code which has to be corrected by hand each time the code generator runs, to semantically dysfunctional code that causes serious damage to the target platform (e.g., a safety-critical embedded system). Several techniques and mechanisms can by employed in order to improve a code generator's reliability. Stürmer et al. [38] divide those techniques into

- *constructive procedures*, that focus on the adoption of standards and guidelines such as Software Process Improvement and Capability determination (SPiCE), and

---

[1] Please note that in this paper, we use the term "target platform" in the sense of a software platform rather than a hardware platform.

T. Margaria and B. Steffen (Eds.): ISoLA 2014, Part I, LNCS 8802, pp. 425–444, 2014.

– *analytical procedures* such as verification and testing.

In this paper, we focus on *testing* of code generators. When writing tests for a given code generator, a common approach is the application of *unit testing* [3], as depicted in Fig. 1.

Typically, in unit-based testing, test cases steer the system under test (SUT) by means of API calls. Each test case may be parameterized, and the aggregate of available parameter configurations is called the test vector. When running the test, each test case is run repeatedly for each parameter configuration in the test vector associated with that test case. With each test run, the SUT produces an output. Along with the actual test case and the test vector, the test designer also specifies the expected output of the SUT. The expected output is then compared to the actual output by means of a Matcher component, which typically performs one or more asserts. Finally, the test results are summarized in a report. For instance, in the Java world, typical unit testing frameworks that support these steps are JUnit and TestNG.

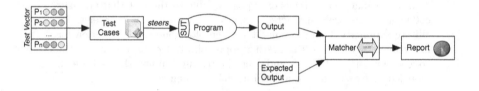

Fig. 1. Classical Unit Testing

When applying this testing approach to a code generator as the SUT, the output that is examined is typically source code in some programming language. Consequently, the specification of the expected output also resembles source code. The Matcher then performs a string comparison, i.e., the test is successful if the output equals the expected output. This testing approach clearly focuses on the syntactic aspects of the code produced by the code generator.

Although this approach works to some extent, it has several disadvantages and is, according to Stahl et al. [34, pp. 166f], rather unfeasible in practice:

– It may lead to many false positives, as a simple change in the formatting of the generated code (e.g. replacing blanks with tabs for indentation) already leads to test failure. This happens although the generated code might still be compilable, executable and semantically correct.
– The approach relies on the test designer who has to specify a correct output expectation. Though the test might validate that this output expectation is met in syntactic terms, it does not provide any information on whether the resulting code *semantically* behaves as intended.

Consequently, Stahl et al. recommend testing the generated code's *effect* (i.e., its behavior when it is executed) instead of its concrete syntax.

In this paper, we present a testing approach that applies this idea in the context of the Genesys Framework [15]. Genesys differs from other code generation frameworks, as it provides a toolbox for constructing code generators as *graphical, hierarchical models* that are composed of reusable *services*.

Genesys provides two mechanisms for ensuring the reliability of code generators, which both belong to the category of analytical procedures. First, as code generators in Genesys are constructed as models, they are amenable to formal methods. In [15], we showed Genesys' support for the *formal verification* of code generators via model checking [6], based on a reusable library of constraints.

This paper focuses on the second mechanism, which is Genesys' support for *testing* code generators. The employed approach is based on *back-to-back-testing* [40], which tests the translation performed by a code generator from a semantic perspective rather than just checking for syntactic correctness of the generation result. Basically, Genesys realizes back-to-back testing by executing both the source model as well as the code generated from it. Both executions produce traces, the *execution footprints*, which are then compared. For all artifacts involved in this testing approach, Genesys consistently employs one single notation: Test data, test cases, the code generators under test, and even the testing framework itself are all modeled using the same graphical modeling language.

In [15], we presented a basic version of this testing approach. In this paper, we further elaborate on it, and we show that the approach scales in at least three dimensions:

1. *Parameterized tests:* Tests can be parameterized in order to increase the overall test coverage.
2. *Multi-platform testing:* The retention of execution semantics can be validated even across different target platforms.
3. *Multi-meta-level testing:* The testing approach can be naturally employed on multiple meta-levels.

The remainder of this paper is structured as follows: In the following Sect. 2, we briefly describe the basics of the Genesys Framework along with its facilities for verification and testing of code generators. Afterwards, Sect. 3 presents the testing approach employed in Genesys and elaborates on the three dimensions mentioned above. Finally, Sect. 4 discusses related work, and Sect. 5 concludes the paper and outlines future work.

2   The Genesys Framework

In this section, we briefly describe Genesys as well as its underlying concepts and key technologies. Conceptually and technically, Genesys is based on *jABC*, which is a general and extensible framework for model-driven and service-oriented development. Please note that, for the sake of brevity, the following descriptions are not exhaustive, but only describe the key concepts required in order to comprehend the main contribution of this paper. This introductive section is based on [17].

2.1 jABC

jABC [35,22,21] is an extensible framework for model-driven and service-oriented development. Models built with jABC are called *Service Logic Graphs* (SLGs), which basically are directed graphs that represent the dynamic flow of actions in an application (i.e., its actual business logic). For composing such models, jABC provides a library of ready-made models and services.

The services contained in this library are called *Service Independent Building Blocks* (SIBs). Closely following the ideas of service orientation, a Service Independent Building Block (SIB) represents an atomic, reusable and configurable service, that provides a single functionality of arbitrary granularity. Accordingly, a SIB's behavior may, e.g., range from low-level tasks like string concatenation or displaying a message, to ready-made web services or even the interaction with highly complex systems, such as Enterprise Resource Planning (ERP) software. Consequently, as models are assembled from such fully functional building blocks, SLGs are *executable*. The largest bundle of SIBs included in jABC's library is called the *Common SIBs* which provide an elementary basis for assembling SLGs.

Apart from services, jABC's library also contains models, which in turn may be used as building blocks of other models. Such building blocks are called *macros*. Hence SLGs can be *hierarchical*, which leads to a high reusability not only of the building blocks, but also of the models, particularly within larger systems. Typically, the ready-made SLGs contained in the library represent reusable application aspects (i.e. cross-cutting concerns), such as error handling or security management. Those aspects are modeled once: Afterwards, they are part of the library and can be reused across applications and domains.

jABC provides a tool for graphically modeling SLGs from the repertoire described above. The functional range of the tool can be extended by plugins, which support development phases such as debugging, monitoring, verification and testing [35].

Model Example. We now introduce the essential concepts underlying jABC's models by means of the example SLG depicted in Fig. 2. This SLG is part of a code generator modeled with Genesys. Its purpose is the generation of an HTML documentation for an arbitrary input SLG. As mentioned above, SLGs are directed graphs, which describe a system in a behavioral manner. The nodes in such a graph are SIBs or, in order to facilitate hierarchical modeling, macros that point to other SLGs. For instance, in the example model depicted in Fig. 2, the nodes labeled `Generate Documentation Link` and `Convert Content To Html` are SIBs. Multiple instances of the same SIB can occur in one model: For instance, the nodes labeled `Generate Model Page Entry (Linked)` and `Generate SIB Page` are instances of the SIB `RunStringTemplate`.

`RunStringTemplate` is an example of a SIB that is particularly relevant for constructing template-based [7] code generators: The task of `RunStringTemplate` is to employ the template engine StringTemplate [27] in order to evaluate a template. Such a template is basically a text containing placeholders, which are filled with dynamic content as soon as the template engine is invoked.

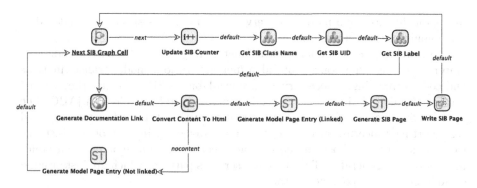

Fig. 2. Example SLG modeling a code generator for HTML documentation

In order to facilitate reusability, each SIB provides a set of *parameters* for configuring the SIB's behavior. For instance, the SIB RunStringTemplate takes four
parameters, one of them (called "template") being the template that should be
evaluated by StringTemplate. For enabling communication among SIB instances
contained in a model (i.e., sharing data), the concrete service implementations
usually keep track of an *execution context*. Technically, this context is like a hash
map, containing simple key-value pairs. Hence a SIB instance is able to read and
manipulate data that has been stored in the context by other SIB instances.

Besides parameters, each SIB also provides a set of so-called *branches*, which
reflect its possible execution results. For instance, the SIB RunStringTemplate
has two branches: *default*, if the template was evaluated successfully, and *error*,
if the template could not be evaluated (e.g., because of syntax errors). Branches
provide the basis for wiring SIB instances in a model via directed edges, as visible
in Fig. 2. Each edge between a source node and its successor directly corresponds
to a branch defined by the source node.

From a technical perspective, a SIB's behavior for a concrete target platform is
implemented by means of a so-called *service adapter* [15]. Particularly, as one SIB
may be executable on multiple target platforms, an arbitrary number of service
adapters can be attached to a SIB. Typically, a service adapter is implemented
in a programming language supported by the desired target platform, so it may,
for instance, be a Java class, a C# class or a Python script.

Decoupling the concrete platform-specific implementations from the SIB description assures that the SIB itself (and thus any SLG that contains the SIB)
is entirely platform independent. The SIB description is specified by means
of a simple Java class that, e.g., defines the corresponding parameters and
branches [35].

2.2   Genesys

Genesys [15] is a framework for the high-level engineering of code generators
based on jABC. Accordingly, with Genesys, code generators are modeled as

SLGs, on the basis of a model and service library that is specifically tailored to the domain of code generation.

The provided services offer typical functionality required for most code generators, such as type conversion, identifier generation, model transformations and code formatting. Those services are available as SIBs, so that they can be used as atomic building blocks for code generator models built with jABC. The models contained in Genesys' library realize further typical functionality and cross-cutting concerns, such as loading and traversing input models. Just like the atomic services, those models can be directly reused as macros when building a new code generator. They can also serve as patterns which are instantiated or adapted for new code generators.

Furthermore, all code generators that have been created with Genesys are included in the library. The rationale behind this is that each new code generator contributes to the library, so that the available repertoire and the potential for reuse is growing continuously. In particular, this facilitates the construction of entire code generator families by deriving new code generators from existing ones [15].

An example for such a code generator family is given by the *jABC code generators* [16]. Code generators in this family support SLGs as their source language, and translate them to desired target platforms. Effectively, the purpose of this code generator family is providing code generation capabilities for jABC. In sum, this family contains 17 code generators, covering a wide range of target platforms, such as Java-based platforms (e.g., plain Java classes, Servlets, JUnit tests), embedded systems (e.g., iOS, the leJOS API for Lego's Mindstorms, Java Micro Edition) and further languages and platforms like Ruby, Perl or C#.

Apart from models and services, Genesys also includes facilities for verification and testing of code generators, which will be addressed in the next section.

Finally, Genesys provides tools that support the usage and the development of code generators. For instance, a jABC plugin allows the configuration and invocation of code generators within the jABC tool, and a Maven plugin enables the integration into a Maven-based tool chain. Tools for generator developers include, e.g., a benchmark framework for examining the performance of code generators, and specialized editors for templates.

2.3   Verification and Testing in Genesys

Fig. 3 shows an overview of the techniques that are employed in Genesys in order to improve the reliability of code generators. As visible in the center of the figure, those techniques are applied to code generator models as well as to the contained services.

Above the dashed line, there are those techniques which support the generator developer while modeling a code generator. The tools that are available for this purpose require a set of local and global constraints, which are checked continuously during the modeling activity. In jABC, local constraints are checked by means of the *LocalChecker* plugin. The scope of local constraints is typically restricted to single SIBs in a model. For instance, such checks include whether a

SIB's parameters have valid values, or whether all required branches are assigned to edges in the model. Local constraints are specified by the SIB expert as corresponding Java code in the SIB. Furthermore, global constraints are checked by means of model checking [6], which is provided by the jABC plugin GEAR [1]. As this paper focuses on testing, please refer to [15] for more details on local checking and model checking in the context of Genesys.

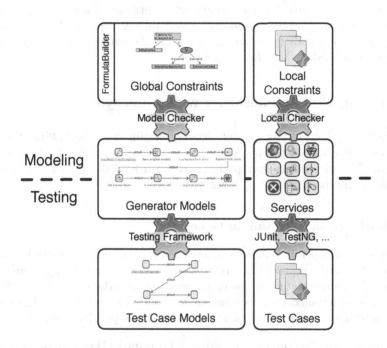

Fig. 3. Verification & Testing in Genesys

Below the dashed line in Fig. 3, testing techniques check whether the code generators and the contained services work as desired (or stipulated). As the services are implemented as code, they can be tested the usual way, e.g., by means of unit tests. For instance, in the case of Java, testing frameworks like JUnit and TestNG are suitable for this purpose.

In order to enable testing entire code generators, Genesys provides a dedicated framework, which will be introduced in Sect. 3. According to the concept underlying this framework, test cases as well as test inputs are, just like the code generators, specified as models in jABC.

Please note the special focus on the simple usage of the supported mechanisms, especially of those working on code generator models. In order to use the model checker or Genesys' testing framework, the generator developer does not have to learn any new language or specification formalisms. The language used for all these tools is given by jABC's SLGs, which is the same language that is used for the development of the actual code generators. The only syntactic difference between those models is that different SIBs are used for their construction.

As constraints and test cases are, once created, added to the Genesys Framework, they form a continuously growing knowledge base for building robust code generators. Consequently, each new code generator has to fulfill all suitable constraints and pass all appropriate tests from the knowledge base, which reduces the likelihood of repeating known mistakes or bugs.

With this holistic and integrated support of verification and testing, Genesys provides powerful mechanisms for the development and quality assurance of robust and reliable code generators, which is (to the authors' knowledge) unique among existing code generation frameworks.

3   Testing Code Generators with Genesys

In the following sections, we present Genesys' testing framework. First, Sect. 3.1 describes how back-to-back testing is realized in Genesys in order to test code generator from a semantic perspective. Afterwards, Sect. 3.2-3.4 elaborate on this testing approach by adding three extensions.

3.1   Back-To-Back-Testing in Genesys

According to Stürmer et al., one "can assume that the code generator is working correctly if invalid test models are rejected by the code generator, [...] and valid test models are translated by the code generator and the code generated from this behaves in a 'functionally equivalent' way" [36]. In more detail, when testing a code generator, usually the following aspects are of peculiar interest:

1. **Appropriate Support of the Source Language**: Does the code generator accept and process all valid (or desired, if the source language should not be supported entirely) inputs in the source language? Are any invalid or undesired inputs rejected?
2. **Correct Translation to the Target Language**: Does the code generator produce syntactically valid source code in the target language? Is the execution behavior specified in the source language retained in the generated code (*execution equivalence*)?
3. **Parametrization of the Code Generator**: Do possible options of the code generator have the expected effects?

Of course, by its very nature, testing only provides incomplete answers to these questions (especially to the one concerning the execution equivalence), relative to the specified test cases. In particular, according to Stürmer et al., the traditional notions of correctness (as, e.g., employed by many of the verification approaches for traditional compilers such as [20,29,25]) cannot be directly applied to code generators, but instead "the definition of correctness has to be based on a notion of sufficiently similar behavior" [37].

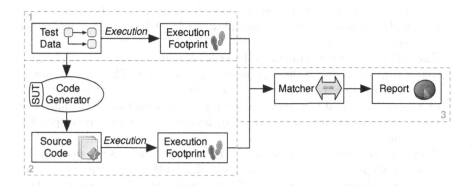

Fig. 4. Back-To-Back-Testing in Genesys

In order to solve this, Genesys provides a back-to-back-testing [40] approach based on execution semantics. In place of a specification of the expected output, this approach uses a given *reference semantics* for comparison with the actual execution semantics of the generated code.

In practice, for modeling languages and Domain Specific Languages (DSLs), this execution semantics is often described by means of natural language, as for instance performed in the Unified Modeling Language (UML) specification. However, in order to avoid the ambiguity and imprecision of natural languages, semantics can also be described formally, e.g., using a denotational [33], operational [28,18], axiomatic [10] or translational approach [19, p. 136f].

In the context of Genesys' testing approach, the latter is most interesting: Following the translational approach, the semantics of a language is given by a translation into another language with well-known semantics. In model-based approaches, such a translation can be provided by a model transformation, which may, e.g., be realized by a code generator.

Fig. 4 shows the testing approach as it has been realized for testing jABC code generators (cf. Sect. 2.3). As the SLG notation is the source language of those code generators, the test inputs for the single test cases are again SLGs (upper left corner of Fig. 4). Such *test models* are constructed on the basis of a small set of dedicated SIBs, which serve a special purpose: Upon execution, each of those SIBs leaves a unique footprint in the execution context (basically a unique string). After executing a test model, the concatenation of the single footprints created by all contained SIBs is the *execution footprint* of the SLG. In other words, such an execution footprint represents a particular trace through a test model.

The execution footprint is used for testing the execution equivalence of the modeled application and its generated counterpart. As depicted in Fig. 4, this test is performed in three main steps:

1. **Direct Execution**: The test model is directly executed with the Tracer, resulting in a corresponding execution footprint. The Tracer plays the role of

a reference implementation that specifies the semantics of SLGs, in contrast to describing the semantics in a formal way. Kleppe [19, p. 135] refers to this as *pragmatic semantics*.

2. **Execution of the Generated Result**: The test model is translated to source code by means of the code generator under test. The resulting source code is either directly executed with an interpreter or an execution engine, or a compiler is used to translate it for a particular runtime environment, in which it can be executed afterwards. Again, both cases yield a corresponding execution footprint.

3. **Test Evaluation**: A Matcher compares the two execution footprints obtained in steps 1 and 2. The requirement of a "sufficiently similar behavior" mentioned above is met by a jABC code generator, if the execution footprints of the modeled application and its generated pendant are equal, i.e., if in both traces the same SIBs were executed in the exact same order. Examining those traces on the granularity of SIBs is a suitable approach, as SIBs are the atomic building blocks of SLGs. The execution of each SIB is represented as a part of the resulting execution footprint (which is stable even across different platforms, cf. Sect. 3.3). The actual implementations of the SIBs are not considered in the test evaluation, as they are transparent to the code generator, which is only concerned with producing the code that orchestrates the SIBs (the *glue code*). The available implementations of a SIB have to be tested by means of classical unit testing.

As the final step of the test evaluation, the test tool reports the test results to the user.

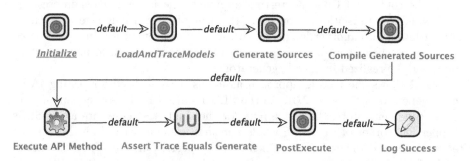

Fig. 5. The testing concept from Fig. 4, modeled in jABC

The testing approach has been realized using jABC, i.e., it has been modeled as an SLG which is depicted in Fig. 5. Most of the SIBs contained in this model are macros, hence the test process is hierarchical, and its single phases are refined by submodels. The basic steps from Fig. 4 are visible in this model:

- The macro `LoadAndTraceModels` obtains the first execution footprint by tracing the model, and thus corresponds to step 1.

- The macros **Generate Sources**, **Compile Generated Sources** as well as the SIB **Execute API Method** correspond to step 2, because they obtain the second execution footprint from the generated pendant.
- Finally, the SIB **Assert Trace Equals Generate** performs the comparison of the two execution footprints, as defined by step 3 in Fig. 4.

The macros **Initialize** and **PostExecute** perform necessary tasks before and after the actual test execution, such as the creation or deletion of required directories. The SIB **Log Success** emits a simple log message once the test execution succeeded. **Execute API Method** executes the generated and compiled result of the previous steps via an API method. Finally, the SIB **Assert Trace Equals Generate** uses JUnit for comparing the obtained execution footprints. Please note that the reporting of the test results is not explicitly modeled in the process, as this task is entirely performed by JUnit as the underlying testing platform.

By means of another code generator developed with Genesys, the *JUnit Generator*, this modeled test process is translated to a test script for JUnit.

By using the testing strategy depicted in Fig. 4, all of the three code generator aspects listed above are tested relative to the available test cases. For instance, if the code generator produces syntactically invalid code from a valid test model (aspect 1), the compilation in step 2, and thus the entire test, will fail. The test for execution equivalence (aspect 2) is realized by comparing the execution footprints in step 3. Finally, the effects of the code generator's options (aspect 3) are tested by multiple executions of the testing procedure with different configurations of the generator in step 2.

Of course, a necessary precondition for this testing strategy is the predictability of the test model's behavior. A repeated execution of one and the same test model should always yield the same execution footprint. Consequently, this approach is not suitable for test inputs with self-adapting or randomized behavior.

Fig. 6 shows some examples of test models from Genesys' testing framework, which serve as a basis for corresponding test cases. The special SIBs mentioned above, which are designed for creating test models and which produce the execution footprints in the execution context, are marked with the word "Test" on their icon.

SLG 1 is a simple sequence which tests the correct translation of different SIB parameters (except for extended SIB parameters like **ContextKey**, which are tested in a separate test model). For this purpose, the SIBs contained in this SLG are equipped with corresponding SIB parameters, such as **CheckCollection-Parameters**, which tests different Java collections like **ArrayList** or **HashMap**. SLGs 2–5 test different control flow mechanisms, such as recursion (2), loops (3), multi-threading (4) and hierarchy (5). As visible from SLG 4, those mechanisms are also tested in combination: Apart from the SIB for forking and joining the control flow, this model also contains macros.

Currently, the test suite for the jABC code generators contains 65 of such test models, which serve as the basis of around 380 test cases, the bulk of which are proceeding according to the testing strategy described above. Please note

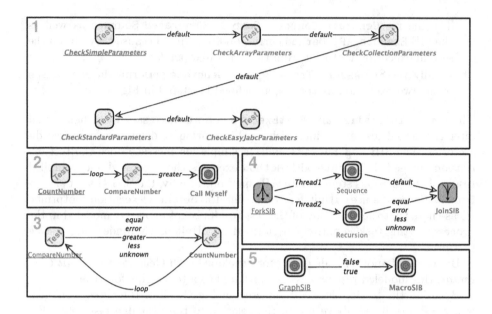

Fig. 6. Example SLGs modeling test inputs

again that the test models, the code generators under test, and even the testing strategy itself are all modeled using SLGs.

3.2   Improving Test Coverage with Parameterized Tests

Beyond the simple examples shown in Fig. 6, test models may resemble complex programs or systems containing a potentially large number of states. Consequently, it is desirable to maximize the number of execution paths in a test model considered by the test, rather than just testing one single execution path per test model.

Parameterized unit tests (PUTs) [39] provide an effective way to support this and are typically well supported by testing frameworks such as JUnit. PUTs generalize test cases by means of parameters, which effectively allow running one single test case repeatedly with different configurations.

In the context of Genesys' testing approach introduced in the previous section, PUTs increase the expressiveness of a test: As the approach is based on the comparison of execution traces (represented by the execution footprints) through a test model and its generated counterpart, the test result gets more precise when considering footprints for *multiple* (ideally all possible) execution paths. If only one exemplary execution footprint is tested for a test model, there may still be other paths for which the code generation does not work properly (i.e., no retainment of execution semantics).

Furthermore, PUTs increase the reusability of test models, as one and the same test model can be used to test multiple issues, steered by corresponding parameterizations.

Fig. 7 shows an extension of Genesys' testing approach, enabling the use of PUTs. For this purpose, each test case is associated with a *test vector* which provides an arbitrary number of *parameter configurations*. When running the test case, the test model is executed repeatedly for each available parameter configuration. Accordingly, this yields a *vector of execution footprints*, the size of which corresponding to the number of available parameter configurations. Each entry in the vector of execution footprints resembles one execution trace through the test model.

Afterwards, the same procedure is performed for the code produced by the code generator (or more general, the model-to-text (M2T) transformation). The generated code is executed using the same test vector, yielding a second vector of execution footprints. Finally, the two resulting execution footprint vectors are compared by the Matcher. To this end, the Matcher compares each entry of the first vector with the entry from the second vector that resulted from the same parameter configuration provided by the test vector. For instance, using the labels from Fig. 7, it compares FP_1 with FP'_1, both resulting from the test run with parameter configuration P_1.

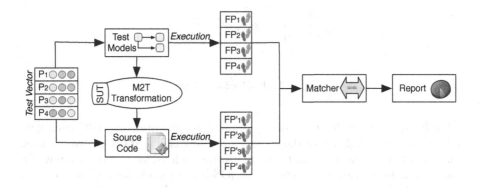

Fig. 7. Extended testing approach with parameterized tests

Effectively, this extended approach results in a two-dimensional notion of test coverage:

1. In the dimension of test models, test coverage depends on a good test vector. This test vector should provide parameter configurations in a way that maximizes the test coverage according to the desired coverage criterion. For instance, test coverage could be defined by means of the coverage of states and transitions that are used when executing the test model.
2. In the dimension of the code generator under test, test coverage is determined by the available test cases (i.e., test models). Remember that in Genesys,

code generators are, just like the test models, modeled by means of the SLG notation. Consequently, test coverage for code generators can be measured in the same way as for the test models.

A good test suite should maximize test coverage in both dimensions.

3.3   Testing across Multiple Target Platforms

The testing approach described in Sect. 3 is also suitable for testing entire code code generator families. Several testing artifacts can be reused among code generator tests, as indicated in Fig. 8.

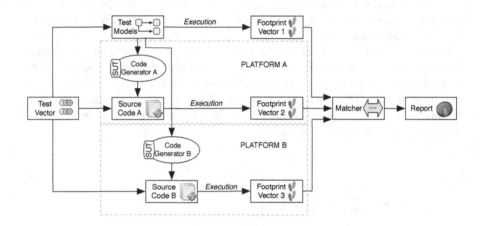

Fig. 8. Multi-Platform Testing

For instance, all code generators contained in the family of jABC code generators (see. Sect. 2.3) share the same source language – SLGs, which are then translated to code for different target platforms such as, for instance, a Java EE container, a JavaScript interpreter, or an iOS-based mobile device. As described in Sect. 2.1, the SLG notation is entirely platform independent. However, in order to be translatable into code that runs on a particular target platform, an SLG requires an appropriate *technical grounding*. Such a technical grounding is established by associating corresponding service adapters for the desired target platform to all SIBs contained in the SLG. Accordingly, given the availability of appropriate technical groundings, test models can be reused for testing all code generators contained in the code generator family.

Moreover, execution footprints can easily be designed in a platform independent way. This is mostly a matter of abstraction: Execution footprints have to be *stable abstractions* [41] of a model's execution behavior (i.e., stable across different platforms). As described in Sect. 3.1, the Genesys testing approach realizes execution footprints as simple (sets of) strings, which can easily be compared across different target platforms.

Technically, in order to enable this platform independent comparison, each SIB contained in the test models has to produce the same footprint chunk for each target platform it supports. For instance, if a SIB provides a service adapter for Java and another one for Python, the execution of the SIB should always yield the same execution footprint for both technical groundings. The execution footprints might, e.g., be stored in a database or in a file, so that they can be accessed by the Matcher for the comparison. This sine qua non has to be considered by the SIB developers and has to be validated by means of classical unit tests, in order to avoid problems like, e.g., the use of different encodings in the considered target platforms.

As indicated by Fig. 8, test vectors can also be reused across different platforms. Typically, the contained parameter configurations consist of data ranging from simple string arguments to complex objects or composite data-types. In order to be utilizable for different platforms, the test vectors have to be provided in available platform independent formats such as XML or JSON. Please note that for clarity, Fig. 8 only shows two code generators for two platforms, however, the approach scales for an arbitrary number of code generators.

3.4   Testing on Multiple Meta-Levels

Finally, the testing approach also works on different meta-levels, as depicted in Fig. 9. This is due to the fact that in Genesys, code generators are themselves created in a model-based fashion.

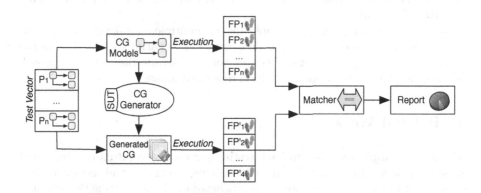

Fig. 9. Multi-Meta-Level Testing

Again, this advantage is particularly visible in the case of jABC code generators (cf. Sect. 2.3). This family contains the *Genesys Code Generator Generator*, which translates any given code generator modeled with Genesys into a plugin for the Genesys jABC Plugin mentioned in Sect. 2.3. Basically, such a plugin is a Java class that implements a particular interface (see [24] for more details on the Genesys Code Generator Generator and the jABC Plugin's architecture).

This Java class can be plugged into the Genesys jABC Plugin, which then allows the direct execution of the code generator from within jABC.

When applying the proposed testing approach to the Genesys Code Generator Generator, the test models are code generators modeled with Genesys, i.e., SLGs. The test vector is given by different jABC models that serve as inputs for the code generators - in fact, these are the same models that played the role of the test models in the previous scenarios. In the resulting test suite, each code generator model resembles a test case for the Genesys Code Generator Generator, and each test case is executed for each model provided by the test vector.

As visible from Fig. 9, the actual test execution remains nearly unchanged: The test cases (i.e. the code generators) are first executed by the Tracer, and afterwards they are translated to code which is also executed, followed by a comparison of the resulting execution vectors performed by a Matcher.

Technically, there is one difference when applying the testing approach on this meta-level: In contrast to the test models described in Sect. 3.1, the code generator models are not specifically created for testing purposes, but instead they are *productive* models. This means that the SIBs contained in those models serve a productive purpose in the code generator, but do not produce any execution footprints that are required for testing.

In order to produce the execution footprints, the SIBs employed in the code generators have to be extended accordingly. For instance, this can be achieved by means of aspect orientation: A suitable aspect is responsible for generating an execution footprint, and is only executed when the SIBs are run in a testing mode. Another possible solution is the extension of the code generator. In this scenario, the generated code is augmented by functionality for producing execution footprints.

In sum, the testing concept is applicable on multiple meta-levels, and is thus suitable for meta-modeling-based code generation scenarios such as [17]. In the current Genesys implementation, we did not yet cascade the testing approach beyond the "Generator Generator" level described above.

4   Related Work

The idea of employing back-to-back testing for code generators can be found in several publications. As already cited above, Stürmer et al. advocate this strategy of testing code generators and incorporate it into a "practice-oriented testing approach for code generation tools" [36]. This testing approach has several similarities to the Genesys testing approach presented in this paper, including the support for PUTs. However, Stürmer et al.'s approach has a focus on the automatic generation of test cases (i.e., test models) on the basis of graph transformation rules [36,37].

Sampath et al. also employ back-to-back-testing in their "behavior directed testing" [32] approach. This approach proposes the use of behavioral test specifications, given as finite-state automatons that model action sequences. Those test specifications plus a metamodel, describing the source language of the code generator under test, are used for generating test cases (i.e. test models, test inputs and expected outputs), forming a test suite that proceeds in a back-to-back manner.

In comparison to the work of Stürmer et al. and Sampath et al., the testing approach presented in this paper does not focus on test case generation, but is instead designed to fit the idea of Genesys as an extensible code generator framework. Test models, test vectors and the SIBs that produce the execution footprints are created by hand, but instantly become part of the Genesys Framework once they are created (cf. Sect. 2.3). In consequence, test developers can often resort to existing items: Test models and test vectors can be reused as described in Sect. 3.3, and SIBs for producing execution footprint only have to be implemented if the target platform under test is not yet supported by the existing SIBs.

As another important difference, both Stürmer et al. and Sampath et al. did not consider the code generators themselves being models, thus not allowing testing on multiple meta-levels (see Sect. 3.4). Genesys also differs in the strong focus on simplicity [23]: All testing artifacts are specified by means of the SLG modeling language (cf. Sect. 3.1), which is also used for modeling the code generators themselves. Thus the code generator developer does not have to learn another specification language in order to create a corresponding test suite.

Test case generation also has a long tradition in compiler testing [4]. In particular, grammar-based testing approaches [2,5,11] typically produce test cases from the grammar (available as, e.g., a context-free grammar or attribute grammar) of the source language. Consequently, such approaches have a focus on the syntactic aspects, whereas the approach presented in this paper tests code generators from a semantic perspective.

In the context of jABC and its precursors, there has been a lot of research concerned with model-based testing in general. A major result is the *Integrated Test Environment* (ITE) [26], which provides a holistic approach for testing modeled systems. According to this approach, test cases and entire test suites are modeled as SLGs, based on a library of test blocks (i.e., SIBs). Further research on testing in jABC and its precursors concerns regression testing and test suite generation via techniques like automata learning [9,31], e.g., for testing legacy or black box systems such as web applications [30] or Computer Telephony Integration systems [8].

Motivated by the need for a framework for the automated test of Genesys code generators, and based on the research experience outlined above, the testing approach presented in this paper has been developed. Essentially, it extends the holistic ITE approach by the dimension of code generation. Prior to the introduction of Genesys and code generation in jABC, the ITE exclusively performed the test execution via direct interpretation of the models.

5   Conclusion and Future Work

In this paper, we presented the testing approach of the Genesys code generator framework. The employed approach is based on back-to-back-testing, which tests the translation performed by a code generator from a semantic perspective rather than just checking for syntactic correctness of the generation result. We described the basic testing framework and showed that it scales in three dimensions: parameterized tests, testing across multiple target platforms and testing on multiple meta-levels.

In particular, the latter is only possible due to the fact that Genesys code generators are constructed as models. Furthermore, in order to facilitate simplicity, Genesys consistently employs one single notation for all artifacts involved in this testing approach: Test data, test cases, the code generators under test, and even the testing framework itself are all modeled using the same graphical modeling language.

Several extensions of the testing approach are imaginable for the future. In particular, automatic test case generation, either "classically" along the lines described in [37] or based on automata learning techniques [9,31], should be integrated. Particularly promising are recent results concerning data handling in automata learning, which range from learning adequate data abstractions [13] to a fully symbolic treatment of data in terms of register automata [12,14]. These results suggest that the bottleneck and deal-breaker of model-based testing, the required test model, can be overcome via integrated testing-based modeling.

Furthermore, a test becomes more expressive if the execution of the generated code on the *real* target system is also included in the comparison of the execution footprints, as proposed in [37] (called processor-in-the-loop, PIL). Currently, all execution runs in the tests (direct execution of the test models as well as the execution of the generated pendants) are performed on the system of the developer who actually runs the tests, or on a corresponding continuous integration server. For instance, in the context of embedded systems, this demands the use of appropriate emulators in order to be able to execute the generated code. By including execution runs on the real target systems in the tests, the complexity of the overall test setup increases in favor of more expressive results, as the tests now are also able to detect, e.g., unexpected side-effects of the target system's runtime environment.

References

1. Bakera, M., Margaria, T., Renner, C.D., Steffen, B.: Tool-supported enhancement of diagnosis in model-driven verification. Innovations in Systems and Software Engineering 5(3), 211–228 (2009)
2. Bazzichi, F., Spadafora, I.: An automatic generator for compiler testing. IEEE Transactions on Software Engineering SE 8(4), 343–353 (1982)
3. Beck, K.: Test Driven Development: By Example. Addison-Wesley (2002)
4. Boujarwah, A.S., Saleh, K.: Compiler test case generation methods: a survey and assessment. Information & Software Technology 39(9), 617–625 (1997)
5. Celentano, A., Crespi-Reghizzi, S., Vigna, P.D., Ghezzi, C., Granata, G., Savoretti, F.: Compiler testing using a sentence generator. Softw., Pract. Exper. 10(11), 897–918 (1980)
6. Clarke, E.M., Grumberg, O., Peled, D.: Model Checking. MIT Press (1999)

7. Czarnecki, K., Helsen, S.: Feature-based survey of model transformation approaches. IBM Systems Journal 45, 621–645 (2006)
8. Hagerer, A., Hungar, H., Margaria, T., Niese, O., Steffen, B., Ide, H.-D.: Demonstration of an Operational Procedure for the Model-Based Testing of CTI Systems. In: Kutsche, R.-D., Weber, H. (eds.) FASE 2002. LNCS, vol. 2306, pp. 336–340. Springer, Heidelberg (2002)
9. Hagerer, A., Hungar, H.: Model Generation by Moderated Regular Extrapolation. In: Kutsche, R.-D., Weber, H. (eds.) FASE 2002. LNCS, vol. 2306, pp. 80–95. Springer, Heidelberg (2002)
10. Hoare, C.A.R.: An axiomatic basis for computer programming. Communications of the ACM 12, 576–580 (1969)
11. Homer, W., Schooler, R.: Independent testing of compiler phases using a test case generator. Softw., Pract. Exper. 19(1), 53–62 (1989)
12. Howar, F., Steffen, B., Jonsson, B., Cassel, S.: Inferring canonical register automata. In: Kuncak, V., Rybalchenko, A. (eds.) VMCAI 2012. LNCS, vol. 7148, pp. 251–266. Springer, Heidelberg (2012)
13. Howar, F., Steffen, B., Merten, M.: Automata learning with automated alphabet abstraction refinement. In: Jhala, R., Schmidt, D. (eds.) VMCAI 2011. LNCS, vol. 6538, pp. 263–277. Springer, Heidelberg (2011)
14. Isberner, M., Howar, F., Steffen, B.: Learning register automata: from languages to program structures. Machine Learning, 1–34 (2013)
15. Jörges, S.: Construction and Evolution of Code Generators. LNCS, vol. 7747. Springer, Heidelberg (2013)
16. Jörges, S., Lamprecht, A.L., Margaria, T., Schaefer, I., Steffen, B.: A constraint-based variability modeling framework. STTT 14(5), 511–530 (2012)
17. Jörges, S., Steffen, B.: Exploiting ecore's reflexivity for bootstrapping domain-specific code-generators. In: 35th Annual IEEE Software Engineering Workshop, SEW 2012, pp. 72–81. IEEE Computer Society (2012)
18. Kahn, G.: Natural Semantics. In: Brandenburg, F.J., Vidal-Naquet, G., Wirsing, M. (eds.) STACS 1987. LNCS, vol. 247, pp. 22–39. Springer, Heidelberg (1987)
19. Kleppe, A.: Software Language Engineering: Creating Domain-Specific Languages Using Metamodels, 1st edn. Addison-Wesley (2008)
20. Leroy, X.: Formal certification of a compiler back-end or: programming a compiler with a proof assistant. In: POPL 2006, pp. 42–54. ACM (2006)
21. Margaria, T., Steffen, B.: Service Engineering: Linking Business and IT. IEEE Computer 39(10), 45–55 (2006)
22. Margaria, T., Steffen, B.: Agile it: Thinking in user-centric models. In: Margaria, T., Steffen, B. (eds.) ISoLA 2008. CCIS, vol. 17, pp. 490–502. Springer, Heidelberg (2008)
23. Margaria, T., Steffen, B.: Simplicity as a driver for agile innovation. IEEE Computer 43(6), 90–92 (2010)
24. Naujokat, S., Neubauer, J., Lamprecht, A.L., Steffen, B., Jörges, S., Margaria, T.: Simplicity-first model-based plug-in development. Softw., Pract. Exper. 44(3), 277–297 (2014)
25. Necula, G.C.: Proof-carrying code. In: Proceedings of the 24th ACM SIGPLAN-SIGACT Symposium on Principles of Programming Languages, POPL 1997, pp. 106–119. ACM (1997)
26. Niese, O., Steffen, B., Margaria, T., Hagerer, A., Brune, G., Ide, H.-D.: Library-Based Design and Consistency Checking of System-Level Industrial Test Cases. In: Hussmann, H. (ed.) FASE 2001. LNCS, vol. 2029, pp. 233–248. Springer, Heidelberg (2001)

27. Parr, T.: Enforcing strict model-view separation in template engines. In: Proceedings of the 13th International Conference on World Wide Web, WWW 2004, pp. 224–233. ACM (2004)

28. Plotkin, G.D.: A Structural Approach to Operational Semantics. Tech. Rep. DAIMI FN–19, Computer Science Department, Aarhus University (1981)

29. Pnueli, A., Siegel, M.D., Singerman, E.: Translation Validation. In: Steffen, B. (ed.) TACAS 1998. LNCS, vol. 1384, pp. 151–166. Springer, Heidelberg (1998)

30. Raffelt, H., Margaria, T., Steffen, B., Merten, M.: Hybrid test of web applications with webtest. In: Proceedings of the 2008 Workshop on Testing, analysis, and Verification of Web Services and Applications, TAV-WEB 2008, pp. 1–7. ACM (2008)

31. Raffelt, H., Merten, M., Steffen, B., Margaria, T.: Dynamic testing via automata learning. International Journal on Software Tools for Technology Transfer (STTT) 11(4), 307–324 (2009)

32. Sampath, P., Rajeev, A.C., Ramesh, S., Shashidhar, K.C.: Behaviour directed testing of auto-code generators. In: Sixth IEEE International Conference on Software Engineering and Formal Methods (SEFM 2008), pp. 191–200. IEEE Computer Society (2008)

33. Schmidt, D.A.: Denotational semantics: a methodology for language development. William C. Brown Publishers (1986)

34. Stahl, T., Völter, M., Efftinge, S., Haase, A.: Modellgetriebene Softwareentwicklung: Techniken, Engineering, Management. dpunkt, 2nd edn. (2007) (in German)

35. Steffen, B., Margaria, T., Nagel, R., Jörges, S., Kubczak, C.: Model-Driven Development with the jABC. In: Bin, E., Ziv, A., Ur, S. (eds.) HVC 2006. LNCS, vol. 4383, pp. 92–108. Springer, Heidelberg (2007)

36. Stürmer, I., Conrad, M.: Code Generator Testing in Practice. In: INFORMATIK 2004 - Informatik verbindet, Band 2, Beiträge der 34. Jahrestagung der Gesellschaft für Informatik e.V (GI), pp. 33–37. GI (2004)

37. Stürmer, I., Conrad, M., Doerr, H., Pepper, P.: Systematic Testing of Model-Based Code Generators. IEEE Transactions on Software Engineering 33, 622–634 (2007)

38. Stürmer, I., Weinberg, D., Conrad, M.: Overview of existing safeguarding techniques for automatically generated code. In: Proceedings of SEAS 2005, pp. 1–6. ACM (2005)

39. Tillmann, N., Schulte, W.: Parameterized unit tests. In: Proceedings of the 10th European Software Engineering Conference, pp. 253–262. ACM (2005)

40. Vouk, M.A.: Back-to-back testing. Information and Software Technology 32, 34–45 (1990)

41. Windmüller, S., Neubauer, J., Steffen, B., Howar, F., Bauer, O.: Active continuous quality control. In: Proceedings of the 16th ACM SIGSOFT Symposium on Component Based Software Engineering (CBSE), pp. 111–120. ACM (2013)

Rewriting Object Models
With Cycles and Nested Collections
A Model-Based Metaprogramming Problem

Markus Lepper[1] and Baltasar Trancón y Widemann[1,2]

[1] <semantics /> GmbH, Berlin, Germany
[2] Ilmenau University of Technology, Ilmenau, Germany
post@markuslepper.eu

Abstract. Metaprogramming with classical compiler technology is similar to model-based code generation. We discuss a particular tool, umod, that generates complex data model implementations in Java, and a particular aspect of its support for declarative programming: The rewriting of data models in object-oriented style, based on the visitor pattern, with support for arbitrary reference graphs and nested collection-valued fields. We demonstrate that concerns of both compiler theory and model-based development apply, and that the distinction is overshadowed by a general commitment to semantic rigour.

1 Introduction: Compilation, Model-Based Code Generation, and Metaprogramming

The disciplines of classical compiler construction and model-based code generation are widely acknowledged, different community viewpoints aside, to address largely the same basic theoretical problems. One commonly cited characteristic difference in practice is the role assigned to the resulting code artifacts in the software development process:

On the one hand, a classical compiler is typically expected to take textual input code written in some more or less well-established programming language and legible for the programmer, and produce output binary code legible for some real or virtual machine, in the successful case without requiring or providing occasion for user interaction. The compiled program is then expected to run out of the box, or in the case of modular separate compilation, to integrate with other compiled modules (in traditional obscurity called "object code") by a comparatively simple cross-referencing procedure performed by a linker tool.

On the other hand, model-based code generators, in their pure form, feature input "languages" or model formats that are not programming languages in the classical sense, because they are defined by metamodelling rather than grammar, presented and edited visually rather than textually[1], and/or arbitrarily "domain-specific", that is specifically created for a small, or even singular, set of projects.

---

[1] Although tools that bridge classical grammar technology and modeling frameworks, such as Eclipse Xtext, are becoming increasingly popular.

T. Margaria and B. Steffen (Eds.): ISoLA 2014, Part I, LNCS 8802, pp. 445–460, 2014.

The output is then expected to be fed into the project repository alongside hand-written code, and integration often requires nontrivial user intervention: for instance by completing stubs and skeletons, actual editing of generated code (frowned upon by software engineering purists, but pragmatically very useful), or using whatever complex interfacing mechanisms of physically disconnected code fragments the target language provides (such as inheritance in the object-oriented world).

In this paper, we present a particular effort in the construction of semantically sound programming language tools. It demonstrates that the distinction suggested by the above summary is blurred, and by far secondary to the distinction of rigorous and ad-hoc approaches. By sharing our experience, we intend to make a modest contribution to the exchange of ideas and techniques between the two disciplines, and general understanding of their relationship. To this end, we shall

1. discuss a subfield of classical compiler construction that predates model-based approaches (or at least their currently associated buzzwords) but has many requirements, problems and strategies in common, namely the implementation of *generative* or *meta*-programming;
2. present a case study from our own research on metaprogramming tools and techniques, which builds on a classical compiler constructors' viewpoint, but is related to mainstream model-based methodology closely enough to carry some illuminating analogies.

We shall start our discussion by refuting more precisely the distinction as outlined simplistically above, giving two particular arguments to the contrary.

The first concerns the often-cited distinction of model inputs having a distinctively higher level of abstraction than mere programs or being characteristically "non-executable". This is difficult to justify precisely:

> [Automated programming] *always has been a euphemism for programming with a higher-level language than was then available to the programmer. Research in AP is simply research in the implementation of higher-level programming languages.* [9]

The second, related argument concerns the level of abstraction of the back-end rather than the front-end. Delegating tedious and banal coding tasks to the computer has, evidently, always in the history of programming technology been a major goal. Examples of ad-hoc solutions abound, especially in self-application contexts (for instance see the GNU compiler collection [11]), but more generic tools (from LISP hygienic macros to parser generators) have also emerged early.

When such program fragment-generating tools, or metaprograms, are seen by the programmer as an *extension of his own productive capabilities beyond manually typing* code in his target language of choice, the essential distinction between programs and models, and the accidental one between compiler output being opaque and model-based generator output being transparent also vanish.

Tools functioning this way can benefit technically and semantically from the vast body of knowledge of classical compiler construction, but at the same time face many of the extra requirements and issues addressed by model-based code generation. We are confident that the investigation of particular problems and solutions in this area, such as the example technique discussed in the main part of this paper, can help to leverage the synergies of the complementary approaches.

1.1   The ^meta^-tools Approach

The example metaprogramming technique to be discussed below is part of the ^meta^-tools suite [12,7], an extensive collection of programming tools which, by its overall design strategy, is placed in the middle ground between classical compilers and model-based approaches.

The ^meta^-tools suite is designed to amplify the productivity of software development centered around the core technologies Java and XML, by leveraging high-level, declarative and semantically rigorous concepts, notations and styles. Technical implementations are provided through a pragmatic combination of libraries and style patterns (where the expressivity of the host platform suffices) and metaprogramming tools (where it must be transcended). Automatically generated code is human-readable throughout, and interfaced cleanly using the two modularity concepts provided by the Java host language: type parameterization and inheritance.

The ^meta^-tools have been validated mainly in self- and cross-application as well as the construction of other compilers, but also in the rapid prototyping of other medium-scale applications, in particular with emphasis on nontrivial algorithms and data structures.

2   The Data Model and Processor Generator umod

2.1   Models

A major component of the ^meta^-tools suite is the data model definition language and implementation generator umod. It provides a concise and expressive notation for specifying complex graph-like data structures. A umod model is a collection of model elements, represented as Java objects. The umod compiler generates Java code for the implementing classes from a model specification. Generated code comes with sophisticated support for many features: element subtyping, complex collection-valued attributes, pervasive early detection of spurious null references, inheritable constructor signatures, combinator-based pretty-printing, reified getters and setters for point-free programming (à la higher-order functional programming), stable deep equality, pattern matching, etc.

The code generated by umod thus emulates many desirable features of algebraic data types, but comes with the full power of object-oriented programming, in particular unrestricted access to low-level (imperative) programming constructs if necessary, and the ability to deal with arbitrary data graphs rather than trees. We have applied umod to generate abstract syntax representations for several other code generator tools, both classical compilers and other ^meta^-tools components.

Figure 1 shows a typical example from a real-word compiler construction project: The umod source text defines a model named Sig, to be translated into a Java package. The top level model element class Statement is realized as an abstract superclass of both Assignment and Block, etcetera. Both subclasses have fields (instance variables) named left, right and stmts, respectively. In the same text line follows an expression, giving the type of the field, and optionally, after the "!" character, a traversal indication (see next section).

```
MODEL Sig
VISITOR 0 Visitor
VISITOR 0 Rewriter IS REWRITER
// ...
TOPLEVEL CLASS
  Statement ABSTRACT
  | Assignment
          left    SEQ Variable                       ! V 0/0
          right   Expression                         ! V 0/1
  | Block
          stmts   SEQ Statement                      ! V 0/0
  Expression ABSTRACT
  | Reference
          var     Variable                           ! V 0/0
  Variable

  Statistics
          vars    Statement -> bool -> SET Variable  ! V 0/0 L RR
```

Fig. 1. Model Definition umod Source (Excerpt)

The syntax of the type declarations and the resulting carrier sets will be discussed in detail in Section 3.1. For practical programming it is important that the type constructors be fully compositional, as shown in the last field definition line of Fig. 1, and are covered by all features listed above.

2.2 Visitors

The umod system also provides code support for, and fine-grained control over, the *visitor* style pattern, the standard high-end control abstraction of traversal strategies for structured data in object-oriented programming [3,8]. The visitor pattern provides a concise, elegant, safe and robust style of associating data elements with effects: hence it is a prime example of *declarative* style (stating the "what" in user code and delegating the "how" to a lower level such as a library provider, or in our case, a generator). For data models that represent programs, the visitor machinery can be seen as the backbone of an *interpreter* (even if most actual visitors in a language processing tool will interpret only a small aspect each.)

Returning to the example, the annotations following the field types in Fig. 1 at the end of the source line, define *traversal plans* as a basis for the generation of visitor code. The slash "/" separates the numeric identifier of a plan and a number controlling the sequential order when visiting the fields on the same level of class definition. The second line in the example requests for the source code of a visitor called "`Visitor`", following the traversal plan "0". (Different visitors can be derived from one particular traversal plan. The requested flavour is indicated by a suffix in the declaration, see the next line.) The generated code is sketched in Fig. 2.

```
abstract class Visitor {                            // traversal plan 0/
  // ...
  void action(final Block b) {
    for (final Statement s : block.get_stmts())     // traversal order /0
      match(s);
  }
  void action(final Assignment a) {
    match(a.get_left());                            // traversal order /0
    match(a.get_right());                           // traversal order /1
  }
}
```

Fig. 2. Generated Visitor Code (Excerpt)

The generated code realizes the pure traversal, according to the selected traversal plan. Any desired effects are added by the user, by subclassing and method overriding. For our example, we consider the task of *copy propagation*, a typical basic compiler pass that recognizes assignments which redundantly copy values, and eliminates them by substitution. The anonymous class in Fig. 3 implements the recognition phase by descending transparently into the depth of a program model (regardless of the intervening path, for instance via nested `Block` elements), processing the model elements of `Assignment` class, and recording those that match a suitable pattern.[2]

The visitor pattern is rooted firmly in the imperative programming paradigm. That is, its semantics are based on sequential side effects, and rarely investigated globally and formally. True to the spirit of the ^meta^-tools emphasis on semantic precision, we have addressed the problem, and demonstrated the benefits of a formal operational model with a nontrivial optimization strategy [4].

2.3   Rewriters

A further issue with visitor is, in their basic form, a strong asymmetry between declarative *input* (essentially type-directed node matching, encoded into method

---

[2] Pattern matching of subgraphs is performed by the ^meta^-tools component Paisley, which is tightly integrated with umod. See [14].

```
Program copyPropagation(Program prog) {
  final Map<Variable, Variable> copies = new HashMap<>();
  new Visitor() {
    @Override void action(Assignment a) {
      // match pattern "Assignment({x}, Reference(y))" against "a"
      if (/* success */)
        copies.put(x, y);
      super.action(a);                           // top-down traversal
    }
  }.match(prog);
  // ... see below ...
}
```

Fig. 3. User-Defined Visitor Code

signatures) and imperative *reaction* (arbitrary method bodies). This resembles the relation between parser code generated from grammar declarations and interspersed "semantic actions". As a more declarative way of writing we have proposed a complementary extension to the visitor pattern that allows for similarly declarative specification of non-destructive data *transformation*, called the *rewriter* pattern [5]. In the language processing scenario, the rewriter machinery can be seen as the backbone of a *compiler* pass.

Returning again to the example, the third line in Fig. 1 requests rewriter code for the same traversal plan. The generated code is much more complex than in the simple visitor case, because its main purpose is not only to traverse the model, but also to propagate all changes consistently throughout. Different flavours are supported, the most sophisticated being the non-destructive type, combining copy-on-need with aggressive sharing and cycle detection.

Figure 4 shows the generated methods, their call graph, and the possible intervening overrides by the user. The method `rewrite(C2)` is the entry point for the rewriting process for all instances of class C2. It decides by means of a cache, whether the object has already been successfully rewritten or, otherwise, whether a clone already exists. The latter case indicates dynamically a cycle in the model reference graph. Otherwise it creates and memorizes a clone "on stock". All these operations employ library methods from the infrastructure.

Then it calls the generated method `rewriteFields(C2)`. This steps through the fields selected by the traversal plan on class definition level C2, calling `rewrite(F)` on each field value recursively. It updates the clone whenever a different value is returned. In this code, for every field of *collection type* one or more program loops are generated, which iterate this process for all values and create the resulting collection. Additionally `rewriteFields()` on the superclass C1 is called, in order to process inherited fields.

On return, `rewrite()` code checks whether changes in field values have occured, and returns either the original or the modified clone accordingly. Change propagation is based not on single objects, but on *strongly connected components* (SCCs), as recognized by above-mentioned cycle detection.

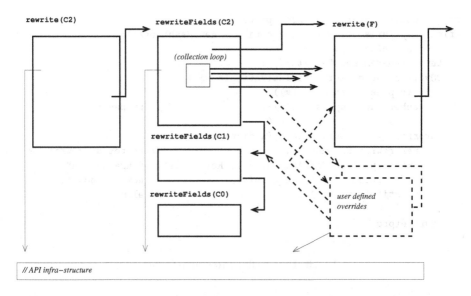

Fig. 4. Control flow in generated rewrite code and user override; cf. Fig. 2 and 3. *Arrow styles:* thick – generated control flow; thin – auxiliary API calls; dashed – interface to user code.

Again, generated code behaves neutrally; the user defines the required transformation by subclassing and overriding, as indicated in Fig. 4. Both levels of generated methods can be overridden, and user code may re-use the generated methods. It also calls the infrastructure library for inquiring and modifying the state of caches and results. There the most important methods are

- substitute(Object o) – sets o as the result of rewriting the currently visited model element;
- substitute_multi(Object... os) – sets a list (of zero, one or more) model elements as the rewriting result.

The anonymous class in Fig. 5 uses the information collected by the code in Fig. 3 to implement the elimination phase of the copy propagation pass.

The rewriter approach to model transformation has many features of high-level declarative programming, notably: robustness against minor changes in the model definition, compositional organization of active code into fragments per model element class, and automated propagation of dynamic changes. But, in contrast to "pure" approaches such as attribute grammars, the declarative paradigm is broken deliberately at the level of user-defined code, where the full powers (and dangers) of the object-oriented host environment are exposed.

This decision, which greatly enlarges the class of expressible rewriting procedures, exposes some technical details. It gives the programmer control over, and responsibility for,

```
Program copyPropagation(Program prog) {
  final Map<Variable, Variable> copies = new HashMap<>();
  // ... see above ...
  return (Program)new Rewriter() {
    @Override void rewriteFields(Variable v) {
      if (copies.containsKey(v))
        substitute(copies.get(v));                    // propagate
    }
    @Override void rewriteFields(Assignment a) {
      super.rewriteFields(a) ;                         // bottom-up rewriting
      // match pattern "Assignment({x}, Reference(y))" against "a"
      if (/* success */ && x.equals(y))               // now redundant?
        substitute_multi() ;                          // eliminate
    }
  }.rewrite(prog);
}
```

Fig. 5. User-Defined Rewriter Code

1. the execution order of rewriting actions in relation to the traversal effected by generated code (see [15] for a theoretical account);
2. the calling context, which may feature mutable state and stipulate restrictions on the type and multiplicity of local rewriting results.

The associated safety conditions can only be expressed partially in the static semantics of a host language such as Java. Our pragmatic solution maps as much to the type system as feasible, checks further conditions at runtime for fail-fast behavior, and leaves more difficult (or undecidable) issues to the user's caution.

So far, we have validated that rewriter-based programming competes favorably with more heavy-weight model transformation frameworks [5], and described very abstract and powerful denotational semantics for "well-behaved" object-oriented rewriters [15]. The overall goal can be described as allowing all kinds of user code in principle, but rewarding disciplined use with beneficial mathematical properties, for a flexible and conscious trade-off between rigor and agility. The following section explicates this strategy by discussing a novel problem, namely, how rewriting carries over to collection types.

3   Rewriting in the Presence of Nested Collections

3.1   Model Definitions in umod, Formally

The mathematical notation used in the following is fairly standard. It is inspired by Z notation [10], as it treats finite maps and sequences as relations with special properties, and thus allows the free application of set and relation operators and functions, as listed in Table 1.

Table 2 shows the components for defining the structure of a model, as far as needed for our problem: C_0 is a finite set of predefined classes, e.g. imported from

Table 1. Mathematical notation

$\mathbb{F}(A)$	Finite power set, the type of all *finite* subsets of the set A.
$A \to B$	The type of the *total* functions from A to B.
$A \nrightarrow B$	The type of the *partial* functions from A to B.
$A \nrightarrow\!\!\!\!\!\rightarrow B$	The type of the *partial and finite* functions from A to B.
$A \leftrightarrow B$	The type of the relations between A and B.
$\operatorname{ran} a, \operatorname{dom} a$	Range and domain of a function or relation.
$S \triangleleft R$	$= R \cap (S \times \operatorname{ran} R)$, i.e. domain restriction of a relation.
$r^{\sim}$	The inverse of a relation
A^*	All possible finite sequences from elements of A, including the empty sequence.
$\mathbf{ID}_A$	$= \{a \in A \bullet (a \mapsto a)\}$, the identity relation.
$r \mathbin{\fatsemi} s$	The composition of two relations: the smallest relation s.t. $a\ r\ b \wedge b\ s\ c \Rightarrow a\ (r \mathbin{\fatsemi} s)\ c$

system libraries, and $\mathcal{T}_{\text{prim}}$ are some primitive data types. Any model declaration defines a finite set of classes C, the *model element classes*, i.e. the classes of the host language objects which together will make up one instance of the model. The total superclass function **extends** must be free of cycles, as usual, and well-founded in $\mathcal{C}_0$. F is the set of all field definitions, each related to one particular model class definition, indicated by *definingClass*; the collection of all fields of a certain class is given by *fields*.

Each field has a type, given by *fieldType*. Types are constructed in generationsas $T = \mathcal{T}_\tau$ for some arbitrary but fixed number τ. The zeroth generation $\mathcal{T}_0$ includes all predefined scalar types $\mathcal{T}_{\text{prim}}$, and non-null references to all external classes $\mathcal{C}_0$ and to all model element classes C. The further generations are made by applying the following *type constructors* in a freely compositional[3] way:

- OPT $\mathcal{T}_n$, – optional type, the special value **null** is allowed additionally.
- SET $\mathcal{T}_n$, – power set, contains all possible finite sets of values of T_n.
- SEQ $\mathcal{T}_n$. – sequence, contains all possible finite lists made of values from T_n.
- MAP $\mathcal{T}_{n,1}$ TO $\mathcal{T}_{n,2}$, abbreviated as $\mathcal{T}_{n,1}$ -> $\mathcal{T}_{n,2}$, – all finite partial mappings from $\mathcal{T}_{n,1}$ to $\mathcal{T}_{n,2}$.
- REL $\mathcal{T}_{n,1}$TO$\mathcal{T}_{n,2}$, abbreviated as $\mathcal{T}_{n,1}$ <-> $\mathcal{T}_{n,2}$, – all finite multi-maps/relations from $\mathcal{T}_{n,1}$ to $\mathcal{T}_{n,2}$.

For every type $t \in T$ there is an *extension* $[\![\,t\,]\!]$, which contains all permitted values for a field declared with type t. For $\mathcal{T}_{\text{prim}}$ and $\mathcal{C}_0$ these are inherited from the host language. For composite **umod** types the extensions are defined in Table 2, creating optional types and finite lists, sets, maps and multimaps as carrier types. The OPT types lead to relaxed getter and setter methods permitting the **null** value, which is otherwise rejected by throwing an exception. The other types are realized by specialized instances of the Java collection framework. The generational way of defining T ensures that every value of a type t

---

[3] Except for OPT which is idempotent.

Table 2. Model Element Classes, Fields and Types of a `umod` Model

$$\text{disjoint}(\mathcal{C}_0, \mathcal{T}_{\text{prim}}, C, F, Q)$$

$$\text{extends} : C \to (C \cup \mathcal{C}_0)$$

$$definingClass : F \to C$$

$$fields(c) = \begin{cases} \{\} & \text{if } c \in \mathcal{C}_0 \\ definingClass^{\sim}(c) \cup fields(\text{extends}(c)) & \text{otherwise} \end{cases}$$

$$fieldType : F \to T$$

$$\exists \tau \bullet T = \mathcal{T}_\tau$$

$$\mathcal{T}_0 = \mathcal{T}_{\text{prim}} \cup \mathcal{C}_0 \cup C$$

$$\mathcal{T}_{n+1} ::= \mathcal{T}_n \mid \text{OPT } \mathcal{T}_n \mid \text{SEQ } \mathcal{T}_n \mid \text{SET } \mathcal{T}_n \mid \text{MAP } \mathcal{T}_n \text{ TO } \mathcal{T}_n \mid \text{REL } \mathcal{T}_n \text{ TO } \mathcal{T}_n$$

$$\texttt{.class} : Q \to C$$

$$fields(q) = fields(\texttt{.class}(q))$$

$$
\begin{aligned}
[\![\, t : \mathcal{T}_{\text{prim}} \,]\!] &= \mathbin{/\!/} \textit{inherited from host language.} \\
[\![\, c : \mathcal{C}_0 \,]\!] &= \mathbin{/\!/} \textit{imported from libraries.} \\
[\![\, \text{OPT } t \,]\!] &= [\![\, t \,]\!] \cup \{\texttt{null}\} \\
[\![\, \text{SEQ } t \,]\!] &= \big([\![\, t \,]\!]\big)^* \\
[\![\, \text{SET } t \,]\!] &= \mathbb{F}[\![\, t \,]\!] \\
[\![\, \text{MAP } t_1 \text{ TO } t_2 \,]\!] &= [\![\, t_1 \,]\!] \nrightarrow [\![\, t_2 \,]\!] \\
[\![\, \text{REL } t_1 \text{ TO } t_2 \,]\!] &= \mathbb{F}\big([\![\, t_1 \,]\!] \times [\![\, t_2 \,]\!]\big) \\
[\![\, c : C \,]\!] &= \{q \in Q \mid \texttt{.class}(q) = c\}
\end{aligned}
$$

is *free of cycles.*[4] It also ensures that all extension sets are disjoint, and we can assume some global "universe" $[\![\, T \,]\!]$. This will be used in few formulas for ease of notation.

Every model is a collection of model elements, i.e. Java objects of model element classes, i.e. values from $[\![\, C \,]\!]$. Each of these is identified by a reference or "pointer value" $q \in Q$, belongs to a certain model class $\texttt{.class}(q)$ and thus has certain fields $fields(q)$. The state of any model is always equivalent to a finite map from all fields of live objects to a permitted value for the respective field type. Field values may directly or indirectly refer to other model elements, and, in contrast to the well-founded collection-based field value world, the resulting graph may contain *arbitrary cycles.*

3.2   Rewriting Collections

The recursive calls to `rewrite()`, as explained informally[5] in Section 2.3, realize and define the rewriting process on the level of single elements and their classes.

---

[4] This is necessary to impose any mathematical semantics on Java collection objects, whose behavior is theoretically undefined, and practically unreliable, in the presence of cyclic containment.

[5] For a formal definition see the forthcoming technical report.

The declarative approach mandates that this point-wise relation is *automatically* lifted to the rewriting of values $v \in [\![\, t \,]\!]$ of a collection type $t \in \mathcal{T}_{n>0}$. Here a potential clash of paradigms can occur: The programmer must rely on the consistency of the collections created by the rewriter. For this, precise semantics are required, based on the *mathematical* notions of sets, sequences, maps, etc.

The host language Java, just like many others, provides an object-oriented collection framework with interfaces called `Set`, `Map`, etc. But the mathematical metaphor is well-known to be lopsided: Their actual behavior relies implicitly on the immutability of contained elements, and explicitly on the order of interfering container mutations, such as `add/remove` or `put`, respectively. Hence the imperative implementation of transformation may be in conflict with the intended mathematics, in particular where control is shared between user-defined and generated code (solid vs. dashed arrows in Fig. 4). It is desirable that the implementation of $[\![\, \texttt{MAP}\,\_\,]\!]$ should detect and signal error conditions whenever a conflict arises. Unfortunately, the corresponding tests are potentially very expensive, and there is no support from the standard libraries.

The following discussion makes two contributions:

1. Precise semantics for the rewriting of freely compositional collections are constructed by (**p1**) to (**p6**) in Table 3. Their implementation is in most cases straight-forward.
2. Second, for the critical case of rewriting maps inference rules are provided which can help to elide costly tests, and hence speed up a reliable implementation significantly.

In a first step we totally forget the structure of the model and the traversal order: We assume the execution of the whole rewriting process has succeeded and delivers k_v, the user defined point-wise map from model elements to (possibly empty) sequences of model elements as their rewriting results, see Table 3. Additionally, $\kappa = \bigcup_{(q,\overline{q}) \in k_v} \{q\} \times \operatorname{ran} \overline{q}$ is a relation which forgets the sequential order of these lists and flattens them into a multi-map. It is important that κ is not necessarily a map, nor total. It will be used in the rewriting of all collections which *directly* contain model elements, except sequences, which use k_v.

The semantics of rewriting collections can now be defined by constructing mappings, i.e. discrete functions $\rho_n : [\![\, \mathcal{T}_n \,]\!] \nrightarrow [\![\, \mathcal{T}_n \,]\!]$, which follow the generational structure of types. These mappings are defined as the family of the smallest relations which satisfy the properties (**p0**) to (**p6**) from Table 3.

The "basic trick" is to encode the collection field values and the rewriting functions themselves *both* as (special cases of) relations. The extension of the sequence type $[\![\, \texttt{SEQ}\, t \,]\!]$ can be encoded as $\mathbb{N} \leftrightarrow [\![\, t \,]\!]$; sets $[\![\, \texttt{SET}\, t \,]\!]$ are encoded by $\{\star\} \leftrightarrow [\![\, t \,]\!]$, and for $[\![\, \texttt{MAP}\, t\, \texttt{TO}\, u \,]\!] \subset [\![\, \texttt{REL}\, t\, \texttt{TO}\, u \,]\!]$ there is a canonical encoding for functions as relations anyhow. This allows the transparent application of the relational composition operator ($\mathring{,}$). This does not only lead to compact formulas, but also induces an intuition which can *easily be explained to programmers* of different skills, e.g. using diagrams.

The properties (**p0**) to (**p4**) suffice for the construction of ρ_n, as long the `MAP` constructor is not involved. These rewriting functions behave nicely: they

Table 3. Rewriting Collections

$$k_v : [\![\,C\,]\!] \to [\![\,C\,]\!]^*$$
$$\kappa : [\![\,C\,]\!] \leftrightarrow [\![\,C\,]\!]$$
$$\rho_n : [\![\,\mathcal{T}_n\,]\!] \nrightarrow [\![\,\mathcal{T}_n\,]\!]$$
$$\mathsf{isMap}(r : A \leftrightarrow B) \stackrel{def}{\Longleftrightarrow} r^{\sim} \,\fatsemi\, r \subseteq \mathbf{ID}_B$$
$$\mathsf{isInj}(r : A \leftrightarrow B) \stackrel{def}{\Longleftrightarrow} r \,\fatsemi\, r^{\sim} \subseteq \mathbf{ID}_A$$
$$\mathsf{isTotal}(r : A \leftrightarrow B, s) \stackrel{def}{\Longleftrightarrow} s \subseteq \mathrm{dom}\, r$$

$$s \in [\![\,\mathcal{T}_{\mathrm{prim}}\,]\!] \cup [\![\,\mathcal{C}_0\,]\!] \cup \{\star\} \implies (s \mapsto s) \in \rho_0 \tag{p0}$$
$$c \in C \land s \in [\![\,\mathtt{SEQ}\ c\,]\!] \implies (s \mapsto \mathsf{flatten}(s \,\fatsemi\, k_v)) \in \rho_1 \tag{p1}$$
$$t \in \mathcal{T}_n \neq C \land s \in [\![\,\mathtt{SEQ}\ t\,]\!] \implies (s \mapsto s \,\fatsemi\, \rho_n) \in \rho_{n+1} \tag{p2}$$
$$t \in \mathcal{T}_n \land s \in [\![\,\mathtt{SET}\ t\,]\!] \implies (s \mapsto s \,\fatsemi\, (\rho_n \cup \kappa)) \in \rho_{n+1} \tag{p3}$$
$$t_1, t_2 \in \mathcal{T}_n \land s \in [\![\,\mathtt{REL}\ t_1\ \mathtt{TO}\ t_2\,]\!] \implies (s \mapsto (\rho_n \cup \kappa)^{\sim} \,\fatsemi\, s \,\fatsemi\, (\rho_n \cup \kappa)) \in \rho_{n+1} \tag{p4}$$

$$\frac{s \in [\![\,\mathtt{MAP}\ t_1\ \mathtt{TO}\ t_2\,]\!] \ \land\ t_1 \in \mathcal{T}_n \ \land\ t_2 \in C \ \land\ \mathsf{isInj}((\mathrm{dom}\, s) \lhd (\rho_n \cup \kappa)) \ \land\ \mathsf{isMap}((\mathrm{ran}\, s) \lhd \kappa)}{(s \mapsto (\rho_n \cup \kappa)^{\sim} \,\fatsemi\, s \,\fatsemi\, \kappa) \in \rho_{n+1}} \tag{p5}$$

$$\frac{s \in [\![\,\mathtt{MAP}\ t_1\ \mathtt{TO}\ t_2\,]\!] \ \land\ t_1, t_2 \in \mathcal{T}_n \ \land\ t_2 \notin C \ \land\ \mathsf{isInj}((\mathrm{dom}\, s) \lhd (\rho_n \cup \kappa))}{(s \mapsto (\rho_n \cup \kappa)^{\sim} \,\fatsemi\, s \,\fatsemi\, \rho_n) \in \rho_{n+1}} \tag{p6}$$

$$\frac{S \subset [\![\,\mathcal{T}_n\,]\!] \ \land\ D = \bigcup_{r \in S} \mathrm{dom}\, r \ \land\ R = \bigcup_{r \in S} \mathrm{ran}\, r \ \land\ \mathsf{isInj}(D \lhd \rho_{n-1}) \ \land\ \mathsf{isInj}(R \lhd \rho_{n-1}) \ \land\ \mathsf{isTotal}(\rho_{n-1}, D \cup R)}{\mathsf{isInj}(S \lhd \rho_n)} \tag{pInj}$$

are total, which means that no typing errors can occur. The cardinality of the user defined rewriting κ (empty, singleton or multiple result) is "automatically absorbed" by the containing collection. This allows to replace one model element by zero or more than one in a $\mathtt{SET}$ or on both sides of a $\mathtt{REL}$.

A special case is the rewriting of $\mathtt{SEQ}\, c$ for $c \in C$, i.e. rewriting $\overline{q} \in Q^*$. Here the sequential order of k_v is respected, and the list $k_v(q)$ is inserted "flattened" into the resulting list. This is described by (**p1**). All other sequences, all sets and all relations are rewritten by simply composing their encoding relation with the rewriting relation ρ_n of their elements' type generation, see rules (**p2**) to (**p4**).

Rewriting $\mathtt{MAP}\, t_1\, \mathtt{TO}\, t_2$ is the real issue: Consider the map of maps $\{\{a \mapsto b\} \mapsto c, \{a \mapsto d\} \mapsto e\}$, where the user's local rules specify d to be rewritten to b. The global rewriting procedure then faces a dilemma, with the following options:

- fail dynamically, e.g. by throwing an exception;
- weaken the type of the result from $\mathtt{MAP}$ to $\mathtt{REL}$, possibly failing later due to violated context conditions;
- silently remove *both* offending pairs;
- silently obey the operational semantics of the underlying object-oriented implementation, thus creating a race condition where *either* of the offending pairs will be overwritten by the other, nondeterministically.

Obviously, the latter two options are unacceptable from a declarative viewpoint, and the possibility of dynamic failure implied by the two former should be contained as much as possible by means of precise diagnostics and static checks.

A given map $m \in [\![\, \mathcal{T}_{n+1} \,]\!] = [\![\, \text{MAP}\, t_1 \,\text{TO}\, t_2 \,]\!]$ is only *guaranteed* to be rewritten to a map m', as opposed to a general relation, if the underlying rewrite relation of all *range* elements is itself a map, and at the same time the rewrite relation of all *domain* elements is *injective*. This is illustrated by the diagram

$$
((\text{dom}\, m) \lhd (\rho_n \cup \kappa))^{\sim} \uparrow \quad \xrightarrow{\ \ m\ \ } \quad \downarrow (\text{ran}\, m) \lhd (\rho_n \cup \kappa)
$$
$$
\xrightarrow{\ \ m'\ \ }
$$

where the relational converse of the left-hand side must be a map.

The right-hand sides fall in two different cases: $t_2 \in C$ covered by rule (**p5**) and $t_2 \notin C$ by (**p6**). The data construction "under the line" is in both cases simple and basically the same as in (**p4**) for unrestricted relations, but he preconditions above the line are critical. For (**p6**) it is clear by construction that every ρ_n is a map. (For every type only one of (**p0**) to (**p6**) matches, and every rule adds exactly one maplet.) In (**p5**) mostly it must be checked dynamically whether $(\text{ran}\, m) \lhd \kappa$ is a map, because this depends on the outcome of the user's code. But it *may* be known statically: A variant of generated rewriter code which does not offer the callback function substitute_multi(Object...) will produce only maps for κ, which are even total.

W.r.t. the left-hand side of the diagram, the check for injectivity (which is the map-ness of the inverse relation) must always be added explicitly, in (**p5**) and in (**p6**). In case of arbitrarily deep nested collection types on the left side of a map, the equality tests involved can be very expensive. Therefore it is necessary to *inherit and infer* the required properties as far as possible.

For injectivity it is clear that the rewriting function of a SET, SEQ, REL and MAP type is injective, if the rewriting function(s) of its element type(s) is (/are both) *injective and total*. Only then it can be guaranteed that different values of the collection type will be mapped to different values. This is formalized as (**pInj**).

For the start of the chain, when the element type is from $\mathcal{T}_{\text{prim}}$ or $\mathcal{C}_0$, it is clear that ρ_0 is total and injective, since it is the identity.

For C, i.e. reference values to model elements, map-ness and totality may be known statically, see remark above, or require explicit testing. Injectivity must always be tested explicitly. Again, SEQ c with $c \in C$ is an exception. In this special case totality and injectivity of the element level do *not* carry over to injectivity of the collection level: e.g., $\rho_0 = \{a \mapsto \langle x \rangle, b \mapsto \langle y, z \rangle, c \mapsto \langle x, y \rangle, d \mapsto \langle z \rangle\}$ leads to $\rho_1 \langle a, b \rangle = \langle x, y, z \rangle = \rho_1 \langle c, d \rangle$.

For the higher levels, the rewriting function $\rho_{n>0}$ is always *total* by construction, since (**p0**) to (**p6**) cover all types. The only "holes" come from the additional conditions in (**p5**) and (**p6**), which detect the typing errors when maps would be rewritten to non-maps. We may assume (w.l.o.g.) that in this case the inference process described here has been aborted anyhow. So the totality of the rewriting function ρ may be assumed and thus *injectivity is completely propagated upward* the type generations, as expressed in (**pInj**). In the optimum case it needs to be checked only once, for κ, and for $[\![\,\text{SEQ}\,c\,]\!] \lhd \rho_1$ with $c \in C$.

For given concrete values, if ρ_n of the components is *not* injective, then ρ_{n+1} of the collections, restricted to those currently alive, still can be. Therefore explicit tests can become necessary also on higher levels, when the values appear on the left side of a map construction. These tests can be very expensive.

In the current implementation all these inferences cannot be leveraged, since the employed standard Java collection implementations do the `equals()` test for every "key" inserted into a map anyhow. But if an implementation were chosen with a "trusted back-door", which allowed to manipulate the underlying data structures with fewer tests, then these inference rules (which e.g. prove that there are never "identical" maps of maps of maps on the left side of a map) will become highly relevant.

Only rewriting algorithms (more or less similar to ours) which treat all values as immutable, can give precise semantics to a point-wise modification of a collection, which is referred to by the left side of a map. With these back-doors this would be possible in acceptable execution time.

If $(\text{dom}\,m) \lhd \rho_n$ is *not* injective, then still a map may result when rewriting the map m, namely iff all values which point to the same value by ρ_n, also have the same value by m. (E.g. rewrite map $\{a \mapsto 2, b \mapsto 2\}$ when the user defines $\{a \mapsto a, b \mapsto a\}$.) For us is it not yet clear how these "accidentally correct" results should be handled. This is both an ergonomic and a philosophic design decision. More practical programming experience is required.

4   Conclusion

Rigorous application of mathematical principles to software design is not just an academic habit and end by itself; it can have very practical and profound impact on the reliability of software and the productivity of the development process. However, rigor comes only easy when a "pure" system can be designed from scratch. Programming tools and systems that build on legacy environments can only go so far. A particular danger to rigor lurks in the double standards of object-orientation with respect to models as transcendental mathematical entities and real, mutable data structures. We have illustrated this by a case study on mathematically sound, dynamic rewriting of complex object models. Where resorting to a pure "sandbox" system is not an option, programming discipline must be exercised carefully. This is made feasible by generating as much code as possible automatically. Using inheritance as the canonical object-oriented technique to interface generated and user code is a generally useful metaprogramming strategy that leverages both a great deal of logical independence of "moving parts", and the opportunity to investigate the remaining interferences systematically, and provide a pragmatic and effective combination of static and dynamic safety nets.

4.1 Related Work

Term rewriting has been one of the earliest subjects of basic research and of practical programming. The foundations have been laid in the early 20th century e.g. Church–Rosser theorem, etc. Since then a broad and thorough theory has evolved. With the upcome of compiler construction in the Nineteen-sixties, implementations became soon necessary, and a large *folklore tradition* began, where term rewriting algorithms were mapped in different ways to concrete programming techniques. Our own development is an attempt of systematizing these well-known programming patterns. Nevertheless, term rewriting in the narrow and classical sense does of course not touch the two problems treated in this paper, cycles in the data and freely compositional collection types.

One of the leading implementations and research tools in term rewriting is *Maude*. The foundation paper [6] is from 1993 and has hardly lost relevance.

Rho-graphs have been developed for combining pattern matching, as known from graph rewriting, and lambda calculus. Recently the treatment of cycles and optimal sharing has been added [1]. We are not aware of any implementation.

A widespread system, well-proven in practice, is Tom [2]. It realizes pattern matching and term rewriting by compiling a mixture of a dedicated control language and a high level hosting language, preferably Java. The problems of cycles and the semantics of maps are not addressed.

All these approaches are different from ours, since they are based on "rewrite-centered" languages specially designed for these techniques, and therefore can come to much stronger theoretical results. On the downside the programmer has to learn a further language and to cope with more or less hidden strategies.

Approaches like the visitor combinators from JJTraveler [13] are different to ours on the other side of the scale: They are more flexible and ad-hoc configurable since they involve no code generation at all, but only (slightly invasive) interface usage. Rewriting and visiting structures with sharing can be implemented on top, in many cases very elegantly, but is not supported initially. The problem of maps is not addressed.

References

1. Baldan, P., Bertolissi, C., Cirstea, H., Kirchner, C.: A rewriting calculus for cyclic higher-order term graphs. Mathematical Structures in Computer Science (2006), https://hal.inria.fr/inria-00110872/en/
2. Balland, E., Brauner, P., Kopetz, R., Moreau, P.E., Reilles, A.: Tom: Piggybacking rewriting on Java. In: Proc. RTA. LNCS, vol. 4533, pp. 36–47. Springer-Verlag (2007), http://hal.inria.fr/inria-00142045
3. Gamma, E., Helm, R., Johnson, R., Vlissides, J.: Design Patterns: Elements of Reusable Object-Oriented Software. Addison-Wesley (1994)
4. Lepper, M., Trancón y Widemann, B.: Optimization of visitor performance by reflection-based analysis. In: Cabot, J., Visser, E. (eds.) Theory and Practice of Model Transformations, ICMT 2011. LNCS, vol. 6707, pp. 15–30. Springer (2011)
5. Lepper, M., Trancón y Widemann, B.: Solving the TTC 2011 compiler optimization task with metatools. In: Van Gorp, P., Mazanek, S., Rose, L. (eds.) Transformation Tool Contest 2011. EPTCS, vol. 74, pp. 70–115 (2011)

6. Martí-Oliet, N., Meseguer, J.: Rewriting logic as a logical and semantic framework. Tech. rep., SRI International (1993)
7. Metatools homepage, http://www.bandm.eu/metatools/
8. Palsberg, J., Jay, C.B.: The essence of the visitor pattern. In: Proc. COMPSAC. pp. 9–15. IEEE Computer Society (1998)
9. Parnas, D.L.: Software aspects of strategic defense systems. Comm. ACM 28(12) (1985)
10. Spivey, J.: The Z Notation: a reference manual. Prentice Hall (1988), http://spivey.oriel.ox.ac.uk/~mike/zrm/
11. Stallman, R.M.: GNU Compiler Collection Internals. Free Software Foundation
12. Trancón y Widemann, B., Lepper, M., Wieland, J.: Automatic construction of XML-based tools, seen as meta-programming. Automated Software Engineering 10(1), 22–38 (2003)
13. Visser, J.: Visitor combination and traversal control. ACM Sigplan Notices, OOPSLA 2001 36(11) (2001)
14. Trancón y Widemann, B., Lepper, M.: Paisley: Pattern matching à la carte. In: Theory and Practice of Model Transformations. LNCS, vol. 7307. Springer (2012)
15. Trancón y Widemann, B., Lepper, M.: Towards (co)algebraic semantics for the object-oriented rewriter pattern. In: Seisenberger, M. (ed.) CALCO Early Ideas (2014)

Compiling SCCharts —
A Case-Study on Interactive Model-Based Compilation*

Christian Motika, Steven Smyth, and Reinhard von Hanxleden

Real-Time and Embedded Systems Group, Department of Computer Science
Christian-Albrechts-Universität zu Kiel, Olshausenstr. 40, 24118 Kiel, Germany
{cmot,ssm,rvh}@informatik.uni-kiel.de
www.informatik.uni-kiel.de/rtsys/

Abstract. SCCharts is a recently proposed statechart language designed for specifying safety-critical reactive systems. We have developed an Eclipse-based compilation chain that synthesizes SCCharts into either hardware or software. The user edits a textual description which is visualized as SCChart and subsequently transformed into VHDL or C code via a series of model-to-model (M2M) transformation steps. An interactive environment gives the user control over which transformations are applied and allows the user to inspect intermediate transformation results. This *Single-Pass Language-Driven Incremental Compilation (SLIC)* approach should conceptually be applicable to other languages as well. Key benefits are: (1) a compact, light-weight definition of the core semantics, (2) intermediate transformation results open to inspection and support for certification, (3) high-level formulations of transformations that define advanced language constructs, (4) a divide-and-conquer validation strategy, (5) simplified language/compiler subsetting and DSL construction.

1 Introduction

Sequentially Constructive Statecharts (SCCharts) are a recently proposed statechart modeling language for reactive systems [13]. SCCharts have been designed with safety-critical applications in mind and are based on the sequentially constructive model of computation (SC MoC) [15]. The SC MoC follows a synchronous approach, which provides semantic rigor and determinism, but at the same time permits sequential assignments within a reaction as is standard in imperative languages. The basis of SCCharts is a minimal set of constructs, termed *Core SCCharts*, consisting of state machines plus fork/join concurrency. Building on these core constructs, *Extended SCCharts* add expressiveness with a rich set of advanced features, such as different abort types, signals, or history transitions. The safety-critical focus of SCCharts is reflected not only in the deterministic semantics, but also in the approach to defining the language, building up on Core SCCharts, which facilitate rigorous formal analysis and verification.

---

* This work was supported by the German Science Foundation (DFG HA 4407/6-1 and ME 1427/6-1) as part of the PRETSY project.

T. Margaria and B. Steffen (Eds.): ISoLA 2014, Part I, LNCS 8802, pp. 461–480, 2014.
© Springer-Verlag Berlin Heidelberg 2014

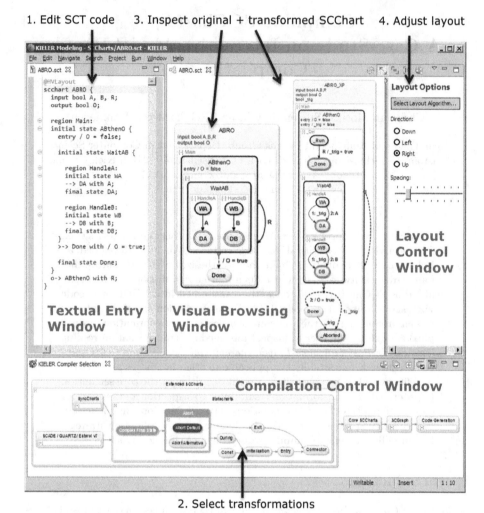

Fig. 1. Screen shot of KIELER SCCharts tool annotated with high-level user story for interactive model-based compilation

The original SCCharts language proposal [13] also presents possible compilation strategies for compiling SCCharts into software (e. g., C code) or hardware (e. g., VHDL). That presentation covers the abstract compilation concepts, largely specific to SCCharts. However, it gives only little detail and motivation on our *incremental, model-based* strategy for realizing these concepts, which is the focus of this paper now.

To get a first idea of this incremental model-based compilation approach and the possibilities it offers, consider the user story depicted in Fig. 1: (1) The user edits a model in a *textual entry window*. In our SCCharts prototype, this is done with the SCCharts Textual Language (SCT). (2) The user selects model-to-model (M2M) transformations to be applied to the model in a *compilation control window*. In our prototype, these transformations are a series of incremental compilation steps from a textual SCChart (SCT) to C or VHDL. (3) The user inspects visual renderings, synthesized by modeling tool in the *visual browsing window*, of both (a) the original SCChart that directly corresponds to the SCT description, before applying the transformation, and (b) the transformed SCChart. (4) The user may fine-tune the graphical views of the SCChart in the *layout control window*. The visual browsing window is updated whenever any input in any of the other three windows changes. For a modeler, the possibility to view not only the original model, but also the effects that different transformation/compilation phases have on the model can help to understand the exact semantics of different language constructs and to fine-tune the original model to optimize the resulting code. Furthermore, the tool smith can validate the compiler one language feature at a time. This compiler validation support is desirable for any language and compiler; it is essential for safety-critical systems.

In contrast, the traditional modeling and software synthesis user story is: (1) The user edits/draws one view of a model. (2) A compiler parses the model and synthesizes code. (3) The user may inspect the final artefacts, such as a C file. This is appropriate for advanced users who are very familiar with the modeling language. However, it offers little guidance for the beginner. Also, this hardly allows to fine-tune and optimize the intermediate and/or resulting artifacts. Furthermore, and perhaps even more importantly, the compiler developer has little support here.

Outline and Contributions

The next section covers the SCCharts language, as far as required for the remainder of this paper, introduces the **ABRO** example, and presents an overview of the compilation of SCCharts.

A main contribution of this paper, which should be applicable outside of SCCharts as well, is the Single-Pass Language-Driven Incremental Compilation (SLIC) approach presented in Sec. 3. We discuss how to determine whether features can be successively transformed in a single sequence, how to derive a transformation schedule, guiding principles for defining transformations and how to build feasible language subsets.

Another contribution of this paper, which is more specific to SCCharts and synchronous languages, is the transformation sequence from **ABRO** to an equivalent SCChart presented in Sec. 4.

We give some implementation notes in Sec. 5, summarize related work in Sec. 6 and conclude in Sec. 7.

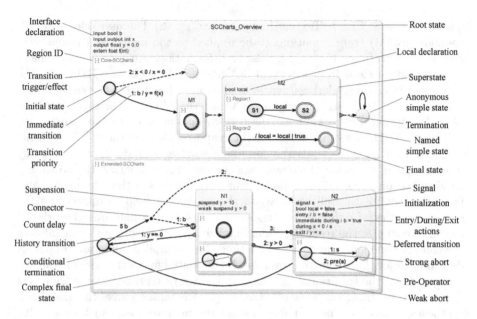

Fig. 2. Syntax overview. The upper region contains Core SCCharts elements only, the lower region illustrates Extended SCCharts.

2   SCCharts and Compilation Overview

An overview of the SCCharts visual language is shown in Fig. 2. The upper part illustrates Core SCCharts; the lower region contains elements from Extended SCCharts.

2.1   Core SCCharts Language Elements

Interface/Local Declarations. An SCChart starts at the top with an *interface declaration* that can declare variables and external functions. Variables can be *inputs*, which are read from the environment, and/or *outputs*, which are written to the environment. At the top level, this means that the environment initializes inputs at the beginning of the tick (stimulus), e.g., according to some sensor data, and that outputs are used at the end of a tick (response), e.g., to feed some actuators. The interface declaration also allows the declaration of local variables, which are neither input nor output. Declarations of local variables may also be attached to inner states as part of a *local declaration*.

States and Transitions. The basic ingredients of SCCharts are *states* and *transitions* that go from a *source state* to a *target state*. When an SCChart is in a certain state, we also say that this state is *active*. Transitions may carry a *transition label* consisting of a *trigger* and an *effect*, both of which are optional. When a transition trigger becomes true and the source state is active, the transition is taken instantaneously, meaning that the source state is left and the target state is entered in the same tick. However, transition triggers are per default *delayed*, meaning that they are disabled in the tick in which the source state just got entered. This convention helps to avoid instantaneous loops, which can potentially result in causality problems. One can override this by making a transition *immediate*, which is indicated graphically by a dashed line. Multiple transitions originating from the same source state are disambiguated with a unique *priority*; first the transition with priority 1 gets tested, if that is not taken, priority 2 gets tested, and so on. If a state has an immediate outgoing transition without any trigger, we refer to this transition as *default transition* because it will always be taken. Furthermore, if additionally there are no incoming *deferred* transitions, we say that the state is *transient* because it will always be left in the same tick as it is entered. When taken, deferred transitions preempt all immediate behavior (including leaving) of the target state they are connected with.

Hierarchy and Concurrency. A state can be either a *simple state* or it can be refined into a *superstate*, which encloses one or several concurrent *regions* (separated region compartments). Conceptually, a region corresponds to a thread. A region gets entered through its *initial state* (thick border), which must be unique to each region. When a region enters a *final state* (double border), then the region *terminates*. A superstate may have an outgoing *termination* transition (green triangle), also called (unconditional) *termination transition*, which gets taken when all regions of this superstate have reached a final state. Termination transitions may be labeled with an action, but do not have an explicit trigger label; they are always immediate (indicated by the dashed line).

2.2   The **ABRO** Example

The **ABRO** SCChart (Fig. 3a and also Fig. 1), the "hello world" [1] of synchronous programming, compactly illustrates concurrency and preemption. The reset signal R triggers a *strong abort* (red circle) of the superstate ABthenO, which means that if R is present, ABthenO is instantaneously re-started.

The execution of an SCChart is divided into a sequence of logical ticks. The interface declaration of **ABRO** states that A and B are Boolean inputs and O is a Boolean output. The execution of this SCChart is as follows. (1) The system enters initial state ABthenO as well as WaitAB. When entering ABthenO the entry action sets the output O to false. WaitAB consists of two regions (threads) HandleA and HandleB. Transitioning into a superstate does not trigger transitions nested within that state unless those transitions are immediate. The initial states WA and WB of both concurrent regions are also entered. (2) HandleA stays in its initial state WA, until the Boolean input A becomes true. Then it transitions to the final state DA. Similary, HandleB stays in its initial state WB, until the Boolean input B becomes true. Then it transitions to the final state DB. (3) When both threads eventually are in their final states DA and DB, immediately the termination transition from WaitAB to Done is taken which is setting the output O to true. (4) The behavior can be reset by setting the input R to true. Then the self-loop

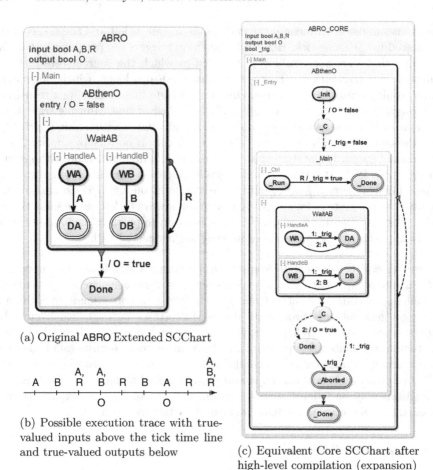

(a) Original ABRO Extended SCChart

(b) Possible execution trace with true-valued inputs above the tick time line and true-valued outputs below

(c) Equivalent Core SCChart after high-level compilation (expansion)

Fig. 3. ABRO, illustrating Extended and Core SCCharts features and the result of consecutive transformations from an Extended SCChart into an equivalent Core SCChart

transition from and to ABthenO is triggered causing a strong preemption and a re-entering of that state. This causes the entry action to reset the output O to false. The strong preemption means that the output O will not be true in case R is true in the same tick when the termination transition from WaitAB to Done is taken.

The exact semantics of ABRO is expressed by the equivalent ABRO_CORE (Fig. 3c), which only uses Core SCCharts language elements.

The ABRO example (Fig. 3a) illustrates some significant concepts of Core and Extended SCCharts. Core features are tick-boundaries (delayed transitions), concurrency (with forking and joining), and deterministic scheduling of shared variable accesses. Extended features are the concept of preemption by using a strong abort transition type for the self-loop transition triggered by R and the entry action for initializing or resetting the output O to false.

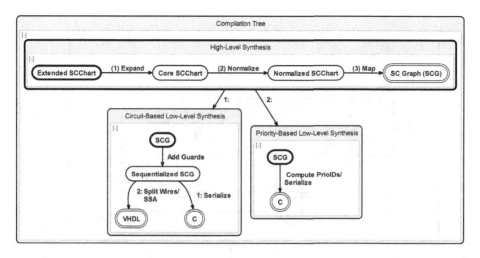

Fig. 4. Full compilation tree from Extended SCCharts to VHDL or C code splits into a high-level part and two different low-level parts

2.3   Compilation Overview

The full compilation tree is illustrated in Fig. 4, using Statecharts notation. In a way, this compilation tree, where incremental compilation steps correspond to the edges, is the dual to the compilation control window (Fig. 1), where the compilation steps correspond to the nodes.

The compilation splits into a high-level and a low-level part. The high-level compilation involves (1) expanding extended features by performing consecutive M2M transformations on Extended SCCharts, (2) normalizing Core SCCharts by using only a small number of allowed Core SCCharts patterns, and (3) straightforward (M2M) mapping of these constructs to an *SC Graph* (*SCG*).

An SCG is a pair (N, E), where N is a set of statement nodes and E is a set of control flow edges. The node types are *entry* and *exit* connectors, *assignments*, *conditionals*, *forks* and *joins*, and *surface* and *depth* nodes that jointly constitute tick-boundaries. The edge types are *flow* edges (solid edges), which denote instantaneous control flow, *pause* tick-boundary edges (dotted lines), and *dependency* edges (dashed edges), added for scheduling purposes. The SCG of **ABRO** that results after applying (2) normalization and (3) mapping to the core version (cf. Fig. 3c) is shown in Fig. 5.

The normalization of Core SCCharts restricts the patterns to be one of the constructs shown in the upper part of Fig. 6, which also illustrates how Normalized SCCharts can be mapped directly to SCG elements.

As illustrated in Fig. 7, the meta models of SCCharts and SCGs are both fairly light-weight, but quite different. Technically, SCGs are just another representation of Normalized SCCharts to facilitate further compilation steps. The low-level transformation steps (cf. Fig. 4) also involve semantics-preserving M2M transformations. Then the resulting sequentialized SCG, e.g., is used directly to derive executable VHDL or C code [13].

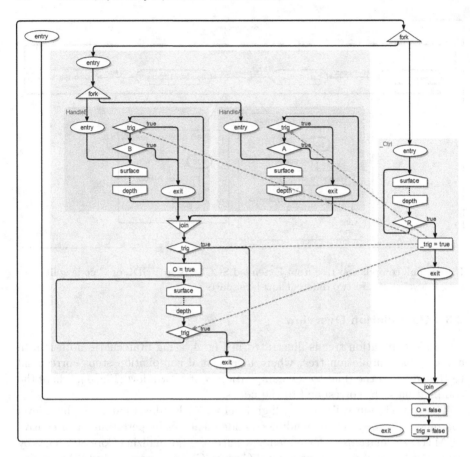

Fig. 5. The ABRO SC Graph (SCG). Dependencies (dashed edges) are used to sequentialize the SCG in further low-level compilation steps.

	Region (Thread)	Superstate (Parallel)	Trigger (Conditional)	Action (Assignment)	State (Delay)
Normalized SCCharts		[-] t1 / [-] t2	1: c 2:	I/x = e	
SCG	entry / exit	fork / join	c true	x = e	surface / depth

Fig. 6. Direct mapping from Normalized (Core) SCCharts constructs to SCG elements

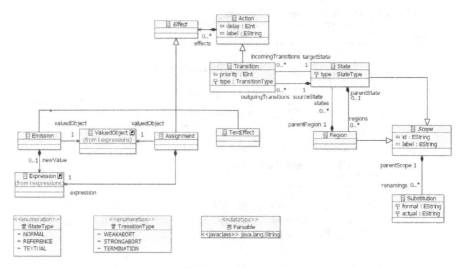

(a) SCCharts Meta Model

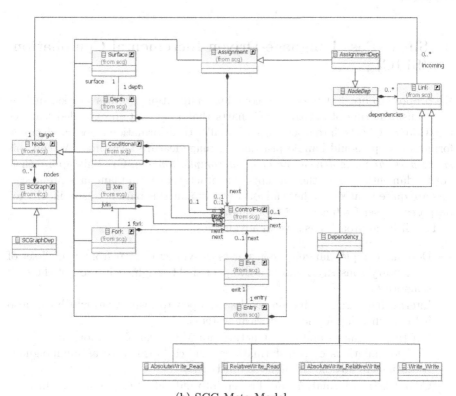

(b) SCG Meta Model

Fig. 7. EMF Meta Models used in SCCharts compilation

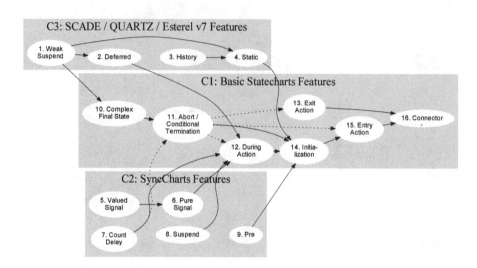

Fig. 8. Extended SCCharts features with their SLIC schedule index and their interdependencies

3 Single-Pass Language-Driven Incremental Compilation (SLIC)

We propose to break down rather complex compilation/synthesis tasks, such as the transformation of arbitrary SCCharts that may contain extended features into Core SCCharts, into a sequence of smaller transformation steps. Each transformation step should handle just one language feature at a time. We call this *single-pass language-driven incremental compilation* (SLIC). This approach is not fundamentally new, the concepts of syntactic sugar and language preprocessors are quite related. We here advocate to exploit this paradigm specifically for purposes of user feedback and tool validation.

The SLIC approach has several advantages:

- Deriving complex language constructs as syntactic sugar from a small set of elementary constructs allows a compact, light-weight definition of the core semantics.
- Intermediate transformation results are open to inspection, which can also help certification for safety-critical systems.
- Existing languages and infrastructures for M2M transformations allow high-level formulations of transformations that can also serve as unambiguous definitions of advanced language constructs.
- Complex transformations are broken into individual components, which allows a divide-and-conquer validation strategy.
- The modularization of the compilation facilitates language/compiler subsetting.

When developing a SLIC transformation sequence, two non-trivial questions arise:

Q1. Does a linear, single-pass transformation sequence suffice?
Q2. If so, how must we order the individual transformation steps?

These questions are answered by the transformation relations presented next.

3.1 Transformation Relations

Given a set of language features F, we propose to define each feature $f \in F$ in terms of a *transformation rule* T_f that expands a model (program) that uses f into another, semantically equivalent model that does not use f. More precisely, T_f produces a model not containing f, but possibly containing features in $Prod_f \subseteq F$. Also, T_f can handle/preserve a certain set of features $Handle_f \subseteq F$. Note that $Handle_f$ must include f.

Based on *Prod* and *Handle*, we define the following relations on F:

Production Order: $f \rightarrow_p g$ iff $g \in Prod_f$. We say that "T_f produces g."
Handling Order: $f \rightarrow_{nhb} g$ iff $f \notin Handle_g$ ("f is not handled by T_g").
SLIC Order: $f \rightarrow g$ iff $f \rightarrow_p g$ or $f \rightarrow_{nhb} g$ ("T_f must precede T_g").

Now we can answer the two questions from above. On Q1: A linear, single-pass transformation sequence suffices iff the SLIC order is acyclic. On Q2: We must order the individual transformation steps according to the SLIC order.

If the SLIC order is acyclic, we can implement a static *SLIC schedule*, which assigns to each $f \in F$ a *schedule index* $i(f)$ such that $f \rightarrow g$ implies $i(f) < i(g)$.

3.2 A SLIC Order for SCCharts Compilation

We now discuss the SLIC order for compiling SCCharts. We focus on the "Expand Extensions" part (see compilation overview, (1) Expand in Fig. 4), but the same principles apply to the other compilation steps as well.

Extended SCCharts provide a set F of *extended features*, listed in Fig. 8. The Extended SCCharts features are grouped into three categories:

C1: Basic Statecharts Features. Common features of various statecharts dialects as known from Harel statecharts [5], e. g., entry actions, exit actions or strong and weak preemption.
C2: SyncCharts Features. Extended SCCharts are quite rich and include, for example, all of the language features proposed for SyncCharts [1], e. g., synchronous signals or suspension.
C3: Further Features. Extended SCCharts include additional features adopted from other synchronous languages such as weak suspension from Quartz [10] or deferred transitions from SCADE. We also categorize History transitions here for language subsetting purposes (cf. Sec. 3.4), even though they were part of the original Harel statecharts.

The transformation rules are not only used to *implement* M2M transformations, but also serve to unambiguously *define* the semantics of the extensions. Each such transformation is of limited complexity, and the results can be inspected by the modeler, or also a certification agency. This is something we see as a main asset of SCCharts for the use in the context of safety-critical systems.

That the SLIC order for SCCharts is acyclic can be validated by visual inspection of Fig. 8, where all features $f \in F$ are ordered left-to-right according to $\rightarrow_p$ (solid arrows) and $\rightarrow_{nhb}$ (dotted arrows). We can also see the SLIC schedule, as each $f \in F$ is prefixed with a "$i(f)$." label that shows its schedule index.

Concerning the feature categories C1, C2, and C3, we observe that inter-category precedence constraints are only of type C2 $\rightarrow$ C1 or C3 $\rightarrow$ C1. Thus we can modularize our schedule according to categories: First transform away all features from C3, then all features from C2, and finally all features from C1.

Referring back to the interactive user story depicted in Fig. 1, note that the compilation control window presents a customizable, slightly abstract view of the transformations and their dependencies depicted in Fig. 8. The user can customize this view by collapsing/expanding parts of the compilation chain. In Fig. 1, the user has chosen to expand the **Statecharts** node, corresponding to C1, and has selected the **Abort Default** transformation to be applied (thus shown in dark blue). The tool automatically selects all "upstream" *required* transformations (light blue) as well, as such that the **Abort Default** transformation is not confronted with any language constructs it cannot handle.

3.3   Designing the Transformation Rules

Whether the SLIC order is acyclic or not is not an inherent property of the language features themselves, but depends on how exactly the transformations for the features are defined. For example, we might have defined our transformation rules T_f such that each extended feature f would be transformed directly into Core SCCharts by T_f alone ($Prod_f = \emptyset$), while preserving all other features ($Handle_f = F$). This would have resulted in an empty SLIC order that would be trivially acyclic. However, this would have defeated the purpose of modularizing the compilation, as at least some of the transformation rules would have to be unnecessary complex.

Instead, we wish the transformation for each f to be rather lean. For that purpose T_f may make use of other features, as reflected by a non-empty $Prod_f$. Furthermore, in defining T_f, we may restrict the models to be transformed to not contain all features in F, meaning that $Handle_f$ may be small. However, care must be taken to not introduce cycles this way. This implies that the more "primitive" a feature f is, the more features T_f it must be able to handle. Furthermore, there is often a trade-off between on the one hand lean transformation rules where some features undergo a long sequence of transformations and on the other hand compact, efficient transformation results.

3.4 Language Subsetting / Constructing DSLs

Given a language L with a set of language features F, a tool smith may wish to offer a derived language L' that offers only a subset $F' \subseteq F$ of language features to the user. For example, the SCCharts language proposal is very rich, which nicely illustrates how a wide range of different features proposed in SyncCharts, SCADE etc. can be grounded in a small set of Core SCCharts features. However, this variety of features may be overwhelming for the user. Also, some features might be rarely used in practice or not be appropriate for certain domains (such as, in our experience, suspension), or might be considered non-desirable for some reasons (such as history transitions, which increase the state space drastically).

Given a feature set F and a production order $\rightarrow_p$, we say that $F' \subseteq F$ is a *feasible subset* iff for all $f \in F'$ and $g \in F$, $f \rightarrow_p g$ implies $g \in F'$. In other words, the transformations of the features in F' do not produce any features outside of F'.

A conservative approach to ensure subset feasibility would include in F' all features whose SLIC schedule index is above a certain value. E.g., for SCCharts, if we define F' such that it includes all features with schedule index 10 and higher, we would obtain all features in category C1, which would be a feasible language subset. However, the definition of subset feasibility permits other subsets as well. E.g., the subset of SCCharts features with indices 11, 14, 15, 16, which includes Aborts (index 11) and all subsequently produced features, would also be feasible.

4 Example: An M2M Transformation Sequence from Extended **ABRO** to Core **ABRO**

This section uses the **ABRO** example to illustrate how selected Extended SCCharts features are incrementally transformed into Core SCCharts. Further details for these transformations and generalizations of the presented transformations are given elsewhere [12].

4.1 Aborts

A hierarchical state can be *aborted* upon some trigger. The ability to specify high-level aborts is one of the most common motivations for introducing hierarchy into statecharts. Aborts are thus a powerful means to specify behavior in a compact manner, but handling them faithfully in simulation and code synthesis is not trivial. There are two cases to consider, *strong aborts*, which get tested before the contents of the aborted superstate gets executed, and *weak aborts*, which get tested after the contents of the aborted state get executed.

Consider the original **ABRO** Extended SCChart as shown in Fig. 3a. **ABthenO** is left by a self-loop strong abort transition triggered by **R**. This abort takes place regardless of which internal state of **ABthenO** is active at the time (tick) of an abort. In case of nested superstates with aborts, this transformation must be applied from the outside in, so that inner aborts can also be triggered by outside abort triggers.

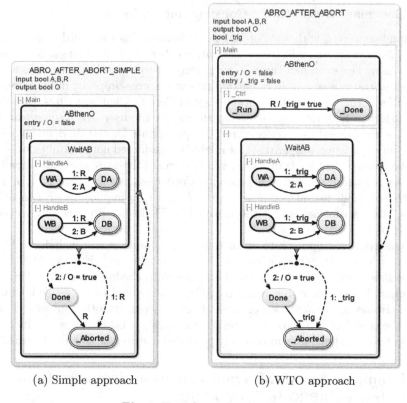

(a) Simple approach   (b) WTO approach

Fig. 9. Transformation for Abort

Fig. 9a illustrates how expanding ABRO results in an equivalent SCChart that
does not use the extended feature Abort anymore. The underlying idea is to make
the internal regions of WaitAB terminate explicitly whenever ABthenO is aborted,
and then use a termination transition to leave WaitAB. Note that strong abortion
has the highest priority and thus the transitions triggered by R have the highest
transition priority 1. Also note that in Fig. 9a the condition R was duplicated 4
times. This may result in multiple evaluations of R and thus violates the *Write-
Things-Once* (WTO) principle. This may not be problematic if the condition
consists a single flag (in this case R), but can be an issue if the condition
consists of a costly expression; down-stream synthesis may or may not be able
to optimize this again by applying, e. g., common subexpression elimination.
Fig. 9b shows an alternative transformation that meets the WTO principle by
concurrently evaluating R just once and triggering the abort using an auxiliary
variable _trig.

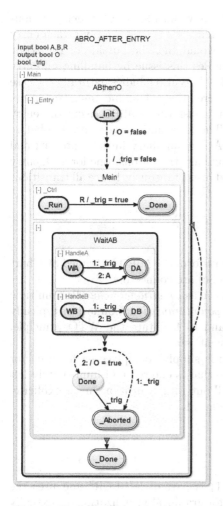

Fig. 10. Transformation for Entry Action

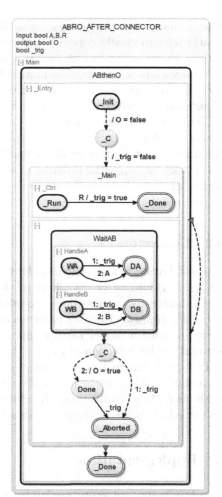

Fig. 11. Transformation for Connector

4.2 Entry Actions

When eliminating the extended abort feature from **ABRO**, the WTO-variant of the Aborts-transformation produced an auxiliary variable _trig together with an entry action for resetting it to false. Entry actions also are extended SCCharts features and hence need to be eliminated during compilation to Core SCCharts. As indicated in Fig. 8, entry actions must be transformed after aborts. Note that entry actions do not get moved outside of the state that they are attached to, hence entry actions can also make use of locally declared variables.

When a state S has an associated entry action A, then A should be performed whenever S is entered, before any internals of S are executed. If multiple entry actions are present, they are performed in sequential order. A non-trivial issue when defining this transformation is that we would like to allow entry actions to still refer to locally declared variables. Hence we cannot simply attach entry actions to incoming transitions, as these would then be outside of the scope of local variables. Our transformation handles this issue by handling all entry actions within the state they are attached to. This also handles naturally the case of initial states, which do not have to be entered through an incoming transition.

The transformation result after further transforming **ABRO** using the entry action transformation is shown in Fig. 10. The entry actions were inserted before the original initial state inside **ABthenO**. A new auxiliary initial state _Init and connectors for sequential ordering of all auxiliary transitions (one for each entry action) are used. Entry actions are executed instantaneously, hence all transitions are immediate.

4.3   Connectors

The last feature to eliminate in order to transform the **ABRO** Extended SCChart (cf. Fig. 3a) into a Core SCChart (cf. Fig. 3c) are connectors.

Connector nodes, sometimes also referenced as *conditional nodes*, link multiple *transition segments* together to form a *compound transition*. Connectors typically serve to make a model more compact, and to facilitate the WTO principle, without the introduction of further (transient) states.

Our approach to transform connectors is simply to replace each connector by a state which must be a transient state that is entered and immediately left again as part of a transition. Therefore, all outgoing transitions must explicitly be made immediate. This can be seen in Fig. 11.

5   Implementation

The SCCharts tool prototype[1] (cf. Fig. 1) is part of KIELER[2] and uses the KLighD diagram synthesis framework [9] for graphical visualization of textually modeled SCCharts. We implemented all transformations from Extended SC-Charts to Core SCCharts, the normalization, the SCG mapping and all SCG transformations (cf. Sec. 2.3) as M2M transformations with Xtend[3]. To illustrate the compact, modular nature of the M2M transformations, Fig. 12 shows the **Connector** transformation described in Sec. 4.3. Xtend keywords and Xtend extension functions are highlighted. The precondition is checked in line 3, i. e., whether the considered state is a connector state. Line 5 sets the type of this state from connector to normal. Finally, lines 7-9 ensure that all outgoing and previously implicit immediate transitions of this state are now being set explicitly to be immediate transitions. As can be seen, the transformation description is straight-forward and of limited complexity.

---

[1] http://www.sccharts.com
[2] http://www.rt.informatik.uni-kiel.de/kieler
[3] http://www.eclipse.org/xtend/

```
1   def void transformConnector(State state) {
2       // If a state is of type connector, then apply the transformation
3       if (state.type == StateType::CONNECTOR) {
4           // Set the state type to normal
5           state.setTypeNormal
6           // Explicitly set all outgoing transitions to be immediate transitions
7           for ( transition : state.outgoingTransitions) {
8               transition.setImmediate(true)
9           }
10      }
11  }
```

Fig. 12. Xtend implementation of transforming connector states

For modeling SCCharts the textual editor shown in Fig. 1 is used. We generated it using the Eclipse based Xtext framework which produces a full-featured textual editor for the SCCharts Textual Language (SCT) with syntax highlighting, code completion and built-in validation. More specifically, this editor is generated from an SCT Xtext grammar description declaring the actual concrete textual syntax for the SCCharts meta model elements (cf. Fig. 7a).

We defined the SCCharts and the SCG transformations on the EMF meta models. The extended and the normalization transformations of the high-level synthesis are so-called "inplace" model transformations because they modify the SCChart model that conforms to the SCCharts meta model shown in Fig. 7a. The SCG mapping transformation is defined on both the SCCharts meta model (cf. Fig. 7a) and the SCG meta model (cf. Fig. 7b). The low-level synthesis, e. g., the sequentialization of SCGs is again defined as several consecutive inplace model transformations all only based on the SCG meta model.

6 Related Work

Statecharts, introduced by Harel in the late 1980s [5], have become a popular means for specifying the behavior of embedded, reactive systems. The visual syntax is intuitively understandable for application experts from different domains and the statechart concepts of hierarchy and concurrency allow the expression of complex behavior in a much more compact fashion than standard, flat finite state machines. However, defining a suitable semantics for the statechart syntax is by no means trivial, as evinced by the multitude of different statechart interpretations. In the 1990s, von der Beeck identified a list of 19 different nontrivial semantical issues, and compared 24 different semantics proposals [11], which did not even include the "official" semantics of the original Harel statecharts (clarified later by Harel [6]) nor the many statechart variants developed since then, including, e. g., UML statecharts with its run-to-completion semantics. One critical issue in defining a statecharts semantics is the proper handling of concurrency, which has a long tradition in computer science, yet, as argued succinctly by Lee [7], has still not found its way into mainstream programming languages such as Java. Synchronous languages were largely motivated by the desire to bring determinism to reactive control flow, which covers concurrency and aborts [2]. SCCharts have taken much inspiration from André's SyncCharts [1], introduced as Safe State Machines (SSMs) in Esterel Studio. However, SCCharts are more liberal that SyncCharts in that they permit multiple variable values per reaction as long as the SC MoC can guarantee determinism.

Edwards [3] and Potop-Butucaru et al. [8] provide good overviews of compilation challenges and approaches for concurrent languages, including synchronous languages. We present an alternative compilation approach that handles most constructs that are challenging for a synchronous languages compiler by a sequence of model-to-model (M2M) transformations, until only a small set of Core SCCharts constructs remains. This applies in particular to aborts in combination with concurrency, which we reduce to terminations.

The incremental, model-based compilation approach using a high-level transformation language (Xtend) allowed us to build a compiler in a matter of weeks and to validate it in a divide-and-conquer manner. Furthermore, the ability to synthesize graphical models, with a high-quality automatic layout, lets the user fully participate in this incremental transformation, as illustrated in the interactive model-based compilation user story in the introduction. This fits very well with the *pragmatics-aware* modeling approach [14], which advocates to separate models from their view and to let the modeling tool generate customized views that highlight certain model aspects. In this light, we might say that the interactive model-based transformation provides the user with different views of one and the same model that differ in abstraction level, from the possibly very abstract model designed by the user all the way down to the implementation level.

7   Conclusions

The incremental, model-based compilation approach presented here did not originate from a desire to develop a new, general approach to synthesis, but rather was the outcome of building a compiler for a specific language, SCCharts. In fact, when building this compiler we did intend to re-use existing approaches and technologies as much as possible. Furthermore, the main purpose of M2M transformation rules that constitute the compiler was originally to unambiguously define the various extended SCCharts features; we were positively surprised to find that they also produce fairly compact, efficient code as well [13]. In the end, the desire to quickly prototype a modular compiler, easy to validate and to customize, prompted us to follow the SLIC approach presented here; and Xtext, Xtend, KIELER and KLighD, all part of Eclipse, were the key enabling technologies for the implementation.

When asking what exactly is "model-based" about the SCCharts compilation approach, one notices that indeed there are many similarities to traditional compilation approaches. For example, the SCCharts with their hierarchical structure might also be considered a form of abstract syntax tree (AST), and the SCG is related to other intermediate formats used in compiling synchronous languages.

However, the SLIC approach is model-driven in the following aspects:

- The compilation steps are M2M transformations where the resulting model contains all information. There are no other, hidden data structures.
- For the most part, the intermediate transformation steps are in the same language as the original model. We just apply a sequence of language sub-setting operations, transforming away one feature at a time. There is a change of language when going from normalized SCCharts to the SCG, but that is mainly for convenience, for example, to be able to separate the surface of a pause from its depth. However, even that step would not have been strictly necessary, we could have stayed with the SCCharts meta model all the way to the final C/VHDL code. In fact, our first implementation had only one meta model.

We see numerous directions for future work. For example, we want to explore further the best ways on how to let the user interact with the compiler and how to manage the model views. Especially for larger models we want to employ techniques like reference states to gain modularization and preserve scalability. Regarding scalability and practicability we hope to report on an ongoing larger case study soon. In this case study our approach is used for designing and implementing a complex model railway controller. The SLIC order for SCCharts, depicted in Fig. 8, has evolved over time, and we expect it to evolve further. For example we currently explore tool support for consistent choices of selected transformations, statically from the SLIC order and dynamically from the features used in concrete models. Also, we are experimenting with alternative transformation rules for one and the same feature, where the choice of the best rule may depend on the original model and overall constraints/priorities. Another active area is that of interactive timing analysis [4], where we investigate how to best preserve timing-information across M2M transformations. The main advantage of our approach is its interactivity. Nonetheless we envision a fully automatic compilation process including the possibility to include our compiler in scripts (e. g., a Makefile) or using it online in the Web.

References

1. André, C.: Semantics of SyncCharts. Technical Report ISRN I3S/RR–2003–24–FR, I3S Laboratory, Sophia-Antipolis, France (April 2003)
2. Benveniste, A., Caspi, P., Edwards, S.A., Halbwachs, N., Guernic, P.L., de Simone, R.: The synchronous languages twelve years later. In: Proc. IEEE, Special Issue on Embedded Systems, vol. 91, pp. 64–83. IEEE, Piscataway (2003)
3. Edwards, S.A.: Tutorial: Compiling concurrent languages for sequential processors. ACM Transactions on Design Automation of Electronic Systems 8(2), 141–187 (2003)
4. Fuhrmann, I., Broman, D., Smyth, S., von Hanxleden, R.: Towards interactive timing analysis for designing reactive systems. Technical Report UCB/EECS-2014-26, EECS Department, University of California, Berkeley (April 2014)
5. Harel, D.: Statecharts: A visual formalism for complex systems. Science of Computer Programming 8(3), 231–274 (1987)

6. Harel, D., Naamad, A.: The STATEMATE semantics of statecharts. ACM Transactions on Software Engineering and Methodology 5(4), 293–333 (1996)
7. Lee, E.A.: The problem with threads. IEEE Computer 39(5), 33–42 (2006)
8. Potop-Butucaru, D., Edwards, S.A., Berry, G.: Compiling Esterel. Springer (May 2007)
9. Schneider, C., Spönemann, M., von Hanxleden, R.: Just model! – Putting automatic synthesis of node-link-diagrams into practice. In: Proceedings of the IEEE Symposium on Visual Languages and Human-Centric Computing (VL/HCC 2013), San Jose, CA, USA, September 15-19, pp. 75–82 (2013)
10. Schneider, K.: The synchronous programming language Quartz. Internal report, Department of Computer Science, University of Kaiserslautern, Kaiserslautern, Germany (2010), http://es.cs.uni-kl.de/publications/datarsg/Schn09.pdf
11. von der Beeck, M.: A comparison of Statecharts variants. In: Langmaack, H., de Roever, W.-P., Vytopil, J. (eds.) FTRTFT 1994 and ProCoS 1994. LNCS, vol. 863, pp. 128–148. Springer, Heidelberg (1994)
12. von Hanxleden, R., Duderstadt, B., Motika, C., Smyth, S., Mendler, M., Aguado, J., Mercer, S., O'Brien, O.: SCCharts: Sequentially Constructive Statecharts for safety-critical applications. Technical Report 1311, Christian-Albrechts-Universität zu Kiel, Department of Computer Science (December 2013) ISSN 2192-6247
13. von Hanxleden, R., Duderstadt, B., Motika, C., Smyth, S., Mendler, M., Aguado, J., Mercer, S., O'Brien, O.: SCCharts: Sequentially Constructive Statecharts for safety-critical applications. In: Proc. ACM SIGPLAN Conference on Programming Language Design and Implementation (PLDI 2014), Edinburgh, UK, ACM (June 2014)
14. von Hanxleden, R., Lee, E.A., Motika, C., Fuhrmann, H.: Multi-view modeling and pragmatics in 2020. In: Calinescu, R., Garlan, D. (eds.) Monterey Workshop 2012. LNCS, vol. 7539, pp. 209–223. Springer, Heidelberg (2012)
15. von Hanxleden, R., Mendler, M., Aguado, J., Duderstadt, B., Fuhrmann, I., Motika, C., Mercer, S., O'Brien, O.: Sequentially Constructive Concurrency—A conservative extension of the synchronous model of computation. In: Proc. Design, Automation and Test in Europe Conference (DATE 2013), Grenoble, France, pp. 581–586. IEEE (March 2013)

Domain-Specific Code Generator Modeling: A Case Study for Multi-faceted Concurrent Systems

Stefan Naujokat[1], Louis-Marie Traonouez[2], Malte Isberner[1],
Bernhard Steffen[1], and Axel Legay[2]

[1] Technische Universität Dortmund, Chair for Programming Systems, Dortmund,
D-44227, Germany
{stefan.naujokat,malte.isberner,steffen}@cs.tu-dortmund.de
[2] IRISA / INRIA, Rennes, F-35042, France
{louis-marie.traonouez,axel.legay}@inria.fr

Abstract. In this paper we discuss an elaborate case study utilizing
the domain-specific development of code generators within the CINCO
meta tooling suite. CINCO is a framework that allows for the automatic
generation of a wide range of graphical modeling tools from an abstract
high-level specification. The presented case study makes use of CINCO to
rapidly construct custom graphical interfaces for multi-faceted, concurrent systems, comprising non-functional properties like time, probability,
data, and costs. The point of this approach is to provide user communities and their favorite tools with graphical interfaces tailored to their
specific needs. This will be illustrated by generating graphical interfaces
for timed automata (TA), probabilistic timed automata (PTA), Markov
decision processes (MDP) and simple labeled transition systems (LTS).
The main contribution of the presented work, however, is the metamodel-
based domain-specific construction of the corresponding code generators
for the verification tools UPPAAL, SPIN, PLASMA-LAB, and PRISM.

1 Introduction

Code generators can be regarded as the enablers for model-driven software engineering (MDSE) [1], as they provide the means to bridging the final gap to
the actual use of a system. Despite this importance the state of the art is still
pretty disappointing: typically, models and code generators in MDSE environments are very generic and only generate partial code which needs to be manually completed. This does not only require a lot of expertise but it also leads
to the typical problems of round-trip engineering whenever the systems evolve.
Domain-specific tools have the potential to overcome this situation by providing
full code generation for their naturally more restrictive contexts.

Metamodeling frameworks support the development of domain-specific modeling environments to great extent, but the development of code generators for
a domain-specific language (DSL) defined in those frameworks is still a complicated task despite the existence of special *code generator DSLs*, such as Xtend [2]

T. Margaria and B. Steffen (Eds.): ISoLA 2014, Part I, LNCS 8802, pp. 481–498, 2014.

for the Eclipse modeling ecosystem [3], the MetaEdit+ Reporting Language (MERL) [4] in the context of Domain-Specific Modeling [5] with MetaEdit+ [6], or the IPTG language of Eli/DEViL [7,8]. These code generator DSLs provide means that extend the possibilities of manual programming with simple string concatenation or template frameworks, but they are difficult to learn and very generic: they are specific to the underlying metamodeling framework, but do not exploit the specifics of the considered problem domain.

The CINCO framework[1] [9] aims at aiding in the development of domain-specific modeling tools in a holistic fashion that in particular comprises code generation. While the domain's metamodel and the graphical editor can be fully generated from higher-level specifications, CINCO additionally provides modeling tool developers with a domain-specific code generator language specifically generated for *their* tool. In fact, this domain-specific code generation language can be automatically obtained from the same abstract specification as the GUI.

In this paper we discuss an elaborate case study utilizing this domain-specific development of code generators within the CINCO meta tooling suite: we show how to rapidly construct custom graphical interfaces for different kinds of concurrent systems, comprising non-functional properties like time, probability, data, and costs. As a result, the corresponding user communities and their favorite tools are provided with graphical interfaces tailored to their specific needs. This will be illustrated by generating graphical interfaces for timed automata (TA) [10], probabilistic timed automata (PTA) [11], Markov decision processes (MDP) [12] and simple labeled transition systems (LTS) [13]. The main contribution of the presented work, however, is the metamodel-based domain-specific construction of the corresponding code generators for the verification tools UP-PAAL [14], SPIN [15], PLASMA-LAB [16], and PRISM [17].

We do not know of any other approach that provides the automatic generation of domain-specific code generator languages. As mentioned before, existing languages are commonly specific to the used modeling framework, but not specific to one's very own metamodel. CINCO's code generation concepts are based on preliminary work [18,19] for the creation of transformation and code generation modeling components for arbitrary Ecore [20] metamodels.

The paper is structured as follows: in order to be able to explain the CIN-CO specification, transformation and code generation concepts using the "PSM" (Parallel Systems Modeling) case study as running example, the upcoming Section 2 motivates and explains it in detail. Section 3 then presents the basic concepts of CINCO and how the specification of the full graphical editor works. Section 4 details on the code generation concepts and how the individual code generators for our target tools are realized, before Section 5 elaborates on the model-to-model transformation of the various source model types into the PSM intermediate language. The paper concludes with a summary and plans for future work in Section 6.

---

[1] CINCO is developed open source under the Eclipse Public License 1.0. The framework as well as example projects are available at the CINCO website: http://cinco.scce.info

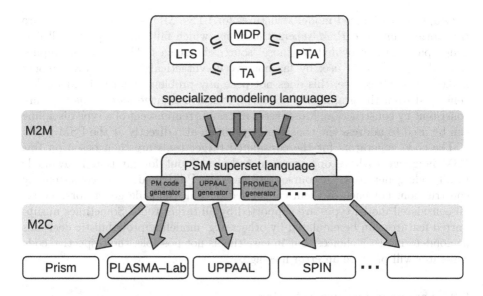

Fig. 1. Model-to-code (M2C) generation of multiple model checkers' input formats from one general model type after model-to-model (M2M) transformations on the specialized model types

2   The PSM Case Study

There is a wealth of model checking tools of concurrent systems, each with their own profile concerning the supported communication paradigm and features like time, probability, data, and costs. It is therefore not surprising that these tools come with dedicated input languages and formats, which can be graphical as in the case of UPPAAL or textual, as in most other cases. This makes it difficult to work with (more than one of) these tools, in particular, as one needs to be aware of their syntactic peculiarities.

The "Parallel Systems Modeling" (PSM) case study therefore facilitates CIN-CO to rapidly construct custom graphical interfaces for the types of concurrent systems supported by those tools. The envisioned realization does not only allow one to customize the graphical interface, but also to generate tool-specific code which can directly be used as input in the considered tool landscape. In fact, it is possible to easily design one's own graphical language which can then be provided at low cost with code generators for the input formats of the considered tools.

2.1   Architecture

In our case study project several different model types (or languages) are involved, each of them represented by an own metamodel generated from a CINCO specification. Fig. 1 illustrates their overall architecture and interplay based on various model to model (M2M) and model to code (M2C) transformations.

Graphically designed model structures for LTSs, MDPs, TAs, and PTAs are transformed into the *PSM superset language* which faithfully captures all language paradigms provided by those 'source' languages. This richness implies some discipline in its use: by far not every syntactically correct PSM model makes sense. Of course, this does not pose any problems for the PSM models generated from the graphically designed 'source' language models, as they are consistent by construction. Moreover, constraints reminiscent of a type discipline can be used to address the consistency problem also directly at the PSM level.

The code generators for the considered target tools are then based on this PSM language to have one common technical input format that is available to all code generators. Of course, although the PSM models are consistent by construction, not each of them can be fed into all the code generators, as not all considered model types are supported by all target tools. Sometimes unsupported features can be emulated by others, e.g. modeling probabilistic decisions as nondeterministic choices, but in case this is not possible, the respective code generator will produce an error message.

2.2   Language Feature Selection

As a starting point, we have begun developing the PSM model type to contain the following language features of LTSs, MDPs, TAs, and PTAs (further features can be added at need):

Modules (or processes) define the concurrent components of the system. Each module is designed with a dedicated automaton.

States are the most fundamental modeling components. Their description typically comprises a name (i.e. a unique identifier), and additional information in terms of atomic propositions like being a start or an accepting state.

Data is stored in local variables (that belong to a module) or global variables. They can be updated with arbitrary expressions using assignments. We assume a C-like syntax for the expressions. Integer and Boolean variables are currently available, with the former one having a defined range (usually smaller than [0,MAXINT]).

Time is modeled using dedicated clock variables that all increase at the same pace. Clocks are always local and can only be reset (i.e. set to 0 using an assignment).

Guards and Invariants are expressions over all the variables that control the possible evolution of a module. Guards are assigned to edges and control which transitions are possible in a given a state. Invariants are assigned to a state and limit the evolution of clock variables in this state.

Probability is frequently used in models to represent uncertain behavior. It can be inserted using probabilistic decision nodes that split a transition into several outcomes according to probability weights. Additionally, a rate can be assigned to each state to model an exponential distribution for modeling the progress of time.

Nondeterminism is allowed whenever two transitions are enabled at the same time.

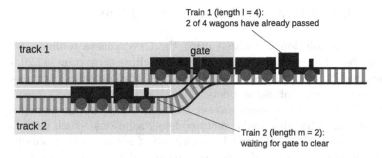

Fig. 2. Train 2 waiting for Train 1 to pass the gate

Arbitrary Code in form of C functions is realized in two ways. In the first case a dedicated node type contains a String attribute where the function body can be inserted. The second case makes use of CINCO's *prime reference* concept: Externally defined components can be placed in the model via drag&drop, creating a different kind of node that is automatically linked to that external element. This way arbitrary external libraries of modeling components can be included without the need to change the tool or metamodel. This closely resembles the concept of Service Independent Building Blocks (SIBs) from jABC [21].

Communication between processes is realized with channels on via transitions may be synchronized. They are declared globally and can be of three types:

- Pairwise (handshake) synchronization involves two transitions (possibly identified with input and output modalities added to the channel) chosen among the possible synchronizations.
- Global synchronization involves all the modules that may synchronize on the channel. Thus it may introduce deadlock in case one of the involved modules is not ready to participate in the corresponding communication.
- Broadcast synchronization involves a sender (identified with an output modality) that synchronizes with all the enabled transitions labeled by an input of the channel.

2.3 Example System

We consider a classical rail road example where two tracks are merged into one at a gate section and a controller of this system must ensure that trains arriving from either track will never collide by blocking one of the trains until the other one has passed (cf. Fig. 2). The time for passing the gate would in reality depend on several factors (e.g. length, speed, acceleration/deceleration etc.), but for our simplified example model we consider the amount of wagons the single factor that determines the passing time.

3 High-Level Graphical Editor Specification

Technically, our solution is realized using the CINCO meta tooling suite [9], a framework based on various libraries from the Eclipse ecosystem [22,20,3]. CINCO is designed to ease the generation of tailored graphical modeling tools from specifications in terms of metamodels.

Metamodeling is the modern answer to the development of domain-specific tools. However, although popular metamodeling solutions – such as the Eclipse Modeling Framework (EMF) and its multitude of accompanying plug-ins – are quite rich in the provision of code generation and transformation features, it is still tedious to develop sophisticated graphical modeling tools on their basis. The goal of CINCO is to simplify this development by providing means to specify a tool's model structure as well as its graphical user interface (and partly also semantics) in an abstract fashion that suffices to automatically generate the whole corresponding modeling tool.

The key to obtaining this degree of automation is the restriction of EMF's generality to focus on graph-based models consisting of various types of nodes and edges. With this reduction, CINCO follows the "easy for the many, difficult for the few"-paradigm that dictates the bulk of problems to be solvable very easily [23]. In our experience, it is surprising how far this paradigm carries and how seldom we need to resort to the difficult for the few part.

At the core of each CINCO product[2] lies a file in the *Meta Graph Language* (MGL) format, which is in fact a domain-specific language for the specification of model types consisting of nodes and edges.[3] Listing 1.1 shows an excerpt from the PSM.mgl: the specified node type State as well as the edge type GuardedTransition have several declared attributes that allow to con-

---

[2] With the term CINCO product (CP) we denote a modeling tool that is developed using CINCO.

[3] This actually makes MGL a meta modeling language or, synonymously, a meta-metamodel for CINCO products.

```
1   @style(state, "${number}")
2   node State {
3       attr EInt as number
4       attr EBoolean as isStartState
5       attr EString as invariant
6       attr EString as exponentialRate
7   }
8
9   @style(guardedTransition, "${guard}", "${channel}")
10  edge GuardedTransition {
11      attr EString as guard
12      attr EString as channel
13      sourceNodes (State)
14      targetNodes (State, Assignment, ProbabilisticDecision)
15
16  }
```

Listing 1.1. Excerpt from the MGL file

figure their instances. Furthermore, the valid source and target node types are configured for the `GuardedTransition`. MGL allows arbitrary annotations to be added to the elements, which are interpreted by *meta plug-ins* during the CINCO tool generation process.

The annotation `@style` is used to refer to an element from the second core DSL of CINCO: the style definition file. Elaborating on the possibilities to describe the nodes' and edges' visual appearance in the generated editor is beyond the scope of this paper.[4] Just note that it is possible to combine different shapes, colors, line types etc. Beyond this static declaration it is also possible to add dynamic elements. For instance, the contents of attributes can be passed as a parameter to the style (as done with the parameters `guard`, `channel`, and `number`). Those parameters are formulated in the Java Expression Language (EL). They are evaluated at runtime and live updated whenever the attribute values change. Furthermore, it is possible to have arbitrary `AppearanceProviders` implemented in Java, which we, for instance, use to dynamically show a small arrow tip in the top left corner of a `State` node's visual representation in case `isStartState` is true.

Overall, the CINCO PSM tool specification that fully realizes the model and its editor only consists of 84 lines of MGL code, 155 lines of Style code, and 19 lines of Java code. In contrast, the generated Graphiti editor alone[5] already consists of over 7,000 lines of code. Of course, generated code tends to be a bit verbose, but it is fair to say that CINCO reduces the amount of code writing by an order of magnitude. Moreover, the required code is much simpler and better structured. In particular it does not require special knowledge about Eclipse and the Graphiti APIs.

Figure 3 shows a screenshot of the generated editor. It consists of some common Eclipse parts (called *views*), such as the Project Explorer, Miniature View, Console, and Properties. In the center is the main editor area showing the model for our train example. It consists of three `Module` containers, one for each train and one for the gate. The gray circles are `State` nodes, of which the one with the arrow tip marker depicts the initial state of the module. The small gray squares represent probabilistic decisions and the blue rectangles are variable assignments. Small circles with different background colors represent clocks, channels, and variables. Variables can either be placed within a module to become local variables, or outside, directly on the diagram canvas to become global variables. Channels are only allowed outside while clocks must be local.

The train model works as follows: in the transition from the initial state 0 to state 1 the train's approach is signaled via channel *appr*1, the local timer x is reset and the length of the train, here modeled as a random decision, is assigned to the variable l. If the train is signaled to stop within 10 time units, it will go to state 2 and wait for the resume signal on channel *go*1. Otherwise, it can pass

---

[4] Please refer to [24] for a detailed explanation on the *Meta Style Language* (MSL) and the other possibilities of the GUI generator.

[5] The Ecore metamodel is generated as well, together with the Java code that implements certain `EOperations`. However, much of the corresponding over 6,000 lines of Java code are generated by the EMF framework without CINCO support.

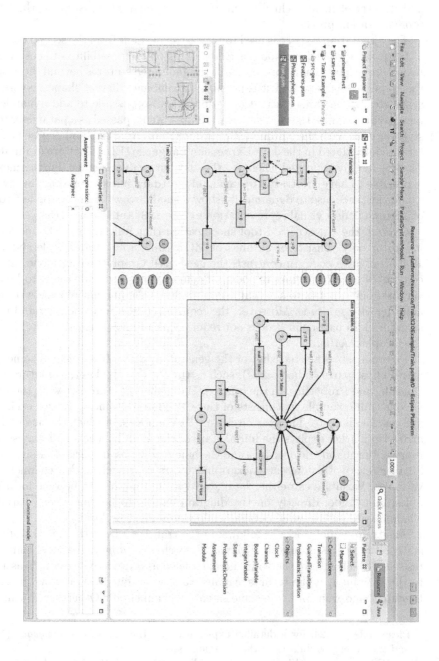

Fig. 3. Screenshot of the generated PSM tool showing the train crossing example

the gate. The second train is modeled analogously. The gate will transition from state 0 to 1 as soon as one of the two trains arrives. If the second train arrives before the first one has left, the local variable *wait* is set to *true*. In the waiting state 1, as soon as the first train has left, the go signal is given to the other one, either via state 2 or 4.

4   Code Generation

So far we have explained how CINCO can be used to easily construct a meta-model and a graphical editor for the PSM superset language. In order to introduce semantics, a code generator needs to be realized, providing a translational semantics for PSM models. In fact, we will have three different code generators, one for each target language.

CINCO comes with a meta plug-in for code generation that interprets a @generate annotation in the MGL file. It generates the required Eclipse code, so that the programmer of the generator does not need to take care of any Eclipse APIs. A *Generate* button is added to the action bar of the CINCO product that triggers the generation of the currently edited model. The generator realization has to implement a certain interface and is then directly provided with the model, leaving all the Eclipse details transparent to the developer.

4.1   Domain-Specific Code Generation

The (main) metamodel of a CINCO product is generated from the MGL specification. This means that we have more precise knowledge on the metamodel's structure than in the standard, purely Ecore-based EMF settings: models always have a graph structure with different node, container and edge types. Thus, the CINCO metamodel generator is directly enabled to generate a library of domain-specific functionality that allows for systematically traversing a given model instance. For example, the following operations are directly supported with a metamodel generated with CINCO:

- Retrieval of successors and predecessors of a given node element. Those specifically generated getters can even be parameterized with a node type to only retrieve successors and predecessors of a given type.
- Access to the source and target nodes with correctly typed getters for every edge type.
- Type sensitive access to all the inner modeling elements of a container (i.e. nodes or other containers).

Please note that these are only some examples and that we constantly enrich the CINCO generator with new domain-specific operations. Of course, similar functionality can also be directly implemented for Ecore metamodels that are not generated with CINCO. However, this would require a lot of tedious code comprising of "instanceof" checks and type casting. In contrast, the CINCO approach allows for the fully automatic generation of this domain-specific functionality.

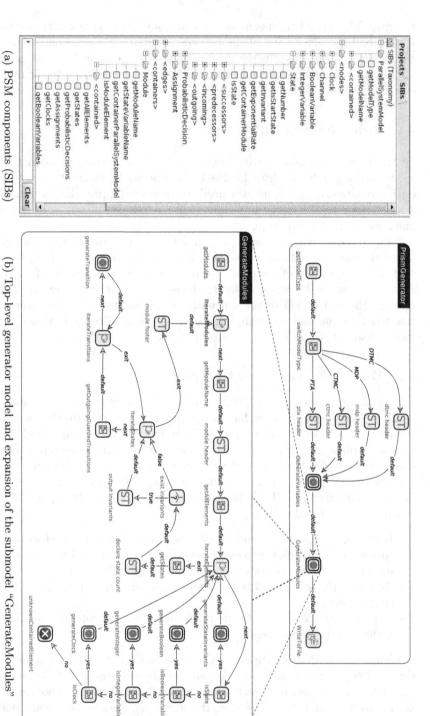

(a) PSM components (SIBs)

(b) Top-level generator model and expansion of the submodel "GenerateModules"

Fig. 4. Excerpts from the modeled PRISM code generator with domain-specific component library

Within the CINCO approach we provide domain-specific functionality for the development of code generators in a twofold fashion: for Java programmers on the one hand a dedicated API is generated. Technically, this is for the most part realized by generating special EOperations and their according implementations into the metamodel. On the other hand, for domain experts who are not necessarily programmers, we generate the same domain-specific functionalities as modeling components for the jABC process modeling framework [21] (cf. Fig. 4(a)). The resulting *Service-Independent Building Blocks* (SIBs) can then easily be combined with SIBs for output generation (e.g. for StringTemplate [25] or Velocity [26]; see also [18]) into a modeled code generator. Figure 4(b) shows an excerpt from the modeled PRISM code generator (cf. upcoming Sec. 4.2) using the generated PSM components as well as some generic components for text generation with StringTemplate (ST on the icon), file I/O, and common tasks such as iterating over elements and error processing. The first model shows the top level of process hierarchy (i.e. the generator root model), while the second one exemplary shows one expanded submodel. While the gain for non-programmers using the jABC is obvious, we think that also people who know programming (which probably can be assumed for developers of modeling tools) strongly benefit from our domain-specific API, as it hides the internal Eclipse structures and is thus also service-oriented in spirit.

Each of the following subsections details on one code generator. As PRISM and PLASMA-LAB use the same input format, they are treated in one section, followed by the UPPAAL generator and the PROMELA generator. The code generators each assume that certain restrictions apply to the model, as the PSM language allows us to build models none of the code generators can handle anymore. Of course, if a new target platform supports more features included in PSM, they would be easy to capture by a corresponding code generator.

4.2   Prism/PLASMA-Lab

The Reactive Module Language (RML) is a textual language based on the Reactive Modules of Alur and Henzinger [27]. The language has been introduced in the model-checker PRISM [17] and is also used by the statistical model-checker PLASMA-LAB [16]. It describes a set of concurrent components with four different semantics:

1. Discrete time Markov chains (DTMCs).
2. Continuous time Markov chains (CTMCs).
3. Markov decision processes (MDPs).
4. Probabilistic timed automata (PTAs).

Each semantics imposes some restrictions on the syntax of the language, although the main elements described below are similar. We present briefly the syntax of the language[6] and then discuss the generation of RML models from our framework.

---

[6] See http://www.prismmodelchecker.org/ for a more complete description.

In RML each component is modeled as a *module* that consists of a set of local declarations of integer and Boolean variables, and a set of *commands*. A command is enabled by a guard and then performs a probability choice among a set of *updates*. An update consists of a set of assignments that update the values of the variables of the model. Commands can be a assigned to a channel, in which case a global synchronization must be performed between all the modules that communicate with the channel. In CTMCs probability choices are governed by rates according to a *race semantics*, whereas in DTMCs, MDPs and PTAs only probability values may be used. The sum of the probabilities of a command must then be equal to 1. RML also allows to model PTAs by introducing real-time clocks as a new type of variables and an invariant expression to each module.

To generate a RML model from our framework, each state is assigned to a value of the state variable of the module. Then each meta-transition from a state to a set of states, passing trough assignments and probability node, is translated in a command. In this process assignments that happen before a probability node are copied in each update. This operation is only safe if these assignments prevent any side effects in the value of the probabilities. Finally, if the model is not a CTMC, all the probabilities of leaving a probabilistic decision node are normalized such that in the generated code the sum of the probabilities is always equal to 1. The resulting generator is able to produce valid RML models from our meta-model under the following restrictions:

- Synchronizations are only global.
- Clocks are only used in the PTA model.
- Synchronized transitions only update local variables.

Example 1. From the model presented in Fig. 3 we generate the following RML code:

```
module Train1
  x : clock;
  l : [0..4] init 0;
  s : [0..4] init 0;

  invariant
  (s=1 => x<=20+1)&(s=3 => x<=15+1)&(s=4 => x<=5+1)
  endinvariant

  [appr1] s=0  -> (2)/((2)+(1)):(s'=1)&(x'=0)&(l'=4) +
                  (1)/((2)+(1)):(s'=1)&(x'=0)&(l'=2);
  [stop1] s=1 & x<=10+1 -> (s'=2);
  [] s=1 & x>=10+1 -> (s'=4)&(x'=0);
  [go1] s=2 -> (s'=3)&(x'=0);
  [] s=3 & x>=7+1 -> (s'=4)&(x'=0);
  [leave1] s=4 & x>=3+1 -> (s'=0);
endmodule
```

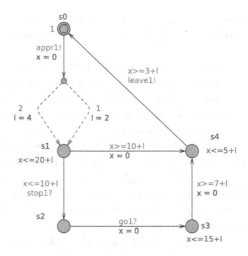

Fig. 5. UPPAAL model of the train

4.3 UPPAAL

UPPAAL [28] allows us to design timed automata models, possibly extended with variables and stochastic features, and load them from XML files. A model in UPPAAL consists of a set of *templates*, each modeled by a timed automaton. Local and global variables can be integers, Booleans, and clocks. A timed automaton consists of a set of control states, called *locations*, to which may be assigned an invariant expression and an exponential rate. UPPAAL also allows us to use probabilistic decision nodes that are used by the statistical model-checker. Then two types of transitions are possible:

- Transitions between two states, or from a state to a probabilistic decision node, may comprise a guard expression, a synchronization channel and a set of assignments.
- Transitions from a probabilistic decision node to a state may comprise a probability weight and a set of assignments.

We can generate UPPAAL models in XML format if the following restrictions apply:

- The model is only a PTA.
- Synchronizations are pairwise or broadcast, with input and output modalities.

Example 2. From the model presented in Fig. 3 we generate the UPPAAL model of Fig. 5. The semantics of colors in this model are the following: invariants are drawn in purple, guards in green, synchronization in light blue, assignments in blue, probability weights in brown and exponential rates in red.

4.4 Promela

PROMELA (short for <u>Pro</u>cess <u>Me</u>ta <u>La</u>nguage) is the input language for the SPIN software model checker [15]. Due to the popularity of SPIN, various other tools have been adapted to accept PROMELA input as well (for instance LTSMIN [29]), making it an attractive choice especially for the comparison of different model checking tools.

The syntax of PROMELA closely resembles that of the C programming language, augmented by inter-process communication constructs such as buffered or unbuffered channels, atomic sections etc. Moreover, unlike C, PROMELA allows for non-deterministic choices via statements with non-disjoint guards.

A PROMELA model consists of one or more *process types* or *process behaviors* (`proctypes`), which may be instantiated to form running processes. These processes can communicate via (buffered or unbuffered) channels or shared (global) variables. A process type can be thought of in analogy to a C function that, when instantiated, is executed in parallel with other running processes. Like C functions, process type declarations may be parameterized, with the actual arguments supplied at instantiation time.

While this would theoretically allow for an unbounded number of instantiated processes (technically, the number of simultaneously running processes is limited to 255 in SPIN), we do not make use of the possibility of run-time process instantiations: the notion of *modules* as set out in Sec. 2.2 requires that there exists an a-priori known, *fixed* set of parallel components (processes). For process type declarations which are used for a single process instance only, PROMELA provides the `active` keyword as a prefix to `proctype` declarations to denote that the corresponding process type is to be instantiated once at the beginning of the program.

Unlike the languages presented in the previous sections, PROMELA neither supports time nor probabilities. While there do exist extensions for both aspects (PROBMELA [30] for probabilistic processes and RT-PROMELA [31] for real-time properties), for this case study we chose to focus on the original PROMELA due to the popularity of the SPIN model checker.

In order to generate PROMELA files, the model has to fulfill the following prerequisites:

- no clocks, invariants, or exit rates occur in the model,
- synchronizations are pairwise only, with input and output modalities,
- each guard only contains either an expression over variables or a synchronization via a specific channel, but not both simultaneously.

The last restriction is due to the fact that in PROMELA, evaluating the synchronization expression `chan ? MSG` is not side-effect free, and thus cannot be performed in conjunction with a simple expression such as `x >= 10`. Note that we do not forbid probabilistic choices in the model. However, as probabilities cannot be expressed in PROMELA, those will be realized as simple non-deterministic choices.

The translation from an automaton-like structure, as is the modeling formalism for process behavior in our tool, to PROMELA code can be realized in a fashion similar to that for PRISM described in Sec. 4.2: each process has a (local) integer variable indicating the current state of the process, initialized to the value corresponding to the respective initial state. The process body then consists of a do...od block, executing transition statements (assignments, non-deterministic choices, and state changes) according to the current state and satisfied guards. In order to be consistent with the RML notion of *updates* (cf. Sec. 4.2), each sequence of transition statements is wrapped in an atomic block.

5 Model-to-Model Transformations

CINCO allows for the easy creation of many different graphical modeling tools. Thus, the so far presented MGL specification of the modeling language PSM can simply be stripped down to the needed parts, fed into the CINCO tool generator, resulting in the automatic creation of a dedicated modeling tool for any language $L \subseteq PSM$. This could, for instance, result in an LTS modeling tool that only contains states and transitions with channels. In fact, the required changes to the code generators would only be marginal, as one only needs to remove those parts of the generator code that handle the no longer present artifacts, like clocks, assignments, variables etc.

The resulting tools look very similar to the full PSM modeler as presented in Fig. 3. The only immediate difference is that the components palette on the right contains fewer elements and that the elements when configured in the Properties view contain fewer parameters. Even though these differences might look marginal at first sight, they may drastically ease the working with the specialized tools.

However, manually changing the code generators is impractical, especially if extensions to PSM are made that would require all derived code generators to be manually adapted again. Therefore, as already introduced before (cf. also Fig. 1), we use only one code generator base and provide model-to-model (M2M) transformations that translate other model types into PSM. As PSM is designed to provide all the required features, these transformations turn out to essentially be simple injective mappings, which may e.g., require renaming channels into alphabet symbols for labeled transition systems.

Figure 6 illustrates this concept in more detail for labeled transition systems. There exist two different MGL specifications and thus two different metamodels (PSM.ecore and LTS.ecore) are generated. As explained before, the code generators operate on the PSM metamodel. Thus the domain-specific LTS models need to be transformed into PSM models, a fact which is hidden to the user, who is only confronted with states and transitions.

Of course, the here depicted LTS instance (Trains.lts) does not contain time, probabilities or variables. Thus, the resulting PSM instance (Trains.psm) semantically differs from the one presented in Fig. 3. It just models the gate as a semaphore preventing both trains to enter simultaneously. It can, however, now be translated into all three target languages.

Technically, the realization of the M2M transformations is a special case of the code generator concepts presented in Sec. 4.1. The only difference is that instead of generating the domain-specific library of components for *one* MGL model, we now have *two*, and that instead of reading one model type and writing text,

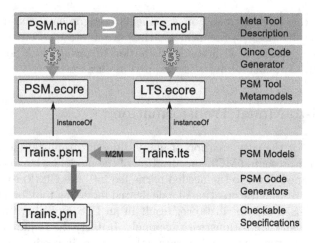

Fig. 6. Multiple products of the PSM family realized as subsets of the full language

we now read one model type and write the other. We are currently investigating ways how these transformations can also be created automatically.

6 Conclusion

We have presented the PSM case study, a generic conceptual framework to rapidly construct custom graphical interfaces with corresponding code generators for multi-faceted, concurrent systems that is based on the CINCO meta tooling suite. The point of the CINCO project is the explicit support of domain-specificity in order to simplify the tailored tool development. The impact of this approach has been illustrated by generating graphical interfaces for timed automata, probabilistic timed automata, Markov decision processes, and simple labeled transition systems, and the corresponding metamodel-based construction of code generators for UPPAAL, SPIN, PLASMA-LAB, and PRISM.

Key to the case study is the development of a 'unifying' super-set parallel systems modeling language (PSM) which serves as a 'mediator' between the multiple 'source' modeling languages and the various targeted input formats for model checking tools. This does not only allow for the generation of the domain-specific tools, but it also provides a means for systematically studying the differences and commonalities of the various system scenarios.

PSM is designed to allow the easy specification of model-to-model transformations from the source models. Moreover, our Eclipse-based framework provides automatically generated domain-specific code that frees the developer of the code generator from dealing with intricate Eclipse APIs. We envision that these features can be combined to further increase the potential of automatic code generation in order to also automatically generate the required model-to-model transformations into the intermediate PSM language.

References

1. Brambilla, M., Cabot, J., Wimmer, M.: Model-Driven Software Engineering in Practice. Morgan & Claypool (2012)
2. Xtend, https://www.eclipse.org/xtend/ (Online; last accessed April 23, 2014)
3. Gronback, R.C.: Eclipse Modeling Project: A Domain-Specific Language (DSL) Toolkit. Addison-Wesley, Boston (2008)
4. MetaEdit+ Version 4.5 Workbench Users Guide - 5.3 MERL Generator Definition Language, https://www.metacase.com/support/45/manuals/mwb/Mw-5_3.html (Online; last accessed July 31, 2014)
5. Kelly, S., Tolvanen, J.P.: Domain-Specific Modeling: Enabling Full Code Generation. Wiley-IEEE Computer Society Press, Hoboken (2008)
6. Kelly, S., Lyytinen, K., Rossi, M.: MetaEdit+: A Fully Configurable Multi-User and Multi-Tool CASE and CAME Environment. In: Constantopoulos, P., Vassiliou, Y., Mylopoulos, J. (eds.) CAiSE 1996. LNCS, vol. 1080, pp. 1–21. Springer, Heidelberg (1996)
7. Kastens, U., Pfahler, P., Jung, M.T.: The Eli System. In: Koskimies, K. (ed.) CC 1998. LNCS, vol. 1383, pp. 294–297. Springer, Heidelberg (1998)
8. Schmidt, C., Cramer, B., Kastens, U.: Generating visual structure editors from high-level specifications. Technical report, University of Paderborn, Germany (2008)
9. Naujokat, S., Lybecait, M., Steffen, B., Kopetzki, D., Margaria, T.: Full generation of domain-specific graphical modeling tools: A meta^{2}modeling approach (under submission, 2014)
10. Alur, R., Dill, D.L.: A theory of timed automata. Theoretical Computer Science 126, 183–235 (1994)
11. Kwiatkowska, M., Norman, G., Segala, R., Sproston, J.: Automatic verification of real-time systems with discrete probability distributions. Theoretical Computer Science 282, 101–150 (2002)
12. Howard, R.A.: Dynamic Programming and Markov Processes. MIT Press (1960)
13. Katoen, J.-P.: Labelled Transition Systems. In: Broy, M., Jonsson, B., Katoen, J.-P., Leucker, M., Pretschner, A. (eds.) Model-Based Testing of Reactive Systems. LNCS, vol. 3472, pp. 615–616. Springer, Heidelberg (2005)
14. Bengtsson, J., Larsen, K.G., Larsson, F., Pettersson, P., Yi, W.: UPPAAL – a Tool Suite for Automatic Verification of Real-Time Systems. In: Alur, R., Sontag, E.D., Henzinger, T.A. (eds.) HS 1995. LNCS, vol. 1066, pp. 232–243. Springer, Heidelberg (1996)
15. Holzmann, G.J.: The SPIN Model Checker - Primer and Reference Manual. Addison-Wesley (2004)
16. Boyer, B., Corre, K., Legay, A., Sedwards, S.: Plasma-lab: A flexible, distributable statistical model checking library. In: Joshi, K., Siegle, M., Stoelinga, M., D'Argenio, P.R. (eds.) QEST 2013. LNCS, vol. 8054, pp. 160–164. Springer, Heidelberg (2013)
17. Kwiatkowska, M., Norman, G., Parker, D.: PRISM 4.0: Verification of probabilistic real-time systems. In: Gopalakrishnan, G., Qadeer, S. (eds.) CAV 2011. LNCS, vol. 6806, pp. 585–591. Springer, Heidelberg (2011)
18. Jörges, S.: Construction and Evolution of Code Generators. LNCS, vol. 7747. Springer, Heidelberg (2013)
19. Lybecait, M.: Entwicklung und Implementierung eines Frameworks zur grafischen Modellierung von Modelltransformationen auf Basis von EMF-Metamodellen und Genesys. diploma thesis, TU Dortmund (2012)

20. Steinberg, D., Budinsky, F., Paternostro, M., Merks, E.: EMF: Eclipse Modeling Framework, 2nd edn. Addison-Wesley, Boston (2008)
21. Steffen, B., Margaria, T., Nagel, R., Jörges, S., Kubczak, C.: Model-Driven Development with the jABC. In: Bin, E., Ziv, A., Ur, S. (eds.) HVC 2006. LNCS, vol. 4383, pp. 92–108. Springer, Heidelberg (2007)
22. McAffer, J., Lemieux, J.M., Aniszczyk, C.: Eclipse Rich Client Platform, 2nd edn. Addison-Wesley Professional (2010)
23. Margaria, T., Steffen, B.: Simplicity as a Driver for Agile Innovation. Computer 43(6), 90–92 (2010)
24. Kopetzki, D.: Model-based generation of graphical editors on the basis of abstract meta model specifications. Master's thesis, TU Dortmund (2014)
25. Parr, T.: String Template, http://www.stringtemplate.org/ (Online; last accessed July 18, 2014)
26. The Apache Software Foundation: Apache Velocity Site, https://velocity.apache.org/ (Online; last accessed July 17, 2014)
27. Alur, R., Henzinger, T.A.: Reactive modules. Formal Methods in System Design 15(1), 7–48 (1999)
28. Behrmann, G., David, A., Larsen, K.G., Håkansson, J., Pettersson, P., Yi, W., Hendriks, M.: Uppaal 4.0. In: QEST, pp. 125–126. IEEE Computer Society (2006)
29. Blom, S., van de Pol, J., Weber, M.: Ltsmin: Distributed and symbolic reachability. In: Touili, T., Cook, B., Jackson, P. (eds.) CAV 2010. LNCS, vol. 6174, pp. 354–359. Springer, Heidelberg (2010)
30. Baier, C., Ciesinski, F., Grosser, M.: PROBMELA: A Modeling Language for Communicating Probabilistic Processes. In: Proceedings of the Second ACM and IEEE International Conference on Formal Methods and Models for Co-Design, MEMOCODE 2004, pp. 57–66. IEEE (2004)
31. Tripakis, S., Courcoubetis, C.: Extending PROMELA and SPIN for Real Time. In: Margaria, T., Steffen, B. (eds.) TACAS 1996. LNCS, vol. 1055, pp. 329–348. Springer, Heidelberg (1996)

Tutorial: Automata Learning in Practice

Falk Howar[1], Malte Isberner[2], and Bernhard Steffen[2]

[1] Carnegie Mellon University Silicon Valley, Moffett Field, CA, USA
falk.howar@gmail.com
[2] Technical University Dortmund, Chair for Programming Systems, Dortmund,
D-44227, Germany
{malte.isberner,steffen}@cs.tu-dortmund.de

Abstract. The paper reviews active automata learning with a particular focus on sources of redundancy. In particular, it gives an intuitive account of TTT, an algorithm based on three tree structures which concisely capture all the required information. This guarantees minimal memory consumption and it drastically reduces the length of membership queries, in particular in application scenarios like monitoring-based learning, where long counter examples arise. The essential steps and the impact of TTT are illustrated via experimentation with *LearnLib*, a free, open source Java library for active automata learning.

1 Introduction

Most systems in use today lack adequate specification or make use of underspecified or even unspecified components. In fact, the much propagated component-based software design style typically leads to under-specified systems, as most libraries only provide partial specifications of their components. Moreover, typically, revisions and last minute changes hardly enter the system specification. This hampers the application of any kind of formal validation techniques like model based testing or model checking. Active automata learning [4] has been proposed as a technique to apply model-based techniques in scenarios where models are unavailable, possibly incomplete, or erroneous [8,26].

Characteristic for active learning automata learning is its iterative alternation between a "testing" phase for completing the transitions relation of the model aggregated from the observed behavior, and an equivalence checking phase, which either signals success or provides a counterexample, i.e., a behavior that distinguishes the current aggregate (called hypothesis) from the system to be learned.

This technique, which originally has been introduced for dealing with formal languages, works very well also for reactive systems, whenever the chosen interpretation of the stimuli and reactions leads to a deterministic language. For such systems, active automata learning can be regarded as *regular extrapolation*, i.e., as a technique to construct the "best" regular model being consistent with the observations made.

In this tutorial we present the state of the art of practice-oriented, active automata learning by using *LearnLib*,[1] a free, open source Java library for active

---

[1] http://www.learnlib.de

T. Margaria and B. Steffen (Eds.): ISoLA 2014, Part I, LNCS 8802, pp. 499–513, 2014.
© Springer-Verlag Berlin Heidelberg 2014

automata learning, as a means to infer models of software systems. The open source version of *LearnLib* is the result of 10 years of research and development: It is the result of a redesign and re-implementation of the closed source *Learn-Lib* [24,28], which has originally been designed to systematically build finite state machine models of unknown real world systems (telecommunications systems, web services, etc.).

A decade of experience in the field led to the construction of a platform for experimentation with different learning algorithms as well as for statistically analyzing their characteristics in terms of learning effort, run time and memory consumption. More importantly, *LearnLib* provides a lot of infrastructure, enabling easy application in the domain of software systems.

Whereas the tutorial is structured in three parts of equal length covering (1) the theoretical foundations, (2) active automata learning algorithms, and (3) applications, the remainder of this paper focuses on providing an intuitive understanding of how to overcome "historical" shortcomings of the original L* algorithm. This results in the TTT algorithm, whose impact is illustrated via experimentation with *LearnLib*.

In the following, Section 2 sketches the basics of active automata learning, before Section 3 discusses various realizations along a concrete example. Subsequently, Section 4, the main part of the paper, intuitively present TTT, a redundancy-free algorithm for active automata learning. The paper closes with a brief discussion of applications in Section 5 and some conclusions and perspectives in Section 6.

2   What Is Active Automata Learning?

We will start by introducing some basic notation and then give a rough sketch of active learning. Let Σ be a finite set of *input symbols* $a_1, \ldots, a_k$. Sequences of input symbols are called *words*. The empty word (of length zero) is denoted by ε. Words can be concatenated in the obvious way: we write uv when concatenating two words u and v. Finally, a *language* $\mathcal{L} \subseteq \Sigma^*$ is a set of words.

Definition 1 (Deterministic finite automaton). *A deterministic finite automaton (DFA) is a tuple* $\langle Q, q_0, \Sigma, \delta, F \rangle$, *where*

- Q *is the finite set of states,*
- $q_0 \in Q$ *is the dedicated initial state,*
- Σ *is the finite input alphabet,*
- $\delta : Q \times \Sigma \to Q$ *is the transition function, and*
- $F \subseteq Q$ *is the set of final states.*

We write $q \xrightarrow{a} q'$ *for* $\delta(q, a) = q'$ *and* $q \xrightarrow{w} q'$ *if for* $w = a_1 \cdots a_n$ *there is a sequence* $q = q^0, q^1, \ldots, q^n = q'$ *of states such that* $q^{i-1} \xrightarrow{a_i} q^i$ *for* $1 \leq i \leq n$. $\qquad\square$

A DFA $\mathcal{A}$ accepts the regular language $\mathcal{L}_\mathcal{A}$ of words that lead to final states on $\mathcal{A}$, i.e, $\mathcal{L}_\mathcal{A} = \left\{ w \in \Sigma^* \mid q_0 \xrightarrow{w} q, \text{ with } q \in F \right\}$.

For words over Σ, we can define their *residual (language)* wrt. $\mathcal{L}$, which is closely related to the well-known Nerode relation [25]: for a language $\mathcal{L}$ let the residual language of a word $u \in \Sigma^*$ wrt. $\mathcal{L}$, denoted by $u^{-1}\mathcal{L}$, be the set $\{v \in \Sigma^* \mid uv \in \mathcal{L}\}$.

Definition 2 (Nerode equivalence). *Two words w, w' from Σ^* are equivalent wrt. $\mathcal{L}$, denoted by $w \equiv_{\mathcal{L}} w'$, iff $w^{-1}\mathcal{L} = w'^{-1}\mathcal{L}$.* □

By $[w]$ we denote the equivalence class of w in $\equiv_{\mathcal{L}}$. For regular languages (where $\equiv_{\mathcal{L}}$ has finite index), a DFA $\mathcal{A}_{\mathcal{L}}$ for $\mathcal{L}$ can be constructed from $\equiv_{\mathcal{L}}$ (cf. [11]): For each equivalence class $[w]$ of $\equiv_{\mathcal{L}}$, there is exactly one state $q_{[w]}$, with $q_{[\varepsilon]}$ being the initial one. Transitions are formed by one-letter extensions, i.e. $q_{[u]} \xrightarrow{a} q_{[ua]}$. Finally, a state is accepting if $[u] \subseteq \mathcal{L}$ (if not, then $[u] \cap \mathcal{L} = \emptyset$, as either ε is in the residual or not). No DFA recognizing $\mathcal{L}$ can have less states than $\mathcal{A}_{\mathcal{L}}$, and since it is unique up to isomorphism, it is called the *canonical* DFA for $\mathcal{L}$. This construction and the Nerode relation are the conceptual backbone of active learning algorithms.

Active learning aims at inferring (unknown) regular languages. Many active learning algorithms are formulated in the MAT-learning model introduced by [4], which assumes the existence of a *Minimally Adequate Teacher* (MAT) answering two kinds of queries.

Membership queries test whether a word $w \in \Sigma^*$ is in the unknown language $\mathcal{L}$. These queries are employed for building hypothesis automata.

Equivalence queries test whether an intermediate hypothesis language $\mathcal{L}_{\mathcal{H}}$ equals $\mathcal{L}$. If so, an equivalence query signals success. Otherwise, it will return a *counterexample*, i.e., a word $w \in \Sigma^*$ from the symmetric difference of $\mathcal{L}_{\mathcal{H}}$ and $\mathcal{L}$.

The key idea of active learning algorithms, the most prominent example being Angluin's L* algorithm, is to approximate the Nerode congruence $\equiv_{\mathcal{L}}$ by some equivalence relation $\equiv_{\mathcal{H}}$ such that $\equiv_{\mathcal{L}}$ (not strictly) refines $\equiv_{\mathcal{H}}$. This approximation is achieved by identifying *prefixes* u, which serve as representatives of the classes of $\equiv_{\mathcal{H}}$, and *suffixes* v, which are used to prove inequalities of the respective residuals, separating classes. Throughout the course of the learning process, the sets of both prefixes and suffixes grow monotonically, allowing for an increasingly fine identification of representative prefixes.

Having identified (some) classes of $\equiv_{\mathcal{L}}$, a hypothesis $\mathcal{H}$ is constructed in a fashion resembling the construction of the canonical DFA (cf. [17] for a detailed account). Of course, some further constraints must be met in order to ensure a well-defined construction. For a more detailed description, also comprising the technical details of organizing prefixes, suffixes and the information gathered from membership queries, we refer the reader to [4].

As sketched above, $\mathcal{H}$ is subjected to an equivalence query, which either signals success (in which case learning terminates) or yields a counterexample. This counterexample serves as a witness that the approximation of $\equiv_{\mathcal{L}}$ is too coarse, triggering a refinement of $\equiv_{\mathcal{H}}$ (and thus $\mathcal{H}$). This alternation of *hypothesis construction* and *hypothesis validation* is repeated until an equivalence query finally signals success. Convergence is guaranteed as $\equiv_{\mathcal{H}}$ is refined with each equivalence query, but always remains a (non-strict) coarsening of $\equiv_{\mathcal{L}}$.

3   Realization: L* and Its Offsprings

In this section, we will discuss briefly (and partially) the lineage of active automata learning algorithms that originated from the seminal L* algorithm and highlight important conceptual improvements of specific contributions.

3.1   Running Example

Fig. 1 shows the smallest deterministic automaton for our running example: a language of all words over the alphabet $\{a, b\}$ with at least two $a's$ and an odd number of $b's$.

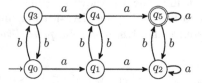

Fig. 1. Minimal acceptor for our running example

3.2   Initial Approach: Observation Table à la Angluin

In her 1987 paper describing the L* algorithm, Angluin [4] introduced the *observation table* data structure as a means to realize the Nerode approximation as described in Section 2. Essentially, an observation table is a two dimensional array partitioned in an upper and a lower part, where the upper part is intended to model the states of a minimal acceptor, whereas the lower part models the transitions. Rows are labeled with reaching words (also called *access sequences*), and columns with distinguishing futures, i.e., words that are used to prove that the residual languages of two reaching words are different, or equivalently, that these reaching words cannot lead to the same state.

Two of the observation tables obtained when learning the running example (Fig. 1) using L* are shown in Figure 2. The first one (Fig. 2, middle) is the initial one, whereas the second one (Fig. 2, right) is the final one, where the word *bbabbab* was used as the first and only counterexample.

The main weakness of this data structure is that it applies the distinguishing power of a certain distinguishing future similarly to all reaching words, which requires a huge number of in a sense "unjustified" membership queries. But also the treatment of counterexamples described in the original L* algorithm has its flaws, which we will discuss in the next section.

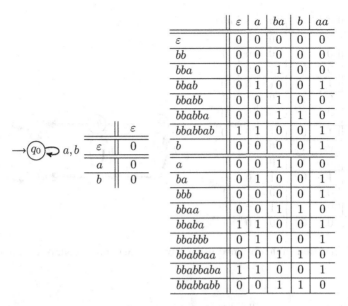

Left observation table:

	ε
ε	0
a	0
b	0

Right observation table:

	ε	a	ba	b	aa
ε	0	0	0	0	0
bb	0	0	0	0	0
bba	0	0	1	0	0
bbab	0	1	0	0	1
bbabb	0	0	1	0	0
bbabba	0	0	1	1	0
bbabbab	1	1	0	0	1
b	0	0	0	0	1
a	0	0	1	0	0
ba	0	1	0	0	1
bbb	0	0	0	0	1
bbaa	0	0	1	1	0
bbaba	1	1	0	0	1
bbabbb	0	1	0	0	1
bbabbaa	0	0	1	1	0
bbabbaba	1	1	0	0	1
bbabbabb	0	0	1	1	0

Fig. 2. Initial 1-state hypothesis, corresponding observation table, and observation table for final hypothesis after processing counterexample $w = bbabbab$

3.3   Improvement 1: Rivest & Schapire's Counterexample Analysis

The observation table depicted in the right of Figure 2 contains a lot of redundancy: several rows in the upper part are completely identical. As a consequence, some of the states in the final hypothesis (Fig. 1) are identified through multiple prefixes. For example, the state q_0 is identified by both ε and bb. Each of these identifying prefixes requires k rows in the lower part of the table. All of these need to be considered for *consistency checking*.

Most of these problems can be alleviated by changing the way how counterexamples are handled. Rivest and Schapire [29] presented a method that adds only a single *suffix* to the observation table. Moreover, this suffix can be found efficiently, using only $O(\log m)$ membership queries for a counterexample of length m. The original algorithm used a binary search for this task (cf. also [31]); however, other search strategies might perform significantly better in practice, while maintaining the worst-case complexity [19].

In fact, the set of suffixes is the only part of the observation table that is explicitly augmented as a result of counterexample analysis. However, this added suffix is guaranteed to lead to the table not being closed, which results in a row being moved from the lower to the upper part of the table.

Using this strategy, rows are only ever moved to the upper part of the table because they represent a previously undiscovered state: otherwise, they would not cause an unclosedness. This in turn means that all upper rows refer to distinct states in the hypothesis, i.e., identifying prefixes are unique! As a direct consequence, this eliminates the need for checking consistency.

	ε	bbab	bab	b	aba
ε	0	0	0	0	1
a	0	1	0	0	1
ab	0	0	1	0	0
aba	1	0	1	0	0
aa	0	1	0	1	1
b	0	0	0	0	0
aab	1	0	1	0	0
abab	0	1	0	1	1
abb	0	1	0	1	1
abaa	1	0	1	0	0
aaa	0	1	0	1	1
ba	0	0	1	0	0
bb	0	0	0	0	1

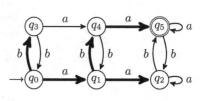

Fig. 3. Observation table obtained using Rivest & Schapire's counterexample analysis method

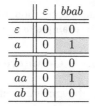

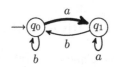

	ε	bbab
ε	0	0
a	0	1
b	0	0
aa	0	1
ab	0	0

Fig. 4. Intermediate (closed) observation table and corresponding non-canonical hypothesis during Rivest&Schapire's algorithm. The highlighted cells induce the counterexamples $a \cdot bbab$ and $aa \cdot bbab$.

An important observation is that the prefix-closedness property of the short prefix set is maintained. Along with the aforementioned uniqueness property, the short prefixes now induce a *spanning tree* on the hypothesis. The corresponding "tree" transitions are shown in bold in Figure 3 (right). The remaining, "non-tree" transitions correspond to the long prefixes.

A Side-Effect: Instable Hypotheses. Using Rivest&Schapire's counterexample analysis results in the suffix set of the observation table no longer being suffix closed, as opposed to the original L* algorithm. This does not affect correctness, as suffix-closedness of the discriminator set is not mandatory for realizing the Nerode approximation described in Section 2. However, there is a curious side effect: in spite of a closed observation table, the hypothesis might no longer be consistent with the observations stored in this table. In fact, it might not even be canonical, as the example of a closed observation table and non-canonical hypothesis shown in Figure 4 shows.

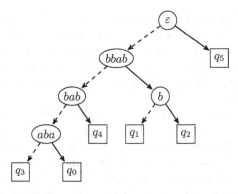

Fig. 5. Discrimination tree for final hypothesis, obtained using the Observation Pack algorithm

Luckily, there is a simple remedy: for each cell in the observation table, we check if its contents match the output predicted by the hypothesis. If this is not the case, we have another counterexample which can be treated in the same fashion as above. Concerns have been voiced that this might lead to an infinite loop, as in some cases neither the counterexample nor the language accepted by the hypothesis changes. However, this is not the case: the counterexample analysis is based on transforming prefixes of the counterexample to access sequences in the hypothesis. Progress is then ensured by the growth of the state and thus access sequence set.

Following [17], we refer to hypotheses that do not predict the observation table contents correctly as *instable* hypotheses. This is due to the fact that they themselves form a source of counterexamples (in conjunction with the underlying data structure), triggering their own refinement without the need for an "external" equivalence query.

3.4 Improvement 2: Discrimination Trees

Rivest&Schapire's counterexample analysis method ensures that the number of both rows and columns is bounded by kn and n, respectively. As every cell in the observation table is filled by performing a membership query, in total $O(kn^2)$ queries are required for constructing the table, plus another $O(n \log m)$ for counterexample analysis (m being the length of the longest counterexample). This constitutes a major improvement over the original L* algorithm, where the number of rows is dominated by knm, resulting in a query complexity of $O(kmn^2)$.

We can also conclude that the *minimum* number of columns is $\lceil \log_2 n \rceil$, as c columns allow distinguishing 2^c states. However, this is a rather hypothetical case: the obtained suffixes will usually not be that "informative". In the example above (cf. Fig. 3), in fact 5 suffixes are required to distinguish 6 states, even though theoretically, 3 could suffice ($2^3 = 8 \geq 6$).

How does this affect the learning process? To answer this question, let us take a closer look of what happens when we add new rows to the observation table after moving a row from the lower to the upper part of the table (i.e., after fixing an unclosedness). The process of filling these new rows with data values through membership queries has the goal of determining the target state of the respective transition.

The contents of row *abaa* can be represented as the 5-dimensional bitvector $1, 0, 1, 0, 0$. However, the first value alone is enough to rule out any other existing state except for q_5! Determining the values for all cells in this row thus is not necessary to accomplish our stated goal of finding the successor state.

The data structure of a *discrimination tree*, introduced into the context of active automata learning by Kearns&Vazirani [21], allows for a more fine-grained classification scheme for distinguishing between states. An example for such a discrimination tree is showed in Figure 5. Leaves in this tree are labeled with states of the hypothesis, while inner nodes are labeled with discriminators. Each inner node has two children, the 0-child (dashed line) and the 1-child (solid line). The semantics of a discrimination tree is best explained in terms of the "sifting" operation: given a prefix $u \in \Sigma^*$, at each inner node labeled with a discriminator v a membership query for $u \cdot v$ is posed. Depending on the outcome of this query (0 or 1), we move on to the respective child of the inner node. This process is repeated until a leaf is reached, which forms the result of the sifting operation. Each state labels the leaf in the discrimination tree which is the outcome of sifting its access sequence into the tree.

For each distinct pair of states, there is exactly one *lowest common ancestor* (LCA) in the discrimination tree. The label of the LCA is sufficient evidence for separating the two states, as it proves them to be Nerode-inequivalent. Discrimination trees are thus redundancy-free in the sense that *exactly one* such separator is maintained for every distinct pair of states. In an observation table, in contrast, the number of discriminators to distinguish any pair of two states is always fixed, regardless of "how different" the states are: state q_5, for example, is very different from the other states due to its being accepting. This is the reason why only a single discriminator is enough to distinguish it from any other state.

The discrimination tree in Figure 5 was obtained through the Observation Pack [12] algorithm, which builds upon Rivest&Schapire's algorithm, but replaces the observation table with a discrimination tree. As such, it is not surprising that the overall set of discriminators is the same as that in Figure 3 (left). Also, the short prefixes (access sequences), along with the spanning tree structure (Fig. 3, right), remains the same.

Does L* "waste" queries? It would be unfair to say that the additional queries posed when using an observation table were wasted, as an "unexpected" outcome still leads to a new state being discovered. However, rigorously speaking, they are misplaced: in the hypothesis construction phase, the prime goal should be to gather enough information to construct a subsequent hypothesis. The search for new states, on the other hand, should be deferred to the *hypothesis validation* phase (i.e., approximating an equivalence query). The results of the ZULU challenge clearly show that membership queries are better spent in the hypothesis validation phase: there the discrimination tree-based Observation Pack algorithm [12] combined with a sophisticated search for counterexamples ("Evolving Hypothesis", cf. [12,16]) performed best among all competing ones.

4 The TTT Algorithm

The discrimination tree approach eliminates a large share of the aforementioned redundancies, as the structure of the discrimination tree ensures that there is exactly *one* discriminator that separates each pair of states. The overall number of membership queries required for hypothesis construction depends on how well the tree is balanced: it is $O(kn^2)$ for a degenerated tree, and $O(kn \log n)$ for a perfectly balanced tree. This makes rebalancing trees seem worthwhile; however, it can be shown that there are automata for which *all* discrimination trees are degenerated. Hence, any queries spent on rebalancing attempts might be in vain.

Nevertheless, there is another aspect, which also exposes a flaw in the complexity measure we have resorted to so far: considering the total number of queries does not take into account the *length* of the involved words. This is despite the fact that the time for processing a membership query *will* inevitably require an amount of time (at least) proportional to its length. From a practical standpoint, this could be justified by the assumption that *resets* often are much more expensive than processing the actual query. However, from an asymptotic perspective, this is just a constant factor. Besides, there are settings where the cost of a single symbol outweighs that of a reset, e.g., when learning web services. A reset can simply be performed by initiating a new connection and creating a new session on the server, but the network latency limits the rate in which the symbols of the respective word can be executed.

Looking at the discrimination tree in Figure 5, one notices that the discriminators are rather long. Since they are derived as suffixes of former counterexamples, their length is bounded by m. Moreover, as the introduction of new transitions in the hypothesis requires sifting through the whole tree, this means that an unfavorably long counterexample obtained in one hypothesis validation round can affect the lengths of membership queries in *all* subsequent hypothesis construction phases. This renders classical learning algorithms near unusable in settings where extremely long counterexamples are the norm, such as in monitoring setups (cf. [6,18]).

4.1 The Big Picture

The TTT algorithm [18] addresses this problem by ensuring that the length of every discriminator in the tree is bounded by n. It does so by re-establishing the suffix-closedness property of the discriminator set. This enables a very compact representation of this set, which can then be stored as a *trie*: a root-directed tree in which each node corresponds to a word, which can be obtained by concatenating the symbols on the path to the root.

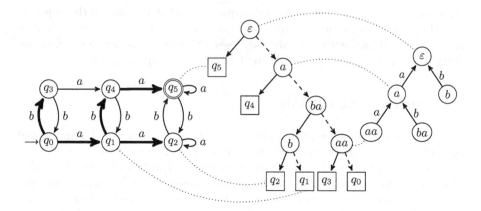

Fig. 6. The three tree-based data structures of TTT: the spanning tree-based hypothesis, the discrimination tree, and the suffix trie. A subset of the connection between the data structures is represented using dotted lines.

An instance of such a trie can be seen in the right of Figure 6, corresponding to the discriminator set $\{\varepsilon, a, ba, b, aa\}$. Note that this discriminator set is the same as that of the classic L* algorithm (cf. Fig. 2).

Figure 6 moreover shows an exemplary view on TTT's data structures, which also explain its name: on the left is the transition graph of the hypothesis, which is constructed around the *spanning tree* (highlighted transitions). Each state in this graph corresponds to a leaf in the *discrimination tree* (middle). The discriminators labeling inner nodes in this tree are then stored in the mentioned *suffix trie*, such that each inner node of the discrimination tree corresponds to a node in the suffix trie.

The redundancy-freeness of this setup is underlined by the fact that the overall space requirement is asymptotically the same as that of the transition graph alone, $O(kn)$. The short-prefix set Sp can be obtained from the spanning tree, and the discriminators can be obtained from the suffix trie. Moreover, the number of nodes in each of the trees is bounded by $2n$.

4.2 Background: Discriminator Finalization

The TTT algorithm is very similar to the Observation Pack algorithm, but extends it by one key step: *discriminator finalization*. This step ensures that every discriminator occurring at an inner node is a suffix of another discriminator, which allows it to be stored in the suffix trie.

The process of obtaining such discriminators by prepending a single symbol to existing discriminators is closely related to the process of *minimization* (cf. [10]). For the technical details, we refer the reader to [18] and focus on the "visible" effect on the internal data structures.

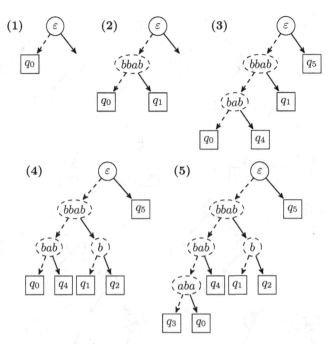

Fig. 7. Sequence of discrimination trees generated during hypothesis stabilization. The dashed inner nodes are temporary, and will be finalized in a later step.

As remarked in Section 3, intermediate (instable) hypotheses might be non-canonical. In these cases, there are pairs of state for which no discriminator can be obtained from the hypothesis, as they might be equivalent. This calls for fully stabilizing the hypothesis first, before discriminators can be finalized. During stabilization, the discrimination tree grows (cf. Fig. 7), but the newly inserted inner nodes are marked as *temporary* (dashed outline). These temporary discriminators are then *finalized* in a second step, which is illustrated in Figure 8. In each of the finalization steps, a temporary discriminator is replaced by a new, final one, which is backed by the hypothesis.

Considering the last discrimination tree shown in Figure 7 (5), only the root (which is always ε) is final. Hence, any new final discriminator has to consist of a single symbol (prepended to the empty word). The leaves in the left ("false") subtree are q_0 through q_4. Looking at the hypothesis (Fig. 3, right), this set of nodes can be partitioned by the discriminators a or b, of which the former is chosen (Fig. 8 (1)). Note that the new, final discriminator is always placed above *all* temporary discriminators, ensuring that all descendant inner nodes of a temporary inner node are also temporary. Also note that the structure of the discrimination tree can change, as is the case here, causing the maximum depth to increase by one. However, experiments have shown that the step of discriminator finalization often *decreases* the average tree depth, leading to not only shorter but also *fewer* membership queries [18].

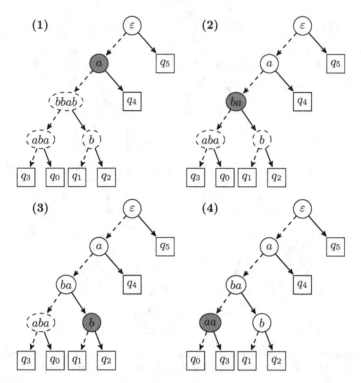

Fig. 8. Sequence of discrimination trees generated during discriminator finalization. The gray node is the inner node with the most recently finalized discriminator.

5   Applications

Active learning has been applied successfully in a number of interesting case studies. It has been used to infer models of CTI systems [8,9], web-applications [27], communication protocol entities [2], the new biometric European passport [3], bot nets [7], a network of integrated controllers in the door of a car [30], and enterprise applications [5]. The particular challenges of practical application are discussed in [14] along with illustrating examples from case studies. The third part of the tutorial focuses on these challenges:

A: Interacting with real systems

   The interaction with a realistic target system comes with two problems. The technical problem of establishing an adequate interface that allows one to apply test cases for realizing so-called membership queries, and a conceptual problem of bridging the gap between the abstract learned model and the concrete runtime scenario. This gap is usually closed by a so-called mapper component, which is placed between a learning algorithm and a system under learning. Mappers translate abstract queries into tests on an actual system [23,20].

B: Membership Queries

Whereas small learning experiments typically require only a few hundred membership queries, learning realistic systems may easily require several orders of magnitude more. One can either use filters that reduce the number of queries (e.g., using domain knowledge to answer queries without tests) [22], or distribute queries to many oracles [13].

C: Reset

Active learning requires membership queries to be independent. Whereas this is no problem for simulated systems, it may be quite problematic in practice. Resetting a system can be an expensive task, e.g., for systems that store state in a database. In such a case it can be beneficial to "re-use" test cases by suspending their execution and continuing it adding suffixes incrementally [5].

D: Parameters and value domains

Active learning classically is based on abstract communication alphabets. Parameters and interpreted values are only treated to an extent expressible within the abstract alphabet. In practice, this typically is not sufficient, not even for systems as simple as communication protocols, where, e.g., increasing sequence numbers must be handled, or where authentication requires matching user/password combinations. There exist multiple approaches that extend active automata learning to classes of languages with data parameters (e.g. [15,1]).

E: Equivalence Queries

Equivalence queries compare a learned hypothesis model with the target system for language equivalence and, in case of failure, return a counterexample exposing a difference. In practice, equivalence queries will have to be approximated using membership queries. Methods from conformance testing have been suggested as approximations but are in general too expensive to be feasible for industry scale applications. Randomized search often proves to be a viable alternative (cf. [16]).

The tutorial will highlight the solutions and support *LearnLib* provides for dealing with these challenges.

6   Conclusions

In this paper and the accompanying tutorial we reviewed active automata learning in three steps. First, we provided some theoretic foundations. In a second step, we discussed important milestones in the development of active automata learning algorithms with a particular focus on sources of redundancy. We gave an intuitive account of TTT, an algorithm based on three tree structures which concisely capture all the required information. The algorithm guarantees minimal memory consumption and drastically reduces the length of membership queries, in particular in application scenarios like monitoring-based learning, where long counter examples arise. Finally, we addressed challenges that usually arise when using active automata learning to infer models of software systems.

References

1. Aarts, F., Heidarian, F., Kuppens, H., Olsen, P., Vaandrager, F.: Automata learning through counterexample guided abstraction refinement. In: Giannakopoulou, D., Méry, D. (eds.) FM 2012. LNCS, vol. 7436, pp. 10–27. Springer, Heidelberg (2012), http://dx.doi.org/10.1007/978-3-642-32759-9_4

2. Aarts, F., Jonsson, B., Uijen, J.: Generating models of infinite-state communication protocols using regular inference with abstraction. In: Petrenko, A., Simão, A., Maldonado, J.C. (eds.) ICTSS 2010. LNCS, vol. 6435, pp. 188–204. Springer, Heidelberg (2010)

3. Aarts, F., Schmaltz, J., Vaandrager, F.: Inference and abstraction of the biometric passport. In: Margaria, T., Steffen, B. (eds.) ISoLA 2010, Part I. LNCS, vol. 6415, pp. 673–686. Springer, Heidelberg (2010)

4. Angluin, D.: Learning Regular Sets from Queries and Counterexamples. Inf. Comput. 75(2), 87–106 (1987)

5. Bauer, O., Neubauer, J., Steffen, B., Howar, F.: Reusing System States by Active Learning Algorithms. In: Moschitti, A., Scandariato, R. (eds.) Eternal Systems. CCSE, vol. 255, pp. 61–78. Springer (2012)

6. Bertolino, A., Calabrò, A., Merten, M., Steffen, B.: Never-Stop Learning: Continuous Validation of Learned Models for Evolving Systems through Monitoring. ERCIM News 2012(88) (2012)

7. Bossert, G., Hiet, G., Henin, T.: Modelling to Simulate Botnet Command and Control Protocols for the Evaluation of Network Intrusion Detection Systems. In: 2011 Conference on Network and Information Systems Security (SAR-SSI), pp. 1–8 (May 2011)

8. Hagerer, A., Hungar, H.: Model generation by moderated regular extrapolation. In: Kutsche, R.-D., Weber, H. (eds.) FASE 2002. LNCS, vol. 2306, pp. 80–95. Springer, Heidelberg (2002)

9. Hagerer, A., Margaria, T., Niese, O., Steffen, B., Brune, G., Ide, H.D.: Efficient regression testing of CTI-systems: Testing a complex call-center solution. Annual review of communication, Int.Engineering Consortium (IEC) 55, 1033–1040 (2001)

10. Hopcroft, J.E.: An $n \log n$ Algorithm for Minimizing States in a Finite Automaton. Tech. rep., Stanford, CA, USA (1971)

11. Hopcroft, J.E., Motwani, R., Ullman, J.D.: Introduction to automata theory, languages, and computation - (2. ed.). Addison-Wesley series in Computer Science. Addison-Wesley-Longman (2001)

12. Howar, F.: Active Learning of Interface Programs. Ph.D. thesis, TU Dortmund University (2012), http://dx.doi.org/2003/29486

13. Howar, F., Bauer, O., Merten, M., Steffen, B., Margaria, T.: The Teachers' Crowd: The Impact of Distributed Oracles on Active Automata Learning. In: Hähnle, R., Knoop, J., Margaria, T., Schreiner, D., Steffen, B. (eds.) ISoLA 2011 Workshops 2011. Communications in Computer and Information Science, vol. 336, pp. 232–247. Springer, Heidelberg (2012)

14. Howar, F., Merten, M., Steffen, B., Margaria, T.: Practical Aspects of Active Automata Learning. In: Formal Methods for Industrial Critical Systems, Wiley-VCH (2012)

15. Howar, F., Steffen, B., Jonsson, B., Cassel, S.: Inferring canonical register automata. In: Kuncak, V., Rybalchenko, A. (eds.) VMCAI 2012. LNCS, vol. 7148, pp. 251–266. Springer, Heidelberg (2012)

16. Howar, F., Steffen, B., Merten, M.: From ZULU to RERS. In: Margaria, T., Steffen, B. (eds.) ISoLA 2010, Part I. LNCS, vol. 6415, pp. 687–704. Springer, Heidelberg (2010)
17. Isberner, M., Howar, F., Steffen, B.: Learning Register Automata: From Languages to Program Structures. Machine Learning 96(1-2), 65–98 (2014), http://dx.doi.org/10.1007/s10994-013-5419-7
18. Isberner, M., Howar, F., Steffen, B.: The TTT algorithm: A redundancy-free approach to active automata learning. In: Bonakdarpour, B., Smolka, S.A. (eds.) RV 2014. LNCS, vol. 8734, pp. 307–322. Springer, Heidelberg (2014)
19. Isberner, M., Steffen, B.: An Abstract Framework for Counterexample Analysis in Active Automata Learning. In: Clark, A., Kanazawa, M., Yoshinaka, R. (eds.) Proc. ICGI 2014. JMLR W&CP (to appear, 2014)
20. Jonsson, B.: Learning of Automata Models Extended with Data. In: Bernardo, M., Issarny, V. (eds.) SFM 2011. LNCS, vol. 6659, pp. 327–349. Springer, Heidelberg (2011)
21. Kearns, M.J., Vazirani, U.V.: An Introduction to Computational Learning Theory. MIT Press, Cambridge (1994)
22. Margaria, T., Raffelt, H., Steffen, B.: Knowledge-based Relevance Filtering for Efficient System-level Test-based Model Generation. Innovations in Systems and Software Engineering 1(2), 147–156 (2005)
23. Merten, M., Isberner, M., Howar, F., Steffen, B., Margaria, T.: Automated learning setups in automata learning. In: Margaria, T., Steffen, B. (eds.) ISoLA 2012, Part I. LNCS, vol. 7609, pp. 591–607. Springer, Heidelberg (2012)
24. Merten, M., Steffen, B., Howar, F., Margaria, T.: Next generation learnLib. In: Abdulla, P.A., Leino, K.R.M. (eds.) TACAS 2011. LNCS, vol. 6605, pp. 220–223. Springer, Heidelberg (2011)
25. Nerode, A.: Linear Automaton Transformations. Proceedings of the American Mathematical Society 9(4), 541–544 (1958)
26. Peled, D., Vardi, M.Y., Yannakakis, M.: Black Box Checking. In: Wu, J., Chanson, S.T., Gao, Q. (eds.) Proc. FORTE 1999, pp. 225–240. Kluwer Academic (1999)
27. Raffelt, H., Merten, M., Steffen, B., Margaria, T.: Dynamic testing via automata learning. Int. J. Softw. Tools Technol. Transf. 11(4), 307–324 (2009)
28. Raffelt, H., Steffen, B., Berg, T., Margaria, T.: LearnLib: a framework for extrapolating behavioral models. Int. J. Softw. Tools Technol. Transf. 11(5), 393–407 (2009)
29. Rivest, R.L., Schapire, R.E.: Inference of Finite Futomata Using Homing Sequences. Inf. Comput. 103(2), 299–347 (1993)
30. Shahbaz, M., Shashidhar, K.C., Eschbach, R.: Iterative refinement of specification for component based embedded systems. In: ISSTA 2011, pp. 276–286 (2011)
31. Steffen, B., Howar, F., Merten, M.: Introduction to active automata learning from a practical perspective. In: Bernardo, M., Issarny, V. (eds.) SFM 2011. LNCS, vol. 6659, pp. 256–296. Springer, Heidelberg (2011)

LNCS Transactions on Foundations
for Mastering Change: Preliminary Manifesto

Bernhard Steffen

Chair of Programming Systems, TU Dortmund, Germany
steffen@cs.tu-dortmund.de

Today's development of modern software-based Systems is characterized by (1) vaguely defined problems (the result of some requirements engineering), (2) typically expressed in natural language or, in the best case, in a semi-formal notation, (3) implementation on top of large software libraries or other third party code as an overall system of millions of lines of code to (4) run on a highly complex enterprise environment, which may even critically involve services connected via wide area networks, i.e., the Internet, and it should, of course, be (5) easily adaptable to changing requests.

Practice answers these requests with quite some success with approaches like extreme programming and Scrum, which essentially replace any kind of foundational method be close cooperation and communication within the team and with the customer, combined with early prototyping and testing. Main critique to this formal methods-free approach is merely its lack of scalability, which is partly compensated by involving increasingly complex third party components, while keeping the complexity of their orchestration at a Srum-manageable level.

Does this state of the art reduce the role of the classical formal methods-based approaches in the sense of Hoare and Dijkstra to the niche of (extremely) safety-critical systems, simply because it is unclear

- What should be formally verified in cases where the problem is not stated precisely upfront? In fact, in most software projects, adapting the development to the changing needs revealed last-minute is the dominating task?
- What does a fully verified program help, if it comes too late? In fact, in many projects the half-life period is far too short to accomodate any verification activities.

In fact, in some sense the opposite is true, namely that the formal methods developed in the last decade are almost everywhere. E.g., type systems are omnipresent, but seemlessly working in the back of most IDE's, which are typically supported by complex data flow analyses and sophisticated code generation methods. In addition, (software) model checking has become popular to control application-specific properties, and even the originally very pragmatic software testing community gradually employs more and more model-based technologies.

However, admittedly, development and debugging as supported by complex integrated development environments (IDEs) like Eclipse and Netbeans or by dedicated bugtracking tools do not attempt to guarantee correctness by construction,

T. Margaria and B. Steffen (Eds.): ISoLA 2014, Part I, LNCS 8802, pp. 514–517, 2014.

the ultimate goal of Dijkstra and Hoare. Rather they are characterized by their community-driven reactiveness:

- What should be formally verified in cases where the problem is not stated precisely upfront? In fact, in most software projects, adapting the development software is developed quickly by large communities,
- documentation is largely replaced by online forums,
- quality assurance is a community effort,
- success of a software depends on the vitality of its community. to the changing needs revealed last-minute is the dominating task?

FoMC intends to establish a forum for formal methods-based research that fosters a discipline for rigorously dealing the nature of today's agile system development, which is characterized by unclear premises, unforeseen change, and the need for fast reaction, in a context of hard to control frame conditions, like third party components, network-problems, and attacks. Submissions are evaluated according to these goals. Papers may well focus on individual techniques, but must clearly position themselves in the FoMC landscape. In particular, FoMC aims at establishing a common nomenclature to overcome the currently quite diverse use of notation.

It is planned to complement FoMaC by a sister journal, the LNBI *Transaction on Managing Change* (ToMaC), which address human factors, project and risk management, as well as methods to control time to market, total cost of ownership and return of investment.

1 Profile of FoMaC

FoMaC is concerned with the foundations of mastering change and variability during the whole system lifecycles at various conceptual levels. It explicitly comprises meta modeling as a means for conceptually addressing domain specialization, which can also be regarded as a technology transfer appoach, where methods are considered to systematically adapt solutions from one (application) domain for another domain. In particular, this comprises the generation of and transformations between domain specific languages, as well as other issues of domain modeling and validation, which FoMaC addresses for every phase of the systems' lifecycles:

Modeling and Design: This is the main level at which 'classical' variability modeling operates. The methods considered here generalize classical modeling to specifically address variability issues, like where and how to change things, and technology to maintain structural and semantical properties within the range of modeled variability. Here methods like feature modeling, '150% modeling', productline management, model to model transformations, constraint-based (requirement) specification, synthesis-based model completion, aspect-oriented transformations, model checking, and feature interaction detection are considered.

Implementation: At this level, FoMaC addresses methods beyond classical parametric and modular programming approaches, like aspect orientation, delta programming, program generation, aspect and generative programming, and program transformation, but also static and dynamic validation techniques, like program verification, symbolic execution, runtime verification, (model-based) testing, and test-based modeling,

Runtime and Use: This is the level of self-X technology, where methods are addressed that allow, steer, and control autonomous evolution of systems during runtime. These methods comprise techniques to achieve fault tolerance, runtime planning and synthesis, higher-order exchange of functionality, hot deployment and fail-over, and they should go hand in hand with the abovementioned dynamic validation techniques, like program verification, symbolic execution, runtime verification, (model-based) testing, test-based modeling, and monitoring.

Maintenance/Evolution/Migration: This level is concerned with the long-term perspective of system evolution, i.e. the part where the bulk of costs is accumulated. Central issues here are the change of platform, the merging of systems of overlapping functionality, the maintenance of downward compatibility, and the support of a continuous (system) improvement process, as well as continuous quality assurance comprising regression testing, monitoring, delta testing, and model-based diagnostic features.

2 People and Perspective

Initiatives are driven by people, their visions, their example, and their support. The very diverse position papers in this track, which range from quite concrete [4,1,9,2,5] proposals to increasingly 'philosophical' statements [8,3,6], provide a flavor of the intended FoMaC spectrum: Everything is allowed, as long as it clearly contributes to the art of mastering change.

Important is that we start freeing ourselves from methods and notions known from classical disciplines: Terms like architecture impose the unnecessary and nightmarish feeling that what we do now is cast in stone and unchangeable forever, garbage collection suggest waste removal problems, and the typical development processes breath the stiffness of classical construction. FoMaC is intended to address these issues not only at the technological level, but also by supporting a change of mindset by changing terminology: What we need to establish is a general attitude and corresponding technology that everything can change at any time in case of need, and that this becomes so easy that most of the required day-to-day changes can be mastered at the application level or is even automatically taken care of via synthesis or runtime-adaptivity [7].

References

1. Felderer, M.: Current Issues on Model-Based Software Quality Assurance for Mastering Change. In: Margaria, T., Steffen, B. (eds.) ISoLA 2014, Part I. LNCS, vol. 8802, pp. 521–523. Springer, Heidelberg (2014)

2. Hähnle, R.: Managing change in formal software analysis: Two research challenges. In: Margaria, T., Steffen, B. (eds.) ISoLA 2014, Part I. LNCS, vol. 8802, pp. 527–529. Springer, Heidelberg (2014)
3. Hinchey, M.: Software (Must) change. In: Margaria, T., Steffen, B. (eds.) ISoLA 2014, Part I. LNCS, vol. 8802, pp. 538–540. Springer, Heidelberg (2014)
4. Wirsing, M., Hölzl, M.: Formal methods for collective adaptive ensembles. In: Margaria, T., Steffen, B. (eds.) ISoLA 2014, Part I. LNCS, vol. 8802, pp. 518–520. Springer, Heidelberg (2014)
5. Legay, A.: Mastering changes: Some research topics. In: Margaria, T., Steffen, B. (eds.) ISoLA 2014, Part I. LNCS, vol. 8802, pp. 530–532. Springer, Heidelberg (2014)
6. Margaria, T.: The change of change. In: Margaria, T., Steffen, B. (eds.) ISoLA 2014, Part I. LNCS, vol. 8802, pp. 541–543. Springer, Heidelberg (2014)
7. Margaria, T., Steffen, B.: Simplicity as a Driver for Agile Innovation. Computer 43 (2010)
8. Rensink, A.: Forever software. In: Margaria, T., Steffen, B. (eds.) ISoLA 2014, Part I. LNCS, vol. 8802, pp. 535–537. Springer, Heidelberg (2014)
9. Tripakis, S.: Compositional model-based system design as a foundation for mastering change. In: Margaria, T., Steffen, B. (eds.) ISoLA 2014, Part I. LNCS, vol. 8802, pp. 524–526. Springer, Heidelberg (2014)

Formal Methods
for Collective Adaptive Ensembles

Martin Wirsing and Matthias Hölzl

Institut für Informatik
Ludwig-Maximilians-Universität München
{martin.wirsing,matthias.hoelzl}@ifi.lmu.de

Modern ICT technologies such as the internet, the cloud, and mobile devices lead to the development of more and more decentralized and distributed systems which operate in open and non-deterministic environments and interact with humans or other devices and systems in elaborate ways. Such systems are often called *ensembles* (for an overview see [9]). Socio-technical systems such as ICT-supported "smart cities" (see e.g. [13]). and cyber-physical systems such as sensory swarm and bio-cyber systems can be seen as special cases of ensembles (for an overview see [4]).

Mastering change is one of the main characteristics and challenges for ensembles: ensembles have to adapt to changing environments and changing requirements. Ensembles have often to cope with the change of their population: members can leave the ensemble whereas other entities can become part of the ensemble. Typically all these changes have to occur without redeployment and without interruption of the ensemble's functionality.

Although more and more ensemble systems are developed, foundations for systematically constructing and analyzing ensembles are missing. The existing foundational methods typically cannot deal with the dynamically changing nature of ensembles and they are difficult to scale to the size of ensembles. Foundations are needed also to ensure security and privacy of the data collected by the ensembles and to analyze and evaluate systemic failure modes, i.e., failures that cannot be traced unambiguously to a single component.

To tackle these challenges several disciplines may contribute foundational methods:

Concurrent Systems: The area of concurrent systems deals with problems such as enabling and limiting concurrency, access to shared resources, avoidance of deadlocks and other anomalies, or communication between processes. Research in concurrent systems often employs formalisms and techniques such as Petri nets, process calculi, coordination models and languages. Logics serve to specify the behaviour systems, ranging from modal and temporal logics to higher-order logics and term rewriting. E.g. recent results include the Linda-based language SCEL [5] for specifying ensembles and approaches for black-box and white-box adaptation [10,3].

Quantitative and Qualitative Analysis: A main focus is the qualitative and quantitative analysis of systems exploiting such notions as bisimilarity of different processes or reasoning on stochastic properties of systems consisting of many equivalent processes. Challenges and a promising approach for dealing

T. Margaria and B. Steffen (Eds.): ISoLA 2014, Part I, LNCS 8802, pp. 518–520, 2014.

with adaptation of ensembles are described in [8] and [2]. Example results include applications to robot swarms [20] to smart cities [7].

Adaptive Systems: The area of adaptive systems is increasingly inspired by nature- or socially-inspired solutions, such as swarm computing [6] and electronic institutions [14], and also focuses on systems consisting of interacting entities, but is more concerned with the reaction of whole systems or individual actors in a system to a changing environment. Research in this area is often focused on the control of a dynamically changing system by feedback loops [17], on the emergence and control of self-organized behaviours [11], and in general on the "laws" and contexts that influence the evolution of the systems properties and the individuals' behaviour [16].

Self-Awareness: Concentrating more closely on the individual entities in a system, research in self-awareness investigates models needed by agents operating in an open and changing environment to successfully achieve their goals and to cooperate with other agents. Many formalisms from artificial intelligence, knowledge representation and reasoning, or machine learning are used, e.g., logical and action calculi [15], Bayesian networks [12] or reinforcement learning [19], and research often focuses on the application of metacognitive methods to improve the behaviour of individual agents or the social interactions between agents [1].

While these methods provide starting points for further investigations, none of them is currently capable of addressing the scale and amount of dynamic change in ensembles. FOMAC [18] will be an ideal venue to publish further foundational research that contributes to mastering these challenges.

Acknowledgements. This work has been partially sponsored by the FET-IST project FP7-257414 ASCENS.

References

1. Anderson, M.L., Perlis, D.: Logic, self-awareness and self-improvement: the metacognitive loop and the problem of brittleness. J. Log. Comput. 15(1), 21–40 (2005)
2. Bortolussi, L., Nicola, R.D., Gast, N., Gilmore, S., Hillston, J., Massink, M., Tribastone, M.: A Quantitative Approach to the Design and Analysis of Collective Adaptive Systems. In: 1st FoCAS Workshop on Fundamentals of Collective Systems, Taormina, Sicily, Italy (September 2013)
3. Bruni, R., Corradini, A., Gadducci, F., Lluch Lafuente, A., Vandin, A.: A Conceptual Framework for Adaptation. In: de Lara, J., Zisman, A. (eds.) Fundamental Approaches to Software Engineering. LNCS, vol. 7212, pp. 240–254. Springer, Heidelberg (2012)
4. Cengarle, M.V., Trngren, M., Bensalem, S., McDermid, J., Sangiovanni-Vincentelli, A., Passerone, R.: Structuring of CPS Domain: Characteristics, Trends, Challenges and Opportunities associated with CPS (2014), http://www.cyphers.eu/sites/default/files/D2.2.pdf (last accessed: August 03, 2014)

5. De Nicola, R., Lluch Lafuente, A., Loreti, M., Morichetta, A., Pugliese, R., Senni, V., Tiezzi, F.: Programming and Verifying Component Ensembles. In: Bensalem, S., Lakhneck, Y., Legay, A. (eds.) From Programs to Systems. LNCS, vol. 8415, pp. 69–83. Springer, Heidelberg (2014)
6. Dorigo, M., Stützle, T.: Ant Colony Optimization. The MIT Press (2004)
7. Fricker, C., Gast, N.: Incentives and redistribution in homogeneous bike-sharing systems with stations of finite capacity. EURO Journal on Transportation and Logistics, 1–31 (2014), http://dx.doi.org/10.1007/s13676-014-0053-5
8. Hillston, J.: Challenges for Quantitative Analysis of Collective Adaptive Systems. In: Abadi, M., Lluch Lafuente, A. (eds.) TGC 2013. LNCS, vol. 8358, pp. 14–21. Springer, Heidelberg (2014)
9. Hölzl, M., Rauschmayer, A., Wirsing, M.: Engineering of Software-Intensive Systems: State of the Art and Research Challenges. In: Wirsing, M., Banâtre, J.-P., Hölzl, M., Rauschmayer, A. (eds.) Soft-Ware Intensive Systems. LNCS, vol. 5380, pp. 1–44. Springer, Heidelberg (2008)
10. Hölzl, M., Wirsing, M.: Towards a system model for ensembles. In: Agha, G., Danvy, O., Meseguer, J. (eds.) Formal Modeling: Actors, Open Systems, Biological Systems. LNCS, vol. 7000, pp. 241–261. Springer, Heidelberg (2011)
11. Kauffman, S.: Origins of Order: Self-Organization and Selection in Evolution. Oxford University Press (1993)
12. Koller, D., Friedman, N.: Probabilistic Graphical Models - Principles and Techniques. MIT Press (2009)
13. Miorandi, D., De Pellegrini, F., Mayora, O., Giaffreda, R.: Collective Adaptive Systems: Scenarios, Approaches and Challenges (2010), ftp://ftp.cordis.europa.eu/pub/fp7/ict/docs/fet-proactive/shapefetip-cas10_en.pdf (last accessed: August 3, 2014)
14. Pitt, J., Schaumeier, J., Artikis, A.: Coordination, conventions and the self-organisation of sustainable institutions. In: Kinny, D., Hsu, J.Y.-j., Governatori, G., Ghose, A.K. (eds.) PRIMA 2011. LNCS, vol. 7047, pp. 202–217. Springer, Heidelberg (2011)
15. Reiter, R.: Knowledge in Action: Logical Foundations for Specifying and Implementing Dynamical Systems. MIT Press (July 2001)
16. Schuster, D., Rosi, A., Mamei, M., Springer, T., Endler, M., Zambonelli, F.: Pervasive social context: Taxonomy and survey. ACM TIST 4(3), 46 (2013)
17. Serbedzija, N. (ed.): Reflective Approach for Real-Life Computing. Reflect Project (2011), http://reflect.pst.ifi.lmu.de/images/pdf/D7.3A-REFLECT-Monograph.pdf
18. Steffen, B.: LNCS Transaction on Foundations for Mastering Change: Preliminary Manifesto. In: Margaria, T., Steffen, B. (eds.) ISoLA 2014. LNCS, vol. 8802, pp. 514–517. Springer, Heidelberg (2014)
19. Sutton, R.S., Barto, A.G.: Reinforcement Learning: An Introduction. MIT Press (1998)
20. Wirsing, M., Hölzl, M., Tribastone, M., Zambonelli, F.: ASCENS: Engineering Autonomic Service-Component Ensembles. In: Beckert, B., Bonsangue, M.M. (eds.) FMCO 2011. LNCS, vol. 7542, pp. 1–24. Springer, Heidelberg (2012)

Current Issues on Model-Based Software Quality Assurance for Mastering Change

Michael Felderer

University of Innsbruck, Innsbruck, Austria
michael.felderer@uibk.ac.at

Quality of software and software-based systems is playing an increasingly important role for the success of products [1]. As requirements to products inevitably change over time, for instance, new or adapted functionalities, technologies or regulations have to be taken into account, also software has to change or its quality decays. As software also becomes more complex and interconnected, mastering software quality for rapidly changing software products is challenging and proactive measures are needed to counter quality decay during software evolution. A promising cornerstone to continuously control quality in this dynamic and evolving context are quality models which provide an abstract and analyzable view of software artifacts with the objective to describe, assess and/or predict quality [2,3]. Quality models in this broad sense comprise all types of models supporting analytical quality assurance like hierarchical quality models, test models, defect models or reliability growth models. These models have a high potential to improve effectiveness and efficiency of analytical quality assurance to cope with software change, as they for instance support decisions, automation and re-use. Nevertheless, their acceptance and spread in the software industry is still rather low, as there are several unresolved issues that have to be addressed by upcoming research. Suitable solutions to model-based software quality assurance for analysing the state of the software quality are especially required for the following current issues:

- *Creation and maintenance of models*: One main obstacle to dissemination of model-based approaches in general, is the overhead to initially create and to continuously maintain models. To lower this barrier, support to either automatize model creation and maintenance or to clearly simplify these tasks is required. Former, can for instance be supported by machine learning technologies and formal methods. A promising approach in this direction is Active Continuous Quality Control [4], where incremental active automata learning technology is applied to infer evolving behavioral automata. Latter, can be supported by modern modeling workbenches for domain specific languages [5] which provide powerful model engineering support to simplify manual model creation and maintenance. In quality assurance, domain specific languages have recently been applied for modeling tests [6,7].
- *Integration of analytics*: Software analytics, i.e., the use of analysis, software data, and systematic reasoning for managers and software engineers with the aim of empowering stakeholders of software development to make better decisions is an area of explosive growth [8]. Especially, for software quality

T. Margaria and B. Steffen (Eds.): ISoLA 2014, Part I, LNCS 8802, pp. 521–523, 2014.

purposes analytics is promising to evaluate the current quality status, to predict future statuses, and to continuously monitor quality. Analytics normally combines some degree of automation with human involvement. The integration of analytics with available quality models could foster this combination and lead to new visualization and interpretation of software engineering data to control quality of evolving software.

– *Alignment of quality models with unstructured artifacts*: In an industrial setting, quality models never capture relevant quality information completely, but have to be aligned with material (usually documents) of an unstructured nature (usually text) like requirements specifications or test reports. Information retrieval, as for instance applied in [9] is a promising approach to support this alignment for mastering change.

– *Support for extra-functional aspects*: Extra-functional aspects like security, safety, performance, or sustainability [10] require specific modeling approaches to cope with change. So far, this problem has not adequately been tackled for all types of quality models. For instance, further research on model-based (regression) testing of extra-functional aspects is required [11].

– *Balance between quality and risk*: Risk is the degree to which a product does not satisfy the stated and implied needs of its various stakeholders and thus represents potential damages and losses [12]. The concept of risk supports decisions on good enough quality for software release or changes and relates quality investments to budget and time. Recently, risk has especially been applied to support testing in so called risk-based testing approaches [13], but further research on the balance between quality and risk is required.

– *Justification by empirical evidence*: For industrial application, evidence following the strict guidelines of empirical software engineering [14] has to be provided to show in which context specific model-based quality assurance approaches actually provide support to master change, and what the practical limitations of these approaches are. Empirical studies on model-based quality assurance in general and especially also on its effectiveness and efficiency are still rare. An exemplary empirical investigation for hierarchical quality models is provided in [15] and for test models in [16].

Suitable solutions to the issues mentioned before will heavily improve model-based quality assurance of software and contribute to mastering change in terms of the manifesto of the LNCS Transactions on Foundations for Mastering Change (FoMaC) [17]. FoMaC is concerned with mastering change during the whole system lifecycle at various conceptual levels, in particular during meta modeling, modeling and design, implementation, runtime, as well as maintenance, evolution and migration. Solutions to the issues raised in this paper support mastering change in all these areas. For instance, the creation and maintenance of quality models as well as their alignment with requirements address change aspects during meta modeling, modeling and design, but also during implementation; support for extra-functional aspects and analytics as well as balance between quality promote chanage aspects at runtime as well as during maintenance, evolution and migration. Finally, the justification by empirical evidence is a cross-cutting issue to evaluate technology transfer in any of these areas.

References

1. Breu, R., Kuntzmann-Combelles, A., Felderer, M.: New perspectives on software quality. IEEE Software 31(1), 32–38 (2014)
2. Breu, R., Agreiter, B., Farwick, M., Felderer, M., Hafner, M., Innerhofer-Oberperfler, F.: Living models-ten principles for change-driven software engineering. Int. J. Software and Informatics 5(1-2), 267–290 (2011)
3. Wagner, S.: Software Product Quality Control. Springer (2014)
4. Windmüller, S., Neubauer, J., Steffen, B., Howar, F., Bauer, O.: Active continuous quality control. In: Proceedings of the 16th International ACM Sigsoft Symposium on Component-Based Software Engineering, pp. 111–120. ACM (2013)
5. Voelter, M., Benz, S., Dietrich, C., Engelmann, B., Helander, M., Kats, L.C., Visser, E., Wachsmuth, G.: DSL Engineering-Designing, Implementing and Using Domain-Specific Languages (2013) dslbook.org
6. Baker, P., Dai, Z.R., Grabowski, J., Haugen, Ø., Schieferdecker, I., Williams, C.: Model-driven testing. Springer (2008)
7. Felderer, M., Breu, R., Chimiak-Opoka, J., Breu, M., Schupp, F.: Concepts for model-based requirements testing of service oriented systems. In: Proceedings of the IASTED International Conference, vol. 642, p. 018 (2009)
8. Menzies, T., Zimmermann, T.: Software analytics: So what? IEEE Software 30(4), 31–37 (2013)
9. Yadla, S., Hayes, J.H., Dekhtyar, A.: Tracing requirements to defect reports: an application of information retrieval techniques. Innovations in Systems and Software Engineering 1(2), 116–124 (2005)
10. Penzenstadler, B., Raturi, A., Richardson, D., Tomlinson, B.: Safety, security, now sustainability: the non-functional requirement for the 21st century (2014)
11. Häser, F., Felderer, M., Breu, R.: Software paradigms, assessment types and non-functional requirements in model-based integration testing: a systematic literature review. In: Proceedings of the 18th International Conference on Evaluation and Assessment in Software Engineering, p. 29. ACM (2014)
12. Wieczorek, M., Vos, D., Bons, H.: Systems and Software Quality. Springer (2014)
13. Felderer, M., Schieferdecker, I.: A taxonomy of risk-based testing. STTT (2014), doi: 10.1007/s10009-014-0332-3
14. Wohlin, C., Runeson, P., Höst, M., Ohlsson, M.C., Regnell, B., Wesslén, A.: Experimentation in software engineering. Springer (2012)
15. Wagner, S., Lochmann, K., Heinemann, L., Kläs, M., Trendowicz, A., Plösch, R., Seidl, A., Goeb, A., Streit, J.: The quamoco product quality modelling and assessment approach. In: Proceedings of the 2012 International Conference on Software Engineering, pp. 1133–1142. IEEE (2012)
16. Pretschner, A., Prenninger, W., Wagner, S., Kühnel, C., Baumgartner, M., Sostawa, B., Zölch, R., Stauner, T.: One evaluation of model-based testing and its automation. In: Proceedings of the 27th International Conference on Software Engineering, pp. 392–401. ACM (2005)
17. Steffen, B.: LNCS Transactions on Foundations for Mastering Change: Preliminary Manifesto. In: Margaria, T., Steffen, B. (eds.) ISoLA 2014, Part I. LNCS, vol. 8802, pp. 514–517. Springer, Heidelberg (2014)

Compositional Model-Based System Design
as a Foundation for Mastering Change

Stavros Tripakis

UC Berkeley and Aalto University
stavros.tripakis@gmail.com

Building large and complex *cyber-physical systems*, from automotive controllers, to pacemakers, to smart power grids, cannot be done by trial-and-error, as this is neither cost effective nor safe. *Model-based design* (e.g., see [10]) is a system design approach which advocates building models of the system under design, instead of system prototypes. Models are cheaper and faster to build than prototypes, thus yielding a more efficient design process.

Research-wise, model-based design has three elements:

1. *Modeling*, which addresses the problem of how to express in the best possible way the system that we want to design. Coming up with the right languages to capture different types of systems from a variety of domains (automotive, electronics, energy, health care, biology, etc.) is a major research challenge.
2. *Analysis*, which addresses the problem of how to ensure that what we designed is really what we want. A variety of analysis techniques are available to achieve this goal, starting with simulation, the workhorse of system design, all the way to exhaustive techniques such as formal verification and model checking (e.g., see [14] for a survey of verification techniques for timed and hybrid automata, or the textbooks [5,2] for a thorough presentation of the topic). These techniques allow to test the model, discover bugs, and fix them early enough in the design process.
3. *Implementation*, which addresses the problem of how to generate, ideally fully automatically, working systems from the design models. The goal is that the resulting system preserves the properties of the original model. This is important, since we would like to avoid as much as possible having to test the system itself. Ideally, the system should be equivalent to the model, so that, assuming that the model is correct, and that the generation process is not buggy, the generated system is *correct by construction*. The challenge in achieving this goal is that there is often a semantic gap between high-level models and low-level implementations. For instance, the model may assume a synchronous semantics, whereas the implementation is asynchronous. Some preliminary research toward bridging such gaps can be found in [4,17,16].

Model-based design raises a number of significant research challenges (what are the right modeling languages? how to combat state explosion during analysis? how to bridge the semantic gaps during implementation? etc.). Making progress in addressing these challenges is necessary, but by no means sufficient. Systems are rarely built from scratch. They evolve. New systems are built as newer versions of older systems. The new system reuses many of the components of one

T. Margaria and B. Steffen (Eds.): ISoLA 2014, Part I, LNCS 8802, pp. 524–526, 2014.
© Springer-Verlag Berlin Heidelberg 2014

or more existing systems. Systems are often built by many people organized in teams with different backgrounds. Communication between such teams is often difficult. Some systems are developed by open communities of volunteers with loose organization. In most cases systems are *open* in the sense that they must inter-operate with other (existing or to be developed) systems, about which little is known. This is one of the reasons why system requirements often change. The assumptions about the environment in which the system is supposed to operate change over time, and therefore the requirements must change as well. In a world of millions of programmers and billions of inter-connected devices, these trends can only intensify. Consequently, the science of system design must encompass variety and change as its primary goals. This is why a journal on the *Foundations of Mastering Change* [13] is timely.

Compositionality is a key element for mastering change. Compositionality is a heavily used term with many meanings. It can be seen as a cross-cutting concern, affecting all elements of model-based design. We need compositional modeling methods, since large and complex models cannot be built monolithically, but by somehow assembling submodels (e.g., see [18,3,12]). We also need compositional analysis frameworks such as *assume-guarantee reasoning* (e.g., see [11,6,8,1]) or *interface theories* (e.g., see [7,15]) in order to break up large verification tasks into smaller and computationally easier subtasks. We also need compositional implementation methods, for instance, *modular code generation* [9], which allows to generate code from part of a model, say, when this part is modified, without having to re-generate code from the entire model.

The above are some of the topics that could be addressed in this new journal.

Acknowledgements. This work was partially supported by the Academy of Finland and by the NSF via projects *COSMOI: Compositional System Modeling with Interfaces* and *ExCAPE: Expeditions in Computer Augmented Program Engineering*. This work was also partially supported by IBM and United Technologies Corporation (UTC) via the iCyPhy consortium.

References

1. Alur, R., Henzinger, T.: Reactive modules. Formal Methods in System Design 15, 7–48 (1999)
2. Baier, C., Katoen, J.-P.: Principles of Model Checking. MIT Press (2008)
3. Broman, D., Brooks, C., Greenberg, L., Lee, E.A., Tripakis, S., Wetter, M., Masin, M.: Determinate Composition of FMUs for Co-Simulation. In: 13th ACM & IEEE Intl. Conf. on Embedded Software, EMSOFT 2013 (2013)
4. Caspi, P., Scaife, N., Sofronis, C., Tripakis, S.: Semantics-Preserving Multitask Implementation of Synchronous Programs. ACM Transactions on Embedded Computing Systems (TECS) 7(2), 1–40 (2008),
   http://www.eecs.berkeley.edu/~stavros/papers/acm-tecs08.pdf
5. Clarke, E., Grumberg, O., Peled, D.: Model Checking. MIT Press (2000)
6. Clarke, E.M., Long, D.E., McMillan, K.L.: Compositional model checking. In: Fourth Annual Symposium on Logic in Computer Science (1989)

7. de Alfaro, L., Henzinger, T.: Interface automata. In: Foundations of Software Engineering (FSE). ACM Press (2001)
8. Henzinger, T., Qadeer, S., Rajamani, S.: You assume, we guarantee: Methodology and case studies. In: Vardi, M.Y. (ed.) CAV 1998. LNCS, vol. 1427, pp. 440–451. Springer, Heidelberg (1998)
9. Lublinerman, R., Szegedy, C., Tripakis, S.: Modular Code Generation from Synchronous Block Diagrams – Modularity vs. Code Size. In: 36th ACM Symposium on Principles of Programming Languages (POPL 2009), pp. 78–89. ACM (2009)
10. Nicolescu, G., Mosterman, P.J.: Model-Based Design for Embedded Systems. CRC Press (2009)
11. Pnueli, A.: In transition from global to modular temporal reasoning about programs. In: Logics and Models of Concurrent Systems, sub-series F: Computer and System Science, pp. 123–144. Springer (1985)
12. Reineke, J., Tripakis, S.: Basic Problems in Multi-View Modeling. In: Tools and Algorithms for the Construction and Analysis of Systems – TACAS (2014)
13. Steffen, B.: LNCS transactions on foundations for mastering change: Preliminary manifesto. In: Margaria, T., Steffen, B. (eds.) ISoLA 2014, Part I. LNCS, vol. 8802, pp. 514–517. Springer, Heidelberg (2014)
14. Tripakis, S., Dang, T.: Modeling, Verification and Testing using Timed and Hybrid Automata. In: Mosterman, P., Nicolescu, G. (eds.) Model-Based Design for Embedded Systems. CRC Press (2009)
15. Tripakis, S., Lickly, B., Henzinger, T.A., Lee, E.A.: A Theory of Synchronous Relational Interfaces. ACM Transactions on Programming Languages and Systems (TOPLAS) 33(4) (2011)
16. Tripakis, S., Limaye, R., Ravindran, K., Wang, G.: On tokens and signals: Bridging the semantic gap between dataflow models and hardware implementations. In: International Conference on Embedded Computer Systems: Architectures, Modeling and Simulation – SAMOS XIV (2014)
17. Tripakis, S., Pinello, C., Benveniste, A., Sangiovanni-Vincentelli, A., Caspi, P., Natale, M.D.: Implementing Synchronous Models on Loosely Time-Triggered Architectures. IEEE Transactions on Computers 57(10), 1300–1314 (2008)
18. Tripakis, S., Stergiou, C., Shaver, C., Lee, E.A.: A modular formal semantics for Ptolemy. Mathematical Structures in Computer Science 23, 834–881 (2013)

Managing Change in Formal Software Analysis: Two Research Challenges

Reiner Hähnle

Technische Universität Darmstadt
Department of Computer Science
haehnle@cs.tu-darmstadt.de

In the field of formal analysis of software systems dramatic progress could be witnessed in the last decade or so. Formal verification of simple safety properties often can be achieved in a fully automated manner for non-trivial, commercial code [3]. It can be expected that the verification of generic safety properties (for example, buffer under-/overflows, null pointer accesses) will soon become part of the compilation tool chain. Changing compilation targets tend to be managed simply by recompilation, so: where is the need for managing change in formal software analysis? Let us try to give an answer in the form of two research challenges.

Functional Verification. In contrast to checking of safety properties, functional verification still requires vast efforts. True, even highly complex system software can be formally verified when sufficient effort is spent, as is demonstrated (for example) by the L4.verified [5] and Verisoft [2] projects. However, this typically requires serious effort (ranging between several person months and person decades), involving formal specification and verification specialists. Even if some effort can be spent, it remains a central problem of current verification methods that they are not robust in presence of changes in the verification target: already small changes can invalidate large parts of an existing verification argument and might require to redo much of the verification effort. But, as clearly spelled out in the *FoMaC Manifesto* [6], change occurs continually during software development, and formal methods must cope with it, if they are to be relevant. Based on current technology, formal verification is simply far too disruptive in the context of agile development processes and can only be considered as a *post hoc* activtity. This renders functional verification impractical for any application outside extremely safety-critical systems. Therefore, we pose the following challenge:

> *Make formal specification and verification non-disruptive in the presence of changes in the verification target. Specifically, integrate formal verification with standard change management mechanisms such as version control, regression testing, etc.*

As one recent example of the line of work we have in mind, consider [4], which presents a technique for compositional, contract-based, formal verification in presence of constant evolutionary changes to the verification target.

T. Margaria and B. Steffen (Eds.): ISoLA 2014, Part I, LNCS 8802, pp. 527–529, 2014.
© Springer-Verlag Berlin Heidelberg 2014

Resource Analysis. Resource analysis is typically fully automatic and requires little or only generic specifications [1]. This makes it a highly interesting and useful alternative to full verification in case when the latter cannot be achieved or is too expensive. But resource analysis became a central issue also for a different reason: requirememts and code are not the only aspects of a system that can change. In recent years, the need to deal with dynamically changing computing environments, i.e., resources, became a pivotal issue. This is caused by three nearly parallel developments: the move from single- to multi-core architectures to compensate for the breakdown of Moore's law; the advent of cloud computing technology that renders available resources highly elastic; and the availability of sensing, computing, and networking capabilities in just any kind of technical artifact (*"cyber-physical system"*). As a consequence, modern software must be able to take advantage of different resource profiles that even might change dynamically during execution. To this end it is of prime importance to be able to analyze and optimize the resource consumption of software. This goes far beyond the classical topics of worst-case execution time and memory allocation, but includes parameters such as bandwidth, latency, degree of parallelism, and, of growing importance, energy consumption. It must be possible to connect the results of resource analysis with optimization of system configurations and, ultimately, with dynamic adaptation mechanisms. Hence, our second research challenge:

> *Extend resource analysis to a comprehensive set of environmental parameters including network and energy aspects. Make analysis methods incremental and change-aware. Use analysis results to generate optimized system configurations. Align these with dynamic software adaptation mechanisms with the aim of optimized resource consumption in a dynamically changing environment.*

References

1. Albert, E., Arenas, P., Flores-Montoya, A., Genaim, S., Gómez-Zamalloa, M., Martin-Martin, E., Puebla, G., Román-Díez, G.: SACO: Static analyzer for concurrent objects. In: Ábrahám, E., Havelund, K. (eds.) TACAS 2014 (ETAPS). LNCS, vol. 8413, pp. 562–567. Springer, Heidelberg (2014)
2. Alkassar, E., Hillebrand, M.A., Paul, W., Petrova, E.: Automated verification of a small hypervisor. In: Leavens, G.T., O'Hearn, P., Rajamani, S.K. (eds.) VSTTE 2010. LNCS, vol. 6217, pp. 40–54. Springer, Heidelberg (2010)
3. Beyer, D.: Status report on software verification. In: Ábrahám, E., Havelund, K. (eds.) TACAS 2014 (ETAPS). LNCS, vol. 8413, pp. 373–388. Springer, Heidelberg (2014)
4. Bubel, R., Hähnle, R., Pelevina, M.: Fully abstract operation contracts. In: Margaria, T., Steffen, B. (eds.) ISoLA 2014, Part II. LNCS, vol. 8803, pp. 120–134. Springer, Heidelberg (2014)

5. Klein, G., Andronick, J., Elphinstone, K., Heiser, G., Cock, D., Derrin, P., Elkaduwe, D., Engelhardt, K., Kolanski, R., Norrish, M., Sewell, T., Tuch, H., Winwood, S.: seL4: Formal verification of an operating system kernel. Communications of the ACM 53(6), 107–115 (2010)
6. Steffen, B.: LNCS transaction on foundations for mastering change: Preliminary manifesto. In: Margaria, T., Steffen, B. (eds.) ISoLA 2014, Part I. LNCS, vol. 8802, pp. 514–517. Springer, Heidelberg (2014)

Mastering Changes: Some Research Topics

Axel Legay

INRIA Rennes - Bretagne Atlantique

1 Position

Over the past, system design was mostly organized around a vertically integrated development, supporting in-house activities. There, the system was defined as a stone-block entity impermeable to changes. In this context, rigorous software design was a very static process which mostly consisted in exploring parts of the system via techniques known as testing or formal verification [CGP99].

Nowadays, the situation has drastically changed. Indeed, several industrial sectors involving, e.g, complex (embedded, or cyber physical) systems have recently experienced deep changes in their organization, aerospace and automotive being the most prominent examples. These sectors have now evolved into more specialized, horizontally structured companies: *E*quipment *S*uppliers (ESs) and *O*riginal *E*quipment *M*anufacturers (OEMs). OEMs perform system design and integration by importing/combining/reusing entire subsystems (also called components) provided by ESs. Depending of the situation and the needs of the client, different subsystems can be added/removed on demand during the entire lifetime of a product. In this context, the ability to efficiently mastering changes becomes as central as the verification problem. This situation will, at minimum, generates the following research activities already outlined in [Ste].

- The separation of concerns calls for new system models and high level languages that allows us not only to capture the behavior of a global entity, but also to reason (at fine granularity) on the relationship between its components. In this context, the use of meta models, interfaces [LKF02, AH01], or contracts [SBW11, EFN$^+$14] to reason at a high level and separate the concerns will become crucial. In the same spirit, synthesis will definitively play a crucial role. Particularly, we forseen the use of such technique to synthesize the possibly dynamic interactions between components of a given system with the objective of satisfying a given property [BBB$^+$11, ?]. Synthesis will also be used to reduce the burden in verifying complex systems [GMS14]. Still in the same spirit, we will have to take into account that large-size systems are now deployed over the internet (medical devices, energy saving systems, ...). This calls for new language paradigm and new models that take the resource constraints of this material into account.
- As the relationship between components may be variable and/or adaptive and dynamic, we also forseen that the combination of models used to describe components's behaviors (transition systems, etc) with those used to describe variability (feature diagrams [Bat05, CBH11], ...) and adaptive changes will

T. Margaria and B. Steffen (Eds.): ISoLA 2014, Part I, LNCS 8802, pp. 530–532, 2014.

become central. Initial move in the context of product lines was taken with Feature Transition Systems [CHS+10]. Other works can be found, e.g, [CA05, JLM+12], or in [CdLG+09] that poses the foundations for adaptivity. The challenge is that those new models should be flexible enough so that adding/ removing parts of the system (or parts of its behavior) does not call for an entirely new modelisation – hence gaining in productivity. This vision, combined with the one in the previoius item, should be impacted at the high language level, and formalism such as UML will certainly encompass more and more variability aspects in a near future.

- New metrics will be needed to quantify the impact of changes [vBKPR14]. This will be important when the designer will have to decided which change is best for her design (cost, reliability, ...). Existing methodologies mostly rely on qualitative or Boolean metrics, but in a world of compromises and optimizations, it is likely that quantities become a first citizen.
- New runtime monitoring techniques [?] that are able to detect changes on the fly and to react when needed (correction, information, counter example, ...), see e.g., [GMS12]. Such techniques will be of particular interest when the whole state-space of the system cannot be characterized in advance, which is the case for most CPS or Systems of Systems. There the principle of self-adaptivity to potentially unknown changes becomes crucial [FDC14]. Observe that those techniques will certainly have to be combined with more accurate verification techniques as this is the case in [SS12].
- The design of new verification techniques that not only allows us to verify parts of the system in an efficient manner, but also quantify the satisfaction with respect to a set of requirements. There, techniques such as statistical model checking [LDB10] and prediction/learning algorithms may be exploited at runtime and/or to overcome undecidability and state-space explosion. Additionally, new formal techniques that are able to take into account the impact of changes will be needed. The latter will avoid us to re-perform the entire verication process for each changes. This is particularly crucial as the system may be part of a line of similar products (for which the work should be done at a high granularity level) and many changes may be applied to the system during its lifetime. Also, some product may be deployed on limited resources, which call for a new dimension in terms of efficiency.

References

[AH01]   de Alfaro, L., Henzinger, T.A.: Interface theories for component-based design. In: Henzinger, T.A., Kirsch, C.M. (eds.) EMSOFT 2001. LNCS, vol. 2211, pp. 148–165. Springer, Heidelberg (2001)

[Bat05]   Batory, D.S.: Feature Models, Grammars, and Propositional Formulas. In: Proceedings of the 9th Int. Software Product Line Conference (SPLC), pp. 7–20 (2005)

[BBB+11]   Basu, A., Bensalem, S., Bozga, M., Combaz, J., Jaber, M., Nguyen, T., Sifakis, J.: Rigorous component-based system design using the bip framework. IEEE Software 28(3), 41–48 (2011)

[CA05]   Czarnecki, K., Antkiewicz, M.: Mapping features to models: A template
            approach based on superimposed variants. In: Glück, R., Lowry, M. (eds.)
            GPCE 2005. LNCS, vol. 3676, pp. 422–437. Springer, Heidelberg (2005)
[CBH11]   Classen, A., Boucher, Q., Heymans, P.: A text-based approach to feature
            modelling: Syntax and semantics of tvl. Sci. Comput. Program. 76(12),
            1130–1143 (2011)
[CdLG⁺09]   Cheng, B.H.C., et al.: Software engineering for self-adaptive systems: A re-
            search roadmap. In: Cheng, B.H.C., de Lemos, R., Giese, H., Inverardi, P.,
            Magee, J. (eds.) Software Engineering for Self-Adaptive Systems. LNCS,
            vol. 5525, pp. 1–26. Springer, Heidelberg (2009)
[CGP99]   Clarke, E., Grumberg, O., Peled, D.: Model Checking. MIT Press (1999)
[CHS⁺10]   Classen, A., Heymans, P., Schobbens, P.-Y., Legay, A., Raskin, J.-F.:
            Model checking lots of systems: Efficient verification of temporal prop-
            erties in software product lines. In: ICSE 32, pp. 335–344. IEEE (2010)
[EFN⁺14]   Estler, H.-C., Furia, C.A., Nordio, M., Piccioni, M., Meyer, B.: Contracts
            in practice. In: Jones, C., Pihlajasaari, P., Sun, J. (eds.) FM 2014. LNCS,
            vol. 8442, pp. 230–246. Springer, Heidelberg (2014)
[FDC14]   Fredericks, E.M., De Vries, B., Cheng, B.H.C.: Towards run-time adapta-
            tion of test cases for self-adaptive systems in the face of uncertainty. In:
            SEAMS, pp. 17–26. ACM (2014)
[GMS12]   Ghezzi, C., Mocci, A., Sangiorgio, M.: Runtime monitoring of component
            changes with spy@runtime. In: ICSE, pp. 1403–1406. IEEE (2012)
[GMS14]   Ghezzi, C., Mocci, A., Sangiorgio, M.: Synthesis of infinite-state abstrac-
            tions and their use for software validation. In: Iida, S., Meseguer, J.,
            Ogata, K. (eds.) Specification, Algebra, and Software. LNCS, vol. 8373, pp.
            276–295. Springer, Heidelberg (2014)
[JLM⁺12]   Jörges, S., Lamprecht, A.-L., Margaria, T., Schaefer, I., Steffen, B.: A
            constraint-based variability modeling framework. STTT 14(5), 511–530
            (2012)
[LDB10]   Legay, A., Delahaye, B., Bensalem, S.: Statistical model checking: An
            overview. In: Barringer, H., Falcone, Y., Finkbeiner, B., Havelund, K.,
            Lee, I., Pace, G., Roşu, G., Sokolsky, O., Tillmann, N. (eds.) RV 2010.
            LNCS, vol. 6418, pp. 122–135. Springer, Heidelberg (2010)
[LKF02]   Li, H.C., Krishnamurthi, S., Fisler, K.: Interfaces for modular feature ver-
            ification. In: ASE, pp. 195–204 (2002)
[SBW11]   Schroeder, A., Bauer, S.S., Wirsing, M.: A contract-based approach to
            adaptivity. J. Log. Algebr. Program. 80(3-5), 180–193 (2011)
[SS12]   Sharifloo, A.M., Spoletini, P.: LOVER: Light-weight fOrmal verification
            of adaptivE systems at run time. In: Păsăreanu, C.S., Salaün, G. (eds.)
            FACS 2012. LNCS, vol. 7684, pp. 170–187. Springer, Heidelberg (2013)
[Ste]   Steffen, B.: LNCS transactions on foundations for mastering change: Pre-
            liminary manifesto. In: Margaria, T., Steffen, B. (eds.) ISoLA 2014, Part
            I. LNCS, vol. 8802, pp. 514–517. Springer, Heidelberg (2014)
[vBKPR14]   van Breugel, F., Kashefi, E., Palamidessi, C., Rutten, J. (eds.): Horizons
            of the Mind. LNCS, vol. 8464. Springer, Heidelberg (2014)

Mastering Change @ Runtime*

Klaus Havelund

Jet Propulsion Laboratory
California Institute of Technology
California, USA

This brief paper is a response to a call [7] for opinion statements from members of the editorial board of the upcoming journal: *LNCS Transactions on Foundations for Mastering Change (FoMaC)*. In the call it says:

> *FoMaC intends to establish a forum for formal methods-based research that fosters a discipline for rigorously dealing with the nature of today's agile system development, which is characterized by unclear premises, unforeseen change, and the need for fast reaction, in a context of hard to control frame conditions, like third party components, network-problem, and attacks.*

The phases covered span from meta modeling to modeling and design, implementation, runtime and finally evolution/migration. In the extreme, all software correctness issues can be considered as purely change issues, where the fundamental question is the following: given a program P, potentially empty, will the addition of the program fragment Δ make $P + \Delta$ satisfy a property ψ? Program fragments Δ can here be understood liberally, as for example edit commands (replace these lines of code with these lines of code), refinements - as in stepwise program refinement suggested for wide-spectrum development languages such as VDM [2], aspects - as in aspect oriented programming, plans - as in planning (the Δ is a new plan), etc. As such, in the extreme, the topic of correctness under change can be considered as the well known topic of correctness. An interesting question is: what is the connection between the concept of change as a special topic and then the more general and traditional software correctness issue?

As is well known, analysis for insurance of correctness as well as security can be performed statically (of code structure) or dynamically (of execution traces). In the realm of static analysis, version control is of course a basic very useful technology. One can imagine version control systems being brought to the next level by being integrated with static analysis tools, explicitly supporting program refinement, as well as smart IDEs, which visually highlight changes as they are made in the editor. In general, the integration of specification, programming and verification, as explored for example in DAFNY [3], as well as in the earlier VDM [2], should in principle make change easier. This includes adoption of high-level programming languages such as SCALA [6].

However, we observe that ensuring correctness of software using static methods is extremely challenging, and therefore our systems should be constructed

---

* The work described in this publication was carried out at Jet Propulsion Laboratory, California Institute of Technology, under a contract with the National Aeronautics and Space Administration.

T. Margaria and B. Steffen (Eds.): ISoLA 2014, Part I, LNCS 8802, pp. 533–534, 2014.

to be robust in the face of errors at *runtime*. In the realm of dynamic analysis, one can distinguish between *detection* of change during runtime, and *causing* change during runtime. Detection of change can occur by monitoring a system's execution while checking its behavior against a formalized specification of expected behavior. Here a system can be considered as emitting a sequence of observable events, which are fed into a monitor, which as a second input takes a specification of expected behavior. The trace is then matched against the specification. Events in practice will carry data, and it must be possible to refer to data in specifications [4]. The specification can be written by humans, or it can be learned from nominal executions, also referred to as specification mining [5]. Properties can be expressed in various specification languages, ranging from state machines, regular expressions, temporal logics, rule-based systems to also include refinement-based notations as discussed previously.

Detection of a property violation can be used to cause a change of behavior by triggering fault-protection code, which steers the application out of a bad situation. The simplest possible fault-protection strategy is to reboot the system, a strategy which in practice is very common. At the other end of the scale is planning and scheduling techniques, which continuously adapt to the current situation. A planner, upon request, generates a new program (plan) to be executed for the next time period in order to achieve a given goal. Planning is related to program synthesis. In contrast to planning, program synthesis usually occurs before deployment and has more static nature, but in theory the two topics are closely related. The common theme for planning and synthesis is the exploration of new ways to write programs that make the correctness question, and thereby change question, less of an issue. For a survey relating verification and validation to planning and scheduling, see [1].

References

1. Bensalem, S., Havelund, K., Orlandini, A.: Verification and validation meet planning and scheduling. Software Tools for Technology Transfer (STTT) 16(1), 1–12 (2014)
2. Bjørner, D., Jones, C.B.: Formal Specification and Software Development. Prentice Hall International (1982) ISBN 0-13-880733-7
3. Dafny website, http://research.microsoft.com/en-us/projects/dafny
4. Havelund, K.: Monitoring with data automata. In: Margaria, T., Steffen, B. (eds.) ISoLA 2014, Part II. LNCS, vol. 8803, pp. 254–273. Springer, Heidelberg (2014)
5. Isberner, M., Howar, F., Steffen, B.: Learning register automata: from languages to program structures. Machine Learning 96(1-2), 65–98 (2014)
6. Scala website, http://www.scala-lang.org
7. Steffen, B.: LNCS Transactions on Foundations for Mastering Change: Preliminary manifesto. In: Margaria, T., Steffen, B. (eds.) ISoLA 2014, Part I. LNCS, vol. 8802, pp. 514–517. Springer, Heidelberg (2014)

Forever Software

Arend Rensink

University of Twente,
arend.rensink@utwente.nl

Any attempt to explain software engineering to a lay audience soon falls back on analogy: building software is like building a bridge, a car, a television set. A large part of the established practice within software engineering is also based on this premise. However, the analogy is false in some important ways, and herein originate many of the problems that have bugged the software industry since its birth.

Software is never finished. Early process models of software engineering, based on conventional wisdom from other engineering disciplines, imagined it as a cascade of phases, in which there would not be any going back: requirements capturing, analysis, design, implementation, testing and maintenance. After all, once a bridge is built, you do not have to redesign it, right?

Wrong — for software. Though these phases exist and it is important to distinguish them, it has now been known for a long time that things are not that clear-cut: a software project does not move as a whole from one phase to the next. More importantly, the process is not that linear: for any serious piece of software, *every single one* of these phases is passed through again and again. Software is never finished, and we'd better accept that and rethink our methods accordingly.

Of course, software *projects* do finish (possibly less quickly than foreseen); but the software *product* stays. However, it does not stay like a bridge, majestically, unchanging and for all to use and admire: it is copied and re-used in contexts it was not developed for, it is extended with little useful bits and pieces of functionality, it is ported to new platforms, cut up and partially rewritten, until it ends up in that black zone we call legacy code — for the next project team to try to understand, curse at and be secretly afraid of.

Verification is never finished. The central belief in the formal methods community, voiced strongly and eloquently by its pioneers, is that programs should not be deployed, maybe not even written, unless and until they are provably and totally correct. Establishing correctness is usually called *verification*. We have since seen that this very hard for practical software, for a large variety of reasons ranging from fundamental to pragmatic; however, watered-down versions, involving approximative methods for weaker notions of correctness, have been reasonably successful; an example are the type systems referred to in the manifesto [10], but in specialised contexts also more sophisticated methods such as model checking [2].

Given that software is never finished, however, and that all phases of development are passed through again and again, it follows that verification is never finished either. Every extension, every modification, every partial reuse needs to

T. Margaria and B. Steffen (Eds.): ISoLA 2014, Part I, LNCS 8802, pp. 535–537, 2014.

be re-verified in order to uphold the claim of correctness. Well-known is the case of the Ariane 5, which failed due to the reuse of a fragment of software that was correct in its original context. Especially in such a situation, where the original context is lost and the original design team is no longer around, re-verification can be even harder than the first time around.

Transformation as a way of life. In software engineering, change is the norm, not the exception. That being the case, we should also put change at the centre of our development methods. This is what is proposed under the header of *model transformation* [9]. To appreciate what this entails, one first has to broaden the mind: from software equating (textual) programs, to software consisting of all digital resources involved, including programs but also design documents, scripts, libraries, auxiliary inputs, configuration settings and whatnot: everything that is required to actually deploy the software. We use the term "model" to encompass each and every such artefact. Now, every change can be understood as a transformation of one set of models to another.

If we know the source model(s) of a given transformation to be correct — for instance because we made a dedicated verification effort — then ideally we should be able to conclude, without further ado, that the target model(s) are as well. For this to be true, it is enough to know that the change does not destroy correctness. If the change is ad hoc, say a textual edit to some input file, then this is in general impossible to know. Therefore, model transformation focusses on the concept of *rules* as the motor behind changes: every individual change is then an instance of a general rule. The preservation of correctness under change can now ideally be shown on the level of the transformation rules.

Challenges. Model transformation is a very active field of research. The ideal of correctness-preserving transformation [7] is one aspect of that research. Also growing is the insight that transformations often need to be invoked backwards, imposing a bidirectionality constraint [11,1]. To realise this, *graph transformation* is widely considered to be a good formal basis [3,4,5]; a lot of recent effort has been dedicated to lifting existing verification methods to that setting [8,6].

Model transformation as a means of mastering change offers a lot of promise. To fulfil that promise, further research is sorely needed. We will never go back to a world without software; so we'd better make sure it is long-lasting, forever software!

References

1. Anjorin, A., Cunha, A., Giese, H., Hermann, F., Rensink, A., Schürr, A.: BenchmarX. In: Hidaka, S., Terwilliger, J. (eds.) Bidirectional Transformations (BX 2014). CEUR Workshop Proceedings, vol. 1133, pp. 82–86 (2014)
2. Baier, C., Katoen, J.P.: Principles of model checking. MIT Press (2008)
3. Czarnecki, K., Helsen, S.: Feature-based survey of model transformation approaches. IBM Systems Journal 45(3), 621–646 (2006)

4. Ehrig, H., Ehrig, K., Prange, U., Taentzer, G.: Fundamentals of Algebraic Graph Transformation. Monographs in Theoretical Computer Science. An EATCS Series. Springer (2006)
5. Ghamarian, A.H., de Mol, M.J., Rensink, A., Zambon, E., Zimakova, M.V.: Modelling and analysis using GROOVE. International Journal on Software Tools for Technology Transfer 14(1), 15–40 (2012)
6. Ghamarian, A.H., Rensink, A.: Generalised compositionality in graph transformation. In: Ehrig, H., Engels, G., Kreowski, H.-J., Rozenberg, G. (eds.) ICGT 2012. LNCS, vol. 7562, pp. 234–248. Springer, Heidelberg (2012)
7. Hülsbusch, M., König, B., Rensink, A., Semenyak, M., Soltenborn, C., Wehrheim, H.: Showing full semantics preservation in model transformation - A comparison of techniques. In: Méry, D., Merz, S. (eds.) IFM 2010. LNCS, vol. 6396, pp. 183–198. Springer, Heidelberg (2010)
8. Rensink, A., Zambon, E.: Pattern-based graph abstraction. In: Ehrig, H., Engels, G., Kreowski, H.-J., Rozenberg, G. (eds.) ICGT 2012. LNCS, vol. 7562, pp. 66–80. Springer, Heidelberg (2012)
9. Sendall, S., Kozaczynski, W.: Model transformation: The heart and soul of model-driven software development. IEEE Software 20(5), 42–45 (2003), full report at http://infoscience.epfl.ch/record/52559
10. Steffen, B.: LNCS Transactions on Foundations for Mastering Change: Preliminary Manifesto. In: Margaria, T., Steffen, B. (eds.) ISoLA 2014, Part I. LNCS, vol. 8802, pp. 514–517. Springer, Heidelberg (2014)
11. Stevens, P.: A landscape of bidirectional model transformations. In: Lämmel, R., Visser, J., Saraiva, J. (eds.) Generative and Transformational Techniques in Software Engineering II. LNCS, vol. 5235, pp. 408–424. Springer, Heidelberg (2008)

Software (must) Change

Mike Hinchey

Lero–the Irish Software Engineering Research Centre
University of Limerick, Limerick, Ireland
Mike.Hinchey@lero.ie

1   Introduction

Software is pervasive. It impacts almost every aspect in our lives. It wakes us in the morning; it cooks our food; it entertains us; it gets us to work; it is involved in almost every aspect of our working day. It is impossible to lead a software-free life.

Software is the driving force in almost any new technological innovation. It is integral to innovations in medicine, manufacturing, transport, space exploration, etc.; almost every field is dependent on software for new innovations and new developments, leading to economic growth and advancement.

More and more organizations are—while not in the software business—turning to software. Many companies are finding that they are becoming software companies, even though that is not how they started out. For example, the use of software in cars has increased dramatically since the early 1990s, albeit starting from a very low level. Nowadays, high-end cars may have upwards of 70 processors on board, with everything from cruise control to entertainment systems controlled by software. In fact, car manufacturer BMW predicts that soon it will employ more software engineers than other engineers. Even computer hardware manufacturers are finding that more and more of their business is software.

2   Software Change

The great advantage of software is that it can be changed. If it weren't to change, then we would do things in hardware (where, traditionally, we've had better successes). This is also a disadvantage, however. Since software is perceived as easy to change, it is often changed, and changed badly.

Changes in software have resulted in the introduction of errors, performance degradation, architectural drift, lack of maintainability, and other problems [1], with a number of well-cited failures in the literature.

Our software systems may have evolved from legacy code or legacy systems, or may be the result of a combination of existing component-based systems, possibly over significant periods of time. Alternatively they may have evolved as a result of a focused and intentional change in the organization and the architecture in order to exploit newer technologies and paradigms (e.g., cloud) believed to be beneficial.

More and more, our software systems are required to adapt and evolve at run-time in order to react to changes in the environment or to meet necessary constraints on the system that were not previously satisfied and possibly not previously known. This is the domain of self-managing software [2].

T. Margaria and B. Steffen (Eds.): ISoLA 2014, Part I, LNCS 8802, pp. 538–540, 2014.
© Springer-Verlag Berlin Heidelberg 2014

3   Evolving Critical Systems

In order to manage change in our software systems that are critical to industry and to society as a whole, there is a need for further research in the area of *Evolving Critical Systems* [3].

Our systems must be described in a manner that enables developers to understand the necessary functionality of the system, which is expressed in a clear and precise manner, while yet offering sufficient flexibility to follow the processes and practices within the organization or necessitated by (possibly regulated) development processes. Our belief is that, as much as possible, a formal approach, as advocated in the FoMaC vision [4] is the most appropriate.

The architecture of the system must be well understood as it will form the basis for future decisions on changes to be made as part of the evolution process. This is particularly true where the system evolves at run-time [2]. Models of the system are a key component which will change over time and offer insights into potential areas of difficulty and as the basis for (possibly automated) code generation.

The system must be structured in a way that change can be managed, and controlled in a clear manner. The core functionality of the system will be fixed while features may be changed, added, adapted, and even deleted, in order to support any necessary evolution.

It is essential that we determine, as part of our change management processes, that quality and reliability are not impaired. This requires continual overview of the development and evolutionary processes. We must ensure that policies and constraints are met, while collection and recording data and evidence and computing a range of reliability measures at various points in time, which will be appropriately analyzed.

4   Conclusions

With good management of change, the quality of software need not deteriorate. In fact, with judicious choices, software quality can be improved as we evolve it [5]. However, this requires us to be conscious of our processes, the changes we make and of the important of software as a key resource for all organizations.

Acknowledgements. This work was supported, in part, by Science Foundation Ireland grant 10/CE/I1855 to Lero - the Irish Software Engineering Research Centre (www.lero.ie)

References

1. Hinchey, M., Coyle, L.: Evolving Critical Systems, Technical Report Lero-TR-2009-00, Lero-the Irish Software Engineering Research Centre (2009)
2. Dobson, S., Sterritt, R., Nixon, P., Hinchey, M.: Fulfilling the Vision of Autonomic Computing. Computer 43(1), 35–41 (2010)
3. Coyle, L., Hinchey, M., Nuseibeh, B., Fiadeiro, J.L.: Evolving Critical Systems. Computer 43(5), 28–33 (2010)

4. Steffen, B.: LNCS transaction on foundations for mastering change: Preliminary manifesto. In: Margaria, T., Steffen, B. (eds.) ISoLA 2014, Part I. LNCS, vol. 8802, pp. 514–517. Springer, Heidelberg (2014)
5. Hinchey, M., Coyle, L.: Preface. In: Hinchey, M., Coyle, L. (eds.) Conquering Complexity, pp ix-xii. Springer, London (2012)

The Change of Change

Tiziana Margaria

Lero and Chair of Service and Software Engineering, University of Limerick, Ireland
tiziana.margaria@lero.ie

1   Change Is not Always Just Change

As we have observed at the International Symposium On Leveraging Applications (ISoLA) conference over the course of its 10 years and six occurrences, research and adoption of new technologies, design principles, and tools in the software design area at large happen, but at a different pace and with different enthusiasm in different domains.

While the internet-dominated branches have adopted apps, the cloud, and thinking in collaborative design and viral distribution models, counting among the enthusiasts those who make a business out of innovation, other markets have adopted novelties either forced by need, like the transportation-related sectors, or by law, like the US government mandated higher auditing standards related to Sarbanes-Oxley, and the financial sector.

Other areas have readily adopted hardware innovation but have tried to deny, resist, and otherwise oppose software-driven agility deriving from the internet economy. An illustrative example is the traditional telecommunication companies, cornered in several markets by the technology that came together with the social networks wave.

Still others are undecided on what to do but for different reasons; mostly they are stuck into oligopolies such as in the ERP and business information system-related enterprise management software industry. These oligopolies set the pace of adoption: they try on one hand to slowdown change in order to protect their old products and on the other hand they try with little success to jump on the internet wagon but failing repeatedly. A prominent example is SAP with their "On demand" offers, whose development was recently stopped.

One other cause of current indecision, as prominently found in the healthcare industry, is an unhealthy combination of concurring factors which include:

- the *fragmentation* of the software and IT market where big players occupy significant cornerstones,
- the *cultural distance* between the care providers (doctors, nurses, therapists, chemists...) and care managers (hospital administrators, payers, and politicians) from the IT professionals and their way of thinking in general and the software design leading-edge reality in particular,
- and the *hyperregulation* in several undercorrelated layers of responsibility by laws as well as by professional organizations and other networks that represent and defend specific interests of niche actors.

T. Margaria and B. Steffen (Eds.): ISoLA 2014, Part I, LNCS 8802, pp. 541–543, 2014.
© Springer-Verlag Berlin Heidelberg 2014

2   Change at Large

In this very diverse context, we see that change in these different domains faces an amazing diversification of challenges. These challenges are never addressed in simple, rational decisions of adoption based on factual measurements of improvement of some metric such as cost, efficiency, or performance as in the ideal world every engineer fancies. Instead, they involve complex processes of a socio-technical character, where a wealth of organizational layers and both short and long term interests must be aligned in order to create a sufficiently scoped backing to some envisaged change management measure.

Once this is achieved (good luck with that!), there is the operationalization problem of facing the concrete individuals that need to be retrained, the concrete systems that need to be overhauled (or substituted), and the concrete ecosystem surrounding these islands of change: they need to support or at least tolerate the intrusion of novelty in a possibly graceful way.

Seen this way, it does not surprise anymore that the success rate of software projects stagnates in the low double digit quartile. It is also clear that the pure technical prowess of the staff and team, while a necessary condition for success, is by far not sufficient to achieve a successful end of a new IT-related project.

While we, within IT, are used to smirk at cartoons that depict traits of the inner software development teams facets[1] , we are not used to look at ourselves from the "outside". For example from the point of view of those other professionals we de facto closely work with, and whose professional and societal life we directly or indirectly influence - to the point of true domination[2]. As Mike Hinchey writes [4], there is hardly anything today that is not software-impacted. As Arend Rensink writes [5], software is never finished.

I use to tell my students that creating a piece of software is like getting a baby. First of all, it takes a couple for it: IT and those who (also) wish this piece of software and provide their contribution. Although, technically, an initial seed is enough, the outcome is better if the heterogeneous team collaborates all the time during the creation, and to prepare a welcoming environment for the new system in its future home. While we in Software Development care a lot about the (9 months equivalent of the) creation time and what can go wrong during this relatively short build period spent in the lab, we hardly practice as much care and foresight as optimal parents do for the delivery itself and its acclimation in the operational environment. This phase is called installation or implementation, depending on whether you are a software engineer or an information system person, resp. In addition, we fail quite miserably short when considering the subsequent 18-21 years of nurturing, care, and responsibility. Concerning maintenance and product evolution, in fact, our practice is still trailing the care and dedication of good parents. The Manifesto of FoMaC [6] addresses in fact

---

[1] For instance, in the famous "tree-swing-comic". Here [2] you find a commented version and also its derivation history, dating back to the '70s.

[2] This is genuine bidirectional incomprehension: as aptly captured in [1]

this phase, and what can be done before in order to face it in the most adequate and informed fashion.

The successive step hinges on the realization that we intrinsically depend upon the understanding and informed support and collaboration of a huge cloud of other professionals, without which no software system can be successful in the long term. As explained in this other story [3], in any IT-related project, we need the right marketing, the right press releases, the right communication, the right bosses and the right customers to achieve what can only be a shared, co-owned success. This is the scope of ToMaC, the sister Transactions o Managing Change that we are going to launch shortly, concerning this collaborative endeavour within enterprises and organizations to *manage change as an asset*.

We really hope, in a few years from now, to be able to look back at this collection of position statements and see how much changed in the way we deal with change in IT, economy, and society.

References

1. The business-it gap illustrated, http://modeling-languages.com/how-users-and-programmers-see-each-other/
2. The tree-swing cartoon, http://www.businessballs.com/treeswing.htm
3. The tree-swing cartoon, http://www.businessballs.com/businessballs_treeswing_pictures.htm
4. Hinchey, M.: Software (Must) change. In: Margaria, T., Steffen, B. (eds.) ISoLA 2014, Part I. LNCS, vol. 8802, pp. 538–540. Springer, Heidelberg (2014)
5. Rensink, A.: Forever software. In: Steffen, B., Margaria, T. (eds.) ISoLA 2014, Part I. LNCS, vol. 8802, pp. 535–537. Springer, Heidelberg (2014)
6. Steffen, B.: LNCS Transactions on Foundations for Mastering Change: Preliminary Manifesto. In: Steffen, B., Margaria, T. (eds.) ISoLA 2014, Part I. LNCS, vol. 8802, pp. 514–517. Springer, Heidelberg (2014)

Author Index